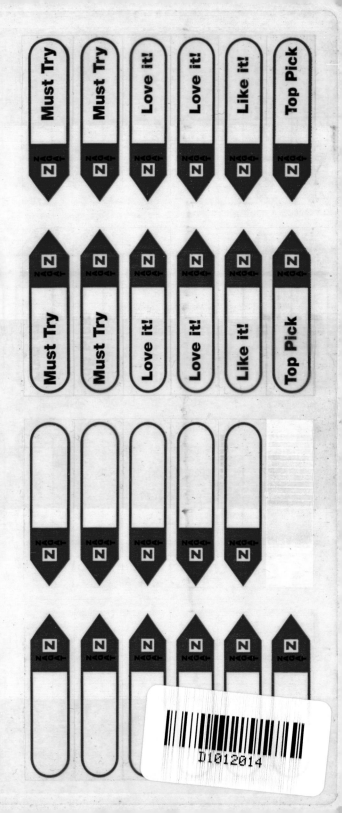

Use these handy Zagat bookmarks to mark your favorites and the places you'd like to try. Plus, we've included re-useable blank bookmarks for you to write on (and wipe off). Browsing through your Zagat guide has never been easier!

Back in 1979, we never imagined that an idea born during a wine-fueled dinner with friends would take us on an adventure that's lasted three decades – and counting.

The idea – that the collective opinions of avid consumers can be more accurate than the judgments of an individual critic – led to a hobby involving friends rating NYC restaurants. And that hobby grew into Zagat Survey, which today has over 350,000 participants worldwide weighing in on everything from airlines, bars, dining and golf to hotels, movies, shopping, tourist attractions and more.

By giving consumers a voice, we – and our surveyors – had unwittingly joined a revolution whose concepts (user-generated content, social networking) were largely unknown 30 years ago. However, those concepts caught fire with the rise of the Internet and have since transformed not only restaurant criticism but also virtually every aspect of the media, and we feel lucky to have been at the start of it all.

And that wasn't the only revolution we happily stumbled into. Our first survey was published as a revolution began to re-shape the culinary landscape. Thanks to a host of converging trends – the declining supremacy of old-school formal restaurants; the growing sophistication of diners; the availability of ever-more diverse cuisines and techniques; the improved range and quality of ingredients; the rise of chefs as rock stars – dining out has never been better or more exciting, and we've been privileged to witness its progress through the eyes of our surveyors. And it's still going strong.

As we celebrate Zagat's 30th year, we'd like to thank everyone who has participated in our surveys. We've enjoyed hearing and sharing your frank opinions and look forward to doing so for many years to come. As we always say, our guides and online content are really "yours."

Nina and Tim Zagat

New York City
Restaurants
2009

EDITORS
Curt Gathje and Carol Diuguid
COORDINATOR
Larry Cohn

Published and distributed by
Zagat Survey, LLC
4 Columbus Circle
New York, NY 10019
T: 212.977.6000
E: newyork@zagat.com
www.zagat.com

ACKNOWLEDGMENTS

We thank Leigh Crandall, Mikola De Roo, Randi Gollin, Lynn Hazlewood, Carolyn Koo, Bernard Onken, Mary Phillips-Sandy, Laura Siciliano-Rosen, Carla Spartos, Kelly Stewart, Gabby Stein and Miranda Van Gelder, as well as the following members of our staff: Josh Rogers (associate editor), Christina Livadiotis (assistant editor), Brian Albert, Sean Beachell, Maryanne Bertollo, Amy Cao, Jane Chang, Sandy Cheng, Reni Chin, Bill Corsello, John Deiner, Caitlin Eichelberger, Alison Flick, Jeff Freier, Shelley Gallagher, Sharon Gintzler, Michelle Golden, Justin Hartung, Karen Hudes, Roy Jacob, Ashunta Joseph, Cynthia Kilian, Natalie Lebert, Mike Liao, Allison Lynn, Dave Makulec, Chris Miragliotta, Andre Pilette, Kimberly Rosado, Becky Ruthenburg, Troy Segal, Aleksandra Shander, Stacey Slate, Jacqueline Wasilczyk, Donna Marino Wilkins, Liz Borod Wright, Yoji Yamaguchi, Sharon Yates, Anna Zappia and Kyle Zolner.

The reviews published in this guide are based on public opinion surveys. The numerical ratings reflect the average scores given by all survey participants who voted on each establishment. The text is based on direct quotes from, or fair paraphrasings of, participants' comments. Phone numbers, addresses and other factual information were correct to the best of our knowledge when published in this guide.

Maps © 2008 GeoNova Publishing, Inc., except for p. 299, provided by Steven Shukow.

Contents

Ratings & Symbols

Zagat Top Spot	Name	Symbols		Cuisine	Zagat Ratings			
					FOOD	DECOR	SERVICE	COST

Area, Address & Contact

Z Tim & Nina's ☽ *Deli*   ▽ 23 | 9 | 13 | $15

W 50s | 4 Columbus Circle (8th Ave.) | 212-977-6000 | www.zagat.com

Review, surveyor comments in quotes

Open 24/7 (some say that's 168 hours too much), this literal "deep dive" (in the CC IRT Station) started the 2008 election sandwich craze, e.g. bits of field-dressed moose on stale Arizona bread vs. Delaware crab on health loaf; though American flags cover the walls, underneath them the place resembles "a derelict hunting cabin" and T&N act like they'd prefer to shoot you than serve you; sure it's "dirt cheap", but you get what you pay for in life.

Ratings

Food, Decor and **Service** are rated on the Zagat 0 to 30 scale.

0	– 9	poor to fair
10	– 15	fair to good
16	– 19	good to very good
20	– 25	very good to excellent
26	– 30	extraordinary to perfection
▽		low response | less reliable

Cost

Our surveyors' benchmark estimate of the price of a dinner with one drink and tip. Lunch is usually 25 to 30% less. At prix fixe–only places we show the charge for the lowest-priced menu plus 30%. For **newcomers** or **write-ins** listed without ratings, the price range is as follows:

I	$25 and below	E	$41 to $65
M	$26 to $40	VE	$66 or more

Symbols

Z	Zagat Top Spot (highest ratings, popularity and importance)
☽	serves after 11 PM
Ⓢ	closed on Sunday
Ⓜ	closed on Monday
⌀	no credit cards accepted

Maps

Index maps show restaurants with the highest Food ratings in those areas.

About This Survey

Here are the results of our 30th annual **New York City Restaurants Survey,** covering 2,073 eateries throughout the five boroughs. Like all our guides, this one is based on the collective opinions of avid consumers – 38,128 all told.

WHO PARTICIPATED: Input from these enthusiasts forms the basis for the ratings and reviews in this guide (their comments are shown in quotation marks within the reviews). These surveyors are a diverse group: 53% are women, 47% men; 10% are in their 20s; 23%, 30s; 20%, 40s; 22%, 50s; and 25%, 60s or above. Collectively they bring roughly 6.6 million annual meals' worth of experience to this Survey. We sincerely thank each of these participants – this book is really "theirs."

HELPFUL LISTS: Our top lists and indexes can help you find exactly the right place for any occasion. See Key Newcomers (page 11), Most Popular (page 12), Top Ratings (pages 13–24), Best Buys (pages 25–28) and the handy indexes starting on page 278.

OUR TEAM: Special thanks go to our editors, Curt Gathje and Carol Diuguid, for their hard work over the years; this is the eighth edition of this guide that they have collaborated on. Thanks also to Larry Cohn, who has coordinated data collection for this book since 1994.

ABOUT ZAGAT: This marks our 30th year reporting on the shared experiences of consumers like you. What started in 1979 as a hobby has come a long way. Today we have over 350,000 surveyors and now cover airlines, bars, dining, entertaining, fast food, golf, hotels, lounges, movies, music, resorts, shopping, spas, theater and tourist attractions in over 100 countries.

INTERACTIVE: Up-to-the-minute news about restaurant openings plus menus, photos and more are free on **ZAGAT.com** and the award-winning **ZAGAT.mobi** (for web-enabled mobile devices). They also enable reserving at thousands of places with just one click.

VOTE AND COMMENT: We invite you to join in any of our surveys at **ZAGAT.com.** There you can rate and review establishments year-round. In exchange for doing so, you'll receive a free copy of the resulting guide when published.

AVAILABILITY: Zagat guides are available in all major bookstores as well as on **ZAGAT.com.** You can also access our content when on the go via **ZAGAT.mobi** and **ZAGAT TO GO** (for smartphones).

FEEDBACK: There is always room for improvement, thus we invite your comments about any aspect of our performance. Did we miss anything? Just contact us at **newyork@zagat.com.**

New York, NY
October 7, 2008

Nina and Tim

Nina and Tim Zagat

What's New

Despite rising food costs and a pervading uneasiness about the economy, NY remains the world's best dining city, continuing to diversify with 119 new openings this year vs. 88 closings. Though it was far from a banner year for major new arrivals, a spate of economical restaurants continued to pop up, reflecting locals' desire for BATH eateries (i.e. Better Alternatives to Home) like pizzerias, burger joints, BBQ places and noodle shops.

OPULENCE ENDURES: Swank was not completely dead, however: Alain Ducasse opened **Adour,** a nouvelle French showplace in the St. Regis that was easily the year's poshest arrival. And restaurateur Drew Nieporent and cutting-edge chef Paul Liebrandt are collaborating on **Corton** (in the former Montrachet digs), while David Bouley reshuffles his culinary empire, moving his eponymous flagship to a grand new setting down the block, doubling the space of **Bouley Upstairs** and adding two newcomers to his ever expanding portfolio, **BrushStroke** and **Secession.**

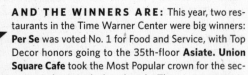

AND THE WINNERS ARE: This year, two restaurants in the Time Warner Center were big winners: **Per Se** was voted No. 1 for Food and Service, with Top Decor honors going to the 35th-floor **Asiate.** Union Square Cafe took the Most Popular crown for the second year running, its sixth win in the last decade. There were upsets in several casual cuisine categories, with first-time winners in three hotly contested genres: Top Hamburger went to **DuMont,** Top Pizza to **Lucali** and Top BBQ to **Fette Sau.** Interestingly enough, all three are located in the rapidly burgeoning borough of Brooklyn.

COST CONTROL: The average dinner cost went up to $40.78 from $39.46 last year, an increase of 3.3%. Although that doesn't appear to be a steep rise, it is up significantly relative to the average inflation rate for a meal, which has hovered around 1% annually since 2001. Indeed, 55% of surveyors say they are spending more dining out than last year, while only 9% say they are spending less; nonetheless, 26% say they are eating out more, while 21% say less.

DELUXE DINING: The average cost for dinner at NYC's Top 20 most expensive restaurants is $156.49, up from last year's $143.06 average. (As recently as 2004, this average was only $91.73.) In this high-end category, inflation since 2001 has averaged an astonishing 12% annually, yet it barely registered on the radar screens of the deep-pocketed clientele, domestic and foreign, who keep these restaurants full.

NEIGHBORHOOD HEAT: While voters named the West Village their favorite dining neighborhood, the Upper West Side was clearly this year's winner for the most noteworthy new arrivals given the debuts of **Bar Boulud, Dovetail, eighty one, Madaleine Mae** and **Mermaid Inn.** Furthermore, UWS spin-offs of **Fatty Crab** and **Shake Shack** are in the works, along with **West Branch,** a new eatery from the area's favorite son, Tom Valenti of **Ouest.**

GOING GREEN: Echoing the ever-growing awareness of the earth's resources, diners are favoring healthier, more environmentally friendly food. Some examples: only 10% order bottled water, now preferring a filtered version of what comes out of the tap. Sixty-seven percent say that eating locally grown food is "important." Given reports of rising mercury levels in fish, 34% are cutting down on or avoiding seafood altogether. And as for the trans-fat issue, 71% support the NYC Health Department's decision to ban them.

OVERVIEW: Service remains the prime restaurant annoyance, followed by noise/crowds and prices. Still, surveyors say that 56% of their meals are prepared outside the home. As for the increasing impact of the Internet, 48% visit an eatery's website before dining there, and 24% report making their reservations online, a substantial increase over 17% in 2008, 12% in 2007 and 9% in 2006. Indeed, seats at Top Newcomer **Momofuku Ko** can be reserved *only* online.

BIG CHEFS, SMALLER SCALE: Reflecting the more casual dining mood, a number of celeb chefs opened places with a decidedly downmarket feel. Daniel Boulud begat **Bar Boulud,** a wine bar specializing in charcuterie; Alain Ducasse brought forth **Benoit,** a French bistro meant to recall its famed Parisian namesake; Anita Lo rolled out **bar Q,** specializing in Asian barbecue; and Jean-Georges Vongerichten debuted a soba shop, **Matsugen.**

FAREWELL: Notable closings included Aix Brasserie, Bette, Bolo, Coco Pazzo, Columbus Bakery, Country, Danube, El Cid, Le Madeleine, Le Tableau, O.G., Sapa, Tasting Room and Tuscan Square. Especially saddening are the losses of **Café Gray, Coco Pazzo, Danube, Florent, L'Impero, Rain, René Pujol** and **San Domenico.**

 WHO'S IN THE KITCHEN? Celebrity chefs who open a restaurant with much fanfare and then are never seen again were the subject of debate in the press this year. Surveyors split on the subject: 41% report that a famous toque lures them in, while 55% say it doesn't affect them.

RANDOM NOTES: The noodle, a staple of Asian diets for centuries, got hot thanks to two key new arrivals, **Ippudo** and **Matsugen,** joining such popular stalwarts as **Minca, Momofuku Noodle Bar** and **Ramen Setagaya** . . . Tipping remained steady at 19%, right on par with the national average . . . Rating the overall dining experience on Zagat's 30-point scale, voters awarded NYC a 24 for culinary creativity and a 27 for diversity, but only a 15 for hospitality and a 13 for table availability . . . Communal tables got lukewarm voter response: 38% are willing to share a table if there is no other option, but 37% would do so "only as a last resort" . . . West Harlem saw the birth of a new Restaurant Row around 135th Street and 12th Avenue. Spacious, spiffy newcomers **Covo** and **Talay** joined pioneers **Dinosaur BBQ** and **Hudson River Café** in what's shaping up to be a bona fide scene.

New York, NY
October 7, 2008

Nina and Tim Zagat

30 Years Later

Sea changes have occurred in the world of food and restaurants since our first survey in 1979. We've moved from a universe in which "fine dining" mostly meant formal and Classic French to one in which just about anything goes. Today the hottest places tend to be stylishly casual, with bare tables, open kitchens and no dress code, serving cuisines that span Afghan to Yemenite. Also, traditionally structured menus are increasingly rare, while small plates are becoming ever more popular.

The diners have also undergone a transformation: exploding public interest in all things culinary – and the consequent proliferation of food magazines, TV shows, websites and blogs – means restaurant-goers are more savvy than ever. And chefs, who once labored anonymously behind the kitchen door, can now aspire to having multiple restaurants as well as their own TV shows and product lines.

But although much has changed, some things remain constant. Thirty-four of the places in our 1979 survey defied the odds and are in the guide today. Some things we said about them back then still hold true:

Algonquin	"Circle gone; nice for a drink"
Barbetta	"Favorite setting and garden"
Brasserie	"Really a pretentious coffee shop"
Café des Artistes	"Pleasant dining among naked ladies"
Da Silvano	"Popular Village Italian"
Four Seasons	"A NYC must"
La Grenouille	"Watch out Lutèce!"
Le Cirque	"Very Upper East Side French"
Le Veau d'Or	"Old standby with loyal following"
One if By Land	"Romance; fireplace on wintry nights"
Oyster Bar	"Outstanding seafood; large and noisy"
Peter Luger	"Uniformly praised; super steaks and no more"
P.J. Clarke's	"Crowded old NYC bar; beer and burger"
Tavern on the Green	"If only food equaled setting"
21 Club	"Favored by pols, press and VIPs"

Survey Stats Then and Now

	1979	2009
No. of Cuisines	19	84
No. of Restaurants	121	2,073
Most Popular	Lutèce	Union Square Cafe
Top Food	Lutèce	Per Se
Top American	Coach House	Per Se
Top Chinese	Ho's Pavilion	Oriental Garden
Top French	Lutèce	Le Bernardin
Top Italian	Parioli Romanissimo	Babbo
Top Japanese	Kitcho	Sushi Yasuda
Top Decor	Windows on the World	Asiate
Top Service	The Palace	Per Se
Average Cost	$26	$40.78*
Most Expensive	The Palace	Masa

*Average annual inflation 1.9% over period

Menus, photos, voting and more – free at ZAGAT.com

30 Dining Trends Then and Now

1979	2009
Bartender	Mixologist
Bread	Amuse-bouche
Oversized pepper mill	Salt tasting course
Nouvelle cuisine	Molecular gastronomy
Châteaubriand	Kobe beef
Pub	Gastropub
2nd Ave. Deli on Second Ave.	2nd Ave. Deli off Third Ave.
Tablecloth	Table
Supermarket	Greenmarket
Screwdriver	Mojito
Smoking between courses	Texting between courses
Toque	Shorts and clogs
Mac 'n' cheese	Truffled mac 'n' cheese
Bottled water	House-filtered water
Prix Fixe	Omakase
$20 meal	$20 appetizer
Estate wine	Estate chocolate
Gambling in Vegas	Dining in Vegas
Shirley Temple	Mocktail
Reservationist	Open Table
Sommelier	Interactive wine menu
Chefs cook for celebrities	Chefs are celebrities
Joe Baum	Danny Meyer
Carnivore	Locavore
Shrimp cocktail	Tuna carpaccio
Julia Child	Rachael Ray
Waiter/waitress	Service professional
Baked	Al forno
La Côte Basque	Benoit
Peter Luger	Peter Luger

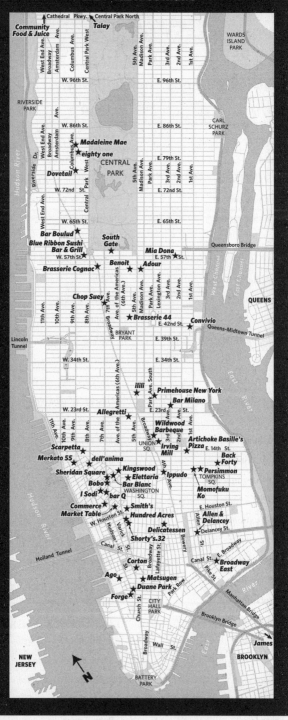

KEY NEWCOMERS

Community
Food & Juice

Talay

Madaleine Mae

eighty one

Dovetail

Bar Boulud

Blue Ribbon Sushi
Bar & Grill

South
Gate

Mia Dona

Adour

Benoit

Brasserie Cognac

Chop Suey

Brasserie 44

Convivio

ilili

Primehouse New York

Bar Milano

Allegretti

Wildwood
Barbeque

Artichoke Basille's
Pizza

Scarpetta

Irving
Mill

Back
Forty

Merkato 55   dell'anima

Kingswood

Persimmon

Ippudo

Sheridan Square

Elettaria

Momofuku
Ko

Bobo   Bar Blanc

I Sodi   bar Q

Allen &
Delancey

Commerce
Market Table

Smith's

Hundred Acres

Delicatessen

Shorty's.32

Broadway
East

Corton

Ago   Matsugen

Duane Park

Forge

James

NEW
JERSEY

BROOKLYN

Key Newcomers

Our editors' take on the year's top arrivals. See page 336 for a full list.

Adour | *French*

Ago | *Italian*

Allegretti | *French*

Allen & Delancey | *American*

Artichoke Basille's | *Pizza*

Back Forty | *American*

Bar Blanc | *French/Italian*

Bar Boulud | *French*

Bar Milano | *Italian*

bar Q | *Pan-Asian*

Benoit | *French*

Blue Ribbon Sushi B&G | *Japanese*

Bobo | *European*

Brasserie Cognac | *French*

Brasserie 44 | *American*

Broadway East | *Vegetarian*

Chop Suey | *Pan-Asian*

Commerce | *American*

Community Food | *American*

Convivio | *Italian*

Corton | *French*

Delicatessen | *American*

dell'anima | *Italian*

Dovetail | *American*

Duane Park | *American*

eighty one | *American*

Elettaria | *American*

Forge | *American*

Hundred Acres | *American*

ilili | *Lebanese*

Ippudo | *Japanese*

Irving Mill | *American*

I Sodi | *Italian*

James | *American*

Kingswood | *Australian*

Madaleine Mae | *Southern*

Market Table | *American*

Matsugen | *Japanese*

Merkato 55 | *African*

Mia Dona | *Italian*

Momofuku Ko | *American*

Persimmon | *Korean*

Primehouse NY | *Steak*

Scarpetta | *Italian*

Sheridan Square | *American*

Shorty's.32 | *American*

Smith's | *American*

South Gate | *American*

Talay | *Pan-Latin/Thai*

Wildwood BBQ | *BBQ*

The year to come shows promise with a number of high-profile projects in the works: Michael White (Alto, Convivio) will open Italian seafooder **Marea** in the former San Domenico space; April Bloomfield and Ken Friedman (the Spotted Pig) are planning a new West Chelsea seafooder, **John Dory**; Toronto star chef Susur Lee will open his first U.S. venture, the Modern Chinese **Shang,** in the Thompson Lower East Side hotel; long-delayed **10 Downing** will debut with Jason Neroni behind the burners; Todd English (Olives) will unveil **Libertine** in the Financial District; **A Voce** will branch out with a second location in the Time Warner Center's former Café Gray space, while Michael Psilakis will bring back his original Greek favorite, **Kefi,** in bigger UWS digs; and redos of stalwarts **Minetta Tavern** and the **Oak Room** are in the works. Of course, **ZAGAT.com** offers daily, up-to-the-minute details on NYC's latest openings.

Most Popular

Plotted on the map at the back of this book.

1. Union Square Cafe | *American*
2. Gramercy Tavern | *American*
3. Babbo | *Italian*
4. Le Bernardin | *French/Seafood*
5. Gotham Bar & Grill | *American*
6. Jean Georges | *French*
7. Daniel | *French*
8. Peter Luger | *Steak*
9. Bouley | *French*
10. Eleven Madison Park | *French*
11. Balthazar | *French*
12. Blue Water Grill | *Seafood*
13. Per Se | *American/French*
14. Del Posto | *Italian*
15. Becco | *Italian*
16. Atlantic Grill | *Seafood*
17. Rosa Mexicano | *Mexican*
18. Modern, The | *Amer./French*
19. Café Boulud | *French*
20. Aureole | *American*
21. Nobu | *Japanese*
22. Carmine's | *Italian*
23. Felidia | *Italian*
24. Buddakan | *Asian Fusion*
25. Palm, The | *Steak*
26. Picholine | *French/Med.*
27. Artisanal | *French*
28. Four Seasons | *Continental*
29. Aquagrill | *Seafood*
30. Del Frisco's | *Steak*
31. Tabla | *American*
32. Chanterelle | *French*
33. Aquavit | *Scandinavian*
34. Blue Hill | *American*
35. Telepan* | *American*
36. Il Mulino | *Italian*
37. Ouest | *American*
38. Spice Market | *SE Asian*
39. davidburke/dona. | *Amer.*
40. Café des Artistes | *French*
41. Lupa | *Italian*
42. Craft | *American*
43. Bar Americain | *American*
44. One if by Land | *American*
45. Al Di La | *Italian*
46. La Grenouille | *French*
47. db Bistro Moderne | *French*
48. Sushi Yasuda | *Japanese*
49. Mesa Grill | *Southwestern*
50. L'Atelier/Joël Robuchon | *French*

It's obvious that many of the above restaurants are among NYC's most expensive, but if popularity were calibrated to price, we suspect that a number of other restaurants would join their ranks. Thus, we have added several lists of Best Buys on pages 25-28.

* Indicates a tie with restaurant above

Top Food Ratings

Excludes places with low votes.

28| Per Se | *American/French*
Le Bernardin | *French/Seafood*
Daniel | *French*
Jean Georges | *French*
Sushi Yasuda | *Japanese*
Bouley | *French*
Mas | *American*
L'Atelier/J. Robuchon | *French*
Garden Cafe (Bklyn) | *American*
Gramercy Tavern | *American*

27| Chanterelle | *French*
Sasabune | *Japanese*
Gotham Bar & Grill | *American*
Sushi Seki | *Japanese*
Café Boulud | *French*
Degustation | *French/Spanish*
Peter Luger (Bklyn) | *Steak*
Sugiyama | *Japanese*
Nobu | *Japanese*
Saul (Bklyn) | *American*
Aureole | *American*
Lucali (Bklyn) | *Pizza*
Masa/Bar Masa | *Japanese*
Babbo | *Italian*
Grocery (Bklyn) | *American*
La Grenouille | *French*

Annisa | *American*
Union Square Cafe | *American*
Il Mulino | *Italian*
Di Fara (Bklyn) | *Pizza*
Tratt. L'incontro (Qns) | *Italian*
Sripraphai (Qns) | *Thai*
Scalini Fedeli | *Italian*
Milos | *Greek/Seafood*
Eleven Madison Park | *French*

26| Aquagrill | *Seafood*
Picholine | *French/Med.*
Momofuku Ko | *American*
Blue Hill | *American*
Tanoreen (Bklyn) | *Med./
Mideastern*
Gari/Sushi | *Japanese*
Four Seasons | *American*
Soto | *Japanese*
Nobu 57 | *Japanese*
Scarpetta | *Italian*
Al Di La (Brooklyn) | *Italian*
Roberto (Bronx) | *Italian*
Pearl Oyster Bar | *Seafood*
Poke | *Japanese*
Adour | *French*
Aki | *Japanese*

BY CUISINE

AMERICAN
28| Per Se
Mas
Garden Cafe
Gramercy Tavern
27| Gotham Bar & Grill
Saul

AMERICAN (REGIONAL)
26| Pearl Oyster Bar/NE
24| Roy's NY/Hawaiian
23| Ed's Lobster Bar/NE
22| Mara's Homemade/Cajun
Michael's/CA
21| Carl's Steaks/Philly

BARBECUE
24| Fette Sau
22| Smoke Joint
Dinosaur BBQ
Daisy May's
21| Blue Smoke
Hill Country

BURGERS
24| DuMont
23| Shake Shack
burger joint
22| Corner Bistro
Island Burgers
21| J.G. Melon

CARIBBEAN
23| Cuba/Cuban
22| Victor's Cafe/Cuban
21| Sofrito/Puerto Rican
Son Cubano/Cuban
El Malecon/Dominican
Maroons/Jamaican

CHINESE
24| Oriental Garden
Tse Yang
Shun Lee Palace
23| Philippe
Fuleen Seafood
Spicy & Tasty

COFFEEHOUSES
- <u>22</u> Ferrara
- <u>20</u> Once Upon a Tart
- <u>19</u> Cafe Lalo
- <u>18</u> Le Pain Quotidien
- Omonia Cafe
- <u>17</u> Edgar's Cafe

DELIS
- <u>24</u> Barney Greengrass
- <u>23</u> Ess-a-Bagel
- Katz's Deli
- <u>22</u> 2nd Ave Deli
- Mill Basin Deli
- <u>21</u> PicNic Market

DESSERT
- <u>25</u> ChikaLicious
- Chocolate Room
- <u>24</u> La Bergamote
- <u>23</u> Payard Bistro
- L & B Spumoni
- <u>22</u> Ferrara

DIM SUM
- <u>24</u> Oriental Garden
- <u>21</u> Mandarin Court
- Ping's Seafood
- Chinatown Brasserie
- Dim Sum Go Go
- <u>20</u> Shun Lee Cafe

FRENCH
- <u>28</u> Le Bernardin
- Daniel
- Jean Georges
- Bouley
- L'Atelier/Joël Robuchon
- <u>27</u> Chanterelle
- Café Boulud
- Degustation
- La Grenouille
- Eleven Madison Park
- <u>26</u> Picholine
- Adour

FRENCH (BISTRO)
- <u>25</u> Tournesol
- db Bistro Moderne
- <u>24</u> JoJo
- Le Gigot
- <u>23</u> Capsouto Frères
- Payard Bistro

GREEK
- <u>27</u> Milos
- <u>25</u> Taverna Kyclades
- Eliá
- Pylos
- <u>24</u> Avra
- Anthos

HOTEL DINING
- <u>28</u> Jean Georges
  (Trump Int'l Hotel)
- L'Atelier/Joël Robuchon
  (Four Seasons Hotel)
- <u>27</u> Café Boulud
  (Surrey Hotel)
- <u>26</u> Adour
  (St. Regis Hotel)
- eighty one
  (Excelsior Hotel)
- <u>25</u> Gordon Ramsay
  (London NYC)

INDIAN
- <u>25</u> Tamarind
- <u>24</u> Amma
- <u>23</u> Chola
- dévi
- Dawat
- <u>22</u> Banjara

ITALIAN
- <u>27</u> Babbo
- Il Mulino
- Trattoria L'incontro
- Scalini Fedeli
- <u>26</u> Scarpetta
- Al Di La
- Roberto
- Del Posto
- Felidia
- Scalinatella
- <u>25</u> Spigolo
- Don Peppe

JAPANESE/SUSHI
- <u>28</u> Sushi Yasuda
- <u>27</u> Sasabune
- Sushi Seki
- Sugiyama
- Nobu
- Masa/Bar Masa
- <u>26</u> Gari/Sushi
- Soto
- Nobu 57
- Poke
- Aki
- Blue Ribbon Sushi

KOREAN

24 Bann
Moim
Hangawi
23 Cho Dang Gol
22 Woo Lae Oak
21 Kang Suh

KOSHER

22 Chennai Garden
2nd Ave Deli
Mill Basin Deli
Prime Grill
21 Pongal
20 Caravan of Dreams

MEDITERRANEAN

26 Picholine
Tanoreen
25 Little Owl
Convivium Osteria
Taboon
24 Tempo

MEXICAN

24 Itzocan
Pampano
Maya
Mexicana Mama
23 Hell's Kitchen
Toloache

MIDDLE EASTERN

26 Tanoreen
25 Taboon
23 ilili
Hummus Place
22 Sahara
Turkish Kitchen

NEWCOMERS

26 Momofuku Ko
Scarpetta
Adour
Dovetail
eighty one
25 Duane Park
24 Shorty's.32
dell'anima
Blue Ribbon Sushi B&G
Artichoke Basille's
South Gate
Allen & Delancey
23 Community Food
Market Table
ilili

NOODLE SHOPS

23 Momofuku Noodle Bar
Soba-ya
22 Great NY Noodle
21 Rai Rai Ken
20 Ramen Setagaya
Pho Bang

PIZZA

27 Lucali
Di Fara
25 Denino's
Grimaldi's
Franny's
24 Artichoke Basille's

RAW BARS

26 Aquagrill
Pearl Oyster Bar
25 Esca
fresh
24 Blue Ribbon
23 BLT Fish

SEAFOOD

28 Le Bernardin
27 Milos
26 Aquagrill
Pearl Oyster Bar
Oceana
25 Taverna Kyclades

SMALL PLATES

28 L'Atelier/Joël Robuchon
27 Degustation
25 Maze
Sakagura
Perbacco
24 Frankies Spuntino

SOUTH AMERICAN

25 Caracas
23 Churrascaria
22 Pio Pio
Empanada Mama
Buenos Aires
SushiSamba

SOUTHERN/SOUL

24 Egg
21 Amy Ruth's
Miss Mamie's/Maude's
20 Mo-Bay
19 Pink Tea Cup
Rack & Soul

SOUTHWESTERN

23 Mesa Grill
19 Canyon Road
   Agave
18 Miracle Grill
   Santa Fe
17 Cilantro

SPANISH/TAPAS

25 Casa Mono
24 Las Ramblas
   Tía Pol
23 Pamplona
22 Mercat
   El Pote

STEAKHOUSES

27 Peter Luger
25 Del Frisco's
   Strip House
   BLT Prime
   Wolfgang's
   Sparks Steak
24 Palm, The
   BLT Steak
   Ruth's Chris
   Keens
   Christos
   Pietro's

THAI

27 Sripraphai
24 Kuma Inn
23 Joya
   Erawan
   Song
   Wondee Siam

TURKISH

22 Sahara
   Turkish Kitchen
   Pera
   Ali Baba
21 Beyoglu
   Akdeniz

VEGETARIAN

24 Hangawi
23 Candle 79
   Candle Cafe
   Pure Food & Wine
   Hummus Place
22 Chennai Garden

VIETNAMESE

23 Omai
22 Nicky's Viet.
21 Nha Trang
   Saigon Grill
   Nam
   Indochine

BY SPECIAL FEATURE

BREAKFAST

Balthazar
Bubby's
Clinton St. Baking Co.
Egg
Good Enough to Eat
Morandi
Norma's
Popover Cafe
Regency
Sarabeth's

BRUNCH DOWNTOWN

Aquagrill
Balthazar
Blue Ribbon Bakery
Bubby's
Clinton St. Baking Co.
Essex
Five Points
Jane
Pastis
Prune

BRUNCH MIDTOWN

Artisanal
Cafeteria
Eatery
elmo
Friend of a Farmer
L'Express
Norma's
Penelope
Rainbow Room
Water Club

BRUNCH UPTOWN

Atlantic Grill
Café des Artistes
Carlyle
Isabella's
Miss Mamie's/Maude's
Nice Matin
Ouest
Popover Cafe
Sarabeth's
Telepan

Menus, photos, voting and more – free at ZAGAT.com

BUSINESS LUNCH/ DOWNTOWN

- Bouley
- City Hall
- Delmonico's
- Gotham Bar & Grill
- Harry's
- Les Halles
- MarkJoseph Steak
- Nobu
- Union Square Cafe
- Wolfgang's

BUSINESS LUNCH/ MIDTOWN

- Alto
- Aquavit
- Bar Americain
- Four Seasons
- Jean Georges
- Le Bernardin
- Lever House
- Michael's
- Modern, The
- 21 Club

CELEBRATIONS

- Bouley
- Cru
- Daniel
- FireBird
- Four Seasons
- Le Bernardin
- Rainbow Room
- River Café
- Tavern on the Green

CELEBRITY SCENES

- Balthazar
- Cipriani Downtown
- Da Silvano
- Joe Allen
- Nobu
- Pastis
- Per Se
- Rao's
- Spotted Pig
- Waverly Inn

CHILD-FRIENDLY

- American Girl Place
- Benihana
- Bubby's
- Carmine's
- Cowgirl
- Landmarc
- Moxie Spot

- Ninja
- Serendipity 3
- Two Boots

DINING AT THE BAR

- Babbo
- Centro Vinoteca
- Del Posto
- Gotham Bar & Grill
- Gramercy Tavern
- Hearth
- Perry Street
- Picholine
- Red Cat
- Union Square Cafe

GROUP DINING

- Asia de Cuba
- Buddakan
- Carmine's
- China Grill
- Churrascaria Plataforma
- Hill Country
- Rosa Mexicano
- Ruby Foo's
- Stanton Social
- Tao

HIPSTER HANGOUTS

- Allen & Delancy
- Delicatessen
- dell'anima
- Employees Only
- Fette Sau
- Freemans
- La Esquina
- Schiller's
- Spotted Pig
- Tailor

HISTORIC PLACES

- Algonquin
- Fraunces Tavern
- Keens
- Landmark Tavern
- Old Homestead
- Oyster Bar
- Pete's Tavern
- P.J. Clarke's
- Rainbow Room
- 21 Club

HOTTEST SERVERS

- Brother Jimmy's
- Buddakan
- Cafeteria
- Coffee Shop
- Del Frisco's

44/44½
Hawaiian Tropic Zone
Indochine
Pastis
Tao

LATE DINING
Baraonda
Blue Ribbon
Delicatessen
DuMont
Frank
'ino
La Esquina
Pastis
Raoul's
Spotted Pig

MEET FOR DRINK/DTN
Balthazar
Bond Street
Buddha Bar
Employees Only
Gotham Bar & Grill
Harry's
Odeon
Rayuela
Spice Market
Stanton Social

MEET FOR DRINK/MIDTWN
Barbounia
Blue Fin
Django
Grayz
Koi
Maze
Michael Jordan's
Modern, The
Nobu 57
Town

MEET FOR DRINK/UPTWN
Atlantic Grill
Cafe Luxembourg
Compass
Daniel
Demarchelier
Geisha
J.G. Melon
Landmarc
Orsay
Ouest

MILESTONES
75th   Rainbow Room
50th   Brasserie

Four Seasons
25th   Garden Cafe
Gotham Bar & Grill
Indochine
Petrossian
Rosa Mexicano
20th   Lucky Strike
Michael's

POWER SCENES
Daniel
Elio's
Four Seasons (Grill Room)
Jean Georges
Le Bernardin
Michael's
Regency
Smith & Wollensky
Sparks Steak
21 Club

QUICK BITES
Amy's Bread
Azuri Cafe
BLT Burger
Caracas
Fresco
'ino
Nicky's Viet.
Shake Shack
Westville
'wichcraft

SENIOR APPEAL
Barbetta
Barney Greengrass
Bravo Gianni
Café des Artistes
Chez Napoléon
Elaine's
Felidia
Mr. K's
Russian Tea Room
Sal Anthony's

SINGLES SCENES
Baraonda
Buddakan
Buddha Bar
Butter
Employees Only
'inoteca
La Esquina
STK
SushiSamba
Tao

Menus, photos, voting and more – free at ZAGAT.com

SOCIETY WATCH

- Four Seasons (Pool Room)
- Geisha
- Harry Cipriani
- La Goulue
- Le Bilboquet
- Lusardi's
- Nello
- Primavera
- Sant Ambroeus
- Swifty's

TRANSPORTING EXPERIENCES

- Balthazar
- Boathouse
- Buddakan
- Chez Josephine
- FireBird
- Il Buco
- Matsuri
- Suba
- Tao
- Tavern on the Green

24-HOUR

- Bereket
- Bún
- Cafeteria
- Empire Diner
- French Roast

- Kum Gang San
- L'Express
- R&L Restaurant
- Sarge's Deli
- Veselka

VISITORS ON EXP. ACCT.

- Bouley
- Chanterelle
- Craft
- Daniel
- Four Seasons
- Gordon Ramsay
- Jean Georges
- Masa
- Nobu
- Per Se

WINNING WINE LISTS

- Alto
- Babbo
- Cru
- Daniel
- Del Posto
- Harry's
- Modern, The
- Per Se
- Sparks Steak
- Union Square Cafe
- Veritas

BY LOCATION

CHELSEA

- 26 Scarpetta
- Del Posto
- 25 Morimoto
- Da Umberto
- 24 Tía Pol
- La Bergamote

CHINATOWN

- 24 Oriental Garden
- 23 Fuleen Seafood
- Nice Green Bo
- 22 Peking Duck
- Joe's Shanghai
- Grand Sichuan

EAST 40s

- 28 Sushi Yasuda
- 25 Sakagura
- Aburiya Kinnosuke
- Sparks Steak
- 24 Megu Midtown
- Palm, The

EAST 50s

- 28 L'Atelier/Joël Robuchon
- 27 La Grenouille
- 26 Four Seasons
- Adour
- Oceana
- Felidia

EAST 60s

- 28 Daniel
- 27 Sushi Seki
- Aureole
- 26 Scalinatella
- 25 davidburke/donatella
- 24 JoJo

EAST 70s

- 27 Sasabune
- Café Boulud
- 26 Gari/Sushi
- 24 Campagnola
- 23 Lusardi's
- Sette Mezzo

EAST 80s

26	Poke
25	Spigolo
	Erminia
24	Etats-Unis
	Sistina
23	Elio's

EAST 90s & EAST 100s

24	Sfoglia
	Itzocan
23	Nick's
22	Pio Pio
	El Paso Taqueria
21	Pinocchio

EAST VILLAGE

27	Degustation
26	Momofuku Ko
	Kanoyama
25	Caracas
	Hearth
	Jewel Bako

FINANCIAL DISTRICT

24	MarkJoseph Steak
	Roy's NY
	Adrienne's Pizza
23	Fresco
22	Delmonico's
	Bobby Van's

FLATIRON/UNION SQ.

28	Gramercy Tavern
27	Union Square Cafe
26	Veritas
	Craft
	15 East
25	Fleur de Sel

GARMENT DISTRICT

24	Keens
23	Uncle Jack's
22	Cho Dang Gol
	Osteria Gelsi
	Kati Roll Co.
21	Kang Suh

GRAMERCY

27	Eleven Madison Park
25	Tabla
	Casa Mono
	A Voce
	BLT Prime
24	Novitá

GREENWICH VILLAGE

28	Mas
27	Gotham Bar & Grill
	Babbo
	Annisa
	Il Mulino
26	Blue Hill

HARLEM

23	Community Food
22	Dinosaur BBQ
21	Amy Ruth's
	Hudson River Café
	Miss Mamie's/Maude's
	Papaya King

LITTLE ITALY

24	Pellegrino's
23	Il Cortile
	Angelo's, Mulberry St.
22	Il Palazzo
	La Esquina
	Ferrara

LOWER EAST SIDE

25	Clinton St. Baking
24	Frankies Spuntino
	ápizz
	Falai
	Kuma Inn
	Allen & Delancey

MEATPACKING

24	Valbella
	Old Homestead
22	Spice Market
21	Merkato 55
	Son Cubano
	STK

MURRAY HILL

25	Wolfgang's
24	Sushi Sen-nin
	Hangawi
23	Vezzo
	Artisanal
	Asia de Cuba

NOHO

24	Bond Street
	Aroma
	Il Buco
23	Bianca
22	Five Points
	Mercat

Menus, photos, voting and more – free at ZAGAT.com

NOLITA

- **24** Lombardi's
- Peasant
- **23** Ed's Lobster Bar
- **22** Public
- **20** Café Habana
- **19** Le Jardin Bistro

SOHO

- **26** Aquagrill
- Blue Ribbon Sushi
- **25** L'Ecole
- Aurora
- **24** Shorty's.32
- Blue Ribbon

TRIBECA

- **28** Bouley
- **27** Chanterelle
- Nobu
- Scalini Fedeli
- **25** Bouley, Upstairs
- fresh

WEST 40s

- **26** Gari/Sushi
- **25** Del Frisco's
- Esca
- db Bistro Moderne
- Sushi Zen
- **24** Triomphe

WEST 50s

- **28** Le Bernardin
- **27** Sugiyama
- Milos
- **26** Nobu 57
- Yakitori Totto
- Modern, The

WEST 60s

- **28** Per Se
- Jean Georges
- **27** Masa/Bar Masa
- **26** Picholine
- **25** Telepan
- **24** Asiate

WEST 70s

- **26** Gari/Sushi
- Dovetail
- **23** Ocean Grill
- 'Cesca
- Hummus Place
- Tenzan

WEST 80s

- **26** eighty one
- **25** Ouest
- **24** Barney Greengrass
- Celeste
- **23** Nëo Sushi
- **22** Land

WEST 90s & UP

- **24** Gennaro
- Pisticci
- **23** Terrace in the Sky
- **22** Pio Pio
- Indus Valley
- Max SoHa

WEST VILLAGE

- **26** Perry Street
- Wallsé
- **25** Little Owl
- Piccolo Angolo
- **24** dell'anima
- Mary's Fish Camp

OUTER BOROUGHS

BRONX

- **26** Roberto
- **24** Patricia's
- **23** Enzo's
- Dominick's
- Jake's
- Artie's

BROOKLYN: BAY RIDGE

- **26** Tanoreen
- **25** Areo
- Eliá
- Fushimi
- **24** Agnanti
- Tuscany Grill

BROOKLYN: HTS/DUMBO

- **26** River Café
- **25** Grimaldi's
- **24** Noodle Pudding
- Henry's End
- Queen
- **22** Jack the Horse

BKLYN: CARROLL GDNS./ BOERUM & COBBLE HILL

- **27** Saul
- Lucali
- Grocery, The
- **25** Chocolate Room
- **24** Frankies Spuntino
- Chestnut

BKLYN: FT. GREENE/ PROSPECT HTS.

28 Garden Cafe
25 Franny's
22 Smoke Joint
21 Ici
   67 Burger
20 Zaytoons

BROOKLYN: PARK SLOPE

26 Al Di La
   Blue Ribbon Sushi
25 Convivium Osteria
   applewood
   Chocolate Room
24 Tempo

BKLYN: WILLIAMSBURG

27 Peter Luger
26 Dressler
25 Aurora
24 Egg
   Fette Sau
   DuMont

BROOKLYN: OTHER

27 Di Fara (Midwood)
25 Good Fork (Red Hook)
23 Joe's Pizza (Midwood)

   L & B Spumoni (Bensonhurst)
   Tenzan (Bensonhurst)
22 Farm on Adderley (Ditmas Pk.)

QUEENS: ASTORIA/L.I.C.

27 Trattoria L'incontro
25 Taverna Kyclades
   Piccola Venezia
   Tournesol (L.I.C.)
24 Christos
   Agnanti

QUEENS: OTHER

27 Sripraphai (Woodside)
25 Don Peppe (Ozone Park)
   Sapori D'Ischia (Woodside)
   Danny Brown (Forest Hills)
24 La Flor Bakery (Woodside)
   Park Side (Corona)

STATEN ISLAND

25 Denino's
   Trattoria Romana
   Bocelli
   Fushimi
24 Carol's Cafe
23 Da Noi

Menus, photos, voting and more - free at ZAGAT.com

Top Decor Ratings

29 Asiate	Modern, The
28 Per Se	Gramercy Tavern
Daniel	Boathouse
Four Seasons	Aureole
27 La Grenouille	25 FireBird
Adour	Kings' Carriage
River Café	Park Ave . . .
Rainbow Room	South Gate
Buddakan	Piano Due
Kittichai	Matsuri
Terrace in the Sky	Water Club
Gilt	Perry Street
Del Posto	L'Atelier/Joël Robuchon
One if by Land	EN Japanese
Le Bernardin	View, The*
26 Buddha Bar	Water's Edge
Tao	Gotham Bar & Grill
Carlyle	Le Cirque
Megu	Grand Tier
Spice Market	eighty one
Chanterelle	Town
Cávo	Tabla
Eleven Madison Park	Dressler
Morimoto	Wakiya
Café des Artistes	24 Public
Jean Georges	Rayuela

GARDENS

Barbetta	I Trulli
Barolo	Jolie
Battery Gardens	Park, The
Bryant Park Grill	Pure Food & Wine
I Coppi	Tavern on the Green

PRIVATE PARTIES

(max. capacity)

Barbetta (140)	Matsuri (56)
Blue Water Grill (300)	Megu (600)
Buddakan (700)	Modern, The (80)
City Hall (415)	Oceana (60)
Craftsteak (300)	Park, The (1200)
Daniel (250)	Patroon (100)
Del Frisco's (75)	Per Se (60)
Del Posto (1,200)	Picholine (22)
Fiamma (80)	Redeye Grill (400)
Four Seasons (350)	River Café (125)
Grayz (100)	Spice Market (150)
Harry's Café (80)	Tao (500)
Keens (500)	Tavern on the Green (2,500)
Landmark Tavern (50)	Thalassa (450)
Le Bernardin (130)	21 Club (150)
Le Cirque (240)	Water Club (1000)

ROMANCE

Allen & Delancey	Le Refuge
Bouley	Mas
Café des Artistes	One if by Land
Chanterelle	Petrossian
Convivium Osteria	Rainbow Room
Daniel	Raoul's
Del Posto	River Café
Erminia	Scalini Fedeli
Gascogne	Suba
Il Buco	Terrace in the Sky
Kings' Carriage	Wallsé
La Grenouille	Water's Edge

VIEWS

Alma	Porter House NY
Asiate	Rainbow Room
Battery Gardens	River Café
Boathouse	Sea Grill
Chop Suey	Terrace in the Sky
Gigino Wagner Park	View, The
Modern, The	Water Club
Per Se	Water's Edge

Top Service Ratings

28 Per Se	Scalini Fedeli
Daniel	River Café
Chanterelle	Carlyle
27 Le Bernardin	Blue Hill
Jean Georges	Valbella
La Grenouille	Cru
Gramercy Tavern	Del Posto
Bouley	Grocery, The
Four Seasons	15 East
26 Eleven Madison Park	Veritas*
Café Boulud	Perry Street
Adour	**24** Gordon Ramsay
Aureole	Erminia
L'Atelier/Joël Robuchon	Aquavit
Union Square Cafe	Babbo
Garden Cafe	Asiate
Mas	Il Tinello
Gotham Bar & Grill	Oceana
Masa/Bar Masa	One if by Land
Tom's	Tocqueville
Annisa	Piano Due
Sugiyama	Craft
25 Picholine	Rossini's
Gilt	eighty one
Antica Venezia	Pinocchio

Menus, photos, voting and more – free at ZAGAT.com

Best Buys

Everyone loves a bargain, and NYC offers plenty of them. Three things to bear in mind: lunches typically cost 25 to 30% less than dinners, dining in the outer boroughs is a bit less costly than in Manhattan and biannual Restaurant Weeks (usually in January and July) offer some of the city's best for big bargain prix fixes.

ALL YOU CAN EAT

23] Chola
    Churrascaria
    Becco
22] Chennai Garden
    La Baraka
21] Utsav
    Yuka
    Dakshin Indian
    Diwan
    Darbar
20] Porcão Churrascaria
18] Green Field▽

BYO

27] Lucali
26] Tanoreen
    Poke
24] Kuma Inn
23] Wondee Siam
    Phoenix Garden
22] Cube 63
    Peking Duck
    Grand Sichuan
    Tartine
    Nook
21] Meskerem (G Vill)

FAMILY-STYLE

26] Roberto
25] Don Peppe
    Piccolo Angolo
24] Oriental Garden
    Pisticci
    Patricia's
23] Nick's
    Rao's
    Asia de Cuba
    Dominick's

PRE-THEATER/EARLY-B

27] Sugiyama
25] Ouest
    Del Frisco's
    Pepolino
    db Bistro Moderne
24] Palm, The

Bann
Henry's End
Avra
Anthos
23] Ocean Grill
    dévi

PRIX FIXE LUNCH

28] Jean Georges ($24)
    Sushi Yasuda ($23)
27] Gotham Bar & Grill ($31)
    Milos ($24)
26] Oceana ($33)
    Perry Street ($24)
    Felidia ($30)
    15 East ($29)
25] Tabla ($35)
    Maze ($28)
    Fleur de Sel ($29)
    Del Frisco's ($32)

PRIX FIXE DINNER

28] Sushi Yasuda ($23)
    Garden Cafe ($32)
26] Dovetail ($38)
24] Tempo ($32)
    JoJo ($35)
    Rose Water ($28)
    Bond Street ($40)
    Aroma ($35)
    Hangawi ($35)
    Sushiden ($35)

PUB GRUB

22] Corner Bistro
21] J.G. Melon
20] 8 Mile Creek
19] ChipShop
18] Elephant & Castle
    E.U., The
17] Joe Allen
    Landmark Tavern
    Walker's
    Jackson Hole
    O'Neals'
    P.J. Clarke's

BEST BUYS: FULL MENU

Alice's Tea Cup | *American*
Bereket | *Turkish*
Big Wong | *Chinese*
Brennan & Carr | *Sandwiches*
Congee | *Chinese*
Cubana Café | *Cuban*
Dim Sum Go Go | *Chinese*
El Malecon | *Dominican*
Energy Kitchen | *Health Food*
Excellent Dumpling | *Chinese*
Fette Sau | *BBQ*
Great NY Noodle | *Noodle Shop*
Hummus Place | *Israeli/Veg.*
Joe & Pat's | *Italian/Pizza*
Joya | *Thai*
Land | *Thai*
L & B Spumoni | *Dessert/Pizza*
La Taqueria | *Mexican*
La Taza de Oro | *Diner*
Mama's Food | *American*
Mandoo Bar | *Korean*
Mill Basin Deli | *Deli*
Mill Korean | *Korean*
Nha Trang | *Vietnamese*

Nyonya | *Malaysian*
Penelope | *American*
Pepe | *Italian*
Pho Bang | *Vietnamese*
Pink Tea Cup | *Soul/Southern*
Pio Pio | *Peruvian*
Pump Energy | *Health Food*
Quantum Leap | *Health/Veg.*
Rai Rai Ken | *Noodle Shop*
Ramen Setagaya | *Noodle Shop*
Rice | *Eclectic*
Saigon Grill | *Vietnamese*
SEA | *Thai*
Smoke Joint | *BBQ*
Song | *Thai*
Sripraphai | *Thai*
Sweet-n-Tart | *Chinese*
Thai Pavilion | *Thai*
Tierras | *Colombian*
Veselka | *Ukrainian*
Wo Hop | *Chinese*
Wondee Siam | *Thai*
X.O. | *Chinese*
Zaytoons | *Mideastern*

BEST BUYS: SPECIALTY SHOPS

Amy's Bread | *baked goods*
Artichoke Basille's | *pizza*
Better Burger | *burgers*
brgr | *burgers*
burger joint | *burgers*
Burritoville | *Mexican*
Caracas | *arepas*
Carl's | *cheese steaks*
ChikaLicious | *desserts*
Chipotle | *Mexican*
Chocolate Room | *desserts*
Chop't Creative | *salads*
Coals | *pizza*
Corner Bistro | *burgers*
Denino's | *pizza*
Di Fara | *pizza*
Dirty Bird to-go | *chicken*
Dishes | *sandwiches*
Dumpling Man | *dumplings*
Empanada Mama | *empanadas*
Ess-a-Bagel | *deli*
Ferrara | *Italian pastries*
Five Guys | *burgers*
goodburger | *burgers*

Gray's Papaya | *hot dogs*
Grimaldi's | *pizza*
Hale & Hearty | *soup*
Hampton Chutney | *Indian*
Joe's Pizza | *pizza*
Kati Roll Co. | *Indian*
La Bergamote | *French pastries*
La Flor Bakery | *Mexican*
Lenny's | *sandwiches*
Lucali | *pizza*
Nicky's Viet. | *sandwiches*
99 Miles to Philly | *cheese steaks*
Once Upon a Tart | *baked goods*
Papaya King | *hot dogs*
Peanut Butter | *sandwiches*
Pizza 33 | *pizza*
Press 195 | *sandwiches*
Rickshaw | *dumplings*
Roll-n-Roaster | *sandwiches*
Shake Shack | *burgers*
67 Burger | *burgers*
S'MAC | *mac 'n' cheese*
Sweet Melissa | *pastries*
Waldy's | *pizza*

BEST BUYS: PRIX FIXE MENUS

LUNCH: $35 OR LESS

Abboccato	$24	La Petite Auberge	20
A.J. Maxwell's	25	Le Cirque	28
Al Bustan	25	L'Ecole	28
Amalia	24	Le Perigord	32
Angelo & Maxie's	21	Le Veau d'Or	20
Anthos	28	Lumi	25
Aroma	18	Maze	28
Artisanal	25	Megu	25
Asiate	24	Megu Midtown	29
Atlantic Grill	24	Mercer Kitchen	24
Avra	29	Mia Dona	25
Barbounia	20	Michael Jordan's	24
Becco	18	Milos	24
Bistro du Nord	18	Molyvos	25
Cafe de Bruxelles	15	Montparnasse	20
Cafe Luxembourg	30	Mr. K's	28
Cafe Un Deux Trois	18	Oceana	33
Capsouto Frères	24	Ocean Grill	24
Chiam	21	Olives	24
Chin Chin	28	Orsay	24
Cibo	32	Osteria del Circo	28
davidburke/donatella	24	Pampano	26
Dawat	16	Parlor Steakhouse	25
Del Frisco's	32	Patroon	27
Demarchelier	16	Periyali	26
Django	24	Perry Street	24
Duane Park	24	Petrossian	35
etcetera etcetera	24	Porca Churrascaria	23
Felidia	30	Post House	25
15 East	29	Remi	26
FireBird	30	Roc	30
Five Points	20	Solera	29
Fleur de Sel	29	Spice Market	17
Gallagher's Steak	28	Sushi Yasuda	23
Gascogne	21	Tabla	35
Gavroche	20	Tamarind	24
Geisha	29	Tao	24
Giorgio's/Gramercy	18	Thalia	17
Gotham Bar & Grill	31	Tía Pol	16
Green Field	17	Tocqueville	24
Hangawi	20	Toloache	26
Il Bastardo	15	Trata Estiatorio	25
I Trulli	24	Tribeca Grill	29
Jean Georges	24	Tse Yang	28
JoJo	24	Turkish Kitchen	17
Josephina	24	21 Club	35
Kellari Taverna	25	Uskudar	19
Kings' Carriage	19	ViceVersa	24
Korea Palace	18	Vong	24
La Boîte en Bois	26	Water's Edge	29
La Mangeoire	20	Zarela	17

PT = pre-theater only; where two prices are listed, the first is pre-theater and the second for normal dinner hours.

Abboccato/PT $35	Kellari Taverna 35
Akdeniz. 22	Kittichai/PT 30
Aki/PT 28	La Baraka 27/39
Alouette/PT 25	La Boîte en Bois/PT 38
Amalia. 35	La Bonne Soupe 24
Artisanal/PT. 35	La Mangeoire 28/35
Atlantic Grill/PT 28	La Mediterranée 32
Avra/PT 39	La Petite Auberge 28
Bacchus. 25	Le Refuge 32
Bay Leaf/PT 21	Le Singe Vert/PT 29
Becco. 23	Levana 38
Bistro du Nord/PT 20	Madison Bistro. 32
Bistro Ten 18/PT 29	Maria Pia 22
Bombay Palace 24/30	Marseille 35
Brasserie Julien/PT 25	McCormick/Schmick's/PT. . . 30
Bryant Park Grill/PT. 35	Métisse/PT 22
B. Smith's 32	Metrazur 35
Cafe Centro. 35	Molyvos/PT 37
Cafe Cluny/PT 30	Montparnasse 23
Cafe de Bruxelles/PT. 25	Notaro 26
Cafe des Artistes 35	Ocean Grill/PT 25
Café du Soleil/PT. 22	Osteria del Circo 38
Cafe Loup 28	Ouest/PT. 34
Cafe Un Deux 29	Pascalou/PT. 20
Caffè Grazie 35	Pasha/PT 24
Capsouto Frères 39	Patroon. 39
Cascina/PT. 25	Payard Bistro 37
Caviar Russe/PT 30	Persimmon 37
Cebu/PT 21	Pietrasanta 22
Chez Napoléon. 30	Pigalle/PT 26
Chin Chin 35	Quercy 28
Cibo 35	Remi 38
Cipriani Dolci 40	Savann/PT 21
Cipriani Downtown 39	Sharz Cafe/PT 22
Compass. 35	Sugiyama/PT 32
Cornelia St. Cafe 25	Sushi Yasuda 23
Del Frisco's/PT. 40	Table d'Hôte. 24/29
Demarchelier 26	Tempo. 32
Dervish Turkish/PT 28	Thalia/PT. 35
Divino 27	Toloache/PT 35
etcetera etcetera 35	Tommaso 25
Franchia 30	Trata Estiatorio/PT 25
Garden Cafe 32	Turkish Cuisine 27
Gascogne/PT 28	21 Club/PT 40
Gavroche/PT 20	Utsav/PT 30
Gigino 30	ViceVersa 35
Green Field 28	Village. 29
Hangawi 35	Vincent's 28
Indochine/PT 35	Vivolo/PT. 29
Jarnac 37	Vong/PT. 35
Jewel of India/PT 28	Water Club. 40

RESTAURANT
DIRECTORY

	FOOD	DECOR	SERVICE	COST

Abboccato *Italian*

| | 21 | 19 | 20 | $62 |

W 50s | Blakely Hotel | 136 W. 55th St. (bet. 6th & 7th Aves.) | 212-265-4000 | www.abboccato.com

"Interesting" Italian food, "lovely" digs and a "convenient" location "across from City Center" add up to "delightful" dining at this "discreet" Midtown sibling of Oceana and Molyvos; alright, it's "kinda pricey", but "wonderful" lunch/pre-theater prix fixes are good "value."

Abigael's *Pan-Asian*

| | 19 | 15 | 18 | $52 |

Garment District | 1407 Broadway (bet. 38th & 39th Sts.) | 212-575-1407 | www.abigaels.com

"Upscale kosher" sums up the scene at Jeffrey Nathan's Garment District eatery, a bi-level affair featuring "well-presented" Pan-Asian items as well as steaks and sushi; critics claim it "lacks sparkle", citing "tired" decor and sometimes "spotty" service.

Abigail *American*

| | - | - | - | M |

Prospect Heights | 807 Classon Ave. (St. Johns Pl.) | Brooklyn | 718-399-3200 | www.abigailbrooklyn.com

Chef Abigail Hitchcock (CamaJe) goes outer-borough via this spacious, brick-lined New American in Prospect Heights, offering three squares a day including midpriced small plates at dinner that can be paired with an extensive wine list; N.B. cooking classes in the downstairs lounge are in the works.

Aburiya Kinnosuke *Japanese*

| | 25 | 20 | 21 | $50 |

E 40s | 213 E. 45th St. (bet. 2nd & 3rd Aves.) | 212-867-5454 | www.aburiyakinnosuke.com/aburiya.htm

"Original" is the word for this "offbeat", sushi-free Midtown Japanese grill known for "authentic" robata dishes and "homemade fresh tofu"; "polite" service, fair pricing and meticulous "attention to detail" make for consistently "satisfying" dining.

Acappella *Italian*

| | 24 | 21 | 24 | $70 |

TriBeCa | 1 Hudson St. (Chambers St.) | 212-240-0163 | www.acappella-restaurant.com

"One of TriBeCa's fanciest Italians", this "special-occasion" Tuscan features "excellent" food served by a "fawning" staff skilled in "old-school" tableside preparation; "low lighting", "pretty" decor and "amazing" gratis grappa "make the hefty tabs easier to digest."

Accademia di Vino *Italian*

| | 20 | 19 | 18 | $51 |

E 60s | 1081 Third Ave. (bet. 63rd & 64th Sts.) | 212-888-6333 | www.accademiadivino.com

A "vibrant addition" to the UES, this "hopping" Italian enoteca/trattoria serves everything from "delicious small plates" to "big tasty meals", washed down with an "epic wine list"; the "service could be better" and the meandering, "cavernous" setting can get "crazy noisy", yet most call it a "keeper."

Acqua *Italian*

| | 18 | 16 | 17 | $37 |

W 90s | 718 Amsterdam Ave. (bet. 94th & 95th Sts.) | 212-222-2752 | www.acquanyc.com

"Neighborhood folks" tout this "trusty" UWS Italian "standby" where the eats are "reliable", the vibe "relaxed" and the "price is right"; occasionally service can be "thinner than the pizza crust", but it's still more than "decent all around."

Acqua at Peck Slip *Italian*   ▽ 19 | 17 | 18 | $37

Seaport | 21 Peck Slip (Water St.) | 212-349-4433 | www.acquarestaurantnyc.com

Set in a "prize location on a cobblestoned street", this "unpretentious" Seaport Italian offers "hearty", "modestly priced" dishes in "laid-back" environs; regulars cite a "Euro feel" and add it's best when you can "sit outside with a view of the harbor."

Z NEW Adour *French*   26 | 27 | 26 | $120

E 50s | St. Regis Hotel | 2 E. 55th St. (bet. 5th & Madison Aves.) | 212-710-2277 | www.adour-stregis.com

A "triumph for Monsieur Ducasse", this "glamorous" new Midtown French in the St. Regis offers "sophisticated", "wine-centric" dining in a "sumptuous" David Rockwell makeover of the former Lespinasse space; chef Tony Esnault's "approachable" yet *très*-haute menu is "sublime on all counts" and service is equally "flawless", so even though it "wallops the wallet", most agree it's nothing less than "wonderful."

Adrienne's Pizzabar ☻ *Pizza*   24 | 16 | 15 | $24

Financial District | 87 Pearl St. (bet. Coenties Slip & Hanover Sq.) | 212-248-3838 | www.adriennespizzabar.com

"Addictive", "crispy" pies for "bargain" tabs draw hordes to this "happening" Financial District pizzeria that's a suits "zoo" at prime times; "subpar" service and "nothing-special" decor are trumped by outdoor seating that feels like a "movie set of old NY."

Aesop's Tables ⓜ *American/Mediterranean*   ▽ 22 | 20 | 20 | $42

Staten Island | 1233 Bay St. (Maryland Ave.) | 718-720-2005

"Manhattan style" comes to Staten Island via this "semi-upscale" Med–New American offering a variety of "interesting" repasts and "attentive service"; it's especially "enjoyable" in the summer when you can "sit in the garden."

Afghan Kebab House *Afghan*   19 | 10 | 17 | $25

E 70s | 1345 Second Ave. (bet. 70th & 71st Sts.) | 212-517-2776
W 50s | 764 Ninth Ave. (bet. 51st & 52nd Sts.) | 212-307-1612
Jackson Heights | 74-16 37th Ave. (bet. 74th & 75th Sts.) | Queens | 718-565-0471

"Flavorful" eats led by "succulent" kebabs turn up at this "no-frills" Afghan trio; sure, the "dingy" looks and "harried" staff may be "too authentic", but the "bargain" tabs – and BYO policy – win most over.

Agave *Southwestern*   19 | 18 | 16 | $37

W Village | 140 Seventh Ave. S. (bet. Charles & W. 10th Sts.) | 212-989-2100 | www.agaveny.com

The mood's "festive" at this "reasonably priced" West Villager serving "reliably spicy" Southwestern grub in a "laid-back", whitewashed room; though the tequila list is "impressive", the same can't be said for the "loud" acoustics and "hit-or-miss" service.

Agnanti *Greek*   24 | 15 | 18 | $35

Bay Ridge | 7802 Fifth Ave. (78th St.) | Brooklyn | 718-833-7033 ☻

(continued)

(continued)

Agnanti

Astoria | 19-06 Ditmars Blvd. (19th St.) | Queens | 718-545-4554
www.agnantimeze.com

"Out of the way but closer than Greece", these "unpretentious" tavernas in Astoria and Bay Ridge draw crowds with "delectable", "down-home" Hellenic fare, "gracious" service and "decent prices"; cognoscenti show up "when the weather's nice" for alfresco seating.

	FOOD	DECOR	SERVICE	COST

NEW Ago *Italian* | 17 | 21 | 18 | $79

TriBeCa | The Greenwich Hotel | 379 Greenwich St. (N. Moore St.) | 212-925-3797

Robert De Niro's latest TriBeCa endeavor is an "attractive" Tuscan spin-off of siblings in Hollywood, Vegas and South Beach; the food is "good", but not good enough to justify the "expensive" tabs and service still working out "early-days" kinks, though a bar scene for "young, fabulous" types helps.

Aja ● *Pan-Asian* | 20 | 21 | 18 | $43

E 50s | 1068 First Ave. (58th St.) | 212-888-8008 | www.ajaasiancuisine.com
NEW G Village | 432 Sixth Ave. (bet. 9th & 10th Sts.) | 212-253-7100

"Something a little different", these "dark", "sleek" dens offer "appealing" Pan-Asian fare that's priced to suit a "young crowd" that can abide "unZen-like" noise; sure, they have "a lot of style", but the "flashy" decor (giant Buddhas and ponds with live fish) leads some to label them "Tao wannabes."

A.J. Maxwell's Steakhouse *Steak* | 22 | 19 | 22 | $65

W 40s | 57 W. 48th St. (bet. 5th & 6th Aves.) | 212-262-6200 | www.ajmaxwells.com

"Midtown suits" gnaw on *Flintstone*-size" steaks at this "above-average" Rock Center chophouse set in a "sparse" room decorated with a mural left from its days as the "Forum of the Twelve Caesars"; "accommodating" service makes the "expense-account" tabs easier to digest.

Akdeniz ⑤ *Turkish* | 21 | 13 | 19 | $31

W 40s | 19 W. 46th St. (bet. 5th & 6th Aves.) | 212-575-2307 | www.akdenizturkishusa.com

"Mideast meets Midtown" at this "tiny" Turk offering "precisely cooked, delicately seasoned" dishes served by an "efficient" staff; the "no-ambiance" setting is "not made for lingering", but it's a "solid" option for "bargain"-hunters thanks to a $21.95 dinner prix fixe.

Aki *Japanese* | 26 | 13 | 20 | $44

G Village | 181 W. Fourth St. (bet. Barrow & Jones Sts.) | 212-989-5440

"Tables fill early" at this "tiny", nondescript Village Japanese known for "imaginative" sushi "beautifully presented" with "Caribbean flair"; devotees dub it a "Nobu-like experience on a small scale", enhanced by "gracious service" and a "bargain" $28 pre-theater prix fixe.

A La Turka ● *Turkish* | 18 | 12 | 16 | $35

E 70s | 1417 Second Ave. (74th St.) | 212-744-2424 | www.alaturkarestaurant.com

"Well-prepared, no-surprises" Turkish fare turns up at this UES "neighborhood" joint offering a "wide range" of "gently priced" kebabs, meze

	FOOD	DECOR	SERVICE	COST

and the like; the decor "won't whirl your turban", but at least you'll "eat in peace" since it can be "hard to flag down a waiter."

Alberto *Italian* | 22 | 19 | 22 | $46 |

Forest Hills | 98-31 Metropolitan Ave. (70th Ave.) | Queens | 718-268-7860
"Classic" Italian dishes "prepared with care", "terrific service" and a "warm", "old-world" vibe have made this Forest Hills vet a "longtime standby"; maybe "seniors rule the roost", but everyone "feels at home" at this "reliable" place.

Al Bustan *Lebanese* | 19 | 14 | 17 | $45 |

E 50s | 827 Third Ave. (bet. 50th & 51st Sts.) | 212-759-5933 | www.albustanny.com
"Reasonably authentic Lebanese" dishes lie ahead at this "old-school" Midtowner that's either "decent" or "going downhill", depending who's talking; "uninspiring" decor and "up-and-down" service are overlooked thanks to "ok" pricing.

Alcala *Spanish* | ▽ 22 | 18 | 20 | $52 |

E 40s | 342 E. 46th St. (bet. 1st & 2nd Aves.) | 212-370-1866 | www.alcalarestaurant.com
An "international" crowd peppered with "U.N. diplomats" convenes at this "charming" Midtowner for Spanish cuisine with "Basque variations"; service manages to be both "friendly" and "unobtrusive", while "eating in the garden makes the tapas taste even better."

Alchemy *American* | 17 | 17 | 18 | $32 |

Park Slope | 56 Fifth Ave. (bet. Bergen St. & St. Marks Pl.) | Brooklyn | 718-636-4385 | www.alchemybrooklyn.com
"Bringing the gastropub to Brooklyn", this "cute", "jam-packed" Park Slope New American has quickly turned to gold thanks to "good burgers" and a "great beer selection"; service "hiccups" notwithstanding, it's a "welcome addition" for its moderate pricing alone.

☑ Al Di La *Italian* | 26 | 18 | 22 | $46 |

Park Slope | 248 Fifth Ave. (Carroll St.) | Brooklyn | 718-783-4565 | www.aldilatrattoria.com
"Paradise" – save for the "no-reservations policy" – this "exceptional" Park Slope Venetian is always "mobbed", so insiders "dine early or late to avoid the crush", or cool their heels at the "cute" wine bar around the corner; the cooking is "transcendent", the service "professional" and the cost so much less than Manhattan that some surveyors are "considering moving to Brooklyn."

Aleo *Mediterranean/Italian* | 19 | 16 | 19 | $44 |

Flatiron | 7 W. 20th St. (5th Ave.) | 212-691-8136 | www.aleorestaurant.com
"Tasty", "simply prepared" Med-Italian dishes turn up at this "pleasant" Flatiron venue where moderate tabs and "helpful" servers enhance the "neighborhood feel"; insiders say the "outdoor garden is hard to beat."

Alfama *Portuguese* | 21 | 19 | 21 | $49 |

W Village | 551 Hudson St. (Perry St.) | 212-645-2500 | www.alfamarestaurant.com
This "genteel" Village Portuguese lined in "pretty tile" is "NY's answer to Lisbon" thanks to "authentic" dishes ("bring on the bacalao!") and

an "amazing port selection"; "gracious" service and a "charming" vibe make it right for a "romantic evening", especially during Wednesdays' live *fado* sessions.

Al Forno Pizzeria *Pizza* | 20 | 12 | 17 | $24 |

E 70s | 1484 Second Ave. (bet. 77th & 78th Sts.) | 212-249-5103

"Family-friendly" and "reasonably priced", this "basic" UES pizza purveyor rolls out "tasty" brick-oven thin-crust pies as well as "better-than-average" traditional fare; a "noisy", "more-diner-than-restaurant" ambiance makes it an "eat-and-run kind of place."

Alfredo of Rome *Italian* | 18 | 19 | 18 | $49 |

W 40s | 4 W. 49th St. (bet. 5th & 6th Aves.) | 212-397-0100 | www.alfredos.com

No surprise, the "incredibly rich" fettuccine Alfredo is *molto bene* at this "sleek" Rock Center Italian with "Hirschfeld drawings" on the walls and "tourists with fanny packs" in the seats; it may be "pricey" and "service could be better", but you can't beat the location.

Algonquin Hotel Round Table *American* | 16 | 23 | 19 | $55 |

W 40s | Algonquin Hotel | 59 W. 44th St. (bet. 5th & 6th Aves.) | 212-840-6800 | www.algonquinhotel.com

The place may be "full of NY literary history", but the American grub's "rather ho-hum" at this "clubby" Theater District "throwback"; ergo, some suggest "skipping dinner" and having "classic cocktails" in the comfortable, wood-paneled lobby or checking out the "cabaret in the Oak Room" instead.

Alias *American* | 21 | 15 | 19 | $36 |

LES | 76 Clinton St. (Rivington St.) | 212-505-5011 | www.aliasrestaurant.com

"Something for everyone" could be the motto of this "casual" LES American purveying "gourmet comfort food" in a "funky" storefront setting; you can count on staffers to serve with "verve", and the "excellent" pricing is a plus (especially Sunday evening's "bargain" $30 prix fixe).

Ali Baba *Turkish* | 22 | 14 | 18 | $31 |

NEW **E 40s** | 862 Second Ave. (46th St.) | 212-888-8622
Murray Hill | 212 E. 34th St. (bet. 2nd & 3rd Aves.) | 212-683-9206
www.alibabaturkishcuisine.com

"Popular" is putting it mildly at this "fez-tastic" Murray Hill Turk that's "always crowded to the bursting point" thanks to "deelish" dishes at "can't-be-beat" prices; service is "warm" and the garden a "delight", so even if you "wait 1,001 nights for a table", it's "worth it"; N.B. the new U.N.-area offshoot opened post-Survey.

Alice's Tea Cup *American* | 19 | 20 | 17 | $25 |

E 60s | 156 E. 64th St. (Lexington Ave.) | 212-486-9200
E 80s | 220 E. 81st St. (bet. 2nd & 3rd Aves.) | 212-734-4832
W 70s | 102 W. 73rd St. (bet. Amsterdam & Columbus Aves.) | 212-799-3006
www.alicesteacup.com

A "fantasy world" for "ladies and little ladies", these "darling" tearooms offer American finger sandwiches, "scrumptious scones" and "giggly chitchat" over an "extravagant assortment" of cuppas; it may be a "madhouse" with "sluggish service" and "ridiculous waits", but ultimately it's "so cute you can't resist."

NEW Allegretti ⓈFrench | - | - | - | E |

Flatiron | 46 W. 22nd St. (bet. 5th & 6th Aves.) | 212-206-0555 |
www.allegrettinyc.com

Chef Alain Allegretti (ex Le Cirque, Atelier) strikes out on his own with
this Flatiron arrival offering elegant, pricey French fare from his native
Nice; housed in the sleekly redone former Arezzo space, it retains the
wood-burning oven ideal for roasted fish and meat dishes, and has already become a hot ticket for power couples like Bill and Hillary.

NEW Allen & Delancey ● American | 24 | 24 | 20 | $67 |

LES | 115 Allen St. (Delancey St.) | 212-253-5400 | www.allenanddelancey.net
Neil Ferguson (ex Gordon Ramsay) brings "luxury dining to the LES"
with this "edgy" yet "polished" New American turning out "marvelous"
"high-end" meals in a "divine", brick-walled setting "lit with many candles"; "amiable service" enhances a mood so "seductive" that romeos
report "if you can't seal the deal here, you may as well quit."

Alma Mexican | 20 | 21 | 18 | $35 |

Carroll Gardens | 187 Columbia St., 2nd fl. (Degraw St.) | Brooklyn |
718-643-5400 | www.almarestaurant.com

"Upscale" Mexican grub for "reasonable" dough "justifies the trek" to
this "popular" Carroll Gardens cantina with "drop-dead Manhattan
skyline views" from its roof deck as a bonus; "iffy service" and "long
waits" are blunted by "enormous mojitos" and "killer" margs.

Alouette ● French | 20 | 17 | 20 | $44 |

W 90s | 2588 Broadway (bet. 97th & 98th Sts.) | 212-222-6808 |
www.alouettenyc.com

"Tiny and atmospheric", this "genteel" UWS "neighborhood standby"
matches "classic *bonne femme*" French cooking with a "Left Bank" vibe
and "welcoming" service; though tables are "tight", "decent" pricing
and a $25 early-bird prix fixe "steal" seal the deal.

Alta Mediterranean | 23 | 22 | 20 | $46 |

G Village | 64 W. 10th St. (bet. 5th & 6th Aves.) | 212-505-7777 |
www.altarestaurant.com

An "inviting fireplace" lends a "ski lodge" feel to this "romantic" Village
"hideaway" specializing in "inventive" Med small plates; service is
"rapid" and the wine list "fabulous", but the price of these "delicious
morsels" can "add up quickly"; P.S. "order the Brussels sprouts."

Alto Ⓢ Italian | 25 | 23 | 23 | $83 |

E 50s | 11 E. 53rd St. (bet. 5th & Madison Aves.) | 212-308-1099 |
www.altorestaurant.com

Ideal for "special occasions", this "top-drawer" Midtowner "reaches
for world-class" via chef Michael White's "sublime" Italian cooking
showcased in a "sleek" space dominated by a "backlit wall of wine bot-
tles"; despite "alto prices", the "smooth" service and "relaxing" mood
make this one a "destination" for "elite" types.

Ama Italian | 23 | 19 | 21 | $52 |

SoHo | 48 MacDougal St. (bet. King & Prince Sts.) | 212-358-1707 |
www.amanyc.com

"Quiet and elegant", this white-walled SoHo Southern Italian specializes in "zesty" Puglian dishes that arrive "impeccably prepared" with

"original flourishes"; though service can range from "casual" to "thoughtful", it's generally "excellent" and "you can always get a table."

Amalia *Mediterranean*
21 | 23 | 19 | $58

W 50s | 204 W. 55th St. (bet. B'way & 7th Ave.) | 212-245-1234 | www.amalia-nyc.com

"Flavorful" Mediterranean dishes compete with an "ornate", "urban cave" setting (think black-glass chandeliers, distressed brick walls) at this "stylish" Midtowner; "service could be better" and the pricing's "a tad high", but its "hip, trendy" patrons "don't mind going for broke" here.

Amaranth ● *Mediterranean*
18 | 17 | 18 | $55

E 60s | 21 E. 62nd St. (bet. 5th & Madison Aves.) | 212-980-6700 | www.amaranthrestaurant.com

"People-watching counts more than eating" at this "pricey", "very UES" Mediterranean; its "loyal local" following – heavy on the "sugar daddies" and "affectation aficionados" – likes its "clubby" mood and "flattering lighting", not the "tight", "loud" setting.

Amarone ● *Italian*
18 | 14 | 18 | $40

W 40s | 686 Ninth Ave. (bet. 47th & 48th Sts.) | 212-245-6060 | www.amaronenyc.com

"Daily fresh pastas" take center stage on the "basic Italian" menu of this "can't-go-wrong" Hell's Kitchen "mainstay"; "nothing-fancy" decor doesn't keep fans from piling into its "snug" space – it's "always busy" pre-theater, thanks to a "quick" staff and "reasonable" tabs.

Amazing 66 *Chinese*
21 | 10 | 12 | $25

Chinatown | 66 Mott St. (bet. Bayard & Canal Sts.) | 212-334-0099

This C-town Cantonese "lives up to its name" with "consistently high-quality" eats served in "generous" portions; a "fantastic" $5.25 lunch special and "interesting" menu items like conch and frog outweigh the "rush-rush", "marginal"-English servers.

Amber ● *Pan-Asian*
20 | 20 | 19 | $38

E 80s | 1406 Third Ave. (80th St.) | 212-249-5020
NEW W 70s | 221 Columbus Ave. (70th St.) | 212-799-8100

"Full of energy", this Upper East Side "hot spot" and its new crosstown twin offer Pan-Asian plates, "decent sushi and "tasty" drinks, though the main draw is the "trendy", "Tao"-esque vibe; the "young" following tolerates "deafening" decibels in exchange for "eager" service and "moderate" pricing.

American Girl Place Cafe *American*
12 | 22 | 19 | $36

E 40s | American Girl Place | 609 Fifth Ave., 3rd fl. (49th St.) | 212-644-1145 | www.americangirlplace.com

Mothers and daughters share a "bonding experience" at this American cafe in a Midtown toy store where the meals play second fiddle to "the dolls, the decor and the memories"; the "high tea" is especially "fun", despite "overpriced", "nothing-special" food.

Amma *Indian*
24 | 17 | 20 | $46

E 50s | 246 E. 51st St. (bet. 2nd & 3rd Aves.) | 212-644-8330 | www.ammanyc.com

"*Amma mia!*" – the "talented kitchen" at this "haute" Midtowner turns out "subtly spiced" Northern Indian cuisine that's right "up there with the best"; the townhouse setting may be getting "tired", but the "helpful" staff helps make it "worth the extra rupees."

Ammos *Greek*
21 | 21 | 19 | $53

E 40s | 52 Vanderbilt Ave. (bet. 44th & 45th Sts.) | 212-922-9999 🗷
Astoria | 20-30 Steinway St. (bet. 20th Ave. & 20th Rd.) | Queens | 718-726-7900 ●Ⓜ
www.ammosnewyork.com

These "chic" Greeks in Astoria and opposite Grand Central have added some Med items to their "delightful" lineup of "nouveau" Hellenica and "incredibly fresh" seafood; an "island holiday" vibe and "friendly" service amm-eliorate the "by-the-pound" pricing.

Amorina *Pizza*
▽ 24 | 16 | 21 | $24

Prospect Heights | 624 Vanderbilt Ave. (Prospect Pl.) | Brooklyn | 718-230-3030 | www.amorinapizza.com

"Perfect" Roman-style pizzas come adorned with "adventuresome" toppings (think "cherries") at this "unassuming" Prospect Heights Italian that also turns out a variety of "rustic dishes"; "pleasant service" and pleasing pricing make it particularly "family-friendly."

Amy Ruth's *Soul Food*
21 | 12 | 17 | $24

Harlem | 113 W. 116th St. (bet. Lenox & 7th Aves.) | 212-280-8779 | www.amyruthsharlem.com

"Stick-to-your-ribs" soul food "with a capital S" translates into "long waits" at this Harlem "staple" famed for its "fabulous" fried chicken, waffles and cornbread at "real-deal" prices; it may resemble a "large cafeteria", but the vibe is more like "grandma's kitchen in Alabama."

Amy's Bread *Bakery/Sandwiches*
23 | 11 | 16 | $13

Chelsea | Chelsea Mkt. | 75 Ninth Ave. (bet. 15th & 16th Sts.) | 212-462-4338
G Village | 250 Bleecker St. (bet. Carmine & Leroy Sts.) | 212-675-7802
W 40s | 672 Ninth Ave. (bet. 46th & 47th Sts.) | 212-977-2670
www.amysbread.com

Expect "long breadlines" at these bakery/sandwich shop/"carb heaven" combos where fans would "pay for the smell alone"; while the service is appropriately "flaky", "tight" setups make these "utilitarian" pit stops best for "takeout."

Angelica Kitchen ⊘ *Vegan/Vegetarian*
20 | 15 | 17 | $26

E Village | 300 E. 12th St. (bet. 1st & 2nd Aves.) | 212-228-2909 | www.angelicakitchen.com

It's "impossible to eat anything unhealthy" at this "creative", cash-only East Village vegan where "earthy" staffers vend "virtuous" vittles "good enough for omnivores"; maybe the "bland" digs need "sprucing up", but the BYO policy helps keep costs low.

Angelina's *Italian*
23 | 19 | 19 | $59

Staten Island | 26 Jefferson Blvd. (Annadale Rd.) | 718-227-7100
NEW **Staten Island** | 399 Ellis St. (off Arthur Kill Rd.) | 718-227-2900 Ⓜ
www.angelinasristorante.com

"Staten Island's version of Il Mulino", this "top-notch" Italian rolls out "great food", "live music" and "Manhattan-esque" decor, though some debate the "Central Park prices" given the Annadale strip-mall setting; the new Tottenville outpost (opened post-Survey) boasts water views and a sprawling triplex setting.

	FOOD	DECOR	SERVICE	COST

Angelo & Maxie's *Steak*
21 | **18** | **19** | **$56**

Flatiron | 233 Park Ave. S. (19th St.) | 212-220-9200

NEW Maxie's Bar & Grill ● *American*

Flatiron | 233 Park Ave. S. (enter on 19th St., bet. Irving Pl. & Park Ave. S.) | 212-979-7800

www.angelo-maxies.com

"Not for the faint of heart", this "hopping" Flatiron "carnivore cavern" lures "ravenous suits" with "gargantuan" steaks and an "achingly noisy" "nightclub atmosphere"; for "a little less craziness", there's now its "inexpensive" new next-door bar-and-grill spin-off focusing on burgers.

Angelo's of Mulberry Street Ⓜ *Italian*
23 | **16** | **20** | **$46**

Little Italy | 146 Mulberry St. (bet. Grand & Hester Sts.) | 212-966-1277 | www.angelomulberry.com

"One of the few Little Italy originals left", this "tried-and-true" Neapolitan "mainstay" has been dishing out "red-sauce classics" for the "right price" since 1902; an "on-the-ball" staff, "tacky" decor and "touristy crowd" are all part of the package, ditto the "lines out the door" most weekends.

Angelo's Pizzeria *Pizza*
19 | **11** | **14** | **$24**

E 50s | 1043 Second Ave. (55th St.) | 212-521-3600
W 50s | 117 W. 57th St. (bet. 6th & 7th Aves.) | 212-333-4333
W 50s | 1697 Broadway (bet. 53rd & 54th Sts.) | 212-245-8811
www.angelospizzany.com

Midtowners dig this "easy, breezy" pizzeria trio dispensing "solid" pies with "nicely charred crusts" as well as a "limited menu" of "hit-the-spot" Italian standards; "good-value" prices trump the "laughable service" and "typical" surroundings.

Angus McIndoe ● *American*
17 | **15** | **19** | **$41**

W 40s | 258 W. 44th St. (bet. B'way & 8th Ave.) | 212-221-9222 | www.angusmcindoe.com

"Post-theater" central for off-duty "Broadway stars", this "cheerful" Times Square triplex is the kind of place where the "celebrity quotient" outshines the "straightforward", "reasonably priced" American eats; P.S. your "waiter's mood may depend on how his audition went."

ⓩ Annisa *American*
27 | **22** | **26** | **$77**

G Village | 13 Barrow St. (bet. 7th Ave. S. & W. 4th St.) | 212-741-6699 | www.annisarestaurant.com

A "Village destination for foodies", Anita Lo's "civilized" New American "boutique" showcases her "remarkable", "complex" dishes in "hushed", "minimalist" environs; "cordial service" adds gloss to the "sensual experience", and though "over-the-top" tabs may break the spell, the $75 tasting menu lets you "treat yourself" to a glimpse of "gustatory heaven" for a bit less.

Anthony's *Italian*
19 | **15** | **20** | **$27**

Park Slope | 426A Seventh Ave. (bet. 14th & 15th Sts.) | Brooklyn | 718-369-8315 | www.anthonysbrooklyn.com

"Crispy, tasty pizza" is the main attraction at this "low-key" Park Slope Southern Italian, a "red-sauce kind of place" with a "friendly", "feel-at-home" vibe; "when you don't want to cook" and "don't want to pay a whole lot", look no further.

	FOOD	DECOR	SERVICE	COST

Anthos ☒ *Greek*

24 | **20** | **21** | **$69**

W 50s | 36 W. 52nd St. (bet. 5th & 6th Aves.) | 212-582-6900 |
www.anthosnyc.com

"Brilliant flavor combinations" underlie the "thrilling" menu of this
"nouvelle Greek" "class operation" from chef Michael Psilakis and restaurateur Donatella Arpaia; it's already a "Midtown business standby"
owing to the "adult" mood, "formal" service and "Aristotle Onassis"-
worthy bills, though a few say the "rather bland decor" needs work.

Antica Venezia *Italian*

22 | **21** | **25** | **$52**

W Village | 396 West St. (W. 10th St.) | 212-229-0606 | www.avnyc.com

"Solicitous" service sets the "affable" tone at this "off-the-beaten-
path" Village Italian purveying "pricey", "well-prepared" pastas plus
"grilled delights" with lots of "little extras" (like gratis "after-dinner
cordials"); romantics tout its "dimly lit" room and time their visit to
catch the "lovely" sunset over the Hudson.

Antonucci *Italian*

21 | **15** | **17** | **$52**

E 80s | 170 E. 81st St. (bet. Lexington & 3rd Aves.) | 212-570-5100

A "real neighborhood sleeper", this "charming" UES Italian serves "interesting twists on typical dishes" in an "upbeat" storefront enhanced
by "pleasant" service; "noisy" acoustics make the sidewalk seats "on
a quiet street" particularly enticing.

A.O.C. ❶ *French*

19 | **17** | **17** | **$38**

W Village | 314 Bleecker St. (Grove St.) | 212-675-9463 | www.aocnyc.com

A.O.C. Bistro ❶ *French*

Park Slope | 259 Fifth Ave. (Garfield Pl.) | Brooklyn | 718-788-1515

"More than respectable" bistro fare turns up at this "appealing" West
Village "taste of Paris" that has spawned a "welcome" Park Slope offshoot; "good value" and "adorable" back gardens make for "A.O.K."
dining, provided you don't mind "playing find the waiter."

NEW Apiary *American*

- | **-** | **-** | **M**

E Village | 60 Third Ave. (bet. 10th & 11th Sts.) | 212-254-0888 |
www.apiarynyc.com

This stylish newcomer feels more grown-up than most of its East
Village neighbors, thanks to its design partner, Ligne Roset, the
high-end French furniture retailer; the sophistication continues with a
midpriced, globally influenced New American menu paired with a
sizable wine list.

ápizz ☒ *Italian*

24 | **21** | **21** | **$45**

LES | 217 Eldridge St. (bet. Rivington & Stanton Sts.) | 212-253-9199 |
www.apizz.com

Despite a "not-great" LES location, this "cozy little hideaway" draws
in-the-know types with "delightful", "hearth-fired" Italiana straight
from a huge brick oven; given the "romantic", "toasty" vibe and "accommodating" service, fans find it "hard to believe it's still a secret."

applewood Ⓜ *American*

25 | **20** | **22** | **$48**

Park Slope | 501 11th St. (bet. 7th & 8th Aves.) | Brooklyn | 718-768-2044 |
www.applewoodny.com

"Intensely flavored" New American plates are assembled from organic, sustainably grown ingredients "fresh off the farm" at this "charm-

ing", "country inn"–like Park Sloper; "scanty portions" at Manhattan prices are offset by "civilized service", "relaxed" vibrations and an "out-of-this-world" brunch.

AQ Cafe 🛇 *Scandinavian* ▽ 22 | 14 | 14 | $23

Murray Hill | Scandinavia House | 58 Park Ave. (bet. 37th & 38th Sts.) | 212-847-9745 | www.scandinaviahouse.org

"Change-of-pace" seekers like the "tasty" Scandinavian fare proffered at Marcus Samuelsson's lunch-only Murray Hill cafeteria; despite "Ikea" decor and "glacier-slow service", it provides an "Aquavit"-esque experience at a much "lower price"; N.B. a spin-off is coming to Columbus Circle.

🗹 Aquagrill *Seafood* 26 | 19 | 23 | $58

SoHo | 210 Spring St. (6th Ave.) | 212-274-0505 | www.aquagrill.com

"Seafood right off the boat" prepared by chef Jeremy Marshall plus "oysters galore" from a "knockout raw bar" are served by "spot-on" staffers at this "love-at-first-bite" SoHo piscatorium where's it's "fun to sit at the bar and watch the shuckers"; "crowbar" seating and "high prices" aside, it's only "getting better with age."

Aquamarine ● *Pan-Asian* 20 | 21 | 19 | $37

Murray Hill | 713 Second Ave. (bet. 38th & 39th Sts.) | 212-297-1880

Pretty "trendy" for Murray Hill, this popular Pan-Asian purveyor provides everything from sizzling platters to "imaginative" sushi in a "glitzy" space that includes a "water wall" and a "busy bar"; service can be "inconsistent" when it gets "hectic", but rates are always "reasonable."

🗹 Aquavit *Scandinavian* 25 | 24 | 24 | $109

E 50s | 65 E. 55th St. (bet. Madison & Park Aves.) | 212-307-7311 | www.aquavit.org

"Still working his Scandinavian magic", Marcus Samuelsson turns out "exquisite" meals paired with "sublime" namesake cocktails at this "handsome", "highbrow" Midtowner manned by a "meticulous" crew; "be prepared to spend a small fortune" on the prix fixe–only dinner, though the stripped-down, à la carte front cafe is "just as good" and "costs less."

Arabelle *American/French* ▽ 22 | 25 | 24 | $96

E 60s | Plaza Athénée Hotel | 37 E. 64th St. (bet. Madison & Park Aves.) | 212-606-4647 | www.arabellerestaurant.com

"Special occasions with your significant other" are made for this prix fixe–only French-American "stunner" in the Plaza Athénée, where "classic" food, "tuxedoed waiters" and "swank surroundings" can make one feel like an "old-world aristocrat"; indeed, everything here is "beautifully old-fashioned", save for the contemporary "high-end" pricing that may account for the lack of crowds.

Areo ● 🅼 *Italian* 25 | 19 | 21 | $51

Bay Ridge | 8424 Third Ave. (bet. 84th & 85th Sts.) | Brooklyn | 718-238-0079

Set in the "real Little Italy – Bay Ridge" – this "old-time" Italian offers "wonderful" fare in "classic" digs tended by an "excellent" staff; still, the "food is only part of the show" what with all the "singles on the loose" sporting "gold chains" and "heavy cologne."

Arirang Hibachi Steakhouse *Japanese*

20	18	20	$37

Bay Ridge | 8814 Fourth Ave. (bet. 88th & 89th Sts.) | Brooklyn | 718-238-9880

Staten Island | 23A Nelson Ave. (Locust St.) | 718-966-9600
www.partyonthegrill.com

"Corny" it may be, but the hibachi "chef theatrics" at these "lively" Japanese steakhouses are "always a blast", especially for the kiddies; despite the "typical", "Benihana-wannabe" offerings, they're usually "crowded" and "noisy" – maybe because prices are so "decent."

Arno ⊠ *Italian*

▽ 20	17	20	$47

Garment District | 141 W. 38th St. (bet. B'way & 7th Ave.) | 212-944-7420 | www.arnoristorante.com

Now celebrating its 25th anniversary, this "steady" Northern Italian "institution" offers "traditional" eats for a "not bad" price in the "restaurant-challenged" Garment District; "excellent" service helps patrons overlook the "no ambiance" problem.

Aroma ● *Italian*

24	18	23	$40

NoHo | 36 E. Fourth St. (bet. Bowery & Lafayette St.) | 212-375-0100 | www.aromanyc.com

"Pleasant" is the word on this "charming", "bread box-size" NoHo Italian known for its "extensive wine list" and a menu culled from the day's "farmer's market"; it's a "tight" squeeze and "always filled", but "warm service" and modest pricing are ample distractions.

Arqua *Italian*

22	20	21	$60

TriBeCa | 281 Church St. (White St.) | 212-334-1888 | www.arquaristorante.com

"Around for a long time" and "as good as ever", this TriBeCa Northern Italian serves "satisfying", "upscale" fare in a beautifully "minimalist" room recalling a town square in Tuscany; it's "not cheap, but well worth it" for the "gracious service" and "adult atmosphere" alone.

Arté *Italian*

17	16	19	$43

G Village | 21 E. Ninth St. (bet. 5th Ave. & University Pl.) | 212-473-0077 | www.arterestaurant.com

"One of a vanishing breed", this "traditional" Village Italian draws "neighborhood" types with "simple", "old-style" eats and a "cozy fireplace"; perhaps it's "seen better days" decorwise, but "amiable" service and "reasonable" costs make it a "keeper."

Arté Café *Italian*

18	17	16	$36

W 70s | 106 W. 73rd St. (bet. Amsterdam & Columbus Aves.) | 212-501-7014 | www.artecafenyc.com

"Solid red-sauce" meals are the "staple" of this "serviceable" UWS Italian, home to "good values", "hectic" service and a "lovely garden"; "lunch is quiet, dinner is not", and the $15.95 early-bird is a "bargain."

NEW Artichoke Basille's Pizza ●≠ *Pizza*

24	8	12	$13

E Village | 328 E. 14th St. (bet. 1st & 2nd Aves.) | 212-228-2004

"Patience is a virtue" at this tiny new East Village slice joint that's drawn "huge lines down the block" from day one thanks to a signature "artichoke dip"-topped pie so "spectacular" that the "closet"-size di-

| | FOOD | DECOR | SERVICE | COST |

mensions and "snarky" service are forgotten; P.S. it's already notorious
for keeping "crazy hours", so call ahead.

Artie's Seafood/Steak
| 23 | 17 | 20 | $38 |

Bronx | 394 City Island Ave. (Ditmars St.) | 718-885-9885 |
www.artiesofcityisland.com

"City Island locals" convene for "superior seafood" and "tasty" steaks,
"plated with pizzazz", at this "down-to-earth" surf 'n' turfer on the
scene since 1967; despite "outdated" decor and "no water view",
"reasonable" tabs and "caring service" keep regulars regular.

Artie's Deli Deli
| 18 | 10 | 14 | $23 |

W 80s | 2290 Broadway (bet. 82nd & 83rd Sts.) | 212-579-5959 |
www.arties.com

To relive "old times", try this "industrial-strength", low-budget UWS
deli known for its "two-hands-on sandwiches" and "penicillin"-like
matzo ball soup; despite the "fluorescent" decor and servers "as salty
as the pickles", purists pout it "feels inauthentic."

☑ Artisanal French
| 23 | 20 | 20 | $54 |

Murray Hill | 2 Park Ave. (enter on 32nd St., bet. Madison & Park Aves.) |
212-725-8585 | www.artisanalbistro.com

A "mind-boggling mecca" for "cheese mavens", Terrance Brennan's
French brasserie in Murray Hill (aka "fondue heaven") also provides
"fairly priced" "comfort food à la français" and "charmant" service;
regulars brush up on their "lip reading" ahead of time since the "good-
looking" space tends toward "cacophonous."

Arturo's Pizzeria ● Italian
| 21 | 12 | 16 | $26 |

G Village | 106 W. Houston St. (Thompson St.) | 212-677-3820

"Old Greenwich Village" lives on via this "speakeasy"-style Italian zip-
ping out "zesty", "tasty" pies from its coal-fired oven; though well
"worn around the edges" after 50-odd years in operation, it's beloved
for its "quirky staff", "cheap" tabs and "wonderful live jazz."

Asia de Cuba Asian/Cuban
| 23 | 24 | 20 | $61 |

Murray Hill | Morgans Hotel | 237 Madison Ave. (bet. 37th & 38th Sts.) |
212-726-7755 | www.chinagrillmgt.com

There's "glitz on both ends of the fork" as "eye candy" and "exotic"
Asian-Cubana collide at this "chichi" Murray Hiller where the "communal table is the best place in town to chat with strangers"; Philippe
Starck's "stunning", all-white *Miami Vice* decor still impresses, ditto
pricing as "high" as the decibels, yet some say the scene is "getting
a little old."

Asiakan Japanese/Pan-Asian
| 19 | 18 | 20 | $32 |

W 90s | 710 Amsterdam Ave. (bet. 94th & 95th Sts.) | 212-280-8878

"Artistic sushi" and "new-wave" Pan-Asian items fill out the menu of
this "snazzy" Upper Westsider; service is "courteous" and the "neon"
ambiance "fun", provided "you can get over the TV screens."

☑ Asiate American/Asian
| 24 | 29 | 24 | $111 |

W 60s | Mandarin Oriental Hotel | 80 Columbus Circle, 35th fl.
(60th St. at B'way) | 212-805-8881 | www.mandarinoriental.com

"Dead-on" Central Park views and a dining room so "gorgeous" that
it's rated No. 1 for Decor add "wow" to this "tranquil haven" high in

Columbus Circle's Mandarin Oriental Hotel; new chef Toni Robertson offers a near "flawless" menu of Asian–New American dishes, while "top-notch service" adds to the "knockout" experience; true, the "splurge"-worthy tabs are stunning in their own right, but the $24 prix fixe "lunch is a deal."

Aspen ●☒ *American* | 18 | 23 | 16 | $48 |

Flatiron | 30 W. 22nd St. (bet. 5th & 6th Aves.) | 212-645-5040 | www.aspen-nyc.com

"Wear black", "be young" and "drop names" to fit in at this "clublike" Flatiron New American offering "delicious" tapas and "après-work" scenery in a faux "Swiss chalet" setting complete with "roaring log fire"; too bad the "high prices" match the staff's "high attitude."

Atlantic Grill *Seafood* | 23 | 19 | 20 | $53 |

E 70s | 1341 Third Ave. (bet. 76th & 77th Sts.) | 212-988-9200 | www.brguestrestaurants.com

"So fresh you want to slap it", the "sure-bet" seafood at Steven Hanson's UES "classic" continues to draw "teeming throngs" with "friendly" service and "almost reasonable" tabs; when the "festive" goings-on reach "rugby-scrum" proportions, regulars head for the "back room for conversation."

August *European* | 21 | 20 | 19 | $47 |

W Village | 359 Bleecker St. (bet. Charles & W. 10th Sts.) | 212-929-4774 | www.augustny.com

Maybe the menu "feels more like autumn", but this "intimate" Villager appeals year-round thanks to midpriced "modern" European fare from a "well-utilized wood-burning oven"; service is a tad "casual" and the quarters "tight", but the "greenhouselike" back garden is a "winner."

Au Mandarin *Chinese* | 18 | 14 | 17 | $32 |

Financial District | World Financial Ctr. | 200-250 Vesey St. (West St.) | 212-385-0313 | www.aumandarin.com

Corporate types tuck into "solid" business eats at this WFC Chinese "standby", aka the "Merrill Lynch kitchen"; despite "cloth napkins", its "bright" mall setting lends a "fast-food" feel, so insiders opt for take-out or the "carpeted back room."

☑ Aureole ☒ *American* | 27 | 26 | 26 | $109 |

E 60s | 34 E. 61st St. (bet. Madison & Park Aves.) | 212-319-1660 | www.charliepalmer.com

A "foodie mecca", Charlie Palmer's "joyous" East Side New American is known for "paradise-on-a-plate" repasts, "chic people-watching" and blessedly "easy-to-come-by reservations"; "stellar" service and a "posh", flower-filled townhouse setting cushions the fact that the prix fixe–only dinners are priced like "Picassos" – though there's a more reasonable $38 lunch; N.B. it's set to relocate opposite Bryant Park in the new Bank of America building in spring 2009.

Aurora *Italian* | 25 | 21 | 20 | $47 |

SoHo | 510 Broome St. (bet. Thompson St. & W. B'way) | 212-334-9020
Williamsburg | 70 Grand St. (Wythe Ave.) | Brooklyn | 718-388-5100 ⌂ www.auroraristorante.com

These "mellow marvels" in Williamsburg and SoHo draw fans with "moderately priced" Italian cooking with "fresh-from-the-garden taste", "efficiently served" in "cozy", brick-walled digs; while the Billyburg original earns points for its "attitude-changing garden", the "cash-only" policy loses them.

Austin's Steakhouse *Steak*   ▽ 21 | 19 | 21 | $57

Bay Ridge | 8915 Fifth Ave. (90th St.) | Brooklyn | 718-439-5000 | www.austinssteakhouseny.com

"Peter Luger it's not", yet this "unpretentious" Bay Ridge chop shop is a "favorite with locals" who tout its "solid" steaks, "well-chosen wine list" and "attentive" service; somewhat "pricey" tabs and "out-of-date decor" come with the territory.

A Voce *Italian*   25 | 21 | 21 | $68

Gramercy | 41 Madison Ave. (26th St.) | 212-545-8555 | www.avocerestaurant.com

"Sybaritic" dining awaits at this Italian "heavy hitter" off Madison Square Park, where "pasta like silk" and other "luscious" dishes are presented by a "pro" crew; while the "midcentury modern" decor splits voters ("attractive" vs. "antiseptic"), there's concurrence on the "loud" decibels and "daunting" tabs; N.B. the departure of chef Andrew Carmellini puts its Food score in question.

NEW Avon Bistro **☒** *American*   - | - | - | M

E 50s | 155 E. 52nd St. (bet. Lexington & 3rd Aves.) | 212-752-9587 | www.avonbistro.com

Snappy design sets the chic mood at this new Midtowner looking to up the ante on New American cuisine in an area better known for its happy hours, burgers and steaks; moderate pricing and a private dining space make it a natural for nearby corporate types.

Avra **●** *Greek*   24 | 21 | 21 | $56

E 40s | 141 E. 48th St. (bet. Lexington & 3rd Aves.) | 212-759-8550 | www.avrany.com

"If you can't get to the Aegean", there's always this "animated" Midtown Hellenic specializing in "fabulous", "simply grilled" whole fish and other "chic Greek" items; "per-pound pricing" means the "pennies do add up", but the cost is incidental if you snag one of the "great outdoor seats."

Awash *Ethiopian*   21 | 11 | 15 | $24

E Village | 338 E. Sixth St. (bet. 1st & 2nd Aves.) | 212-982-9589 **●**

W 100s | 947 Amsterdam Ave. (bet. 106th & 107th Sts.) | 212-961-1416 www.awashnyc.com

"Bold, delicious Ethiopian food" that you "eat with your hands" pleases folks "willing to experiment" at this "interactive" twosome; "lethargic" service and a "dearth of decor" are trumped by tabs so "affordable" that it's usually full of "students on dates."

Azul Bistro **●** *Argentinean/Steak*   ▽ 23 | 18 | 19 | $40

LES | 152 Stanton St. (Suffolk St.) | 646-602-2004 | www.azulnyc.com

It's "all about meat" at this "low-key" LES Argentinean, a "charming" little locus for "flavorful" steaks and "great gaucho" grub that's "sanely priced"; the "cool", "dark" digs lure "arty, sexy" types who wish the staff weren't so "overworked."

	FOOD	DECOR	SERVICE	COST

Azuri Cafe ☞ *Israeli* ▽ 25 | 3 | 10 | $14

W 50s | 465 W. 51st St. (bet. 9th & 10th Aves.) | 212-262-2920
Some of the "best falafel around" turns up at this "teensy" Hell's Kitchen "hole-in-the-wall" where the Israeli kosher eats are both "delicious" and "cheap"; downsides include "next to no seating" and a "cantankerous owner" who's "fanatic about quality" but "rude to everyone."

☑ Babbo ● *Italian* 27 | 23 | 24 | $79

G Village | 110 Waverly Pl. (bet. MacDougal St. & 6th Ave.) | 212-777-0303 | www.babbonyc.com
Only "getting better with age", Mario Batali and Joe Bastianich's Village flagship offers "brilliant" repasts backed by an "unparalleled wine list" and "exemplary service" in a handsome carriage house setting; prices are high, but since it's NYC's No. 1 Italian, reservations are nearly "impossible"; to avoid waiting for a seat until the "next geological epoch", come early and "dine at the bar"; still, some say "overhyped."

Bacchus *French* ▽ 19 | 18 | 19 | $35

Boerum Hill | 409 Atlantic Ave. (bet. Bond & Nevins Sts.) | Brooklyn | 718-852-1572 | www.bacchusbistro.com
"Very French, but in a good way", this "sweet" little Boerum Hill "favorite" on "bustling" Atlantic Avenue supplies "excellent" bistro fare along with an approachable wine list; prices are "reasonable", and ooh-la-la, what a "wonderful garden."

Baci & Abbracci ● *Italian* ▽ 22 | 19 | 22 | $32

Williamsburg | 204 Grand St. (bet. Bedford & Driggs Aves.) | Brooklyn | 718-599-6599 | www.baciny.com
While most everything is "delicious", the brick-oven pizza is simply "*fantastico*" at this "nifty" Williamsburg Italian where the "inventive" fare comes with a Neapolitan twist; "jovial" service and a "spacious garden" has patrons sending it "hugs and kisses."

NEW Back Forty *American* 19 | 17 | 18 | $38

E Village | 190 Ave. B (bet. 11th & 12th Sts.) | 212-388-1990 | www.backfortynyc.com
"They do simple things well" at Peter Hoffman's "affordable", "ingredient-conscious" East Villager where "locavores" laud the "farm-fresh" New American menu built around a "fab" burger; still, the "minimalist" decor and "service issues" need tweaking.

NEW Bagatelle ● *French* ▽ 22 | 24 | 22 | $68

Meatpacking | 409 W. 13th St. (bet. 9th Ave. & Washington St.) | 212-675-2400
"Beautiful room, beautiful people" and "outstanding" French fare keep things "hoppin'" at this "trendy" new Meatpacking District boîte; prices are as "high" as the music is "loud", but the "scene is oh-so-entertaining" and the staff "as attractive as the customers."

Baldoria *Italian* 21 | 17 | 20 | $56

W 40s | 249 W. 49th St. (bet. B'way & 8th Ave.) | 212-582-0460 | www.baldoriamo.com
Spun off from Rao's yet still "under the radar in the crowded Theater District", Frank Pellegrino Jr.'s "convivial", "old-school" Italian wins kudos for "meatballs like mama used to make"; the "Sinatra-

"era" duplex setting may be "tired" and tabs "not cheap", but "at least you can get in" without having to kiss anyone's ring.

☑ Balthazar ● French | 23 | 23 | 19 | $55 |

SoHo | 80 Spring St. (bet. B'way & Crosby St.) | 212-965-1414 | www.balthazarny.com

"More juggernaut than restaurant", Keith McNally's "action-packed" SoHo "beehive" offers "toothsome" French food, "deft" service and a "pitch-perfect" rendering of a Parisian brasserie; expect lots of "hub-bub", "tough reservations", moderately "pricey" tabs and a "loud" crowd that runs the gamut from "skeletal models" and fat cats to "celebs" and starstruck "tourists"; in sum, it's *presque* Paris.

Baluchi's Indian | 17 | 13 | 15 | $27 |

E 50s | 224 E. 53rd St. (bet. 2nd & 3rd Aves.) | 212-750-5515
E 80s | 1724 Second Ave. (bet. 89th & 90th Sts.) | 212-996-2600
Gramercy | 329 Third Ave. (bet. 24th & 25th Sts.) | 212-679-3434
G Village | 361 Sixth Ave. (Washington Pl.) | 212-929-2441
G Village | 90 W. Third St. (bet. Sullivan & Thompson Sts.) | 212-529-5353
SoHo | 193 Spring St. (bet. Sullivan & Thompson Sts.) | 212-226-2828
TriBeCa | 275 Greenwich St. (Warren St.) | 212-571-5343
W 50s | 240 W. 56th St. (bet. B'way & 8th Ave.) | 212-397-0707
Forest Hills | 113-30 Queens Blvd. (bet. 76th Ave. & 76th Rd.) | Queens | 718-520-8600
www.baluchis.com

"Consistent if not outstanding", this "workmanlike", all-over-town Indian chain vends "solid", "generic" eats for "modest" sums; "dingy" decor and "below-par" service make them "better for takeout" – except at lunchtime, when the dine-in deal is "half-price."

Bamonte's Italian | 22 | 16 | 21 | $42 |

Williamsburg | 32 Withers St. (bet. Lorimer St. & Union Ave.) | Brooklyn | 718-384-8831

"When you're tired of hipsters", this vintage-1900 Williamsburg "trip back in time" is just the ticket for "delicious, old-world" Italian grub served by career waiters who've "been there forever"; maybe the "faded" decor "hasn't changed since day one", but the price is right at this "must-see" place.

Banjara ● Indian | 22 | 15 | 18 | $31 |

E Village | 97 First Ave. (6th St.) | 212-477-5956 | www.banjarany.com

"Much better than the run-of-the-mill Indians" on nearby Sixth Street, this "authentic" East Villager parlays "zesty, well-spiced" food that's worth the "extra rupees"; the staff is "pleasant", and even if the decor's "drab", at least there are "no Christmas lights."

Bann Korean | 24 | 24 | 22 | $50 |

W 50s | Worldwide Plaza | 350 W. 50th St. (bet. 8th & 9th Aves.) | 212-582-4446 | www.bannrestaurant.com

"Nouvelle Korean" food served in a "modern", "elegant" setting is yours at this "roomy" Hell's Kitchen "sleeper" that's a sibling of Downtown favorite Woo Lae Oak; hidden in an "out-of-the-way" site in Worldwide Plaza, it's "never crowded" but ever "lovely – except for the bill."

	FOOD	DECOR	SERVICE	COST

Bann Thai *Thai* | 19 | 18 | 18 | $28

Forest Hills | 69-12 Austin St. (Yellowstone Blvd.) | Queens | 718-544-9999 |
www.bannthairestaurant.com

The food is "spicy" but the mood "mellow" at this Forest Hills Thai, a
"no-brainer" thanks to "authentic" cooking and "fanciful" decor; better yet, the prices "won't kill your wallet", another reason why it's a
"favorite of the locals."

Bao Noodles *Vietnamese* | 18 | 12 | 15 | $25

Gramercy | 391 Second Ave. (bet. 22nd & 23rd Sts.) | 212-725-7770 |
www.baonoodles.com

"Un-pho-gettable pho" and other "authentic" dishes fill out the menu
of this Gramercy Vietnamese that's particularly "easy on the wallet";
"indifferent" service and "bare-bones" looks don't deter fans seeking
something "totally tasty" and totally affordable.

Bar Americain *American* | 22 | 22 | 21 | $62

W 50s | 152 W. 52nd St. (bet. 6th & 7th Aves.) | 212-265-9700 |
www.baramericain.com

Bobby Flay adds his signature "flay-re" to "well-turned-out" American
classics at this Midtown "mega-bistro", a "big, airy" thing overseen by a
"good-natured" crew; sure, the "expense account"–priced grub comes
with a "side order of noise", but the overall experience is "invigorating."

Baraonda ● *Italian* | 18 | 17 | 16 | $49

E 70s | 1439 Second Ave. (75th St.) | 212-288-8555 | www.baraondany.com
More about "meeting than eating", this "swinging" UES Italian serves
"ok", "high-priced" eats but its "Eurotrash" following is more preoccupied with the "party atmosphere" and late-night "dancing on tabletops"
to notice; unfortunately, the "noncaring service" is often overwhelmed
by the "noisy", "energetic" scene.

Barbès ● *French/Moroccan* | 20 | 18 | 19 | $43

Murray Hill | 21 E. 36th St. (bet. 5th & Madison Aves.) | 212-684-0215 |
www.barbesrestaurantnyc.com

"Stodgy Murray Hill" gets a jolt via this "unexpected" French-
Moroccan "jewel" where "complex" dishes brimming with "novel flavors" are presented in "dark, sexy" digs; the tabs are "affordable" and
the service "cheerful", so even when it's busy, the mood seems more
"cozy" than "cramped."

Barbetta ●⊠Ⓜ *Italian* | 20 | 22 | 21 | $62

W 40s | 321 W. 46th St. (bet. 8th & 9th Aves.) | 212-246-9171 |
www.barbettarestaurant.com

"Old-world elegance" turns up at this "venerable" Theater District
Northern Italian, the "grande dame" of Restaurant Row since 1925;
though some find it a bit "formal", there's praise for the "stellar" cuisine, smooth service, "beautiful brownstone" setting and that "gorgeous garden" that lends a literal breath of fresh air.

NEW **Bar Blanc** *French/Italian* | 23 | 23 | 20 | $65

G Village | 142 W. 10th St. (bet. Greenwich Ave. & 7th Ave. S.) |
212-255-2330 | www.barblanc.com

A trio of Bouley alums are off to a "strong" start at this "chic"
Village newcomer purveying "inventive", "skillfully prepared" French-

Italian dishes; the "slinky", white-on-white space draws a "sophisti-cated" following that tolerates tabs that are "a little pricier than they need to be."

Barbone ● *Italian*　　▽ 23 | 18 | 21 | $43

E Village | 186 Ave. B (bet. 11th & 12th Sts.) | 212-254-6047 | www.barbonenyc.com

"Decadent" pastas may be its "highlight", but everything's "delicious" at this "homey" East Village Italian presided over by a "charming" chef-owner; "affordable" costs, "treat-you-like-a-king" service and a "heaven-sent garden" are making it almost "too popular."

NEW Bar Boulud *French*　　22 | 20 | 20 | $63

W 60s | 1900 Broadway (bet. 63rd & 64th Sts.) | 212-595-0303 | www.danielnyc.com

Daniel Boulud goes "casual" at this new French wine bar facing Lincoln Center serving a rustic bistro menu topped off by a "much-vaunted" selection of charcuterie; as expected, the wine list is "excellent" and pricing "over-the-top", but the "simple" decor gets mixed marks ("wonderfully minimalist" vs. "upmarket tunnel") and the service is "still finding its way"; N.B. check out the private party spaces downstairs.

Barbounia *Mediterranean*　　20 | 21 | 17 | $50

Flatiron | 250 Park Ave. S. (20th St.) | 212-995-0242 | www.barbounia.com

"Killer cocktails", an "attractive" crowd and a "big", "breezy" setting amp up the decibels at this "fresh" Flatiron Mediterranean where the "flavorful" food plays second fiddle to the "booming" scene; even "uneven" service and "spendy" tabs can't dampen the "party atmosphere" here.

Barbuto *Italian*　　21 | 17 | 17 | $51

W Village | 775 Washington St. (bet. Jane & W. 12th Sts.) | 212-924-9700 | www.barbutonyc.com

Set in a revamped garage, Jonathan Waxman's "industro-chic" West Village Italian is "best in summer" when the "doors are open", but year-round you'll find "market-fresh" meals "simply but stunningly prepared" for an "affordable" cost; but even though the eats are up to speed, some say the "absent-minded" staff could use a tune-up.

Barking Dog *American*　　15 | 13 | 15 | $24

E 70s | 1453 York Ave. (77th St.) | 212-861-3600
E 90s | 1678 Third Ave. (94th St.) | 212-831-1800 ⊟
Murray Hill | Affinia Dumont | 150 E. 34th St. (bet. Lexington & 3rd Aves.) | 212-871-3900 ●

These "glorified diners" packed with "strollers" and pooch "paraphernalia" put out plentiful American comfort chow at "palatable prices"; they're also brunch destinations for "hair-of-the-dog-that-bit-you" types who can abide the "doggone waits" and "hectic" vibes.

barmarché ● *American*　　▽ 19 | 19 | 17 | $41

NoLita | 14 Spring St. (Elizabeth St.) | 212-219-2399 | www.barmarche.com

"Low-key yet stylish" dining turns up at this "affordable" NoLita New American where the "tasty" eats are enhanced by "perfect cocktails"; it's a "solid first-date place", and even though the staff is "not bad to look at", the pace is too "leisurely" for some.

	FOOD	DECOR	SERVICE	COST

NEW Bar Milano ● *Italian* — 22 | 22 | 21 | $61

Gramercy | 323 Third Ave. (24th St.) | 212-683-3035 | www.barmilano.com

The Denton brothers ('ino, 'inoteca, Lupa) bring Milan chic to Gramercy with this new, three-meals-a-day Northern Italian complete with a "happening" bar, "spot-on" menu, "excellent" wine list and "attentive" staff; despite its "ambitious" aspirations, the "high decibels" and "high prices" need some finessing.

Z Barney Greengrass M⊅ *Deli* — 24 | 7 | 14 | $27

W 80s | 541 Amsterdam Ave. (bet. 86th & 87th Sts.) | 212-724-4707 | www.barneygreengrass.com

"As good as NY deli gets" (and voted No. 1 in the genre), this 101-year-old UWS "shrine" to "Jewish soul food" reeks of "retro charm" with a "harried" mood and "deliciously dumpy" decor in need of a "schmear of paint"; though it's "cash only" and service is "as salty as the lox", the "smells alone are worth the price of admission."

Barolo *Italian* — 19 | 21 | 18 | $52

SoHo | 398 W. Broadway (bet. Broome & Spring Sts.) | 212-226-1102 | www.nybarolo.com

You'll "forget you're in Manhattan" in the "close-to-paradise" garden that's the "real attraction" at this SoHo magnet for "groups" and "tourists"; the Italian menu is "solid" enough – if a tad "pricey for what it is" – ditto the "efficient" service.

Bar Pitti ●⊅ *Italian* — 22 | 15 | 17 | $40

G Village | 268 Sixth Ave. (bet. Bleecker & Houston Sts.) | 212-982-3300

"Bodaciously tasty pastas" draw both "Village celebs" and ordinary mortals to this "cash-only" Italian where "who's sitting next to you" trumps what you're eating; "gentle prices" and primo "sidewalk seating" make up for the "absentee service", "long waits" and "what-decor?" decor.

NEW bar Q *Pan-Asian* — ∇ 20 | 18 | 21 | $53

W Village | 308-310 Bleecker St. (bet. Grove St. & 7th Ave. S.) | 212-206-7817 | www.barqrestaurant.com

Anita Lo's "distinctive" cooking has a new Village showcase at this "casual" Asian barbecue-cum-raw bar set in "minimalist", "stark white" digs with a greenhouse atrium; overall, this enterprise is "almost there."

NEW Barrio *Mexican* — ∇ 19 | 16 | 14 | $32

Park Slope | 210 Seventh Ave. (3rd St.) | Brooklyn | 718-965-4000 | www.barriofoods.com

Slopers seeking another open-air dining option are packing this Mexican newcomer, aptly named 'neighborhood' in Spanish; it wins favor with its midpriced menu, festive background music and low-lit setting with dark-wood accents and ceramic tile floors – as well as plenty of seats on the covered patio.

Bar Stuzzichini *Italian* — 20 | 17 | 18 | $44

Flatiron | 928 Broadway (bet. 21st & 22nd Sts.) | 212-780-5100 | www.barstuzzichini.com

"Terrific", "bite-size" tapas arrive in a "huge" setting at this "dark wood"–lined Flatiron Italian yearling that also offers an "extensive" wine list; despite "skimpy" portions and somewhat "distracted" service, it's already so "popular" that you may need to brush up on your "sign language."

Basilica ● *Italian* — 20 | 13 | 19 | $32

W 40s | 676 Ninth Ave. (bet. 46th & 47th Sts.) | 212-489-0051
"Solid", "no-nonsense" Italiana comes "fast enough to let you make your show" at this "friendly" but "frenetic" Hell's Kitchen "hole-in-the-wall"; the "narrow" digs may have "bowling-alley-lane" dimensions, but the tabs are "modest", especially the $28 prix fixe "deal" that "includes a bottle of wine."

Basso56 ● *Italian* — 21 | 17 | 22 | $48

W 50s | 234 W. 56th St. (bet. B'way & 8th Ave.) | 212-265-2610 | www.basso56.com
Still turning out *"delizioso"* Italian dishes, this former Downtowner relocated to the Theater District may be "undiscovered" but is "quickly becoming a favorite", particularly for "pre-Carnegie Hall" dining; expect "cordial" service, fair prices and a "long, thin" setting.

Basta Pasta *Italian* — 22 | 17 | 20 | $43

Flatiron | 37 W. 17th St. (bet. 5th & 6th Aves.) | 212-366-0888 | www.bastapastanyc.com
"Venice meets Tokyo" at this "hip", midpriced Flatiron venue that takes pasta to "another level" via "detail-oriented" Italian cooking "with a Japanese twist"; "adventurous" fusion fans tout the "cool" open kitchen and the spaghetti "served in a Parmesan wheel", not the plain ambiance.

Battery Gardens *American/Continental* — 18 | 23 | 19 | $48

Financial District | SW corner of Battery Park (State St.) | 212-809-5508 | www.batterygardens.com
"No matter what the season", the "breathtaking" views of Lady Liberty and the Hudson make the food taste better at this American-Continental "hidden in a corner of Battery Park"; "caring service" and "reasonable prices" also earn kudos, but nothing beats its "outdoor tables" on a summer evening.

Bay Leaf *Indian* — 20 | 16 | 17 | $39

W 50s | 49 W. 56th St. (bet. 5th & 6th Aves.) | 212-957-1818 | www.bayleafnyc.com
At this "mellow" Indian near Carnegie Hall, you can count on "all the classics", "economically priced" and served in "plentiful" portions by "solicitous" (if "slow") staffers; apart from white tablecloths, it's a "no-frills" affair, jazzed up by a "killer" $14.95 lunch buffet.

Bayou *Cajun* — ∇ 22 | 19 | 21 | $33

Staten Island | 1072 Bay St. (bet. Chestnut & St. Mary's Aves.) | 718-273-4383 | www.bayoustatenisland.com
"Every night feels like Mardi Gras" at this Staten Island "homage to New Orleans", where "tasty" Cajun-Creole eats are served in "tiny", brick-walled digs by a crew that "tries hard to keep customers happy"; add "bargain" rates and it's no wonder the "good times roll" here.

B. Café *Belgian* — 22 | 18 | 20 | $39

E 70s | 240 E. 75th St. (bet. 2nd & 3rd Aves.) | 212-249-3300
This "hidden" UES Belgian bistro purveys "amazing moules frites" and an "excellent beer selection" in "ultra-intimate", brick-walled digs; a

"gracious owner" sets the "feel-at-home" mood, and even though the offerings are "not dietetic", they are well priced.

Beacon *American* | 22 | 21 | 21 | $60 |

W 50s | 25 W. 56th St. (bet. 5th & 6th Aves.) | 212-332-0500 | www.beaconnyc.com

"Terrific wood-grilled" grub is the calling card of Waldy Malouf's "relaxed" Midtown New American that lures expense account–bearing suits "like moths to a flame" for "power-lunching"; the "enormous", multilevel space is "chic", service "considerate" and at least the "prix fixe meals" are a "bargain."

Beast *Mediterranean* | ▽ 22 | 17 | 19 | $29 |

Prospect Heights | 638 Bergen St. (Vanderbilt Ave.) | Brooklyn | 718-399-6855 | www.brooklynbeast.com

"Tempting tapas" pair well with "great drinks" at this "low-key" Prospect Heights Mediterranean, a "dark little joint" perfect for "nibbling" and "leisurely conversation"; there's also a "fantastic brunch" for patient types who can abide "slow" service.

Ⓩ Becco ◑ *Italian* | 23 | 17 | 21 | $44 |

W 40s | 355 W. 46th St. (bet. 8th & 9th Aves.) | 212-397-7597 | www.becco-nyc.com

Simply a "sensation", Joe Bastianich's Restaurant Row Italian is famed for its all-the-carbs-you-can-eat $22.95 "pasta orgy" (accompanied by a "brilliant, $25-per-bottle wine list"); an "aim-to-please" staff ensures a "rollicking good time", no matter how "crowded" or "noisy" it gets.

Beccofino *Italian* | 21 | 17 | 19 | $33 |

Bronx | 5704 Mosholu Ave. (bet. Fieldston Rd. & Spencer Ave.) | 718-432-2604

Folks looking for a "fresh carb fix" like this "charming" Bronx Italian that may have "small" dimensions but offers red-sauce portions "so big that everyone leaves with leftovers"; the "no-reservations" policy results in prime-time "waits", yet overall it's "good news for Riverdale."

NEW Belcourt *European* | 20 | 18 | 18 | $42 |

E Village | 84 E. Fourth St. (2nd Ave.) | 212-979-2034 | www.belcourtnyc.com

Though it looks like an "East Village take on a Paris bistro", this "casual" newcomer offers a "trendy" Pan-European menu; the staff is "still finding its groove" and some wish they could "muffle the din", but nonetheless it's fast becoming a neighborhood "favorite."

Bella Blu ◑ *Italian* | 20 | 17 | 18 | $50 |

E 70s | 967 Lexington Ave. (bet. 70th & 71st Sts.) | 212-988-4624 | www.baraondany.com

"Socialites", "youngish Euros" and other "pretty people" frequent this "upbeat" UES Northern Italian for "flavorful" pastas and "wonderful" brick-oven pizza served in a room adorned with "groovy murals"; brace yourself for a "noisy", "busy" scene, centered around the "lively bar."

Bella Via *Italian* | 21 | 17 | 19 | $32 |

LIC | 47-46 Vernon Blvd. (48th Ave.) | Queens | 718-361-7510 | www.bellaviarestaurant.com

Evidence of the "gentrifying" LIC scene, this "solid" Italian vends "tasty" pastas and "wonderful" brick-oven pizza in a smallish space with "big glass windows"; fans say the "pleasant" service and "reasonable" prices will "satisfy the most discerning yuppie."

Bellavitae ● Italian | 23 | 18 | 19 | $52 |

G Village | 24 Minetta Ln. (bet. MacDougal St. & 6th Ave.) | 212-473-5121 | www.bellavitae.com

"Still under the radar", this "small but mighty" Village enoteca dishes out "heavenly" small plates paired with an "excellent wine list"; sure, the "staff could learn from Emily Post" and "boy, do those prices add up", yet for most it's a "winner."

Belleville ⊟ French | 17 | 19 | 15 | $36 |

Park Slope | 350 Fifth Ave. (5th St.) | Brooklyn | 718-832-9777 | www.bellevillebistro.com

It "really feels like France" at this "comfortable" Park Slope bistro, a "remarkable replica" of the "namesake Parisian neighborhood" with "haughty service" adding to the authenticity; while the food could be better, the "great atmosphere" and gentle pricing keep regulars regular.

NEW Bellini Italian | ▽ 18 | 16 | 17 | $31 |

W 80s | 483 Columbus Ave. (bet. 83rd & 84th Sts.) | 212-724-4615 | www.bellininyc.com

Set in a diminutive galleylike space, this new neighborhood UWS Italian offers wallet-friendly, pasta-focused entrees that can be ordered in individual or family-style portions, and already has a following for its thin-crust brick-oven pizza; though it's named for the famous Venetian cocktail, it's BYO for now.

Bello Italian | 20 | 16 | 20 | $48 |

W 50s | 863 Ninth Ave. (56th St.) | 212-246-6773 | www.bellorestaurant.com

"Hip it ain't", but this "pleasant" Hell's Kitchen Italian "standby" does come across with "well-presented" traditional fare for "midscale" costs; "old-school service" matches the "old-world" mood, though it's best known for the "ultimate NYC perk" – "free parking" after 5 PM.

Bello Sguardo ● Mediterranean | 19 | 14 | 17 | $38 |

W 70s | 410 Amsterdam Ave. (bet. 79th & 80th Sts.) | 212-873-6252

Upper Westsiders report "good grazing" at this "low-key" Med with an "interestingly varied menu" of small plates and mains; "reasonable" prices and a "conversation-conducive" setting make for a "relaxing night out."

Ben & Jack's Steak House Steak | 23 | 17 | 21 | $68 |

E 40s | 219 E. 44th St. (bet. 2nd & 3rd Aves.) | 212-682-5678 | www.benandjackssteakhouse.com

"Business professionals" wolf down "perfectly cooked" steaks and "classic sides" at this Luger-copy Midtown chop shop that may be "so-so" on looks but saves "going to Brooklyn"; "expensive" tabs and "quick" service come with the "masculine" territory.

Ben Benson's Steak | 23 | 18 | 21 | $69 |

W 50s | 123 W. 52nd St. (bet. 6th & 7th Aves.) | 212-581-8888 | www.benbensons.com

"Testosterone fills the air" at this "old-time" Midtown steakhouse where "tip-top" slabs of beef, "potent" martinis and "macho" "wood-

and-brass" decor combine for a "real boys' night out"; despite the "gruff" service and "ear-splitting" din, "you get what you pay for" here – and "you'll be paying a lot."

Benihana *Japanese*
17 | 15 | 19 | $43

W 50s | 47 W. 56th St. (bet. 5th & 6th Aves.) | 212-581-0930 | www.benihana.com

"Showmanship" is the thing at this midpriced Midtown Japanese steakhouse where "entertaining" chefs slice up "food tossed into the air" with "festive" results; sure, it's "cheesy" and the cooking only "acceptable", but the "chop-chop never goes out of style", especially for "children's birthday parties."

Benjamin Steak House *Steak*
23 | 21 | 22 | $72

E 40s | 52 E. 41st St. (bet. Madison & Park Aves.) | 212-297-9177 | www.benjaminsteakhouse.com

A "pleasant change" in the dining-deprived area around Grand Central, this typically "expensive" chop shop allows fans to wallow in "cholesterol bliss" with "marvelous steaks" served by "nice waiters"; even better, it "actually has decor", set in a "spacious" former clubroom with "high ceilings" and a "fireplace."

NEW Benoit *French*
18 | 20 | 16 | $69

W 50s | 60 W. 55th St. (bet. 5th & 6th Aves.) | 646-943-7373 | www.benoitny.com

Despite its pedigree as a spin-off of a wonderful old Parisian bistro and ownership by Alain Ducasse, this "middling" new Midtown eatery leaves surveyors "disappointed"; comments such as "underwhelming", "pedestrian" and "seriously average, except for the price" indicate that diners expected a lot more than "just another French bistro."

Ben's Kosher Deli *Deli*
18 | 11 | 15 | $25

Garment District | 209 W. 38th St. (bet. 7th & 8th Aves.) | 212-398-2367
Bayside | Bay Terrace | 211-37 26th Ave. (211th St.) | Queens | 718-229-2367
www.bensdeli.net

"If you arrive before five, it's like being in Florida" at these "busy brisket-fests" in Bayside and the Garment District that specialize in "plenteous"-portioned kosher deli items; they're vestiges of a "dying breed", so few kvetch about the "abrupt" service and "nothing-fancy" decor.

Beppe ☒ *Italian*
22 | 19 | 20 | $56

Flatiron | 45 E. 22nd St. (bet. B'way & Park Ave. S.) | 212-982-8422 | www.beppenyc.com

"Consistently busy", this "top-notch" Flatiron Tuscan turns out "earthy" if "pricey" Italian fare in a "farmhouse"-esque setting enhanced by a "warming glow" from the fireplace; an equally "warm welcome" from the staff adds to the "jovial ambiance."

Bereket ●♉ *Turkish*
19 | 3 | 12 | $12

LES | 187 E. Houston St. (Orchard St.) | 212-475-7700

"Everything seems delicious after a night of drinking", and this 24/7 LES "snack king" is renowned as a place "where the cabbies go" for "cheap, fast" Turkish eats; ok, "not a dime was spent on decor", but it's still an "excellent late-night" pit stop.

Better Burger *Burgers*

| 15 | 9 | 13 | $14 |

Chelsea | 178 Eighth Ave. (19th St.) | 212-989-6688 ◐
Murray Hill | 561 Third Ave. (37th St.) | 212-949-7528
W 40s | 587 Ninth Ave. (bet. 42nd & 43rd Sts.) | 212-629-6622
www.betterburgernyc.com

"Fast food without the guilt" sums up the appeal of this "virtuous" mini-chain serving "organic burgers" and air-baked fries in "bright", "plain" settings; but those who think it "doesn't live up to its name" find the goods "underwhelming in flavor and above-average in cost", yet "better than a sharp stick in the eye."

Bettola ◐ *Italian*

| 20 | 14 | 17 | $35 |

W 70s | 412 Amsterdam Ave. (bet. 79th & 80th Sts.) | 212-787-1660 | www.bettolanyc.com

With "crusts so thin you can't gain weight", the "distinctive" pizzas fired in a wood-burning oven are the thing to order at this "low-cost" UWS Italian that also offers "reliable" rustic dishes; insiders prefer the "sidewalk" seats over the "small, noisy" interior.

Beyoglu *Turkish*

| 21 | 16 | 18 | $35 |

E 80s | 1431 Third Ave. (81st St.) | 212-650-0850

Regulars "make a meal of the meze" at this "budget-friendly", "high-energy" UES Turk where everything's "memorable" including the "frazzled" staff that still manages to "bring the food out zippy quick"; P.S. downstairs is usually a "madhouse", but upstairs is "more civilized."

Bianca ⊄ *Italian*

| 23 | 17 | 20 | $34 |

NoHo | 5 Bleecker St. (bet. Bowery & Elizabeth St.) | 212-260-4666

Partial to "delicious" cooking from Italy's Emilia-Romagna region, this "unassuming" NoHo spot also boasts "attentive" service and "remarkable prices"; it's "everything a downtown restaurant should be" from the "cramped" seating to the cash-only rule.

Bice ◐ *Italian*

| 20 | 19 | 19 | $62 |

E 50s | 7 E. 54th St. (bet. 5th & Madison Aves.) | 212-688-1999 | www.bicenewyork.com

"Still packing them in", this Midtown magnet for the "Botox crowd" offers "surprisingly good" Northern Italiana served by an "efficient" if "perfunctory" crew; bring "wads of money" to settle the check, though the "Eurotrendy" people-watching and "oh-so-chic" vibe just might be worth it.

Big Nick's Burger Joint ◐ *Burgers*

| 17 | 5 | 13 | $17 |

W 70s | 2175 Broadway (77th St.) | 212-362-9238
W 70s | 70 W. 71st St. (Columbus Ave.) | 212-799-4444 | www.bignicksny.com

"Supreme burgers", some up to a pound, take the cake on the "mile-long menus" of these separately owned UWS "gourmet greasy spoons"; expect "crusty service", "dingy" digs and "lots of food" for "minimum bucks" – plus a 24/7 open-door policy at the Broadway outpost.

Big Wong ⊄ *Chinese*

| 22 | 5 | 11 | $14 |

Chinatown | 67 Mott St. (bet. Bayard & Canal Sts.) | 212-964-0540

"Cheap Chinese chow" arrives "piping hot" at "unbeatable" rates at this unfortunately named, "been-around-forever" relic of "pure

Chinatown"; despite the "mayhem", the "Formica" and the "service with a grunt", it's "so worth it", especially when the yen for "delicious barbecue" and "genuine" congee strikes.

Biricchino ☒ *Italian* | 19 | 11 | 18 | $38 |

Chelsea | 260 W. 29th St. (8th Ave.) | 212-695-6690 | www.biricchino.com
"Sumptuous" homemade sausages are the specialty of this "handy" Northern Italian parked in the MSG "culinary desert"; it may be a bit "short on charm", but "moderate prices" and "friendly" service carry the day.

Bistro Cassis *French* | 20 | 17 | 16 | $44 |

W 70s | 225 Columbus Ave. (bet. 70th & 71st Sts.) | 212-579-3966 | www.bistrocassisnyc.com
Like an "ersatz trip to Paris", this "casual" Westsider is close to the "real thing", purveying "almost-France" eats and service *avec* "attitude" in a "bustling" milieu; the no-reservations policy may be "frustrating", but the "affordable" tabs are *très bonnes*.

Bistro Chat Noir *French* | 19 | 18 | 20 | $56 |

E 60s | 22 E. 66th St. (bet. 5th & Madison Aves.) | 212-794-2428 | www.bistrochatnoir.com
From the La Goulue team comes this "good-vibed" UES French bistro where the "expected" dishes arrive in a "casual" townhouse setting; a "gracious host" and "treat-you-like-a-family-member" service make the "high prices" more palatable.

Bistro Citron *French* | 20 | 18 | 19 | $42 |

W 80s | 473 Columbus Ave. (bet. 82nd & 83rd Sts.) | 212-400-9401 | www.bistrocitronnyc.com
All the "classic French bistro hits" turn up at this "charming" UWS sibling of Bistro Cassis, a "genteelly boisterous" place with "moderate" pricing and a "welcoming atmosphere"; though service veers from "helpful" to *comme ci comme ça*, overall it's a "real neighborhood asset."

Bistro du Nord *French* | 18 | 15 | 16 | $45 |

E 90s | 1312 Madison Ave. (93rd St.) | 212-289-0997
A "touch of Paree" lands in Carnegie Hill via this "quaint" French boîte known for its "fine" bistro standards and "terrific" prix fixes; its negatives include "bumper-to-bumper tables", an "awkward" duplex setting and "indifferent" service – yet locals are still "glad to have it."

Bistro Les Amis ❶ *French* | 21 | 17 | 21 | $42 |

SoHo | 180 Spring St. (Thompson St.) | 212-226-8645 | www.bistrolesamis.com
"Well named", this *charmant* SoHo "neighborhood favorite" boasts a "helpful" staff delivering "top-notch" French bistro classics in "tiny", "romantic" digs that make plenty of *amis*; everything's "on the money", starting with the "fair prices", at this perfect "place to unwind."

Bistro 61 *French* | 19 | 15 | 19 | $40 |

E 60s | 1113 First Ave. (61st St.) | 212-223-6220 | www.bistro61.com
"Lots of French speakers" in the crowd add some "Left Bank" flair to this *"pas mal"* Eastsider near the Queensboro Bridge; "satisfying" bistro fare, a "comfortable", brick-walled setting and "warm" service add to the "friendly" mood.

	FOOD	DECOR	SERVICE	COST

Bistro Ten 18 *American* | 18 | 17 | 17 | $38 |

W 100s | 1018 Amsterdam Ave. (110th St.) | 212-662-7600 |
www.bistroten18.com

"Columbia kids" bring their parents to this "relaxing" Morningside
Heights New American for "reliable" eats at a "reasonable price"; the
staffers are "pleasant" (if you can "flag them down"), and there's a
"sweet fireplace" and view of St. John the Divine to boot.

Bistro 33 *French/Japanese* ∇ 24 | 18 | 22 | $36 |

Astoria | 19-33 Ditmars Blvd. (21st St.) | Queens | 718-721-1933 |
www.bistro33nyc.com

"Astoria's on the upswing" thanks to this Japanese-French "gem" dispensing "creative" bistro eats for a price that "won't break the bank";
sidewalk seating helps ease the crush in the "intimate" dining room,
but no matter where you're parked, the service "shines."

Black Duck *American/Seafood* | 20 | 18 | 19 | $47 |

Gramercy | Park South Hotel | 122 E. 28th St. (bet. Lexington Ave. &
Park Ave. S.) | 212-448-0888 | www.blackduckny.com

"Tucked away in a Gramercy boutique hotel", this New American can
be counted on for midpriced, "well-presented" seafood in a "dimly lit",
"London pub" setting; weekend jazz and a chance to "sit by the fire on
chilly nights" add a note of "romance."

Black Pearl *Seafood* | 18 | 13 | 16 | $40 |

Chelsea | 37 W. 26th St. (bet. B'way & 6th Ave.) | 212-532-9900 |
www.blackpearlonline.com

"Lobster rolls rule" at this "touch-of-New-England" Chelsea seafood
joint that reels 'em in with "good", "simple" fin fare for "reasonable"
sums; apart from the "funky", "coffee-shop" looks and "inconsistent"
service, it's an "easy place to go with friends."

Blaue Gans ● *Austrian/German* | 21 | 18 | 19 | $47 |

TriBeCa | 139 Duane St. (bet. Church St. & W. B'way) | 212-571-8880 |
www.wallse.com

"Sublime schnitzel" highlights the menu of this "casual" TriBeCa establishment where chef Kurt Gutenbrunner offers "delectable",
"affordable" takes on Austro-German cooking; the "low-tech, low-
stress" setting emits an "intellectual" vibe, ditto the "polite" if
somewhat "distracted" staff.

Blockheads Burritos *Mexican* | 16 | 10 | 14 | $19 |

E 50s | 954 Second Ave. (bet. 50th & 51st Sts.) | 212-750-2020
E 80s | 1563 Second Ave. (bet. 81st & 82nd Sts.) | 212-879-1999
Murray Hill | 499 Third Ave. (bet. 33rd & 34th Sts.) |
212-213-3332
W 50s | Worldwide Plaza | 322 W. 50th St. (bet. 8th & 9th Aves.) |
212-307-7029
NEW **W 100s** | 951 Amsterdam Ave. (bet. 106th & 107th Sts.) |
212-662-8226
www.blockheads.com

"Yule log"–size burritos and "$3 margaritas" make this ultra-
"informal" Mexican chain a serviceable "quick fix" providing plenty of
"bang for your peso"; "noisy", "barrio"-like digs make takeout and
"prompt delivery" the way to go.

	FOOD	DECOR	SERVICE	COST

Blossom *Vegan/Vegetarian* | **22** | **18** | **20** | **$36** |

Chelsea | 187 Ninth Ave. (bet. 21st & 22nd Sts.) | 212-627-1144

NEW **Cafe Blossom** *Vegetarian*

W 80s | 466 Columbus Ave. (bet. 82nd & 83rd Sts.) | 212-875-2600
www.blossomnyc.com

Even carnivores tout the "original" fare at these "virtuous vegans" where
the "innovative" menu "doesn't skimp on flavor"; both the "sparse"
UWS branch and "cozier" Chelsea original are "worth sussing out."

BLT Burger *Burgers* | **19** | **14** | **16** | **$25** |

G Village | 470 Sixth Ave. (bet. 11th & 12th Sts.) | 212-243-8226 |
www.bltburger.com

The "BLT empire's bargain branch", this "fun" if "frenetic" Villager
showcases Laurent Tourondel's "innovative" spins on "upscale" burgers, fries and "boozy shakes"; it may "fall short" in the service and decor departments, but few mind since the "price is right."

BLT Fish ⓩ *Seafood* | **23** | **20** | **21** | **$63** |

Flatiron | 21 W. 17th St. (bet. 5th & 6th Aves.) | 212-691-8888 |
www.bltfish.com

"Just-off-the-boat-fresh" fish "cooked to perfection" reels in fans at
Laurent Tourondel's "lovely" Flatiron "seafood shrine"; "spot-on service"
distracts from pricing that's "as high as the tide", though one floor below, the "Cape Cod"-like fish shack is sure alot "cheaper."

BLT Market *American* | **24** | **21** | **22** | **$71** |

W 50s | Ritz-Carlton | 1430 Sixth Ave. (CPS) | 212-521-6125 |
www.bltmarket.com

Laurent Tourondel's latest "charmer" in Midtown's Ritz-Carlton offers
"eclectic", ever-changing New Americana made from "market-fresh ingredients"; maybe the "steep" tabs don't jibe with the "informal country vibe", but this "celebration of the seasons" is an "instant favorite."

Ⓩ BLT Prime *Steak* | **25** | **21** | **22** | **$71** |

Gramercy | 111 E. 22nd St. (bet. Lexington Ave. & Park Ave. S.) |
212-995-8500 | www.bltprime.com

"Mouthwatering" steaks and "heavenly popovers" draw kudos at
Laurent Tourondel's "modern take" on the American steakhouse in
Gramercy; "smooth service" and a "superb wine list" beef up the "so-
phisticated" air, so even if tabs are "prime", it's worth the "indulgence."

BLT Steak ⓩ *Steak* | **24** | **21** | **21** | **$75** |

E 50s | 106 E. 57th St. (bet. Lexington & Park Aves.) | 212-752-7470 |
www.bltsteak.com

You can "taste the aging" in the "incredible steaks" at this "exceptional" Midtown chophouse, the "original in Laurent Tourondel's BLT
empire" that stays "hopping" thanks to "top-notch" cooking, "knowledgeable" service and an "oh-so-chic" atmosphere; "go early to avoid
the din" and "BLC (bring lots of cash)."

bluechili ◑ *Pan-Asian* | **20** | **17** | **18** | **$39** |

W 50s | 251 W. 51st St. (bet. B'way & 8th Ave.) | 212-246-3330 |
www.bluechilinyc.com

Going "beyond the ordinary", this "modern" Theater District Pan-
Asian shakes things up with an "inventive", "flavorful" menu that lures

"young" types; still, the "sleek" setting with "bizarre" lighting that changes color is a bit too "tacky" for some.

Blue Fin ● *Seafood* | 21 | 22 | 19 | $56 |

W 40s | W Times Sq. | 1567 Broadway (47th St.) | 212-918-1400 | www.brguestrestaurants.com

Bringing "destination" dining to Times Square, Steve Hanson's "popular" seafooder vends "swimmingly fresh" fish in its "lively" street-level cafe as well as a "more relaxed" upstairs room; despite "high decibels" and "uneven service", fans are willing to "pay the premium" for the "primo location" alone.

Blue Ginger *Japanese/Pan-Asian* | 20 | 15 | 18 | $35 |

Chelsea | 106 Eighth Ave. (bet. 15th & 16th Sts.) | 212-352-0911

"Inventive rolls", "fresh sushi" and "well-prepared" Pan-Asian dishes elevate this "relaxed" Chelsea spot a "step above the run-of-the-mill"; "quick, no-frills service" and "price-is-right" costs compensate for the ho-hum atmosphere.

Z Blue Hill *American* | 26 | 22 | 25 | $76 |

G Village | 75 Washington Pl. (bet. MacDougal St. & 6th Ave.) | 212-539-1776 | www.bluehillfarm.com

"Produce so fresh it hasn't been planted yet" is the secret ingredient of "wizard" Dan Barber's "organic chic" New American, specializing in "exquisite seasonal creations" emphasizing "local artisanal" items; throw in a "tranquil" Village setting, "gracious" service and a "romantic garden", and it's easy to see why this "locavore's dream" is worth the "hedge-fund" pricing.

Blue Ribbon ● *American* | 24 | 18 | 22 | $51 |

SoHo | 97 Sullivan St. (bet. Prince & Spring Sts.) | 212-274-0404
Park Slope | 280 Fifth Ave. (bet. 1st St. & Garfield Pl.) | Brooklyn | 718-840-0404
www.blueribbonrestaurants.com

At these "always busy", "night owl"–friendly New Americans, the Bromberg brothers purvey "eclectic", "ridiculously extensive" menus that "satisfy cravings" from "the simple to the sublime"; an "unfailingly friendly" staff sets a mood so "cheerful" that admirers overlook the "hefty waits" and "pricey" tabs for "gourmet dining, even at midnight."

Blue Ribbon Bakery ● *American* | 24 | 18 | 20 | $41 |

G Village | 35 Downing St. (Bedford St.) | 212-337-0404 | www.blueribbonrestaurants.com

"Amazing smells" issue from this "classic" Village New American from the Bromberg brothers, where a "working bakery" and a "bustling bistro" put out "fresh-baked bread" and "down-home delicious" meals; sure, it can be "noisy and crowded", but it's ever a "standout" for "terrific" brunching – "if you can get a seat."

Z Blue Ribbon Sushi ● *Japanese* | 26 | 19 | 21 | $54 |

SoHo | 119 Sullivan St. (bet. Prince & Spring Sts.) | 212-343-0404
Park Slope | 278 Fifth Ave. (bet. 1st St. & Garfield Pl.) | Brooklyn | 718-840-0408
www.blueribbonrestaurants.com

Like "pieces of heaven on a plate", the "super-fresh" sushi and "unusual rolls" are nothing less than "sumptuous" at these "service-oriented" twins from the Bromberg brothers; just "bring lots of cash" and "prepare to wait", though the payoff is a dining experience that could be "better than therapy."

NEW Blue Ribbon Sushi Bar & Grill ❶ *Japanese*

| 24 | 21 | 21 | $61 |

W 50s | 6 Columbus Hotel | 308 W. 58th St. (bet. 8th & 9th Aves.) | 212-397-0404 | www.blueribbonrestaurants.com
The Bromberg brothers "finally" make the psychic leap to Midtown at this "happening" Columbus Circle outpost featuring both "upscale sushi" and Eastern-accented grilled items from a "dumbfoundingly long" menu (it's open for breakfast, lunch and dinner); while "service is as friendly as the fish is fresh", the pricing is strictly "special occasion."

Blue Smoke *BBQ*

| 21 | 17 | 19 | $42 |

Gramercy | 116 E. 27th St. (bet. Lexington Ave. & Park Ave. S.) | 212-447-7733 | www.bluesmoke.com
It's ok to "lick your fingers" at Danny Meyer's "civilized" Gramercy BBQ "mecca", turning out "serious", "falling-off-the-bone" ribs, "excellent beers" and "fab sides" in a bustling setting; while purists protest "NYC prices" and its "high-end lowbrow" dichotomy, there's agreement that the sounds from the downstairs Jazz Standard will "heal your soul."

⊿ Blue Water Grill ❶ *Seafood*

| 23 | 22 | 21 | $54 |

Union Sq | 31 Union Sq. W. (16th St.) | 212-675-9500 | www.brguestrestaurants.com
"Fish fanatics" angle over to Steve Hanson's "upbeat" Union Square "seafood haven" for "consistently delicious" catches plated in a "handsome" remodeled bank setting ringed by a "can't-be-beat" outdoor veranda (there's also an "intimate jazz room" downstairs); despite "splurge" pricing and a "cacophonous din", chances are you'll "swim home happy."

Boathouse *American*

| 17 | 26 | 17 | $54 |

E 70s | Central Park | Central Park Lake, enter on E. 72nd St. (Central Park Dr. N.) | 212-517-2233 | www.thecentralparkboathouse.com
Right out of a "Monet painting", this "magical" lakeside New American in Central Park feels like an "elegant country retreat in the heart of Manhattan"; too bad about the "expensive", "catering-hall" food and "somewhat forced" service, but ultimately the "view trumps all" here.

Bobby Van's Steakhouse *Steak*

| 22 | 19 | 21 | $66 |

E 40s | 230 Park Ave. (46th St.) | 212-867-5490 🖫
E 50s | 131 E. 54th St. (bet. Lexington & Park Aves.) | 212-207-8050
Financial District | 25 Broad St. (Exchange Pl.) | 212-344-8463 🖫
Bobby Van's Grill ❶🖫 *Steak*
W 50s | 135 W. 50th St. (bet. 6th & 7th Aves.) | 212-957-5050 www.bobbyvans.com
"Beef lovers unite" at this "clubby" quartet where "attentive" staffers vend "vantastic", "ranch-size" steaks in "loud", "testosterone-laden" settings; for "real atmosphere", visit the Downtown branch's "bank vault" room – a fitting setting given the "big bucks" you'll shell out.

	FOOD	DECOR	SERVICE	COST

NEW Bobo *European* | 21 | 23 | 20 | $66

W Village | 181 W. 10th St. (7th Ave. S.) | 212-488-2626 | www.bobonyc.com

Set in a "beautiful brownstone", this soigné new Villager offers lots of "romantic" potential, with a moody subterranean bar, antiques-bedecked dining room and alfresco terrace; despite many "changes in the kitchen", the European fare is "delicious" and the "cool young" crowd doesn't seem to mind the upscale tabs.

Boca Chica *Pan-Latin* | 20 | 15 | 17 | $29

E Village | 13 First Ave. (1st St.) | 212-473-0108

"Party-in-a-glass" cocktails are the draw at this "funky" East Villager where folks able to "remember the food" report "tasty" Pan-Latin eats; if you can get over the "loud twentysomething" crowd and "killer lines", it's "one of the best deals in town."

Bocca Lupo ● *Italian* | 23 | 20 | 19 | $31

Cobble Hill | 391 Henry St. (Warren St.) | Brooklyn | 718-243-2522

"Gentle on the wallet and awesome on the palate", this "casual" Italian pairs "fabulous small plates" with "good wine choices" on a "picturesque" Cobble Hill side street; despite the "noisy", "barlike atmosphere", most agree it's "just what the neighborhood needed."

Bocelli *Italian* | 25 | 22 | 23 | $48

Staten Island | 1250 Hylan Blvd. (bet. Clove & Old Town Rds.) | 718-420-6150 | www.bocellirest.com

Long a Staten Island "institution", this "old-world" Italian is known for its "delicious" seafood menu plied in "copious" servings by a "dependable" crew; maybe it's "a bit expensive", but in return there's a "romantic atmosphere", weekly entertainment and valet parking.

Bodrum *Mediterranean/Turkish* | 20 | 14 | 18 | $38

W 80s | 584 Amsterdam Ave. (bet. 88th & 89th Sts.) | 212-799-2806 | www.bodrumnyc.com

"Authentic", "reasonably priced" Med cuisine jazzed up with "Turkish tastes" draws applause at this UWS yearling known for a "wood-burning oven" turning out "fine pizzas" and "to-die-for" baked breads; "snappy service" and sidewalk seats make up for the "cramped" digs.

Bogota Latin Bistro *Pan-Latin* | 20 | 17 | 18 | $28

Park Slope | 141 Fifth Ave. (bet. Lincoln & St. Johns Pls.) | Brooklyn | 718-230-3805 | www.bogotabistro.com

"Filling a void" in Park Slope, this "popular" Pan-Latin offers "tropical fun" via "flavorful" food, "creative" drinks and "spunky" staffers, all for "reasonable" dough; those not in the mood for a "loud" "party atmosphere" take refuge in its all-seasons "back garden."

Bôi *Vietnamese* | 19 | 14 | 17 | $28

E 40s | 246 E. 44th St. (bet. 2nd & 3rd Aves.) | 212-681-6541

Bôi to Go 🗷🍴 *Vietnamese*

E 40s | 800 Second Ave. (bet. 42nd & 43rd Sts.) | 212-681-1122 | www.boi-restaurant.com

A "cool alternative" near Grand Central, this "upscale" but "low-key" Vietnamese vends "fresh", "spicy" dishes and "fabulous" desserts in "dark", "unobtrusive" digs; its nearby take-out site offers a "limited menu" of "quick-bite" sandwiches, all at "decent" prices.

	FOOD	DECOR	SERVICE	COST

Bombay Palace *Indian* | 18 | 17 | 17 | $38 |

W 50s | 30 W. 52nd St. (bet. 5th & 6th Aves.) | 212-541-7777 | www.bombay-palace.com

"Flavorful, curry-laden" dishes and "well-choreographed" service are routine at this regal Midtown Indian standby; though it's "a bit pricey" for the genre and has seen better days, the $14.95 "all-you-can-eat" lunch buffet is a must-try.

Bombay Talkie *Indian* | 19 | 18 | 16 | $36 |

Chelsea | 189 Ninth Ave. (bet. 21st & 22nd Sts.) | 212-242-1900 | www.bombaytalkie.com

"Clever" takes on Indian street food fill the menu of this "buzzy" Chelsea duplex where "playful cocktails" and a "loungey" setting bring in a "young" crowd; though the "Bollywood poster" decor is "fun", the place won't inspire any sequels with its "tiny portions" and "airhead" service.

Bond 45 ◗ *Italian* | 19 | 17 | 18 | $50 |

W 40s | 154 W. 45th St. (bet. 6th & 7th Aves.) | 212-869-4545 | www.bond45.com

As "brassy" and "boisterous" as its Times Square neighborhood, this "big" Italian brasserie via Shelly Fireman is carved out of the "old Bond's clothing store" and revered for its "great antipasto"; maybe it's a bit "pricey" and "impersonal", but "they understand curtain time."

Bondi Road ◗ *Australian* ▽ | 18 | 15 | 19 | $31 |

LES | 153 Rivington St. (bet. Clinton & Suffolk Sts.) | 212-253-5311 | www.bondiroad.com

Known for its "fish 'n' chips, mate", this "easygoing" LES Aussie also offers "simply prepared" pub grub with a Down Under spin for "reasonable" sums; "powerful cocktails", "surf-themed" decor and "hottie" staffers make it a nexus for "rowdy folk."

Bond Street ◗ *Japanese* | 24 | 22 | 19 | $65 |

NoHo | 6 Bond St. (bet. B'way & Lafayette St.) | 212-777-2500

The "food is as good as the scene" at this ever "chic" NoHo Japanese serving sushi "so fresh you barely have to chew" in a "highly stylized setting" tended by a "fashion shoot"-ready crew; just plan to "spend a fortune" for the chance to "hobnob with fabulous people" in its "cozy alcoves" or "sexy" downstairs lounge.

Bonita ◗ *Mexican* | 19 | 16 | 17 | $24 |

Fort Greene | 243 DeKalb Ave. (Vanderbilt Ave.) | Brooklyn | 718-622-5300
Williamsburg | 338 Bedford Ave. (bet. S. 2nd & 3rd Sts.) | Brooklyn | 718-384-9500
www.bonitanyc.com

These "hip" Brooklyn Mexicanos sling "cheap" tacos and other "south-of-the-border" classics "just like *abuelita* made" in "laid-back", "no-frills" digs; there's "not much space" and the staff may be on "permanent siesta", yet they do "hit the spot."

Boqueria ◗ *Spanish* | 22 | 18 | 19 | $46 |

Flatiron | 53 W. 19th St. (bet. 5th & 6th Aves.) | 212-255-4160 | www.boquerianyc.com

Think "Barcelona in Manhattan" to get the idea behind this "irresistible" Flatiron Spaniard that lures a "young" crowd with ultra-"creative" takes on Basque and Catalonian tapas; no, it "ain't cheap", the dimensions are "tiny" and that "no-reservations policy" is a "bummer", but ultimately it's a kick "rubbing elbows with the people here."

Borgo Antico ● *Italian*   17 | 16 | 18 | $42

G Village | 22 E. 13th St. (bet. 5th Ave. & University Pl.) | 212-807-1313 | www.borgoanticony.com

"As comfortable as a pair of old slippers", this "unassuming" double-decker Villager offers "good value" via "homey" Italian offerings served by "agreeable" waiters; alright, there are "no fireworks" and it's time to "refresh" the decor, but fans say this "sleeper" is "pleasant" enough.

Bottega del Vino *Italian*   21 | 20 | 21 | $67

E 50s | 7 E. 59th St. (bet. 5th & Madison Aves.) | 212-223-3028 | www.bottegadelvinonyc.com

Replicating its "home base in Verona", this "white-glove" Midtown Italian with a "charming Alps atmosphere" matches "wonderful" food with a "veritable tome" of a wine list; given the "high rollers" it attracts, the "Fifth Avenue prices" are no surprise.

Bottino *Italian*   19 | 18 | 17 | $44

Chelsea | 246 10th Ave. (bet. 24th & 25th Sts.) | 212-206-6766 | www.bottinonyc.com

West Chelsea "gallery-hoppers" plug this "appealing" Tuscan for "simple" fare that's especially "comforting after you've spent thousands on a multimedia installation"; service can be "indifferent" and its popularity may be "cooling a bit", but the back garden remains as "divine" as ever.

Bouchon Bakery *American/French*   23 | 14 | 17 | $29

W 60s | Time Warner Ctr. | 10 Columbus Circle, 3rd fl. (60th St. at B'way) | 212-823-9366 | www.bouchonbakery.com

For a "decadent" shopping break, Thomas Keller's New American cafe/patisserie in the Time Warner Center injects a bit of "food heaven into everyday life" with its "sophisticated sandwiches" and "sublime" French pastries; despite the "food court" feel and "inconsistent" service, its "pedigree is obvious."

☑ Bouley ● *French*   28 | - | 27 | $98

TriBeCa | 120 W. Broadway (Duane St.) | 212-964-2525 | www.davidbouley.com

"After all these years", "dining doesn't get any more sophisticated" than at David Bouley's "transcending" TriBeCa experience where the French cooking is "fantastic" and the "unobtrusive" staff "knows exactly what to do" and does it; sure, the tabs are "splurge"-worthy, but in return you can expect "special-occasion" meals every night of the week and the $38 prix fixe lunch is an "all-time fave"; N.B. it's due to move around the corner to spiffy new digs at 163 Duane Street.

☑ Bouley, Upstairs *Eclectic*   25 | 16 | 18 | $50

TriBeCa | 130 W. Broadway (Duane St.) | 212-608-5829 | www.davidbouley.com

Have a "bite of Bouley flavor at a fraction of the price" at this TriBeCa Eclectic that will offer more "elbow room" once it expands downstairs from its original second-floor location; maybe the "decor's not the reason to visit", but the "cuisine-crossing" menu (including sushi) is so "creative" you won't care.

NEW Bourbon Street Bar & Grille *Cajun*

FOOD	DECOR	SERVICE	COST
-	-	-	M

W 40s | 346 W. 46th St. (bet. 8th & 9th Aves.) | 212-245-2030 | www.bourbonny.com

N'Awlins lands on Restaurant Row via this new Cajun-Creole whose chef previously manned the stoves at the Big Easy's famed Commander's Palace; set in a soaring, double-height space, it sports a wrought iron-railed mezzanine overlooking the main floor, as well as a streetside balcony and a long mahogany bar topped by a stuffed alligator.

Bourbon Street Café *Cajun/Southern*

18	16	17	$31

Bayside | 40-12 Bell Blvd. (bet. 40th & 41st Aves.) | Queens | 718-224-2200 | www.bourbonstreetny.com

"Surprisingly tasty" Cajun dishes as well as pub-grub standards turn up at this "cheerful" Bayside "staple" where "if they say it's spicy, you'd better believe them"; while there are "no bells and whistles" here, the bar scene is "very active" and quite affordable.

NEW Braai ● *South African*

-	-	-	M

W 50s | 329 W. 51st St. (bet. 8th & 9th Aves.) | 212-315-3315 | www.braainyc.com

From the owners of nearby Xai Xai Wine Bar comes this affordable Hell's Kitchen arrival, a South African *braai* (or BBQ) joint plying game meats like ostrich and venison; housed in a hutlike space done up in thatched bamboo, it's well located for a pre-theater meal.

Brasserie ● *French*

20	21	19	$52

E 50s | Seagram Bldg. | 100 E. 53rd St. (bet. Lexington & Park Aves.) | 212-751-4840 | www.patinagroup.com

Whether for "power breakfasts" or late-night bites, Midtowners flock to this 50-year-old "Gotham classic" for "reliable" French fare served in a "Space Age Modern" setting; while "noisy and expensive", it's "always fun", though some wish the menu were as "cutting-edge" as the decor.

NEW Brasserie Cognac ● *French*

▽ 19	16	16	$53

W 50s | 1740 Broadway (55th St.) | 212-757-3600 | www.cognacrestaurant.com

Though this "airy" Midtowner from the Serafina team may be brand-new, its old-school design incorporating mirrors, pressed-tin ceilings and lots of dark-wood paneling feels time-tested; in addition to cognac-based cocktails at the bar, there's a variety of cheese and charcuterie on offer, as well as "authentic" French brasserie items.

Brasserie 8½ *French*

22	23	22	$59

W 50s | 9 W. 57th St. (bet. 5th & 6th Aves.) | 212-829-0812 | www.brasserie812.com

A "grand staircase" worthy of "Gloria Swanson" greets you at this "glam-orous" Midtowner where "contemporary" French cuisine and an "affable staff" make for "adult" dining; "expensive price tags" and a "hidden" subterranean location may explain why it's relatively "undiscovered."

NEW Brasserie 44 *American*

19	21	18	$57

W 40s | Royalton Hotel | 44 W. 44th St. (bet. 5th & 6th Aves.) | 212-944-8844 | www.brasseriefortyfour.com

One of the most "well-kept secrets" in the Theater District, this "re-cently redone" New American (née 44) features "better food than you'd expect in a hip hotel", along with a vaguely nautical redesign, "not-cheap" pricing and a crowd as "beautiful" as ever.

Brasserie Julien *French*

18	19	17	$45

E 80s | 1422 Third Ave. (bet. 80th & 81st Sts.) | 212-744-6327 | www.brasseriejulien.com

Bringing "France" to Yorkville, this "charming" brasserie offers "solid" Gallic grub in "congenial" deco digs, where the "Parisian flair" extends to the "uneven service"; insiders say it's best experienced on weekends when there's "live jazz", but it's "*très* enjoyable" any day of the week.

Brasserie Ruhlmann *French*

18	21	18	$55

W 50s | 45 Rockefeller Plaza (enter on 50th St., bet. 5th & 6th Aves.) | 212-974-2020 | www.brasserieruhlmann.com

An "incredible" art deco room "straight out of Paris in the '20s" is the highlight of this Rock Center brasserie featuring "quality" French fare overseen by executive chef Laurent Tourondel and a "spacious" outdoor terrace; service is "pleasant" and the tabs "expensive", yet for some it's all about "location."

Bravo Gianni ● *Italian*

21	14	21	$66

E 60s | 230 E. 63rd St. (bet. 2nd & 3rd Aves.) | 212-752-7272

"Everyone makes you feel at home" at this UES trip "back in time" known for its "fine" Northern Italian fare; it attracts an "older set" that can handle the "expense account"-worthy tabs, and though the decor's "tired", the "food's so good you won't care."

Bread Tribeca *Italian*

19	15	15	$34

TriBeCa | 301 Church St. (Walker St.) | 212-334-8282 | www.breadtribeca.com

Bread ● *Sandwiches*

NoLita | 20 Spring St. (bet. Elizabeth & Mott Sts.) | 212-334-1015

It's all about the "tasty fresh bread" at this "fashionable" TriBeCan specializing in sandwiches and "simple" Italian dishes served in "bare", "loftlike" digs; "indifferent" service is trumped by "affordable" tabs, and there's also a pint-size, separately owned NoLita affiliate.

Breeze *French/Thai*

21	14	18	$33

W 40s | 661 Ninth Ave. (bet. 45th & 46th Sts.) | 212-262-7777 | www.breezenyc.com

"Upbeat" is the mood at this "trendy" Thai-French "find" in Hell's Kitchen where "light" fusion bites arrive in a "modern diner" setting; the "prices are good", and it gets bonus points for being "near the theaters."

Brennan & Carr ●⊟ *Sandwiches*

20	8	15	$17

Sheepshead Bay | 3432 Nostrand Ave. (Ave. U) | Brooklyn | 718-646-9559

"Nothing changes" at this "decades-old" Sheepshead Bay "blue-collar" landmark famed for its "messy" roast beef sandwiches "double-dipped" in au jus; the "same low prices" compensate for the "mediocre service" and "Dark Ages" decor.

brgr *Burgers*

18	13	14	$16

Chelsea | 287 Seventh Ave. (bet. 26th & 27th Sts.) | 212-488-7500 | www.brgr.us

"Have it your way" at this Chelsea eatery where "build-it-yourself" burgers are "made to order" from "juicy" beef, turkey and veggie patties; though it's "a tad expensive" given the "cafeteria-counter service", the "Fresca on tap" is simply "priceless."

Bricco *Italian*   19 | 17 | 19 | $43

W 50s | 304 W. 56th St. (bet. 8th & 9th Aves.) | 212-245-7160 |
www.bricconyc.com

At this "intimate" Hell's Kitchen Italian, "wonderful" brick-oven pizzas and pastas are served for "decent" costs; it's best remembered for its "famous ceiling" embedded with lipsticked kiss marks, and some would like to smooch the "warm staff" for assuring that you "make the curtain."

Brick Cafe *French/Italian*   19 | 20 | 17 | $32

Astoria | 30-95 33rd St. (31st Ave.) | Queens | 718-267-2735 |
www.brickcafe.com

A "solid local choice" for a drink, "quick bite" or full-fledged Franco-Italian dining, this "popular" Astoria bistro is a "reliably good" option for "basic", "affordable" food; "softly flickering candlelight" within and seating outside add to the "relaxed" mood.

Brick Lane Curry House *Indian*   21 | 14 | 17 | $32

E Village | 306-308 E. Sixth St. (2nd Ave.) | 212-979-2900 |
www.bricklanecurryhouse.com

"Fiery", "flavorful" curries in the style of London's "real Brick Lane" head up the get-out-the-"fire-extinguisher" menu of this Sixth Street Indian; the "generous portions" are "fairly priced" (especially the lunch buffets), even if the decor and "sluggish" service are not so hot.

Bridge Cafe *American*   21 | 19 | 22 | $44

Financial District | 279 Water St. (Dover St.) | 212-227-3344 |
www.bridgecafenyc.com

"Old NY" gets an "updated menu" at this "back-in-time", circa-1794 tavern near the "foot of the Brooklyn Bridge" serving "well-prepared" New Americana; "accommodating" staffers, "moderate" tabs and a "congenial" crowd make it a great "nontouristy find."

Brio *Italian*   18 | 15 | 17 | $41

E 60s | 137 E. 61st St. (Lexington Ave.) | 212-980-2300
NEW **E 80s** | 1725 Second Ave. (89th St.) | 212-289-8944 ◖
www.brionyc.com

These "ultrabusy" Eastsiders serve "basic" Italian grub, including a notably "crispy" pizza at the Bloomingdale's-area original (the new Second Avenue spin-off features more of a wine-bar menu); despite "noisy" environs and "average" service, "fair prices" keep the trade brisk.

Brioso *Italian*   ▽ 24 | 19 | 23 | $44

Staten Island | 174 New Dorp Ln. (9th St.) | 718-667-1700 |
www.briosoristorante.com

Staten Islanders "skip the drive into the city" thanks to the standout "robust" Italian cooking and "pro" service at this longtimer; "loud" and deservedly "crowded on weekends", it's "reasonably priced" all the time.

NEW Broadway East Ⓜ *Vegetarian*   ▽ 21 | 23 | 19 | $45

LES | 171 E. Broadway (bet. Jefferson & Rutgers Sts.) | 212-228-3100 |
www.broadwayeast.com

Sustainability gets a stylish twist at this LES "nouveau vegetarian" set in a "drop-dead-gorgeous" space complete with a plant-sprouting wall; the "delicious" seasonal offerings range from grilled pizzas to macrobiotic plates (and even some fish and poultry), while the green/locavore ethos extends to the local beers and wines on offer.

Brooklyn Diner USA ☻ *Diner* | 17 | 14 | 15 | $31 |

W 40s | 155 W. 43rd St. (bet. B'way & 6th Ave.) | 212-265-5400
W 50s | 212 W. 57th St. (bet. B'way & 7th Ave.) | 212-977-2280
www.brooklyndiner.com

"Hefty portions" of "elevated diner" food at affordable prices draw "animated" crowds to these "fast-paced" American "throwbacks" from Shelly Fireman; despite "theme-park decor" and "preoccupied" staffers, they're "well located" and you certainly "won't leave hungry."

Brooklyn Fish Camp ⓜ *Seafood* | 22 | 15 | 19 | $41 |

Park Slope | 162 Fifth Ave. (Degraw St.) | Brooklyn | 718-783-3264 | www.brooklynfishcamp.com

"Killer lobster rolls" are the bait at this Park Slope seafooder, a Mary's Fish Camp spin-off offering the same "consistently high quality" for slightly "pricey" tabs (though still "cheaper than driving to Maine"); the ho-hum interior is trumped by a "delightful" warm-weather garden and year-round "wisecracking" waitresses.

Brother Jimmy's BBQ *BBQ* | 16 | 11 | 14 | $25 |

E 40s | Grand Central | lower level (42nd St. & Vanderbilt Ave.) | 212-661-4022
E 70s | 1485 Second Ave. (bet. 77th & 78th Sts.) | 212-288-0999 ☻
E 90s | 1644 Third Ave. (92nd St.) | 212-426-2020 ☻
Garment District | 416 Eighth Ave. (31st St.) | 212-967-7603 ☻
NEW **Murray Hill** | 181 Lexington Ave. (31st St.) | 212-779-7427
W 80s | 428 Amsterdam Ave. (bet. 80th & 81st Sts.) | 212-501-7515 ☻
www.brotherjimmys.com

"Young and loud" but "tasty as hell", these "guy-oriented" BBQ joints serve "not-bad" eats to "beer-soaked frat boys" lured in by "cheap" tabs, "fishbowl"-size drinks and "hot little waitresses" flashing "bare midriffs"; in short, "if you're over 30, have it delivered."

Brown Café *American* | ∇ 22 | 15 | 20 | $30 |

LES | 61 Hester St. (bet. Essex & Ludlow Sts.) | 212-477-2427

Exuding a whiff of "downtown bohemia", this "low-tech", under-the-radar LES cafe draws "casual hipsters" with "well-priced" seasonal New Americana; despite "tiny" digs and "uncomfortable", "lumberjack-chic" furnishings, this sleeper remains a "neighborhood" favorite.

Bryant Park Grill/Cafe *American* | 17 | 21 | 17 | $47 |

W 40s | behind NY Public Library | 25 W. 40th St. (bet. 5th & 6th Aves.) | 212-840-6500 | www.arkrestaurants.com

An "unbeatable setting" – "scenic" Bryant Park – is the thing at this "touristy" twosome where the "casual" alfresco Cafe is reminiscent of an "upscale picnic" and the more formal indoor Grill has a "greenhouse feel"; sadly, the "star" setting supersedes the "adequate" American eats.

B. Smith's Restaurant Row *Southern* | 18 | 19 | 19 | $47 |

W 40s | 320 W. 46th St. (bet. 8th & 9th Aves.) | 212-315-1100 | www.bsmith.com

A "solid" pre-theater choice, this "cheerful" Restaurant Row "standby" serves midpriced, "stick-to-your-ribs" Southern grub in an "earthy, welcoming" room; customers "love it", especially when charming TV celeb/owner Barbara Smith is around.

Bubba Gump Shrimp Co. ◑ *American/Seafood* | 14 | 16 | 16 | $31 |

W 40s | 1501 Broadway (bet. 43rd & 44th Sts.) | 212-391-7100 | www.bubbagump.com

"More kitsch than kitchen", this "downscale" Times Square American theme eatery draws "tourists and Forrest Gump lovers" with its "decent shrimp" and "folksy" service; though "gimmicky" and "designed for the masses", at least it's "relatively easy on the wallet."

Bubby's *American* | 17 | 13 | 15 | $29 |

TriBeCa | 120 Hudson St. (N. Moore St.) | 212-219-0666
Dumbo | 1 Main St. (bet. Plymouth & Water Sts.) | Brooklyn | 718-222-0666 Ⓜ⇗
www.bubbys.com

These "sunny" neighborhood "staples" purvey "routine" American comfort food for "decent prices", though they're best known for "legendary brunches"; despite "loud" decibels and "lacking service", they're usually "ridiculously busy" with lots of "children underfoot."

☒ Buddakan ◑ *Asian* | 23 | 27 | 21 | $63 |

Chelsea | 75 Ninth Ave. (16th St.) | 212-989-6699 | www.buddakannyc.com
"Putting the awe in awesome", Stephen Starr's "opulent" Chelsea "pleasure dome" features an "impressive" modern Asian menu that plays second fiddle to the "glitzy" setting, an "ambitiously staged series of spaces" replete with "incredible chandeliers" and "soaring ceilings"; "steep prices", "loud" noise and "consistent waits" to the contrary, it's a "NY must" for "the young and hip."

Buddha Bar ◑ *Asian Fusion* | 19 | 26 | 17 | $63 |

Meatpacking | 25 Little W. 12th St. (bet. 9th Ave. & Washington St.) | 212-647-7314 | www.buddhabarnyc.com

"Quite the scene", this "big, brassy" Meatpacking restaurant-cum-nightclub is known for its "over-the-top" looks incorporating "way-cool jellyfish tanks", koi ponds and a 17-ft.-tall Buddha; too bad the "usual" Asian fusion fare doesn't live up to the scenery, though the place does provide "all the elements of a wild night out": "loud music", "snooty" attitude and "humbling" tabs.

Buenos Aires ◑ *Argentinean* | 22 | 14 | 18 | $38 |

E Village | 513 E. Sixth St. (bet. Aves. A & B) | 212-228-2775 | www.buenosairesnyc.com

Still "under the radar" in the East Village, this "authentic" Argentine steakhouse is a "win-win" choice with its "wrap-around-the-plate" grilled meats, "fantastic empanadas" and "well-priced Malbecs"; add in "gracious" service and a garden to augment the "bare-bones" interior, and it's a "true find."

Bukhara Grill *Indian* | 22 | 16 | 19 | $36 |

E 40s | 217 E. 49th St. (bet. 2nd & 3rd Aves.) | 212-888-2839 | www.bukharany.com

The $15.95 lunch buffet is a "reasonably priced" "spice delight" at this U.N.-area Indian that curries favor with "tasty" vittles and "calm" atmospherics; maybe the "interior could use an upgrade", but the small second-floor terrace is fine as is.

	FOOD	DECOR	SERVICE	COST

Bull and Bear ● *Steak* — 19 | 21 | 20 | $64

E 40s | Waldorf-Astoria | 570 Lexington Ave. (49th St.) | 212-872-4900 | www.bullandbearsteakhouse.com

There's "nothing bearish" going on at this "expensive", "old-fashioned" Waldorf-Astoria chop shop where "classy steaks", "clublike" looks and a "beautiful mahogany bar" add up to "macho power dining"; look for a "man-in-the-gray-flannel-suit" crowd and "service like it used to be."

Bull Run *American* — 17 | 16 | 17 | $43

Financial District | Club Quarters Hotel | 52 William St. (Pine St.) | 212-859-2200

"Convenient" is the word for this Financial District New American where the "good to average" grub is ferried by a "prompt" crew; still, "anonymous" looks and "predictable" dining make some say it's worthwhile only "if you're in the neighborhood."

NEW Bún ● *Vietnamese* — ▽ 21 | 17 | 18 | $31

SoHo | 143 Grand St. (bet. Crosby & Lafayette Sts.) | 212-431-7999 | www.eatbun.com

"High-concept creations" at "great prices" lure fans to this "innovative" new 24/7 SoHo Vietnamese where the "flavorful" namesake staple (rice vermicelli) appears in many forms on the menu; too bad the "modern", stylishly spare decor seems at odds with the "clunky" service.

Burger Heaven *Burgers* — 16 | 8 | 14 | $19

E 40s | 20 E. 49th St. (bet. 5th & Madison Aves.) | 212-755-2166
E 40s | 291 Madison Ave. (bet. 40th & 41st Sts.) | 212-685-6250 ⊠
E 50s | 536 Madison Ave. (bet. 54th & 55th Sts.) | 212-753-4214
E 50s | 9 E. 53rd St. (bet. 5th & Madison Aves.) | 212-752-0340
E 60s | 804 Lexington Ave. (62nd St.) | 212-838-3580
E 80s | 1534 Third Ave. (bet. 86th & 87th Sts.) | 212-722-8292
www.burgerheaven.com

Positioned somewhere "between diners and coffee shops", these "Middle America" patty palaces purvey "good sloppy burgers" for folks who like it "fast and cheap"; despite "variable" service and "time-machine" decor, they're a magnet for business-lunchers on the run.

**burger joint at
Le Parker Meridien** ●⊅ *Burgers* — 23 | 9 | 11 | $15

W 50s | Le Parker Meridien | 119 W. 56th St. (bet. 6th & 7th Aves.) | 212-708-7414

For "top-class burgers" in the "most unlikely" setting, check out this "old-school" hamburger joint incongruously "tucked away behind a curtain" in a "swank" Midtown hotel lobby; while the chow scores well, the "intimidating service", "lowbrow decor", "minimal seating" and "unbearable" lunch lines don't; P.S. the secret's out, "even Oprah knows."

NEW Burger Shoppe ●⊠ *Burgers* — ▽ 18 | 13 | 11 | $14
(aka Wall Street Burger Shoppe)

Financial District | 30 Water St. (bet. Broad St. & Coenties Slip) | 212-425-1000 | www.burgershoppenyc.com

Bringing a '50s feel to the Financial District, this nostalgic burger joint is outfitted as a retro diner on the first floor and a vintage taproom on the second; midpriced patties and takeaway/delivery options keep it buzzing through lunch, while a simple beer and wine list lures after-work types.

	FOOD	DECOR	SERVICE	COST

Burritoville *Tex-Mex*   17 | 7 | 13 | $13

Chelsea | 264 W. 23rd St. (bet. 7th & 8th Aves.) | 212-367-9844 ☽

E 50s | 866 Third Ave. (52nd St.) | 212-980-4111

E 70s | 1487 Second Ave. (bet. 77th & 78th Sts.) | 212-472-8800 ☽

Financial District | 36 Water St. (Broad St.) | 212-747-1100

Financial District | 80 Nassau St. (bet. Fulton & John Sts.) | 212-285-0070

Garment District | 352 W. 39th St. (9th Ave.) | 212-563-9088

TriBeCa | 116 Chambers St. (Church St.) | 212-566-2300

W 40s | 625 Ninth Ave. (44th St.) | 212-333-5352 ☽

W 70s | 166 W. 72nd St. (bet. Amsterdam & Columbus Aves.) | 212-580-7700 ☽

W Village | 298 Bleecker St. (7th Ave. S.) | 212-633-9249
www.burritoville.com

An "empty stomach" is a prerequisite at this all-over-town Tex-Mex chain vending "hefty", "can't-go-wrong" burritos and other "cheap college food" (including some "vegetarian options"); "so-so service" and "zero decor" make a strong case for takeout or delivery.

Butai *Japanese*   ▽ 21 | 20 | 19 | $47

Gramercy | 115 E. 18th St. (bet. Irving Pl. & Park Ave. S.) | 212-387-8885 | www.butai.us

Fans of "something different" like the "delicious" robata grill offerings at this "chic" Gramercy Japanese where there's "always space" and the staff is always "helpful with the plethora of choices"; the rather "pricey" small plates do "add up quickly", but they're "terrific" (and intended) for sharing.

Butter ⓩ *American*   20 | 23 | 18 | $57

E Village | 415 Lafayette St. (bet. Astor Pl. & 4th St.) | 212-253-2828 | www.butterrestaurant.com

"Trendy" is the word for this "stylish" duplex near the Public Theater where the focus is not on the "surprisingly good" New American food but rather on "who's walking in the door"; "hoity-toity" service and "expensive" tabs put off "mere mortals", while "celebs" head downstairs to "hobnob."

Cabana ☽ *Nuevo Latino*   21 | 17 | 17 | $36

E 60s | 1022 Third Ave. (bet. 60th & 61st Sts.) | 212-980-5678

Seaport | Pier 17 | 89 South St. (Fulton St.) | 212-406-1155

Forest Hills | 107-10 70th Rd. (bet. Austin St. & Queens Blvd.) | Queens | 718-263-3600

www.cabanarestaurant.com

Take a "vacation on a plate" via the "delicious" Nuevo Latino *comida* washed down with "addictive mojitos" at this "vibrant" Cuban mini-chain; ok, the "long waits" and "too-laid-back" service are "no day at the beach", but "moderate prices" (and "wonderful views" at the "waterfront" Seaport branch) compensate.

NEW Cabrito *Mexican*   - | - | - | M

G Village | 50 Carmine St. (bet. Bedford & Bleecker Sts.) | 212-929-5050 | www.cabritonyc.com

Rib-sticking Mexicana in the form of affordably priced tacos, *cemitas* (sandwiches) and the namesake slow-roasted goat turn up on the menu of this new Village cantina; it's set in a snug tile-and-stucco interior with a lengthy bar as its focus, but in warmer months the back patio is a welcome alternative.

Cacio e Pepe *Italian*

| 21 | 16 | 19 | $39 |

E Village | 182 Second Ave. (bet. 11th & 12th Sts.) | 212-505-5931 | www.cacioepepe.com

The "must-order" item at this "neighborhood" East Village trattoria is its "standout" signature pasta dish served in a Parmesan wheel, though its Roman specialties are equally "excellent"; "decor isn't the greatest", but it does deliver "modest" prices, "service with a smile" and a "lovely back garden."

Cacio e Vino ◐ *Italian*

| ▽ 21 | 15 | 17 | $38 |

E Village | 80 Second Ave. (bet. 4th & 5th Sts.) | 212-228-3269 | www.cacioevino.com

Look for a "high authenticity factor" at this "little" East Village Sicilian known for "real Italian" cooking and "delicious wood-fired pizzas" for "reasonable" dough; "fresh-off-the-boat" service means there are "no clichés" here, save for the "boring red-sauce-joint" decor.

Cafe Asean ⇄ *SE Asian*

| 20 | 12 | 17 | $28 |

G Village | 117 W. 10th St. (bet. Greenwich & 6th Aves.) | 212-633-0348 | www.cafeasean.com

"Leisurely" grazing on "inspired" Southeast Asian fare is yours at this "quiet" Villager where the staff's "friendly" and the "rustic" digs exude "shabby charm" (there's also a more "pleasant garden"); though many "wish they took credit cards", it's hard to "eat out much cheaper."

Cafe Bar ◐ *Greek/Mediterranean*

| ▽ 20 | 18 | 15 | $25 |

Astoria | 32-90 36th St. (34th Ave.) | Queens | 718-204-5273

"Hipsters" dig this "cool" Astorian for its "delicious", fairly priced Greek-Med menu and "art house–cum–coffee shop" vibe (it "looks like it belongs in San Francisco"); it's a "fun place to lounge and relax", a sentiment that the "snail's-pace" service seems to echo.

☑ Café Boulud *French*

| 27 | 23 | 26 | $84 |

E 70s | Surrey Hotel | 20 E. 76th St. (bet. 5th & Madison Aves.) | 212-772-2600 | www.danielnyc.com

"Comfortable" yet "civilized", Daniel Boulud's "sophisticated" Upper East Side satellite provides "glorious" dining thanks to chef Gavin Kaysen's "exquisite" French cuisine, "interesting" wines and "seamless service"; though decidedly "costly", prices are "less astronomical" than at the flagship, especially for the "bargain" $40 lunch prix fixe; N.B. the somewhat "dated" interior is undergoing renovations in summer 2008.

Cafe Centro ◩ *Mediterranean*

| 19 | 18 | 19 | $48 |

E 40s | MetLife Bldg. | 200 Park Ave. (45th St.) | 212-818-1222 | www.patinagroup.com

The "classic business lunch" is in full swing at this "vibrant" brasserie near Grand Central that lures throngs with "dependable" Med meals, "efficient" service and "commuter convenience"; those seeking "more relaxed", crowd-free dining report that "dinner's a delight."

	FOOD	DECOR	SERVICE	COST

Cafecito ☞ *Cuban*

▽ 21 | 15 | 15 | $27

E Village | 185 Ave. C (bet. 11th & 12th Sts.) | 212-253-9966 |
www.cafecitonyc.com

Latin lovers get their "Cuban fix" at this "out-of-the-way" East Villager
where the "quality" cooking "transports you" to Havana; though
there's "little going on by way of decor or service", "reasonable prices"
and "fab mojitos" save the day.

Cafe Cluny ● *American/French*

20 | 19 | 19 | $49

W Village | 284 W. 12th St. (W. 4th St.) | 212-255-6900 | www.cafecluny.com

Popular with "wafer-thin" models and "arty celebs", this "sunny",
"sceney" Village bistro serves a "simple but delicious" French-American
menu; devotees report this "instant classic" is especially "popular"
(read: "cramped") for brunch.

Cafe Colonial *Brazilian*

▽ 18 | 16 | 15 | $30

NoLita | 276 Elizabeth St. (Houston St.) | 212-274-0044 |
www.cafecolonialny.com

"Fun people-watching" comes in "close" quarters at this "hip" NoLita
Brazilian known for doing "really good chow at reasonable prices"; too
bad about the "thrown-together" decor and "English"-challenged service, but that doesn't diminish the "good vibe."

Cafe Con Leche *Cuban/Dominican*

17 | 11 | 15 | $24

W 80s | 424 Amsterdam Ave. (bet. 80th & 81st Sts.) | 212-595-7000
W 90s | 726 Amsterdam Ave. (bet. 95th & 96th Sts.) | 212-678-7000
www.cafeconlechenyc.com

As "close to Miami" as the UWS gets, these "lively" "neighborhood
fixtures" serve "tasty" Cuban-Dominican chow as well as some of the
"best coffee in town"; forget about the "*mañana*" service and "divey"
settings: the payoff is "lots of food for small prices."

Café d'Alsace ● *French*

20 | 18 | 18 | $47

E 80s | 1695 Second Ave. (88th St.) | 212-722-5133 | www.cafedalsace.com

Aside from its midpriced, "stick-to-your-ribs" French menu featuring
"unusual" Alsatian specialties, this "upbeat" UES brasserie also features
a "phenomenal" beer menu (and even a suds sommelier); "deafening"
decibels and "cramped" quarters make the patio "the place to be."

Café de Bruxelles ● *Belgian*

20 | 15 | 19 | $42

W Village | 118 Greenwich Ave. (13th St.) | 212-206-1830

"There's more to the menu than moules frites" at this "venerable"
West Villager that also offers seldom-seen "Belgian favorites" and an
"extensive selection" of Trappist beer; prices are "modest" and service
"relaxed", so despite the "stodgy" feel, most report "life is good" here.

☑ Café des Artistes ● *French*

22 | 26 | 23 | $69

W 60s | 1 W. 67th St. (bet. Columbus Ave. & CPW) | 212-877-3500 |
www.cafenyc.com

The "older the violin, the sweeter the music" says it all about this
"classy" UWS "grande dame" via George and Jenifer Lang that "still
seduces" with an "oh-so-romantic setting" that combines "beautiful
flowers" and "sensual murals" of wood nymphs with "delicious" French
dishes and "excellent service"; a "feast for the eyes and palate", it's
"quintessential NYC" and worth every penny.

	FOOD	DECOR	SERVICE	COST

Café du Soleil   *French/Mediterranean*
19 | 18 | 15 | $39

W 100s | 2723 Broadway (104th St.) | 212-316-5000

"Re-creating the French bistro experience on the UWS", this "cozy" spot serves "tasty" French-Med dishes in atmospheric digs for a "surprisingly affordable" price; while the "truly Parisian" service can be "condescending", the "outdoor seating is a plus."

Cafe Español ◐ *Spanish*
20 | 14 | 19 | $34

G Village | 172 Bleecker St. (bet. MacDougal & Sullivan Sts.) | 212-505-0657
G Village | 78 Carmine St. (bet. Bedford St. & 7th Ave. S.) | 212-675-3312
www.cafeespanol.com

"Old-world" is the word on these "welcoming", separately owned Villagers purveying "honest" Spanish fare in "plentiful" portions; "charming" service, "low prices" and "many sangrias" on offer make them "longstanding gems."

Café Evergreen   *Chinese*
20 | 12 | 19 | $32

E 60s | 1288 First Ave. (bet. 69th & 70th Sts.) | 212-744-3266

"Who needs Chinatown?" when there's this "reliably good" UES Cantonese serving some of the "best dim sum north of Canal" backed up by an "amazing wine list" and "understanding" service; maybe the decor's "uninspired", but the pricing's "reasonable" and "delivery is fast."

Cafe Fiorello ◐ *Italian*
20 | 16 | 18 | $50

W 60s | 1900 Broadway (bet. 63rd & 64th Sts.) | 212-595-5330 |
www.cafefiorello.com

Just a "stone's throw from Lincoln Center", this "finely tuned" Italian is applauded for its "extraordinary" antipasto bar, "amazing thin-crust pizzas" and "zippy" staffers who "ensure you won't be late for *Falstaff*"; regulars sidestep the "noisy" pre-theater "bustle" at its "wonderful" people-watching sidewalk tables.

Café Frida   *Mexican*
20 | 15 | 17 | $38

W 70s | 368 Columbus Ave. (bet. 77th & 78th Sts.) | 212-712-2929 |
www.cafefrida.com

"Excellent" made-to-order guacamole and "hallucinatory margaritas" collide at this "unpretentious" UWS Mexican that's usually "bustling and noisy"; the staff may be on "Mexico time", but "reasonable" prices and a "fun" feel keep it *mucho* "popular."

Cafe Gitane ◐⌿ *French/Moroccan*
19 | 15 | 14 | $26

NoLita | 242 Mott St. (Prince St.) | 212-334-9552

"Skinny models" and "Euro" types meet cute at this ever-"trendy", cash-only NoLita cafe where "you may feel out of place if you weigh over 100 pounds"; the French-Moroccan eats are "wonderfully light" (and not badly priced), though the "pretentious" staff can make you "feel as if you should serve them."

Café Habana ◐ *Cuban/Mexican*
20 | 14 | 14 | $22

NoLita | 17 Prince St. (Elizabeth St.) | 212-625-2001
Habana Outpost ⌿ *Cuban/Mexican*
Fort Greene | 755-757 Fulton St. (S. Portland Ave.) | Brooklyn | 718-858-9500
www.ecoeatery.com

Mexico and Cuba form a "harmonious union" at this "groovy" NoLita "hole-in-the-wall" where a "cool crowd" congregates for "cheap", "down-home" Latin cooking; the "daunting lines", "beyond-tight fit" and "rushed service" can be avoided at the nearby take-out annex or the eco-conscious Fort Greene satellite.

Cafe Joul *French*

| 18 | 13 | 17 | $43 |

E 50s | 1070 First Ave. (bet. 58th & 59th Sts.) | 212-759-3131

This Sutton Place "sleeper" offers "moderately priced" French bistro items and "decent service" in "friendly" environs; maybe the "spare setting" is "not exciting", but regulars find it's "just right" in a "neighborhood thin on options."

NEW Café Katja *Austrian*

| ▽ 24 | 20 | 23 | $30 |

LES | 79 Orchard St. (bet. Broome & Grand Sts.) | 212-219-9545

"Different and delicious", this "cozy" new LES Austrian "sliver" of a cafe vends "perfect sausages", spaetzle and the like paired with "terrific wines and tasty brews"; a "sweet staff" and "affordable" tabs mean it's usually "crowded."

Cafe Lalo ●⇕ *Coffeehouse/Dessert*

| 19 | 19 | 13 | $21 |

W 80s | 201 W. 83rd St. (bet. Amsterdam Ave. & B'way) | 212-496-6031 | www.cafelalo.com

"Still trading" on its *You've Got Mail* cameo, this "quintessential" UWS dessert dispenser lures "crowds" with a "decadent selection" of "naughty" treats; too bad "indifferent" service, a "touristy scene" and that "cash-only" policy detract from the otherwise "sweet" experience.

Cafe Loup ● *French*

| 19 | 17 | 19 | $43 |

G Village | 105 W. 13th St. (bet. 6th Ave. & 7th Ave. S.) | 212-255-4746

"Your favorite pair of shoes in restaurant form", this "steady" French bistro brings "a bit of the Left Bank to the Village" via its "grown-up atmosphere", "not fussy" traditional menu and "easily digestible bills."

Cafe Luluc ●⇕ *French*

| 20 | 16 | 17 | $28 |

Cobble Hill | 214 Smith St. (Baltic St.) | Brooklyn | 718-625-3815

"When you can't get to Paris", there's always this cash-only outpost of "French bohemia" in Cobble Hill serving "solid" bistro fare at a "fraction of what it would cost in Manhattan"; though the "excellent brunch" can get as "crowded as the Champs-Élysées", off-peak it's as "cozy as they come."

Cafe Luxembourg ● *French*

| 20 | 18 | 18 | $53 |

W 70s | 200 W. 70th St. (bet. Amsterdam & West End Aves.) | 212-873-7411 | www.cafeluxembourg.com

There's still "good energy" aplenty at this "vibrant" UWS French "institution" where the "reliable" bistro chow and "occasional star sightings" make for "enjoyable" repasts with a side of "rubbernecking"; true, it can be "noisy" and "cramped", with "pretty lofty" tabs, but ultimately "it still swings."

Cafe Mogador ● *Moroccan*

| 21 | 16 | 17 | $28 |

E Village | 101 St. Marks Pl. (bet. Ave. A & 1st Ave.) | 212-677-2226 | www.cafemogador.com

With "no pretensions", just "inexpensive", "hit-the-spot" Moroccan eats, this "insanely popular" East Villager has provided "good bang for the buck" since 1983; despite "flighty" service and "nothing-fancy" looks, it's an "everyday place" for "hip" locals.

	FOOD	DECOR	SERVICE	COST

Cafe Ronda *Mediterranean/S American*   19 | 15 | 15 | $36

W 70s | 249-251 Columbus Ave. (bet. 71st & 72nd Sts.) | 212-579-9929 | www.caferonda.com

"Excellent tapas" are the draw at this "inviting" UWS Med–South American where regulars wager the "outdoor seats are the best bet"; if the service "sometimes feels lost" and the noise level is "bothersome", at least the "people-watching" is prime.

Café Sabarsky/Café Fledermaus *Austrian*   21 | 23 | 19 | $42

E 80s | Neue Galerie | 1048 Fifth Ave. (86th St.) | 212-288-0665 | www.wallse.com

"Divine" desserts begging the question "art or tart?" are yours at Kurt Gutenbrunner's "charming" Austrian *kaffeehaus* in the UES Neue Galerie, where "fin de siècle Vienna comes alive" via a "sinful array" of "otherworldly" treats; as a result, "long queues" are common, though the "more casual" Fledermaus downstairs is usually less packed.

Cafe S.F.A. *American*   18 | 17 | 18 | $36

E 40s | Saks Fifth Ave. | 611 Fifth Ave., 8th fl. (bet. 49th & 50th Sts.) | 212-940-4080

A "calming" respite for "power-shoppers", Saks' "recently renovated" eighth-floor cafe offers "reliable" Americana made tastier by views of "St. Patrick's spires" and the "Rock Center rooftop gardens"; "forgetful" service and "expensive-for-what-it-is" pricing are the downsides.

NEW **Cafe Society** ❷ *Eclectic*   - | - | - | E

Union Sq | 9 E. 16th St. (bet. 5th Ave. & Union Sq. W.) | 212-675-4700 | www.cafesocietynyc.com

Set in the former Steak Frites space off Union Square, this Eclectic newcomer named for a famed 1940s nightclub is quite a stylish affair, with backlit mirrors, salmon-hued walls and a prominent silver bar; foodwise, expect a premium-priced list of goods from around the globe, ranging from sushi to spareribs.

Cafe Spice *Indian*   18 | 13 | 15 | $27

E 40s | Grand Central | lower level (42nd St. & Vanderbilt Ave.) | 646-227-1300
G Village | 72 University Pl. (bet. 10th & 11th Sts.) | 212-253-6999
www.cafespice.com

"Filled with NYU students around the clock", this "handy" Villager curries favor with "tasty", "American-accented" Indian fare that's "attractively priced"; the takeout-only satellite in Grand Central's food court is just the ticket "when you're waiting for a train."

Cafe Steinhof *Austrian*   18 | 16 | 18 | $27

Park Slope | 422 Seventh Ave. (14th St.) | Brooklyn | 718-369-7776 | www.cafesteinhof.com

"Huge portions" of "inexpensive" Austrian comfort food "done right" turn up at this "publike" Park Sloper that ups the ante with live music on Wednesday and Sunday "movie nights"; throw in "$6 goulash on Mondays" and no wonder it's "usually hopping."

Cafeteria ❷ *American*   18 | 15 | 14 | $32

Chelsea | 119 Seventh Ave. (17th St.) | 212-414-1717

The "people-watching may be more delicious than the food" at this "boisterous" Chelsea American where everyone from "brunch-seekers"

	FOOD	DECOR	SERVICE	COST

to "club bunnies" pile in for midpriced comfort grub ferried by a staff with "heavy-duty attitude"; even though it's open "24 hours a day", some find it "a bit five minutes ago."

Cafe Un Deux Trois ◑ *French*   16 | 15 | 17 | $43
W 40s | 123 W. 44th St. (bet. B'way & 6th Ave.) | 212-354-4148 | www.cafeundeuxtrois.biz

Though the overall experience is debatable – "enjoyable" vs. "uninspiring" – this "noisy", "family-oriented" Times Square bistro supplies "accessible" French food, "decent" pricing and a "chaotic" mien; maybe the "tired" decor needs work, but you may not notice as they "zoom you in and out to make the curtain."

Caffe Bondi *Italian*   ∇ 19 | 16 | 19 | $40
Staten Island | 1816 Hylan Blvd. (bet. Buel & Dongan Hills Aves.) | 718-668-0100

"Everyone knows your name" at this SI Italian where the "solid" Sicilian cuisine comes with a side of "outer-borough friendliness"; if the "dark" interior disappoints, there's always "outside dining in good weather."

Caffe Buon Gusto *Italian*   17 | 14 | 17 | $32
E 50s | 1009 Second Ave. (bet. 53rd & 54th Sts.) | 212-755-1476
E 70s | 236 E. 77th St. (bet. 2nd & 3rd Aves.) | 212-535-6884
Brooklyn Heights | 151 Montague St. (bet. Clinton & Henry Sts.) | Brooklyn | 718-624-3838
www.cafebuongusto.com

It's the "hearty Italian fare", "not glitz or glitter", that draws "neighborhood" types to this "low-key" trio; "you can't go wrong" with the "create-your-own" combos of pasta and sauce, nor with the "inexpensive" cost.

Caffe Cielo ◑ *Italian*   19 | 16 | 19 | $46
W 50s | 881 Eighth Ave. (bet. 52nd & 53rd Sts.) | 212-246-9555

"Convenient to theaters" and Upper Eighth Avenue's burgeoning scene, this "white-tablecloth" Northern Italian provides "tasty" "traditional" cooking at tabs that "won't break the bank"; weekenders tout its "delicious" $12.95 prix fixe brunch.

Caffe Grazie *Italian*   18 | 16 | 19 | $47
E 80s | 26 E. 84th St. (bet. 5th & Madison Aves.) | 212-717-4407 | www.caffegrazie.com

Museum Mile–goers and "older" locals "refuel" at this UES Italian duplex, a "pleasant option" set in a "subdued" townhouse; the food is "consistently good", the service "courteous" and the mood "slightly north of casual" – ditto the "somewhat high" tabs.

Caffe Linda 🅂 *Italian*   ∇ 19 | 12 | 17 | $29
E 40s | 145 E. 49th St. (bet. Lexington & 3rd Aves.) | 646-497-1818

"Bustling" at lunch and more "quiet" at dinner, this "decent" Italian offers "reliable" fare in a "heart-of-Midtown" locale; while "you can't beat the price for the quality of food", the same can't be said of the "bland" decor.

Caffé on the Green 🅼 *Italian*   21 | 22 | 21 | $51
Bayside | 201-10 Cross Island Pkwy. (bet. Clearview Expwy. & Utopia Pkwy.) | Queens | 718-423-7272 | www.caffeonthegreen.com

"Queens' version of Tavern on the Green", this Bayside Italian "gem" set in "Rudolph Valentino's former home" is "special-occasion" central, with "excellent" cooking, "careful service" and "beautiful" grounds enhanced by "spectacular views"; sure, "it'll cost you", but it's not that much for an "impressive evening."

Calle Ocho *Nuevo Latino*

22	22	19	$45

W 80s | 446 Columbus Ave. (bet. 81st & 82nd Sts.) | 212-873-5025 | www.calleochonyc.com

"*Caliente*" is the word for this "zingy" UWS Nuevo Latino that "feels like a vacation", from the "party" atmosphere to the "young", "eye-candy" crowd; thanks to "inventive" food and some of the "best mojitos ever", it's often "jam-packed."

CamaJe ● *American/French*

22	15	19	$37

G Village | 85 MacDougal St. (bet. Bleecker & Houston Sts.) | 212-673-8184 | www.camaje.com

Chef Abigail Hitchcock's "creative" menu supplies a true "foodie experience" for "good value" at this "small" Franco-American that's a "welcome escape from the MacDougal Street madness"; extras include "cooking classes", "wine tastings" and blindfolded "dining-in-the-dark" nights.

NEW Cambodian Cuisine *Cambodian*

-	-	-	M

E 90s | 1664 Third Ave. (bet. 93rd & 94th Sts.) | 212-348-9100 | www.cambodiancuisinenyc.com

Transplanted to the UES from Fort Greene, this casual new Cambodian features midpriced spicy specialties like its popular chicken ahmok (chicken with coconut milk curd and red pepper); despite not much decor save for exposed-brick walls and a bit of artwork, the unusual offerings are enough to keep diners occupied.

Campagnola ● *Italian*

24	18	22	$67

E 70s | 1382 First Ave. (bet. 73rd & 74th Sts.) | 212-861-1102

"Wall Street meets Little Italy" at this "top-notch" UES Italian where a "cliquey" "badda-bing" crowd of "regulars", "celebs" and "folks who couldn't get into Rao's" gathers; don't forget to "bring your wallet" and don't expect much service "unless they know you" – then "they do everything but spoon-feed you."

NEW Campo *Italian*

∇ 18	17	20	$31

W 100s | 2888 Broadway (bet. 112th & 113th Sts.) | 212-864-1143 | www.camponyc.com

Bringing some zip to Upper Broadway, this new trattoria features moderately priced Italian classics served in spacious, retro-rustic digs with exposed-brick walls and a tin ceiling; people-watchers campo out at the marble-topped bar near the big glass windows that open onto the sidewalk.

NEW Canaille M⊄ *French*

∇ 23	17	21	$41

Park Slope | 78 Fifth Ave. (bet. Prospect & St. Marks Pls.) | Brooklyn | 718-789-8899 | www.canaillebistro.com

The latest "vest-pocket bistro" to pop up on Park Slope's burgeoning Fifth Avenue Restaurant Row, this "small place with a big heart" offers moderately priced Gallic grub in "quaint" environs; so long as you don't mind the "chatty" owner, it's a "welcome" addition to the area.

	FOOD	DECOR	SERVICE	COST

Canaletto *Italian*
21 | **16** | **21** | **$52**

E 60s | 208 E. 60th St. (bet. 2nd & 3rd Aves.) | 212-317-9192

"Old-world" East Side Northern Italian that purveys "dependable", "ungussied-up" grub served by a "cordial" crew in a "white-tablecloth" setting; maybe there are "few surprises", but when it comes to "reliable neighborhood standbys", it remains "tried-and-true."

Candle Cafe *Vegan/Vegetarian*
23 | **13** | **19** | **$32**

E 70s | 1307 Third Ave. (bet. 74th & 75th Sts.) | 212-472-0970 | www.candlecafe.com

Vegans and vegetarians are "in their glory" at this "down-home" UES cafe that may be "more casual" and "economical" than its sister, Candle 79, but has food that's "equally good"; indeed, the "fantastic" offerings snuff out complaints of "long waits" and "uninspired decor."

☑ Candle 79 *Vegan/Vegetarian*
23 | **20** | **22** | **$46**

E 70s | 154 E. 79th St. (bet. Lexington & 3rd Aves.) | 212-537-7179 | www.candlecafe.com

This "haute", meat-free Upper Eastsider comes "to the rescue" for "upscale" vegetarians and vegans seeking "sophisticated" "culinary creations" presented in an "elegant" setting; a "solicitous" staff rounds out an overall "healthy", "guilt-free" experience.

Canyon Road *Southwestern*
19 | **16** | **17** | **$37**

E 70s | 1470 First Ave. (bet. 76th & 77th Sts.) | 212-734-1600 | www.arkrestaurants.com

"Attractive" UES "whippersnappers" seeking "lethal" margaritas and "rock-solid", low-cost Tex-Mex eats keep this Southwesterner "swinging", especially "on weekends"; though it's a natural for "match.com dates", just "make sure you aren't in a hurry – the staff never is."

Capital Grille *Steak*
23 | **22** | **22** | **$67**

E 40s | 155 E. 42nd St. (bet. Lexington & 3rd Aves.) | 212-953-2000 | www.thecapitalgrille.com

"Suits" say this Grand Central–area chain link "doesn't feel like a chain", but rather is a "capital" place to chow down on "outstanding" cuts of beef with "superb" service that "bucks the gruff" steakhouse norm; few mind paying for the experience.

Capsouto Frères *French*
23 | **22** | **23** | **$57**

TriBeCa | 451 Washington St. (Watts St.) | 212-966-4900 | www.capsoutofreres.com

"Bring your GPS" – this "middle-of-nowhere" TriBeCa "mainstay" is "worth seeking out" for "classic" French bistro fare (including "sublime" soufflés); "friendly" staffers preside over a "quiet", "beautifully unstuffy room" that manages to be "cozy despite the high ceilings"; thankfully, there's easy parking.

Caracas Arepa Bar *Venezuelan*
25 | **13** | **16** | **$19**

E Village | 93½ E. Seventh St. (bet. Ave. A & 1st Ave.) | 212-529-2314

Caracas to Go *Venezuelan*
E Village | 91 E. Seventh St. (1st Ave.) | 212-228-5062 www.caracasarepabar.com

"Creative gourmet riffs" on "unusual" stuffed arepas are a "steal" at this "tiny sliver of Venezuela" in the East Village; since service runs on

"South American time" and there's often a "long wait", try takeout next door for a "cheap", "filling" fix.

Cara Mia *Italian* | 19 | 14 | 17 | $37 |

W 40s | 654 Ninth Ave. (bet. 45th & 46th Sts.) | 212-262-6767 | www.caramianyc.com

A "safe bet" pre- or post-theater, this Hell's Kitchen Italian "fills up quickly" with folks seeking "satisfying" homemade pastas and the like at affordable prices; seating is "cramped", but service is brisk.

Caravan of Dreams *Vegan/Vegetarian* | 20 | 14 | 17 | $26 |

E Village | 405 E. Sixth St. (1st Ave.) | 212-254-1613 | www.caravanofdreams.net

"Bohemian hip" is alive and well at this kosher vegan "oasis" that's become an East Village "institution"; "picky palates" praise the "cheap", "delicious" offerings, though the "hippie decor", "out-there" service and "hit-or-miss" live music are less dreamy.

Carino *Italian*   ∇ | 20 | 12 | 20 | $36 |

E 80s | 1710 Second Ave. (bet. 88th & 89th Sts.) | 212-860-0566

"Classic" all the way, this "old-style" UES Southern Italian features "solid", "home-cooked" staples seemingly straight from "grandma's kitchen"; maybe the "checkered-tablecloth" decor "won't win any awards", but at least the tabs make you a winner.

Carl's Steaks *Cheese Steaks* | 21 | 5 | 12 | $13 |

Murray Hill | 507 Third Ave. (34th St.) | 212-696-5336 ◐
TriBeCa | 79 Chambers St. (bet. B'way & Church St.) | 212-566-2828
www.carlssteaks.com

"Yo, Philly fans", this Murray Hill–TriBeCa duo dishes out "cheap", "sloppy" cheese steaks smothered in Cheez Whiz that are as close to "authentic" "as you'll find in NYC"; since there's not much service, decor or seating, either "eat standing up" or get it to go.

☒ Carlyle Restaurant *French* | 22 | 26 | 25 | $82 |

E 70s | Carlyle Hotel | 35 E. 76th St. (Madison Ave.) | 212-570-7192 | www.thecarlyle.com

Evoking a world "that's almost gone" (i.e. jackets required at dinner), this "gracious" UES dining room offers "impeccably prepared" New French cuisine in a "civilized" milieu; such "rarefied" supping can cost a "small fortune", though breakfast, brunch and lunch are a better "bargain."

☒ Carmine's *Italian* | 20 | 15 | 18 | $40 |

W 40s | 200 W. 44th St. (bet. B'way & 8th Ave.) | 212-221-3800 ◐
W 90s | 2450 Broadway (bet. 90th & 91st Sts.) | 212-362-2200
www.carminesnyc.com

The "more the merrier" could be the motto of these "jumping" West Side eatfests where "gargantuan", family-style portions of "budget"-priced Southern Italian grub can feed "an army"; it's "always fun" and always "packed", despite "choppy service", "long waits" and "tourist throngs"; just "bring your family and friends" and "come hungry."

Carnegie Deli ◐⊄ *Deli* | 21 | 9 | 13 | $28 |

W 50s | 854 Seventh Ave. (55th St.) | 212-757-2245 | www.carnegiedeli.com

For "sandwiches piled to the ceiling" and "marvelous cheesecake", check out this "NY classic" (circa 1937) Midtown deli; decor is "sparse", service "wiseacre" and payment cash-only, but that doesn't keep "tourists", "natives" and *Broadway Danny Rose* fans from squeezing in to those long communal tables for what may be "too much of a good thing" – "oy vey."

Carol's Cafe 🅂Ⓜ Eclectic

FOOD	DECOR	SERVICE	COST
24	19	21	$55

Staten Island | 1571 Richmond Rd. (bet. Four Corners Rd. & Seaview Ave.) | 718-979-5600 | www.carolscafe.com

"Haute cuisine" comes to "little old Staten Island" at this "unique" Eclectic where "top-notch" chef Carol Frazzetta displays an "artistic" touch with her "inventive" offerings; though it's a "beautiful dining experience for any borough", prices tend toward "Manhattan."

Casa 🅂 Brazilian

FOOD	DECOR	SERVICE	COST
∇ 24	20	21	$42

W Village | 72 Bedford St. (Commerce St.) | 212-366-9410 | www.casarestaurant.com

Though this Village "find" may "inspire a flight to Rio", its "authentic" Brazilian menu requires no passport; the "perpetually packed" conditions feel congenial after a couple of their "don't-miss caipirinhas."

Ⓩ Casa Mono ❶ Spanish

FOOD	DECOR	SERVICE	COST
25	17	19	$52

Gramercy | 52 Irving Pl. (17th St.) | 212-253-2773 | www.casamononyc.com

"Like Spain on Irving Place", Mario Batali's "mind-blowing" Gramercy tapas bar offers "grilled exotica" and "dazzling wines" in "tiny", "closet"-size digs; score a "seat at the bar facing the open kitchen" where you can "watch the chefs work their magic" and you'll forget about the "cheek-by-jowl" seating and "sticker shock."

Cascina ❶ Italian

FOOD	DECOR	SERVICE	COST
19	16	18	$40

W 40s | 647 Ninth Ave. (bet. 45th & 46th Sts.) | 212-245-4422 | www.cascina.com

With "homey food" and an "unassuming" attitude, this "safe-bet" Hell's Kitchen Italian "knows what it is" – a "handy" choice for locals and theatergoers seeking "good value"; a "wood-burning stove" and wines from their own vineyard add to the experience.

Casellula ❶ American

FOOD	DECOR	SERVICE	COST
∇ 21	19	22	$38

W 50s | 401 W. 52nd St. (bet. 9th & 10th Aves.) | 212-247-8137 | www.casellula.com

"Fabulous fromage" highlights the menu of this "cozy" Hell's Kitchen spot where "informed" staffers pair "cheese flights" with an "excellent" wine list; the rest of the American offerings can be "hit-or-miss", but at least everything is "reasonably priced."

Casimir ❶ French

FOOD	DECOR	SERVICE	COST
20	20	14	$37

E Village | 103-105 Ave. B (bet. 6th & 7th Sts.) | 212-358-9683 | www.casimirrestaurant.com

"Dark and moody", this "bohemian cool" East Villager "feels like a real French bistro" with a "surprisingly good" menu; though service is "sketchy", a "chill back garden" makes this a "great first date" option.

Caviar Russe American

FOOD	DECOR	SERVICE	COST
24	22	22	$95

E 50s | 538 Madison Ave., 2nd fl. (bet. 54th & 55th Sts.) | 212-980-5908 | www.caviarrusse.com

Vending a "perfect marriage of caviar and sushi", this "grown-up" Midtown American offers "sublime" dining in a "casually elegant" room overseen by "pro" staffers; sure, it's "expensive" and the mezzanine location "quirky", but it's hard to beat for "sophisticated" supping.

Cávo ● *Greek*   20 | 26 | 19 | $44

Astoria | 42-18 31st Ave. (bet. 42nd & 43rd Sts.) | Queens | 718-721-1001 | www.cavocafelounge.com

"Amazing" for Astoria, this "posh" Greek "restaurant-cum-nightclub" serves "good", slightly "pricey" food in a "cavernous" interior or in a "beautiful", "waterfall"-equipped outdoor garden; after 11 PM, it morphs into an "electric" scene for the "21-to-35-year-old" set.

Cebu ● *Continental*   21 | 19 | 19 | $38

Bay Ridge | 8801 Third Ave. (88th St.) | Brooklyn | 718-492-5095

Bay Ridge's "first choice" for "late-night" dining (till 3 AM), this "always crowded" Continental purveys a "tasty", midpriced menu that's especially "delicious" for weekend brunch; regulars eschew the "din at the bar" and head for the "intimate" back room.

Celeste ⊅ *Italian*   24 | 11 | 16 | $33

W 80s | 502 Amsterdam Ave. (bet. 84th & 85th Sts.) | 212-874-4559

Despite "no credit cards, no reservations" and "no elbow room", there's always a "brutal line" at this UWS "worst-kept secret" for one simple reason: "mouthwatering" Neapolitan meals at "great prices"; its colorful owner is full of "great patter" – ask him about the "secret cheese plate."

Cellini *Italian*   21 | 18 | 22 | $56

E 50s | 65 E. 54th St. (bet. Madison & Park Aves.) | 212-751-1555 | www.cellinirestaurant.com

"Everything clicks" at this Midtown Northern Italian "power-lunch" destination thanks to "ample portions" of "on-point" food served by a "gracious" staff; at dinner, it's more "quiet", "romantic" and expensive.

Cendrillon Ⓜ *Asian/Filipino*   21 | 18 | 20 | $42

SoHo | 45 Mercer St. (bet. Broome & Grand Sts.) | 212-343-9012 | www.cendrillon.com

"Dressed-up" Filipino favorites and "imaginative" Pan-Asian dishes make for "intriguing combinations" at this "friendly", "family-run" SoHo venue that's much "loved by locals"; a "warm" staff and "homey", "hospitable" environs add value to the midpriced tabs.

Centolire *Italian*   21 | 21 | 20 | $61

E 80s | 1167 Madison Ave. (bet. 85th & 86th Sts.) | 212-734-7711 | www.pinoluongo.com

"Elegant" Carnegie Hill types get "suited up" for this "special" "night-out-in-the-neighborhood" place where chef Pino Luongo's "*veramente Italiano*" Tuscan specialties are served by an "on-point" crew; the "airy" duplex setting is more "upscale" upstairs, but it's "expensive" throughout, so bargain-hunters tout the $27.50 prix fixe lunch.

Centovini *Italian*   20 | 22 | 20 | $57

SoHo | 25 W. Houston St. (bet. Greene & Mercer Sts.) | 212-219-2113 | www.centovininyc.com

It's a "marriage of food and design" at this SoHo enoteca where "creative" Italian eats are offset by Murray Moss' "stunningly spartan" decor – though the "masterful" wine list just might eclipse both; overall, both the quality and the cost are "high."

	FOOD	DECOR	SERVICE	COST

Centrico *Mexican* — 19 | 18 | 17 | $45

TriBeCa | 211 W. Broadway (Franklin St.) | 212-431-0700 |
www.myriadrestaurantgroup.com
Aarón Sanchez devises "high-end" "twists" on Mexican standards at
Drew Nieporent's "spacious", "big-windowed" TriBeCan where a
"stylish young crowd" drops by for the "happening" bar scene; any
lapses seem inconsequential after a couple of "terrific" margaritas.

Centro Vinoteca ◐ *Italian* — 22 | 19 | 19 | $51

W Village | 74 Seventh Ave. S. (Barrow St.) | 212-367-7470 |
www.centrovinoteca.com
"Batali protégé" Anne Burrell is "usually visible" at this "trendy", midpriced West Village Italian "scene" where "superb *piccolini*" (small
plates) and vino in quartinos encourage sharing; the "cute" servers
may "still need some polish" and the "lively" room verges on "deafening", but upstairs is "more subdued."

Cercle Rouge ◐ *French* — 19 | 20 | 17 | $46

TriBeCa | 241 W. Broadway (bet. Beach & White Sts.) | 212-226-6252 |
www.cerclerougeresto.com
"Tried-and-trusted" French favorites have significantly "improved" at
this "low-key" brasserie that some dub "TriBeCa's answer to
Balthazar"; "tight" seating and "inconsistent" service are offset by a
"perfect summer terrace" and midrange pricing.

'Cesca *Italian* — 23 | 22 | 21 | $60

W 70s | 164 W. 75th St. (Amsterdam Ave.) | 212-787-6300 |
www.cescanyc.com
As "popular" as ever, this UWS Southern Italian attracts "all ages and
types" with "bold, hearty" food and "sharp", "solicitous" service; a "vibrant bar scene" fronts a "classy" yet "comfortable" dining room –
both can be "costly" but the payoff is "tip-top" dining.

Chadwick's *American* — 22 | 19 | 22 | $45

Bay Ridge | 8822 Third Ave. (89th St.) | Brooklyn | 718-833-9855 |
www.chadwicksny.com
For "real Brooklyn dining and decor", follow the "locals" to this "social
club"-like Bay Ridge American vending "large portions" of steak and
seafood plus other "honest" vittles, all served "with care"; it's an
"oldie but goodie" that's much appreciated for its $17 lunch prix fixe
and $23 early-bird "values."

Chance *Pan-Asian* — ∇ 20 | 18 | 18 | $32

Boerum Hill | 223 Smith St. (Butler St.) | Brooklyn | 718-242-1515 |
www.chancecuisine.com
A "novelty" on Smith Street, this "solid" Pan-Asian flaunts "slick",
"modern" looks (including a "lovely waterfall behind the bar") in a
"small" setting; it's also vaunted for "value" – those under-$10 lunch
boxes are an "absolute steal."

🆉 Chanterelle *French* — 27 | 26 | 28 | $127

TriBeCa | 2 Harrison St. (Hudson St.) | 212-966-6960 |
www.chanterellenyc.com
"Adult perfection" sums up the scene at David and Karen Waltuck's
30-year-old French "destination", bringing "ethereal", "transcendent"

cuisine to TriBeCa; "anticipatory" service and a "large", "flower"-filled room have diners "floating on air", though the "big", prix fixe–only bills may keep them tethered to earth; N.B. the set-price $42 lunch (when dishes are also available à la carte) is more affordable.

Charles' Southern-Style Kitchen ⓜ *Southern* | ▽ 22 | 6 | 13 | $17 |

Harlem | 2839 Frederick Douglass Blvd. (151st St.) | 212-926-4313
Don't worry about the "calorie count" at this "sinful" Harlem Southerner slinging real-deal "homestyle" cooking – starring some "great fried chicken" – at "can't-be-beat" prices; there's "no ambiance", but there is "takeout", and that all-you-can-eat buffet just might "make you whistle 'Dixie'"

Chef Ho's Peking Duck Grill *Chinese* | 22 | 13 | 18 | $30 |

E 80s | 1720 Second Ave. (bet. 89th & 90th Sts.) | 212-348-9444
The "name says it all" at this "semi-upscale" UES Chinese where the "fantastic" signature dish is "as good as Chinatown" and the tabs are "bargain" priced; even if the atmosphere's "ordinary", the "accommodating" staff makes sure the "welcome is warm."

Chennai Garden *Indian/Vegetarian* | 22 | 10 | 14 | $23 |

Gramercy | 129 E. 27th St. (Park Ave. S.) | 212-689-1999
"Solid vegetarian" food that's "kosher to boot" is yours at this "tasty" Gramercy Parker where the "spicy" South Indian specialties come out "quick and easy" (not to mention "cheaply"); though there's "not much decor", the $6.95 all-you-can-eat lunch buffet more than compensates.

Chestnut ⓜ *American* | 24 | 19 | 22 | $44 |

Carroll Gardens | 271 Smith St. (bet. Degraw & Sackett Sts.) | Brooklyn | 718-243-0049 | www.chestnutonsmith.com
Despite New American "cooking with heart", "congenial" service and "relaxing" atmospherics, this Carroll Gardens neighborhood "treasure" somehow remains "under the radar"; it may be "a bit expensive" for these parts, but the "inspired" Tuesday–Wednesday prix fixe is a bona fide "good deal."

Chez Jacqueline *French* | 20 | 18 | 20 | $48 |

G Village | 72 MacDougal St. (bet. Bleecker & Houston Sts.) | 212-505-0727
A "*très bien*" Village "veteran" that would be at home in "Provence", this "quiet French bistro" is known for "tasty", "dependable" cooking "like you remember"; locals laud the "quality service" and "old-world charm" that's made it "stand the test of time."

Chez Josephine ●ⓜ *French* | 20 | 21 | 21 | $51 |

W 40s | 414 W. 42nd St. (bet. 9th & 10th Aves.) | 212-594-1925 | www.chezjosephine.com
An "homage to Josephine Baker", this "haute camp" Theater District French cafe is run by her adopted son, Jean-Claude, who's a "whole Broadway show all by himself"; while the piano player is "entertaining" and the bistro fare "surprisingly good", the "heavily decorated" setting – a "cross between a bordello and *La Cage Aux Folles*" – is most memorable.

	FOOD	DECOR	SERVICE	COST

Chez Napoléon ⊠ *French*
| | 21 | 15 | 21 | $45 |

W 50s | 365 W. 50th St. (bet. 8th & 9th Aves.) | 212-265-6980 | www.cheznapoleon.com

Sure, it's a real "throwback", but "that's the attraction" at this circa-1960 Theater District "old-timer" whose French cooking is more "*grand-mère*" than haute; though it could stand some "refurbishing", the "reasonable" pricing and "family-owned" feeling are fine as is.

Chez Oskar ⦿ *French*
| | ▽ 17 | 16 | 16 | $31 |

Fort Greene | 211 DeKalb Ave. (Adelphi St.) | Brooklyn | 718-852-6250 | www.chezoskar.com

"Familiar" French bistro classics arrive in "funky" digs at this Fort Greene "mainstay" whose "great value" makes it a hit with "young" types; the "shabby-chic" interior may be "a bit tight", but "fantastic energy" and a "great" weekend brunch make up for it.

Chiam Chinese Cuisine *Chinese*
| | 22 | 17 | 20 | $44 |

E 40s | 160 E. 48th St. (bet. Lexington & 3rd Aves.) | 212-371-2323

"Corporate" types like this Midtown Cantonese "crowd-pleaser" for its "fancy", fairly "Americanized" dishes served in "comfortable upscale" digs; though it's a tad "pricey" for the genre, the $20.50 prix fixe lunch is "well worth the money."

Chianti ⓜ *Italian*
| | 21 | 16 | 20 | $39 |

Bay Ridge | 8530 Third Ave. (bet. 85th & 86th Sts.) | Brooklyn | 718-921-6300 | www.chianti86.com

"Reliable red-sauce" favorites served "individually or family-style" keep the trade brisk at this Bay Ridge "neighborhood" Italian where locals admit to "fasting the day prior to dining"; it's particularly "great with a group" what with the "reasonable" prices and "patient" staff.

ChikaLicious *Dessert*
| | 25 | 17 | 22 | $23 |

E Village | 203 E. 10th St. (bet. 1st & 2nd Aves.) | 212-995-9511 ⓜ
NEW | **E Village** | 204 E. 10th St. (bet. 1st & 2nd Aves.) | 212-475-0929 ⦿ www.chikalicious.com

"Delectable desserts" are the thing at this "pint-size" East Village sweet specialist offering three-course prix fixes along with optional wine pairings; although it's "pricey for the portion size", the "long lines" out front speak for themselves; N.B. the new across-the-street offshoot doing takeout only may help curtail the queues.

Chiles & Chocolate Oaxacan Kitchen *Mexican*
| | 18 | 13 | 16 | $30 |

Park Slope | 54 Seventh Ave. (bet. Lincoln & St. Johns Pls.) | Brooklyn | 718-230-7700

Bringing a "dash of innovation" to Park Slope, this "modest" Mexican specializing in "uncompromisingly authentic" Oaxacan cuisine is "not run-of-the-mill"; the "mole is incomparable" and the price is right, but the "postage stamp" space can get so "cramped" that many suggest "takeout or delivery."

Chimichurri Grill ⦿ *Argentinean/Steak*
| | 20 | 13 | 19 | $46 |

W 40s | 606 Ninth Ave. (bet. 43rd & 44th Sts.) | 212-586-8655 | www.chimichurrigrill.com

Carnivores crowd into this "tight" Hell's Kitchen Argentinean steakhouse for "beef, of course", namely its "generous portions" of "tender" meats slathered with that "delicious" signature sauce; moderate tabs and "good pre-theater" turnaround make this one a "great find."

Chimu *Peruvian*　　　　　　　　▽ 23 | 17 | 19 | $30

Williamsburg | 482 Union St. (bet. Bond & Nevins Sts.) | Brooklyn | 718-349-1208

"Unique" Peruvian coastal cuisine surfaces at this seafood-based Williamsburger set in an "inconspicuous location just off the BQE"; "like so many neighborhood joints", it's "small and crowded", but you "won't be disappointed" when the "affordable" bill arrives.

China Fun *Chinese*　　　　　　　15 | 9 | 13 | $24

E 60s | 1221 Second Ave. (64th St.) | 212-752-0810 ◐
W 70s | 246 Columbus Ave. (bet. 71st & 72nd Sts.) | 212-580-1516
www.chinafun-ny.com

No kidding, this "busy" crosstown Chinese duo "does great business" thanks to modest pricing and an "enormous" menu with plenty of options, "even sushi"; still, many sigh it's just "ordinary" with rushed service and "does the trick" only when you need to "eat and run."

China Grill *Asian*　　　　　　　22 | 21 | 19 | $58

W 50s | 60 W. 53rd St. (bet. 5th & 6th Aves.) | 212-333-7788 |
www.chinagrillmgt.com

"Still going strong", this "stylish" Midtown Asian is a "place to be seen and not heard" given the "boisterous" crowd tucking into "excellent", "expensive" dishes; modernists find it as "dated as a '70s disco ball", but diehards declare "old hat never tasted so good."

Chinatown Brasserie ◑ *Chinese*　　21 | 22 | 17 | $48

NoHo | 380 Lafayette St. (Great Jones St.) | 212-533-7000 |
www.chinatownbrasserie.com

"Artistic" dim sum "at any hour" is the calling card of this "high-style" NoHo Chinese where "fairly authentic" dishes – from Peking duck to BBQ ribs – receive "elegant" presentations; "prices are a little steep", but the "stunning", bi-level space is "full of action" nonetheless.

Chin Chin ◑ *Chinese*　　　　　　23 | 18 | 21 | $51

E 40s | 216 E. 49th St. (bet. 2nd & 3rd Aves.) | 212-888-4555 |
www.chinchinny.com

For a taste of "emperor's dining", this longtime Midtown Chinese offers "delicate, satisfying" dishes including a "must-try" Grand Marnier shrimp; its "corporate" following feels it's "worth the premium" prices given such "refined" fare and "courteous" service.

Chinese Mirch *Asian Fusion*　　　19 | 11 | 15 | $27

Gramercy | 120 Lexington Ave. (28th St.) | 212-532-3663 |
www.chinesemirch.com

"China meets India" at this "unconventional" Curry Hill fusion spot that marries the two nations' cuisines with "super-spicy" results; despite some menu "misses" and "service issues", it's "like nothing else" around.

Chino's *Asian*　　　　　　　　　▽ 19 | 15 | 18 | $30

Gramercy | 173 Third Ave. (bet. 16th & 17th Sts.) | 212-598-1200 |
www.chinosnyc.com

Having abandoned its small-plates concept, this Gramercy Asian now purveys "flavorful fusion" in entree-size portions accompanied by "delicious cocktails"; "reasonable" tabs and "solicitous" service keep it "popular" with "many locals."

Chipotle *Mexican*
18 | 10 | 14 | $12

E 40s | 150 E. 44th St. (bet. Lexington & 3rd Aves.) | 212-682-9860
E 50s | 150 E. 52nd St. (bet. Lexington & 3rd Aves.) | 212-755-9754
E Village | 19 St. Marks Pl. (bet. 2nd & 3rd Aves.) | 212-529-4502
Financial District | 2 Broadway (Stone St.) | 212-344-0941
Flatiron | 680 Sixth Ave. (bet. 21st & 22nd Sts.) | 212-206-3781
G Village | 55 E. Eighth St. (bet. B'way & University Pl.) | 212-982-3081
Murray Hill | Empire State Bldg. | 350 Fifth Ave. (34th St.) | 212-695-0412
SoHo | 200 Varick St. (bet. Houston & King Sts.) | 646-336-6264
W 40s | 9 W. 42nd St. (bet. 5th & 6th Aves.) | 212-354-6760
Brooklyn Heights | 185 Montague St. (Clinton St.) | Brooklyn | 718-243-9109
www.chipotle.com
Additional locations throughout the NY area

This "guilty pleasure" Mexican chain "does one thing, and does it right" – "super-size", "tailor-made" burritos assembled from "fresh ingredients" for "affordable" dough; insiders dodge the "epic" lines during the "lunch rush" by "ordering online."

ChipShop *British*
19 | 14 | 17 | $21

NEW **Bay Ridge** | 7215 Third Ave. (bet. 72nd & 73rd Sts.) | Brooklyn | 718-748-0594 ⊟
Brooklyn Heights | 129 Atlantic Ave. (bet. Clinton & Henry Sts.) | Brooklyn | 718-855-7775
Park Slope | 383 Fifth Ave. (bet. 6th & 7th Sts.) | Brooklyn | 718-832-7701 ⊟
www.chipshopnyc.com

Peddling "real-deal fish 'n' chips" plus "deep-fried" desserts, this low-cost, "no-frills" Brooklyn trio offers a genuine British "cholesterolfest" with some "whimsy" on the side; the new Bay Ridge branch is especially "family-friendly", but all are "bloody lovely" so long as you "don't bother looking for healthy items on the menu."

NEW Cho Cho San *Japanese*
- | - | - | M

G Village | 15 W. Eighth St. (bet. 5th & 6th Aves.) | 212-473-3333 | www.chochosanrestaurant.com

Set on Eighth Street's burgeoning Restaurant Row, this minimally dressed Japanese newcomer delivers standard sushi at standard prices, along with some interesting twists: a diverse selection of vegetable rolls, plus a variety of cooked entrees from rice bowls to stir-fry to Japanese-style pasta.

Chocolate Room, The Ⓜ *Dessert*
25 | 18 | 20 | $17

NEW **Cobble Hill** | 269 Court St. (bet. Butler & Douglass Sts.) | Brooklyn | 718-246-2600
Park Slope | 86 Fifth Ave. (bet. Prospect Pl. & St. Marks Ave.) | Brooklyn | 718-783-2900
www.thechocolateroombrooklyn.com

"Transcendent chocolate experiences" lie in store at these "heavenly" Brooklyn dessert emporiums (aka "endorphin central") where the "sinful" choices can be paired with wine; still, the "ice-cream parlor" feel and "chipper" service can't shake many out of their "sugar-induced comas."

	FOOD	DECOR	SERVICE	COST

Cho Dang Gol *Korean* — 23 | 15 | 17 | $29

Garment District | 55 W. 35th St. (bet. 5th & 6th Aves.) | 212-695-8222 |
www.chodanggolny.com

The "signature tofu dishes are a must" at this "authentic" Garment
District Korean popular with "young" expats lured in by "cleanly prepared" dishes that are "good for your taste buds and your soul"; the
"value" pricing is pretty "comforting" too.

Chola *Indian* — 23 | 16 | 20 | $37

E 50s | 232 E. 58th St. (bet. 2nd & 3rd Aves.) | 212-688-4619 |
www.fineindiandining.com

"Pitch-perfect" Indian cuisine mixing the "traditional" with "offbeat regional" dishes awaits at this "adventurous" Eastsider that
dares to go "beyond tikka masala"; while the "variety" and "knowledgeable" service earn kudos, it's the "superb" $13.95 lunch buffet
that's most applause-worthy.

NEW Chop Suey *Pan-Asian* — ∇ 15 | 22 | 17 | $56

W 40s | Renaissance Times Square Hotel | 714 Seventh Ave., 2nd fl.
(bet. 47th & 48th Sts.) | 212-261-5200

A "stunning Times Square" view is about the only draw at this new,
window-lined Pan-Asian (in the former Foley's Fish House space); otherwise, the food's "uninspiring" and "overpriced", service "confused"
and the second-floor location hard to find.

Chop't Creative Salad *American* — 19 | 9 | 13 | $13

E 50s | 165 E. 52nd St. (bet. Lexington & 3rd Aves.) |
212-421-2300 🗷
E 50s | 60 E. 56th St. (bet. Madison & Park Aves.) | 212-750-2467 🗷
Union Sq | 24 E. 17th St. (bet. B'way & 5th Ave.) | 646-336-5523
NEW W 50s | 145 W. 51st St. (bet. 6th & 7th Aves.) |
212-974-8140 🗷
www.choptsalad.com

Lettuce lovers can't resist the "siren song" of these "efficient", modern
salad shops that crank out "custom" combos of "amazingly fresh"
greens and toppings; "insane" lunchtime lines and "pricey" tabs for
the genre come with the territory.

Chow Bar *Asian Fusion* — 19 | 17 | 19 | $39

W Village | 230 W. Fourth St. (W. 10th St.) | 212-633-2212

"Great specialty drinks" and "solid" Asian fusion at "fair prices" have
made this West Villager a "popular" stop for 10 years now; a "hip atmosphere" where "lingering is never a problem" overcomes the
"noisy" sound levels and decor in need of "renovation."

Christos Steak House ☻ *Steak* — 24 | 18 | 21 | $54

Astoria | 41-08 23rd Ave. (41st St.) | Queens | 718-777-8400 |
www.christossteakhouse.com

The "top-of-the-line" surf 'n' turf "rocks" at this smartly served Astoria
steakhouse that's "worth a trip over the bridge"; a "large selection of
prime-aged meats" comes "prepared to perfection" backed up with
"traditional Greek sides", while "valet parking" is an extra perk.

Z Churrascaria Plataforma ☻ *Brazilian* — 23 | 19 | 22 | $71

W 40s | 316 W. 49th St. (bet. 8th & 9th Aves.) | 212-245-0505 |
www.churrascariaplataforma.com

(continued)

☑ Churrascaria TriBeCa ◑ *Brazilian*

TriBeCa | 221 W. Broadway (bet. Franklin & White Sts.) | 212-925-6969 |
www.churrascariatribeca.com

Gluttons "eat their body weight in beef" at these "rambunctious"
Brazilian meatfests where "spirited" waiters keep the skewers coming
till patrons finally "surrender"; though the "gustatory challenge" is
"pricey", it's "paradise" even for vegetarians given the all-you-can-
eat salad bar.

Cibo *American/Italian*

19	17	20	$46

E 40s | 767 Second Ave. (41st St.) | 212-681-1616
"Comfortable" and "accommodating", this Tuscan–New American offers "hearty servings" of midpriced, reliably good food ferried by an
"attentive" crew; proximity to Grand Central makes it a "fine fallback"
for "relaxed business lunching."

Cilantro *Southwestern*

17	14	16	$29

E 70s | 1321 First Ave. (71st St.) | 212-537-4040 ◑
E 80s | 1712 Second Ave. (bet. 88th & 89th Sts.) | 212-722-4242 ◑
W 80s | 485 Columbus Ave. (bet. 83rd & 84th Sts.) | 212-712-9090
www.cilantronyc.com

"Lively" is putting it mildly at this "loud" Southwestern trio where the
"vibrant" mood is fueled by "big servings" of "reliable" grub paired
with "zingy" margaritas; maybe the decor and service are "nothing
fancy", but the "prices are right on the money."

Cipriani Dolci ◑ *Italian*

19	19	18	$52

E 40s | Grand Central | West Balcony (42nd St. & Vanderbilt Ave.) |
212-973-0999 | www.cipriani.com

"Sip a Bellini" and "enjoy the people-watching" at this unique Venetian
"perched on a mezzanine" overlooking Grand Central Station's "hustle
and bustle"; sure, it's "spendy" and there's the "typical Cipriani attitude", but it's a natural when "waiting for a train."

Cipriani Downtown ◑ *Italian*

20	18	17	$72

SoHo | 376 W. Broadway (bet. Broome & Spring Sts.) | 212-343-0999 |
www.cipriani.com

"Somebodies and nobodies" converge at this "show-off-ish" SoHo
Italian with a "high scene factor", drawing "models and the men who
buy them salad" as well as assorted "Euros", "poseurs" and "snappy
dressers"; the Bellinis and food are "always excellent", but the "triple-
markup" prices and "snotty" staff are another story.

Circus *Brazilian*

20	18	19	$55

E 60s | 132 E. 61st St. (bet. Lexington & Park Aves.) | 212-223-2965 |
www.circusrestaurante.com

There's "more than just grilled meats" on tap at this "neighborhoody"
Brazilian Eastsider, namely "wonderful caipirinhas", "festive" decor
and a staff that "couldn't be nicer"; regulars report it's "overlooked"
(despite 15 years in business), maybe since it's "a bit pricey."

Citrus Bar & Grill *Asian/Nuevo Latino*

19	18	17	$40

W 70s | 320 Amsterdam Ave. (75th St.) | 212-595-0500 | www.citrusnyc.com
"Good times" lie ahead at this "upbeat" UWS Latin-Asian that offers
an "interesting mix of options" – sushi or paella? – for "fair" prices and

a "pleasant" brunch to boot; just be aware that the "happy young crowd" can generate "LaGuardia-taxiway" noise levels.

City Bakery *Bakery* | 21 | 11 | 12 | $19 |

Flatiron | 3 W. 18th St. (bet. 5th & 6th Aves.) | 212-366-1414 | www.thecitybakery.com

Though its "distinctive" salad bar/buffet is "always fresh", Maury Rubin's Flatiron "staple" is best known for its "superlative" baked goods and "addictive hot chocolate"; prices can be as "painful" as the "search for a seat", yet word is you "can't go wrong" here.

City Crab & Seafood Co. *Seafood* | 17 | 15 | 17 | $44 |

Flatiron | 235 Park Ave. S. (19th St.) | 212-529-3800 | www.brandedrestaurants.com

Crustacean cravers dig the "succulent", "reasonably priced" shellfish at this "cavernous" Flatiron seafooder with an equally jumbo-size menu; although some crab about "formulaic" decor and "erratic" service, it's usually "packed" to the gills regardless.

City Hall 🗷 *Seafood/Steak* | 20 | 21 | 20 | $57 |

TriBeCa | 131 Duane St. (bet. Church St. & W. B'way) | 212-227-7777 | www.cityhallnyc.com

The "red-suspender set" – think "local pols" and other city "bigwigs" – wheel and deal at this "standout" TriBeCa surf 'n' turfer from Henry Meer, where "terrific", "top-dollar" grub is served in "spiffy digs" (or in "great party rooms" downstairs); the mood is "historic" and "fast-moving", kinda "like NYC" itself.

City Island Lobster House ● *Seafood* | 20 | 16 | 18 | $44 |

Bronx | 691 Bridge St. (City Island Ave.) | 718-885-1459 | www.cilobsterhouse.com

City Island's "small-town" feel makes it "easy to forget you're in NY" at this midpriced "family favorite" famed for "ocean-fresh" seafood served by a "chipper" crew; no surprise, the deck's delightful sunset-over-the-Sound views drub the "drab" digs inside.

City Lobster & Crab Co. *Seafood* | 18 | 15 | 16 | $50 |

W 40s | 121 W. 49th St. (6th Ave.) | 212-354-1717

"Surprisingly good" aquatic eats make this Midtown seafooder popular with "tourists" who show up for the "uncramped" seating and "fair" pricing; most overlook the "plain-Jane" ambiance ("Maine, it's not") given its Radio City/Broadway theater "convenience."

Clinton St. Baking Co. *American* | 25 | 13 | 16 | $27 |

LES | 4 Clinton St. (bet. Houston & Stanton Sts.) | 646-602-6263 | www.greatbiscuits.com

It's worth braving the "looong" lines for "pancakes from Cloud Nine" at this exceptional LES American bakery/cafe justifiably renowned for its "killer" weekend brunch; it's so "small" that "only the slim may dine comfortably", though access is easier at the calmer dinner hour.

Coals 🗷 *Pizza* | ▽ 23 | 15 | 17 | $21 |

Bronx | 1888 Eastchester Rd. (Morris Park Ave.) | 718-823-7002 | www.coalspizza.com

Distinguished by its "novel" concept – "irresistible" *grilled* pizzas – this "unique" Bronx joint also offers a "limited", "inexpensive" selection of soup, salad and panini; "friendly" service and a "youthful vibe" keep it popular with "mainly locals"; N.B. closed weekends.

Coco Roco *Peruvian*

| 21 | 14 | 15 | $26 |

Cobble Hill | 139 Smith St. (bet. Bergen & Dean Sts.) | Brooklyn | 718-254-9933
Park Slope | 392 Fifth Ave. (bet. 6th & 7th Sts.) | Brooklyn | 718-965-3376

There's "a lot happening on the plate" at these "festive" Brooklyn Peruvians where "little coin" buys "plentiful" portions and an especially "heavenly" rotisserie chicken; "slow" service and not much decor don't hamper the "hopping" scene.

Coffee Shop ● *American/Brazilian*

| 15 | 12 | 12 | $29 |

Union Sq | 29 Union Sq. W. (16th St.) | 212-243-7969

Food, decor and service are pretty much "afterthoughts" at this "cheap and cheerful" Union Square Brazilian-American best known for its "statuesque" staff and their "who-cares attitude"; "late-night" hours, "sexy" people-watching and "clublike" decibels are all part of the package.

Cole's Dock Side *Continental/Seafood*

| ∇ 22 | 20 | 23 | $39 |

Staten Island | 369 Cleveland Ave. (Hylan Blvd.) | 718-948-5588 | www.colesdockside.com

"Delicious" fresh fish is the bait at this Staten Island Continental seafooder situated "right by the water" on Great Kills Harbor; it's especially "wonderful" when "outside dining" is an option, but the "attentive" service and decent prices are "enjoyable year-round."

Colors *Eclectic*

| ∇ 18 | 18 | 19 | $46 |

E Village | 417 Lafayette St. (bet. Astor Pl. & 4th St.) | 212-777-8443 | www.colors-nyc.com

"Established and owned" by former Windows on the World employees, this East Village Eclectic offers a midpriced menu that "spans the globe", served by an "accommodating" team; most "enjoy supporting" this "cooperative venture", but it's a case of "love the concept, like the food."

Comfort Diner *Diner*

| 16 | 11 | 15 | $21 |

E 40s | 214 E. 45th St. (bet. 2nd & 3rd Aves.) | 212-867-4555
Flatiron | 25 W. 23rd St. (bet. 5th & 6th Aves.) | 212-741-1010
www.comfortdiner.com

It's "Thanksgiving every day" at this "old-timey", "just-what-the-name-says" duo slinging "better-than-average diner food" that "sticks to your ribs" but won't empty your wallet; too bad the "indifferent service" and "tired" "'50s-style" decor make some uncomfortable.

NEW Commerce *American*

| 22 | 21 | 18 | $61 |

W Village | 50 Commerce St. (Barrow St.) | 212-524-2301

A "worthy renovation" of a "storied" West Village location (the former Grange Hall), this "sceney" New American offers "carefully conceived" dishes in "beautiful" digs adorned with a "WPA-style mural" and "deco bar"; downsides are "service kinks" and "deafening" acoustics.

NEW Community Food & Juice *American*

| 23 | 19 | 17 | $32 |

W 100s | 2893 Broadway (bet. 112th & 113th Sts.) | 212-665-2800 | www.communityrestaurant.com

From the Clinton St. Baking Co. crew comes this new American cafe-cum–juice bar, a "breath of fresh air" for Morningside Heights, where "organic ingredients" take comfort food to the "next level"; given the "airy", "tall-windowed" space, "fair" pricing and "no-reservations" policy, there's "always a line."

Compass *American*   22 | 23 | 21 | $59

W 70s | 208 W. 70th St. (bet. Amsterdam & West End Aves.) | 212-875-8600 | www.compassrestaurant.com

"Civil acoustics" permit "quiet conversation" at this "comfortable" UWS New American that hits "all the right points" with "first-rate" food and "beautiful" looks; tabs tend to skew up, but on Sundays the "tremendous" wine list is half-price, an "amazing deal."

Congee ◐ *Chinese*   20 | 13 | 13 | $22

Little Italy | 98 Bowery (bet. Grand & Hester Sts.) | 212-965-5028

Congee Bowery ◐ *Chinese*

LES | 207 Bowery (bet. Rivington & Spring Sts.) | 212-766-2828

Congee Village ◐ *Chinese*

LES | 100 Allen St. (bet. Broome & Delancey Sts.) | 212-941-1818 | www.congeevillagerestaurants.com

You can "eat till you drop" for "super-value" prices at these separately owned Downtown Cantonese specializing in the eponymous rice porridge that's the equivalent of "Chinese chicken soup"; all locations sport "kitschy" decor, but Congee Village looks like a "set from *Indiana Jones and the Temple of Doom.*"

NEW Convivio ☒ *Italian*   - | - | - | M

E 40s | 45 Tudor City Pl. (42nd St., bet. 1st & 2nd Aves.) | 212-599-5045 | www.convivionyc.com

Reinventing L'Impero's former digs, this new Tudor City Southern Italian from restaurateur Chris Cannon and chef Michael White has gotten a snazzy, *La Dolce Vita*-esque redo; the menu's been similarly rejiggered – and the overall price point lowered – with more antipasti and a variety of snacklike *sfizi*; to get an overview, try the four-course, $59 prix fixe extravaganza.

Convivium Osteria *Mediterranean*   25 | 23 | 23 | $51

Park Slope | 68 Fifth Ave. (bet. Bergen St. & St. Marks Ave.) | Brooklyn | 718-857-1833 | www.convivium-osteria.com

Like a "mini–European vacation", this "magical" Park Slope Med offers a transporting menu of "full, bold flavors" served in a romantically "rustic" setting (that includes a "lovely garden" and a "best-kept-secret wine cellar"); prices may be "inflated" for Brooklyn, but the overall experience is "fabulous."

Cookshop ◐ *American*   23 | 19 | 21 | $52

Chelsea | 156 10th Ave. (20th St.) | 212-924-4440 | www.cookshopny.com

"Locavores" love the "ever-changing", "market-driven" menu at this "clever" Chelsea American that's designed "with foodies in mind"; sure, prices are "high" and the "hustle and bustle" can get "loud", but a "pleasant" ambiance, "down-to-earth" service and a "diverse" crowd make for "terrific" supping.

Coppola's *Italian*   19 | 15 | 18 | $37

Gramercy | 378 Third Ave. (bet. 27th & 28th Sts.) | 212-679-0070 ◐

(continued)

Coppola's

W 70s | 206 W. 79th St. (bet. Amsterdam Ave. & B'way) | 212-877-3840
www.coppolas-nyc.com

There's "something for everyone" on the menu of these "casual" neighborhood Italians, peddling "red-sauce" favorites in "bountiful" portions; the perennially "crowded" conditions reflect their "reasonable" costs.

Cornelia Street Cafe ◐ *American/French*
| 19 | 16 | 18 | $35 |

G Village | 29 Cornelia St. (bet. Bleecker & W. 4th Sts.) | 212-989-9319 | www.corneliastreetcafe.com

It doesn't get more "Village-y" than this French-American "old friend", dishing out "home-cooked meals" and "fantastic brunches" since 1977; "decent prices", "cool vibes" and eclectic entertainment in its downstairs performance space have made it a bona fide neighborhood "haunt."

Corner Bistro ◐≢ *Burgers*
| 22 | 9 | 12 | $16 |

W Village | 331 W. Fourth St. (Jane St.) | 212-242-9502

"Grimy" decor is "part of the charm" at this "genuine" Village tavern famed for its "thick", "messy" burgers, "paper-plate" china and "dirt-cheap beer"; expect "long lines" of "frat boys" with "impending hangovers" who don't mind the "military service" or "truck stop restrooms."

NEW Corton *French*
| - | - | - | VE |

TriBeCa | 239 W. Broadway (bet. Walker & White Sts.) | 212-219-2777 | www.cortonnyc.com

Restaurateur Drew Nieporent (Nobu, Tribeca Grill) and avant-garde chef Paul Liebrandt (Atlas, Gilt) join forces at this New French due to arrive in TriBeCa's former Montrachet space; look for exotic takes on classical French cuisine – served in pricey, prix fixe-only menus starting at $76 – paired with a wine list concentrating on the Burgundy region.

Cosette *French*
| 21 | 16 | 22 | $39 |

Murray Hill | 163 E. 33rd St. (bet. Lexington & 3rd Aves.) | 212-889-5489 | www.cosette-bistro.com

"Small-town France" alights in Murray Hill via this ultra-"snug" bistro "sleeper" featuring "dependably delicious" *cuisine grand-mère*; the "mom-and-pop" ambiance is reflected in the "'80s pricing", "personal service" and digs so "cozy" that some want to "sleep over."

Così *Sandwiches*
| 16 | 10 | 11 | $14 |

E 40s | 38 E. 45th St. (bet. Madison & Vanderbilt Aves.) | 212-370-0705
E 50s | 60 E. 56th St. (bet. Madison & Park Aves.) | 212-588-1225
Financial District | World Financial Ctr. | 200 Vesey St. (West St.) | 212-571-2001
Flatiron | 700 Sixth Ave. (bet. 22nd & 23rd Sts.) | 212-645-0223
Garment District | 498 Seventh Ave. (bet. 36th & 37th Sts.) | 212-947-1005
G Village | 53 E. Eighth St. (bet. B'way & Mercer St.) | 212-260-1507
G Village | 841 Broadway (13th St.) | 212-614-8544 ◐
W 40s | 11 W. 42nd St. (bet. 5th & 6th Aves.) | 212-398-6662
W 50s | Paramount Plaza | 1633 Broadway (50th St.) | 212-397-9838
W 70s | 2186 Broadway (bet. 76th & 77th Sts.) | 212-595-5616
www.getcosi.com
Additional locations throughout the NY area

"Addictive" flatbread "just out of the oven" stuffed with "tasty" fillings is the "main event" at these "ubiquitous" sandwich shops specializing in "upscale fast food"; despite "crazy" lines and "assembly-line" service, it's still relatively easy to "grab and go."

Counter ● *Vegan/Vegetarian*

21	20	20	$39

E Village | 105 First Ave. (bet. 6th & 7th Sts.) | 212-982-5870 |
www.counternyc.com

Eluding the "granola-and-Birkenstocks stigma", this chic East Village vegetarian vends "healthy, delicious" cuisine that will satisfy both vegans and omnivores; a "tastefully hip" setting, "helpful" staffers and moderate tabs enhance the "orgasmic organic" experience.

Country, Café at ● *American*

20	21	18	$54

Gramercy | Carlton Hotel | 90 Madison Ave. (bet. 26th & 27th Sts.) |
212-889-7100 | www.countryinnewyork.com

"Modern American fare with flair" turns up at this subterranean room in Gramercy's Carlton Hotel, a "fine-looking" space built around a "crowded" central bar; "quiet" at lunch and "noisy" for supper, it boasts an "upscale" air that's reflected in its somewhat "inflated" pricing; N.B. its more formal upstairs sibling, Country, has closed.

NEW Covo ● *Italian*

▽ 24	25	20	$31

Harlem | 701 W. 135th St. (12th Ave.) | 212-234-9573 |
www.covony.com

The latest arrival to West Harlem's budding Restaurant Row on 12th Avenue (aka Manhattanville) is this "huge", loftlike Italian known for "terrific pizzas" straight from a showpiece brick oven; "friendly service", "reasonable prices" and a "fun" upstairs lounge keep locals "coming back for more."

Cowgirl *Southwestern*

16	17	16	$28

W Village | 519 Hudson St. (W. 10th St.) | 212-633-1133 |
www.cowgirlnyc.com

All about "kitschy flair", this overdecorated West Village "hoot" has a "split personality": by day, families "bring the kids" for "heaping plates" of Southwestern grub (think "Frito pies" and other "guilty pleasures"), but after sunset, singles ride in for "pitchers of margaritas" and "group celebrations."

Ⓩ Craft *American*

26	24	24	$77

Flatiron | 43 E. 19th St. (bet. B'way & Park Ave. S.) | 212-780-0880 |
www.craftrestaurant.com

A "minimalist star" in the NYC firmament, *Top Chef* Tom Colicchio's "upscale, not uptight" Flatiron New American proffers "pure, clean flavors" via "build-your-own" menus crafted with "impeccable" ingredients; smooth service seconded by a super-"stylish" setting secure its "well-deserved reputation", but be prepared to "pay dearly" for this "deceptively simple" "complete restaurant experience."

Craftbar *American*

21	19	19	$50

Flatiron | 900 Broadway (bet. 19th & 20th Sts.) | 212-461-4300 |
www.craftrestaurant.com

"More laid-back" than its 'round-the-corner Flatiron sibling, "Craft's little brother" still "hits the right notes" with "simple, tasty" New Americana at a "more affordable" price point; while the room "lacks magic" and the menu's "limited", "you can actually get a reservation" without planning weeks ahead.

	FOOD	DECOR	SERVICE	COST

Craftsteak *Steak*
23 | 24 | 23 | $80

Chelsea | 85 10th Ave. (bet. 15th & 16th Sts.) | 212-400-6699 |
www.craftrestaurant.com

Ordering can be "complicated" at Tom Colicchio's "chic", high-ceilinged
West Chelsea steakhouse where diners choose "what the cow ate and
where it came from" aided by "patient" servers; the gimmick may be
"a bit precious" for some, but ultimately the "gorgeous cuts of meat"
(at "home equity loan" prices) make for "justifiable excess."

NEW Crave on 42nd Ⓜ *American*
∇ 19 | 13 | 16 | $45

W 40s | 650 W. 42nd St. (bet. 11th & 12 Aves.) | 212-564-9588 |
www.craveon42nd.com

Top Chef finalist Dave Martin brings his "famous truffled mac 'n'
cheese" to the "far western" reaches of Hell's Kitchen via this "fine"
new American; though it's "still finding its groove" in the service and
decor departments, locals find it a "welcome addition" to the scene.

Crema *Mexican*
22 | 18 | 19 | $45

Chelsea | 111 W. 17th St. (bet. 6th & 7th Aves.) | 212-691-4477 |
www.cremarestaurante.com

Chef Julieta Ballesteros whips up "creative" Nuevo Mexican meals at
this "cute" Chelsea cantina that mixes "traditional and modern" fare
for "surprising", "gourmet" results; "indulgent" drinks, "upbeat" atmospherics and "pleasant" staffers more than justify the tabs.

Crispo ● *Italian*
23 | 19 | 20 | $47

W Village | 240 W. 14th St. (bet. 7th & 8th Aves.) | 212-229-1818 |
www.crisporestaurant.com

"Popularity has led to crowds" at this "former hidden gem" in the West
Village offering "honest" Northern Italian cooking for "affordable"
rates; "cozy" digs, "attentive" service and a "magical", all-seasons
garden add up to "reliably good" dining.

Ⓩ Cru 🄴 *European*
26 | 23 | 25 | $109

G Village | 24 Fifth Ave. (bet. 9th & 10th Sts.) | 212-529-1700 |
www.cru-nyc.com

A "cast-of-thousands" wine list draws "vinophiles" to this "outstanding"
Villager, backed up by "sublime" Modern European cooking, "impeccable" service and a "pleasant" if "sterile" setting; prix fixe–only menus
($84 and up) make for "blow-the-kids'-college-fund" dining, but cheaper
à la carte options are available in the walk-ins-only front room.

Ⓩ Cuba *Cuban*
23 | 18 | 20 | $39

G Village | 222 Thompson St. (bet. Bleecker & W. 3rd Sts.) | 212-420-7878 |
www.cubanyc.com

"Enticingly spicy aromas" are a preview of the "authentic island
tastes" turning up at this "tiny little" Village Cuban; "fab" mojitos,
"live Latin music" and free homemade cigars fuel the "loud", "bustling
scene", and it's "affordable" to boot.

Cuba Cafe *Cuban*
20 | 16 | 18 | $31

Chelsea | 200 Eighth Ave. (bet. 20th & 21st Sts.) | 212-633-1570 |
www.chelseadining.com

Muy bien eating lies ahead at this "venerable" Chelsea Cuban that's
a long-standing destination for "satisfying" grub and "punchy" cock-

tails at *"muy cheapo"* tabs; "engaging" service and "campy decor" enhance the "festive" feel.

Cubana Café ●⇄ *Cuban*

FOOD	DECOR	SERVICE	COST
19	15	15	$23

G Village | 110 Thompson St. (bet. Prince & Spring Sts.) | 212-966-5366
Carroll Gardens | 272 Smith St. (bet. Degraw & Sackett Sts.) | Brooklyn | 718-858-3980

"Hearty" Cuban eats for really "inexpensive" dough keep this "folksy" Village-Carroll Gardens duo popular with a "cool young crowd"; "ridiculously small" settings, a "cash-only" policy and "iffy" service are the downsides.

Cube 63 *Japanese*

FOOD	DECOR	SERVICE	COST
22	14	16	$34

LES | 63 Clinton St. (bet. Rivington & Stanton Sts.) | 212-228-6751 ●🄱
Cobble Hill | 234 Court St. (bet. Baltic & Warren Sts.) | Brooklyn | 718-243-2208
www.cube63.com

"Good, well-priced sushi" and "creative" specialty rolls are the bait at these LES–Cobble Hill Japanese that are on the "tiny" side, hence the "loud" decibels; "BYO is key" at keeping prices low in Manhattan, while the Brooklyn branch pours beer, wine and sake.

Cucina di Pesce ● *Italian*

FOOD	DECOR	SERVICE	COST
18	14	18	$27

E Village | 87 E. Fourth St. (bet. Bowery & 2nd Ave.) | 212-260-6800 | www.cucinadipesce.com

A "no-fuss" East Village "standby", this "quaint" Italian specializes in "seafood with a distinctly Italian flair" served in "decent"-size portions at an "inexpensive" price; no one minds the "average" decor and service given that "amazing" $12.95 early-bird.

Curry Leaf *Indian*

FOOD	DECOR	SERVICE	COST
20	10	16	$27

Gramercy | 99 Lexington Ave. (27th St.) | 212-725-5558 | www.curryleafnyc.com

Whether you like "subtle spicing" or "real heat", Kalustyan's Curry Hill Indian does it "authentically" and for an "oh-so-affordable" tab; "indifferent" service and "not-the-best" decor can be bypassed by "prompt, reliable delivery."

Da Andrea *Italian*

FOOD	DECOR	SERVICE	COST
23	14	21	$36

W Village | 557 Hudson St. (bet. Perry & W. 11th Sts.) | 212-367-1979 | www.biassanot.com

"Narrow on space but broad in appeal", this longtime West Village Italian boasts "flavorful" Emilia-Romagna "home cooking" served by an "easygoing" crew that treats patrons "like family"; though "not much on looks", few notice given the "low prices" and "happy" mood.

Da Ciro *Italian/Pizza*

FOOD	DECOR	SERVICE	COST
22	16	20	$46

Murray Hill | 229 Lexington Ave. (bet. 33rd & 34th Sts.) | 212-532-1636 | www.daciro.com

Regulars report it's all about the "out-of-this-world" focaccia Robiola at this under-the-radar Murray Hill Italian that also purveys "excellent" Italian standards and pizza in a duplex setting; upstairs is "more relaxing" than the "noisy" ground floor, but either way expect "great service and value."

Dae Dong ● *Korean*   ▽ 18 | 13 | 15 | $29
Bayside | 220-15 Northern Blvd. (220th St.) | Queens |
718-631-7100
"Seoul food" fanciers salute this Bayside spot where "solid" Korean
barbecue "cooked at table hibachis" is accompanied by random
Japanese items; though "nothing distinguishes" the functional service and decor, dae hards declare it a "reliable" choice, in spite of
the unfortunate name.

Da Filippo *Italian*   21 | 16 | 20 | $56
E 60s | 1315 Second Ave. (bet. 69th & 70th Sts.) | 212-472-6688 |
www.dafilipporestaurant.com
The "old-world atmosphere" "never changes" at this "consistent" UES
Northern Italian where larger-than-life owner Carlo Meconi and his
"warm" staff "make you feel at home"; the pricing may be "a bit
high for a neighborhood restaurant", but the "delicious" result is
"well worth it."

Daisy May's BBQ USA *BBQ*   22 | 6 | 12 | $23
W 40s | 623 11th Ave. (46th St.) | 212-977-1500 |
www.daisymaysbbq.com
Hog-wild fans of this "no-frills", cafeteria-style smoke hut in Hell's
Kitchen "hunker down" at "communal" picnic tables over "succulent
ribs" and other "knockout" BBQ, bolstered by "right tasty" fixin's, all
at tabs that Li'l Abner could afford; a Midtown satellite lunch cart
saves admirers the "trek" to the Way West Side.

Dakshin Indian Bistro *Indian*   21 | 11 | 18 | $26
E 80s | 1713 First Ave. (bet. 88th & 89th Sts.) | 212-987-9839 |
www.dakshintogo.com
Maybe the sari decor "could use some Botox", but otherwise this "tiny"
UES "neighborhood Indian" is a "real pleaser" when it comes to "delicious", "affordable" food and "pleasant service"; at $7.95, no gour-
mand can afford to miss the midday buffet.

Dallas BBQ ● *BBQ*   14 | 9 | 13 | $22
Chelsea | 261 Eighth Ave. (23rd St.) | 212-462-0001
E 70s | 1265 Third Ave. (bet. 72nd & 73rd Sts.) | 212-772-9393
E Village | 132 Second Ave. (St. Marks Pl.) | 212-777-5574
Washington Heights | 3956 Broadway (bet. 165th & 166th Sts.) |
212-568-3700
W 40s | 241 W. 42nd St. (bet. 7th & 8th Aves.) | 212-221-9000
W 70s | 27 W. 72nd St. (bet. Columbus Ave. & CPW) |
212-873-2004
Downtown Bklyn | 180 Livingston St. (bet. Hoyt & Smith Sts.) | Brooklyn |
718-643-5700
www.dallasbbq.com
"Serious eaters" "belly up to the trough" at this "mass-market" BBQ
chain where "acceptable" 'cue in "behemoth portions" is chased with
"colossal" drinks; folks on a "tight budget" show up for "bargain"
binges, ignoring the "frenetic" feel and "eyesore" decor.

Danal *Mediterranean*   20 | 20 | 19 | $41
G Village | 59 Fifth Ave. (bet. 12th & 13th Sts.) | 212-982-6930
Newly moved to a "more expansive" Village duplex, this French-Med
preserves its "special charm" by keeping its "quaint provincial" vibe,

"flavorful" food and "reasonable" cost intact; while the "loss of the garden" is bemoaned, it's still as "comfortable" as ever.

Da Nico *Italian*

21 | 17 | 19 | $41

Little Italy | 164 Mulberry St. (bet. Broome & Grand Sts.) | 212-343-1212 | www.danicoristorante.com

"Touristy Mulberry Street" is home to this Little Italy "mainstay" where "waiters with great accents" purvey "large portions" of "delicious" red-sauce Italiana for "moderate" sums; the "fantastic" back patio is the place to be in temperate weather.

☑ Daniel ⑤ *French*

28 | 28 | 28 | $137

E 60s | 60 E. 65th St. (bet. Madison & Park Aves.) | 212-288-0033 | www.danielnyc.com

Home to what could be "heaven's kitchen", Daniel Boulud's eponymous East Side "masterpiece" exudes "true class" with "matchless" staffers serving "incomparable" New French prix fixes and a "definitive" wine list in a "sumptuous", jackets-required milieu (the lounge also offers à la carte dining); it may cost a "king's ransom", but appropriately enough, most "feel like royalty" at meal's end; N.B. a full renovation is slated for autumn 2008.

Danny Brown
Wine Bar & Kitchen Ⓜ *European*

25 | 22 | 23 | $45

Forest Hills | 104-02 Metropolitan Ave. (71st Dr.) | Queens | 718-261-2144 | www.dannybrownwinekitchen.com

Forest Hills "holds its own with Manhattan" via this "much-needed addition" that pairs "superb" European fare with a "well-thought-out" wine list in "stylish" environs; tended by an "accommodating" staff, it strikes the "perfect balance" between "classy" and "relaxed."

Da Noi *Italian*

23 | 19 | 22 | $43

Staten Island | 138 Fingerboard Rd. (Tompkins Ave.) | 718-720-1650
Staten Island | 4358 Victory Blvd. (Service Rd.) | 718-982-5040
www.danoirestaurant.com

"Stylish" yet still "traditional", these "exceptionally run" SI Northern Italians "aim to please" with an "extensive menu" of "delectable" items plus "personable" service; they're particularly "crowded on weekends", so insiders drop by on school nights.

Darbar *Indian*

21 | 16 | 18 | $33

E 40s | 152 E. 46th St. (bet. Lexington & 3rd Aves.) | 212-681-4500 | www.darbarny.com

"Reliably fine" cooking allows this "modest" Indian to "curry favor" with "U.N. folks" and other East Midtown locals; the split-level setting may be "nothing to write home about", but "the price is right", especially that "super" $11.95 lunch buffet.

Darna *Moroccan*

▽ 21 | 17 | 17 | $42

W 80s | 600 Columbus Ave. (89th St.) | 212-721-9123 | www.darnanyc.com

As an "interesting" kosher option, this Upper Westsider provides "plenty of choice" via "surprisingly tasty" Moroccan specialties that make its "simple, quiet" locale a "worthy destination"; however, many maintain that service is too darna "slow."

	FOOD	DECOR	SERVICE	COST

Da Silvana Ⓜ *Italian*
▽ 22 | 15 | 20 | $48

Forest Hills | 71-51 Yellowstone Blvd. (bet. Clyde & Dartmouth Sts.) | Queens | 718-268-7871

A "longtime staple" in Forest Hills, this "newly renovated" Italian has been a "neighborhood favorite" for 25 years thanks to "generous" helpings of "good" red-sauce dishes; moderate prices and "wonderful" service are further reasons why it "never disappoints."

Da Silvano ● *Italian*
21 | 16 | 18 | $64

G Village | 260 Sixth Ave. (Bleecker St.) | 212-982-2343 | www.dasilvano.com

Silvano Marchetto's "high-octane" Village Tuscan is "definitely an experience", what with its "da-licious" Tuscan grub, "charming" staff and "steep" tabs; but it's the "Page Six factor" – i.e. NYC "celeb watching at its best" – that keeps it crowded, particularly at the coveted sidewalk tables where "more stars than the Planetarium" hold court.

Da Tommaso ● *Italian*
19 | 13 | 20 | $46

W 50s | 903 Eighth Ave. (bet. 53rd & 54th Sts.) | 212-265-1890

"Tried-and-true" for "most satisfactory" Northern Italian basics, this Theater District fixture will "fill you up and get you on your way" in time to make the curtain; the "tight" quarters are "nothing fancy", but when the yen for an "old-fashioned" meal strikes, "this is 'da' place."

Da Umberto Ⓢ *Italian*
25 | 18 | 23 | $62

Chelsea | 107 W. 17th St. (bet. 6th & 7th Aves.) | 212-989-0303

An "oldie but goodie", this "traditional" Chelsea Tuscan "never loses its touch" for "perfectly executed" dishes and "gracious service" in a room where you almost "expect Jerry Vale to walk in"; still, given the high pricing, aesthetes argue the decor "needs freshening."

Ⓩ davidburke & donatella *American*
25 | 23 | 22 | $75

E 60s | 133 E. 61st St. (bet. Lexington & Park Aves.) | 212-813-2121 | www.dbdrestaurant.com

"Air kissers" "rub elbows" and rave about chef David Burke's "imaginative", "not-to-be-missed" cooking at this "delightful" New American where privileged Upper Eastsiders gather for "classy" repasts; expect a "professional" staff and a "chichi" but "cheery" townhouse setting, and while it's "not cheap", the $24 "prix fixe lunch is a steal"; N.B. Donatella Arpaia's departure puts its front-of-the-house performance (and name) in question.

David Burke at Bloomingdale's *American*
18 | 13 | 14 | $31

E 50s | Bloomingdale's | 159 E. 59th St. (bet. Lexington & 3rd Aves.) | 212-705-3800 | www.burkeinthebox.com

Shoppers seeking an "energy" boost take a break at David Burke's "creative" New American cafe and adjacent "fancy fast-food" shop that are both affordable and "conveniently" sited inside Bloomie's; critics aren't buying the "overcrowded" layout and "disorganized" service, but it sure "beats the local deli."

Dawat *Indian*
23 | 18 | 20 | $49

E 50s | 210 E. 58th St. (bet. 2nd & 3rd Aves.) | 212-355-7555

Long a "best bet" for "gourmet Indian" dining, this East Midtowner showcases actress/chef Madhur Jaffrey's "blissful" takes on classic dishes, abetted by "fine service" and a "soothing" ambiance; even though some say the "bloom is off" the somewhat "staid" surroundings, it's still "worth every rupee."

☑ db Bistro Moderne *French*   25 | 21 | 22 | $65

W 40s | City Club Hotel | 55 W. 44th St. (bet. 5th & 6th Aves.) | 212-391-2400 | www.danielnyc.com

Daniel Boulud "gets it right" at this "Theater District godsend", a "knockout" French bistro where a "buzzy" crowd savors a "fabulous" menu led by a "vaunted" $32 burger; it's "worth the splurge" for the "swift, cordial" service and sophisticated setting alone, though showgoers cite the $45 dinner prix fixe as an "unbeatable bargain."

Dean's *Pizza*   17 | 15 | 15 | $27

E 40s | 801 Second Ave. (bet. 42nd & 43rd Sts.) | 212-878-9600
NEW TriBeCa | 349 Greenwich St. (bet. Harrison & Jay Sts.) | 212-966-3200
W 80s | 215 W. 85th St. (bet. Amsterdam Ave. & B'way) | 212-875-1100
www.deansnyc.com

Locals with "kids in tow" welcome this "family-oriented" pizzeria trio as a "boon" for their brick-oven pies, especially the "old-fashioned square" variety; maybe service is "in the clouds" and the setups "big", "busy" and "bland", but "fair prices" compensate.

Deborah ⓜ *American*   20 | 13 | 19 | $36

G Village | 43 Carmine St. (bet. Bedford & Bleecker Sts.) | 212-242-2606 | www.deborahlifelovefood.com

"Inventive" chef Deborah Stanton takes a "fresh approach" to "homey food" at this ultra-"cozy" Villager that lures "neighborhood" folk with "delish" New Americana and "sweet service"; the narrow space and "squashed" seating are alleviated in the summer by a secret "back patio."

Dee's Brick Oven Pizza ⓜ *Mediterranean/Pizza*   22 | 18 | 19 | $28

Forest Hills | 107-23 Metropolitan Ave. (74th Ave.) | Queens | 718-793-7553 | www.deesnyc.com

This Forest Hills "favorite" consistently dee-livers "wonderful", "well-crafted" pizza and "tasty" Mediterranean pastas in "spacious", "kid-friendly" quarters; given the "warm atmosphere" and "reasonable" cost, it's always "extremely busy."

DeGrezia Ⓢ *Italian*   22 | 20 | 23 | $59

E 50s | 231 E. 50th St. (bet. 2nd & 3rd Aves.) | 212-750-5353 | www.degreziaristorante.com

Although "below street level", this "old-fashioned" East Midtown Italian rises "way above" the norm with a "top-notch" "traditional" menu matched with "gracious" service and a "peaceful" ambiance; but note, all that "charm" "doesn't come cheap."

☑ Degustation Ⓢ *French/Spanish*   27 | 21 | 24 | $61

E Village | 239 E. Fifth St. (bet. 2nd & 3rd Aves.) | 212-979-1012

The "lucky" few parked at the 16-seat tasting bar at Jack and Grace Lamb's "unique" East Villager have the chance to observe "masterful chefs" concocting "heavenly" Franco-Spanish small plates from the best possible ingredients; it's an "unforgettable experience" for "serious foodies" who "only wish the space were bigger", and perhaps that the price was a bit lower.

☑ Del Frisco's ◐ *Steak* — 25 | 23 | 23 | $72

W 40s | 1221 Sixth Ave. (49th St.) | 212-575-5129 | www.delfriscos.com
Nirvana for "white-collar alpha males", this "top-flight" Midtown chophouse supplies "gut-busting" slabs of "extraordinary", "buttery" beef in "grand" style; the "spot-on" service and "mahogany-walled" "Texas elegance" make for an "impressive" way to "blow a bundle", though non-expense accounters plug the $39.95 pre-theater menu as a "great buy."

Delhi Palace *Indian* — ▽ 20 | 13 | 16 | $23

Jackson Heights | 37-33 74th St. (bet. 37th Ave. & 37th Rd.) | Queens | 718-507-0666
Although "overshadowed" by its neighbor, Jackson Diner, this Jackson Heights Indian runs a "close second" according to locals who tout its "solid" cooking and all-you-can-eat $8.95 lunch buffet; "inexpensive" tabs make the "simple" digs and "curt" service bearable.

NEW Delicatessen ◐ *American* — - | - | - | M

NoLita | 54 Prince St. (Lafayette St.) | 212-226-0211 | www.delicatessennyc.com
Spun off from the longtime Chelsea favorite Cafeteria, this NoLita newcomer boasts a similarly deadpan moniker along with the same slick modern looks, jazzed up American comfort-food eats and late-night hours; retractable streetside walls that open up in temperate weather make dropping in easy.

NEW dell'anima ◐ *Italian* — 24 | 18 | 21 | $54

W Village | 38 Eighth Ave. (bet. Jane & W. 12th Sts.) | 212-366-6633 | www.dellanima.com
"Trendiness" has made this "intimate" West Village newcomer a "cheek-by-jowl" experience thanks to its "superlative" rustic Italian grub ("dell'icious pastas") and "impressive", "well-priced" vinos; it's "worth the effort" to score a table, and you can "see all the action" from the kitchen-side "chef's counter."

Delmonico's ☒ *Steak* — 22 | 22 | 22 | $65

Financial District | 56 Beaver St. (S. William St.) | 212-509-1144 | www.delmonicosny.com
Twenty-first-century "robber barons" assemble at this 1830s-era Financial District steakhouse, a "broker's haven" that "continues to impress" with "first-class cuts" and "pro" service; the "old-world ambiance" preserves all the "charm of days gone by", though pricing is decidedly more up to date.

☑ Del Posto *Italian* — 26 | 27 | 25 | $91

Chelsea | 85 10th Ave. (16th St.) | 212-497-8090 | www.delposto.com
A "large-scale" "sensory experience" from the Batali-Bastianich team, this Way West Chelsea "haute Italian" "wows" with "delectable" cuisine and an "off-the-charts" wine list presented in a "lavish", marble-and-mahogany room recalling a "majestic palazzo"; "exceptional service" rounds out the "tour de force" dining experience, and though "sticker shock" is likely, the "enoteca is a total bargain."

	FOOD	DECOR	SERVICE	COST

Delta Grill ● *Cajun/Creole*
| | 19 | 16 | 18 | $32 |

W 40s | 700 Ninth Ave. (48th St.) | 212-956-0934 | www.thedeltagrill.com
"If you're craving NOLA", this "casual" Cajun-Creole joint in Hell's Kitchen is a "pretty authentic" substitute with its funky "bayou" vibe and "big portions" of "satisfying", "fairly priced" home cookin'; on weekends, free live music ratchets up the "Southern comfort."

Demarchelier *French*
| | 17 | 15 | 16 | $47 |

E 80s | 50 E. 86th St. (bet. Madison & Park Aves.) | 212-249-6300 | www.demarchelierrestaurant.com
Upper Eastsiders make this "relaxed" French bistro a "hopping hang-out" for "solid" comfort food and "active bar" scenery at prices that are "*très raissonnables*" for the neighborhood; though cynics nix the "plain setting", "tight tables" and "snooty staff", regulars say that's what makes it "authentic."

Demaré *French*
| | 19 | 17 | 19 | $47 |

E 70s | 181 E. 78th St. (bet. Lexington & 3rd Aves.) | 212-744-1800 | www.bandolbistro.com
"Surprisingly undiscovered", this "small", "serene" Upper Eastsider (the rechristened Bandol Bistro) furnishes "fine" French bistro standards at a "fair price" plus an "extensive" selection of by-the-glass wines; "warm service" cements its rep as a "reliable" "local" retreat.

Denino's Pizzeria ⊅ *Pizza*
| | 25 | 10 | 17 | $20 |

Staten Island | 524 Port Richmond Ave. (bet. Hooker Pl. & Walker St.) | 718-442-9401
A Staten Island mainstay since 1937, this "old-time" pizza parlor plies "addictive" thin-crust pies washed down with "cheap beer"; the "bare-bones" decor and "family atmospherics" may "leave plenty to be desired", but "be prepared to fight crowds on weekends" all the same.

Dennis Foy *American*
| | 24 | 20 | 20 | $64 |

TriBeCa | 313 Church St. (bet. Lispenard & Walker Sts.) | 212-625-1007 | www.dennisfoynyc.com
One of TriBeCa's "best-kept secrets", Dennis Foy's New American "stands out" with "inventive" cooking, a "well-chosen" wine list and "knowledgeable" staffers; fans feel this venture (adorned with the chef's own artwork) deserves "more recognition", even if it's pricey for the locale.

Dervish Turkish ● *Turkish*
| | 19 | 15 | 18 | $36 |

W 40s | 146 W. 47th St. (bet. 6th & 7th Aves.) | 212-997-0070 | www.dervishrestaurant.com
"Something different" in the Theater District, this "handy" Turk offers "tasty" standards and "swift service" that will whirl you out "before the curtain goes up"; the bi-level space could stand a "makeover", but most focus on the "affordable" cost, notably that $25 early-bird dinner.

DeStefano's Steakhouse Ⓜ *Steak*
| | ▽ 23 | 17 | 20 | $62 |

Williamsburg | 89 Conselyea St. (Leonard St.) | Brooklyn | 718-384-2836
The old school rules at this Williamsburg chop shop set in a compact, tin-ceilinged space that recalls a "Scorsese movie set"; "choice cuts" of beef and "excellent" Italian sides make it "worth a visit", despite "expensive" tabs.

	FOOD	DECOR	SERVICE	COST

Destino ⓧ *Italian*
20 **18** **19** **$55**

E 50s | 891 First Ave. (50th St.) | 212-751-0700 |
www.destinony.com

"Worth trying" for the "killer meatballs" alone, this "neighborhoody" Sutton Place Italian features "above-average" red-sauce dishes for folks who "can't get into Rao's"; even though it "ain't cheap", with celeb co-owner Justin Timberlake on board, most are "ok" with it.

Deux Amis *French*
19 **16** **19** **$46**

E 50s | 356 E. 51st St. (bet. 1st & 2nd Aves.) | 212-230-1117

A "friendly" East Midtown "haunt", this "local" bistro serves "solid French comfort food" with a side of "homey charm" via its "caring" owner; seating is usually "a bit tight" given the "big repeat crowd", but is alleviated by outdoor tables that simulate a "Parisian side street."

dévi *Indian*
23 **21** **21** **$57**

Flatiron | 8 E. 18th St. (bet. B'way & 5th Ave.) | 212-691-1300 |
www.devinyc.com

Achieving "new heights" that "you won't find on Sixth Street", this recently reopened, "high-style" Flatiron Indian helmed by chefs Suvir Saran and Hemant Mathur flaunts "flavorful" spicing in its ultra-"refined" cuisine; given "solicitous" service and an "exotic", "dimly lit" setting, the "steep prices" don't deter dévotees.

Devin Tavern *American*
18 **21** **19** **$54**

TriBeCa | 363 Greenwich St. (bet. Franklin & Harrison Sts.) | 212-334-7337 |
www.devintavern.com

An alternative to "too-cool TriBeCa", this "comforting", bi-level New American "sleeper" is a "spacious", "Aspen"-esque retreat serving "hearty" seasonal fare along with "amazing" cocktails in its "great bar"; even holdouts harping on "inconsistent" execution grant its "potential."

Ⓩ Di Fara Ⓜ✄ *Pizza*
27 **4** **8** **$14**

Midwood | 1424 Ave. J (bet. 14th & 15th Sts.) | Brooklyn |
718-258-1367

"Di-licious" is the word on this Midwood "Holy Grail of pizza", a circa-1963 "hole-in-the-wall" where "master" chef Dominic De Marco rewards "insane waits" with "sublime" "handcrafted" pies; sure, it's "four bucks a slice", but admirers aver "there's no better on the planet."

Dim Sum Go Go *Chinese*
21 **12** **14** **$22**

Chinatown | 5 E. Broadway (Chatham Sq.) | 212-732-0797

"Nontraditional" dim sum "prepared to order" and served all day means "no carts" and "less chaos" at this Chinatown novelty; purists protest "it's not the same experience" sans trolleys and nix the "sterile decor", but admit the "tranquil" mood is a "relief."

Diner ☽ *Diner*
21 **17** **17** **$33**

Williamsburg | 85 Broadway (Berry St.) | Brooklyn | 718-486-3077 |
www.dinernyc.com

"Cool but approachable", this "offbeat" South Williamsburg "favorite" lures "hipsters" with "homespun" New American diner chow served by "tattooed girls" in a "funky", "pre-war" dining car; just "be prepared to wait" on weekends, when "brunch is what it's all about."

	FOOD	DECOR	SERVICE	COST

Dinosaur Bar-B-Que ⓜ BBQ
| 22 | 16 | 17 | $29 |

Harlem | 646 W. 131st St. (12th Ave.) | 212-694-1777 |
www.dinosaurbarbque.com

"Yabba dabba doo"–size portions of "bodacious", "butt-kicking BBQ"
chased with "awesome" microbrews keep this "rollicking" West
Harlem honky-tonk "crazy busy" with curious 'cue connoisseurs cag-
ing a "real-deal bargain"; just make sure to "have a reservation" to
avoid the "mad scramble to get a seat."

Dirty Bird to-go *American*
| 19 | 6 | 14 | $16 |

W Village | 204 W. 14th St. (7th Ave.) | 212-620-4836 |
www.dirtybirdtogo.com

"Urban picnic" types say this West Village "takeaway" specialist is their
"go-to" for "delish" fried and rotisserie versions of "free-range chicken"
paired with "down-home sides"; it's a "worthwhile" fast-food "alternative", though some cluck it's a "tad expensive for the portion size."

Dishes *Sandwiches*
| 21 | 12 | 11 | $17 |

E 40s | 6 E. 45th St. (bet. 5th & Madison Aves.) | 212-687-5511 🅢
E 40s | Grand Central | lower level (42nd St. & Vanderbilt Ave.) |
212-808-5511
E 50s | Citigroup Ctr. | 399 Park Ave. (53rd St.) | 212-421-5511 🅢

"Wildly popular" with Midtown's "upwardly mobile" nine-to-fivers,
this threesome's "mouthwatering array" of "high-class" sandwiches,
soups and salads attracts "madhouse hordes" at lunch; but as ratings
show, decor and service aren't their strong suit.

District *American*
| 20 | 19 | 20 | $55 |

W 40s | Muse Hotel | 130 W. 46th St. (bet. 6th & 7th Aves.) | 212-485-2999 |
www.districtnyc.com

Show-goers applaud this "tucked-away" Times Square New American
as a "tranquil" overture featuring "enticing" food, "efficient" service
and a "delightful" David Rockwell–designed room with a theatrical
motif; the $45 pre-theater prix fixe caps an "on-point" performance.

Ditch Plains ❶ *Seafood*
| 16 | 16 | 17 | $35 |

G Village | 29 Bedford St. (Downing St.) | 212-633-0202 |
www.ditch-plains.com

Named after a Montauk "surfing community", Marc Murphy's "laid-
back" Village seafooder has tides of "young, pretty" things stoked
about its "simple" "beach-shack" fare; though some swells are "not
impressed", at least there's "less of a wait than at Pearl Oyster Bar."

Divino ⓜ *Italian*
| 18 | 14 | 19 | $42 |

E 80s | 1556 Second Ave. (bet. 80th & 81st Sts.) | 212-861-1096 |
www.divinoristorante.net

This midpriced UES "fixture" still "hits the spot" with "hearty" Northern
Italian fare ferried by "courtly" staffers; the interior may seem a bit
"dowdy", but live music most nights "adds a little something."

Diwan *Indian*
| 21 | 17 | 18 | $37 |

E 40s | Helmsley Middletowne | 148 E. 48th St. (bet. Lexington & 3rd Aves.) |
212-593-5425

"Corporate" types vouch for the "high standards" at this East Midtown
Indian that "satisfies" with "flavorful" fare and "friendly" service; it's

best known for an "excellent, varied" $13.95 buffet lunch that "leaves you and your wallet full."

Django ⚑ *French/Mediterranean*

	FOOD	DECOR	SERVICE	COST
	20	21	19	$54

E 40s | 480 Lexington Ave. (bet. 46th & 47th Sts.) | 212-871-6600 | www.djangorestaurant.com

Djazzed up with "groovy", "harem"-like decor, this "modern" Midtowner offers "sophisticated" French-Med dishes in its upstairs dining room along with an "amusing after-work scene" in its street-level lounge; it's a magnet for "finance" types who aren't djarred by its "expensive" tabs.

Docks Oyster Bar *Seafood*

19	16	17	$50

E 40s | 633 Third Ave. (40th St.) | 212-986-8080
W 80s | 2427 Broadway (bet. 89th & 90th Sts.) | 212-724-5588
www.docksoysterbar.com

"Still going strong", these "consistent" crosstown "standbys" retain a "fail-safe" rep for "reliably fresh" raw bars and "ample" servings of "straightforward" seafood; "fair prices" are an additional lure, though detractors dock them for "noisy" acoustics and "offhand" service.

Do Hwa *Korean*

▽ 21	17	18	$38

G Village | 55 Carmine St. (Bedford St.) | 212-414-1224 | www.dohwanyc.com

As "close to authentic" as Korean food gets in the Village, this "flavorful" BBQ specialist puts out "tasty" chow at "K-town comparable" prices in a "chic", "modern-ish" setting; "interactive" types say it's even more "fun" if you "sizzle your own" at a grill table.

Dok Suni's ●⌀ *Korean*

▽ 22	13	17	$34

E Village | 119 First Ave. (bet. St. Marks Pl. & 7th St.) | 212-477-9506

"Downtown types" dock at this "cash-only" East Villager for "kickin'" "Korean comfort food" that "fills you up without breaking the bank"; "excellent" cocktails ratchet up the "lively" vibe, even if the space "needs more seating" and decor.

Dominick's ⌀ *Italian*

23	10	17	$38

Bronx | 2335 Arthur Ave. (bet. Crescent Ave. & E. 187th St.) | 718-733-2807

"Nobody goes home hungry" from this "legendary", cash-only Bronx Italian where "scrumptious" cooking is served at shared tables with "no menu" ("just ask what's good") and "no check" (they'll "tell you what you owe"); the "decor's better" following a recent renovation, but the no-reservations policy means the same "crazy long waits."

Don Giovanni ● *Italian*

17	11	14	$26

Chelsea | 214 10th Ave. (bet. 22nd & 23rd Sts.) | 212-242-9054
W 40s | 358 W. 44th St. (9th Ave.) | 212-581-4939
www.dongiovanni-ny.com

"Quick", "casual" and "convenient", these West Side Italians sling "satisfactory" pastas and pizzas for "budget" tabs; the settings and service are "nothing to rave about", but they're "usually buzzing" all the same.

Donguri Ⓜ *Japanese*

▽ 27	16	26	$63

E 80s | 309 E. 83rd St. (bet. 1st & 2nd Aves.) | 212-737-5656 | www.dongurinyc.com

A "real Japanese" that doesn't slice sushi, this UES "gem" "astounds the palate" via "superb" specialties from Japan's Kansai region (many based on soba and udon noodles), served by a "doting" staff; given the "culinary greatness", most have "no complaints" about the "high prices" and "tiny", "plain-Jane" setting.

Don Pedro's *Caribbean/European*   20 | 16 | 19 | $40

E 90s | 1865 Second Ave. (96th St.) | 212-996-3274 | www.donpedros.net

For a "refreshing change of pace" on the Upper East Side, this "comfortable" Euro-Caribbean dishes out "tasty", "original" dishes in "huge portions"; throw in "friendly service" and "lively" vibes fueled by "killer cocktails", and it's a "worthwhile stop."

Don Peppe Ⓜ ⌿ *Italian*   25 | 10 | 18 | $44

Ozone Park | 135-58 Lefferts Blvd. (bet. 135th & 149th Aves.) | Queens | 718-845-7587

Garlic lovers relish the "superior red-sauce" Italiana plated at this Ozone Park "institution" where the "enormous", "family-style" portions are washed down with "homemade wine"; "wear loose clothes", "bring cash" (they don't take plastic) and be prepared for "no frills."

Dos Caminos *Mexican*   20 | 20 | 18 | $44

E 50s | 825 Third Ave. (bet. 50th & 51st Sts.) | 212-336-5400
Gramercy | 373 Park Ave. S. (bet. 26th & 27th Sts.) | 212-294-1000
SoHo | 475 W. Broadway (bet. Houston & Prince Sts.) | 212-277-4300
www.brguestrestaurants.com

A "total good time" awaits at this "festive" threesome from Steve Hanson that matches "modern", midpriced Mexican meals with "attractive", "upscale" surroundings; known for their "must-have" guacamole whipped up tableside and "killer margaritas", they're "loud and hectic" with "spotty" service, yet compadres "can't get enough" of them.

NEW Dovetail *American*   26 | 21 | 23 | $71

W 70s | 103 W. 77th St. (Columbus Ave.) | 212-362-3800 | www.dovetailnyc.com

Quite simply a "stunner", this new, "high-end" UWS duplex "soars" thanks to John Fraser's "masterful", global-inflected New American cooking that dovetails perfectly with "seamless service" to justify every "pricey" penny spent; set in an "austere but elegant" space, it gives "adult" diners "lots to coo about"; P.S. downstairs is Siberia.

Downtown Atlantic Ⓜ *American*   19 | 15 | 18 | $34

Boerum Hill | 364 Atlantic Ave. (bet. Bond & Hoyt Sts.) | Brooklyn | 718-852-9945 | www.downtownatlantic.com

Parked in an "old-school Brooklyn setting", this "welcoming" Boerum Hill New American is a "neighborhood standard", providing a "varied menu" of "straightforward", "reasonably priced" goods plus "sublime desserts" from an "on-premises bakery"; locals like it because it "feels like home", except the food is better.

Doyers Vietnamese *Vietnamese*   ▽ 21 | 4 | 13 | $18

Chinatown | 11-13 Doyers St., downstairs (Chatham Sq.) | 212-513-1521

The Chinatown basement locale may be "hard to find", but this "windowless dive" is one of the "best Vietnamese bargains" around; "somnambulant service" and "zero ambiance" are reflected in the rock-bottom pricing.

			FOOD	DECOR	SERVICE	COST

Dressler *American*

26 | 25 | 23 | $52

Williamsburg | 149 Broadway (bet. Bedford & Driggs Aves.) | Brooklyn | 718-384-6343 | www.dresslernyc.com

"Williamsburg's answer to Gramercy Tavern", this "standout" New American "puts it all together" with "stellar" seasonal fare, an "eager-to-please staff" and "beautifully handcrafted" surroundings festooned with "exquisite ironwork from the Brooklyn Navy Yard"; it "can compete with any venue across the river", thus the "718 prices" are a "steal."

NEW Duane Park *American*

25 | 22 | 22 | $56

TriBeCa | 157 Duane St. (bet. Hudson St. & W. B'way) | 212-732-5555 | www.duaneparknyc.com

Replacing Duane Park Cafe, this new TriBeCan offers "wonderful" Southern-accented New American food, a "beautiful" chandeliered interior and "quietly efficient" service; since it retains its precursor's "serene" vibe, it's shaping up to be a bona fide "neighborhood sleeper."

Due ◑ *Italian*

21 | 15 | 21 | $47

E 70s | 1396 Third Ave. (bet. 79th & 80th Sts.) | 212-772-3331

"Respectable" dining with "no pretenses" makes this UES spot a "favorite" for "toothsome" Northern Italian fare and "committed" service; loyal locals laud it for "keeping the comfort level high" at a "gentle price."

DuMont *American*

24 | 17 | 18 | $27

Williamsburg | 432 Union Ave. (bet. Devoe St. & Metropolitan Ave.) | Brooklyn | 718-486-7717 | www.dumontrestaurant.com

DuMont Burger ◑ *American*

Williamsburg | 314 Bedford Ave. (bet. S. 1st & 2nd Sts.) | Brooklyn | 718-384-6127 | www.dumontnyc.com

Williamsburgers can "stop cooking at home" thanks to this "easygoing joint" serving "artful" yet "cheap" New American standards; a "hip crowd" convenes in the "inviting" interior or "Zen-like garden", or hits the Bedford Avenue mini spin-off for "awesome" burgers and sandwiches.

Dumpling Man ◑ *Chinese*

18 | 7 | 12 | $12

E Village | 100 St. Marks Pl. (bet. Ave. A & 1st Ave.) | 212-505-2121 | www.dumplingman.com

When it comes to a "cheap" quickie, this "painless" East Village Chinese offers "lots to choose from" via a "flavorful" roster of "substantial dumplings", all "freshly made" right in front of you; but given the "hole-in-the-wall" setting, "takeout is the best bet."

Dylan Prime *Steak*

24 | 22 | 21 | $67

TriBeCa | 62 Laight St. (Greenwich St.) | 212-334-4783 | www.dylanprime.com

"Snazzier than your average steakhouse", this "hip" TriBeCan draws "youthful" types with "fabulous" fare served "without attitude" in a "dark", "nontraditional" setting; add in a "wonderful" separate bar area, and it's easy to see why it's "worth the hefty price" and is always full.

Earthen Oven *Indian*

20 | 12 | 17 | $36

W 70s | 53 W. 72nd St. (bet. Columbus Ave. & CPW) | 212-579-8888 | www.earthenovennyc.com

"Marvelous" regional dishes not found in the typical tandoori lineup turn up on the menu of this UWS Indian vending "enticing eats" for "decent" dough; the digs may be "low on atmosphere", but the "high culinary standards" leave most more than "satisfied."

East Manor *Chinese*   19 | 12 | 12 | $25

Flushing | 46-45 Kissena Blvd. (bet. Kalmia & Laburnum Aves.) | Queens | 718-888-8998

"Hong Kong–style" carts provide "lots of selection" at this "huge" Flushing Chinese that specializes in "tantalizing" dim sum at lunchtime and on weekends; low prices and "fast (if not friendly)" service keep things "bustling" here, though it's "less hectic" on weekdays.

East of Eighth ● *Eclectic*   17 | 15 | 19 | $32

Chelsea | 254 W. 23rd St. (bet. 7th & 8th Aves.) | 212-352-0075

"Popular" Chelsea Eclectic "mainstay" with "decent chow" at "moderate prices", a *très gay* bar scene and "cute garden"; bargain-hunters report the $18 early-bird prix fixe is quite a "deal."

E.A.T. *American*   19 | 10 | 13 | $41

E 80s | 1064 Madison Ave. (bet. 80th & 81st Sts.) | 212-772-0022 | www.elizabar.com

"Mobbed at lunch", Eli Zabar's UES New American stalwart is a "beacon" for "mighty delicious" sandwiches and other "gourmet" deli fare; supporters tolerate the "brusque service", "tight quarters" and "insane prices" since it's "one of the few places to get a decent bite" in the neighborhood.

Eatery ● *American*   19 | 16 | 17 | $33

W 50s | 798 Ninth Ave. (53rd St.) | 212-765-7080 | www.eaterynyc.com

"Good times abound" at this "friendly" Hell's Kitchen New American, a "cool white" destination for locals digging into a "crowd-pleasing" menu of "affordable" "modern diner" items like its "famous mac 'n' jack"; just be ready for "loud", "cramped" conditions and weekend brunch "waits."

Ecco ⊠ *Italian*   22 | 17 | 21 | $52

TriBeCa | 124 Chambers St. (bet. Church St. & W. B'way) | 212-227-7074

Like a "trip back in time", this TriBeCa Italian is a "consistently solid" source of "classic" cuisine and "attentive" service in "genuine throwback" environs; admirers aver its "old-fashioned", pre-Prohibition style and "comfort" are "worth the money", while that "live piano" on weekends adds an appealing echo.

Edgar's Cafe ●⇄ *Coffeehouse*   17 | 16 | 15 | $23

W 80s | 255 W. 84th St. (bet. B'way & West End Ave.) | 212-496-6126

Edgar Allan Poe inspired the "Gothic" look of this namesake UWS coffeehouse, celebrated for its "wide variety" of "decadent desserts" sold for "cash only"; "easily distracted" service sets the "leisurely" pace, so it's an "isle of calm" for a "chat" or a midnight snack.

Edison Cafe ⇄ *Coffee Shop*   15 | 7 | 13 | $21

W 40s | Edison Hotel | 228 W. 47th St. (bet. B'way & 8th Ave.) | 212-840-5000

A haunt for "Broadway honchos" and members of the chorus, this "retro" Theater District coffee shop (aka the 'Polish Tea Room') plies "cheap" Jewish eats like matzo ball soup and blintzes; despite decidedly "dumpy decor" and "crusty servers", it's lauded as both a "survivor" and a "hoot."

Ed's Lobster Bar Ⓜ *Seafood*

23	16	19	$42

NoLita | 222 Lafayette St. (bet. Kenmare & Spring Sts.) | 212-343-3236 | www.lobsterbarnyc.com

For cooking that "reminds you of Maine", check out the "succulent" lobster rolls and other "New England classics" at this "casual" NoLita seafood shack, renowned as a "Pearl Oyster Bar copycat"; its "inviting" but "narrow" quarters are "usually crowded", so insiders "go early" for a "quieter experience."

Egg ⊘ *Southern*

24	11	16	$18

Williamsburg | 135A N. Fifth St. (bet. Bedford Ave. & Berry St.) | Brooklyn | 718-302-5151 | www.pigandegg.com

"True Southern fare" is the hallmark of this cash-only Williamsburg cubbyhole, home to "killer" "comfort breakfasts" and lunches and now a Wednesday–Sunday dinner menu led by an "astonishing fried chicken"; it's "nothing to look at" and seating's "scarce", but at least you won't be shelling out much.

Eight Mile Creek ⓞ *Australian*

▽ 20	13	18	$39

NoLita | 240 Mulberry St. (bet. Prince & Spring Sts.) | 212-431-4635 | www.eightmilecreek.com

Plucky patrons "jump at the chance to try kangaroo" at this NoLita Australian featuring a "well-prepared" sampling of "authentic", low-priced grub; the double-decker "pub" setting also sports a "garden area" and so many "Aussie accents" you'll "swear you're Down Under."

🆕 eighty one *American*

26	25	24	$80

W 80s | Excelsior Hotel | 45 W. 81st St. (bet. Columbus Ave. & CPW) | 212-873-8181 | www.81nyc.com

Proof of the ongoing UWS fine-dining renaissance, this new "class act" from the "dedicated" Ed Brown (ex Sea Grill) serves "superb" seasonal New Americana in a "chic", velvety setting; the "remarkable staff" tends to a "sophisticated" clientele that doesn't mind paying "high-end" prices for "true luxury."

EJ's Luncheonette ⊘ *American*

16	9	14	$22

E 70s | 1271 Third Ave. (73rd St.) | 212-472-0600
W 80s | 447 Amsterdam Ave. (bet. 81st & 82nd Sts.) | 212-873-3444

Ever "crowded" with the "stroller set", this "traditional diner" duo is best known for its "can't-be-beat" breakfasts and "blue-plate specials" piled high with "hearty" "all-American" chow; "no-frills" settings, "ridiculous" weekend waits and a "cash-only" policy are trumped by a "speedy" pace and "good value."

Elaine's ⓞ *American/Italian*

12	13	13	$55

E 80s | 1703 Second Ave. (bet. 88th & 89th Sts.) | 212-534-8103

Long renowned as *the* "literary crowd haunt" and book party central, Elaine Kaufman's UES Italian-American endures despite "pricey", "pedestrian" fare, "indifferent" service and "tired" decor; "clubby", "older" writers argue "it isn't about the food", but ultimately "if they don't know you, they don't want to know you"; as one surveyor says, "a would-be, for has-beens."

	FOOD	DECOR	SERVICE	COST

El Centro ◐ *Mexican*
▽ 20 | 18 | 18 | $30

W 50s | 824 Ninth Ave. (54th St.) | 646-763-6585 | www.elcentro-nyc.com
Hell's Kitchen amigos applaud this "colorful", "upbeat" Mexican for "tasty-as-all-get-out" dishes washed down with "killer margaritas"; *sí*, the "close quarters can be noisy" and the decor verges on "tacky", but with prices this "low", no one cares.

El Charro Español *Spanish*
▽ 22 | 14 | 21 | $42

G Village | 4 Charles St. (bet. Greenwich Ave. & Waverly Pl.) | 212-242-9547
Parked in the same "rustic basement" since 1925, this "authentic" Village Spaniard remains "tried-and-true" for "plentiful" portions of "medium"-priced grub ("heavy on the garlic") served by an "attentive" crew; the atmosphere's "nothing fancy", but there's a reason it's been around "as long as anyone can remember."

Elementi *Italian*
▽ 18 | 20 | 19 | $42

Park Slope | 140 Seventh Ave. (Carroll St.) | Brooklyn | 718-788-8388 | www.elementirestaurant.com
Park Slopers yearning for "more upscale" options are in their element at this new Italian "oasis" supplying "fresh", "fairly priced" food in "comfortable", "beige"-toned surroundings; a few find the going "uneven", but most say it's off to a "promising" start.

Elephant, The ◐ *French/Thai*
▽ 21 | 16 | 15 | $35

E Village | 58 E. First St. (bet. 1st & 2nd Aves.) | 212-505-7739 | www.elephantrestaurant.com
Though this ironically named East Villager has "sardine-can" dimensions, it keeps the crowds coming with its "delightful" Thai-French fare and "potent cocktails"; the "funky" quarters and "laid-back" service are "not for older folks", but twentysomethings trumpet that it's "totally worth" trying.

Elephant & Castle ◐ *Pub Food*
18 | 15 | 18 | $28

G Village | 68 Greenwich Ave. (bet. Perry St. & 7th Ave. S.) | 212-243-1400 | www.elephantandcastle.com
On the Village scene since 1974, this "comforting" joint still "hits the spot" with "enjoyable" pub "basics" and a "hearty brunch"; though "snug to the point of claustrophobic", it offers "value" "without pretense" and "you can always get a seat."

NEW Elettaria ◐ *American*
▽ 23 | 21 | 21 | $54

G Village | 33 W. Eighth St. (bet. 5th & 6th Aves.) | 212-677-3833 | www.elettarianyc.com
A "welcome change", this "trendy" Village newcomer with an "open kitchen" spices up its "terrific" New American lineup with a "hint of India"; the rustic room's "close seating" has everyone "rubbing elbows", but with "amazing mixology" and "sweet" service, surveyors sense a "hit."

⛁ Eleven Madison Park *French*
27 | 26 | 26 | $107

Gramercy | 11 Madison Ave. (24th St.) | 212-889-0905 | www.elevenmadisonpark.com
The "epitome of class", Danny Meyer's "magnificent" New French fronting Madison Square Park "wows the palate" with Daniel Humm's cuisine, following through with "sterling" service and a "stately",

"soaring" art deco space; despite snipes at "elf"-size portions and "stratospherically priced" prix fixes, a clear majority is "happy to pay" for such "effortless indulgence."

El Faro ❷ Ⓜ *Spanish* | 21 | 11 | 18 | $39

W Village | 823 Greenwich St. (bet. Horatio & Jane Sts.) | 212-929-8210 | www.elfaronyc.com

On the scene since 1927, this "vintage" Village Spaniard "still pleases" with "traditional", "reasonably priced" grub seasoned with "garlic for days"; sure, it's "frayed around the edges", but its fans shrug "if it ain't broke, don't fix it."

Eliá Ⓜ *Greek* | 25 | 20 | 22 | $51

Bay Ridge | 8611 Third Ave. (bet. 86th & 87th Sts.) | Brooklyn | 718-748-9891

Thanks to "remarkable takes on typical Greek dishes" – including fish so "fresh" it "practically jumps off your plate" – this "quality" Bay Ridge Hellenic is a "real find"; add "charming" decor, "hospitable" service and a "great outdoor garden", and "you'll think you're in Santorini."

Elias Corner ❷⇗ *Greek/Seafood* | 22 | 8 | 14 | $37

Astoria | 24-02 31st St. (24th Ave.) | Queens | 718-932-1510

It's ultra-"plain" and "only takes cash", but this menuless Greek seafooder in Astoria is a "savvy" choice for "super-fresh" fish "grilled to perfection" at a "good price"; "grumpy" service goes with the "no-frills" style, so it's best in summer "when you can sit outside."

Elio's ❷ *Italian* | 23 | 16 | 19 | $63

E 80s | 1621 Second Ave. (bet. 83rd & 84th Sts.) | 212-772-2242

The "strong buzz" endures at this "upscale" Upper Eastsider, a "Tom Wolfe–ish scene" where "celebs" and "snappy" locals meet cute over "expensive", "top-notch" Italian fare; be prepared for lots of "hustle and bustle" and service that runs the gamut from "welcoming" to "gruff if they don't know you."

El Malecon ❷ *Dominican* | 21 | 9 | 14 | $18

Washington Heights | 4141 Broadway (175th St.) | 212-927-3812
W 90s | 764 Amsterdam Ave. (bet. 97th & 98th Sts.) | 212-864-5648
Bronx | 5592 Broadway (231st St.) | 718-432-5155

Made for "empty stomachs", this Uptown/Bronx trio puts out "stick-to-your-ribs" servings of "mouthwatering rotisserie chicken" and other Dominican "comfort food" for "can't-be-beat" dough; "drab" decor detracts, so regulars often "opt for takeout."

elmo ❷ *American* | 16 | 18 | 16 | $34

Chelsea | 156 Seventh Ave. (bet. 19th & 20th Sts.) | 212-337-8000 | www.elmorestaurant.com

This "lively", "loungey" Chelsea New American may serve only "average" eats but still lures a "beefcake" crowd with its *Sex and the Gay City* vibe; "cute waif" waiters and "affordable" tabs help make it a "local go-to" and a brunch "favorite."

El Parador Cafe *Mexican* | 22 | 16 | 21 | $43

Murray Hill | 325 E. 34th St. (bet. 1st & 2nd Aves.) | 212-679-6812 | www.elparadorcafe.com

"Hidden" and "underappreciated", this 50-year-old Murray Hill Mexican is a "funky throwback" for "excellent" "old-school" dishes served by a staff that "couldn't be nicer"; the "homey" interior is "nothing fancy", but "warm and fuzzy" vibes prevail, especially after a "strong margarita" or two.

El Paso Taqueria *Mexican*

22	12	17	$23

E 100s | 1642 Lexington Ave. (104th St.) | 212-831-9831 ☽
E 90s | 64 E. 97th St. (Park Ave.) | 212-996-1739
Harlem | 237 E. 116th St. (3rd Ave.) | 212-860-4875 ☽
www.elpasotaqueria.com

These Upper Eastsiders "remind you of Mexico" with "tasty", *"muy auténtico"* taqueria items that come at an "amazing price"; service is "sweet" and "fairly quick", though picky eaters eschew the "tight tables" and "cheesy" decor for takeout.

El Pote ⊠ *Spanish*

22	12	21	$41

Murray Hill | 718 Second Ave. (bet. 38th & 39th Sts.) | 212-889-6680 |
www.elpote.com

Murray Hill "neighborhood" types confirm that this "small", "old-school" Spaniard still "stands up" as a supplier of "outstanding paella" and other "traditional" staples; maybe the interior's "kind of shabby", but the staff is "eager to please" and it's "priced right."

El Quijote ☽ *Spanish*

19	13	17	$41

Chelsea | 226 W. 23rd St. (bet. 7th & 8th Aves.) | 212-929-1855

Celebrated as a "kitschy" lobster-and-sangria destination, this "ebullient" Chelsea "old-timer" (since 1930) is "still kicking" thanks to "huge portions" of "dependable" Spanish grub; the "tacky" space may be "showing its age", but it's such a "good buy" there's "always a mob."

NEW El Quinto Pino ☽ *Spanish*

▽ 23	18	21	$34

Chelsea | 401 W. 24th St. (bet. 9th & 10th Aves.) | 212-206-6900

Squeezing the feel of "Barcelona" into a very "small package", this new Chelsea tapas bar from the Tía Pol team plies an "intriguing" roster of "fantastic" finger food accompanied by "terrific" Spanish wines; but given the "midget", table-free setting, expect "trouble finding seats."

Embers *Steak*

21	12	17	$44

Bay Ridge | 9519 Third Ave. (bet. 95th & 96th Sts.) | Brooklyn | 718-745-3700

This Bay Ridge "steakhouse staple" gets glowing reviews for its "mammoth" cuts of "premium" beef served "without the attitude" (or price point) of tonier joints; not so hot is the "dated" room and "tight tables", but ultimately "the lines say it all."

Empanada Mama ☽ *S American*

22	12	16	$16

W 50s | 763 Ninth Ave. (bet. 51st & 52nd Sts.) | 212-698-9008

For a "quickie treat", this Hell's Kitchen South American purveys "freshly made", "come-to-mama" empanadas for all tastes (dessert varieties included) "without breaking the bank"; the "tiny" "hole-in-the-wall" space fills up fast, so many are glad the goods are "portable."

Empire Diner ☽ *Diner*

15	14	14	$25

Chelsea | 210 10th Ave. (22nd St.) | 212-243-2736

Like a "time machine", this "Chelsea fixture" slings "competent" diner grub 24/7 to everyone from "gallery-hoppers" to "clubbers" drawn to its 1929 "deco charm" and "great outside seating"; it's particularly "cool" at 3 AM, when its young, highly watchable crowd is especially oblivious to the prices and "aloof servers."

Empire Szechuan ● *Chinese* | 15 | 9 | 14 | $24 |

G Village | 15 Greenwich Ave. (bet. Christopher & W. 10th Sts.) | 212-691-1535 | www.empiretogo.com
G Village | 173 Seventh Ave. S. (bet. Perry & W. 11th Sts.) | 212-243-6046
Washington Heights | 4041 Broadway (bet. 170th & 171st Sts.) | 212-568-1600
W 60s | 193 Columbus Ave. (bet. 68th & 69th Sts.) | 212-496-8778 | www.empiretogo.com
W 100s | 2642 Broadway (100th St.) | 212-662-9404

"They get the job done" at these "go-to" Chinese purveyors of a "wide variety" of "dependable" dishes for a "decent price" (including "cheap sushi" at some branches); still, the "forgettable decor" has many endorsing their "fast delivery."

Employees Only ● *European* | 19 | 20 | 19 | $45 |

W Village | 510 Hudson St. (bet. Christopher & W. 10th Sts.) | 212-242-3021 | www.employeesonlynyc.com

"Young" types get "social" over "handcrafted cocktails" at this "lively" West Villager, a "fantastic little speakeasy" replica with a "charming" garden; while best "known for the drinks", it also serves "quite good" European fare into the wee hours, when some "wish it were half as full."

Energy Kitchen *Health Food* | 15 | 4 | 12 | $14 |

Chelsea | 307 W. 17th St. (bet. 8th & 9th Aves.) | 212-645-5200
E 40s | 300 E. 41st St. (2nd Ave.) | 212-687-1200
E 50s | 1089 Second Ave. (bet. 57th & 58th Sts.) | 212-888-9300
🆕 **Financial District** | 71 Nassau St. (bet. Fulton & John Sts.) | 212-577-8989 🕿
W 40s | 417 W. 47th St. (9th Ave.) | 212-333-3500
W Village | 82 Christopher St. (bet. Bleecker St. & 7th Ave. S.) | 212-414-8880
www.energykitchen.com

A "gym bunny's best friend", this "no-guilt fast-food" chain offers an "easy" way to "reenergize" on "healthful" burgers, wraps and other "fairly tasty" grub "without making your wallet lose weight"; but given the spartan setups and second-class service, many see the "fitness" of takeout.

EN Japanese Brasserie *Japanese* | 23 | 25 | 21 | $57 |

W Village | 435 Hudson St. (Leroy St.) | 212-647-9196 | www.enjb.com

En-thusiasts en-dorse this "spacious" West Village "eye-opener" for its "swank"-meets-"Zen" ambiance and equally "impressive" menu of "different" Japanese small plates (many showcasing "superb fresh tofu"); an "endless sake list" and "lovely" service encourage "tranquility" – at least until the check arrives.

Ennio & Michael *Italian* | 21 | 16 | 22 | $45 |

G Village | 539 La Guardia Pl. (bet. Bleecker & W. 3rd Sts.) | 212-677-8577 | www.ennioandmichael.com

"Year in, year out", Village regulars turn to this Italian for "*delizioso*", "down-home" dishes delivered by "solicitous" staffers who "make you feel at home"; the decor is "nothing special", so come summer the "outdoor seating is a real plus."

	FOOD	DECOR	SERVICE	COST

Enzo's ⓜ *Italian* | 23 | 14 | 20 | $38

Bronx | 1998 Williamsbridge Rd. (Neill Ave.) | 718-409-3828
Bronx | 2339 Arthur Ave. (bet. Crescent Ave. & E. 186th St.) | 718-733-4455
www.enzosofthebronx.com

Italian dishes "the way momma made them" are yours at this "homey" Bronx duo that proffers "abundant" servings of "flavorful" "red-sauce" favorites; a recent redo on Williamsbridge Road addresses the "minimal" decor issue, though no reservations and "good prices" mean the "long lines" endure.

Epices du Traiteur *Mediterranean/Tunisian* | 21 | 16 | 19 | $44

W 70s | 103 W. 70th St. (Columbus Ave.) | 212-579-5904

An "imaginative alternative" to the "usual Lincoln Center choices", this "cozy oasis" provides a "delightful" Med-Tunisian "mélange" along with "efficient service" at "fair prices"; still, the "secret seems to be out", so to avoid epic "crowding", insiders head for "the garden when possible."

Erawan *Thai* | 23 | 20 | 20 | $37

Bayside | 213-41 39th Ave. (Bell Blvd.) | Queens | 718-229-1620
Bayside | 42-31 Bell Blvd. (bet. 42nd & 43rd Aves.) | Queens | 718-428-2112

The "tantalizing Thai" menu ranges from "subtle to spicy" at this Bayside twosome that also features Siamese surf 'n' turf at the "nicer", roomier 39th Avenue outlet; "courteous" staffers and "Manhattan quality for Queens prices" explain the "weekend waits."

Erminia ⓩ *Italian* | 25 | 24 | 24 | $62

E 80s | 250 E. 83rd St. (2nd Ave.) | 212-879-4284

Perhaps the "ultimate date restaurant", this rustic UES Italian set in "intimate", candlelit digs offers an "enchanting" backdrop for "all things lovey-dovey"; given the "top-of-the-line" Roman fare and "impeccable" service, it's a "fabulous" (if "pricey") way to "celebrate any occasion – especially getting engaged."

Esca ❶ *Italian/Seafood* | 25 | 20 | 22 | $69

W 40s | 402 W. 43rd St. (9th Ave.) | 212-564-7272 | www.esca-nyc.com

"If fish is your thing", the Batali-Bastianich-Pasternack crew's "bustling" Theater District port of call "will esca-late your expectations" with its *supremo* Italian seafood (and "excellent pasta"), "informed" service and "urbane" environs; prices are "extravagant", but the "irresistible" eats "keep reeling 'em in."

Esperanto ❶ *Nuevo Latino* | 20 | 18 | 17 | $31

E Village | 145 Ave. C (9th St.) | 212-505-6559 | www.esperantony.com

For a "spicy" meal that "won't burn a hole in your wallet", this "bright" East Villager supplies "satisfying" Nuevo Latino dishes and "festive" atmospherics fueled by "excellent caipirinhas"; live music and sidewalk seating distract from "lethargic" service.

Ess-a-Bagel *Deli* | 23 | 6 | 13 | $11

E 50s | 831 Third Ave. (bet. 50th & 51st Sts.) | 212-980-1010
Gramercy | 359 First Ave. (21st St.) | 212-260-2252
www.ess-a-bagel.com

"Fresh", "dense" and topped with "whatever your heart desires", the "life preserver"–size bagels vended at this East Side deli duo are "even better when warm out of the oven"; "curmudgeonly" counter service, "bare-bones" decor and "zoo"-like crowds are all "part of the charm."

Essex ● _American_　　　　　18 | 16 | 15 | $32

LES | 120 Essex St. (Rivington St.) | 212-533-9616 | www.essexnyc.com

A "hip" nexus on weekends thanks to its "boozy brunch deal", this "airy" LES New American is favored by "twentysomethings" for its "reliable food", "trendy vibe" and modest prices; dinner features riffs on "pleasing" Jewish-Latin variations, but "don't expect speedy service."

Estancia 460 _Argentinean/Italian_　　▽ 20 | 15 | 18 | $40

TriBeCa | 460 Greenwich St. (bet. Desbrosses & Watts Sts.) | 212-431-5093 | www.estancia460.com

TriBeCans feel "at home" at this "quiet" Italian-Argentinean that serves "dependable", "fairly priced" dishes in a "simple", "rustic" setting enhanced by "outside seating"; "attentive" staffers keep it "comfortable" any time, including "brunch on weekends."

Etats-Unis _American_　　　　　24 | 16 | 22 | $60

E 80s | 242 E. 81st St. (bet. 2nd & 3rd Aves.) | 212-517-8826 | www.etatsunisrestaurant.com

It's a "squeeze" at this "postage stamp-size" Upper Eastsider but the payoff is an "impeccable" New American menu served by a "winning" team; it's an "expensive" but "worthy indulgence", though the "warm wine bar" across the street offers the same kind of food for "less dough."

etcetera etcetera Ⓜ _Italian_　　　21 | 19 | 21 | $47

W 40s | 352 W. 44th St. (bet. 8th & 9th Aves.) | 212-399-4141 | www.etcrestaurant.com

As a "relaxed alternative" to sibling ViceVersa, this Theater District "price performer" proffers "imaginative", "well-prepared" Italian food and "warm" service in an "upbeat", "urban-modern" setting; it can get quite "noisy", so for quieter dining, "request a table upstairs."

Ethos ● _Greek_　　　　　　　22 | 16 | 18 | $38

Murray Hill | 495 Third Ave. (bet. 33rd & 34th Sts.) | 212-252-1972 | www.ethosnyc.com

"Grilled fish par excellence" is the focus of this Murray Hill Hellene where "simple" Greek "favorites" are priced for "value" in an "inconspicuous" taverna setting; "relaxed" service to the contrary, it's typically "packed" with "contented" customers.

E.U., The ● _European_　　　　18 | 21 | 17 | $44
(aka European Union)

E Village | 235 E. Fourth St. (bet. Aves. A & B) | 212-254-2900 | www.theeunyc.com

The "gastropub phenom" gets a "hip" spin at this East Villager where the "wonderfully inventive" European fare is served in an "attractive rustic" setting; given the choice of small or large plates and a "killer brunch", it's "interesting" dining, if a tad "pricey for the locale."

Euzkadi _Spanish_　　　　　▽ 19 | 17 | 18 | $38

E Village | 108 E. Fourth St. (bet. 1st & 2nd Aves.) | 212-982-9788 | www.euzkadirestaurant.com

Aka "bachelorette party" central, this East Village "Basque bastion" keeps the "energy high" with "tasty tapas" and "friendly", "flirty" service in a "funky little" space; "bargain" rates and live flamenco Tuesday nights add to the "festive" feel.

Evergreen Shanghai ⌧ Chinese
19 | 12 | 15 | $29

Murray Hill | 10 E. 38th St. (bet. 5th & Madison Aves.) | 212-448-1199
Sinophiles "don't have to go to Chinatown" anymore for "traditional Shanghainese cooking" thanks to this Murray Hill Chinese, also known for its dim sum and "juicy" soup dumplings; an "atmosphere made for takeout" is offset by "reasonable" costs.

Excellent Dumpling House ⌇ Chinese
19 | 4 | 11 | $15

Chinatown | 111 Lafayette St. (bet. Canal & Walker Sts.) | 212-219-0212
"Named right", this Chinatown "stalwart" is known for its "fantastic" dumplings and "super-cheap" Shanghai specialties that "make jury duty a pleasure"; be prepared for a "utilitarian" setup with "packed communal tables", but then again "you're not there for the atmosphere."

Extra Virgin Mediterranean
21 | 18 | 18 | $42

W Village | 259 W. Fourth St. (bet. Charles & Perry Sts.) | 212-691-9359 | www.extravirginrestaurant.com
Extra "fabulosity" marks this "trendy" West Villager, a "tightly packed" destination for "attractive young" things hobnobbing over "delightful" Med dishes that "won't break the bank"; "spotty" service aside, it's a "favorite" for its "sidewalk tables" and "excellent brunch", so expect extra "long lines."

Fabio Piccolo Fiore Italian
∇ 22 | 21 | 22 | $49

E 40s | 230 E. 44th St. (bet. 2nd & 3rd Aves.) | 212-922-0581 | www.fabiopiccolofiore.com
A "quiet sleeper" near Grand Central, this "attractive" Italian pleases patrons with "congenial service" and "marvelous" food from a chef-owner so "accommodating" he'll "make anything you can dream up"; in a neighborhood with "too few good choices", it's an affordable "find."

Fairway Cafe American
18 | 8 | 10 | $27

W 70s | 2127 Broadway, 2nd fl. (74th St.) | 212-595-1888
Red Hook | 480-500 Van Brunt St. (Reed St.) | Brooklyn | 718-694-6868
www.fairwaymarket.com
Extend a "shopping expedition" at these "tucked-away", low-budget cafes serving "above-average" American eats ("or a steak dinner on the UWS"); plan on "absentee service" and "nonexistent" decor, except for Red Hook's "picture-perfect" harbor view.

Falai Italian
24 | 18 | 19 | $50

LES | 68 Clinton St. (bet. Rivington & Stanton Sts.) | 212-253-1960 | www.falainyc.com
Falai Panetteria Italian
LES | 79 Clinton St. (Rivington St.) | 212-777-8956
Caffe Falai Italian
SoHo | 265 Lafayette St. (Prince St.) | 212-274-8615
There are three ways to catch the "buzz" on chef Iacopo Falai's "innovative" cooking: the original LES flagship offering "amazingly accomplished" Italian dinners, or the "more informal" Panetteria and Caffe (both decorated in trademark "stark white" fashion) for "first-rate" breakfasts and lunches.

	FOOD	DECOR	SERVICE	COST

F & J Pine Restaurant *Italian*   21 | 19 | 19 | $37

Bronx | 1913 Bronxdale Ave. (bet. Matthews & Muliner Aves.) |
718-792-5956 | www.fjpine.com

Folks pining for "*abbondanza*" head to this "huge" Bronx Italian for "super" red-sauce standards plated in "ginormous portions"; you may "see a Yankee or two" in the "raucous" digs, and since it's "quite popular" on weekends and game days, "expect to wait."

Farm on Adderley *American*   22 | 19 | 21 | $37

Ditmas Park | 1108 Cortelyou Rd. (bet. Stratford & Westminster Rds.) |
Brooklyn | 718-287-3101 | www.thefarmonadderley.com

Bringing a "breath of fresh air" to "up-and-coming" Ditmas Park, this New American "pioneer" sows loyalty with "lip-smacking", "market-driven" fare at a "great value" served by "warm" staffers; add a "congenial" setting and "lovely garden" and, no surprise, it's "going strong."

Fatty Crab ● *Malaysian*   21 | 12 | 16 | $40

W Village | 643 Hudson St. (bet. Gansevoort & Horatio Sts.) | 212-352-3590 |
www.fattycrab.com

Think "Kuala Lumpur on the Hudson" to get the gist of Zak Pelaccio's "rockin'" West Village "hole-in-the-wall" where a "slow", "surfer-dude" staff serves "intensely flavored" Malaysian street fare; despite "loud music" and "shoehorned" seating, "long lines" are the norm.

Fatty's Cafe *American/Eclectic*   ▽ 22 | 17 | 20 | $23

Astoria | 25-01 Ditmars Blvd. (Crescent St.) | Queens | 718-267-7071 |
www.fattyscafenyc.com

"You're in good hands" at this "cheap 'n' cheery" Astorian, serving "Latin-influenced" American food minus "any sort of pretension"; it's a "go-to" brunch spot with "bohemian" digs "decorated with art for sale" and a bonus "back garden."

☑ Felidia *Italian*   26 | 22 | 24 | $75

E 50s | 243 E. 58th St. (bet. 2nd & 3rd Aves.) | 212-758-1479 |
www.lidiasitaly.com

TV guru Lidia Bastianich "lives up to her reputation" at this "*magnifico*" East Side Italian, an "elegant" but "nonintimidating" "benchmark" for "sumptuous cuisine" paired with an "excellent wine list" in a "lovely townhouse" setting; "first-class", "black-tie" service caps a "memorable" performance that "doesn't come cheap" yet "never fails to impress."

Félix ● *French*   16 | 16 | 14 | $42

SoHo | 340 W. Broadway (Grand St.) | 212-431-0021 |
www.felixnyc.com

It's "all about the scene" at this SoHo "magnet" for "gorgeous Euros" and "trust-fund kids" who show up for the "party", not the "nonchalant service" or "just ok" French eats; it's best for brunch and "people-watching", especially when "all the doors open to the street."

Ferrara ● *Bakery*   22 | 16 | 16 | $22

Little Italy | 195 Grand St. (bet. Mott & Mulberry Sts.) | 212-226-6150 |
www.ferraracafe.com

"Holy cannoli!", you can "gain weight just by breathing the air" at this circa-1892 Little Italy "icon", a "classic" after-dinner stop for "delectable Italian desserts" and "wonderful" espresso at semi-"pricey" tabs; just bear with the "rushed" service and "full-contact" throngs of "locals, tourists and everyone in between"; it's also called "too commercial."

☑ Fette Sau *BBQ* | 24 | 17 | 14 | $25 |

Williamsburg | 354 Metropolitan Ave. (bet. Havemeyer & Roebling Sts.) | Brooklyn | 718-963-3404

Proof that "hipsters do eat meat", this "garage"-like Williamsburg BBQ (voted No. 1 in this Survey) offers a chance to "pig out" on "mouthwatering" 'cue "purchased by weight" in a "cafeteria-type line"; fans perched on "picnic benches" swilling "local lagers" and "smoky bourbons" consider it a bargain "blast."

Fiamma ☑ Ⓜ *Italian* | 24 | 23 | 23 | $111 |

SoHo | 206 Spring St. (bet. 6th Ave. & Sullivan St.) | 212-653-0100 | www.brguestrestaurants.com

Now showcasing the "superior" skills of chef Fabio Trabocchi, Steve Hanson's "reborn" SoHo Italian remains a "deluxe experience" that lures fans with "brilliant food" and a "refined" townhouse setting; "you'll feel classy" just being there, but remember to "line up financing" in advance.

15 East ☑ *Japanese* | 26 | 21 | 25 | $84 |

Union Sq | 15 E. 15th St. (bet. 5th Ave. & Union Sq. W.) | 212-647-0015 | www.15eastrestaurant.com

Ranked in the "top echelon" of Japanese eateries, this "special" Union Square sushi shrine from the Tocqueville team purveys "absolutely delicious morsels" sliced by a "skilled, friendly" chef and served in a "spare", "hushed" setting; indeed, the "beautiful Zen feeling" is broken only when the bill arrives.

57 *American* | 23 | 24 | 24 | $78 |

E 50s | Four Seasons Hotel | 57 E. 57th St. (Madison Ave.) | 212-829-3859 | www.fourseasons.com

Overlooking the Four Seasons' I.M. Pei-designed lobby is this "classic" New American, serving three meals daily in a "minimalist", "high-ceilinged" setting that works for both "business and pleasure"; "extravagant" pricing and "polished service" come with the territory, even if a minority sees "no flair" here.

Fig & Olive *Mediterranean* | 20 | 20 | 18 | $45 |

NEW **E 50s** | 10 E. 52nd St. (bet. 5th & Madison Aves.) | 212-319-2002 ◐
E 60s | 808 Lexington Ave. (bet. 62nd & 63rd Sts.) | 212-207-4555
Meatpacking | 420 W. 13th St. (bet. 9th Ave. & Washington St.) | 212-924-1200 ◐
www.figandolive.com

With "artisanal olive oils" as its focal point, this "sprightly" Med trio is known for "deliciously light" small plates paired with "fairly priced" vino; a *Real Housewives* crowd" convenes Uptown while the "lofty" Meatpacking District outpost is more "convivial if a bit loud."

Filippo's Ⓜ *Italian* | ∇ 26 | 21 | 24 | $50 |

Staten Island | 1727 Richmond Rd. (bet. Buel & Seaver Aves.) | 718-668-9091 | www.filipposrestaurant.com

Bring a "recording device" to keep track of the "long list" of "inventive" specials at this Staten Island Italian where the classic cooking "never disappoints" and the service is "personable"; though expensive by area standards, nevertheless it's "always abuzz" and there's "always a wait."

			FOOD	DECOR	SERVICE	COST

F.illi Ponte Ⓢ *Italian* — 22 | 19 | 21 | $69

TriBeCa | 39 Desbrosses St. (bet. Washington & West Sts.) | 212-226-4621 | www.filliponte.com

In Way West TriBeCa (you almost have to swim there), this "old-world" Italian serves "wonderful food" (its signature 'angry lobster') in "clubby", brick-lined digs blessed with a "view of the Hudson"; the "checks are big" and the crowd heavily "bridge-and-tunnel", but to traditionalists that's beside the ponte.

Finestra *Italian* — ∇ 17 | 15 | 18 | $40

E 70s | 1370 York Ave. (73rd St.) | 212-717-8594

Yorkville denizens who "want to fill up" head for this "neighborhood" Italian, a "low-key", "comforting haven" that offers the "expected" staples in "well-sized portions"; live music diverts attention from a room that "could use some updating."

Fino Ⓢ *Italian* — 19 | 15 | 21 | $48

Financial District | 1 Wall Street Ct. (Pearl St.) | 212-825-1924 | www.finony.com
Murray Hill | 4 E. 36th St. (bet. 5th & Madison Aves.) | 212-689-8040 | www.fino36.com

"Old-school in every way", this "steady" duo springs "no surprises" as "gracious" staffers bring on "quality" Italian favorites for midrange sums; their "quiet" charms appeal to the corporate class, though hedgers warn of "lacking decor" at the Murray Hill outpost.

Fiorentino's *Italian* — 20 | 14 | 18 | $33

Gravesend | 311 Ave. U (bet. McDonald Ave. & West St.) | Brooklyn | 718-372-1445

"When nonna isn't available", this Gravesend "gathering place" is a "tried-and-true" destination for "copious" portions of "homestyle" Neapolitan *cucina* at a "great price"; the "deafening" digs are always crowded with regulars, so on weekends "you'll have to wait."

Fiorini Ⓢ *Italian* — 20 | 19 | 21 | $55

E 50s | 209 E. 56th St. (bet. 2nd & 3rd Aves.) | 212-308-0830 | www.fiorinirestaurant.com

"Veteran" restaurateur Lello Arpaia "pulls off another winner" at this "civilized" East Midtowner, a "neighborhood hit" for "top-notch" Neapolitan cuisine served with "professional" poise in "spacious" surroundings; all told, locals laud it as a "worthy" arrival.

FireBird Ⓜ *Russian* — 19 | 25 | 21 | $62

W 40s | 365 W. 46th St. (bet. 8th & 9th Aves.) | 212-586-0244 | www.firebirdrestaurant.com

Like a trip "back to St. Petersburg", this "opulent" Restaurant Row Russian duplex "dazzles" with "indulgent caviar blini and "honey-infused vodka" "served with flair" by "costumed" waiters in a "pomp-and-circumstance", "Fabergé-egg" setting; the tabs are equally "extravagant", though the $49 EarlyBird is a way to try it for less.

Firenze ⓞ *Italian* — 21 | 19 | 22 | $49

E 80s | 1594 Second Ave. (bet. 82nd & 83rd Sts.) | 212-861-9368

"Cozy" quarters add to the "intimate" aura of this UES "date place" where the "terrific" Tuscan fare and "quiet, candlelit" ambiance are so "romantic" that the "only thing missing is the violins"; the "simpatico" style extends to the "complimentary house grappa" at the finale.

Fish *Seafood*

FOOD	DECOR	SERVICE	COST
20	12	17	$40

G Village | 280 Bleecker St. (Jones St.) | 212-727-2879

"Fresh fish" in the window display adds "authenticity" to this ersatz New England "seaside shack" in the Village, where pescavores squeeze in for "casual" fin fare presented in an equally "simple" setting; if you're looking to net a "bargain", the "oyster special can't be beat."

Five Front *American*

FOOD	DECOR	SERVICE	COST
20	18	18	$40

Dumbo | 5 Front St. (Old Fulton St.) | Brooklyn | 718-625-5559 | www.fivefrontrestaurant.com

A "low-key" front-runner in a "limited" neighborhood, this "homey" Dumbo bistro "flatters your palate" with "creative" New Americana at "reasonable prices"; followers "can't wait for summer" to hit its "charming" bamboo garden nestled "right under the Brooklyn Bridge."

Five Guys *Burgers*

FOOD	DECOR	SERVICE	COST
20	7	13	$12

NEW **G Village** | 496 La Guardia Pl. (bet. Bleecker & Houston Sts.) | 212-228-6008 ●

NEW **W 50s** | 43 W. 55th St. (bet. 5th & 6th Aves.) | 212-459-9600

NEW **W Village** | 296 Bleecker St. (7th Ave. S.) | 212-367-9200

Brooklyn Heights | 138 Montague St. (bet. Clinton & Henry Sts.) | Brooklyn | 718-797-9380

NEW **Park Slope** | 284 Seventh Ave. (bet. 6th & 7th Sts.) | Brooklyn | 718-499-9380

College Point | 132-01 14th Ave. (132nd St.) | Queens | 718-767-6500 www.fiveguys.com

"Super-fresh burgers" accessorized with "tons of toppings" "raise the bar for fast food" at this burgeoning DC-based chain that also offers "swoon"-worthy fries and "free peanuts while you wait"; the ambiance is barely "basic", but "budget" diners are "glad to have them here."

NEW 5 Napkin Burger ● *Burgers*

FOOD	DECOR	SERVICE	COST
-	-	-	M

W 40s | 630 Ninth Ave. (45th St.) | 212-757-2277

Spun off from Nice Matin, this new Hell's Kitchen burger joint features a menu built around its super-sized, Comté cheese–topped namesake; subway-tiled walls and meat hooks dangling from the ceiling lend a butcher-shop feel, though the tabs won't cost you an arm and a leg.

5 Ninth ● *Eclectic*

FOOD	DECOR	SERVICE	COST
20	21	18	$54

Meatpacking | 5 Ninth Ave. (bet. Gansevoort & Little W. 12th Sts.) | 212-929-9460 | www.5ninth.com

Set in the "trend-heavy Meatpacking District", this "beautiful" 19th-century townhouse draws crowds with an "edgy but recognizable" Eclectic menu washed down with "stiff drinks"; while the back garden is "charming", the staff "attitude" and "pocketbook-pinching" tabs aren't.

Five Points ● *American/Mediterranean*

FOOD	DECOR	SERVICE	COST
22	21	21	$49

NoHo | 31 Great Jones St. (bet. Bowery & Lafayette St.) | 212-253-5700 | www.fivepointsrestaurant.com

"Popular" with "hipster" locals, this "modern" NoHo Med–New American plies "inspired" seasonal dishes and "spot-on" service in a "pretty room" with a "bubbling brook" running through it; the

| | FOOD | DECOR | SERVICE | COST |

"noise level" aside, it's a "treat" that scores extra points with its "what-a-scene brunch."

Fives *American*   ▽ 23 | 24 | 25 | $69

W 50s | Peninsula Hotel | 700 Fifth Ave. (55th St.) | 212-903-3918 | www.peninsula.com

"Posh", "sotto-voce" atmospherics attract an "older business crowd" to this "upscale" spot in the Peninsula Hotel, where the "well-prepared" New American menu is "served beautifully" in "dignified" environs; it's plainly out to "impress", not least with its "steep" prices.

Flatbush Farm *American*   19 | 19 | 17 | $35

Park Slope | 76 St. Marks Ave. (Flatbush Ave.) | Brooklyn | 718-622-3276 | www.flatbushfarm.com

Cultivating a "solid neighborhood" rep, this Park Slope New American lures "locavores" with a modestly priced market menu in "inviting", "low"-lit digs; true, the service is sometimes "absent", but there's also a "garden that lulls you" in fair weather.

Flea Market Cafe ● *French*   19 | 18 | 16 | $34

E Village | 131 Ave. A (bet. 9th St. & St. Marks Pl.) | 212-358-9282

"East Village to the max", this "quaint" French bistro "standby" gratifies its "oh-so-boho" following with "decent", "moderately priced" eats and an "offbeat" display of knickknacks for sale; being "trustworthy" means it's "often overcrowded", especially for brunch.

Fleur de Sel *French*   25 | 21 | 23 | $99

Flatiron | 5 E. 20th St. (bet. B'way & 5th Ave.) | 212-460-9100 | www.fleurdeselnyc.com

"Excellence continues" at Cyril Renaud's "classy" Flatiron French, a "treat" for "discriminating" types with prix fixe–only repasts showcasing "*magnifique*" Breton fare paired with "top-of-the-line" wines; "solicitous service" and a "civilized" milieu help justify the high cost, while the $29 lunch deal pleases the "budget-impaired."

Flor de Mayo ● *Chinese/Peruvian*   20 | 8 | 16 | $22

W 80s | 484 Amsterdam Ave. (bet. 83rd & 84th Sts.) | 212-787-3388
W 100s | 2651 Broadway (bet. 100th & 101st Sts.) | 212-663-5520

"Succulent", "perfectly seasoned" rotisserie chicken keeps locals flocking to these "dependable" UWS "fallbacks" for "cheap" Chinese-Peruvian eats; "hectic" vibes, "rushed" service and "diner" decor make a strong case for takeout.

Flor de Sol 🅈 *Spanish*   21 | 21 | 19 | $46

TriBeCa | 361 Greenwich St. (bet. Franklin & Harrison Sts.) | 212-366-1640 | www.flordesolnyc.com

"Castanets" and candlelight set the "festive" mood at this TriBeCa Spaniard that entices "cool" customers with "kick-ass" tapas, "lethal" sangria and a "jaw-droppingly good-looking" staff; just be prepared for "loud" acoustics when the "flamenco dancing" kicks in.

NEW Forge 🅈 *American*   - | - | - | E

TriBeCa | 134 Reade St. (bet. Greenwich & Hudson Sts.) | 212-941-9401 | www.forgenyc.com

Hearty, seasonally oriented New Americana turns up at this new TriBeCan from Marc Forgione, son of legendary toque Larry Forgione

(An American Place); a dark, stylish interior done up with exposed brick and reclaimed cedar lends romantic appeal, while the pricey tabs don't faze its youngish, well-heeled crowd.

Forlini's ● *Italian* | 19 | 14 | 19 | $39 |

Chinatown | 93 Baxter St. (Walker St.) | 212-349-6779
"Judges and lawyers" grab "honest meals" at this longtime Northern Italian vet near Foley Square, a "friendly", "family-run" spot for "reliable" "old-school" cooking; the "retro" digs may be "tired", but it "keeps on trucking" nonetheless.

Fornino *Pizza* | ▽ 23 | 17 | 18 | $22 |

Williamsburg | 187 Bedford Ave. (bet. 6th & 7th Sts.) | Brooklyn | 718-384-6004
"Pizza is an art form" at this Williamsburg "wood-fired" pie parlor where the "gourmet" lineup of "delectable toppings" includes herbs "grown in the garden out back"; if the service and setting "could be snappier", the eating "more than makes up for it."

44 & X Hell's Kitchen ● *American* | 22 | 19 | 20 | $45 |

W 40s | 622 10th Ave. (44th St.) | 212-977-1170 | www.44andX.com

44½ ● *American*

W 40s | 626 10th Ave. (bet. 44th & 45th Sts.) | 212-399-4450
"Haute versions of comfort food" are ferried by "model-gorgeous" waiters at these "happening" Hell's Kitchen storefronts, known for "tempting" mac 'n' cheese and other American standards; fans ignore the "view of a gas station" and focus on the "hot crowd" and "lively" bar instead.

☑ Four Seasons ☒ *American* | 26 | 28 | 27 | $96 |

E 50s | 99 E. 52nd St. (Park Ave.) | 212-754-9494 | www.fourseasonsrestaurant.com
It "doesn't get any classier" than this 200-season-old Midtown "gold standard" where host-owners Alex von Bidder and Julian Niccolini present "sublime" New American cuisine and "exceptional" service in a "breathtaking", Philip Johnson–designed space; whether for the Grill Room's lunchtime "power scene" or the Pool Room's "drop-dead" evening "elegance", this is "one to write home about"; N.B. jackets (with "deep pockets") required.

Fragole *Italian* | 22 | 18 | 20 | $31 |

Carroll Gardens | 394 Court St. (1st Pl.) | Brooklyn | 718-522-7133 | www.fragoleny.com
Pastaphiles deem this "inviting" Carroll Gardens Italian a "neighborhood sweet spot" for its "delicious" menu (jazzed up with the "freshest" daily specials), "no-attitude" service and "affordable" tabs; since its repute "continues to grow", it's "not always easy to get in."

Franchia *Korean/Tearoom* | ▽ 19 | 19 | 19 | $30 |

Murray Hill | 12 Park Ave. (bet. 34th & 35th Sts.) | 212-213-1001 | www.franchia.com
The "perfect place to veg out", this "tranquil" "Zen teahouse" in Murray Hill serves "imaginative" vegetarian Korean fare that complements its "exotic" brews; it's a "stylish" setup given the fair pricing, and the "efficient" staffers ensure "you're never rushed."

	FOOD	DECOR	SERVICE	COST

Francisco's Centro Vasco *Spanish*
| 22 | 12 | 19 | $47 |

Chelsea | 159 W. 23rd St. (bet. 6th & 7th Aves.) | 212-645-6224 | www.centrovasco.ypguides.net

"Roll up your sleeves" for a Spanish "lobsterfest" at this "longtime Chelsea favorite" where "gigantic crustaceans" are "cooked to perfection" for "rock-bottom prices"; the "pace is frenetic" and it's "not the classiest" joint, but the "value-seeking crowds" don't seem to mind.

Frank ●🔂 *Italian*
| 23 | 14 | 16 | $33 |

E Village | 88 Second Ave. (bet. 5th & 6th Sts.) | 212-420-0202 | www.frankrestaurant.com

"Size doesn't matter" at this ultra-"tiny", no-reservations East Villager offering "simply amazing" "homestyle" Italian food served in "scruffy", "bustling" quarters with "rock-concert" noise levels; considering that the cash-only costs are such a "steal", "long waits" are "inevitable."

Frankie & Johnnie's Steakhouse 🅂 *Steak*
| 21 | 15 | 20 | $61 |

Garment District | 32 W. 37th St. (bet. 5th & 6th Aves.) | 212-947-8940
W 40s | 269 W. 45th St., 2nd fl. (bet. B'way & 8th Ave.) | 212-997-9494 ●
www.frankieandjohnnies.com

Ever "steady", these "old-time" chop shops still "hit the mark" with "solid steaks" and "accommodating" service; the "past-its-prime" 1926 Times Square original is right out of "Damon Runyon", while the roomier Garment District spin-off exudes a tony "townhouse feel."

Frankies Spuntino *Italian*
| 24 | 20 | 20 | $36 |

LES | 17 Clinton St. (bet. Houston & Stanton Sts.) | 212-253-2303 ●
Carroll Gardens | 457 Court St. (bet. 4th Pl. & Luquer St.) | Brooklyn | 718-403-0033 🔂
www.frankiesspuntino.com

"Lovingly crafted" small plates are the specialty at this "rustic" Carroll Gardens Italian and its LES "walk-in-closet" spin-off; "good value" keeps their "tight" spaces "jam-packed", though the Brooklyn original offers extra breathing room in its "gorgeous garden."

Franny's *Pizza*
| 25 | 17 | 20 | $40 |

Prospect Heights | 295 Flatbush Ave. (bet. Prospect Pl. & St. Marks Ave.) | Brooklyn | 718-230-0221 | www.frannysbrooklyn.com

"Not your ordinary pizza place", this "charming" Prospect Heights venue employs "seasonal" ingredients to create "brilliant" thin-crust pies backed up by "fab pastas" and "amazing cocktails"; no surprise, it draws "killer crowds" despite its fairly "high prices."

Fratelli *Italian*
| ▽ 21 | 15 | 21 | $39 |

Bronx | 2507 Eastchester Rd. (Mace Ave.) | 718-547-2489

So "accommodating" that it feels "like home", this Bronx "local" is favored for "waist-buster" portions of "old-fashioned" Italian grub for "decent" dough; it may be "predictable", but its "family-oriented" clientele wouldn't have it any other way.

Fraunces Tavern 🅂 *American*
| 16 | 22 | 17 | $44 |

Financial District | 54 Pearl St. (Broad St.) | 212-968-1776 | www.frauncestavern.com

It's all about the "history" at this circa-1762 Financial District tavern, a "quaint" Colonial artifact where "Washington bid his troops farewell";

the American grub is "acceptable at best", but "Revolutionary War–era" enthusiasts and "tourists" say it's worth visiting – "at least once."

Frederick's Downtown ◐ *French/Mediterranean*   17 | 17 | 16 | $57

W Village | 637 Hudson St. (Horatio St.) | 212-488-4200

Frederick's Madison *French/Mediterranean*

E 60s | 768 Madison Ave. (bet. 65th & 66th Sts.) | 212-737-7300
www.fredericksnyc.com

"Euro types" dig the "scene" at this "civilized" duo where the "satisfactory" French-Med fare takes a backseat to the "good-looking", "Prada"-clad crowds; "non-bargain prices" leave some miffed, especially given the "snooty" service.

Fred's at Barneys NY *American/Italian*   20 | 17 | 17 | $47

E 60s | Barneys NY | 660 Madison Ave., 9th fl. (60th St.) | 212-833-2200
To see "how the other half" lunches, try this "Beverly Hills"–esque Midtowner where "pretty folk" nibble "tasty" Tuscan–New American bites while assessing the "size-zero" competition; sure, it's "pricey" and "jammed", though the "buzz" abates at the dinner hour.

Freemans ◐ *American*   21 | 22 | 18 | $45

LES | Freeman Alley (off Rivington St., bet. Bowery & Chrystie St.) |
212-420-0012 | www.freemansrestaurant.com
Accessed via an obscure LES "back alley", this New American "hideaway" exudes "hipster cool" backed up by "outstanding" "down-home cooking" and "rustic" digs heavy on the "taxidermy"; since the "secret is long out", "brutal waits" come with the territory.

French Roast ◐ *French*   15 | 14 | 13 | $28

G Village | 78 W. 11th St. (bet. 5th & 6th Aves.) | 212-533-2233
W 80s | 2340 Broadway (85th St.) | 212-799-1533
www.frenchroastny.com
"No-brainers" for "casual schmoozing", this "faux" Parisian cafe duo supplies "run-of-the-mill" French fare 24/7 for "modest" costs; despite the "canned ambiance", "crowded" seating and "checked-out" service, they're "easy if not terribly exciting choices."

Fresco by Scotto 🅂 *Italian*   23 | 19 | 21 | $62

E 50s | 34 E. 52nd St. (bet. Madison & Park Aves.) | 212-935-3434

Fresco on the Go *Italian*

E 50s | 40 E. 52nd St. (bet. Madison & Park Aves.) | 212-754-2700 🅂
NEW **Financial District** | 114 Pearl St. (Hanover Sq.) | 212-635-5000
www.frescobyscotto.com
"The Scottos will take care of you" at their "welcoming" Midtown Tuscan, a "bustling" nexus for "excellent" food, "professional" service and "TV celebrity-spotting"; tabs are decidedly "upmarket", but so is its performance and its carry-out counterparts provide the "same quality for a fraction of the price."

fresh *Seafood*   25 | 21 | 23 | $60

TriBeCa | 105 Reade St. (bet. Church St. & W. B'way) | 212-406-1900 |
www.freshrestaurantnyc.com
The "name says it all" at this "civilized" TriBeCan, where the "perfectly prepared" seafood is "super-fresh" while the "professional service" is anything but; its "under-the-radar" status keeps the mood "subdued", and although "pricey", "you get what you pay for" and then some.

	FOOD	DECOR	SERVICE	COST

NEW **Friedman's Delicatessen** *Deli* ▽ 21 | 10 | 16 | $23

Chelsea | Chelsea Mkt. | 75 Ninth Ave. (bet. 15th & 16th Sts.) | 212-929-7100
Chelsea Market's new kosher deli "fills a long-standing need" in the area, serving "serious" Jewish staples including sandwiches piled high with "quality" meats; while the setting's "authentic" enough, it's somehow "not a relaxing place."

Friend of a Farmer *American*   18 | 17 | 17 | $31

Gramercy | 77 Irving Pl. (bet. 18th & 19th Sts.) | 212-477-2188 | www.friendofafarmernyc.com
Like a trip to the "countryside", this "comforting" Gramercy fixture offers "down-home-in-the-city" American cooking for "reasonable" sums amid "cute" "farmhouse decor"; service may be "harried", but that doesn't keep "ridiculously long lines" from forming for weekend brunch.

FROG ⑤ *Eclectic/French*   19 | 20 | 17 | $55

SoHo | 71 Spring St. (bet. Crosby & Lafayette Sts.) | 212-966-5050 | www.frognyc.com
This "glam" SoHo yearling "sure does leap out at you" with its "mod decor" and "fanciful", "French-inspired" global eats matched with "tasty drinks"; the "loopy" service and "silly name" aside, it's an always hopping "treat" even if some critics croak all that "flash" somehow "doesn't gel" at their price level.

Fuleen Seafood ❶ *Chinese/Seafood*   23 | 8 | 15 | $29

Chinatown | 11 Division St. (Bowery) | 212-941-6888
"Slam-dunk" seafood with "bold flavors" even lures landlubbers to this "real-deal" Hong Kong–style fish joint in Chinatown; despite "rec-room" ambiance and "bring-an-interpreter" service, the payoffs are a "great bang for your buck" and late-night hours (till 3 AM).

Fushimi *Japanese*   25 | 24 | 21 | $46

Bay Ridge | 9316 Fourth Ave. (bet. 93rd & 94th Sts.) | Brooklyn | 718-833-7788
Staten Island | 2110 Richmond Rd. (Lincoln Ave.) | 718-980-5300
There's "no need to go to Manhattan" for "amazing" sushi and "top-notch" Japanese fare thanks to this "hip" outer-borough duo with "trendy" looks, "attentive" service and hopping "bar scenes"; they're "pricey but worth it" for the "fabulous presentation" alone.

Gabriela's *Mexican*   18 | 17 | 17 | $35

W 90s | 688 Columbus Ave. (bet. 93rd & 94th Sts.) | 212-961-0574 | www.gabrielas.com
"Good", "inexpensive" Mexicana plus a "kick-back-and-relax" mood make this "casual" Upper Westsider a "neighborhood favorite"; bonus points go to the "covered outdoor seating" and "snappy margaritas", though the "flighty" service is another story.

Gabriel's ⑤ *Italian*   22 | 19 | 22 | $59

W 60s | 11 W. 60th St. (bet. B'way & Columbus Ave.) | 212-956-4600 | www.gabrielsbarandrest.com
A "long-standing favorite" among the "media crowd" – it's the site of the East Coast Oscar party – Gabriel Aiello's "warm" UWS Tuscan boasts "top-of-the-line" cooking, "excellent wine", "diligent" service and "convenience" to both Lincoln Center and the Time Warner

colossus; granted, it may be a bit "pricey", but it's sure alot cheaper and "less crowded" at lunch, and Gabriel "couldn't be nicer."

Gahm Mi Oak ● Korean | ∇ 20 | 12 | 13 | $25 |

Garment District | 43 W. 32nd St. (bet. B'way & 5th Ave.) | 212-695-4113
"Late-night cravings" are answered at this 24/7 Garment District Seoul-fooder best known for its "tasty" *sollongtang* beef soup that some say is "Korean for 'hangover cure'"; "bare-bones" decor and "surly service" to the contrary, it's "fast", "simple" and "always a bargain."

Gallagher's Steak House ● Steak | 21 | 18 | 18 | $65 |

W 50s | 228 W. 52nd St. (bet. B'way & 8th Ave.) | 212-245-5336 | www.gallaghersnysteakhouse.com
"Serious meat eaters" tout this Theater District stalwart, a "bastion of steak" since 1927 that still offers "massive" chops served by "crusty" waiters around "since Prohibition"; the checkered-tablecloth decor may be "a bit tired", but the "expensive" tabs will wake you up.

☑ Garden Cafe ☒Ⓜ American | 28 | 21 | 26 | $54 |

Prospect Heights | 620 Vanderbilt Ave. (St. Marks Pl.) | Brooklyn | 718-857-8863
"Like being invited to someone's house for dinner" – "except that someone is a gourmet chef" – this "tiny" Prospect Heights "treasure" is a "charming, intimate" enterprise thanks to the efforts of owners John and Camille Policastro; look for "spectacular" New American food, "perfect hospitality" and prices that are low for the quality.

Gargiulo's Italian | 22 | 18 | 21 | $46 |

Coney Island | 2911 W. 15th St. (bet. Mermaid & Surf Aves.) | Brooklyn | 718-266-4891 | www.gargiulos.com
"Old Coney Island" lives on at this barnlike, circa-1907 Southern Italian "throwback" where "generous portions" of red-sauce fare are served by tuxedoed waiters; prices are "reasonable" enough, but if you "pick the right number after the meal" you just may "win a free dinner."

☑ Gari Japanese | 26 | 14 | 20 | $76 |

W 70s | 370 Columbus Ave. (bet. 77th & 78th Sts.) | 212-362-4816

☑ Sushi of Gari Ⓜ Japanese

E 70s | 402 E. 78th St. (bet. 1st & York Aves.) | 212-517-5340

☑ Sushi of Gari 46 Ⓜ Japanese

W 40s | 347 W. 46th St. (bet. 8th & 9th Aves.) | 212-957-0046 www.sushiofgari.com
"Gari Sugio works magic" at his ultra-"innovative" Japanese trio known for "transcendent", "work-of-art" sushi that "couldn't be any fresher", even though the decor could be; purists say the "omagod" omakase is "the way to go", although a "flight to Tokyo may be cheaper."

Gascogne French | 21 | 19 | 20 | $49 |

Chelsea | 158 Eighth Ave. (bet. 17th & 18th Sts.) | 212-675-6564 | www.gascognenyc.com
"French expats add atmosphere" to this "quaint" Chelsea bistro purveying "authentic" Southwestern Gallic food and "hospitable" service for fairly "affordable" fares; while the decor's debatable (either "cozy" or "cramped"), there's agreement that the "back garden is perfect" for a "romantic" meal *à deux*.

	FOOD	DECOR	SERVICE	COST

Gavroche *French* | 17 | 15 | 19 | $44

W Village | 212 W. 14th St. (bet. 7th & 8th Aves.) | 212-647-8553 | www.gavroche-ny.com

"Comfortable" and "moderately priced", this "homey" West Village bistro presents "better-than-average" French comfort food in a room that "needs some updating"; still, the "alfresco dining" on its "peaceful" patio "more than makes up for" any shortcomings.

NEW Gazala Place *Mideastern* | ▽ 25 | 10 | 19 | $22

W 40s | 709 Ninth Ave. (bet. 48th & 49th Sts.) | 212-245-0709 | www.gazalaplace.com

Reputedly NYC's only eatery offering Middle Eastern Druse cooking, this "tiny" Hell's Kitchen storefront showcases made-from-scratch falafel and hummus platters, along with signature thin wheat pita; the "informal" setting is reflected in the "cheap" cost and "BYO" policy.

Geisha 🈲 *Japanese* | 23 | 22 | 20 | $62

E 60s | 33 E. 61st St. (bet. Madison & Park Aves.) | 212-813-1113 | www.geisharestaurant.com

"Cool sushi" meets "hot babes" at this "upscale" UES Japanese-French fusion practitioner where the "energetic Madison Avenue scene" nearly overwhelms the "adventurous" cooking; be prepared for a "fashionable", "well-dressed" crowd toying with "tiny portions" at "big prices"; it's something of a squeeze, but given your fellow patrons, you won't mind.

Gemma ● *Italian* | 19 | 22 | 17 | $47

E Village | Bowery Hotel | 335 Bowery (bet. 2nd & 3rd Sts.) | 212-505-9100 | www.theboweryhotel.com

Parked on the burgeoning Bowery, this Italian "hot spot" draws a "young crowd" that reports the food is "surprisingly good" though the rustic "atmosphere is better" (think "dark wood, copper pots, dripping candles"); service is "on cue" and prices "decent", leaving the "no-reservations policy" as the only drawback.

NEW General Greene Ⓜ *American* | - | - | - | M

Fort Greene | 229 DeKalb Ave. (Clermont Ave.) | Brooklyn | 718-222-1510

The general idea at this Fort Greene newcomer is stylish, seasonal spins on hearty American comfort dishes (think deviled eggs, ribs) in both small-plate and entree-size portions; the narrow, minimalist-chic setting is focused around a long bar turning out classic cocktails.

Gennaro 🚫 *Italian* | 24 | 14 | 17 | $39

W 90s | 665 Amsterdam Ave. (bet. 92nd & 93rd Sts.) | 212-665-5348

Upper Westsiders "can't get enough" of this Italian "neighborhood knockout" famed for "outstanding" cooking at "modest" prices; too bad about the "harried" service, "crunch" seating and no-reservations/"cash-only" rules, but in gennar-al it's worth the "ever-present lines."

Ghenet *Ethiopian* | ▽ 21 | 13 | 14 | $30

NoLita | 284 Mulberry St. (bet. Houston & Prince Sts.) | 212-343-1888
NEW Park Slope | 348 Douglass St. (bet. 4th & 5th Aves.) | Brooklyn | 718-230-4476
www.ghenet.com

Folks who are "up for anything" tout this "different" NoLita Ethiopian offering "delicious", "wonderfully spiced" dishes served family-style, sans utensils (you eat with your hands, scooping up the food with injera bread); "value" pricing trumps the iffy service and "tired" decor; N.B. the new Park Slope outpost opened post-Survey.

Giambelli ● *Italian*

FOOD	DECOR	SERVICE	COST
22	16	22	$62

E 50s | 46 E. 50th St. (bet. Madison & Park Aves.) | 212-688-2760 | www.giambelli50th.com

A "reliable old standard" on the scene "since the Ice Age", this circa-1957 Midtown Italian purveys "wonderful" cooking (especially if "you like garlic") served by a "nonintrusive" staff; still, critics contend it's "resting on its laurels", citing "tired looks" and "overpriced" tabs.

Gigino Trattoria *Italian*

FOOD	DECOR	SERVICE	COST
20	18	17	$43

TriBeCa | 323 Greenwich St. (bet. Duane & Reade Sts.) | 212-431-1112 | www.gigino-trattoria.com

Gigino at Wagner Park *Italian*

Financial District | 20 Battery Pl. (West St.) | 212-528-2228 | www.gigino-wagnerpark.com

Locals seeking a "casual sit-down" like this TriBeCa trattoria for its "reasonably priced" menu highlighted by "to-die-for thin-crust pizza"; its Wagner Park sibling is a "sunset" destination given an alfresco patio with "breathtaking" views of the harbor and the Statue of Liberty – your cousin from Little Rock will love it.

Gilt ⊠Ⓜ *American*

FOOD	DECOR	SERVICE	COST
25	27	25	$111

E 50s | NY Palace Hotel | 455 Madison Ave. (bet. 50th & 51st Sts.) | 212-891-8100 | www.giltnewyork.com

The "talented" Christopher Lee mans the stoves at this New American "stunner" in Midtown's Palace Hotel, where "flawless" food, a "superb sommelier", "seamless service" and "opulent" decor merge for a "sumptuous" dining experience; however, the prix fixe–only menu is priced for "special occasions", so don't forget to bring "deep pockets."

Gino ⊅ *Italian*

FOOD	DECOR	SERVICE	COST
19	11	18	$49

E 60s | 780 Lexington Ave. (bet. 60th & 61st Sts.) | 212-758-4466

"Straight out of a Woody Allen movie", this circa-1945, cash-only Italian "warhorse" near Bloomie's is renowned for "retro Brooklyn Italian" dishes slathered in "red sauce"; "ancient waiters" and "anachronistic zebra print wallpaper" lend "time-warp" appeal to its "three generations of regulars", who show up like clockwork once a week.

Giorgione *Italian*

FOOD	DECOR	SERVICE	COST
22	19	18	$50

SoHo | 307 Spring St. (bet. Greenwich & Hudson Sts.) | 212-352-2269 | www.giorgionenyc.com

"Sophisticated" Italian grub "done right" is yours at this "out-of-the-way" West SoHo "gem" from celeb grocer Giorgio DeLuca; though it "doesn't look like much from the outside", its "cool" "young crowd" digs the "low-key" vibe and "high-quality" product.

Giorgio's of Gramercy *American*

FOOD	DECOR	SERVICE	COST
21	17	20	$47

Flatiron | 27 E. 21st St. (bet. B'way & Park Ave. S.) | 212-477-0007 | www.giorgiosofgramercy.com

For "cozy" dining "amid the Flatiron bustle", check out this "unpretentious" New American, a relatively "well-kept secret" despite "solid" food at "fair prices"; refurbished decor and "personable" service keep the mood "pleasant" here.

	FOOD	DECOR	SERVICE	COST

Giovanni Venticinque *Italian*
▽ 22 | 20 | 21 | $62

E 80s | 25 E. 83rd St. (bet. 5th & Madison Aves.) | 212-988-7300
"Mature, Rockefeller-esque" types patronize this "cocooning" UES Tuscan parked a "stone's throw from the Met" that's a natural "after a museum tour"; the "refined" cooking reflects its "unhurried" pace and "quiet", "grown-up" air, even if the prices break the spell.

Girasole *Italian*
21 | 15 | 20 | $59

E 80s | 151 E. 82nd St. (bet. Lexington & 3rd Aves.) | 212-772-6690
An "old standby" for the "50-plus crowd", this "homey", 20-year-old Upper Eastsider plies "dependable" Italian fare ferried by waiters who treat regulars "like family"; fans don't mind the "costly" tabs or "nothing-special" decor, though the "noise level" is another story.

Gnocco Caffe ● *Italian*
22 | 17 | 19 | $37

E Village | 337 E. 10th St. (bet. Aves. A & B) | 212-677-1913 | www.gnocco.com
"Sinfully good" namesake appetizers and thin-crust pizzas highlight the "tasty" Emilian *cucina* offered at this "relaxed" East Village Italian; service is "pleasant but scattered", and there's a "divine garden" and "great value" pricing to boot.

Gobo *Vegan/Vegetarian*
22 | 18 | 18 | $33

E 80s | 1426 Third Ave. (81st St.) | 212-288-5099
G Village | 401 Sixth Ave. (bet. 8th St. & Waverly Pl.) | 212-255-3242
www.goborestaurant.com
Vegan/vegetarian fare "with carnivore appeal" turns up at this "approachable" duo where the "delicious", Asian-accented offerings are both "inventive and virtuous"; tabs are mild, and the chance to "dine with Buddhist monks across from your table" provides an "element of enlightenment" to the meal.

Golden Unicorn *Chinese*
20 | 12 | 13 | $25

Chinatown | 18 E. Broadway, 2nd fl. (Catherine St.) | 212-941-0911 | www.goldenunicornrestaurant.com
It's "dim sum madness" at this "huge" Chinatown "grande dame" where customers "point at items" on the "carts speeding by", or just "eat and guess"; the "bargain" pricing makes the "rude service" and "long lines" more tolerable, though it's "less crazy" if you "go early."

Gonzo *Italian/Pizza*
20 | 16 | 18 | $43

G Village | 140 W. 13th St. (bet. 6th & 7th Aves.) | 212-645-4606
A "well-kept secret" where you can "eat well for less", this Village Italian is lauded for its thin-crust pizza that's "worth a trip from anywhere"; service is "friendly" and the atmosphere "upbeat", sometimes so much so that it results in "deafening" decibels.

good *American*
21 | 14 | 17 | $35

W Village | 89 Greenwich Ave. (bet. Bank & W. 12th Sts.) | 212-691-8080 | www.goodrestaurantnyc.com
"Aptly named", this "cozy" West Village New American radiates "neighborhood charm", serving "fabulous baked goods" and other "comfort treats" for fair prices; regulars report that the "unbeatable" brunch is worth the inevitable "long wait"; non-regulars cite the decor and service as not so good.

	FOOD	DECOR	SERVICE	COST

goodburger *Burgers* | 18 | 9 | 13 | $14 |

E 40s | 800 Second Ave. (42nd St.) | 212-922-1700
E 50s | 636 Lexington Ave. (54th St.) | 212-838-6000
NEW Flatiron | 870 Broadway (bet. 17th & 18th Sts.) | 212-529-9100
NEW W 40s | 23 W. 45th St. (bet. 5th & 6th Aves.) | 212-354-0900
www.goodburgerny.com

The "old-fashioned", "made from scratch" burgers at this "extremely casual" mini-chain can be paired with "better-than-good" fries and shakes; too bad the decor and service are barely up to scratch and at times the "loud music prohibits conversation."

Good Enough to Eat *American* | 20 | 15 | 17 | $26 |

W 80s | 483 Amsterdam Ave. (bet. 83rd & 84th Sts.) | 212-496-0163 | www.goodenoughtoeat.com

A slice of "Vermont" on the UWS, this "home-away-from-home" eatery with a "white picket fence" outside offers "stick-to-your-ribs" Americana at "small-town" prices; it's best known for its "outstanding brunch" and "outrageous waits" – its setting is "too small for its fan base."

Good Fork 🄼 *Eclectic* | 25 | 19 | 23 | $42 |

Red Hook | 391 Van Brunt St. (bet. Coffey & Dikeman Sts.) | Brooklyn | 718-643-6636 | www.goodfork.com

Hidden "near the end of the world in Red Hook", this "destination" Eclectic thrills fans with "sophisticated", Asian-accented cuisine paired with "perfectly crafted cocktails"; other reasons it's "usually packed" include "moderate" pricing and the "attentive" service of its "charming" husband-and-wife team.

Gordon Ramsay *French* | 25 | 24 | 24 | $130 |

W 50s | The London NYC | 151 W. 54th St. (bet. 6th & 7th Aves.) | 212-468-8888 | www.gordonramsay.com

Famously "creative", infamously "temperamental" chef Gordon Ramsay displays his "meticulous attention to detail" – "maybe yelling does make food taste better" – at this New French in Midtown's London NYC Hotel; the "phenomenal", prix fixe–only meals are "beautifully presented", the service "world-class" and the ambiance "tranquil", leaving only the decor debatable ("classy" vs. "cruise ship"); in sum, everything's totally "tip-top" – the tabs too.

🅉 Gotham Bar & Grill *American* | 27 | 25 | 26 | $77 |

G Village | 12 E. 12th St. (bet. 5th Ave. & University Pl.) | 212-620-4020 | www.gothambarandgrill.com

"Everything's just right" at this "amazingly consistent" Village "special-occasion spot" helmed by chef Alfred Portale, whose "architectural" New American "tall food" is "every bit as thrilling" as when it opened 25 years ago; the staff is "on its game", the room "majestic" and the prices as "sky-high" as ever (though the $31 prix fixe lunch is a "bargain"); in short, it "makes you glad you live in this great town."

Grace's Trattoria *Italian* | 19 | 16 | 18 | $43 |

E 70s | 201 E. 71st St. (bet. 2nd & 3rd Aves.) | 212-452-2323 | www.gracestrattoria.net

"Owned by the high-end retail market next door", this local "favorite" lures Upper Eastsiders with "dependable" Pugliese dishes and "friendly, efficient" service; the decor may be a tad "dated", but overall it's a "good casual standby."

Gradisca *Italian*   21 | 17 | 17 | $45

G Village | 126 W. 13th St. (bet. 6th Ave. & 7th Ave. S.) | 212-691-4886 | www.gradiscanyc.com

The "homemade pastas" shine at this "dark" and "cozy" Village Italian, an "adult" neighborhood nexus parked on a quiet cross street; "inventive" specials, "moderate" tabs and a "relaxed" vibe keep locals loyal despite "inconsistent service" and "noisy weekends."

NEW Graffiti Ⓜ *Eclectic*   ▽ 24 | 20 | 23 | $40

E Village | 224 E. 10th St. (bet. 1st & 2nd Aves.) | 212-677-0695 | www.graffitinyc.com

"Adventurous" is the word on this new "sweet-and-savory" East Village spot via pastry chef Jehangir Mehta, who serves an Indian-inflected Eclectic menu of "unique" small plates; while the 18-seat setting divides voters ("cute as a button" vs. "not so comfy"), all agree the "excellent" food "makes up for the lack of space."

Ⓩ Gramercy Tavern *American*   28 | 26 | 27 | $107

Flatiron | 42 E. 20th St. (bet. B'way & Park Ave. S.) | 212-477-0777 | www.gramercytavern.com

A "not-to-be-missed restaurant experience", Danny Meyer's "special-occasion" Flatiron "powerhouse" still "fires on all cylinders" thanks to chef Michael Anthony's "heavenly" New American food, "treat-you-like-royalty" service and an "upscale rustic" ambiance right out of 18th-century New England; sure, the prix fixe–only tabs can "break the bank", but in return you "honestly get everything you pay for", and the "less expensive" upfront tavern is a "great alternative."

Grand Sichuan *Chinese*   22 | 7 | 13 | $24

Chelsea | 229 Ninth Ave. (24th St.) | 212-620-5200 ◗
Chinatown | 125 Canal St. (Chrystie St.) | 212-625-9212 ⌘
E 50s | 1049 Second Ave. (bet. 55th & 56th Sts.) | 212-355-5855
E Village | 19-23 St. Marks Pl. (bet. 2nd & 3rd Aves.) | 212-529-4800
NEW **G Village** | 15 Seventh Ave. S. (bet. Carmine & Leroy Sts.) | 212-645-0222
Murray Hill | 227 Lexington Ave. (bet. 33rd & 34th Sts.) | 212-679-9770
Rego Park | 98-108 Queens Blvd. (bet. 66th Rd. & 67th Ave.) | Queens | 718-268-8833
www.thegrandsichuan.com

"Richly flavored" Sichuan dishes so "unapologetically spicy" you'll be "sweating like you're in aerobics class" take center stage at this "cheap", "real-McCoy" mini-chain; "worn-out" looks and "service with a smirk" lead some to opt for "delivery."

Grand Tier Ⓢ *Italian*   19 | 25 | 23 | $83

W 60s | Metropolitan Opera House | Lincoln Center Plaza, 2nd fl. (bet. 63rd & 65th Sts.) | 212-799-3400 | www.patinagroup.com

An "overture to the evening's musical enjoyment", this "luxurious" (read: "costly") Met venue "can't be beat for convenience" when at Lincoln Center; ticket-holders tout the "beautiful setting" and "amazingly precise timing" that allows you to "return for dessert at intermission"; N.B. an Italian menu is set to debut when the Opera's new season commences.

	FOOD	DECOR	SERVICE	COST

Grano Trattoria ◐ *Italian* — ▽ 23 | 18 | 21 | $40

G Village | 21 Greenwich Ave. (W. 10th St.) | 212-645-2121 | www.granonyc.com

"Devoted neighborhood regulars" plug this well-kept Village "secret" for its "authentic" Italian menu led by "perfect brick-oven pizzas"; "quaint" digs, "friendly" staffers and midrange tabs round out the overall "delightful" experience.

Gray's Papaya ◐⊖ *Hot Dogs* — 21 | 4 | 13 | $6

Garment District | 539 Eighth Ave. (37th St.) | 212-904-1588
G Village | 402 Sixth Ave. (8th St.) | 212-260-3532
W 70s | 2090 Broadway (72nd St.) | 212-799-0243

Not to be missed, these quintessential 24/7 frank phenomena provide "snappy" hot dogs and "delish" tropical drinks to a "truly democratic" NY crowd; its $3.50 "recession special" may be the best deal in town, trumping the "spartan" digs and "brusque", whaddya-want service.

Grayz ◐⊠ *Eclectic* — 23 | 21 | 22 | $73

W 50s | 13-15 W. 54th St. (bet. 5th & 6th Aves.) | 212-262-4600 | www.grayz.net

"Imaginative" Eclectic food enhanced by Gray Kunz's "Midas touch" is served in this "classy" Midtown townhouse where savvy sorts "request the top floor"; the concept has moved away from its original small-plates-and-drinks idea to a more traditional appetizer/entree arrangement, but it remains as "pricey" as ever.

Great Jones Cafe ◐ *Cajun* — 19 | 13 | 16 | $29

NoHo | 54 Great Jones St. (bet. Bowery & Lafayette St.) | 212-674-9304 | www.greatjones.com

The "South rises again" at this "chill" NoHo Cajun slinging "down-to-earth comfort cooking" for "good prices"; a particularly "excellent brunch" makes the "tiny", "funky" space ultra-"cramped" on weekends, though it's more "relaxed" during the week.

Great NY Noodle Town ◐⊖ *Noodle Shop* — 22 | 5 | 11 | $17

Chinatown | 28½ Bowery (Bayard St.) | 212-349-0923

Insiders recommend the "salt-baked anything" at this "reliable" Chinatown seafood "standby" also known for its "wonderful" noodle soups and "laughably cheap" tabs; "tacky" decor, "nonexistent" service and "contortionist" seating are the downsides.

Greek Kitchen *Greek* — 20 | 11 | 17 | $30

W 50s | 889 10th Ave. (58th St.) | 212-581-4300 | www.greekkitchennyc.com

Its Way West Hell's Kitchen neighborhood may be "offbeat", but this "quality" Hellenic is a "close walk to Lincoln Center" and offers good, "simple" Greek "standards" for easily "affordable" dough; "prompt service" is another plus, though the ambiance is strictly coffee shop.

Green Field Churrascaria *Brazilian* — ▽ 18 | 14 | 17 | $38

Corona | 108-01 Northern Blvd. (108th St.) | Queens | 718-672-5202

Both a "carnivore's fantasy" and "glutton's paradise", this all-you-can-eat Corona Brazilian BBQ offers an "awe-inspiring amount of food" served by skewer-wielding waiters in "bustling", "stadium"-size digs; "nothing fancy" sums up the football field–like decor and fumbling service, but you "certainly get your money's worth" here.

	FOOD	DECOR	SERVICE	COST

Greenhouse Café *American*

Bay Ridge | 7717 Third Ave. (bet. 77th & 78th Sts.) | Brooklyn | 718-833-8200 | www.greenhousecafe.com

| 18 | 19 | 19 | $38 |

"Still kicking" after 30 years, this Bay Ridge New American serves "dependable" chow in a "charming" setting complete with a glass-clad rear atrium; "fair prices", "down-to-earth service" and a "low-key" ambiance have made it a "local institution."

NEW Greenwich Grill *Japanese/Mediterranean*

TriBeCa | 428 Greenwich St. (bet. Laight & Vestry Sts.) | 212-274-0428 | www.greenwichgrill.com

| - | - | - | M |

Set in a slick duplex space, this new TriBeCan has a split personality, with a Japanese-accented Mediterranean menu served on the street level while its basement houses a sushi bar stocked with fish flown in from Japan; either way, tabs are moderate.

Grifone 🗷 *Italian*

E 40s | 244 E. 46th St. (bet. 2nd & 3rd Aves.) | 212-490-7275 | www.grifonenyc.com

| 23 | 17 | 24 | $62 |

Transporting you "back to the home country", this "sedate" Northern Italian near the U.N. features an "upscale", "melt-in-your-mouth" menu served by "extremely attentive" staffers; while the "time-warp" decor won't wow you, the "high prices" just might.

Grimaldi's 🗷 *Pizza*

Dumbo | 19 Old Fulton St. (bet. Front & Water Sts.) | Brooklyn | 718-858-4300 | www.grimaldis.com

| 25 | 11 | 14 | $21 |

Just "this side of perfection", the "heavenly thin-crusted" pies piled with "high-quality toppings" make for pizza "masterpieces" at this cash-only Dumbo "stronghold"; long lines are part of this "Brooklyn experience", ditto the "rushed service" and "ordinary" decor.

☒ Grocery, The 🗷🖩 *American*

Carroll Gardens | 288 Smith St. (bet. Sackett & Union Sts.) | Brooklyn | 718-596-3335 | www.thegroceryrestaurant.com

| 27 | 16 | 25 | $60 |

You may "never venture into Manhattan again" after a visit to this "tiny but charming" Carroll Gardens storefront where a "solicitous" staff serves "knock-your-socks-off" New Americana made from "local, seasonal ingredients"; the setting's too "minimalist" for some (the "garden is better") and it's a little "pricey", but overall it's "totally worth the splurge" for food that would cost twice as much in Manhattan.

Grotta Azzurra ● *Italian*

Little Italy | 177 Mulberry St. (Broome St.) | 212-925-8775 | www.grottaazzurrany.com

| 19 | 15 | 17 | $46 |

Channeling "old-school Little Italy", this "reasonable imitation" of the 1908 original offers "classic", midpriced Southern Italian grub in "schmaltzy" digs; though "not what it used to be" and "quite the tourist destination", it's still worth a try to "relive your youth."

Guantanamera *Cuban*

W 50s | 939 Eighth Ave. (bet. 55th & 56th Sts.) | 212-262-5354 | www.guantanameranyc.com

| 20 | 16 | 18 | $37 |

A "little piece of Cuba in Midtown", this "authentic" Latin can get "crowded" thanks to its "tasty" cooking, "fab cocktails" and "reasonable prices"; the "energetic" vibe is ratcheted up by "live bands" and dancing, and there's also a free "hand-rolled cigar on the way out."

Gus' Place ◑ *Greek/Mediterranean* | 19 | 14 | 20 | $38

G Village | 192 Bleecker St. (bet. MacDougal St. & 6th Ave.) | 212-777-1660 | www.gusplacenyc.com

Locals "feel like family" at this "gracious" Villager where the host/namesake is "on hand to make sure you're happy"; the "delicious, expertly prepared" Greek-Med offerings are "more than acceptable" for the price, leaving "tiny" dimensions as the only downside.

Gusto ◑ *Italian* | 22 | 20 | 19 | $53

G Village | 60 Greenwich Ave. (Perry St.) | 212-924-8000 | www.gustonyc.com

Despite "chef turnover", this "vibrant" Villager now helmed by Anne Burrell still supplies a "good feed" with Italian cooking that's "complex" but "accessible"; its "see-and-be-seen" crowd likes the "intelligent" service, "upscale" decor and "vibrant" feel – in short, "the name suits the place."

Gyu-Kaku *Japanese* | 22 | 20 | 19 | $45

E 40s | 805 Third Ave., 2nd fl. (50th St.) | 212-702-8816
E Village | 34 Cooper Sq. (bet. Astor Pl. & 4th St.) | 212-475-2989
www.gyu-kaku.com

"Interactive" types who want to "play with fire" are hot for these "entertaining" branches of the Japanese BBQ chain where you "grill your own food" on charcoal braziers; nightclub looks, "prompt" service and an upbeat vibe help justify the slightly "pricey" tabs.

Hacienda de Argentina ◑ *Argentinean/Steak* | 18 | 17 | 17 | $54

E 70s | 339 E. 75th St. (bet. 1st & 2nd Aves.) | 212-472-5300

"Serious carnivores" can "taste the difference" that grass-fed beef makes at this UES Argentinean steakhouse that's also "less expensive" for the genre than the norm; some say the brick-lined, "candlelit" setting is "dark and romantic", but others advise "bring a flashlight."

Hale & Hearty Soups *Sandwiches/Soup* | 19 | 7 | 12 | $11

Chelsea | Chelsea Mkt. | 75 Ninth Ave. (bet. 15th & 16th Sts.) | 212-255-2400
E 40s | 685 Third Ave. (43rd St.) | 212-681-6460
E 40s | Grand Central | lower level (42nd St. & Vanderbilt Ave.) | 212-983-2845
E 60s | 849 Lexington Ave. (bet. 64th & 65th Sts.) | 212-517-7600
Financial District | 55 Broad St. (Beaver St.) | 212-509-4100
Garment District | 462 Seventh Ave. (35th St.) | 212-971-0605
W 40s | Rockefeller Plaza | 30 Rockefeller Plaza (49th St.) | 212-265-2117
W 40s | 49 W. 42nd St. (bet. 5th & 6th Aves.) | 212-575-9090
W 50s | 55 W. 56th St. (bet. 5th & 6th Aves.) | 212-245-9200
Brooklyn Heights | 32 Court St. (Remsen St.) | Brooklyn | 718-596-5600
www.haleandhearty.com
Additional locations throughout the NY area

"Fast, fresh" sandwiches, salads and a "mind-boggling variety" of "satisfying soups" make up the menu of this "true-to-its-name" chain; despite "AWOL" service and "no decor whatsoever", "long lines" persist at lunchtime, especially during "bikini season."

Hallo Berlin *German*

19 | 10 | 12 | $23

W 40s | 626 10th Ave. (bet. 44th & 45th Sts.) | 212-977-1944 |
www.halloberlinrestaurant.com

"*Wunderbar*" wursts washed down with "hearty" German brews are
yours at this Hell's Kitchen *brauhaus*; sure, das tabs are "cheap", but
there are downsides: "picnic-table decor" and "inattentive" service.

Hampton Chutney Co. *Indian*

19 | 9 | 13 | $16

SoHo | 68 Prince St. (bet. Crosby & Lafayette Sts.) | 212-226-9996
W 80s | 464 Amsterdam Ave. (bet. 82nd & 83rd Sts.) | 212-362-5050
www.hamptonchutney.com

Offering "cheap, delicious dosas", these Indian fusion practitioners
are highly touted as "healthful" alternatives to fast food; while the
SoHo branch is a hipster scene and the UWS more of a "mommy-and-
me" magnet, both provide big "bang for your buck."

☑ Hangawi *Korean*

24 | 24 | 24 | $46

Murray Hill | 12 E. 32nd St. (bet. 5th & Madison Aves.) | 212-213-0077 |
www.hangawirestaurant.com

A "peaceful reprieve from the craziness" of city life, this Murray Hill
Korean offers a "unique" vegetarian menu in a "soothing", "shoe-free"
environment that recalls a "spa"; "quiet" decibels and "customer-is-
king" service help you forget the slightly "expensive" tabs.

Hard Rock Cafe ● *American*

12 | 19 | 14 | $31

W 40s | 1501 Broadway (43rd St.) | 212-343-3355 | www.hardrock.com

"Food isn't the attraction" at this "memorabilia"-laden, rock 'n' roll-
themed chain link in Times Square; though its "burgers are decent"
enough, "tourists" and "kids of all ages" show up mainly to commune
with "Elvis' spirit" or to "sit next to their favorite guitar."

Harrison, The *American*

24 | 21 | 23 | $61

TriBeCa | 355 Greenwich St. (Harrison St.) | 212-274-9310 |
www.theharrison.com

New chef Amanda Freitag (ex Gusto) is cooking at this "classy" TriBeCa
New American, and her "delightful", Med-inspired dishes are already
winning raves; "smooth" service and "Hamptons-in-the-city" decor add
to the "cool, casual" feel, making the "upscale" pricing easy to digest.

Harry Cipriani ● *Italian*

19 | 21 | 19 | $91

E 50s | Sherry Netherland | 781 Fifth Ave. (bet. 59th & 60th Sts.) |
212-753-5566 | www.cipriani.com

The "scene outshines the food" at this "clubby" Venetian in the Sherry
Netherland, where the "just ok" cooking pales in comparison to the
revved-up "power people–watching"; the "Bellinis are a must", and
you'll need a few before the "obscenely expensive" bill arrives – "flying
to Italy might be cheaper."

Harry's Cafe ●☒ *Eclectic*

22 | 20 | 20 | $53

Financial District | 1 Hanover Sq. (bet. Pearl & Stone Sts.) | 212-785-9200

Harry's Steak ☒ *Steak*

Financial District | 97 Pearl St. (bet. Broad St. & Hanover Sq.) | 212-785-9200
www.harrysnyc.com

Full of "memories for older Wall Streeters", this Financial District duo
in the landmark India House "still packs 'em in"; the subterranean

chop shop serves "high-quality" beef and wines in clubby, "old-school" environs, while the Eclectic cafe above is centered around a "fun", "noisy" bar; both offer great bang for the buck.

Haru *Japanese*

	21	17	17	$41

E 40s | 280 Park Ave. (48th St.) | 212-490-9680
E 70s | 1327 Third Ave. (76th St.) | 212-452-1028 ◗
E 70s | 1329 Third Ave. (76th St.) | 212-452-2230 ◗
NEW Financial District | 1 Wall Street Ct. (bet. Beaver & Pearl Sts.) | 212-785-6850
Flatiron | 220 Park Ave. S. (18th St.) | 646-428-0989 ◗
W 40s | 205 W. 43rd St. (bet. B'way & 8th Ave.) | 212-398-9810 ◗
W 80s | 433 Amsterdam Ave. (bet. 80th & 81st Sts.) | 212-579-5655 ◗
www.harusushi.com

"Swimmingly good sushi" surfaces at this "safe-bet" Japanese mini-chain renowned for its "unusually large" portions, "concert"-level acoustics and "clublike" vibes; prices are "reasonable", but the "harried" servers keep the tables turning, so "don't expect to linger."

Hasaki ◗ *Japanese*

	22	13	19	$40

E Village | 210 E. Ninth St. (bet, 2nd & 3rd Aves.) | 212-473-3327 | www.hasakinyc.com

"Consistent quality" has kept this "old-faithful" East Villager in business for 25 years vending "impeccable sushi" and other "delicious" Japanese items for "solid-value" prices; "no reservations" are accepted, so insiders "arrive early or late" to sidestep the "masses" on line.

Hatsuhana ⌧ *Japanese*

	24	15	20	$52

E 40s | 17 E. 48th St. (bet. 5th & Madison Aves.) | 212-355-3345
E 40s | 237 Park Ave. (46th St.) | 212-661-3400
www.hatsuhana.com

The 48th Street "original" introduced sushi to Midtown in 1976, and this "quality" chainlet remains ever "reliable" for "top-of-the-line" Japanese fare (at equally "upscale" prices); maybe the decor's getting "stale", but at least the fish is "always fresh" and the staffers know their jobs after all those years.

Havana Alma de Cuba *Cuban*

	20	18	19	$36

W Village | 94 Christopher St. (bet. Bedford & Bleecker Sts.) | 212-242-3800 | www.havananyc.com

"Tasty" Cuban *comida* is served by a "friendly" crew at this "little Village jewel" that supplies "fun" atmospherics with "live music" for low dough; when it gets too "noisy" and "cramped", regulars retreat to the "nice garden" out back.

Havana Central *Cuban*

	17	16	16	$31

Union Sq | 22 E. 17th St. (bet. B'way & 5th Ave.) | 212-414-2298
W 40s | 151 W. 46th St. (bet. 6th & 7th Aves.) | 212-398-7440
W 100s | 2911 Broadway (bet. 113th & 114th Sts.) | 212-662-8830
www.havanacentral.com

It's "hearty" Cuban chow, tropical decor and "terrific drinks" times *tres* at this "sassy" Cuban trio where "affordable" tabs and "live music" ratchet up the "lively" mood; too bad "slow service" can put a damper on all the "fun."

	FOOD	DECOR	SERVICE	COST

Haveli ● *Indian* — 21 | 17 | 20 | $33

E Village | 100 Second Ave. (bet. 5th & 6th Sts.) | 212-982-0533
Partisans praise this longtime East Village Indian as "a cut above" its neighbors, pointing to "perfectly spiced" creations, "attentive" service and "Christmas light–free" decor; though "priced a bit higher" than the competition, it's still an "excellent value."

Hawaiian Tropic Zone ● *American* — ▽ 15 | 17 | 16 | $43

W 40s | 729 Seventh Ave. (49th St.) | 212-626-7312 | www.hawaiiantropiczone.com
"Bikini-clad waitresses" strut their stuff at this "bachelor party"–ready Times Square American with a "gimmicky" beauty-and-the-beach theme; while the fairly "good" cooking "doesn't justify" the "strip-club prices", most show up "for the babes", not the grub.

Hearth *American/Italian* — 25 | 20 | 23 | $65

E Village | 403 E. 12th St. (1st Ave.) | 646-602-1300 | www.restauranthearth.com
"Casual yet sophisticated", Marco Canora's "adult" East Villager is "everything dining should be" thanks to "uniquely subtle" Tuscan-American cooking served by an "enthusiastic staff" in "warm" digs (the best seats are at the counter overlooking the open kitchen's "wood-burning oven"); granted, it's "expensive", but the overall "fantastic experience" is well "worth the price."

Heartland Brewery *Pub Food* — 14 | 13 | 15 | $29

Garment District | Empire State Bldg. | 350 Fifth Ave. (34th St.) | 212-563-3433
Seaport | 93 South St. (Fulton St.) | 646-572-2337
Union Sq | 35 Union Sq. W. (bet. 16th & 17th Sts.) | 212-645-3400
W 40s | 127 W. 43rd St. (bet. B'way & 6th Ave.) | 646-366-0235
W 50s | 1285 Sixth Ave. (51st St.) | 212-582-8244
www.heartlandbrewery.com
Hopsheads "seeking a pint" head for this "convenient" microbrewery chain where the "tasty" house brews "hit the spot"; the "typical" pub grub, "nonchalant" service and "shopping-mall" decor are another story, but most agree they're "bearable" for an "after-work burger and beer."

Heidelberg *German* — 18 | 16 | 16 | $36

E 80s | 1648 Second Ave. (bet. 85th & 86th Sts.) | 212-628-2332 | www.heidelbergrestaurant.com
Deutschland devotees dig das "remnant of old Yorkville", a circa-1938 "time warp" famed for "satisfying schnitzel" and "giant boots of beer"; maybe the "lederhosen-clad staff" and "Disney-does-Bavarian-beer-hall" decor are a little "hokey", but the "inexpensive" tabs and "party atmosphere" sure are a "treat."

Hell's Kitchen *Mexican* — 23 | 16 | 18 | $42

W 40s | 679 Ninth Ave. (bet. 46th & 47th Sts.) | 212-977-1588 | www.hellskitchen-nyc.com
"Unexpected" dishes with "kick" and "*delicioso*" drinks make this Clinton "Nuevo Mexicano" a "must try"; though popular "pre-theater" owing to "prompt" service and "reasonable" tabs, the "no-reservations policy" and "small" setting can translate into "long waits."

Henry's End *American*
24 | 15 | 23 | $46

Brooklyn Heights | 44 Henry St. (bet. Cranberry & Middagh Sts.) | Brooklyn | 718-834-1776 | www.henrysend.com

"Adventurous" types who "love wild game" tout this "quirky" Brooklyn Heights New American where "unique", "savory" meats are paired with an "extensive wine list"; "cozy closet"–size quarters are trumped by "value" pricing and an "exceptional proprietor."

Hibino 🗷 *Japanese*
▽ 26 | 19 | 22 | $33

Cobble Hill | 333 Henry St. (Pacific St.) | Brooklyn | 718-260-8052 | www.hibino-brooklyn.com

"Daily changing" Kyoto-style *obanzai* (small plates) star at this "destination-worthy" Cobble Hill Japanese, an "authentic yet approachable" place also featuring "super-fresh" sushi and "epiphany"-worthy housemade tofu; what with the "sweet staff" and "lovely" setting, fans "can't believe it's not more expensive."

Highline ● *Thai*
19 | 21 | 18 | $35

Meatpacking | 835 Washington St. (Little W. 12th St.) | 212-243-3339 | www.nychighline.com

Over-the-top "futuristic design" is the main draw at this "trendy" Thai triplex in the Meatpacking District; since the "tasty" chow is "deliciously underpriced", brace yourself for a "hip young crowd" and a "late-night bar/lounge" scene.

Hill Country *BBQ*
21 | 16 | 13 | $33

Chelsea | 30 W. 26th St. (bet. B'way & 6th Ave.) | 212-255-4544 | www.hillcountryny.com

Texas Hill Country lands in Chelsea via this "cavernous" BBQ specialist in a "beat-up honky-tonk" setting where the food is ordered "cafeteria-style", "served on butcher paper" and consumed at long "communal tables"; fans find it "seriously delicious", but foes fret it's "kinda pricey" given the "tedious" "serve-yourself" process.

Hispaniola ● *Dominican*
▽ 20 | 20 | 17 | $41

Washington Heights | 839 W. 181st St. (bet. Cabrini Blvd. & Pinehurst St.) | 212-740-5222 | www.hispaniolarestaurant.com

"Huge portions" of "flavorful", Asian-accented Dominican chow are yours at this "upscale" fusion practitioner in Washington Heights; while the upstairs "view of the GW bridge" is a "treat", the "spotty service" and "high prices" for the neighborhood are less so.

HK ● *American*
▽ 17 | 18 | 17 | $34

Garment District | 523 Ninth Ave. (39th St.) | 212-947-4208 | www.hkhellskitchen.com

A "bright" spot on an "unremarkable stretch" near the Lincoln Tunnel, this "trendy" American dishes out "fancy comfort food" in "chic", minimalist environs; while the "service could use some fine tuning", the "hip scene", "pretty" patrons and "reasonable" costs are fine as is.

Holy Basil ● *Thai*
21 | 17 | 17 | $31

E Village | 149 Second Ave., 2nd fl. (bet. 9th & 10th Sts.) | 212-460-5557 | www.holybasilrestaurant.com

"High-end" food meets "low-end" pricing at this "terrific" Thai, a "soothing" place hidden "upstairs and away" from the East Village "bustle"; the "low-lit" setting and "balcony" seating are "sorta roman-tic", but the "bargain" tabs get the most love here.

House, The ● *Mediterranean*
▽ 20 | 24 | 19 | $48

Gramercy | 121 E. 17th St. (bet. Irving Pl. & Park Ave. S.) | 212-353-2121 | www.thehousenyc.com

Nestled in a "beautifully renovated" 1850s carriage house, this "sweet little" Gramercy Med is made for "romantics" given its "showplace" looks alone; an "eclectic", small plates–centric menu, "knowledgeable staff" and "reasonable" pricing add to the overall "charming" experience.

Houston's *American*
20 | 18 | 19 | $39

E 50s | Citigroup Ctr. | 153 E. 53rd St. (enter at 3rd Ave. & 54th St.) | 212-888-3828
Gramercy | NY Life Bldg. | 378 Park Ave. S. (27th St.) | 212-689-1090 www.hillstone.com

"Delish" American pub grub at "fair prices" results in "hour-plus" hang times at this "surprisingly good chain"; still, the thought of its "legend-ary spinach dip" combined with the "bustling singles scene" at the bar "makes the waiting less painful."

HSF ⊘ *Chinese*
19 | 10 | 12 | $24

Chinatown | 46 Bowery (bet. Bayard & Canal Sts.) | 212-374-1319

An "amazing variety" of "fresh", "cheap" dim sum is rolled out at this not-what-it-used-to-be "point-and-eat" C-town Cantonese vet; given "no decor", "communal tables" and rather dim service, it's "in-and-out" eating for most.

Hudson Cafeteria *American/Eclectic*
20 | 24 | 19 | $47

W 50s | Hudson Hotel | 356 W. 58th St. (bet. 8th & 9th Aves.) | 212-554-6000 | www.morganshotelgroup.com

While "long past its trendy phase", this "stylish" American-Eclectic off Columbus Circle still vends midpriced "upscale comfort food" in a "gorgeous" "Gothic dining hall" setting (think "Vincent Price" meets Ivy League refectory); in the summer, a "breezy" outdoor terrace dis-tracts from the "not-great service."

Hudson River Café ● *American/Seafood*
21 | 22 | 19 | $43

Harlem | 697 W. 133rd St. (12th Ave.) | 212-491-9111 | www.hudsonrivercafe.com

West Harlem's "gentrifying" 12th Avenue strip is home to this "up-town novelty", an "all-seasons" affair with several "off-the-hook" pa-tios as well as a coolly chic indoor space; the "creative", well-priced New American seafood menu shines, abetted by "eager" service and occasional "live jazz."

Hummus Place ● *Israeli/Vegetarian*
23 | 9 | 15 | $16

E Village | 109 St. Marks Pl. (bet. Ave. A & 1st Ave.) | 212-529-9198
NEW **G Village** | 71 Seventh Ave. S. (bet. Barrow & Bleecker Sts.) | 212-924-2022
G Village | 99 MacDougal St. (bet. Bleecker & W. 3rd Sts.) | 212-533-3089
W 70s | 305 Amsterdam Ave. (bet. 74th & 75th Sts.) | 212-799-3335 www.hummusplace.com

"World class hummus" is "all they have and all they need" at this Israeli trio where the namesake dish "puts the supermarket version to shame"; despite "crowded", "bare-bones" settings and "oblivious" (albeit "fast") service, the "dirt-cheap prices" make fans "hope they never pita out."

NEW Hundred Acres ● *American* ▽ 18 | 21 | 19 | $46

SoHo | 38 MacDougal St. (Prince St.) | 212-475-7500 | www.hundredacresnyc.com

A "more casual remake" of the former Provence, this "pleasant" new SoHo venue from the owners of Cookshop and Five Points specializes in seasonal, "reasonably priced" New Americana; it comes with "friendly" service, "laid-back" ambiance and a "lovely" back garden.

Ichiro ● *Japanese* 21 | 13 | 20 | $33

E 80s | 1694 Second Ave. (bet. 87th & 88th Sts.) | 212-369-6300

"Imaginative", "substantially sized" sushi sold for surprisingly small sums establishes this UES Japanese as a "solid" neighborhood choice; since the decor's rather "ordinary", aesthetes opt for "delivery so fast you'll think they made it outside your front door."

Ici ☒ *American/French* 21 | 19 | 19 | $42

Fort Greene | 246 DeKalb Ave. (bet. Clermont & Vanderbilt Aves.) | Brooklyn | 718-789-2778 | www.icirestaurant.com

A "rarity in hipsterland", this Fort Greene Franco-American fashions "memorable meals" from seasonal, locally grown goods; moderate pricing, a "lovely garden" and "attentive" service cancel out the "small" digs.

I Coppi *Italian* 22 | 19 | 20 | $48

E Village | 432 E. Ninth St. (bet. Ave. A & 1st Ave.) | 212-254-2263 | www.icoppinyc.com

It's all about the "wonderful" year-round garden at this "classic" East Village Tuscan, though the "rustic, gutsy" menu is equally "delicious"; "gracious owners", an "extensive wine list" and midrange tabs complete the overall "charming" package.

Ideya *Caribbean* ▽ 19 | 15 | 18 | $33

SoHo | 349 W. Broadway (bet. Broome & Grand Sts.) | 212-625-1441 | www.ideya.net

"Everyone's having a good time" at this "casual" SoHo Caribbean where a "pretty crowd" surrenders to "mojito madness"; the "simple" menu is "light and creative", but still plays second fiddle to the "loud" scene, "actor/model" staff and "cool Latin vibe."

Il Bagatto ●☒ *Italian* 23 | 16 | 17 | $38

E Village | 192 E. Second St. (bet. Aves. A & B) | 212-228-0977 | www.ilbagattonyc.com

"Mobbed" for a good reason, this East Village "favorite" is famed for "delicious homemade pastas" at really "reasonable" rates; trade-offs include "long waits", "tight" seats and so-so service, but most agree it's "worth the hassle" to sample "heaven on a plate."

Il Bastardo ● *Italian/Steak* 19 | 17 | 17 | $40

Chelsea | 191 Seventh Ave. (bet. 21st & 22nd Sts.) | 212-675-5980 | www.ilbastardonyc.com

"Better-than-expected" food and a pleasant setting make this Chelsea Tuscan steakhouse a neighborhood "default" for "easy" dining; fans "love the name", the "generous portions" and "decent" prices, and tout its adjoining enoteca, Bar Baresco, for "low-key" tippling.

	FOOD	DECOR	SERVICE	COST

Il Buco ◐ *Italian/Mediterranean*

| 24 | 22 | 21 | $61 |

NoHo | 47 Bond St. (bet. Bowery & Lafayette St.) | 212-533-1932 | www.ilbuco.com

"Sophisticated" meets "earthy" on the "magic" menu of this "original" NoHo Med-Italian where a "beautiful", "bubbly" crowd is "transported" by an antiques-laden "farmhouse setting" (and "romantic" wine cellar); throw in "superb service" and the "big prices" are easy to swallow.

Il Cantinori *Italian*

| 22 | 21 | 21 | $62 |

G Village | 32 E. 10th St. (bet. B'way & University Pl.) | 212-673-6044 | www.ilcantinori.com

"Sure bets" don't come any "classier" than this "old-school" Village "stalwart" supplying "upscale" Northern Italiana and "impeccable service"; the "gorgeous", flower-filled setting works well for either "romantic" or "relaxed" supping, but don't forget to bring along plenty of dough.

Il Corallo Trattoria *Italian*

| 22 | 14 | 20 | $27 |

SoHo | 176 Prince St. (bet. Sullivan & Thompson Sts.) | 212-941-7119

"Top-notch" Italian fare and "bargain basement" bills keep regulars regular at this "simple" SoHo trattoria known for its "infinite number" of "awesome pastas"; despite "cramped" quarters and that "no-reservations" policy, it's a "can't-be-beat value."

Il Cortile ◐ *Italian*

| 23 | 20 | 21 | $52 |

Little Italy | 125 Mulberry St. (bet. Canal & Hester Sts.) | 212-226-6060

You'll *mangia bene* at this "first-rate" Mulberry Street Italian where "experienced waiters" tote "big portions" of "classic" red-sauce dishes that are "rich" – and richly priced; while the interior is "pretty", insiders say the "food tastes even better in the garden room."

Il Fornaio *Italian*

| 22 | 15 | 19 | $34 |

Little Italy | 132A Mulberry St. (bet. Grand & Hester Sts.) | 212-226-8306 | www.ilfornaionyc.com

"Bright, innovative cooking" is the draw at this Little Italy "red-sauce heaven" that's something of a "local secret" in a land of "tourist traps"; a "homey" atmosphere, "dependable" service and "good value" make it a "great little treasure."

Il Gattopardo ◐ *Italian*

| 23 | 18 | 23 | $64 |

W 50s | 33 W. 54th St. (bet. 5th & 6th Aves.) | 212-246-0412 | www.ilgattopardonyc.com

A "convenient" Midtown location ("opposite MoMA" and adjoining "Manolo Blahnik") lures patrons to this Neapolitan "sleeper" featuring "delectable" food and "attentive" service in a "sleek" white townhouse setting; granted, an "expense account" helps when it comes time to settle the bill, but the payoff is *fabuloso* dining.

Il Giglio ⊠ *Italian*

| 25 | 18 | 24 | $71 |

TriBeCa | 81 Warren St. (bet. Greenwich St. & W. B'way) | 212-571-5555 | www.ilgigliorestaurant.com

You should "skip lunch" before trying this "terrific" TriBeCa Tuscan that's touted for its "delicious", filling freebies followed by "large portions" of sensational Italiana; the "tuxedoed" staff make everyone "feel important", so the "robust checks" are easier to digest.

	FOOD	DECOR	SERVICE	COST

NEW ilili *Lebanese*   23 23 21 $57

Gramercy | 236 Fifth Ave. (bet. 27th & 28th Sts.) | 212-683-2929 |
www.ililinyc.com

An "all-around winner", this "trendy" new Lebanese brings a "breath
of fresh air" to Gramercy Park, purveying a "well-executed", small
plates-focused menu mixing "classic and innovative" tastes; a handsome, wood-beamed" setting and "thumping house music" burnish
the "happening" vibe, and help justify the bilili.

Il Menestrello ◙ *Italian*   ▽ 21 16 22 $60

E 50s | 50 E. 50th St. (bet. Madison & Park Aves.) | 212-421-7588

"Good old-fashioned" dining is yours at this "reliable" Midtown Italian
boasting "solid" eats and a "pleasant staff"; it's popular with the "business crowd" at lunchtime and more "quiet" at the dinner hour, but either way don't be surprised by the "expensive" tabs.

Z Il Mulino ◙ *Italian*   27 17 23 $87

G Village | 86 W. Third St. (bet. Sullivan & Thompson Sts.) | 212-673-3783 |
www.ilmulinonewyork.com

"Subtlety is not the strong suit" of this "old-world" Village "bacchanal"
where "last meal"-worthy Italian dining begins with plentiful "freebie
appetizers" and the food "just keeps on coming", served by a "pro"
team in "dark", "crowded" digs; sure, it's a "difficult reservation" to
snag and the "price tag is as big as the portions", but ultimately it's a
"not-to-be-missed experience", and hey, "you won't have to eat for
days after"; N.B. lunch is cheaper and easier to book.

Il Nido ◙ *Italian*   23 18 22 $69

E 50s | 251 E. 53rd St. (bet. 2nd & 3rd Aves.) | 212-753-8450 |
www.ilnidonyc.com

"Harking back to the good old days", this 30-year-old Midtown Northern
Italian serves "excellent" standards toted by a "skilled" staff in a "soothing" setting; though the prices are the only thing "not from another era",
given the overall "lovely experience" there are no complaints.

Il Palazzo *Italian*   22 19 22 $45

Little Italy | 151 Mulberry St. (bet. Grand & Hester Sts.) | 212-343-7000

The "pasta is fresh, but the waiters aren't" at this "authentic" Little
Italy trattoria offering an "extensive", seafood-heavy Italian menu
that's "superior" to most of the local competition; "affordable" checks
and a lovely glass-enclosed "garden room" add to the "great value."

NEW Il Passatore ⊅ *Italian*   ▽ 25 21 23 $27

Williamsburg | 14 Bushwick Ave. (bet. Devoe St. & Metropolitan Ave.) |
Brooklyn | 718-963-3100 | www.ilpassatorebrooklyn.com

"Charming" is the word for this new East Williamsburg Italian specializing in the "wonderful" cooking of the Emilia-Romagna region; the "simple" rustic digs (think exposed brick, tin ceiling) open onto a swell
outdoor deck, and "reasonable" prices trump the "cash-only" policy.

Il Postino ● *Italian*   23 18 22 $67

E 40s | 337 E. 49th St. (bet. 1st & 2nd Aves.) | 212-688-0033 |
www.ilpostinorestaurant.com

An endless list of specials recited by "amusing" waiters is the hook at
this "fine" Italian near the U.N., but you need to "take a notepad" to

keep track; the "quiet" room works equally well for business or plea-sure, but be prepared to "spend like it's the '80s" either way.

Il Riccio ● *Italian*

FOOD	DECOR	SERVICE	COST
20	15	19	$54

E 70s | 152 E. 79th St. (bet. Lexington & 3rd Aves.) | 212-639-9111 | www.ilriccionyc.com

"Busy" is putting it mildly at this UES "neighborhood staple" for the "well-heeled", where the Italian cooking makes "prosaic dishes taste original" and the staff successfully "aims to please"; sure, it's "small and crowded", but hey, isn't that "Mayor Bloomberg in the back room"?

Il Tinello ⊠ *Italian*

FOOD	DECOR	SERVICE	COST
24	20	24	$69

W 50s | 16 W. 56th St. (bet. 5th & 6th Aves.) | 212-245-4388

"Experienced diners" who like to "dress up and spend money" tout this "old-school" Midtown Italian for its "excellent" food, "tuxedoed staff" and "starched-tablecloth" setting; as for the admittedly "expensive" tabs, supporters shrug "you only live once."

Il Vagabondo *Italian*

FOOD	DECOR	SERVICE	COST
18	15	18	$47

E 60s | 351 E. 62nd St. (bet. 1st & 2nd Aves.) | 212-832-9221 | www.ilvagabondo.com

With "red sauce" on the plate and "red-checkered cloths" on the ta-bles, this UES Italian "oldie but goodie" (since 1965) caters to fans of "throwback" dining and pricing; its "novelty" attraction – an "indoor bocce ball court" – outweighs the "tired" ambiance.

Il Valentino *Italian*

FOOD	DECOR	SERVICE	COST
∇ 18	19	20	$58

E 50s | Sutton Place Hotel | 330 E. 56th St. (bet. 1st & 2nd Aves.) | 212-355-0001 | www.ilvalentinony.com

"Old-fashioned but serviceable", this Sutton Place Northern Italian is a "quiet" nexus for "simple food" backed by weekend piano music; it caters to an "older clientele" that doesn't mind the "special-occasion" pricing but can't fathom "why it's not more crowded."

Inagiku *Japanese*

FOOD	DECOR	SERVICE	COST
22	20	21	$62

E 40s | Waldorf-Astoria | 111 E. 49th St. (bet. Lexington & Park Aves.) | 212-355-0440 | www.inagiku.com

"Deferential" waitresses in "kimonos" set the "calm" tone at this long-time Waldorf-Astoria Japanese where "top-quality" sushi is purveyed in "elegant" environs; while the $35 prix fixe lunch is a relative "bar-gain", dinner is best savored on an "expense account."

Indochine ● *French/Vietnamese*

FOOD	DECOR	SERVICE	COST
21	21	18	$53

E Village | 430 Lafayette St. (bet. Astor Pl. & 4th St.) | 212-505-5111 | www.indochinenyc.com

Once "impossibly chic" and now simply "classic", this 25-year-old French-Vietnamese near the Public Theater offers "exceptional" din-ing (and "people-watching") in a setting that's "pretty" to some, but "cheesy" to others; while a few feel it's "lost its mojo", they're easily outvoted year after year.

Industria Argentina ● *Argentinean/Steak*

FOOD	DECOR	SERVICE	COST
19	18	19	$48

TriBeCa | 329 Greenwich St. (bet. Duane & Jay Sts.) | 212-965-8560 | www.iatribeca.com

To experience "Buenos Aires without packing your bags", check out this "inviting" TriBeCa Argentinean vending "excellent" steaks and a "good wine list" in "modern", "high-style" digs; locals report the "reasonable prices" are a welcome "change of pace" in this tony part of town.

Indus Valley *Indian*
22 | 15 | 19 | $32

W 100s | 2636 Broadway (100th St.) | 212-222-9222 | www.indusvalleyusa.com

"Fragrant, flavorful" Indian food with "just the right amount of heat" turns up at this "elite" Upper Westsider flaunting plenty of "downtown style"; though you'll "spend more than on Sixth Street", the $12.95 prix fixe lunch buffet is a bona fide "bargain."

'ino ● *Italian*
24 | 15 | 18 | $27

G Village | 21 Bedford St. (bet. Downing St. & 6th Ave.) | 212-989-5769 | www.cafeino.com

Despite a "postage stamp" setting, this "delectable" Village Italian wine bar continues to pack 'em in; "tiny" tabs echo the dimensions, and the "most amazing panini on earth" seals the deal.

'inoteca ● *Italian*
23 | 18 | 20 | $39

LES | 98 Rivington St. (Ludlow St.) | 212-614-0473 | www.inotecanyc.com

"Exceptional small plates" and a "cocktail-party" vibe lure "the young and vibrant" to this "casual" LES panini-and-vino specialist, where patient staffers "translate the Italian menu"; expect the same "long waits", "high volume" and "decent pricing" as at its sibling, 'ino, but more room.

Insieme *Italian*
24 | 20 | 22 | $70

W 50s | The Michelangelo Hotel | 777 Seventh Ave. (bet. 50th & 51st Sts.) | 212-582-1310 | www.restaurantinsieme.com

A "real gem in a rhinestone neighborhood", this "swank" Times Square Italian showcases the cooking of chef Marco Canora, whose "first-rate" mix of the "classic" and the "contemporary" makes it "hard not to lick the plate"; all agree it's "spendy", though the "modern" decor gets mixed reviews – "chic" vs. "cold."

Intermezzo *Italian*
17 | 15 | 17 | $35

Chelsea | 202 Eighth Ave. (bet. 20th & 21st Sts.) | 212-929-3433

"What you see is what you get" at this Chelsea Italian, an "old standby" for "tasty", "straightforward" dining at "moderate" sums; the simple storefront setting satisfies "trendy" types, but the pounding "club music" is "too loud" for some.

NEW Ippudo ● *Japanese*
▽ 25 | 23 | 22 | $26

E Village | 65 Fourth Ave. (bet. 9th & 10th Sts.) | 212-388-0088 | www.ippudo.com/ny

Famed for its "silky" signature tonkotsu ramen, this "real-deal" East Village link of a Japanese chain is the latest contender for the title of "Noodle Heaven"; "inexpensive" costs and a "cool" setting make it a "force to be reckoned with", hence the "long waits."

Iron Sushi *Japanese*
19 | 12 | 17 | $29

E 70s | 355 E. 78th St. (bet. 1st & 2nd Aves.) | 212-772-7680
Murray Hill | 440 Third Ave. (bet. 30th & 31st Sts.) | 212-447-5822
www.ironsushiny.com

"Quick and easy" says it all about these satisfying East Side "sushi standbys" slicing "large portions" of "fresh" fish for a "fair price"; aesthetes put off by the "generic" looks note that "delivery is a plus."

	FOOD	DECOR	SERVICE	COST

NEW Irving Mill *American*
Gramercy | 116 E. 16th St. (bet. Irving Pl. & Park Ave. S.) | 212-254-1600 | www.irvingmill.com

21 | 23 | 21 | $60

From the "woody", "haute farmhouse" decor to the "seasonal", Greenmarket-inspired menu, this New American comer off Union Square has already been dubbed "Gramercy Tavern lite", given its "toothsome" grub, "friendly vibe" and "spacious" setting; maybe it's "kinda pricey" and "not on many radar screens", but fans feel it's "just what the neighborhood needed."

Isabella's *American/Mediterranean*
W 70s | 359 Columbus Ave. (77th St.) | 212-724-2100 | www.brguestrestaurants.com

20 | 19 | 19 | $43

Ever "bustling", this longtime Upper West Side "default" from Steve Hanson is "always crowded" thanks to "delicious", well-priced Mediterranean–New American fare with "something to please everyone"; "pleasant" service and a "mainstay brunch" add to its appeal, along with "revered sidewalk seating" perfect for Columbus Avenue "people-watching."

Ise *Japanese*
E 40s | 151 E. 49th St. (bet. Lexington & 3rd Aves.) | 212-319-6876
Financial District | 56 Pine St. (bet. Pearl & William Sts.) | 212-785-1600 | www.iserestaurant.com 🈂
W 50s | 58 W. 56th St. (bet. 5th & 6th Aves.) | 212-707-8702

21 | 13 | 17 | $38

This "reliable" izakaya trio offers "affordable" sushi, sashimi and katsu that's "authentic" enough to satisfy a "Japanese expat" following; regulars tout the "attentive service", ignore the "forgettable decor" and report that the "daily lunch specials" are a "must-try."

Island Burgers & Shakes *Burgers*
W 50s | 766 Ninth Ave. (bet. 51st & 52nd Sts.) | 212-307-7934 | www.islandburgersny.com

22 | 8 | 15 | $17

Big "messy burgers" with a "seemingly infinite choice of toppings" washed down with "dreamy shakes" are the hooks at this surf-themed Hell's Kitchen "staple"; "low costs" distract from the "no-frills" decor and the much-lamented "lack of french fries."

NEW I Sodi ● *Italian*
W Village | 105 Christopher St. (bet. Bleecker & Hudson Sts.) | 212-414-5774

∇ 21 | 18 | 22 | $53

A massive bar of reclaimed chestnut wood dominates this smart sliver of a newcomer in the West Village offering a short but serious menu of rustic Tuscan specialties; the "appealing" grub is best accompanied with house-specialty Negronis or selections from the predominantly Italian wine list, all delivered by a smooth crew.

Italianissimo *Italian*
E 80s | 307 E. 84th St. (bet. 1st & 2nd Aves.) | 212-628-8603 | www.italianissimonyc.net

∇ 24 | 19 | 24 | $49

"Small" but "classy", this UES Italian "rare find" offers "delicious" dishes "cooked to perfection" and presented by "caring" staffers in a "cozy", brick-lined room; though it "can get expensive", there's a $21.75 early-bird for the budget-minded.

	FOOD	DECOR	SERVICE	COST

Ithaka ● *Greek/Seafood* — 21 | 17 | 20 | $46

E 80s | 308 E. 86th St. (bet. 1st & 2nd Aves.) | 212-628-9100 |
www.ithakarestaurant.com
A "taste of Athens" in Yorkville, this "low-key" Greek seafooder puts
out "tasty" grilled fish in a whitewashed, "Santorini"-esque setting for
a moderate cost; "gracious service" and "pleasant guitar music" up
the appeal for its "older, family-oriented" crowd.

I Tre Merli ● *Italian* — 17 | 17 | 17 | $44

SoHo | 463 W. Broadway (bet. Houston & Prince Sts.) | 212-254-8699
W Village | 183 W. 10th St. (W. 4th St.) | 212-929-2221
www.itremerli.com
Long a SoHo "standard", this "pleasant" trattoria is better known for
its "dramatic, high-ceilinged" space and "pretty Euro" people-
watching than its "good" if "routine" Italian menu; while its Village sibling is considerably "smaller", both share fairly "affordable" tabs and
so-so service.

I Trulli *Italian* — 23 | 21 | 20 | $58

Gramercy | 122 E. 27th St. (bet. Lexington Ave. & Park Ave. S.) |
212-481-7372 | www.itrulli.com
On its way to "becoming an institution", this 15-year-old Gramercy
Italian specializes in "authentic Pugliese" cuisine served in rustically
"romantic" environs enhanced by a "cozy" fireplace in winter and a
"lovely garden" in summer; a "brilliant wine list" (decanted at the adjoining enoteca) helps distract from the "upscale" pricing.

Itzocan ⊅ *Mexican* — 24 | 10 | 18 | $34

E 100s | 1575 Lexington Ave. (101st St.) | 212-423-0255
E Village | 438 E. Ninth St. (bet. Ave. A & 1st Ave.) | 212-677-5856 ●
"Affable" and "unpretentious", these "top-notch" Mexicans share
"tiny", "hole-in-the-wall" settings, though the UES branch gives a "sophisticated", French-influenced spin to its dishes, while the East
Village original offers more straightforward, "south-of-the-border"
presentations; both are "reasonably priced", but accept cash only.

Ivo & Lulu ⊅ *Caribbean/French* — ▽ 24 | 13 | 20 | $29

SoHo | 558 Broome St. (bet. 6th Ave. & Varick St.) | 212-226-4399
"Cheap in cost, rich in flavor", this "off-the-beaten-path" SoHo French-
Caribbean enjoys a strong "local" following; recent renovations have
expanded the formerly "tight space" somewhat, while its much beloved "BYO policy" remains intact.

Jack's Luxury Oyster Bar Ⓩ *Continental/French* — ▽ 26 | 18 | 22 | $67

E Village | 101 Second Ave. (bet. 5th & 6th Sts.) | 212-979-1012
"Memorable" dining awaits at this "creative" East Village French-
Continental where "sublime" bivalves and other "delicious morsels" are
"expensive but worth it"; loyalists lament its move to a "tiny", "bland"
storefront, but admit there's "never a missed cue" servicewise.

Jackson Diner ⊅ *Indian* — 21 | 10 | 15 | $23

Jackson Heights | 37-47 74th St. (bet. Roosevelt & 37th Aves.) |
Queens | 718-672-1232 | www.jacksondiner.com
Fans "savor the flavors" at this "lively" Jackson Heights Indian that's best
known for its "exceptional" $9.95 brunch buffet; "patience-testing

	FOOD	DECOR	SERVICE	COST

lines" and "no charm" in the looks department are downsides, but the
low prices and fine food "go a long way" to make up for it.

Jackson Hole *American*
	17	10	14	$21

E 60s | 232 E. 64th St. (bet. 2nd & 3rd Aves.) | 212-371-7187 ◑
E 80s | 1611 Second Ave. (bet. 83rd & 84th Sts.) | 212-737-8788 ◑
E 90s | 1270 Madison Ave. (91st St.) | 212-427-2820
Murray Hill | 521 Third Ave. (35th St.) | 212-679-3264 ◑
W 80s | 517 Columbus Ave. (85th St.) | 212-362-5177
Bayside | 35-01 Bell Blvd. (35th Ave.) | Queens | 718-281-0330 ◑
Jackson Heights | 69-35 Astoria Blvd. (70th St.) | Queens | 718-204-7070 ◑
www.jacksonholeburgers.com

"Ginormous", "juicy" burgers and "artery-clogging fries" are all you
need to know about this American mini-chain that also offers "pig-
out" portions and "get-your-money's-worth" tabs; they're particularly
"child-friendly", so parents ignore the "greasy-spoon" decor and "disorganized" service on the theory that "red meat is good for you."

Jack the Horse Tavern *American*
	22	20	19	$41

Brooklyn Heights | 66 Hicks St. (Cranberry St.) | Brooklyn | 718-852-5084 |
www.jackthehorse.com

"Tucked away on a tree-lined street", this "much needed" Brooklyn
Heights New American turns out "excellent" food and grog in a "welcoming", "laid-back" environment enhanced by "cordial service";
"reasonable" tabs cement the all-around "pleasant" experience.

Jacques *French*
	19	17	17	$43

E 80s | 206 E. 85th St. (bet. 2nd & 3rd Aves.) | 212-327-2272
NoLita | 20 Prince St. (bet. Elizabeth & Mott Sts.) | 212-966-8886
www.jacquesnyc.com

"Mouthwatering" moules frites are the draw at these Gallic brasseries
with a "real French feel", right down to the service *avec* "Parisian indif-
ference"; while the UES menu tends toward the "classic", the NoLita
outpost adds a North African spin, but both share "good value."

Jaiya Thai *Thai*
	22	9	15	$29

Gramercy | 396 Third Ave. (28th St.) | 212-889-1330 | www.jaiya.com
They "really turn up the heat" at this "authentic" Gramercy Thai where
even mild dishes tend toward the "spicier end of the spectrum";
though "bargain" bills blunt below-standard decor and service, many
still prefer takeout or delivery.

Jake's Steakhouse *Steak*
	23	18	20	$48

Bronx | 6031 Broadway (242nd St.) | 718-581-0182 |
www.jakessteakhouse.com

"Excellent steaks" are a given at this "upscale" Riverdale chop shop
since it's run by meat wholesalers, while "Bronx prices" throw some
"value" into the mix; insiders add that in addition to smart service, the
second-floor dining room boasts "great views" of Van Cortlandt Park.

NEW James Ⓜ *American*
	-	-	-	E

Prospect Heights | 605 Carlton Ave. (St. Marks Ave.) | Brooklyn |
718-942-4255 | www.jamesrestaurantny.com

To a leafy Prospect Heights corner comes this upscale New American
arrival whose elegant, seasonally oriented fare stands out in the area;
it's stylish from its pressed-tin ceilings and nifty Lucite chandelier

to the dark-wood bar mixing au courant cocktails, but it exudes a welcoming neighborhood vibe.

Jane *American* | 21 | 17 | 19 | $40 |

G Village | 100 W. Houston St. (bet. La Guardia Pl. & Thompson St.) | 212-254-7000

"Popular for good reason", this Village "find" offers an "imaginative", "moderately priced" New American menu with "enough variety to please everyone"; throw in "personable" service and a "relaxed" ambiance, and it's no surprise the "killer" brunch is such a "scene."

Japonais Ⓢ *Japanese* | 20 | 23 | 18 | $60 |

Gramercy | 111 E. 18th St. (bet. Irving Pl. & Park Ave. S.) | 212-260-2020 | www.japonaisnewyork.com

"Creative", French-inflected Japanese dishes play second fiddle to the "dazzling", red-lacquered setting at this "hip" Gramercy Japanese where the food is "worth every penny"; the "expansive" setting also includes two "sexy", "sceney" lounges.

Japonica *Japanese* | 22 | 14 | 20 | $45 |

G Village | 100 University Pl. (12th St.) | 212-243-7752 | www.japonicanyc.com

Maintaining its "serious" reputation for over three decades, this "reliable" Village Japanese slices its sushi in "gargantuan" portions presented with "pride and flair"; despite the "unexciting" decor, it's not at all overpriced for what it is.

Jarnac Ⓜ *Mediterranean* | 23 | 20 | 23 | $53 |

W Village | 328 W. 12th St. (Greenwich St.) | 212-924-3413 | www.jarnacny.com

Ever-present owners "make you feel at home" at this "cute as a button" Village French-Med known for its "simple", "scrumptious" cooking (notably a "great cassoulet"); the "cozy" setting is *très romantique*, but the "tabs are higher than you'd expect."

Jasmine *Thai* | 19 | 14 | 17 | $27 |

E 80s | 1619 Second Ave. (84th St.) | 212-517-8854

"Solid" standards for "cheap" make this "neighborhood" Thai an UES "staple"; while "helpful" service and "ample space" abet its rep for "casual dining", "noisy" acoustics lead some to opt for "super-fast delivery."

Jean Claude ∅ *French* | ▽ 21 | 16 | 19 | $41 |

SoHo | 137 Sullivan St. (bet. Houston & Prince Sts.) | 212-475-9232

For French fare "so authentic you expect to pay in euros", check out this "small" SoHo bistro that also boasts "lovely service" and a "low-key" vibe; sure, "it's a drag they don't take credit cards", but good value makes up for it.

ⓩ Jean Georges Ⓢ *French* | 28 | 26 | 27 | $127 |

W 60s | Trump Int'l Hotel | 1 Central Park W. (bet. 60th & 61st Sts.) | 212-299-3900 | www.jean-georges.com

A "class act from start to finish", Jean-Georges Vongerichten's Columbus Circle flagship "continues to dazzle" with "top-rung", "ever-evolving" New French prix fixes that "simultaneously comfort and excite", served by a "read-your-mind" staff in a "modern" setting; jackets are required for this "practically perfect" dining experience, and though prices are "not for the weak of pocketbook", most agree it's "worth every cent" and say the $24 set-price lunch (in the "more casual" Nougatine Room) is the "best deal in town."

Jewel Bako ●⊠ *Japanese* | 25 | 22 | 23 | $80 |

E Village | 239 E. Fifth St. (bet. 2nd & 3rd Aves.) | 212-979-1012
"Hidden away" in a "tiny" East Village storefront, this chic Japanese enjoys a "well-deserved reputation" for "sexy sushi" served in "fashionable", bamboo-lined digs; the "terrific service" is overseen by "hosts-with-the-most" Jack and Grace Lamb, and the overall mood is "serene – until the check arrives."

Jewel of India *Indian* | 19 | 17 | 19 | $39 |

W 40s | 15 W. 44th St. (bet. 5th & 6th Aves.) | 212-869-5544 | www.jewelofindiarestaurant.com
"Affordable", "above-average" Indian standards, "attentive" service and a "comfortable" setting have made this bi-level Midtowner a "reliable" stop for 20 years; insiders say downstairs is "better" than upstairs and the $16.95 "lunch buffet deal" is most "satisfying" of all.

J.G. Melon ●⊅ *Pub Food* | 21 | 12 | 15 | $26 |

E 70s | 1291 Third Ave. (74th St.) | 212-744-0585
The burgers and cottage fries blow away the rest of the "buttoned-down comfort-food" menu offered at this longtime UES pub; despite "cranky" staffers and a "cash-only" rule, it's a "preppy" magnet thanks to its "college-days"-meets-"country-club" aura.

Jimmy's 43 ● *American*   ▽ | 21 | 17 | 18 | $34 |

E Village | 43 E. Seventh St., downstairs (bet. Bowery & 2nd Ave.) | 212-982-3006 | www.jimmysno43.com
Secreted in an East Village basement, this easy-to-miss pub has an antler-heavy rathskeller setting that's as laid-back as the pricing; look for an assortment of "surprisingly excellent" American small plates paired with an "unbelievable draft beer list."

Jing Fong *Chinese* | 19 | 12 | 11 | $21 |

Chinatown | 20 Elizabeth St. (bet. Bayard & Canal Sts.) | 212-964-5256
You can "feel the floor vibrating" at this "mammoth" Chinatown "dim sum circus" offering a "massive variety" of "tasty" Hong Kong–style treats; "dirt-cheap" tabs, "deafening" decibels and "no-English" service are all part of the "chaotic", "Vegas"-esque package.

JJ's Asian Fusion Ⓜ *Asian Fusion*   ▽ | 24 | 16 | 21 | $29 |

Astoria | 37-05 31st Ave. (bet. 37th & 38th Sts.) | Queens | 718-626-8888 | www.jjsfusion.com
"Fantastic" edamame potstickers are the "must-try" items at this Astoria Asian fusion practitioner where the "innovative" menu includes some mighty "delicious sushi"; no one minds the "modest" looks given the "inexpensive" tabs and "sweet-as-pie" owners.

Joe Allen ● *American* | 17 | 16 | 18 | $42 |

W 40s | 326 W. 46th St. (bet. 8th & 9th Aves.) | 212-581-6464 | www.joeallenrestaurant.com
Long a "theatrical institution", this Restaurant Row American dishes out "reliable" comfort chow to show-goers and "drunk actors" alike; sure, the decor's "stale" and service depends on whether "your waiter

had a good audition that day", but it's always a "safe bet" for "casual" grazing at a "modest" cost.

Joe & Pat's *Italian/Pizza*
22 | 11 | 18 | $21

Staten Island | 1758 Victory Blvd. (Manor Rd.) | 718-981-0887 | www.joeandpatsny.com

"Delicious" pies with "paper-thin crusts" make for "pizza perfection" at this circa-1960 Staten Island "favorite"; despite dinerlike decor and "loud" acoustics, it's a bargain neighborhood "staple."

Joe's Ginger ⊄ *Chinese*
20 | 9 | 14 | $21

Chinatown | 25 Pell St. (Doyers St.) | 212-285-0333 | www.joeginger.com

"Inexpensive, filling and delicious" sums up the meals at this C-town specialist in Shanghai-style cuisine that's mainly patronized for its "great soup dumplings"; "less crowded" than similarly named nearby competitors, it's especially handy for "jury duty."

Joe's Pizza *Pizza*
23 | 5 | 13 | $9

G Village | 7 Carmine St. (bet. Bleecker St. & 6th Ave.) | 212-255-3946 ◐
Midwood | 1621 Kings Hwy. (E. 16th St.) | Brooklyn | 718-339-4525 ⊄
Park Slope | 137 Seventh Ave. (bet. Carroll St. & Garfield Pl.) | Brooklyn | 718-398-9198

These separately owned pizzerias produce "chewy", "fresh-from-the-oven" pies made with "artful crusts" and "fresh mozzarella"; given the "divey", "hole-in-the-wall" setups, takeout is recommended – just "try not to lick the delivery box."

Joe's Shanghai *Chinese*
22 | 9 | 14 | $24

Chinatown | 9 Pell St. (bet. Bowery & Mott St.) | 212-233-8888 ⊄
W 50s | 24 W. 56th St. (bet. 5th & 6th Aves.) | 212-333-3868
Flushing | 136-21 37th Ave. (bet. Main & Union Sts.) | Queens | 718-539-3838 ⊄
www.joeshanghairestaurants.com

"Unbeatable soup dumplings" are the "highlight" of this Shanghainese trio that's usually "crowded with tourists and Zagat readers"; "greasy-spoon" decor, "long lines" and "shared tables" come with the territory, but all is forgiven after one bite of its "cheap", "tasty" morsels.

Johnny Utah's ◐⊠ *BBQ/Southwestern*
∇ 13 | 19 | 16 | $40

W 50s | 25 W. 51st St., downstairs (bet. 5th & 6th Aves.) | 212-265-8824 | www.johnnyutahs.com

Bringing "Texas to Manhattan", this midpriced Midtown BBQ joint is better known for its "mechanical bull" and faux Wild West ambiance than its just "ok" food and "so-so" service; still, it's always good "for a laugh" watching people who think they're in *"Urban Cowboy"* "making fools of themselves" and then suing when they fall off.

John's of 12th Street ⊄ *Italian*
19 | 14 | 18 | $32

E Village | 302 E. 12th St. (2nd Ave.) | 212-475-9531

A "throwback" to the days of cheap plates of "red gravy" and "gooey cheese", this circa-1908 East Village Italian comes with an "old-school" crew; "dripping candles" cast a "romantic" glow, though the mood may vanish "if you could actually see the place."

John's Pizzeria *Pizza*
22 | 13 | 15 | $23

E 60s | 408 E. 64th St. (bet. 1st & York Aves.) | 212-935-2895

(continued)

John's Pizzeria

G Village | 278 Bleecker St. (bet. 6th Ave. & 7th Ave. S.) |
212-243-1680 ●⊟
W 40s | 260 W. 44th St. (bet. B'way & 8th Ave.) |
212-391-7560 ●
www.johnspizzerianyc.com

"Long lines" prove that this "classic" pizzeria trio "deserves its rep" as the "granddaddy" of "crispy, brick-oven perfection" – even if "molasses"-slow service and a "no-slices" policy detract; though purists plainly prefer the 80-year-old Village original, Midtown's "converted church" setting is "perfect" pre-theater.

JoJo *French*

24	22	23	$70

E 60s | 160 E. 64th St. (bet. Lexington & 3rd Aves.) | 212-223-5656 |
www.jean-georges.com

"Magnifique" is the word on Jean-Georges Vongerichten's original UES bistro where "sublime" French fare is buttressed by silken service; romantics debate which floor of the "rococo" townhouse has more "mojo", but all agree the $24 prix fixe lunch is highly "attractive."

Jolie *French*

21	20	20	$40

Boerum Hill | 320 Atlantic Ave. (bet. Hoyt & Smith Sts.) | Brooklyn |
718-488-0777 | www.jolierestaurant.com

A "must-visit" for locals, this "inviting" Boerum Hill boîte lives up to its name with "pretty" French cooking, "friendly" service and modest pricing; it's especially "delightful" for dinner *à deux*, particularly in the "lovely" back garden.

Josephina ● *American*

18	16	17	$48

W 60s | 1900 Broadway (bet. 63rd & 64th Sts.) | 212-799-1000 |
www.josephinanyc.com

Waiters "whisk" you through dinner so efficiently that this "spacious" spot opposite Lincoln Center is ever "popular" with time-sensitive ticket-holders; "reliable" New Americana transcends the "hectic" vibe and "close quarters."

Josie's *Eclectic*

19	15	16	$34

Murray Hill | 565 Third Ave. (37th St.) | 212-490-1558
W 70s | 300 Amsterdam Ave. (74th St.) | 212-769-1212

Josie's Kitchen *Eclectic*

E 80s | 1614 Second Ave. (84th St.) | 212-734-6644
www.josiesnyc.com

"Virtuous", mostly organic grub makes for "sin-free" dining at this well-priced Eclectic trio that's particularly popular with "girls'-night-out" groups; however, "patience is needed" at peak times when the "minimalist" digs get "noisy" and the "frazzled" staff seems to "take forever."

Joya ⊟ *Thai*

23	17	18	$22

Cobble Hill | 215 Court St. (bet. Warren & Wyckoff Sts.) | Brooklyn |
718-222-3484

"Better-than-Bangkok" Thai food at "bargain" tabs keeps this "hip", cash-only Cobble Hiller "always mobbed"; "strong" drinks, "quick" service and a "sexy industrial" setting fuel the "vibrant buzz", but if "blaring" dance music ain't your thing, "try for a table in the garden."

	FOOD	DECOR	SERVICE	COST

Jubilee *French*   **22** | **16** | **19** | **$49**

E 50s | 347 E. 54th St. (bet. 1st & 2nd Aves.) | 212-888-3569 |
www.jubileeny.com

An "older" crowd crams into this "classic" Sutton Place French bistro
for its "superb" signature mussels and "caring" service; however, upmarket tabs, "tired" decor and "herring tin"–tight seating are no
cause for jubilation.

Jules ● *French*   ▽ **18** | **16** | **15** | **$39**

E Village | 65 St. Marks Pl. (bet. 1st & 2nd Aves.) | 212-477-5560 |
www.julesbistro.com

"Nestled among the tattoo parlors" on St. Marks Place, this "easygoing" East Villager offers "simple", well-priced Gallic grub along with
"authentic French" (i.e. "attitude"-ridden) service; nightly live jazz
lends a *Casablanca* atmosphere" to the proceedings.

Junior's *Diner*   **17** | **11** | **15** | **$26**

E 40s | Grand Central | lower level (42nd St. & Vanderbilt Ave.) |
212-983-5257

W 40s | Shubert Alley | 1515 Broadway (enter on 45th St., bet. B'way &
8th Ave.) | 212-302-2000 ●

Downtown Bklyn | 386 Flatbush Ave. Ext. (DeKalb Ave.) | Brooklyn |
718-852-5257 ●

www.juniorscheesecake.com

"Sublime cheesecake" is all you need to know about this Downtown
Brooklyn "classic" dispensing "giant" portions of "the usual" deli offerings in "schmaltzy" digs; the less atmospheric Manhattan branches
are "convenient" if catching a show or train.

NEW Kafana Ⓜ⇄ *Serbian*   **-** | **-** | **-** | **M**

E Village | 116 Ave. C (bet. 7th & 8th Sts.) | 212-353-8000 |
www.kafananyc.com

Possibly the only Serbian eatery in the city, this diminutive Alphabet
City arrival – whose name translates as 'neighborhood restaurant' –
should be a boon to local carnivores given the menu's high pork quotient; fair prices and a warm, brick-lined space add to its appeal.

Kai ⊠Ⓜ *Japanese*   ▽ **25** | **23** | **25** | **$72**

E 60s | Ito En | 822 Madison Ave., 2nd fl. (bet. 68th & 69th Sts.) |
212-988-7277 | www.itoen.com

Aficionados "appreciate the subtleties" of Japanese cuisine on display
at this "superb" UES kaiseki experience, located in a "serene" setting
above tea boutique Ito En; expect "Zen-like" dining, starting with
"small portions" and ending with "big" bills.

Kampuchea Ⓜ *Cambodian*   ▽ **21** | **17** | **17** | **$31**

LES | 78 Rivington St. (Allen St.) | 212-529-3901 | www.kampucheanyc.com

"Flavorful" noodles, sandwiches and other Khmer street food make
up the menu of this Lower East Side Cambodian "find"; the "uncomfortable seating" and "loud" acoustics are tempered by "relaxed" service and "inexpensive" tabs.

Kang Suh ● *Korean*   **21** | **11** | **15** | **$35**

Garment District | 1250 Broadway (32nd St.) | 212-564-6845

"Tasty at all hours", this 24/7 Garment District Korean offers "sizzling", do-it-yourself BBQ as well as a host of other "reliable" menu op-

tions (including sushi) at low cost; it's been a "Manhattan fixture" for 25 years, despite "no atmosphere" and "rushed service."

Kanoyama ● *Japanese* | 26 | 16 | 20 | $53 |

E Village | 175 Second Ave. (11th St.) | 212-777-5266 | www.kanoyama.com

"Hard-to-find cuts" of "Masa-level" fish are fashioned into tiny "pieces of art" at the sushi bar of this East Village Japanese; "casual service", "simple" decor and "fair prices" are added appeals, but "word is getting out", so "long waits" may be expected.

Kati Roll Co. *Indian* | 22 | 6 | 12 | $11 |

Garment District | 49 W. 39th St. (bet. 5th & 6th Aves.) | 212-730-4280
G Village | 99 MacDougal St. (bet. Bleecker & W. 3rd Sts.) | 212-420-6517 ●

"Late-night" revelers seeking "cheap snacks" tout the "fantastic" namesake rolls (aka Indian burritos) at these Midtown/Village storefronts; "long lines", "slow" service and sari decor to the contrary, fans "keep coming back."

Katsu-Hama *Japanese* | 22 | 10 | 15 | $27 |

E 40s | 11 E. 47th St. (bet. 5th & Madison Aves.) | 212-758-5909 | www.katsuhama.com

"Japanese comfort food" in the form of "tender", "tasty" fried cutlets is the hook at this bare-bones Midtown katsu parlor that "goes beyond sushi"; "quick" service and "affordable" tabs make it a prime "lunch spot", complete with midday "waits."

⊠ Katz's Delicatessen *Deli* | 23 | 9 | 12 | $22 |

LES | 205 E. Houston St. (Ludlow St.) | 212-254-2246 | www.katzdeli.com

"Loud and crowded, just like NY", this "frozen-in-time" LES deli "where Harry met Sally" ("I'll have what she's having") is famous for its "unsurpassed" pastrami, service "with a snarl" and total "lack of decor", unless you consider Formica decor; although it can be tough to "find a seat" or get the counterman's attention, it's a slice of "cultural history" that everyone should experience.

Keens Steakhouse *Steak* | 24 | 23 | 22 | $67 |

Garment District | 72 W. 36th St. (bet. 5th & 6th Aves.) | 212-947-3636 | www.keens.com

"Meat lovers" and history lovers praise this circa-1885 Garment District steakhouse/bar/party space where over 80,000 "clay pipes line the ceiling" and the signature "mutton chop is king"; "first-rate service", "manly", "Grover Cleveland"-worthy portions and a "treasure trove" of American memorabilia add to the museum-quality appeal; in sum, it's well worth the splurge.

Kellari Taverna ● *Greek* | 21 | 22 | 20 | $51 |

W 40s | 19 W. 44th St. (bet. 5th & 6th Aves.) | 212-221-0144 | www.kellari.us
NEW Kellari's Parea ● *Greek*

Flatiron | 36 E. 20th St. (bet. B'way & Park Ave. S.) | 212-777-8448 | www.kellari-parea.com

Fans feel like "dancing in the isles" at these "high-style" Hellenics hailed for "outstanding grilled fish", "attentive" service and "lively" dispositions; the "spacious" Theater District branch caters to showgoers with a $29.95 early-bird, while the Flatiron location draws more of a "neighborhood" crowd.

	FOOD	DECOR	SERVICE	COST

Killmeyer's Old Bavaria Inn German
19 | 18 | 19 | $32

Staten Island | 4254 Arthur Kill Rd. (Sharrotts Rd.) | 718-984-1202 | www.killmeyers.com

There's "a bit of the old world" still intact at this cost-efficient Staten Island German known for good grub and a "great beer selection"; its biergarten is a natural for Oktoberfest, while an "oompah band" and "friendly" "costumed waitresses" add to the "kitschy" allure.

Kings' Carriage House American
21 | 25 | 23 | $72

E 80s | 251 E. 82nd St. (bet. 2nd & 3rd Aves.) | 212-734-5490 | www.kingscarriagehouse.com

An "elegant townhouse location" lends this "adult" UES New American a "hideaway" feel, while ultra-"charming" decor, "delicious" prix fixe menus and "gracious service" make it "perfect for celebrations or romance"; sure, it's "expensive", so "value"-seekers show up for high tea or the bargain $18.95 lunch special.

NEW Kingswood Australian
▽ 21 | 20 | 18 | $49

G Village | 121 W. 10th St. (bet. Greenwich & 6th Aves.) | 212-645-0018

"Young", "too-cool-for-school" types are buzzing about this "trendy" new Village gastropub, serving "delicious" Australian-accented Americana; while both the room and crowd are "attractive", the "lively" "table-hopping" makes for "incredibly loud" dining.

King Yum Chinese
▽ 17 | 13 | 18 | $27

Fresh Meadows | 181-08 Union Tpke. (181st St.) | Queens | 718-380-1918 | www.kingyumrestaurant.com

There are "no innovations" and "no need for them" at this circa-1953 Fresh Meadows "institution" purveying an "old-fashioned" mix of Chinese and Polynesian items – "pupu platter, anyone?" – in a "campy luau" setting; karaoke and drinks garnished with umbrellas add to the "kitschy" goings on, and the "throwback" tabs ain't bad either.

Ki Sushi Japanese
▽ 26 | 22 | 23 | $34

Boerum Hill | 122 Smith St. (bet. Dean & Pacific Sts.) | Brooklyn | 718-935-0575

"Fresh fish abounds" at this "hip" Boerum Hill Japanese slicing "impeccable" sushi with "great attention to detail"; "attentive" service, "dark", "chic" digs and modest pricing have made it a "neighborhood hot spot."

Kitchen Club French/Japanese
▽ 21 | 19 | 21 | $48

NoLita | 30 Prince St. (Mott St.) | 212-274-0025 | www.thekitchenclub.com

"Fabulously eccentric" proprietress Marja Samsom and her dog Chibi (a "local institution") set the "charming" mood at this "tiny" NoLita French-Japanese known for its "intriguing", midpriced dishes and particularly "divine dumplings"; it's a "one-of-a-kind" spot that loyal locals "love."

Kitchenette Southern
19 | 15 | 16 | $25

TriBeCa | 156 Chambers St. (bet. Greenwich & W. B'way) | 212-267-6740
W 100s | 1272 Amsterdam Ave. (bet. 122nd & 123rd Sts.) | 212-531-7600
www.kitchenetterestaurant.com

"Wonderfully homey", this "old-timey" Southern duo purveys "great-value" "'50s throwback comfort food" in "colorful, kitschy" digs; it's a "fantastic brunch" destination, but brace yourself for "DMV-like" lines and "so-so" service.

	FOOD	DECOR	SERVICE	COST

☑ Kittichai *Thai*
22 | 27 | 20 | $60

SoHo | 60 Thompson Hotel | 60 Thompson St. (bet. Broome & Spring Sts.) | 212-219-2000 | www.kittichairestaurant.com

"Theatrical" decor (including a "pond with floating candles and orchids") nearly overwhelms the "innovative" food at this "so-hip-it-hurts" Thai where "stylish" sorts struggle to be heard over the "loud music"; sure, "it's pricey" and the "modellike" staff exudes "attitude", but let's face it, "it's SoHo."

Klee Brasserie *American/European*
21 | 19 | 20 | $52

Chelsea | 200 Ninth Ave. (bet. 22nd & 23rd Sts.) | 212-633-8033 | www.kleebrasserie.com

"Brightening up Ninth Avenue", this "no-pretense" Chelsea Euro-American flexes its "culinary potential" with a "well-prepared" menu, "relaxed" setting and "gracious" service; while "a little expensive for a neighborhood place", overall it's a "pleasant surprise."

Klong ● *Thai*
21 | 17 | 15 | $25

E Village | 7 St. Marks Pl. (bet. 2nd & 3rd Aves.) | 212-505-9955 | www.klongnyc.com

"Delicious", "super-cheap" Bangkok street food draws a "young crowd" to this St. Marks Place Thai; despite "spotty service" and too much "noise", the "glitzy", "dimly lit" space reeks of "cool" and stays busy "into the early morning hours" as a hangover antidote.

Knickerbocker Bar & Grill ● *American*
19 | 17 | 19 | $49

G Village | 33 University Pl. (9th St.) | 212-228-8490 | www.knickerbockerbarandgrill.com

A Village "staple" for over three decades, this New American steakhouse stays "crowded" thanks to "dependably delicious" cuts, "low price points", "efficient service" and "live weekend jazz"; though some feel "it's time for a renovation", nostalgists want its "old-school charm" to stay the way it is.

Knife + Fork Ⓜ *European*
▽ 21 | 17 | 19 | $51

E Village | 108 E. Fourth St. (bet. 1st & 2nd Aves.) | 212-228-4885 | www.knife-fork-nyc.com

"Imaginative", "beautifully presented" Modern European fare is the draw at this "rustic" "little" East Villager whose "relaxed" vibe is matched with "friendly but leisurely" service; though meals can be "pricey", the $45 tasting menu is "one of the city's great hidden deals."

Kobe Club Ⓢ *Steak*
23 | 23 | 21 | $108

W 50s | 68 W. 58th St. (bet. 5th & 6th Aves.) | 212-644-5623 | www.kobeclubny.com

The 2,000 swords hanging overhead lend a "dominatrix-samurai" feel to Jeffrey Chodorow's "sexy" Midtown steakhouse that specializes in "amazing" Wagyu and Kobe beef; just be prepared to "spend your paycheck" on what some call a "gimmicky" experience.

Kodama ● *Japanese*
19 | 10 | 17 | $29

W 40s | 301 W. 45th St. (bet. 8th & 9th Aves.) | 212-582-8065

"Going to a show?" – grab some "decent" sushi first at this cheap, "no-frills" Theater District mainstay; it's "hardly luxurious" and often "crowded", but you "never know which actor may be sitting next to you."

	FOOD	DECOR	SERVICE	COST

Koi *Japanese*

24 | 23 | 18 | $65

W 40s | Bryant Park Hotel | 40 W. 40th St. (bet. 5th & 6th Aves.) | 212-921-3330 | www.koirestaurant.com

This "über-trendy" Midtown Japanese offers "creative" sushi and "delicious" fusion dishes in a "sleek", "sophisticated" setting; its "loud, youthful" crowd makes for "good people-watching", offsetting the "silly" prices and sometimes "indifferent" service.

Korea Palace 🖹 *Korean*

18 | 13 | 19 | $36

E 50s | 127 E. 54th St. (bet. Lexington & Park Aves.) | 212-832-2350 | www.koreapalace.com

Midtown office workers look to this "large", "reliable" Korean 'cue purveyor for "consistently" "solid" classics, plus sushi, delivered by a "courteous" crew; most find the "nondescript" digs easy to overlook while scarfing down the "bargain" lunch deal (three courses for $17.95).

Korhogo 126 Ⓜ *French*

▽ 23 | 19 | 18 | $41

Carroll Gardens | 126 Union St. (bet. Columbia & Hicks Sts.) | Brooklyn | 718-855-4405 | www.korhogo126.com

An infusion of West African dishes has enlivened the "delectable", midpriced French menu at this "rustic", "out-of-the-way" Carroll Gardens eatery; for a "romantic" repast, regulars repeatedly recommend the "charming" back garden.

Ko Sushi *Japanese*

20 | 15 | 19 | $32

E 70s | 1329 Second Ave. (70th St.) | 212-439-1678
E 80s | 1619 York Ave. (85th St.) | 212-772-8838

These separately owned UES Japanese "hangouts" are "always crowded" thanks to their "fresh", "honest" fare, low pricing and "attentive" staff; for those who don't like the "spare" digs, takeout is "prompt".

NEW Kouzan ❶ *Japanese*

▽ 20 | 23 | 21 | $35

W 90s | 685 Amsterdam Ave. (93rd St.) | 212-280-8099 | www.kouzanny.com

The "lush", "waterfall"-enhanced interior of this new UWS sushi "haven" distinguishes it from its "not-so-distant kouzan" Yuki a block away; a "soupçon of fusion" tastes all the better given the "friendly" service and "reasonable" prices.

Kuma Inn Ⓜ🖵 *Filipino/Thai*

24 | 13 | 19 | $35

LES | 113 Ludlow St., 2nd fl. (bet. Delancey & Rivington Sts.) | 212-353-8866 | www.kumainn.com

"Don't be put off by the stairwell entrance" of this second-floor LES "hideaway" – it's "worth seeking out" for its "refined" Filipino-Thai small-plate fare; the "friendly" vibe, "reasonable" prices and BYO policy make up for the tiny, no-frills digs.

Kum Gang San ❶ *Korean*

21 | 15 | 16 | $33

Garment District | 49 W. 32nd St. (bet. B'way & 5th Ave.) | 212-967-0909
Flushing | 138-28 Northern Blvd. (bet. Bowne & Union Sts.) | Queens | 718-461-0909
www.kumgangsan.net

These "bustling" 24-hour Koreans offer "tasty" BBQ and other classics; "fast-paced" service means meals may not be leisurely, but they're "lots of fun" thanks to "kitschy" decor elements.

	FOOD	DECOR	SERVICE	COST

Kuruma Zushi ⑤ *Japanese* — ▽ 28 | 15 | 23 | $129

E 40s | 7 E. 47th St., 2nd fl. (bet. 5th & Madison Aves.) | 212-317-2802
Follow "in-the-know Japanese businessmen" to this mezzanine Midtowner and you'll find sushi "heaven" with "exquisite" fish and service that's "beyond attentive"; regulars recommend "going omakase" – and when it's time to settle the check, just "pretend it's Monopoly money."

Kyotofu ●Ⓜ *Dessert/Japanese* — 21 | 20 | 20 | $28

W 40s | 705 Ninth Ave. (bet. 48th & 49th Sts.) | 212-974-6012 | www.kyotofu-nyc.com
"Who knew tofu could taste so good?" marvel foodies who fawn over this affordable Japanese Midtowner that "does amazing things with soy", especially in its "luscious" desserts; its sleek, "tight" space is "always full", but the "hip, happening" vibe overcomes all.

Kyo Ya ● *Japanese* — ▽ 29 | 24 | 26 | $100

E Village | 94 E. Seventh St., downstairs (1st Ave.) | 212-982-4140
Though most surveyors have yet to discover this "sophisticated" East Village Japanese kaiseki specialist, those who know it say it's "one of the best" for "wonderful" multicourse set meals served in "calm", wood-lined environs; "kimono-clad" servers ensure all feel "well-cared-for" here.

La Baraka *French* — 22 | 17 | 24 | $40

Little Neck | 255-09 Northern Blvd. (2 blocks e. of Little Neck Pkwy.) | Queens | 718-428-1461 | www.labarakarest.com
"Gracious" owners "make you feel like part of the family" at this "charming bit of France" in Little Neck, the "real deal" for "old-fashioned" Gallic standards; though the "throwback" decor is "a bit worn", the prices are also pleasingly retro – and the "hospitality makes up for all."

La Belle Vie *French* — 18 | 18 | 18 | $37

Chelsea | 184 Eighth Ave. (bet. 19th & 20th Sts.) | 212-929-4320
Considered a "pleasant neighborhood" fallback, this "cozy" Chelsea French bistro is ideal for "casual" everyday meals given its "relaxing" vibe, "reliable, fairly priced" fare and "warm" service; maybe it's "nothing to write home about", but it does boast "excellent people-watching" from the sidewalk seats.

La Bergamote *Bakery/French* — 24 | 13 | 15 | $14

Chelsea | 169 Ninth Ave. (20th St.) | 212-627-9010
NEW **W 50s** | 515 W. 52nd St. (bet. 10th & 11th Aves.) | 212-586-2429
A "treat every time", this Chelsea bakery/cafe's "splendidly tempting" pastries and other Gallic goods are "exquisite to the eye and the palate"; the "cramped" digs don't deter the faithful, ditto the "politely indifferent" service; N.B. the 52nd Street offshoot opened post-Survey.

La Boîte en Bois *French* — 21 | 15 | 20 | $51

W 60s | 75 W. 68th St. (bet. Columbus Ave. & CPW) | 212-874-2705 | www.laboitenyc.com
Among the city's "best-kept secrets", this "delightful" Lincoln Center-area "gem" plies "well-prepared", "old-fashioned" French fare ferried by a "spirited" staff; given the "pocket-size" digs you may "bump chairs with the next table" and it's not exactly cheap.

	FOOD	DECOR	SERVICE	COST

La Bonne Soupe *French*
`18` `13` `16` `$29`

W 50s | 48 W. 55th St. (bet. 5th & 6th Aves.) | 212-586-7650 |
www.labonnesoupe.com

An "old standby" that "doesn't let you down", this "quaint" Midtown
bistro is "reliable" for "top-notch onion soup" and a roster of "standard"
French fare that's "more diverse than the name" suggests; it's "quick"
and "affordable", but beware "brusque" service and "lackluster" decor.

La Bottega ● *Italian/Pizza*
`16` `20` `15` `$40`

Chelsea | Maritime Hotel | 88 Ninth Ave. (17th St.) | 212-243-8400 |
www.themaritimehotel.com

"If you can snag a table outside" on the "beautiful patio" when the
"weather's fine", this "sceney" Chelsea Italian is "the place to be"; most
"can forgive" the "slow" service and "just-ok" food at "high prices"
here given the "privilege of watching the trendy people" at play.

L'Absinthe *French*
`22` `22` `20` `$68`

E 60s | 227 E. 67th St. (bet. 2nd & 3rd Aves.) | 212-794-4950 |
www.labsinthe.com

Those "pining for Paris" head for this "classy", "old-style" UES brasserie
where the "belle epoque decor hits just the right note" and you're sure
to have a "memorable" meal; you'll feel you "could be in France" when
the check comes – but in this zip code "no one seems to mind."

La Cantina Toscana *Italian*
`24` `15` `21` `$55`

E 60s | 1109 First Ave. (bet. 60th & 61st Sts.) | 212-754-5454

The nearby Queensboro Bridge may start to look like "the hills of
Tuscany" after you've sampled the "amazingly authentic" game dishes
and "fresh pastas" at this "underappreciated" UES trattoria; its "tiny"
digs and "splurge"-size tabs are offset by the "personable" owner.

Lady Mendl's *American*
`▽` `22` `26` `24` `$46`

Gramercy | Inn at Irving Pl. | 56 Irving Pl. (bet. 17th & 18th Sts.) |
212-533-4466 | www.ladymendls.com

It feels like "being transported to an Edith Wharton novel" at this
Gramercy Park tea parlor where "classy" Victorian rooms host "women
of all ages" enjoying "proper cucumber sandwiches" and other New
American bites served by a "wonderful" staff; sure, such ladylike "elegance" is "expensive", but it's hard to top for a "shower" or "afternoon with your daughter."

La Esquina ● *Mexican*
`22` `20` `17` `$43`

Little Italy | 106 Kenmare St. (bet. Cleveland Pl. & Lafayette St.) |
646-613-7100 | www.esquinanyc.com

A "secret-society attitude" and "snooty" bouncer set the tone for the
"speakeasy-style" brasserie/tequila bar downstairs at this Little Italy
Mexican; to "avoid the scene", try the "amazing" take-out taqueria for
"*guapos*" tacos or the "chilled-out" cafe for "tasty", "simple" fare.

La Flor Bakery & Cafe ⊅ *Bakery*
`24` `15` `18` `$24`

Woodside | 53-02 Roosevelt Ave. (53rd St.) | Queens | 718-426-8023

The Mexican chef-owner "brings his homeland to life" through an
eclectic mix of "scrumptious" savories and sweets at this cheap, cash-
only bakery/cafe tucked under the 7 el in Woodside; expect a wait
since it's "too small" and service can be "flaky."

	FOOD	DECOR	SERVICE	COST

La Focaccia ◐ *Italian*
▽ 20 | 18 | 20 | $40

W Village | 51 Bank St. (W. 4th St.) | 212-675-3754

A "sweet corner" on a "beautiful" Village block is home to this "friendly", "often crowded" "favorite" whose "consistent", "hearty" Italian fare (including its "worthy" namesake) "won't break the bank"; tables are "very close together" but it's "romantic" nonetheless.

La Giara *Italian*
19 | 16 | 19 | $37

Murray Hill | 501 Third Ave. (bet. 33rd & 34th Sts.) | 212-726-9855 | www.lagiara.com

On a "strip of unexciting choices" in Murray Hill, this "dependable" Italian stands out with its "authentic" eats at "gentle" prices (including a $19.95 early-bird deal); it's "not much" to look at, but "cheerful" staffers engender a "warm", "relaxed" vibe.

La Gioconda *Italian*
20 | 14 | 20 | $42

E 50s | 226 E. 53rd St. (bet. 2nd & 3rd Aves.) | 212-371-3536 | www.lagiocondany.com

This "quaint" Turtle Bay "hideaway" offers "solid", "home"-style Italian fare at "reasonable" prices, albeit in "cramped" digs that "leave something to be desired"; still, the "friendly" service "never disappoints."

La Goulue ◐ *French*
20 | 19 | 18 | $64

E 60s | 746 Madison Ave. (bet. 64th & 65th Sts.) | 212-988-8169 | www.lagoulrestaurant.com

"Air kisses rule" at this "frenetic", "oh-so-*prétentieux*" UES French bistro where "pearl necklaces" vie with "trendy Eurotrash duds" for the best "real estate", i.e. sidewalk tables for "watching trophy wives walk by"; service can be "haughty" and the food may be "overpriced", but the Gallic standards are reliably "tasty."

☑ La Grenouille 🅢🅜 *French*
27 | 27 | 27 | $104

E 50s | 3 E. 52nd St. (bet. 5th & Madison Aves.) | 212-752-1495 | www.la-grenouille.com

The "second-best thing the French ever gave NYC" is this Midtown "archetype of fine dining", considered the "last" of the city's "great cathedrals of French food"; its "rich", "classic" cuisine "takes you to another plane of consciousness" but also "takes a bite out of your pocket", so make sure to "soak in" the "breathtaking" "flower-filled" room and the staff's "gracious hospitality"; N.B. jackets required.

La Grolla *Italian*
19 | 13 | 18 | $44

W 70s | 413 Amsterdam Ave. (bet. 79th & 80th Sts.) | 212-496-0890 | www.lagrolla.us

This "shoebox-size" Upper Westsider turns out "hearty", "value"-priced specialties from Italy's Valle d'Aosta region; despite the "tight", "uninspired" surroundings, the neighborhood "sorely needs more like this" "unpretentious", "family-friendly" standby.

La Houppa *Italian*
▽ 18 | 18 | 19 | $57

E 60s | 26 E. 64th St. (bet. 5th & Madison Aves.) | 212-317-1999

Relatively "unpublicized", this UES "neighborhood secret" comes as a "pleasant surprise" given its "authentic" Northern Italian fare, "lovely art deco interior" and general "lack of snootiness"; P.S. the "romantic" back garden may help hopeful suitors "close the deal."

| | FOOD | DECOR | SERVICE | COST |

Lake Club *Continental/Seafood* ▽ 22 | 25 | 21 | $47

Staten Island | 1150 Clove Rd. (Victory Blvd.) | 718-442-3600 |
www.lake-club.com

The "superb view" of Clove Lake makes this Continental "lodge"
"one of Staten Island's most beautiful settings"; the seafood-focused
fare is "top notch" with "service to match", and the "cozy yet elegant"
atmosphere is ideal for a "first date", though not surprisingly it's "on
the pricey side" – at least by SI standards.

La Lanterna di Vittorio ● *Italian* 19 | 22 | 17 | $27

G Village | 129 MacDougal St. (bet. W. 3rd & 4th Sts.) | 212-529-5945 |
www.lalanternacaffe.com

You feel you've been "whisked away from the hustle and bustle" at this
"cozy" Village Italian supplying "quality" pizzas, pastas and desserts
that don't "break the bank"; "working fireplaces", a "tranquil" enclosed garden and "cool" live jazz add up to the "perfect date place."

La Lunchonette *French* 21 | 15 | 20 | $43

Chelsea | 130 10th Ave. (18th St.) | 212-675-0342

A "throwback" to when West Chelsea was on the "down and out" side,
this bistro "oasis" offers "honest" French "down-home" cooking at
"reasonable" rates; its "unfailing" friendliness keeps its "bohemian"
regulars coming, even if the "nothing-fussy" digs "perhaps take
shabby-chic too far."

La Mangeoire *French* 19 | 18 | 20 | $47

E 50s | 1008 Second Ave. (bet. 53rd & 54th Sts.) | 212-759-7086 |
www.lamangeoire.com

Regulars have "gone for decades" but "first-timers" also "feel like
family" at this "French country farmhouse"–like East Midtown
"neighborhood standby"; besides its "unpretentious" bistro fare, the
"soothing" space with fresh flowers and Provençal paintings contrib-
ute to the "homey" experience.

La Masseria ● *Italian* 22 | 19 | 22 | $55

W 40s | 235 W. 48th St. (bet. B'way & 8th Ave.) | 212-582-2111 |
www.lamasserianyc.com

"Artfully prepared" food "without pretension" is the forte of this "bustling" Theater District Southern Italian whose relatively "roomy" space
has a "pleasant" "pastoral" look; it's "expensive", but at least you can
count on the "unassuming" staff to "get you to your show on time."

La Mediterranée *French* 19 | 16 | 19 | $48

E 50s | 947 Second Ave. (bet. 50th & 51st Sts.) | 212-755-4155 |
www.lamediterraneeny.com

A "throwback to the way French restaurants used to be", this Midtown
Provençal is an "unassuming", "affordable" choice for "solid" cooking
delivered by a "welcoming" crew; a pianist's "tuneful music" ups the
"romance" quotient (Thursday–Saturday nights).

La Mela ● *Italian* 19 | 12 | 17 | $38

Little Italy | 167 Mulberry St. (bet. Broome & Grand Sts.) | 212-431-9493 |
www.lamelarestaurant.com

Best for "big, boisterous" groups, this Little Italy mainstay dishes up
"heaps" of "nonna's Sunday" Southern Italiana served "family-style";

maybe it's a little "touristy and gaudy", but never mind – it's also "affordable and unpretentious."

La Mirabelle *French*
| 22 | 17 | 23 | $50 |

W 80s | 102 W. 86th St. (bet. Amsterdam & Columbus Aves.) | 212-496-0458
"Run by a family that only wants to see you happily fed", this "delightful" UWS bistro suits diners who "still like a tablecloth and civility" to go with their "scrumptious" "old-French" fare; "blissfully not trendy", it boasts prices that satisfy the "regulars who span three generations."

Lan *Japanese*
| ▽ 25 | 19 | 23 | $53 |

E Village | 56 Third Ave. (bet. 10th & 11th Sts.) | 212-254-1959 | www.lan-nyc.com
A "sleeper on the sushi scene", this "feels-like-Tokyo" East Village Japanese also specializes in "excellent cooked dishes" like sukiyaki and shabu-shabu, backed by a list of artisanal sakes; its "hipster" expat clientele touts the "friendly" service and "serene" vibe, if not the "pricey" checks at meal's end.

Land *Thai*
| 22 | 17 | 18 | $27 |

E 80s | 1565 Second Ave. (bet. 81st & 82nd Sts.) | 212-439-1847
W 80s | 450 Amsterdam Ave. (bet. 81st & 82nd Sts.) | 212-501-8121
www.landthaikitchen.com
You can "expect a wait" at this Crosstown Thai twosome, but "it's worth it" according to admirers who "squeeze in like sardines" for "creative", "spicy" dishes that "make you sweat with joy"; "speedy" service and "cool", "mod" digs are enticements, but it's "bargain prices" that seal the deal.

L & B Spumoni Gardens *Dessert/Pizza*
| 23 | 10 | 15 | $22 |

Bensonhurst | 2725 86th St. (bet. 10th & 11th Sts.) | Brooklyn | 718-449-6921 | www.spumonigardens.com
The "ethereally light" Sicilian squares and "creamy" spumoni inspire hyperbole ("the best ever!") at this Bensonhurst "staple" that has a certain *Saturday Night Fever* vibe though it opened when FDR was in office; "get here early" 'cause "tables inside and out fill up fast."

Landmarc ● *French*
| 20 | 19 | 19 | $48 |

TriBeCa | 179 W. Broadway (bet. Leonard & Worth Sts.) | 212-343-3883
W 60s | Time Warner Ctr. | 10 Columbus Circle, 3rd fl. (60th St. at B'way) | 212-823-6123
www.landmarc-restaurant.com
You "can't go wrong" at Marc Murphy's "bustling" TriBeCa-Time Warner Center "favorites" that pack 'em in with "dependable", "something-for-everyone" French bistro cooking and a "broad", "low-priced" wine list; however, their serious "popularity" and "no-reservations" policy often spell "long waits" and "noisy" crowds.

Landmark Tavern *American/Irish*
| 17 | 18 | 18 | $36 |

W 40s | 626 11th Ave. (46th St.) | 212-247-2562 | www.thelandmarktavern.org
A "vestige of time gone by", this circa-1868 Hell's Kitchen tavern offers Irish-American pub fare that's "only slightly more updated" than the "old NY" digs (and that's a good thing); it's worth a visit for the "history" alone, but it's also an "atmospheric" party venue whose scotch list that "goes on for miles" provides another reason to trek west.

	FOOD	DECOR	SERVICE	COST

La Paella *Spanish*
| | 19 | 16 | 16 | $35 |

E Village | 214 E. Ninth St. (bet. 2nd & 3rd Aves.) | 212-598-4321 | www.lapaellanyc.com

"Crowds", "noise" and so-so service notwithstanding, romeos rate this East Village Spaniard "perfect" for an "intimate date"; its "solid" tapas also work well for "groups" – and by day, the "lunch deal" ($12.99 for three courses) packs plenty of "bang for the buck."

La Palapa ● *Mexican*
| | 19 | 16 | 18 | $34 |

E Village | 77 St. Marks Pl. (bet. 1st & 2nd Aves.) | 212-777-2537
G Village | 359 Sixth Ave. (bet. Washington Pl. & W. 4th St.) | 212-243-6870
www.lapalapa.com

Margaritas that "rock your world" get soaked up with "tasty" (if "predictable") Mexican fare at this cross-Village duo; the "lively" vibe and "hospitable" service make it the kind of "neighborhood place" where locals "just walk in and chill."

La Petite Auberge *French*
| | 19 | 15 | 21 | $47 |

Gramercy | 116 Lexington Ave. (bet. 27th & 28th Sts.) | 212-689-5003 | www.lapetiteaubergeny.com

Meant to evoke an eatery in one of "Brittany's villages", this "quaint" "fixed-in-time" Gramercy French keeps cranking out "reliably appealing" bistro classics; sure, "it could use sprucing up", but "who cares?" – it's mercifully "without the attitude" of its "too-cool" competitors.

La Pizza Fresca Ristorante *Italian*
| | 22 | 16 | 17 | $39 |

Flatiron | 31 E. 20th St. (bet. B'way & Park Ave. S.) | 212-598-0141 | www.lapizzafrescaristorante.com

A "fantastic little find", this Flatiron Italian proffers "surprisingly good" "brick-oven" pizzas and other "straight-off-the-boat" staples, but it's best known for its "impressive" wines; "service can be a bit slow" but at least the staff's "friendly."

La Ripaille *French*
| | ∇ 23 | 20 | 21 | $48 |

W Village | 605 Hudson St. (bet. Bethune & W. 12th Sts.) | 212-255-4406 | www.laripailleny.com

The owner "really goes out of his way to make you feel welcome" at this "old warhorse" that's the "very definition" of a "warm", "cozy" "Village bistro"; with "honest French cooking" considered "worth every penny", it's a cherished "neighborhood" "standby."

La Rivista ●⊠ *Italian*
| | 21 | 17 | 20 | $47 |

W 40s | 313 W. 46th St. (bet. 8th & 9th Aves.) | 212-245-1707

A "longtime" player on the "pre-theater" scene, this "tiny" Restaurant Row "staple" delivers "solid" Italian cooking via a staff bent on "getting you out on time"; the interior "could use updating", but most don't quibble given the "fair" prices and "bargain validated parking."

NEW La Rural ● *Argentinean*
| | ∇ 22 | 18 | 19 | $39 |

W 90s | 768 Amsterdam Ave. (bet. 97th & 98th Sts.) | 212-749-2929

"Fabulous beef at reasonable prices" endears the locals to this "informal", "bustling" new UWS Argentinean in the "tastefully" redone former Pampa space; given its "perfectly done" grill standards and "delicious Malbecs to go with them", it's appealing to "serious carnivores."

	FOOD	DECOR	SERVICE	COST

Las Ramblas ◗ *Spanish* — 24 | 16 | 21 | $38

G Village | 170 W. Fourth St. (bet. Cornelia & Jones Sts.) | 646-415-7924 | www.lasramblasnyc.com

Eat like a "thrifty Barcelonan" at this Village "virtual trip to Spain" where "fantastic", "perfectly priced" tapas and "attentive" service make "cramped quarters" easy to overlook; however, now that "everyone's found" this "neighborhood secret", prepare for a "wait."

La Taqueria *Mexican* — 20 | 12 | 15 | $16

Park Slope | 72 Seventh Ave. (bet. Berkeley & Lincoln Pls.) | Brooklyn | 718-398-4300

Rachel's Taqueria *Mexican*

Park Slope | 408 Fifth Ave. (bet. 7th & 8th Sts.) | Brooklyn | 718-788-1137

"Nothing like an actual Cali-style burrito" enthuse amigos of these laid-back, low-budget Park Slope taquerias where the flavors are "authentic" and the "no-frills" decor is vintage "Grateful Dead"; the cafe at the Seventh Avenue original was redone post-Survey and now features a snazzy bar and a more sophisticated menu.

La Taza de Oro 🗷🗷 *Diner* — 18 | 6 | 17 | $16

Chelsea | 96 Eighth Ave. (bet. 14th & 15th Sts.) | 212-243-9946

Definitely "it's a dive", but this coffee shop is a "true Chelsea original" dishing up "cheap", "satisfying", "down-home" Puerto Rican eats in "easy" environs; a "charming survivor" in an evolving area, this bargain "slice of old New York" "has been around" for 50-plus years for lots of good reasons.

🗷 L'Atelier de Joël Robuchon *French* — 28 | 25 | 26 | $127

E 50s | Four Seasons Hotel | 57 E. 57th St. (bet. Madison & Park Aves.) | 212-350-6658 | www.fourseasons.com

"Exquisite in every way", "genius" chef Joël Robuchon's "stunning" Japanese-influenced Midtown French outpost offers "sublime", "almost-too-beautiful-to-eat" small plates that achieve "absolute purity of flavor"; sit at the "sushi bar"–style counter and "watch the chefs at work" while being attended to by a "pleasant" pro staff – but "be prepared to mortgage your apartment" because "perfection doesn't come cheap."

Lattanzi ◗🗷 *Italian* — 22 | 19 | 21 | $55

W 40s | 361 W. 46th St. (bet. 8th & 9th Aves.) | 212-315-0980 | www.lattanzinyc.com

This "perennial" Theater District pick is "reliable" for "pricey", "*magnifico*" Italian fare "attentively" served in "warm" environs; it gets "even better" post-curtain, when "authentic" Roman-Jewish specialties (e.g. "amazing fried artichokes") are offered and seats in the "beautiful" garden are easier to snag.

Lavagna *Italian* — 25 | 19 | 21 | $43

E Village | 545 E. Fifth St. (bet. Aves. A & B) | 212-979-1005 | www.lavagnanyc.com

"Quaint and cozy", this Alphabet City "gem" is "always crowded" with regulars drawn to its "wonderfully prepared" Italian fare and "little-known, low-priced" wines; its "amiable" service and "romantic" vibe mean it's "perfect" for a "rendezvous with someone special."

	FOOD	DECOR	SERVICE	COST

La Vela *Italian*   18 | 14 | 19 | $36

W 70s | 373 Amsterdam Ave. (bet. 77th & 78th Sts.) | 212-877-7818
"So comfortable you could go in your PJs", this "affordable", "welcoming" UWS Tuscan is a longtime "locals' favorite" thanks to its "solid" basics dispensed in "cheerful" environs; it strikes some as "run-of-the-mill", but for most it's a "homey" "favorite" to "revisit often."

La Villa Pizzeria *Italian*   21 | 15 | 18 | $28

Mill Basin | Key Food Shopping Ctr. | 6610 Ave. U (bet. 66th & 67th Sts.) | Brooklyn | 718-251-8030
Park Slope | 261 Fifth Ave. (bet. 1st St. & Garfield Pl.) | Brooklyn | 718-499-9888 | www.lavillaparkslope.com
Howard Bch | Lindenwood Shopping Ctr. | 82-07 153rd Ave. (82nd St.) | Queens | 718-641-8259
"Divine" "wood-oven" pizza is the thing at this "always-buzzing", "family"-oriented Italian trio, though really there's "no wrong choice" on its "huge menu" of "red-sauce" basics; "generic" decor and prices slightly "high" "for what you get" don't deter the "crowds."

Z Le Bernardin ⑤ *French/Seafood*   28 | 27 | 27 | $139

W 50s | 155 W. 51st St. (bet. 6th & 7th Aves.) | 212-554-1515 | www.le-bernardin.com
"Absolute master" chef Eric Ripert continues to "dazzle the senses" with "final meal"–worthy "piscatorial revelations" at Maguy LeCoze's "matchless" Midtown French "seafood mecca"; "telepathic" service in an "elegant", "understated" setting are reasons why it's "worth dressing up" for (jackets required) and "fishing out your wallet" to settle the whale of a tab; P.S. the $64 prix fixe lunch is a "relative bargain."

Le Bilboquet *French*   22 | 15 | 16 | $60

E 60s | 25 E. 63rd St. (bet. Madison & Park Aves.) | 212-751-3036
It's "tough getting into" this "noisy" "little" bistro where the "authentic" French standards take a backseat to the "flashy, trashy" Euro scene; "expensive" prices and "snobby" service aside, it's just about "the best time you can have on the East Side."

Le Boeuf à la Mode *French*   22 | 20 | 22 | $58

E 80s | 539 E. 81st St. (bet. East End & York Aves.) | 212-249-1473
Things "haven't changed in years – and shouldn't" say loyalists who value this "comfortable" Yorkville classic's "retro" French bistro fare despite its up-to-date prices; its "over-50" crowd also appreciates the "attentive" service and sees "old-world charm" in the somewhat "dated" interior.

Z Le Cirque ⑤ *French*   24 | 25 | 24 | $99

E 50s | One Beacon Court | 151 E. 58th St. (bet. Lexington & 3rd Aves.) | 212-644-0202 | www.lecirque.com
"There's always a show" at "consummate ringmaster" Sirio Maccioni's "fabled" Midtowner, where the "refined" French cuisine and "impeccable" service are the "epitome of NY swank", bested only by the "stunning" "big-top" decor and caravan of "vintage rich-and-famous" faces; just remember to "dress up" (jackets required) and prepare to "pay dearly" (though the $28 prix fixe lunch is a "steal"); P.S. for "less-expensive" tabs "without pomp" try the new adjacent wine-and-tapas lounge that's run by Sirio's talented sons.

L'Ecole ☒ *French*

| 25 | 20 | 23 | $52 |

SoHo | French Culinary Institute | 462 Broadway (Grand St.) | 212-219-3300 | www.frenchculinary.com

"The students try hard to impress" and "it shows" at the French Culinary Institute's SoHo "training ground" for "aspiring chefs"; "earnest service" and "amazing" seasonal prix fixe meals at "bargain" rates make it more than worth "being a test case" – go before they "graduate and charge you double."

Le Colonial *French/Vietnamese*

| 19 | 21 | 18 | $54 |

E 50s | 149 E. 57th St. (bet. Lexington & 3rd Aves.) | 212-752-0808 | www.lecolonialnyc.com

"Step back" into 1920s Saigon at this "exotic" French-Vietnamese Eastsider where the "atmospheric" tropical decor is replete with "fans and flora"; some say the "well-prepared" portions "could be bigger" given the "high prices", but then there's always the "sultry" upstairs bar for a "romantic" drink.

Le Gamin *French*

| 19 | 15 | 16 | $26 |

E Village | 536 E. Fifth St. (bet. Aves. A & B) | 212-529-8933 ◗
G Village | 132 W. Houston St. (bet. MacDougal & Sullivan Sts.) | 212-475-1543 ☞
Prospect Heights | 556 Vanderbilt Ave. (bet. Bergen & Dean Sts.) | Brooklyn | 718-789-5171
www.legamin.com

Francophiles in Manhattan and Brooklyn find that the "simple but tasty" bistro fare ("love the crêpes") at this "laid-back" chainlet "takes them to Paris" without the airfare; everything is "authentic" down to "less-than-attentive" service, but it sure is a "bargain."

Le Gigot Ⓜ *French*

| 24 | 18 | 23 | $54 |

G Village | 18 Cornelia St. (bet. Bleecker & W. 4th Sts.) | 212-627-3737 | www.legigotrestaurant.com

The "superb" Provençal cooking is a "labor of love" at this "tiny", "*charmant*" Village bistro where "knowledgeable", "attentive" service helps make the "cute" but "tight" quarters "acceptable"; prices may be "a little high", but to most the "special experiences" here are certainly "worth it."

Le Grainne Cafe ◗ *French*

| ▽ 19 | 15 | 13 | $26 |

Chelsea | 183 Ninth Ave. (21st St.) | 646-486-3000 | www.legrainnecafe.com

"Café au lait in large bowls", "delicious" crêpes and such and a "just-like-Paris" feel make this Chelsea French cafe a "regular meeting spot" for the "local intelligentsia"; the "value" pricing is another reason it stays "crowded", but those "in a hurry" beware: service is "s-l-o-w."

Le Jardin Bistro *French*

| 19 | 17 | 18 | $43 |

NoLita | 25 Cleveland Pl. (bet. Kenmare & Spring Sts.) | 212-343-9599 | www.lejardinbistro.com

"Sitting under the lush grape arbor" is a "perennial treat" at this "intimate" NoLita bistro boasting a "delightful", "trellised" back garden; "decent" French classics and "friendly" service are year-round draws, with "reasonable prices" sealing its status as "quite a find."

Le Marais *French/Steak* | 20 | 15 | 16 | $52 |

W 40s | 150 W. 46th St. (bet. 6th & 7th Aves.) | 212-869-0900 |
www.lemarais.net
"The place for kosher" in the Theater District, this "no-frills" French
steakhouse is "reliable" for prime, "pricey" beef; it gets "cramped and
noisy", and service really "isn't its thing", but then you can always get
your cuts to go at the "attached butcher shop."

Lemongrass Grill *Thai* | 16 | 12 | 15 | $24 |

Financial District | 84 William St. (Maiden Ln.) | 212-809-8038
Murray Hill | 138 E. 34th St. (bet. Lexington & 3rd Aves.) | 212-213-3317
W 90s | 2534 Broadway (bet. 94th & 95th Sts.) | 212-666-0888
Cobble Hill | 156 Court St. (bet. Dean & Pacific Sts.) | Brooklyn | 718-522-9728
Park Slope | 61A Seventh Ave. (bet. Berkeley & Lincoln Pls.) | Brooklyn |
718-399-7100
www.lemongrassgrill.org
It's "nothing fancy", but this "standard" Thai chain "satisfies" all the
same with "fast, reliable" meals on the "cheap"; the interiors mostly
"could use an update", so some opt for "speedy delivery" – "by the
time you've hung up, they're at your door."

Lenny's *Sandwiches* | 18 | 7 | 14 | $14 |

E 50s | 1024 Second Ave. (54th St.) | 212-355-5700
E 60s | 1269 First Ave. (68th St.) | 212-288-0852
E 70s | 1481 Second Ave. (77th St.) | 212-288-5288
Financial District | 108 John St. (bet. Cliff & Pearl Sts.) | 212-385-2828
Flatiron | 16 W. 23rd St. (5th Ave.) | 212-462-4433
G Village | 418 Sixth Ave. (9th St.) | 212-353-0300
W 40s | 60 W. 48th St. (bet. 5th & 6th Aves.) | 212-997-1969
W 40s | 613 Ninth Ave. (43rd St.) | 212-957-7800
W 70s | 302 Columbus Ave. (74th St.) | 212-580-8300
W 80s | 489 Columbus Ave. (84th St.) | 212-787-9368
www.lennysnyc.com
Additional locations throughout the NY area
"Fresh" "deli-style" sandwiches with "countless toppings" for not a lot
of bread – "what's not to like?" muse groupies of this "lunchtime staple" chain; its "bare-bones" setups can be "uninviting", but "road-
runner" service means you won't linger long.

Leo's Latticini Ⓜ *Deli/Italian* | ▽ 25 | 12 | 21 | $14 |
(aka Mama's of Corona)

Corona | 46-02 104th St. (46th Ave.) | Queens | 718-898-6069
This third-generation "family-run" Italian deli remains a "wonderful" Corona landmark for "unbelievable" heros featuring the "best"
"housemade mozz"; incredibly "cheap" prices for mega-meals and
famously "friendly" service are other "high points" – as for decor,
delis aren't supposed to have much.

Le Pain Quotidien *Bakery/Belgian* | 18 | 15 | 13 | $23 |

E 60s | 833 Lexington Ave. (bet. 63rd & 64th Sts.) | 212-755-5810
E 70s | 252 E. 77th St. (bet. 2nd & 3rd Aves.) | 212-249-8600
E 80s | 1131 Madison Ave. (bet. 84th & 85th Sts.) | 212-327-4900
Flatiron | ABC Carpet & Home | 38 E. 19th St. (bet. B'way & Park Ave. S.) |
212-673-7900
G Village | 10 Fifth Ave. (8th St.) | 212-253-2324
G Village | 801 Broadway (11th St.) | 212-677-5277

(continued)

Le Pain Quotidien

SoHo | 100 Grand St. (bet. Greene & Mercer Sts.) | 212-625-9009
W 50s | 922 Seventh Ave. (58th St.) | 212-757-0775
W 60s | 60 W. 65th St. (bet. B'way & CPW) | 212-721-4001
W 70s | 50 W. 72nd St. (bet. Columbus Ave. & CPW) | 212-712-9700
www.painquotidien.com
Additional locations throughout the NY area

"Fantastique" "European-style" breads, sandwiches and other "wholesome", "largely organic" "light bites" keep this Belgian bakery/cafe chain "bustling and noisy"; the "rustic" interiors outfitted with "wooden communal tables" and "slow", "spacey" service rate a bit less well.

⚡ Le Perigord *French*

| 24 | 20 | 24 | $79 |

E 50s | 405 E. 52nd St. (bet. FDR Dr. & 1st Ave.) | 212-755-6244 | www.leperigord.com

"Old-world" French fine dining is "alive and well" at this "elegant" Sutton Place "grande dame", where "one-of-a-kind" owner Georges Briguet oversees the "traditional haute French" meals featuring "expertly prepared" cuisine and "gracious" tuxedoed service in a "comfortably luxurious" room; loyalists look past the "high prices" and "dated" decor, declaring this "golden oldie" is "still a goodie."

Le Petit Marché *French*

| 22 | 19 | 20 | $44 |

Brooklyn Heights | 46 Henry St. (bet. Cranberry & Middagh Sts.) | Brooklyn | 718-858-9605 | www.bkbistro.com

This "cozy" bistro brings "a bit of France" to Brooklyn Heights with its "crowd-pleasing" Gallic fare and "softly lit", "romantic" milieu; though it gets "a bit cramped", the "good value" and staffers who "sincerely seem to care" make meals here a "genuine delight" all the same.

Le Refuge *French*

| 20 | 19 | 20 | $58 |

E 80s | 166 E. 82nd St. (bet. Lexington & 3rd Aves.) | 212-861-4505 | www.lerefugenyc.com

"You don't have to cross the pond" to "feel like you're in France" thanks to this "time-tested" UES bistro serving "delicious" "provincial" French fare in a "relaxed" "country-house" setting, complete with "pleasant" garden; "charming" service enhances the "old-world" feel, but prices are strictly "up to date."

Le Refuge Inn Ⓜ⊄ *French*

| ∇ 24 | 24 | 23 | $54 |

Bronx | Le Refuge Inn | 586 City Island Ave. (bet. Beach & Cross Sts.) | 718-885-2478 | www.lerefugeinn.com

For "romantic" dining in a "historic" waterside Victorian inn, check out this City Island "charmer"; its "fine French cuisine", "welcoming" service and "beautiful", "country" decor come with a big bonus – the chance to "spend the night" upstairs or make it into a "weekend getaway."

Le Rivage *French*

| 20 | 16 | 20 | $43 |

W 40s | 340 W. 46th St. (bet. 8th & 9th Aves.) | 212-765-7374 | www.lerivagenyc.com

A "longtime favorite" of theatergoers, this "old-line" Restaurant Row Gallic has fans who tolerate its "cramped", "dated" digs in exchange for "reliable", "value"-oriented bistro fare; the meal can feel "rushed", but it's pretty much "guaranteed you'll make your curtain."

	FOOD	DECOR	SERVICE	COST

Les Enfants Terribles ● *African/French*
▽ | 17 | 16 | 16 | $35

LES | 37 Canal St. (Ludlow St.) | 212-777-7518 |
www.lesenfantsterriblesnyc.com

When on the LES, consider this "dark", "funky" standby for its "slightly exotic" "mix of African and French" flavors affordably priced and delivered by a "friendly" staff; "loud (but good) music" and a "sexy" vibe turn the scene "into a party" in later hours.

Les Halles ● *French*
19 | 16 | 16 | $45

Financial District | 15 John St. (bet. B'way & Nassau St.) | 212-285-8585
Gramercy | 411 Park Ave. S. (bet. 28th & 29th Sts.) | 212-679-4111
www.leshalles.net

No, "superstar" chef Anthony Bourdain "doesn't actually cook here" anymore, but these "lively" French bistros' "fantastic" steak frites and "authentic" vibe keep the "crowds" coming; you "may need to shout" over the din, but it's "as Parisian as you can get" without using euros.

Le Singe Vert ● *French*
18 | 16 | 16 | $41

Chelsea | 160 Seventh Ave. (bet. 19th & 20th Sts.) | 212-366-4100 |
www.lesingevert.com

"Close your eyes" and "you're on the Left Bank" at this "*très French*" Chelsea bistro dispensing "decent" classics with "authentic" flair; "crowded", "noisy" quarters are "all part of the experience", though you can "escape" to the sidewalk tables in warm weather.

Levana *Mediterranean*
▽ | 20 | 15 | 21 | $60

W 60s | 141 W. 69th St. (bet. B'way & Columbus Ave.) | 212-877-8457 |
www.levana.com

An "oasis for the orthodox", this Lincoln Center–area Mediterranean is known for its "sophisticated" glatt kosher cooking, including some "interesting items like venison"; "A+ service" takes the sting out of "pricey" tabs and "relic-of-the-'80s" decor.

Le Veau d'Or ⊠ *French*
18 | 12 | 19 | $58

E 60s | 129 E. 60th St. (bet. Lexington & Park Aves.) | 212-838-8133

Harking back to the "good old days" of French dining, this East Side bistro dating from the '30s "still carries the flag" with "supremely tasty" "classic" cuisine and "personable" service; yes, its "frozen-in-time" decor "needs sprucing up", but to most it's "entirely lovable" all the same.

Lever House ⊠ *American*
22 | 22 | 22 | $79

E 50s | 390 Park Ave. (enter on 53rd St., bet. Madison & Park Aves.) |
212-888-2700 | www.leverhouse.com

Longtime chef Dan Silverman has left, but the "see-and-be-seen" scene carries on at this Midtown New American magnet for "media industry mavens" and other "suits"; perhaps its "iconic" "space-age" decor ("like eating on a 747") and "loud" acoustics are better for "business conversation" than "romance" , but whatever the occasion the "food and service are outstanding."

L'Express ● *French*
17 | 14 | 14 | $32

Flatiron | 249 Park Ave. S. (20th St.) | 212-254-5858 |
www.lexpressnyc.com

"Crowded" "around the clock", this "casual-chic" Flatiron "standby" serves its "cheap", "dependable" French bistro standards 24/7; it's

	FOOD	DECOR	SERVICE	COST

"cramped" and "noisy" and service can be "lacking", but for a "quick croque monsieur" or the like "at 3 AM", you "can't beat it."

Le Zie 2000 ● *Italian*

| 21 | 14 | 18 | $40 |

Chelsea | 172 Seventh Ave. (bet. 20th & 21st Sts.) | 212-206-8686 | www.lezie.com

Packed "wall-to-wall" every night, this Chelsea "favorite" has neighbors dropping by regularly for "delectable", "affordable" Venetian dishes served by "friendly folks"; though often "noisy", it's a "pleasant, low-key" kind of place, especially if you "snag a table" in the back room.

Liberty View *Chinese*

| ∇ 19 | 14 | 15 | $28 |

Financial District | 21 South End Ave. (bet. 3rd Pl. & W. Thames St.) | 212-786-1888

Aptly named for its "fabulous views" of the Statue of Liberty, this Battery Park City Chinese is a "decent" choice in a restaurant-challenged zone; even if the service and decor are "mediocre", its low prices and "amazing" outdoor seating alone make it worth considering.

Libretto's Pizza *Italian*

| ∇ 21 | 10 | 16 | $18 |

Murray Hill | 546 Third Ave. (36th St.) | 212-213-6445 | www.librettospizzeria.com

They "know how to make pizza" (including "rare" whole wheat-crusted varieties) at this "low-key" Murray Hill Italian that also plies "delicious" pastas at "reasonable" rates; neighbors also tout the lunch specials and "pleasant" service.

Liebman's *Deli*

| 20 | 9 | 15 | $20 |

Bronx | 552 W. 235th St. (Johnson Ave.) | 718-548-4534 | www.liebmansdeli.com

"All the ingredients of yesteryear" are heaped high on "mouthwatering" sandwiches at this "good ol' Jewish deli" (circa 1953) in the Bronx; sure, service is "surly" and the digs "need a face-lift", but that's the way kosher delis are supposed to be.

Lil' Frankie's Pizza ●⇗ *Pizza*

| 22 | 16 | 16 | $28 |

E Village | 19-21 First Ave. (bet. 1st & 2nd Sts.) | 212-420-4900 | www.lilfrankies.com

This East Village Italian "little brother" to Frank "gets very crowded" thanks to its "fabulous" pizzas and pastas for "cheap"; its "dark" decor is so "cozy" it feels almost "like eating at home" – though "long waits", "cramped" seating and "slapdash" service can dispel the mood.

Lima's Taste ● *Peruvian*

| ∇ 21 | 13 | 14 | $36 |

W Village | 122 Christopher St. (Bedford St.) | 212-242-0010 | www.limastaste.com

"Outstanding" ceviche and grilled meats are among the *muy auténtico* "must-tries" at this West Village Peruvian, which also mixes an "incredible" Pisco sour; "moderate" prices make up for "spotty" service – and anyway it's easy to "flag down your waiter" given its "small" digs.

Lisca *Italian*

| 19 | 15 | 20 | $41 |

W 90s | 660 Amsterdam Ave. (bet. 92nd & 93rd Sts.) | 212-799-3987 | www.liscanyc.com

It's "not fancy", but this "family-run" UWS Tuscan is a "great neighborhood" fallback all the same thanks to its "consistently pleasing" menu and "courteous" service; the manageable prices alone make it "worth putting up with the noise" and "unexciting" setting.

Little D Eatery Ⓜ *American/Eclectic* | ▽ 25 | 18 | 23 | $39 |

Park Slope | 434 Seventh Ave. (bet. 14th & 15th Sts.) | Brooklyn | 718-369-3144 | www.littled-eatery.com

The "little dishes concept" "works to perfection" at this budget-conscious Park Slope Eclectic–New American that delivers both "unusual flourishes" and "familiar favorites" from a "diverse, ever-changing" menu; the "attentive" staff, "unpretentious" vibe and "lovely garden" are other reasons it's so "popular."

Little Giant *American* | 23 | 18 | 19 | $45 |

LES | 85 Orchard St. (Broome St.) | 212-226-5047 | www.littlegiantnyc.com

Sizewise it's "more little than giant", but this "sweet" Lower Eastsider's "deceptively simple" New American cooking based on "fresh", "seasonal" ingredients "makes a big impression"; there are sometimes "waits" and elbow room is scarce, but its "excellent vibe" and "warm" service overcome all.

Little Owl *American/Mediterranean* | 25 | 19 | 23 | $55 |

W Village | 90 Bedford St. (Grove St.) | 212-741-4695 | www.thelittleowlnyc.com

A table at Joey Campanaro's "tiny" West Village Med–New American is "tough to secure" thanks to its "fantastic", "rustic-with-a-refined-edge" cuisine and service "with a huge heart"; the lucky few who snag seats in its "well-appointed" space declare it "truly delightful."

Lobo *Tex-Mex* | 15 | 15 | 15 | $24 |

Cobble Hill | 218 Court St. (bet. Baltic & Warren Sts.) | Brooklyn | 718-858-7739 🈐
Park Slope | 188 Fifth Ave. (Lincoln Pl.) | Brooklyn | 718-636-8886
www.lobonyc.com

"You could swim in the melted cheese" that tops the "gigantic" portions of "ok" Tex-Mex fare at these Brooklyn siblings, best known for their "fun", "rough-and-tumble" vibe, "affordable brunch" and "killer" lobo-tomizing margaritas; N.B. Court Street has a "lovely" back garden that's a perfect prowling ground.

Lobster Box ❶ *Seafood* | 19 | 17 | 18 | $45 |

Bronx | 34 City Island Ave. (bet. Belden & Rochelle Sts.) | 718-885-1952 | www.lobsterboxrestaurant.com

There may be "lobster, lobster everywhere" at this veteran City Island seafooder, but still most agree the "wonderful water views" are the "best thing here"; those who say it's feeling "old" should know it has new owners and recently underwent a redo to give it a fresh, more casual look that goes with the sea breezes.

Locale Café & Bar *Italian* | ▽ 20 | 21 | 19 | $37 |

Astoria | 33-02 34th Ave. (33rd St.) | Queens | 718-729-9080 | www.localeastoria.com

An Astoria "find", this "hip", "modern" Italian keeps "busy" thanks to its "*très* Manhattan" feel and high culinary standards at "Queens prices"; "seating is a bit tight" so "reserve in advance" or be prepared to nurse a martini at the bar.

	FOOD	DECOR	SERVICE	COST

Locanda Vini & Olii ⓜ *Italian* ▽ 25 | 24 | 21 | $48

Clinton Hill | 129 Gates Ave. (bet. Cambridge Pl. & Grand Ave.) | Brooklyn | 718-622-9202 | www.locandany.com

"No eggplant parmigiana here", just "authentic", "delicious" Tuscan fare served in an "atmospheric" converted Clinton Hill pharmacy presided over by a "charming" "husband-and-wife" team; if getting here is a bit of a "trek", most don't mind – after all, "this is not the kind of food you want to rush."

NEW Lokal *Mediterranean* ▽ 22 | 25 | 23 | $21

Greenpoint | 905 Lorimer St. (Bedford Ave.) | Brooklyn | 718-384-6777 | www.lokalbistro.com

Perfect pre-McCarren Park, this "adorable" new Greenpoint bistro and its "marvelous" Med cooking make a "welcome addition to the neighborhood"; in warmer weather its "huge doors open up" and afford leafy views of the park "across the street", while service is "friendly" year-round.

Lombardi's ⵁ *Pizza* 24 | 12 | 15 | $23

NoLita | 32 Spring St. (bet. Mott & Mulberry Sts.) | 212-941-7994 | www.firstpizza.com

For a "slice of pizza history", head to this NoLita "landmark" whose "classic" coal-fired pies are beloved for their "perfectly thin", "crispy, slightly charred" crusts and "fresh, authentic" toppings; however, its perpetual-"favorite" status spells "absurd waits" and "noisy", "cramped" quarters.

NEW Lomito ☽ *Italian* - | - | - | M

SoHo | 300 Spring St. (bet. Greenwich & Hudson Sts.) | 212-929-9494

To SoHo's western edge comes this sultry Italian-Argentinean whose lofty space features vintage film posters and a marble bar; backed by the folks behind Sosa Borella, it offers a midpriced lineup of pastas, pizzettas and *carne*, plus a late-night menu starring the namesake filet mignon sandwich.

Londel's Supper Club ⓜ *Southern* ▽ 20 | 18 | 21 | $35

Harlem | 2620 Frederick Douglass Blvd. (bet. 139th & 140th Sts.) | 212-234-6114 | www.londelsrestaurant.com

There's no mistaking "it's Harlem, baby", at this "classy" Southern joint "jumping" with live weekend jazz and a crowd that "goes to be seen"; there's also a "pleasant" Sunday buffet brunch for those less nocturnally inclined – best of all, it's modestly priced.

London Lennie's *Seafood* 21 | 17 | 19 | $42

Rego Park | 63-88 Woodhaven Blvd. (bet. Fleet Ct. & Penelope Ave.) | Queens | 718-894-8084 | www.londonlennies.com

For a taste of "fresh fish, Queens-style", hit this Rego Park "barn of a restaurant" dishing up "straightforward" seafood "without fancy trimmings"; "noisy" and "family-oriented", it's "better during the week" if you want to "hear anything your tablemates are saying."

Long Tan ☽ *Thai* 18 | 17 | 17 | $28

Park Slope | 196 Fifth Ave. (bet. Berkeley Pl. & Union St.) | Brooklyn | 718-622-8444 | www.long-tan.com

"One of the first" on Park Slope's Fifth Avenue strip, this "reasonable" Thai "standby" is "still going strong" with "creative" fare served in "cool, modern" digs with a "small courtyard seating area"; its "side bar" is popular "for a drink or late bite."

NEW Lookout Hill Smokehouse *BBQ*   – | – | – | M

Park Slope | 230 Fifth Ave. (President St.) | Brooklyn | 718-399-2161 | www.lookouthillsmokehouse.com

The city's BBQ boom continues with the arrival of this Park Sloper, where the daily changing offerings from the smoker – pork, beef, chicken and lamb – are joined by a few sandwiches and appetizers; the garage-chic setting includes a side deck made for people-watching.

Lorenzo's *American*   ∇ 19 | 21 | 20 | $50

Staten Island | Hilton Garden Inn | 1100 South Ave. (Lois Ln.) | 718-477-2400 | www.lorenzosdining.com

Staten Island "bigwigs" convene at this "elegant" dining room inside the Hilton Garden Inn, where the Italian-accented American fare is "pricey", but "everyone is treated like a top customer"; live piano music and special cabaret nights add to an overall "classy" experience.

Los Dados *Mexican*   19 | 18 | 17 | $42

Meatpacking | 73 Gansevoort St. (Washington St.) | 646-810-7290 | www.losdadosmexican.com

Sue Torres "elevates" regional "Mexican street food" at this "fun" Meatpacking District yearling featuring kitschy religious shrines and "fantastic margaritas"; a few shrug "nothing to write home about", but the fact that it's "crowded and noisy" speaks for itself.

Loulou *French*   ∇ 20 | 17 | 18 | $33

Fort Greene | 222 DeKalb Ave. (bet. Adelphi St. & Clermont Ave.) | Brooklyn | 718-246-0633 | www.louloubrooklyn.com

"Consistently good" Gallic "basics" keep 'em coming back to this "friendly" Fort Greene bistro, where the "romantic" mood is abetted by a "cute back garden"; the interior is "charming" or "cramped", depending on who you ask, but no one quibbles about the low tabs.

Z Lucali ⊘ *Pizza*   27 | 19 | 19 | $21

Carroll Gardens | 575 Henry St. (bet. Carroll St. & 1st Pl.) | Brooklyn | 718-858-4086

This Carroll Gardens upstart is voted this year's No. 1 for pizza in NYC thanks to its "sublime", "perfectly thin-crusted" pies and calzones turned out by "brick-oven" maestro/owner Mark Iacono; its "small" space has an "old-world" feel and lots of "local flavor", but "there's always a wait" so "call ahead to get your name on the list."

Lucien ❶ *French*   21 | 17 | 18 | $40

E Village | 14 First Ave. (1st St.) | 212-260-6481 | www.luciennyc.com

"Piaf would approve" of this "bustling", "oh-so-French" East Village bistro serving "reasonably priced" standards "with a little flair" in a room that's "cramped" yet "charming"; its late hours and "raucous" bohemian crowd make it a prime "people-watching" place.

Lucky Strike ❶ *French*   16 | 16 | 16 | $33

SoHo | 59 Grand St. (bet. W. B'way & Wooster St.) | 212-941-0772 | www.luckystrikeny.com

SoHo denizens "can't imagine the 'hood without" Keith McNally's "old faithful", a "favorite" for burgers and other "casual", affordable French bistro fare in appealingly "divey" digs; sure, it's "noisy" and a bit "grungy", but it's hard to beat for a "late-night" bite.

Lucy ⊠ Pan-Latin
∇ 20 | 20 | 18 | $49

Flatiron | ABC Carpet & Home | 35 E. 18th St. (bet. B'way & Park Ave. S.) | 212-475-5829

Tucked inside ABC Carpet & Home, this Flatironer serves "creative, well-prepared" Pan-Latin fare ferried by a "friendly" crew in stylishly "minimalist" digs; it hosts something of a "scene" in its "funky", brightly colored front bar/lounge pouring "excellent" mojitos and sangria.

Lumi ● Italian
18 | 18 | 19 | $53

E 70s | 963 Lexington Ave. (70th St.) | 212-570-2335 | www.lumirestaurant.com

"Perfect for a romantic interlude" or a shopping break, this UES Italian (seen in the *Sex and the City* movie) is set in a "lovely, comfortable" townhouse equipped with two fireplaces; "decent" food, including a "gluten-free" menu, and "pro" service help justify the tabs.

Luna Piena Italian
18 | 15 | 18 | $41

E 50s | 243 E. 53rd St. (bet. 2nd & 3rd Aves.) | 212-308-8882 | www.lunapienanyc.com

"Newly renovated", this Midtown Italian remains a "low-key" "lunch spot" proffering "more-than-adequate" fare at "not-unreasonable" rates; however, those who find it all rather "unmemorable" declare the "beautiful" year-round garden the "only reason to go."

Lunetta Italian
21 | 18 | 19 | $45

NEW **Flatiron** | 920 Broadway (21st St.) | 212-533-3663
Boerum Hill | 116 Smith St. (bet. Dean & Pacific Sts.) | Brooklyn | 718-488-6269 Ⓜ
www.lunetta-ny.com

These "innovative" Italians shine bright with "delicious" seasonal small plates backed by an "interesting" wine selection; their "bistro-like" interiors can get "crowded and noisy" – but there's always the "sweet, informal" garden at the Boerum Hill original or the sidewalk seats at its Flatiron offshoot.

☒ Lupa ● Italian
25 | 18 | 21 | $54

G Village | 170 Thompson St. (bet. Bleecker & Houston Sts.) | 212-982-5089 | www.luparestaurant.com

"Could eat here every day" gush the legions of fans who "love" this "casual", quartino-size Village member of the "Batali-Bastianich-Denton empire" offering its "stunning" "rustic" Roman fare and "fantastic" wines at "tremendous-value" prices; however, it's "always packed" and "noisy", "waits are long" and reservations "hard to come by", so insiders "pop in for lunch" when it's more laid-back.

Lure Fishbar Seafood
23 | 23 | 21 | $57

SoHo | 142 Mercer St., downstairs (Prince St.) | 212-431-7676 | www.lurefishbar.com

They're using "the right bait" at this "pricey" SoHo seafooder that feels "like being on a luxury cruiser" – with "style and service to match"; the "fresh" seafood (including sushi) is "al-lure-ingly wonderful", but it competes with a "hot scene" featuring "thumping" acoustics and "young" things at a "hopping bar."

	FOOD	DECOR	SERVICE	COST

Lusardi's *Italian* — 23 | 18 | 22 | $62

E 70s | 1494 Second Ave. (bet. 77th & 78th Sts.) | 212-249-2020 | www.lusardis.com

"Perfect host" Mario Lusardi makes the "country club set" feel at home at this "old-fashioned" Upper Eastsider plying "excellent" – if "expensive" – Northern Italian fare; a few say it's "starting to sag a bit", but for regulars that's part of its "European charm."

NEW Luxe ☻ *Continental/Italian* — - | - | - | M

Garment District | Wingate by Wyndham | 235 W. 35th St. (bet. 7th & 8th Aves.) | 212-209-6221

Tucked in the Garment District's Wingate by Wyndham is this Italian-Continental eatery serving up wallet-friendly dishes in a roomy, white-tableclothed setting; an equally spacious back garden makes a leafy respite from the touristy buzz of neighboring Herald Square.

Luz *Nuevo Latino* — ▽ 24 | 19 | 20 | $35

Fort Greene | 177 Vanderbilt Ave. (bet. Myrtle Ave. & Willoughby St.) | Brooklyn | 718-246-4000 | www.luzrestaurant.com

"Lots of style but no attitude" endears this "vibrant", "off-the-beaten-path" Fort Greene Nuevo Latino to the neighbors, as does its "fabu-lous", reasonable fare and "prize-worthy" cocktails; its "small" quarters can get "crowded" and "loud", but that's all part of the "fun."

Luzzo's Ⓜ *Italian/Pizza* — ▽ 24 | 14 | 17 | $29

E Village | 211 First Ave. (bet. 12th & 13th Sts.) | 212-473-7447

The "dreamy" thin-crust pizza is "the real thing" at this East Village Sicilian with two coal ovens to ensure a perfectly "crisp and charred crust"; it may be a "hole-in-the-wall" and a bit "expensive" for what it is, but "it's always packed for a reason."

Macelleria ☻ *Italian/Steak* — 19 | 18 | 17 | $54

Meatpacking | 48 Gansevoort St. (bet. Greenwich & Washington Sts.) | 212-741-2555 | www.macelleriarestaurant.com

A former Meatpacking District warehouse done up in faux "butcher shop" style is the "rustic" setting for this "pricey" Italian steakhouse that's usually "crowded" despite "inconsistent" service; it's "great for large groups" and late dining, though "noise" is part of the package.

NEW Madaleine Mae *Southern* — 16 | 15 | 16 | $42

W 80s | 461 Columbus Ave. (82nd St.) | 212-496-3000 | www.madaleinemae.com

Jonathan Waxman's recent contribution to the UWS dishes up its "homey" midpriced Southern fare in "warm" environs centered on a long bar dispensing Caribbean-inspired "rum cures"; however, reports are the overall package "still needs work."

NEW Mad Dog & Beans ☻ *Mexican* — ▽ 19 | 18 | 18 | $33

Financial District | 83 Pearl St. (bet. Coenties Slip & Hanover Sq.) | 212-269-1177 | www.maddogandbeans.com

"Why did it take so long for someone to realize that margaritas mix well with Wall Street?" muse mavens of this "much-needed" Financial District Mexican also known for its "tasty guac"; no wonder most are willing to overlook its "ridiculous name" and prices "high" "for what you get."

	FOOD	DECOR	SERVICE	COST

Madison Bistro *French*

| | 20 | 17 | 20 | $47 |

Murray Hill | 238 Madison Ave. (bet. 37th & 38th Sts.) | 212-447-1919 | www.madisonbistro.com

A "go-to neighborhood" place for many a Murray Hiller, this "small" French bistro plies its "decent" classics in a "quiet" room staffed by an "accommodating" crew; it's not cheap, but the prix fixe is a "bargain."

Madison's *Italian*

| | 21 | 19 | 19 | $37 |

Bronx | 5686 Riverdale Ave. (259th St.) | 718-543-3850

The "Bronx's answer to *Cheers*", this "upscale" Riverdale Italian is a "real neighborhood" hangout particularly beloved for its "excellent bar"; no surprise, waits are "looong", but locals are glad they "don't have to go far" for a "Manhattan-style" experience.

Mai House ● ⑤ *Vietnamese*

| | 20 | 20 | 19 | $51 |

TriBeCa | 186 Franklin St. (bet. Greenwich & Hudson Sts.) | 212-431-0606 | www.myriadrestaurantgroup.com

"Vivid" flavors "wow" the "beautiful people" at Drew Nieporent's "chi-chi" TriBeCa Vietnamese, whose kitchen is now headed by *Top Chef* alum Lisa Fernandes; still, some can't figure out "why it's not more popular" – "hefty prices" by Viet standards may be a clue.

Maison ● *French*

| | 18 | 16 | 15 | $36 |

W 50s | 1700 Broadway (53rd St.) | 212-757-2233 | www.maisonnyc.com

An "awesome" Times Square location complete with outdoor seating and "reasonably priced" fare make this "casual" French bistro a no-brainer pre- or post-theater; it's open 24/7 – and wiseacres quip "they need to be because the service is so slow."

Malagueta Ⓜ *Brazilian*

| | ▽ 23 | 12 | 19 | $31 |

Astoria | 25-35 36th Ave. (28th St.) | Queens | 718-937-4821 | www.malaguetany.com

"So good and so cheap", this Astoria Brazilian is the "closest thing to Rio" this side of the East River; despite decor "in need of sprucing up", it's "not so unknown anymore" and almost "always busy."

Malatesta Trattoria ● ⋻ *Italian*

| | 23 | 16 | 18 | $32 |

W Village | 649 Washington St. (Christopher St.) | 212-741-1207

"Bohemian to the core", this Northern Italian is "pure old West Village" and perfect for pairing "a robust red and a plate of pasta" without breaking the bank; there's no better place to "people-watch" when the "doors open" to the street on warm nights.

Maloney & Porcelli *Steak*

| | 22 | 19 | 21 | $68 |

E 50s | 37 E. 50th St. (bet. Madison & Park Aves.) | 212-750-2233 | www.maloneyandporcelli.com

At this Stillman Midtown meatery you'll find "stockbrokers crying in their martinis" before hunkering down to "huge" hunks of "quality" beef – or the "famous" crackling pork shank; generally it's "expense account all the way", but the weekend "wine dinner is a bargain."

Mamajuana Cafe ● *Caribbean/Dominican*

| | ▽ 21 | 21 | 18 | $37 |

Inwood | 247 Dyckman St. (bet. Payson & Seaman Aves.) | 212-304-0140 | www.mamajuana-cafe.com

A "fantastic addition to Inwood", this "festive" Nuevo Latino "near the Cloisters" is getting noticed for its "chic" "Miami vibe" and "refined"

Dominican-accented cooking; service "can be spotty", but outdoor seating, live music and a "serious" weekend brunch compensate.

Mamá Mexico ● Mexican 19 | 17 | 18 | $36
E 40s | 214 E. 49th St. (bet. 2nd & 3rd Aves.) | 212-935-1316
W 100s | 2672 Broadway (102nd St.) | 212-864-2323
www.mamamexico.com
Folks "get wild" at this Mexican duo where "throw-away-your-inhibitions margs" and "fresh guacamole made tableside" come together in a setting "straight out of Epcot"; some wish the "roving mariachis" would "turn down the volume", but most "don't notice" given the overall "intoxicating" experience.

Mama's Food Shop 図⑦ American 21 | 9 | 13 | $16
E Village | 200 E. Third St. (bet. Aves. A & B) | 212-777-4425 |
www.mamasfoodshop.com
For "heaping portions" of "tasty comfort food" – including "heavenly mac 'n' cheese" – head to this East Village American that's among the "best bargains in town"; those who think the "cafeteria-type" setup and attitudinous "hipster" service "could be better" opt for takeout.

Mancora ● Peruvian ▽ 22 | 14 | 21 | $28
E Village | 99 First Ave. (6th St.) | 212-253-1011
At this "homey" East Village Peruvian, the "delicious", "value"-oriented specialties ("huge, fresh platters of ceviche", the "best chicken I've had in ages") are "presented with pride"; the decor may be "modest", but it "never fails to welcome."

Mandarin Court Chinese 21 | 9 | 13 | $22
Chinatown | 61 Mott St. (bet. Bayard & Canal Sts.) | 212-608-3838
"Cheap, tasty, plentiful – who could ask for more?" muse admirers of this "no-frills" Chinatown dim sum dowager; it's best to "ignore the surly staff, Formica tables" and "weekend crowds" and just focus on those "heavenly" cart-borne tidbits.

Mandoo Bar Korean 20 | 11 | 17 | $20
Garment District | 2 W. 32nd St. (bet. B'way & 5th Ave.) | 212-279-3075
Look for the "cooks making fresh dumplings at the window" and you've found this "tiny", "simple" Garment District Korean known for its namesake bundles "so good you could cry"; it's just the thing for a "quick, cheap" bite, even if purists question its authenticity.

Manducatis Italian 22 | 13 | 20 | $45
LIC | 13-27 Jackson Ave. (47th Ave.) | Queens | 718-729-4602 |
www.manducatis.com
"Every neighborhood should have" a "comfortable, old-style" Italian like this decades-old "institution" in the "boonies of LIC" dishing up classics "just like mama made"; it oozes "unpretentious" hospitality, so most don't mind the "over-the-hill" decor.

Manetta's 図 Italian 22 | 17 | 20 | $35
LIC | 10-76 Jackson Ave. (49th Ave.) | Queens | 718-786-6171
"Amazing" brick-oven pies and "super-rich" pastas in "large portions" add up to serious "value" at this "family-friendly" LIC Italian; all appreciate the "accommodating" service, but the "out-of-the-'70s" decor makes some "wish they delivered."

	FOOD	DECOR	SERVICE	COST

Mangia ☒ *Mediterranean*

19	11	12	$21

E 40s | 16 E. 48th St. (bet. 5th & Madison Aves.) | 212-754-7600
Financial District | Trump Bldg. | 40 Wall St. (bet. Nassau & William Sts.) | 212-425-4040
Flatiron | 22 W. 23rd St. (bet. 5th & 6th Aves.) | 212-647-0200
W 50s | 50 W. 57th St. (bet. 5th & 6th Aves.) | 212-582-5554
www.mangiatogo.com

It's "always a madhouse" but this Med quartet is "worth the aggravation" given its "endless options" of "fresh, delicious" "gourmet" lunch takeout, including one of the town's "best" salad bars; "not-cheap" prices still spell decent "value" once the "high quality" is factored in.

Mara's Homemade *Cajun/Creole*

22	11	20	$34

E Village | 342 E. Sixth St. (bet. 1st & 2nd Aves.) | 212-598-1110 | www.marashomemade.com

Like "eating in the Delta" rather than the East Village, this "down 'n' dirty" Cajun-Creole joint may be the "only reliable place to get fresh crawfish boil" in NYC; it's a refreshing "antidote" to its "Curry Row" neighbors, with "warm" service making up for "cramped" conditions.

Marco Polo Ristorante *Italian*

20	16	20	$46

Carroll Gardens | 345 Court St. (Union St.) | Brooklyn | 718-852-5015 | www.marcopoloristorante.com

At this Carroll Gardens Italian "step back in time", "good" "red-sauce" basics come via "career waiters who know their stuff"; maybe it's "not as cheap as you'd expect", but for a taste of *Sopranos*-esque" Brooklyn "before the yuppies invaded", it's hard to beat.

Maria Pia *Italian*

19	16	18	$39

W 50s | 319 W. 51st St. (bet. 8th & 9th Aves.) | 212-765-6463 | www.mariapianyc.com

"Reliable" "before a Broadway show", this Theater District Italian's "above-average" fare presents solid "value" in a neighborhood short on bargains; with digs on the "small side", it gets "crowded" and "noisy" during pre-curtain hours, so try for the "treasure" of a back garden.

Maria's Mexican Bistro ➊ *Mexican*

19	16	15	$30

Park Slope | 669 Union St. (bet. 4th & 5th Aves.) | Brooklyn | 718-638-2344

"Holy mole!" – this Mexican's "tasty" dishes and "veritable ocean of tequila choices" have amigos trekking to Park Slope's Fourth Avenue frontier; still, a few fret about "spotty" service and say it has all "gone a little downhill since expanding" a while back.

Marina Cafe *Seafood*

20	22	19	$44

Staten Island | 154 Mansion Ave. (Hillside Terr.) | 718-967-3077 | www.marinacafegrand.com

Summer "doesn't get any better" than at this SI seafooder overlooking Great Kills Harbor; it's "lovely" any time of year, but the "decent" fare and so-so service take a back seat to the "unbelievable views" from the expansive deck, which also boasts a tiki bar and nightly live music.

Marinella *Italian*

21	15	22	$42

G Village | 49 Carmine St. (Bedford St.) | 212-807-7472

Everyone "feels like a regular" at this "no-fuss" Village Italian, a supplier of reliably good basics at "reasonable" rates; longtime locals appreciate that its "blackboard menu" and "cozy, tavernlike" digs betray "none of the terminal hipness found elsewhere" in the area.

Mario's ⓜ *Italian*   22 | 15 | 20 | $42

Bronx | 2342 Arthur Ave. (bet. 184th & 186th Sts.) | 718-584-1188 | www.mariosrestarthurave.com

Experience the Bronx's "real Little Italy" at this "friendly" Arthur Avenue "landmark" that has been serving "the best pizza" and other Southern Italian "staples" since 1919; sure, "the look is a little dated" – whaddya expect from a place "where the Rat Pack ate"?

🆕 Market Table ◐ *American*   23 | 19 | 21 | $49

G Village | 54 Carmine St. (Bedford St.) | 212-255-2100 | www.markettablenyc.com

Its brick-lined room is "simple" and "relaxed", the service "warm" and the "constantly evolving" New American fare "delicious" at this new Villager from ex-Mermaid Inn chef Mike Price and Little Owl's Joey Campanaro; though not cheap, it has been "popular" from day one.

MarkJoseph Steakhouse ⓢ *Steak*   24 | 18 | 21 | $68

Financial District | 261 Water St. (off Peck Slip) | 212-277-0020 | www.markjosephsteakhouse.com

"Testosterone rules" at this Financial District steakhouse catering to "loud" Wall Street "guys" with some of the most "glorious" beef "this side of the East River"; if the decor is just ok, the staff is totally "pro" – but no matter what, it's "best if someone else is paying."

Markt *Belgian*   19 | 17 | 17 | $42

Flatiron | 676 Sixth Ave. (21st St.) | 212-727-3314 | www.marktrestaurant.com

It "still delivers the moules" and "fantastic beers", but this Belgian brasserie's move to "smaller" Flatiron digs has split surveyors ("hasn't missed a beat" vs. "lost luster"); however, the "noisy" "crowds" squeezing in, especially for "wonderful brunch", speak for themselves.

Marlow & Sons ◐ *French*   ▽ 23 | 21 | 19 | $38

Williamsburg | 81 Broadway (bet. Berry St. & Wythe Ave.) | Brooklyn | 718-384-1441 | www.marlowandsons.com

The kitchen is "firing on all cylinders" at this tiny Williamsburg "charmer" and Diner sibling that's part "old-style general store", part bar/eatery plying a "limited" roster of "seasonal" French-influenced bites and "rockin'" wine and cocktails; just bear in mind that you "gotta fight with the local hipmongers" for a seat.

Maroons *Jamaican*   21 | 16 | 17 | $36

Chelsea | 244 W. 16th St. (bet. 7th & 8th Aves.) | 212-206-8640 | www.maroonsnyc.com

"Soulful" Jamaican and Southern dishes "priced well" transcend "cramped" quarters and "slow service" at this Chelsea "standby"; party people note that the "low-key" vibe and "comfort food with a capital 'C'" "hit the spot" "after a rough Saturday night."

Marseille ◐ *French/Mediterranean*   20 | 18 | 19 | $47

W 40s | 630 Ninth Ave. (44th St.) | 212-333-3410 | www.marseillenyc.com

For "sophisticated" dining in Hell's Kitchen, try this "informal" yet "civilized" French-Med offering "terrific" eats and an "authentic brasserie" setup complete with "wonderful bar"; it's "fabulous pre-theater" thanks to the "pleasant" staff that "gets you in and out" without making you feel "herded."

Maruzzella ● *Italian* | 22 | 17 | 21 | $42 |

E 70s | 1483 First Ave. (bet. 77th & 78th Sts.) | 212-988-8877 | www.maruzzellanyc.com

They really "roll out the red carpet" at this "warm, inviting" UES Italian, delivering relatively "reasonable", "consistently tasty" standards "with a smile"; "despite the expansion" a couple of years back, it retains its "cozy neighborhood vibe."

Mary Ann's *Tex-Mex* | 14 | 10 | 13 | $26 |

Chelsea | 116 Eighth Ave. (16th St.) | 212-633-0877 ⊟
E Village | 80 Second Ave. (5th St.) | 212-475-5939 ⊟
TriBeCa | 107 W. Broadway (bet. Chambers & Reade Sts.) | 212-766-0911
www.maryannsmexican.com

"Every day can be Cinco de Mayo" at this "boisterous", "no-frills" Tex-Mex chainlet that's "dependable" for a "quick", "cheap" marg-and-chips fix; the "noisy", "cheesy" settings may have "seen better days", but those "potent" cocktails keep the crowd "too drunk to care."

Mary's Fish Camp ⊠ *Seafood* | 24 | 13 | 18 | $43 |

W Village | 64 Charles St. (W. 4th St.) | 646-486-2185 | www.marysfishcamp.com

"Incredible lobster rolls" have legions of fans happily camping out for a place at this "always packed" West Village seafood shack serving some of "the freshest fish" going; prices are "reasonable" and service "friendly", so the only thing missing is a table "overlooking the ocean" – and a few dozen more seats.

☑ Mas ● *American* | 28 | 24 | 26 | $75 |

G Village | 39 Downing St. (bet. Bedford & Varick Sts.) | 212-255-1790 | www.masfarmhouse.com

"Close to dining perfection", this "elegant yet hip" New American Villager is an oasis of "casual" refinement where the "wonderful, market-fresh" cooking by Galen Zamarra is delivered by a "warm" crew in quarters that are "romantic" but nonetheless "not too quiet"; all this "pricey" sophistication means it's "like no *mas*" (farmhouse) most have ever encountered.

☑ Masa ⊠ *Japanese* | 27 | 24 | 26 | $520 |

W 60s | Time Warner Ctr. | 10 Columbus Circle, 4th fl. (60th St. at B'way)
☑ Bar Masa ●⊠ *Japanese*
W 60s | Time Warner Ctr. | 10 Columbus Circle, 4th fl. (60th St. at B'way)
212-823-9800 | www.masanyc.com

Some of the "most expensive" sushi anywhere – but also some of the "absolute best" – can be found at this Zen Time Warner Center Japanese, where "perfectionist" chef Masayoshi Takayama's "exquisite" omakase features course upon course of raw fish "like silk"; at $400 prix fixe it's a major blowout ("I want to thank Gov. Spitzer for putting the price into perspective for me"), but mere mortals can indulge in "almost as good" à la carte offerings at next door's more casual, less expensive (if not exactly cheap) Bar Masa; either way Masa spells mecca.

	FOOD	DECOR	SERVICE	COST

NEW Matilda ⌀ *Italian/Mexican* ▽ 18 | 18 | 20 | $34

E Village | 647 E. 11th St. (bet. Aves. B & C) | 212-777-3355

"Who knew Mexican and Tuscan could work so well together" marvel mavens of this East Village newcomer's "interesting" cuisine that comes together in a "delicate marriage of flavors"; "gracious owners", pleasingly "exotic" decor and eminently affordable tabs mean early-goers are calling it a "gem."

NEW Matsugen *Japanese* ▽ 21 | 19 | 21 | $77

TriBeCa | 241 Church St. (Leonard St.) | 212-925-0202 | www.jean-georges.com

A Japanese soba house gone "upscale", Jean-Georges Vongerichten's TriBeCa newcomer plies "made-on-site" buckwheat noodles in every iteration, plus other "refined" "classics" such as shabu-shabu and sushi, in the sleek "understated" space that formerly housed 66; early reports call it "promising", except for the price.

Matsuri ◑ *Japanese* 23 | 25 | 20 | $61

Chelsea | Maritime Hotel | 369 W. 16th St., downstairs (9th Ave.) | 212-243-6400 | www.themaritimehotel.com

Tadashi Ono's sushi is "incredibly fresh" and the sake selection "endless" at this theatrically "sceney" Japanese "cavern" underneath Chelsea's Maritime Hotel; even if its "fabulous", "larger-than-life" decor has "inspired" many imitators, it remains among the city's more "fashionable" places to "see and be seen."

Max *Italian* 22 | 15 | 16 | $29

E Village | 51 Ave. B (bet. 3rd & 4th Sts.) | 212-539-0111 ◑⌀
TriBeCa | 181 Duane St. (bet. Greenwich & Hudson Sts.) | 212-966-5939
www.max-ny.com

Max SoHa ◑⌀ *Italian*

W 100s | 1274 Amsterdam Ave. (123rd St.) | 212-531-2221 | www.maxsoha.com

For "terrific housemade pastas" and other "hearty", "affordable" Italian staples, you could do far worse than this trattoria trio; the only rubs are the "no-reservations hassle" ("get there early" or expect to "wait") and cash-only policy at the Uptown and East Village locations.

Max Brenner *Dessert* 17 | 18 | 14 | $26

E Village | 141 Second Ave. (9th St.) | 212-388-0030
G Village | 841 Broadway (bet. 13th & 14th Sts.) | 212-388-0030
www.maxbrenner.com

"Must've died and gone to heaven" sigh the "tourists", "teenagers" and "chocoholics" who "pack" into this "Willy Wonka–style" dessert duo for "inventive" cocoa "concoctions" like chocolate pizza; unfortunately, "hit-or-miss" service and "theme park" tendencies aren't so sweet.

Maya *Mexican* 24 | 20 | 20 | $52

E 60s | 1191 First Ave. (bet. 64th & 65th Sts.) | 212-585-1818 | www.modernmexican.com

This "upscale" Eastsider's "nouveau Mexicana" just keeps "getting better", ditto the "superior margaritas"; it's "always bustling" with "beautiful young people", so don't be surprised by the *muy* "noisy" acoustics – or the *gordo* tab.

	FOOD	DECOR	SERVICE	COST

Maze *French*
25 | 20 | 22 | $70

W 50s | The London NYC | 151 W. 54th St. (bet. 6th & 7th Aves.) |
212-468-8889 | www.gordonramsay.com/mazeatthelondonnyc
An "anteroom" to Gordon Ramsay's more formal "inner sanctum",
this "classy" "hotel lobby" eatery offers "well-served", less-
expensive" (but no less "brilliant") New French small plates; if "the
dollar feels weak when the check comes", there's always the $28
lunch prix fixe "deal."

Maz Mezcal *Mexican*
21 | 17 | 19 | $37

E 80s | 316 E. 86th St. (bet. 1st & 2nd Aves.) | 212-472-1599 |
www.mazmezcal.com
There's "no cheesy-queasy" feeling at this UES "standby", a "m'excellent" choice for "inexpensive", "real-deal" south-of-the-border fare
plus a "tequila and mezcal selection" "not to be trifled with"; since it's
"always mobbed" and service can be "spotty", it pays "to be a regular."

McCormick & Schmick's *Seafood*
20 | 18 | 19 | $53

W 50s | 1285 Sixth Ave. (enter on 52nd St., bet. 6th & 7th Aves.) |
212-459-1222 | www.mccormickandschmicks.com
Yes, it's a "chain", but this Midtown seafooder "swims to the top" of
the genre with its "reliable" catch served in "bustling" digs perfect for
"business lunch"; snobs say it would fit better in a "suburban mall" –
but then it wouldn't be so "convenient" "pre-Radio City."

Mediterraneo ◐ *Italian/Pizza*
18 | 14 | 15 | $41

E 60s | 1260 Second Ave. (66th St.) | 212-734-7407 |
www.mediterraneonyc.com
The "cliquey" "scene" suits the "Jimmy Choo-clad" crowd fine at this
"hopping", "noisy" Italian Eastsider where the fairly priced "fresh
pasta" and "thin-crust" pizzas take a backseat to the prime "people-
watching"; ok, the staff "isn't efficient", but "sitting outside sipping
sangria" takes the edge off.

Mee Noodle Shop *Noodle Shop*
18 | 5 | 12 | $16

E 40s | 922 Second Ave. (49th St.) | 212-888-0027
Murray Hill | 547 Second Ave. (bet. 30th & 31st Sts.) |
212-779-1596
W 50s | 795 Ninth Ave. (53rd St.) | 212-765-2929
"Perfect quick noodle" stops, these separately owned Chinese joints
offer supremely "satisfying" soups that are "worth" enduring the "no-
ambiance" digs and "snippy" service; they're "dirt-cheap" – though given
all that slurping you may need to factor "dry-cleaning" into the bill.

Megu *Japanese*
24 | 26 | 23 | $87

TriBeCa | 62 Thomas St. (bet. Church St. & W. B'way)
Megu Midtown ⊠ *Japanese*
E 40s | Trump World Tower | 845 United Nations Plaza (1st Ave. & 47th St.)
212-964-7777 | www.megunyc.com
As "memorable dining experiences" go, it's hard to top this "theatrical"
Japanese duo whose "luxurious" cuisine and "thoughtful" service are
outdone only by the "beautiful", "over-the-top" decor centered around
a "giant Buddha" ice sculpture; the Midtown branch exudes more of a
"business vibe", with "pretty people" gravitating to the TriBeCa original –
both take plenty of yen to enjoy.

	FOOD	DECOR	SERVICE	COST

Melt *American* ▽ 22 | 20 | 21 | $37

Park Slope | 440 Bergen St. (bet. 5th St. & Flatbush Ave.) | Brooklyn | 718-230-5925 | www.meltnyc.com

Simply a "wonderful" "hangout", this Park Sloper plies "delicious", "reasonable" New Americana ferried by a "friendly" staff; the "slick", "ultramodern" decor gets mixed reviews, but all applaud its "lovely brunch."

Menchanko-tei *Noodle Shop* 20 | 9 | 14 | $21

E 40s | 131 E. 45th St. (bet. Lexington & 3rd Aves.) | 212-986-6805
W 50s | 43-45 W. 55th St. (bet. 5th & 6th Aves.) | 212-247-1585
www.menchankotei.com

"Japanese expats" jam these "unassuming", eminently "affordable" Midtown noodle stops for "delicious", "authentic" udon and ramen that will take you back to "Tokyo"; despite "divey" setups, they're always "crowded for lunch" so "get there early."

Mercadito *Mexican* 23 | 16 | 18 | $40

NEW E Village | 172 Ave. B (bet. 10th & 11th Sts.) | 212-388-1750 ●
E Village | 179 Ave. B (bet. 11th & 12th Sts.) | 212-529-6490 ●
W Village | 100 Seventh Ave. S. (bet. Bleecker & Grove Sts.) | 212-647-0830
www.mercaditony.com

"Always buzzing", these "Lilliputian" cross-Villagers offer "out-of-this-world" Mexican fare, notably those "tiny" "tasty tacos"; they're a "tight squeeze" and "not exactly cheap", but chances are you'll "leave happy."

Mercat *Spanish* 22 | 20 | 18 | $51

NoHo | 45 Bond St. (bet. Bowery & Lafayette St.) | 212-529-8600 | www.mercatnyc.com

"Hot from day one", this "like-in-Barcelona" NoHo tapas bar showcases "authentic" Catalan cooking in a "hip", "noisy" setting complete with "open kitchen"; it's a prime "date place" that's also "fun for groups", though service can be "slow" and "tabs mount quickly."

Mercer Kitchen ● *American/French* 21 | 22 | 19 | $56

SoHo | Mercer Hotel | 99 Prince St. (Mercer St.) | 212-966-5454 | www.jean-georges.com

"Still sexy" "after all these years", Jean-Georges Vongerichten's "chic" SoHo hoteler continues to turn out "delicious" French–New American fare in ever-"cool" "subterranean" quarters; "hit-or-miss" service doesn't deter the "crowds", which range from "tourists" to "celebs."

NEW Merkato 55 ● *African* 21 | 23 | 21 | $59

Meatpacking | 55 Gansevoort St. (bet. Greenwich & Washington Sts.) | 212-255-8555 | www.merkato55.com

"Take the classic Pan-Asian restaurant formula and substitute the continent of Africa" and you've got this Meatpacking District arrival featuring "interesting" "Afro-fusion" fare in a "big", "flashy" bi-level space; founding chef Marcus Samuelsson departed post-Survey, leaving the above Food score in question.

Mermaid Inn *Seafood* 21 | 17 | 19 | $46

E Village | 96 Second Ave. (bet. 5th & 6th Sts.) | 212-674-5870
NEW W 80s | 568 Amsterdam Ave. (bet. 87th & 88th Sts.) | 212-799-7400
www.themermaidnyc.com

This "perennial" East Village "favorite" for "solid", "dependable" seafood has taken its "fish shack" formula uptown (finally, "killer" "lobster rolls on the UWS!"); both locations are often "crowded" and "noisy", so, "small seaside town feel" notwithstanding, repasts here are often more "festive" than relaxing.

	FOOD	DECOR	SERVICE	COST

⭐ **Mesa Grill** *Southwestern*
| | 23 | 19 | 20 | $57 |

Flatiron | 102 Fifth Ave. (bet. 15th & 16th Sts.) | 212-807-7400 | www.mesagrill.com

"TV" chef Bobby Flay "gets it right" at this "still-innovative" Flatiron Southwesterner, which was his "first", and his "best" according to boosters of its "big, bold" flavors and "lively" vibe; the "noisy", "dated" digs are less popular, but nevertheless the "crowds" keep coming.

Meskerem *Ethiopian*
| | 21 | 9 | 14 | $23 |

G Village | 124 MacDougal St. (bet. Bleecker & W. 3rd Sts.) | 212-777-8111

W 40s | 468 W. 47th St. (bet. 9th & 10th Aves.) | 212-664-0520 ◗

As "close to Addis Ababa as it comes", this "reliable" Hell's Kitchen–Village duo dishes up "authentic" Ethiopian fare, notably "tasty" stews that you "eat with your hands" using injera bread; "incredible" prices make it easy to overlook the "simple" settings and "slow" service.

Métisse *French*
| | 19 | 16 | 19 | $43 |

W 100s | 239 W. 105th St. (bet. Amsterdam Ave. & B'way) | 212-666-8825 | www.metisserestaurant.com

"One of the best" in the restaurant-challenged area "near Columbia", this "charming" French bistro keeps 'em coming back with "reliable", "reasonably priced" classics and "warm" service; its "comfortable" setting is "nothing fancy", which suits the locals just fine.

Metrazur ⭐ *American*
| | 20 | 21 | 18 | $53 |

E 40s | Grand Central | East Balcony (42nd St. & Vanderbilt Ave.) | 212-687-4600 | www.charliepalmer.com

"Worth missing your train for", Charlie Palmer's "so NYC" New American in Grand Central Terminal is a "magical place" thanks to its "balcony" seating "overlooking the Concourse"; maybe the overall experience is "expensive" "for what you get", but the "people-watching" is beyond compare.

Metro Marché *French*
| | 19 | 15 | 18 | $36 |

W 40s | Port Authority | 625 Eighth Ave. (41st St.) | 212-239-1010 | www.metromarche.com

"Who'd of thunk" you'd find a "quality" French brasserie with "reasonable" prices smack in the middle of "seedy Port Authority"?; the "service keeps pace" with the location's "hurried rhythm", and for those with no time to linger there's a "take-out counter" too.

Mexicana Mama Ⓜ⌿ *Mexican*
| | 24 | 13 | 18 | $34 |

G Village | 47 E. 12th St. (bet. B'way & University Pl.) | 212-253-7594

W Village | 525 Hudson St. (bet. Charles & W. 10th Sts.) | 212-924-4119

"Prepare to wait" at this popular "pint-size" West Village cantina and its slightly roomier crosstown offshoot, both of which dispense "creative", "upscale" Mexican fare in "kitschy", "cramped" digs; pesky "cash-only" and "no-reservations" policies notwithstanding, the hordes keep "squeezing in."

	FOOD	DECOR	SERVICE	COST

Mexican Radio ● *Mexican* — 18 | 13 | 15 | $31

NoLita | 19 Cleveland Pl. (bet. Kenmare & Spring Sts.) | 212-343-0140 | www.mexrad.com
For "basic Mex done right" with "awesome margaritas to match", this NoLita standby fills the bill; it's "cheap", "fun and loud", and even with "hit-or-miss" service, it stands as a "friendly" "alternative" to the area's "snooty hot spots."

Mezzaluna ● *Italian* — 20 | 14 | 17 | $44

E 70s | 1295 Third Ave. (bet. 74th & 75th Sts.) | 212-535-9600 | www.mezzalunany.com
A "hangout" for the *Gossip Girl* crowd by day, at dinner this UES trattoria serves "dependable" pastas and "wood-fired, thin-crust" pies to a "crowded" room of "monied" regulars; while a few complain of "pizza with attitude", loyalists laud it as a "friendly" "neighborhood stalwart."

Mezzogiorno *Italian* — 20 | 17 | 19 | $44

SoHo | 195 Spring St. (Sullivan St.) | 212-334-2112 | www.mezzogiorno.com
With "consistently good" pizzas, pastas and other Tuscan classics, this "reliable" SoHo "staple" is a go-to spot both for "regulars" and "out-of-towners"; if the interior needs a "spruce-up", on a "warm day or evening" it's "wonderful" "out under the awning."

Mezzo Mezzo ● *Greek* — 17 | 15 | 17 | $32

Astoria | 31-29 Ditmars Blvd. (bet. 32nd & 33rd Sts.) | Queens | 718-278-0444
Despite "tough competition in the neighborhood", this Astoria Greek holds its own with "huge portions", "personal service" and "comfortable", "nontraditional" decor; its "loud, familylike atmosphere" gets the added boost of live music on Saturday nights.

NEW Mia Dona *Italian* — 21 | 18 | 19 | $53

E 50s | 206 E. 58th St. (bet. 2nd & 3rd Aves.) | 212-750-8170 | www.miadona.com
Michael Psilakis and Donatella Arpaia "have created another winner" with this "welcoming" East Side Italian featuring "rustic" yet "innovative" fare in "sleek" (some say "sterile") environs; though the staff perhaps is "still getting its footing", most agree that overall it's "off to a good start."

Michael Jordan's
The Steak House NYC *Steak* — 21 | 20 | 19 | $65

E 40s | Grand Central | West Balcony (42nd St. & Vanderbilt Ave.) | 212-655-2300 | www.theglaziergroup.com
You "can't beat" the view of Grand Central's "magnificent" Concourse from this chophouse; "delicious cocktails" and "tasty steaks" have most calling it a "slam dunk", though a few cry foul at "lax" service and "expensive" tabs (aside from the "deal" of a $24 lunch prix fixe).

Michael's ⬛ *Californian* — 22 | 21 | 21 | $69

W 50s | 24 W. 55th St. (bet. 5th & 6th Aves.) | 212-767-0555 | www.michaelsnewyork.com
It's all about the "kiss kiss" factor at this "pretty", art-filled Midtown "media haunt" better known for its "pricey" daylong "power" scene than its "winning" "Cali-chic" cooking and "solid" service; accordingly, don't

expect to get seated in the "cool section" unless "you are a somebody" – and come for breakfast if you want to get published.

Mi Cocina *Mexican*
21 | 17 | 20 | $44

W Village | 57 Jane St. (Hudson St.) | 212-627-8273
For "authentic regional" Mexican tastes and a "high-spirited" good time – especially after sampling the "tequila flights" – this "upscale" West Villager is a safe bet; sure, it's "a little pricey", but the "delightful" staff and "haute" culinary renderings are well worth it.

Mill Basin Kosher Deli *Deli*
22 | 15 | 17 | $25

Mill Basin | 5823 Ave. T (59th St.) | Brooklyn | 718-241-4910 | www.millbasindeli.com
"Humongous sandwiches" are the signature of this "quality kosher deli" in Mill Basin, a "throwback" for "delish" "Jewish specialties" that doubles as a "fine art" gallery with "Ertés and Lichtensteins" on display; maybe it's all that culcha that accounts for prices "on the high side."

Mill Korean *Korean*
18 | 13 | 15 | $22

W 100s | 2895 Broadway (bet. 112th & 113th Sts.) | 212-666-7653
"Students and locals" "don't have to go all the way Downtown" for a "solid" Korean "fix" thanks to this UWS "stalwart"; service is "abrupt" and the "small" setup's "not all that comfortable", but great "value" keeps it "active."

🆕 Milos, Estiatorio ◐ *Greek/Seafood*
27 | 23 | 23 | $79

W 50s | 125 W. 55th St. (bet. 6th & 7th Aves.) | 212-245-7400 | www.milos.ca
It's like "landing in Athens" "without jet lag" at this "top-of-the-line" Midtown Greek, a "superior" source for "fabulously prepared", "fresher-than-fresh" seafood served with "panache" in a "grand", "airy" space; just prepare for pricing "as if Onassis were at your table", especially if you're "paying by the pound."

Minca ◐≠ *Japanese*
▽ 22 | 11 | 17 | $18

E Village | 536 E. Fifth St. (bet. Aves. A & B) | 212-505-8001
Ramen mavens "greedily slurp up" a "lip-smacking" variety of "hearty" noodle soups at this "tiny" East Villager, a "quick", cost-effective choice for "authentic" Japanese "comfort food"; its "neighborhood secret" status means "nabbing a seat" is easier here than at many competitors in the area.

Mingala Burmese *Burmese*
19 | 9 | 17 | $26

E 70s | 1393B Second Ave. (bet. 72nd & 73rd Sts.) | 212-744-8008
E Village | 21-23 E. Seventh St. (bet. 2nd & 3rd Aves.) | 212-529-3656
"For something a little different", this "simple" Burmese duo's "distinctive", veg-friendly dishes offer an "interesting" "Asian variant" served with "no drama"; "low prices" offset the "drab decor" – and aesthetes can always "do takeout" if they don't like mingala-ing with the locals.

Mint *Indian*
▽ 22 | 20 | 19 | $44

E 50s | San Carlos Hotel | 150 E. 50th St. (bet. Lexington & 3rd Aves.) | 212-644-8888 | www.mintny.com
With its "modern" interior bathed in a "mesmerizing green glow", this "upscale" Midtowner draws on "various parts" of the Raj to provide a fresh, "sophisticated taste of India"; it's an "agreeable", if "pricey", option, though the servers may occasionally "drop the ball."

| | FOOD | DECOR | SERVICE | COST |

Miracle Grill *Southwestern* — 18 | 16 | 17 | $32

W Village | 415 Bleecker St. (bet. Bank & W. 11th Sts.) | 212-924-1900
Park Slope | 222 Seventh Ave. (3rd St.) | Brooklyn | 718-369-4541
"Solid standbys" that attract "lively crowds at brunch", these separately owned Southwestern cantinas offer "decent", "really reasonable" food with the bonus of a "cool" "outdoor deck" in Park Slope; despite "iffy" service, they're "dependable" for a "leisurely meal."

Miriam *Israeli/Mediterranean* — 21 | 18 | 19 | $32

Cobble Hill | 229 Court St. (bet. Baltic & Warren Sts.) | Brooklyn | 718-522-2220
Park Slope | 79 Fifth Ave. (Prospect Pl.) | Brooklyn | 718-622-2250
www.miriamrestaurant.com
A "winning meal" at a winning price awaits at this Park Slope–Cobble Hill twosome, where the "savory" Israeli-Med menu takes some "creative twists" and the "welcoming staff" keeps the vibe "relaxed"; weekend brunch is especially "popular" – "for good reason."

Mishima *Japanese* — 22 | 12 | 18 | $36

Murray Hill | 164 Lexington Ave. (bet. 30th & 31st Sts.) | 212-532-9596 | www.mishimany.com
This double-decker "neighborhood Japanese joint" is a "calm" "haven" for Murray Hill sushiphiles, serving "the best cuts" of "amazingly fresh" fish along with "spot-on traditional" cooked dishes; if the "simple setting" "won't wow you", the "affordable" cost just might.

🆕 **Miss Favela** ◗🍴 *Brazilian* — – | – | – | M

Williamsburg | 57 S. Fifth St. (Wythe Ave.) | Brooklyn | 718-230-4040 | www.missfavela.com
At this Williamsburg *botequin,* the Brazilian classics are washed down with fresh caipirinhas and batidas; its casual digs, which open to the street in clement weather, hint at Rio's makeshift urban outskirts, with DJs and live music to keep the mood light.

Miss Mamie's *Soul Food/Southern* — 21 | 11 | 14 | $24

Harlem | 366 W. 110th St. (bet. Columbus & Manhattan Aves.) | 212-865-6744
Miss Maude's *Soul Food/Southern*
Harlem | 547 Lenox Ave. (bet. 137th & 138th Sts.) | 212-690-3100
www.spoonbreadinc.com
"Forget your diet" at these frill-free Harlem staples for "soul food done right", where the "generous", "down-home" servings leave you "completely satisfied"; "service isn't fast-paced", but the "price is right."

Mizu Sushi ⧗ *Japanese* — 23 | 15 | 17 | $38

Flatiron | 29 E. 20th St. (bet. B'way & Park Ave. S.) | 212-505-6688
"From classic rolls to unique combos", the "terrific" sushi has young "hordes" packing this "funky" Flatiron Japanese; it's "energetic", with "blasting music" and "sake bomb" imbibing upping the "noise level."

Mo-Bay *Caribbean/Soul Food* — 20 | 18 | 15 | $32

Harlem | 17 W. 125th St. (bet. 5th & Lenox Aves.) | 212-876-9300 | www.mobayrestaurant.com
This "cozy" Harlem haunt merges Caribbean and soul food into a "tasty" lineup – including a "variety for vegetarians" – that makes for a

"satisfying", economical bite; live jazz adds to the "relaxing vibe", though some expect mo' from the "absentminded" service.

Moda *Italian/Mediterranean*   ▽ 19 | 20 | 23 | $49

W 50s | Flatotel | 135 W. 52nd St. (bet. 6th & 7th Aves.) | 212-887-9880 | www.flatotel.com

"Convenient for pre-theater", this *a la moda* Midtown hotel eatery is a "straightforward" standby for solid, "decently priced" Italian-Med fare and "helpful service"; while the dining room is often "overlooked", the alfresco breezeway area is popular with "socializing" after-workers.

Z Modern, The ⑤ *American/French*   26 | 26 | 24 | $111

W 50s | Museum of Modern Art | 9 W. 53rd St. (bet. 5th & 6th Aves.) | 212-333-1220 | www.themodernnyc.com

Chef Gabriel Kreuther's French–New American cuisine is so "inspired" it "could have been curated" at this MoMA "masterpiece" from Danny Meyer, where the "one-of-a-kind" "luxe setting" with a "splendid view" of the sculpture garden is overseen by a "superb" staff; while it's "well worth" the "platinum" pricing, the "stylish" but "less formal" bar's "exciting" small plates are "easier on the wallet."

Moim Ⓜ *Korean*   24 | 23 | 19 | $41

Park Slope | 206 Garfield Pl. (bet. 7th & 8th Aves.) | Brooklyn | 718-499-8092 | www.moimrestaurant.com

"Super" "modern spins on classic dishes" earn "raves" for this "stylish" Park Slope Korean, a neighborhood "knockout" for "innovative" eating; the "noise level escalates" as "yuppified" fans fill its "chic space", though a garden "oasis" is in the works.

Molyvos 🕗 *Greek*   22 | 19 | 20 | $55

W 50s | 871 Seventh Ave. (bet. 55th & 56th Sts.) | 212-582-7500 | www.molyvos.com

"Roomy" and "convivial", this "marvelous" Midtowner offers a "wide selection" of "top-flight" "traditional" Greek fare just "steps from Carnegie Hall"; it's "not cheap", but the "accommodating" style helps make it "popular for lunch", while the $37 prix fixe keeps the pre-theater scene "going strong."

Z NEW Momofuku Ko *American*   26 | 18 | 22 | $130

E Village | 163 First Ave. (bet. 10th & 11th Sts.) | www.momofuku.com

"David Chang has done it again" at this gustatory "high temple" in a minimalist East Village space, where the "lucky" ko-hort at the "12-seater" tasting bar watches "cutting-edge" chefs prepare "flawless", "adventurous" prix fixe-only Asian-accented New American fare; it's "euphoria" provided you can crack the "radical egalitarian" web-only reservation system and are "prepared to spend" (the price is market-based, but ranges from $85–110); N.B. it recently started serving lunch Friday–Sunday, with a menu more elaborate and expensive than dinner.

Z Momofuku Noodle Bar *Noodle Shop*   23 | 14 | 17 | $31

E Village | 171 First Ave. (bet. 10th & 11th Sts.) | 212-777-7773 | www.momofuku.com

"The hype is justified" at David Chang's "stark", "eternally packed" East Villager, a "casual" communal showcase for Japanese-accented New American fare centered on "ethereal" noodle soups and "transcendent" pork buns; it now occupies "expanded" quarters, but it's still "tight", "rushed" and well "worth the hassle."

Momofuku Ssäm Bar ● *American* | 23 | 15 | 17 | $41 |

E Village | 207 Second Ave. (13th St.) | 212-254-3500 | www.momofuku.com
Admiring multitudes "can't get enough" of David Chang's "brilliant" "flavor combos" at this roomier East Village adjunct of his Noodle Bar, an "informal" destination for "luscious" Asian-influenced New American creations; whether for burrito-esque *ssäms* at lunch or a "more sophisticated" dinner, the "bench seating" "fills up fast" so "be prepared to wait"; N.B. a renovation is in the works that will add a pastry kitchen.

Momoya *Japanese* | 22 | 20 | 19 | $42 |

Chelsea | 185 Seventh Ave. (21st St.) | 212-989-4466
NEW W 80s | 427 Amsterdam Ave. (bet. 80th & 81st Sts.) | 212-580-0007 ●
www.themomoya.com
"A cut above" "the usual sushi joint", this Chelsea Japanese (with an "upbeat" new UWS offshoot) "outclasses the neighborhood competition" with its "fresh", "inventive rolls", "polite" service and "smart" surroundings; if the "high quality" is "surprising", so are the "fair prices."

Mon Petit Cafe *French* | 18 | 15 | 19 | $38 |

E 60s | 801 Lexington Ave. (62nd St.) | 212-355-2233 | www.monpetitcafe.com
"Lunching ladies" on break from shopping Bloomie's "feel right at home" at this "petite" UES bistro, an area "staple" for "well-prepared" French "basics" and "sweet" service; though "nothing fancy", it's "easy on the pocketbook" "so you can shop more."

Monster Sushi *Japanese* | 17 | 11 | 15 | $33 |

Chelsea | 158 W. 23rd St. (bet. 6th & 7th Aves.) | 212-620-9131 ●
W 40s | 22 W. 46th St. (bet. 5th & 6th Aves.) | 212-398-7707
W Village | 535 Hudson St. (Charles St.) | 646-336-1833
www.monstersushi.com
"They ain't lying" about the "super-sized sushi" at this Japanese trio, where "massive" rolls and sashimi "slabs" are served up "fast and easy" in "no-frills" digs; if the experience is "not exactly high-end", the "value" is a "monster hit."

Montparnasse ● *French* | 18 | 18 | 17 | $43 |

E 50s | The Pod Hotel | 230 E. 51st St. (bet. 2nd & 3rd Aves.) | 212-758-6633 | www.montparnasseny.com
"Spacious" and "unpretentious" for a bistro, this Midtowner makes a "comfortable" choice for "quite tasty" French standards and "non-rushed service"; partisans who deem it "dependably" "decent" add the $22.95 pre-theater prix fixe is a "real bargain."

Morandi ● *Italian* | 21 | 20 | 19 | $53 |

G Village | 211 Waverly Pl. (Charles St.) | 212-627-7575 | www.morandiny.com
Impresario Keith McNally "proves himself" again at this "magnetic" Village yearling, where "attractive" trendsters pack the "warm", faux-"weathered" space for "fabulous" "rustic" Italian served by a "genial" staff; the "high-energy" "bustle" is "a little loud", but that's the mark of a "winner."

	FOOD	DECOR	SERVICE	COST

Moran's Chelsea *American*
| 18 | 19 | 20 | $45 |

Chelsea | 146 10th Ave. (19th St.) | 212-627-3030 |
www.moranschelsea.com

"Timeless" "old-world" vibes pervade this Chelsea fixture, a "refuge"
for "quality" American fare in a "classic" "pub-style" setting featuring
an "open fire" and a "vast Waterford collection"; the staff's "lack of
'tude" helps explain why it's "been around for so long."

Morgan, The ⓜ *American*
| 21 | 22 | 20 | $45 |

Murray Hill | The Morgan Library & Museum | 225 Madison Ave.
(bet. 36th & 37th Sts.) | 212-683-2130 | www.themorgan.org

"Dress like a blue blood" for "genteel lunch" at Murray Hill's Morgan
Library, either in the "pleasant" atrium cafe or the "classy" enclave
"converted" from J. Pierpont's dining room; given the "well-executed"
New American food, the "modern"-meets-"historic" atmosphere is
sure to "grow on you."

Morimoto *Japanese*
| 25 | 26 | 23 | $80 |

Chelsea | 88 10th Ave. (bet. 15th & 16th Sts.) | 212-989-8883 |
www.morimotonyc.com

Iron Chef Masaharu Morimoto's "signature flair" is on "electrifying" display at this "stunningly cool" West Chelsea Japanese, which presents
"phenomenal" cuisine and "discreet" service in a space that's "über-
stylish" down to the "high-tech bathrooms"; however, it's a "big-time"
"investment", especially if you "go wild" and order omakase.

Morrell Wine Bar & Cafe *American*
| 18 | 16 | 18 | $48 |

W 40s | 1 Rockefeller Plaza (49th St., bet. 5th & 6th Aves.) | 212-262-7700 |
www.morrellwinebar.com

To "rest your feet and wet your whistle" try this "bustling" Rock
Center hub on prime "real estate" across from the plaza; highlights
include "smart" New American fare, an "amazing" "wine program"
and a "wonderful" patio.

Morton's The Steakhouse *Steak*
| 24 | 20 | 22 | $72 |

E 40s | 551 Fifth Ave. (45th St.) | 212-972-3315 | www.mortons.com

"Expense-account types" "live large" at this "clubby" Midtown meatery,
a "steady" supplier of "top-shelf" steaks, "mammoth sides" and "service
with a smile"; it "doesn't come cheap" and the "tableside preview" of
"beef in plastic wrap" is "way corny", but "the goods themselves deliver."

Moustache ●🌱 *Mideastern*
| 21 | 11 | 15 | $24 |

E Village | 265 E. 10th St. (bet. Ave. A & 1st Ave.) | 212-228-2022
W Village | 90 Bedford St. (bet. Barrow & Grove Sts.) | 212-229-2220

They "don't look like much", but it's worth giving this cross-Village
couple a twirl for "fantastic", "super-fresh" Middle Eastern bites; "bargain prices" "make up for" the "cramped" quarters and "iffy" service,
and at the Eastsider you can "sit in the garden."

Moutarde *French*
| 17 | 19 | 16 | $36 |

Park Slope | 239 Fifth Ave. (Carroll St.) | Brooklyn | 718-623-3600

Channeling "Dijon via Park Slope", this Gallic "charmer" plies "tasty"
"traditional bistro fare" in a "pretty setting" (complete with "sidewalk
tables") that "feels truly French"; service can be "clueless", but at
least "you won't leave broke."

	FOOD	DECOR	SERVICE	COST

NEW Moxie Spot *American/Asian*
| | - | - | - | M |

Brooklyn Heights | 81-83 Atlantic Ave. (bet. Henry & Hicks Sts.) |
Brooklyn | 718-923-9710 | www.themoxiespot.com

"Bring the kids" to this new Brooklyn Heights eatery/harried parent's oasis, serving affordable, healthy, child-friendly American-Asian fare in environs done up with maps, globes and flat-screens playing nature videos; the clincher is its "excellent", well-stocked playroom sure to keep little ones occupied while mom and dad dine at leisure.

Mr. Chow ● *Chinese*
| | 21 | 21 | 18 | $77 |

E 50s | 324 E. 57th St. (bet. 1st & 2nd Aves.) | 212-751-9030

Mr. Chow Tribeca ● *Chinese*

TriBeCa | 121 Hudson St. (N. Moore St.) | 212-965-9500
www.mrchow.com

You feel "trendy just walking in" to Michael Chow's "high-end" Midtown namesake (with a lesser-known, less-trendy TriBeCa outpost), home to "over-the-top everything" from the "celebrity scene" to the "superior" "spin" on Chinese cuisine; just know that it helps to be known here and the "ample" spread may "decimate your budget."

Mr. K's *Chinese*
| | 22 | 23 | 23 | $59 |

E 50s | 570 Lexington Ave. (51st St.) | 212-583-1668 | www.mrks.com

"If you want opulence", this "soothing" Midtowner is a chance to "dine like royalty" on "memorable" "gourmet Chinese" fare served by "courtly" staffers in the "plush", pink-hued "deco interior" "of your dreams"; the prices are accordingly "regal", but the "old-world" "show" is "worth the money" – as long as you're on an expense account.

Mughlai ● *Indian*
| | 19 | 13 | 17 | $34 |

W 70s | 320 Columbus Ave. (75th St.) | 212-724-6363

Followers expect "few surprises" from this UWS Indian, a "been-there-forever" "local favorite" for "authentic", "complexly spiced" cooking in "plain" but "comfortable" digs; if the service is "uneven", the "reasonable" cost compensates.

Nam *Vietnamese*
| | 21 | 17 | 19 | $39 |

TriBeCa | 110 Reade St. (W. B'way) | 212-267-1777 | www.namnyc.com

A "trendy crowd" veers "off the beaten path" to this "hip" TriBeCan to "mix it up" with "excellent", "adventurous" Vietnamese eats in a "lively" setting; overseen by an "efficient" team, it's "worth the trek" for its "appealing" ambiance and "good value."

Nana ⊟ *Asian Fusion*
| | ▽ 20 | 17 | 18 | $29 |

Park Slope | 155 Fifth Ave. (bet. Lincoln & St. Johns Pls.) | Brooklyn |
718-230-3749 | www.nana-parkslope.com

Offering "something for everyone" via a wide-ranging Asian fusion lineup, this "laid-back" Park Sloper is a "nabe fave" for "reliably good" chow on a "budget"; weekend DJs make it "like dining in a disco", but the "music-free" garden is always a "winner."

Nanni Ⓢ *Italian*
| | 24 | 15 | 23 | $60 |

E 40s | 146 E. 46th St. (bet. Lexington & 3rd Aves.) | 212-697-4161 |
www.nannirestaurant.com

"Old-fashioned" is "a compliment" at this Northern Italian "stalwart" near Grand Central, a "legit" source of "wonderful" "standards" served by "pro waiters" who've "worked there forever"; it's high-priced and the "tight quarters" are "long in the tooth", but for its "many regulars" it's forever *perfecto.*"

Naples 45 Ⓢ *Italian* 17 | 14 | 16 | $35

E 40s | MetLife Bldg. | 200 Park Ave. (45th St.) | 212-972-7001 | www.patinagroup.com

"Everyone you've ever worked with" turns up at this "huge" Italian "attached to Grand Central", a "casual" stop for "biz" meals "before jumping on Metro North"; "pizza is the way to go" on the "routine" menu, but know that "hectic" crowds can necessitate "rushed" service.

Natsumi ● *Italian/Japanese* ∇ 22 | 21 | 21 | $42

W 50s | Amsterdam Court Hotel | 226 W. 50th St. (bet. B'way & 8th Ave.) | 212-258-2988

From the team behind Haru comes this "popular" Theater District Italo-Japanese fusion practitioner whose "creative" menu includes the likes of green tea ravioli; "personable servers" man its "trendy" two-part setting featuring a sushi bar/dining room separated by a hotel lobby from the lounge/raw bar.

Neary's ● *Pub Food* 14 | 13 | 19 | $44

E 50s | 358 E. 57th St. (1st Ave.) | 212-751-1434

"Consummate host" and "leprechaun" stand-in Jimmy Neary "acts like he knows you from the old country" at his Midtown pub, a "clublike" "neighborhood haunt" that "hits the spot" with Irish "home cooking"; it's "nothing fancy", but "longtime locals swear by it" all the same.

Negril *Caribbean/Jamaican* 20 | 16 | 16 | $36

Chelsea | 362 W. 23rd St. (bet. 8th & 9th Aves.) | 212-807-6411 ●
G Village | 70 W. Third St. (bet. La Guardia Pl. & Thompson St.) | 212-477-2804 | www.negrilvillage.com Ⓜ

The "hot" spices and "specialty drinks" pack "quite a punch" at these "casual" Caribbeans that "satisfy" with "tasty" jerk chicken and other "Jamaican delicacies" to "get your groove back"; the "Village location is better adorned", but anticipate "less than stellar" service at both.

Nello ● *Italian* 18 | 16 | 15 | $84

E 60s | 696 Madison Ave. (bet. 62nd & 63rd Sts.) | 212-980-9099

"Page Six mentions" abound at this "upmarket" Eastsider, where celebs, "socialites" and their fello "beautiful people" meet over "quality" Italian in a "busy", "very Euro" milieu; meanwhile the "out-of-control pricing" and "snobbery" have commoners bello-ing "who are they kidding?"

Nëo Sushi ● *Japanese* 23 | 15 | 19 | $60

W 80s | 2298 Broadway (83rd St.) | 212-769-1003

"Trying to be Nobu" for the "UWS locals", this "friendly" Japanese standby presents its "delicate", "delicious" sushi "innovations" as "art on a plate"; critics cite the prices as "astronomical" for the locale, but boosters only wish they could afford it "more often."

Neptune Room *Seafood* 21 | 19 | 19 | $49

W 80s | 511 Amsterdam Ave. (bet. 84th & 85th Sts.) | 212-496-4100 | www.theneptuneroom.com

Afishionados "can net fresh seafood" at this UWS "find" that's "always on course" with its "excellent" marine cuisine, raw bar and "surprisingly good brunch"; though it "might seem pricey", its "cheery" service and "quieter" bearing are "a welcome change" in these waters.

Nero ◐ *Italian* | 19 | 18 | 18 | $45 |

Meatpacking | 46 Gansevoort St. (Greenwich St.) | 212-675-5224 | www.neronyc.com

"Hidden" in a "happening area", this Meatpacking District Italian offers "bold" "rustic" cooking at "reasonable prices" in "cool", "candlelit" quarters expanded with "sidewalk seating"; "harried" service aside, it's "enjoyable" "when you can't get a table at Pastis."

New Bo-Ky ⊘ *Noodle Shop* | ▽ 20 | 4 | 9 | $12 |

Chinatown | 80 Bayard St. (bet. Mott & Mulberry Sts.) | 212-406-2292
It's "worth being on jury duty" for a chance to sample the "wide selection" of "out-of-this-world" Chinese and Vietnamese noodle soups at this "real-deal" C-town "staple"; the surroundings and service are "absolutely bare-bones", but you "really can't beat" the cost.

New Leaf Cafe Ⓜ *American* | 20 | 23 | 18 | $41 |

Washington Heights | Fort Tryon Park | 1 Margaret Corbin Dr. (190th St.) | 212-568-5323 | www.nyrp.org
The "perfect place to finish a visit to the Cloisters", this "restful" "oasis" in Fort Tryon Park offers Scott Campbell's "inventive" New American fare in a "sylvan setting" featuring a "scenic patio"; service can be "slow", but then you'll want to linger; P.S. "three cheers for Bette Midler" and her nonprofit that runs this "gem."

Nha Trang *Vietnamese* | 21 | 7 | 15 | $17 |

Chinatown | 148 Centre St. (bet. Walker & White Sts.) | 212-941-9292
Chinatown | 87 Baxter St. (bet. Bayard & Canal Sts.) | 212-233-5948
This "hole-in-the-wall" Chinatown twosome is "well-vetted" for "plentiful" portions of "awesome" "Vietnamese favorites" served in the "blink of an eye" at "low, low prices"; sure, they're seriously "plain", but devotees "don't go for the decor."

Nice Green Bo ⊘ *Chinese* | 23 | 5 | 11 | $18 |
(fka New Green Bo)

Chinatown | 66 Bayard St. (bet. Elizabeth & Mott Sts.) | 212-625-2359

"Juicy soup dumplings" "are the stars" at this "popular" Chinatowner, where the "super" Shanghainese chow comes "practically free"; the new name's a little nicer, but the "dingy" digs, "jammed" "communal seating" and "in-and-out" service are anything but.

Nice Matin ◐ *French/Mediterranean* | 19 | 18 | 17 | $46 |

W 70s | 201 W. 79th St. (Amsterdam Ave.) | 212-873-6423 | www.nicematinnyc.com
"Lively and likable", this UWS "asset" attracts the "trendies" with a "moderately priced" French-Med menu and a "convivial" bistro setting modeled on the "Côte d'Azur"; extras include "outside seating" and a "solid brunch", but beware of sometimes "amateurish service."

NEW Niche *American* | - | - | - | M |

E 80s | 1593 Second Ave. (bet. 82nd & 83rd Sts.) | 212-734-5500
The folks behind Rughetta and Etats-Unis have found an UES niche for this midpriced New American arrival and its upscale comfort fare;

young locals are already filling its chic, narrow space, which has just one long communal marble table – though it's possible to sit *à deux* at a sidewalk table.

Nick & Stef's Steakhouse 🎱 *Steak* | 21 | 18 | 21 | $61 |

Garment District | 9 Penn Plaza (enter on 33rd St., bet. 7th & 8th Aves.) | 212-563-4444 | www.patinagroup.com

Though many go to this Patina-owned Midtown meatery adjoining Penn Station and MSG "for the convenience", its "hearty" grub is considered "surprisingly good"; it's ideal "for pre-Garden events" since there's an "inside passage" to the arena and they "get you out fast."

Nick and Toni's Cafe *Mediterranean* | 17 | 13 | 17 | $48 |

W 60s | 100 W. 67th St. (bet. B'way & Columbus Ave.) | 212-496-4000 | www.nickandtoniscafe.com

There's "no comparison" to the East Hampton original, but this "low-pressure" "standby" "nestled" near Lincoln Center offers "decent" wood-fired Med dishes, minus its forebear's A-list clientele; sporadic service "attitude" can put a nick in the "warm" mood.

Nick's *Pizza* | 23 | 13 | 17 | $24 |

E 90s | 1814 Second Ave. (94th St.) | 212-987-5700 | www.nicksnyc.com
Forest Hills | 108-26 Ascan Ave. (bet. Austin & Burns Sts.) | Queens | 718-263-1126 ⊄

Pizzaphiles "dream about" these "old-fashioned" Forest Hills–UES parlors, home to "sublime" pies sporting "charred thin crusts" and "fresh" toppings – plus "family-style" "red-sauce" fare at the newer Manhattan banch; the decor and service "leave a lot to be desired", but given the "quality" and "value", "who needs anything else?"

Nicky's Vietnamese Sandwiches ⊄ *Sandwiches* | 22 | 5 | 15 | $10 |

E Village | 150 E. Second St. (Ave. A) | 212-388-1088
Boerum Hill | 311 Atlantic Ave. (bet. Hoyt & Smith Sts.) | Brooklyn | 718-855-8838 Ⓜ
www.nickyssandwiches.com

"Addictive" *banh mi* sandwiches are the trademark at this "pint-sized" Vietnamese pair, whose "fresh bread" and "fantastic" fillings are an "absolute delight" for a "bargain" "quick bite"; their "bare-bones" storefronts persuade most junkies to "get takeout."

Nicola's ● *Italian* | 22 | 16 | 20 | $61 |

E 80s | 146 E. 84th St. (bet. Lexington & 3rd Aves.) | 212-249-9850

A "clubby" haven for the well-heeled "local crowd", this "civilized" UES stalwart is "dependable" for "primo" "old-world" Italian cuisine and "pro" service; just keep in mind that the tabs "fit right in" with the "upmarket" zip code and staffers who "cater to regulars" "can be aloof" if you're an inconnu.

99 Miles to Philly ●⊄ *Cheese Steaks* | 18 | 7 | 12 | $12 |

E Village | 94 Third Ave. (bet. 12th & 13th Sts.) | 212-253-2700 | www.99milestophilly.net

"Damn good" Philly cheese steaks "without the 99-mile drive" turn up at this "cash-only" East Villager where aficionados order them "with Cheez Whiz for the real deal"; despite "not much atmosphere" or service, it's popular with "NYU" types given its cheap tabs.

	FOOD	DECOR	SERVICE	COST

Ninja *Japanese* ▽ 16 | 25 | 21 | $67

TriBeCa | 25 Hudson St. (bet. Duane & Reade Sts.) | 212-274-8500 |
www.ninjanewyork.com

Servers in "Ninja outfits" oversee a "Disneyland-esque" "village" at
this TriBeCa themer, providing "decent" Japanese food and "gimmicky" "tableside entertainment" topped with a magic act; though it's
"fun for the kids", grown-ups wish they'd "dial down the cheese factor" and "expensive" tabs.

Nino's ● *Italian* 21 | 19 | 20 | $55

E 70s | 1354 First Ave. (bet. 72nd & 73rd Sts.) | 212-988-0002 |
www.ninosnyc.com

Nino's Bellissima Pizza *Italian*

E 40s | 890 Second Ave. (bet. 47th & 48th Sts.) | 212-355-5540 |
www.ninospositano.com

Nino's Positano *Italian*

E 40s | 890 Second Ave. (bet. 47th & 48th Sts.) | 212-355-5540 |
www.ninospositano.com

Nino's Tuscany *Italian*

W 50s | 117 W. 58th St. (bet. 6th & 7th Aves.) | 212-757-8630 |
www.ninostuscany.com

"Consistently fine dining" marks this "old-school" Italian chainlet, a
source of "super" cuisine and "personal service" for those who can afford the "high-end" pricing; the "classy" First Avenue flagship and its
58th Street outpost host "atmospheric" pianists while Positano and its
adjacent brick-oven pizzeria play it more "casual."

Nippon 🅱 *Japanese* ▽ 22 | 17 | 21 | $64

E 50s | 155 E. 52nd St. (bet. Lexington & 3rd Aves.) | 212-758-0226 |
www.restaurantnippon.com

Established in 1963, this "pioneering" East Midtowner helped introduce
NYC to sushi and remains "dependable" as ever for "high-quality"
"old-line Japanese" served "without the gimmicks"; it's a "venerable"
"standby" despite serious tabs and a setting said to be "showing its age."

NEW Nizza ● *French/Italian* 20 | 18 | 19 | $35

W 40s | 630 Ninth Ave. (bet. 44th & 45th Sts.) | 212-956-1800 |
www.nizzanyc.com

Spun off from neighboring Marseille, this new Hell's Kitchen "price
performer" likewise takes to the Riviera with a "refreshing" Italian-
French lineup focused on "tasty" small plates; the "minimalist-yet-
inviting" space is "popular" with "pre-theater" types who only lament
there aren't "more seats."

Ⓩ Nobu *Japanese* 27 | 22 | 23 | $83

TriBeCa | 105 Hudson St. (Franklin St.) | 212-219-0500

Ⓩ Nobu, Next Door ● *Japanese*

TriBeCa | 105 Hudson St. (bet. Franklin & N. Moore Sts.) |
212-334-4445
www.noburestaurants.com

"Still the gold standard", this TriBeCa "classic" named after founder
Nobu Matsuhisa will "blow you away" with its "phenomenal" Japanese-
Peruvian "creations", "terrific" service and "stratospheric prices"; an
"A-list" assortment of "high rollers" and "celebs" (Robert De Niro is a
partner) makes it "the place to be", and though reservations are "a

nightmare", the "more reasonable" Next Door produces "the same quality" for walk-ins only – and lunch is always a good bet.

☑ Nobu 57 ◑ *Japanese*   26 | 24 | 22 | $82

W 50s | 40 W. 57th St. (bet. 5th & 6th Aves.) | 212-757-3000 | www.noburestaurants.com

Entrée is more "accessible", but otherwise this Midtown "wow" "lives up to the name" of its Downtown forerunner as "bankers" and "beautiful people" "pack" David Rockwell's "cavernous", "high-style" space for "sensational" Japanese-Peruvian cuisine from an "informed" staff; the "celeb"-centric "hot scene" is "everything it's cracked up to be", but prepare to "leave your paycheck" behind.

Nocello *Italian*   20 | 17 | 20 | $49

W 50s | 257 W. 55th St. (bet. B'way & 8th Ave.) | 212-713-0224 | www.nocello.net

"Not fancy but very reliable", this "moderately priced" Midtowner's "quality" Tuscan cooking and swift, "friendly service" make for a "pleasant" meal "close to Carnegie Hall"; modernists dis the "old-fashioned" style, but "you'll never leave hungry."

Noche Mexicana *Mexican*   ▽ 23 | 8 | 18 | $18

W 100s | 852 Amsterdam Ave. (bet. 101st & 102nd Sts.) | 212-662-6900 | www.noche-mexicana.com

It's a "nondescript" "dive", but this Columbia-area "find" takes "the usual Mexican" up a noche with "wondrous" "homestyle" recipes served "without the hoopla" at prices you "can't beat"; regulars who tolerate the "laid-back" pace say it's a "best-kept secret."

NoHo Star ◑ *American*   17 | 14 | 16 | $33

NoHo | 330 Lafayette St. (Bleecker St.) | 212-925-0070 | www.nohostar.com

A "standby" "for all seasons", this longtime NoHo New American "holds its own" with "pleasing" "comfort food" that gets extra glimmer from "Chinese classics" at dinner; "affordability" keeps the "airy yet casual" premises "energetic" and "noisy", "dodgy service" or no.

Nomad *African*   ▽ 20 | 16 | 18 | $31

E Village | 78 Second Ave. (4th St.) | 212-253-5410 | www.nomadny.com

Those in-the-know roam to this "exotic" East Villager to savor "wonderful" North African specialties in a snug but "attractive" setting manned by "personable" expats; in addition to the "interesting" "change from the same-old", admirers are mad about the "reasonable prices."

Nonna *Italian*   18 | 15 | 16 | $32

W 80s | 520 Columbus Ave. (85th St.) | 212-579-3194 | www.nonnarestaurant.com

UWS locals who miss "nonna's cooking" turn to this "unpretentious Italian" as a "satisfying" substitute; if the "hit-or-miss" service and "standard" style are "nothing to rave about", it's a "solid value" – especially the "family-style" Sunday dinner "feast."

Noodle Pudding ▣⇗ *Italian*   24 | 17 | 21 | $37

Brooklyn Heights | 38 Henry St. (bet. Cranberry & Middagh Sts.) | Brooklyn | 718-625-3737

The room's "always packed for a reason" at this "cash-only" Brooklyn Heights trattoria, which "hits the bull's-eye" with "superior", "well-priced" "homestyle" Italiana and "neighborly" service; the only snags are the "high noise level", "no-reservations" rule and "killer" waits.

Nook ◐⊅ *Eclectic* 22 | 11 | 17 | $32

W 50s | 746 Ninth Ave. (bet. 50th & 51st Sts.) | 212-247-5500

This wee Hell's Kitchen Eclectic has found its niche furnishing a "small menu" of "quality" "home cooking" at "recession-friendly" prices; "service is erratic" and "space is tight", but the BYO policy keeps the mood "festive."

Norma's *American* 25 | 18 | 19 | $39

W 50s | Le Parker Meridien | 118 W. 57th St. (bet. 6th & 7th Aves.) | 212-708-7460 | www.parkermeridien.com

Always "eye-opening", this Midtown "champion of breakfasts" and brunches "hits new heights" serving "lavish" New American morning fare (à la the "infamous" $1,000 caviar omelet) in a "cosmopolitan" milieu; its "well-heeled" fans don't mind the "splurge", but report that the crowds can be "out of control."

North Square *American* 22 | 19 | 20 | $45

G Village | Washington Square Hotel | 103 Waverly Pl. (MacDougal St.) | 212-254-1200 | www.northsquareny.com

For "civilized dining", this "favorably priced" Village "sleeper" squarely supplies "delightful" New American fare and "super service" in a "quaint", sunken space that's "conducive to quiet conversation"; local loyalists whisper "let's keep it a secret."

Notaro *Italian* ▽ 18 | 15 | 21 | $38

Murray Hill | 635 Second Ave. (bet. 34th & 35th Sts.) | 212-686-3400 | www.notaroristorante.com

They "make you feel at home" at this "friendly" Murray Hill "neighborhood" Tuscan in Murray Hill, dishing up "satisfying" "comfort food" in a "quiet", "cozy" setting abetted by a "fireplace in back"; its "affordable" prices notably include a $20.95 deal for "the early-bird crowd."

Novecento ◐ *Argentinean/Steak* ▽ 19 | 16 | 17 | $42

SoHo | 343 W. Broadway (bet. Broome & Grand Sts.) | 212-925-4706 | www.novecentogroup.com

"Steak lovers rejoice" over the "excellent meat" and "honest value" at this "SoHo staple", a "safe bet" for Argentine-style beef in "little" "bistro" digs that are like a bit of Buenos Aires; meanwhile, "beautiful Euros" "hang out" at the "vibrant bar."

Novitá *Italian* 24 | 18 | 21 | $54

Gramercy | 102 E. 22nd St. (bet. Lexington Ave. & Park Ave. S.) | 212-677-2222 | www.novitanyc.com

Though somewhat "off the radar" outside the neighborhood, this "neat little" Gramercy "charmer" is a "local favorite" for "delicious" Northern Italian fare smartly served "without attitude"; the "warm" digs are "tight on space", but that hardly dents its sturdy rep.

Nurnberger Bierhaus *German* ▽ 21 | 18 | 21 | $32

Staten Island | 817 Castleton Ave. (Davis Ave.) | 718-816-7461 | www.nurnbergerbierhaus.com

"Oompah comes to Staten Island's North Shore" via this "fun" Teutonic pub, where "hearty" helpings of "old-style" "Bavarian fare" are chased with a "big selection of German beers"; and if the interior gets "cramped", there's always "the biergarten."

Nyonya ● ⊄ *Malaysian* | 22 | 12 | 13 | $21 |

Little Italy | 194 Grand St. (bet. Mott & Mulberry Sts.) | 212-334-3669
Sunset Park | 5323 Eighth Ave. (54th St.) | Brooklyn | 718-633-0808
www.penangusa.com
The "best of Malaysia" is available at this Little Italy-Sunset Park duo that "covers all the bases" with its "excellent", "properly spiced" offerings; the service is "in a rush" and "they still don't take credit cards", but it's "hard to argue" with such "dirt-cheap" tabs.

Oceana 🅱 *American/Seafood* | 26 | 24 | 24 | $101 |

E 50s | 55 E. 54th St. (bet. Madison & Park Aves.) | 212-759-5941 | www.oceanarestaurant.com
It's "all aboard for excellent fish" at this "dreamy" Midtown New American, which "steers a straight course" with "pristine" seafood, "calm" "luxury liner" atmospherics and "service above the call of duty"; the $78 prix fixe-only menu is an "expense-account buster", but all that "elegance" "will leave you floating."

Ocean Grill *Seafood* | 23 | 20 | 21 | $54 |

W 70s | 384 Columbus Ave. (bet. 78th & 79th Sts.) | 212-579-2300 | www.brguestrestaurants.com
UWS finatics "would be lost" without Steve Hanson's "vibrant" seafooder, where the "splendid" fish is "fresh enough to swim away" and there's a "buzz" that swells throughout the "stylish room"; it's "not for quiet conversation", but the "courteous" staff, "fair" prices and "terrific" brunch are "bound to please."

Odeon ● *American/French* | 18 | 17 | 17 | $47 |

TriBeCa | 145 W. Broadway (bet. Duane & Thomas Sts.) | 212-233-0507 | www.theodeonrestaurant.com
An "'80s" "legend" that "just keeps on going", this TriBeCa Franco-American serves its "reliable bistro" bites to "a cross section" of urbanites who keep the deco space "lively"; with its "cool atmosphere" intact, it's still "a safe bet for after-hours" scene scoping.

NEW Olana 🅱 *American* | ▽ 23 | 22 | 22 | $62 |

Gramercy | 72 Madison Ave. (bet. 27th & 28th Sts.) | 212-725-4900 | www.olananyc.com
This "classy", and costly, Gramercy newcomer is out to "wow your palate" with a "complex" New American menu sporting "French and Italian accents" that make "every bite a revelation"; add "gracious" service and a "plush" interior inspired by the "Hudson River School" artists, and it's a "lovely" debut that someday "could be great."

Old Homestead *Steak* | 24 | 17 | 21 | $68 |

Meatpacking | 56 Ninth Ave. (bet. 14th & 15th Sts.) | 212-242-9040 | www.theoldhomesteadsteakhouse.com
Though it's "been there forever" (since 1868), this Meatpacking District cow palace steadily "delivers the goods" with *Flintstone*-size "prime steaks" in a "traditional" "dark-wood" setting; "waiters who know what they're doing" lay on the "old-world charm", and though it's "spendy", "you'll get over it."

	FOOD	DECOR	SERVICE	COST

Olea *Mediterranean* ▽ 23 | 21 | 21 | $36

Fort Greene | 171 Lafayette Ave. (Adelphi St.) | Brooklyn | 718-643-7003 | www.oleabrooklyn.com

"Go nuts" with the "delicious" tapas at this Fort Greene Mediterranean, a "cool haven" for "first-rate" food, "affordable wines" and a "creative brunch"; the "cozy" interior radiates "romance", even if it's often "crowded these days."

Oliva ❶ *Spanish* ▽ 20 | 16 | 17 | $35

LES | 161 E. Houston St. (Allen St.) | 212-228-4143 | www.olivanyc.com

"Solid tapas", "friendly" service and "killer sangria" add up to a "fun" time at this casual, "lively" LES Basque, especially when you factor in the "cheap" tab; its "devoted" followers are a "loud" crowd, but "after a few drinks, it's fine."

Olives *Mediterranean* 22 | 21 | 20 | $58

Union Sq | W Union Sq. | 201 Park Ave. S. (17th St.) | 212-353-8345 | www.toddenglish.com

"Todd English doesn't disappoint" at this "upscale" Med in the W Union Square Hotel, where the "solid", "creative cuisine" is "well worth" the "expense-account" pricing; with a "jumping social scene" in the "bustling bar", "everything is pleasurable" except the "din."

Ollie's *Chinese* 15 | 10 | 13 | $23

W 40s | Manhattan Plaza | 411 W. 42nd St. (bet. 9th & 10th Aves.) | 212-868-6588
W 60s | 1991 Broadway (bet. 67th & 68th Sts.) | 212-595-8181 ❶
W 80s | 2315 Broadway (84th St.) | 212-362-3111 ❶
W 100s | 2957 Broadway (116th St.) | 212-932-3300 ❶

While "satisfying" for "standard" Chinese eats, this "hectic" West Side mini-chain is also "trusty" for "scary-fast" service and "bargain prices"; its "mass-production" MO means "stone-faced" staffers and "basic" surroundings, but fortunately it also delivers in "record time."

Omai *Vietnamese* 23 | 17 | 19 | $40

Chelsea | 158 Ninth Ave. (bet. 19th & 20th Sts.) | 212-633-0550 | www.omainyc.com

"Once you've found it" behind an "unmarked exterior", this "compact" Chelsea Vietnamese aims to please with "terrific" chow served by a "helpful" staff; the "spare" setup is "slightly tight", but those apprised of the "modest cost" say "'oh my' is right."

Omen ❶ *Japanese* ▽ 23 | 16 | 18 | $59

SoHo | 113 Thompson St. (bet. Prince & Spring Sts.) | 212-925-8923

It's "not for those who want routine fare" like sushi, but this "rustic" SoHo Japanese stalwart "astounds" with the "high quality" of its "heavenly" "Kyoto-style" specialties; the "cool" clientele ("incognito" celebs included) hardly minds that it's "esoteric" and ominously "expensive."

Omido ❶ *Japanese* ▽ 24 | 22 | 20 | $51

W 50s | 1695 Broadway (bet. 53rd & 54th Sts.) | 212-247-8110 | www.omidonyc.com

This "upper-end" Japanese Midtowner slices "super-fresh and inventive sushi" in "intimate surrounds" sporting an "eye-catching design" courtesy of AvroKO; the "small" space is warmed with "friendly

Menus, photos, voting and more – free at ZAGAT.com

service" and "wonderful" sakes, and, best of all, even though it's in a touristy area, the "tourists haven't discovered" it yet.

Omonia Cafe ● _Greek_ | 18 | 15 | 14 | $21

Bay Ridge | 7612-14 Third Ave. (bet. 76th & 77th Sts.) | Brooklyn | 718-491-1435

Astoria | 32-20 Broadway (33rd St.) | Queens | 718-274-6650

Serving "fine" java and an "incredible variety" of "heavenly" Hellenic desserts, this Astoria–Bay Ridge Greek coffeehouse duo boasts a "decidedly European feel"; the alfresco tables work for "people-watching", and though service is a "little lax", at least they "never pressure you to leave."

Once Upon a Tart . . . _Coffeehouse_ | 20 | 14 | 13 | $16

SoHo | 135 Sullivan St. (bet. Houston & Prince Sts.) | 212-387-8869 | www.onceuponatart.com

Unsurprisingly, the "delicious tarts" "steal the show" at this SoHo cafe, an "old-fashioned" cubbyhole that also vends "inexpensive" sandwiches, salads and other "well-made" bites; given the "close" quarters and scarce service, many opt for outdoor seating or "takeout."

O'Neals' ● _American_ | 17 | 16 | 18 | $45

W 60s | 49 W. 64th St. (bet. B'way & CPW) | 212-787-4663 | www.onealsny.com

Lincoln Center attendees "can count on" this "rambling" area "standby" for "ample portions" of "straightforward" Americana at "sensible prices"; the "lively bar" contributes to the "congenial", "pubby" atmosphere, though it's "at its best" once the show-goers "clear out."

🆕 1 Dominick ● _Italian_ | – | – | – | I

SoHo | 1 Dominick St. (bet. 6th Ave. & Varick St.) | 212-647-0202, ext. 308

Theatergoers like this new Italian cafe adjoining West SoHo's Here Arts Center, offering reasonably priced fare in a bare-bones, counter-service setting; daytime panini and pastries yield to small plates at night, and although BYO for now, wine and beer is in the works.

One 83 _Italian_ | 20 | 21 | 22 | $49

E 80s | 1608 First Ave. (bet. 83rd & 84th Sts.) | 212-327-4700 | www.one83restaurant.com

Still "barely discovered", this "upscale" UES Northern Italian is nonetheless a "keeper" for "well-executed" cuisine and "courteous" service in a "mercifully" "muted" setting with "plenty of distance between tables"; some favor the "romantic" possibilities, others the "garden in the back."

🅩 One if by Land, Two if by Sea _American_ | 24 | 27 | 24 | $101

G Village | 17 Barrow St. (bet. 7th Ave. S. & W. 4th St.) | 212-228-0822 | www.oneifbyland.com

"Bring the ring" and "hope she says yes" is the theme at this Village New American, which transforms "Aaron Burr's" circa-1767 carriage house into a "romantic landmark"; after the "remarkable" $75 prix fixe menu, "cosseting" service and "classy" backdrop featuring "candlelight" and a pianist, she's bound to accept any proposal; since "they've renovated and brought in a new chef", the "wallet stress" is even more justified.

	FOOD	DECOR	SERVICE	COST

101 *American/Italian* | 19 | 18 | 18 | $41

Bay Ridge | 10018 Fourth Ave. (bet. 100th & 101st Sts.) | Brooklyn | 718-833-1313
Staten Island | 3900 Richmond Ave. (Amboy Rd.) | 718-227-3286
www.101nyc.com

"People-watching at the bar" plays second fiddle to the "surprisingly good" food at this "established", *Goodfellas*-ish Italian–New American duo; while the Staten Island branch is "popular" enough, "it pales in comparison to the Brooklyn one."

107 West *Cajun/Tex-Mex* | 17 | 14 | 17 | $28

Washington Heights | 811 W. 187th St. (bet. Ft. Washington & Pinehurst Aves.) | 212-923-3311
W 100s | 2787 Broadway (bet. 107th & 108th Sts.) | 212-864-1555
www.107west.com

"Acceptable if uninspired", these UWS Cajun-Tex-Mex "neighborhood staples" are "reliable" for "nonadventurous" types hoping to entertain "visiting parents"; maybe the decor is "no-frills" and the service "erratic", but the portions are "good-size" and "not expensive."

Ono *Japanese* | ▽ 19 | 23 | 14 | $72

Meatpacking | Gansevoort Hotel | 18 Ninth Ave. (enter on 13th St., bet. Hudson St. & 9th Ave.) | 212-660-6766 | www.chinagrillmgt.com

At Jeffrey Chodorow's Meatpacking District Japanese, the "cool, hip" space – including an outdoor area complete with reflecting pool, cabanas and bar – overshadows the "really good" sushi and robata grill fare; however, gripes about "major attitude" and "gigantic prices" lead some to suggest this ono is "too sexy for its shirt."

Orchard, The ⊠ *American* | 23 | 22 | 21 | $54

LES | 162 Orchard St. (bet. Rivington & Stanton Sts.) | 212-353-3570 | www.theorchardny.com

"Hip but mature" types find "refuge" at this "soothing" LES New American, where the "fantastic food" takes on Med inflections ("don't miss the flatbreads") and the setting's "mellow orange" tones lend a "sexy vibe"; "attentive service" and "reasonable" wines make this an "excellent" pick for you and your peach.

⊠ Oriental Garden *Chinese/Seafood* | 24 | 12 | 17 | $31

Chinatown | 14 Elizabeth St. (bet. Bayard & Canal Sts.) | 212-619-0085

Seafood "doesn't get any fresher" than when it's plucked "out of the tank" at this "reasonable" Chinatown Cantonese, NYC's No. 1 Chinese, an "old favorite" for "outstanding" eating that includes "high-quality dim sum"; but "abrupt" service and a "simple" space "packed with locals" mean it's "not a place for lingering."

Orsay *French* | 18 | 21 | 17 | $56

E 70s | 1057 Lexington Ave. (75th St.) | 212-517-6400 | www.orsayrestaurant.com

A "social" "staple" for UES swells and "div-orsays", this "bright, bustling" brasserie is an "overall good" source of "classic French bistro fare"; it's "authentic enough" "if you're willing to pay", though some surmise that "attitude was invented here."

	FOOD	DECOR	SERVICE	COST

Orso ● *Italian*
`23` `18` `21` `$56`

W 40s | 322 W. 46th St. (bet. 8th & 9th Aves.) | 212-489-7212 | www.orsorestaurant.com

"Popular as ever", this "accommodating" "Restaurant Row stalwart" is "deserving of a Tony" for its "top-notch" Northern Italian fare and Broadway "clubhouse" vibe, complete with "stargazing" "galore"; but "plan ahead" as pre-show prime time is "usually sold out."

Osso Buco *Italian*
`17` `14` `16` `$36`

E 90s | 1662 Third Ave. (93rd St.) | 212-426-5422
G Village | 88 University Pl. (bet. 11th & 12th Sts.) | 212-645-4525
www.ossobuco2go.com

Prepare for "sharing" at this "casual" duo, which dispenses "family platters" of "dependable" "red-sauce Italian" "at modest prices"; sure, they're "pedestrian" with "haphazard" service, but they're osso convenient "if you can't stand the wait at Carmine's."

Osteria al Doge ● *Italian*
`20` `17` `19` `$49`

W 40s | 142 W. 44th St. (bet. B'way & 6th Ave.) | 212-730-5911 | www.osteria-doge.com

"Deservedly" a "pre-theater fave", this Times Square Italian performs "satisfyingly" with "wonderful" "Venetian-inspired" dishes "that won't break the bank"; the "efficient" staff "gets you out in time", but to avoid the "boisterous" crowd's "wall of noise", "upstairs seating is best."

Osteria del Circo ● *Italian*
`22` `23` `22` `$63`

W 50s | 120 W. 55th St. (bet. 6th & 7th Aves.) | 212-265-3636 | www.osteriadelcirco.com

A "spangly show" awaits at the Maccioni clan's "vibrant" Midtowner, where "big top" decor sets the "whimsical" scene for "cheery" hospitality and "fabulous" Northern Italian fare; while "not cheap", it's "always a treat" for ticket-holders at City Center and Carnegie Hall – and running restaurants well is an inherited skill in this family.

Osteria Gelsi ● *Italian*
`22` `15` `19` `$48`

Garment District | 507 Ninth Ave. (38th St.) | 212-244-0088

Run by an "obliging family", this Garment District "discovery" in the "nowhere land" behind Port Authority is an "unusual" Italian option, preparing "wonderful Puglian" specialties with "creativity and skill"; its "pleasantly quiet" atmosphere repays the "hike over."

Osteria Laguna ● *Italian*
`21` `18` `19` `$47`

E 40s | 209 E. 42nd St. (bet. 2nd & 3rd Aves.) | 212-557-0001 | www.osteria-laguna.com

"Office workers" and "U.N. types" agree that this Midtown Italian is a "solid" choice for "artful" Venetian fare and "genial" service, with "busy 42nd Street" on view through the open front; typically "packed" and "loud" for lunch, it grows "much quieter at dinner."

Otto ● *Pizza*
`23` `19` `19` `$39`

G Village | 1 Fifth Ave. (enter on 8th St., bet. 5th Ave. & University Pl.) | 212-995-9559 | www.ottopizzeria.com

The Batali-Bastianich team's Village enoteca/pizzeria is a "hit" with "the masses", offering "amazing" "designer" pies, "robust" pastas, "unreal gelati" and "incredible" Italian wines in a "raucous" ersatz railway station; it's "jam-packed" with "yuppies", "tourists and the college set", so expect "crazy waits."

☑ Ouest *American*   25 | 21 | 22 | $64

W 80s | 2315 Broadway (bet. 83rd & 84th Sts.) | 212-580-8700 | www.ouestny.com

"Tom Valenti continues to amaze" at this "shining light of the UWS", a "first-class affair" for "richly flavored" New American cuisine and "polished service" in a "stylish" "retro" room featuring "cozy circular booths"; it's an "expensive treat" that's "still going strong" with a best-of-the-West crowd, so be braced for a reservations "gauntlet."

Our Place *Chinese*   20 | 14 | 18 | $34

E 50s | 141 E. 55th St. (bet. Lexington & 3rd Aves.) | 212-753-3900 | www.ourplace-teagarden.com
E 80s | 1444 Third Ave. (82nd St.) | 212-288-4888 | www.ourplaceuptown.com

"Upgrade your Chinese" experience at these separately owned sources of "winning dishes" and "courteous" service, known for "Shanghainese specialties" in Midtown and "weekend dim sum" on the UES; they're "pricey", but "devout regulars" place them "above the crowd."

Outback Steakhouse *Steak*   15 | 12 | 16 | $34

E 50s | 919 Third Ave. (enter on 56th St., bet. 2nd & 3rd Aves.) | 212-935-6400
Flatiron | 60 W. 23rd St. (bet. 5th & 6th Aves.) | 212-989-3122
Dyker Heights | 1475 86th St. (15th Ave.) | Brooklyn | 718-837-7200
Bayside | Bay Terrace | 23-48 Bell Blvd. (26th Ave.) | Queens | 718-819-0908
Elmhurst | Queens Pl. | 88-01 Queens Blvd. (56th Ave.) | Queens | 718-760-7200
www.outback.com

"Take the kids" to this Aussie steakhouse chain, where the "acceptable" grub is "not too costly" and "guaranteed to expand your waistline"; antis argue "Australia should sue" over the "very commercial" style, but c'mon, "who can resist that bloomin' onion?"

Oyster Bar ☒ *Seafood*   21 | 17 | 16 | $48

E 40s | Grand Central | lower level (42nd St. & Vanderbilt Ave.) | 212-490-6650 | www.oysterbarny.com

Traditionalists "treasure" this "time-honored" Grand Central seafood "standard-bearer" for its "amazing assortment" of "impeccable oysters", "classic" pan roasts and "perfectly prepared" fish, paired with "the best" white wines; its "massive" tiled arches may at times echo with the "overwhelming" "din", but it's "hard to top" as a Gotham "must-visit."

Pacificana *Chinese*   ▽ 21 | 19 | 18 | $25

Sunset Park | 813 55th St., 2nd fl. (8th Ave.) | Brooklyn | 718-871-2880

Considering that its "excellent", "inventive" dim sum is on par with "what you'll find in Chinatown", it's no wonder this "cavernous" Sunset Park Cantonese is "so popular"; it's also "friendly" and "reasonably priced" – "what more could you want?"

NEW Padre Figlio *Italian*   - | - | - | E

E 40s | 310 E. 44th St. (bet. 1st & 2nd Aves.) | 212-286-4310 | www.padrefiglio.com

A "quality newcomer" to East Midtown, this father and son-run Italian turns out "excellent" pastas plus red meat that's "better than some

steakhouses'"; "beautiful" banquettes and "book wallpaper" lend a
decorous "library feel" that may distract from the "expensive" tabs.

Paladar *Nuevo Latino*

▽ | 19 | 14 | 17 | $35

LES | 161 Ludlow St. (bet. Houston & Stanton Sts.) | 212-473-3535 |
www.paladarrestaurant.com

Fueled by "masterpiece" mojitos and chef Aarón Sanchez's "flavor-ful", "creative" cooking, this LES Nuevo Latino sustains a "funky",
"younger" "night scene"; a room that's outwardly "nothing special" "is
redeemed" by the "accommodating staff" and "fair prices."

☑ Palm, The *Steak*

24 | 17 | 22 | $69

E 40s | 837 Second Ave. (bet. 44th & 45th Sts.) | 212-687-2953 ☒
E 40s | 840 Second Ave. (bet. 44th & 45th Sts.) | 212-697-5198
W 50s | 250 W. 50th St. (bet. B'way & 8th Ave.) | 212-333-7256
www.thepalm.com

"Still up there" among the "quintessential" "manly" meateries, this
"clamorous", "fast-paced" trio is ever "reliable" for "steaks the
size of cows", "enormous lobsters" and "crusty" "pro" service –
preferably "on somebody else's expense account"; regulars look to the
"unvarnished" 1926 original on the west side of Second Avenue for
"the full experience."

Palma ● *Italian/Mediterranean*

▽ | 23 | 20 | 20 | $48

G Village | 28 Cornelia St. (bet. Bleecker St. & 6th Ave.) | 212-691-2223 |
www.palmanyc.com

"You could walk right past" this "quaint" Village Mediterranean and
miss a "provincial" "charmer" where the "gracious staff" serves up
sensational Sicilian specialties; with a "lovely" "garden out back", it's
even more "enjoyable" "in summer."

Palm Court *French*

▽ | 20 | 26 | 20 | $73

W 50s | Plaza Hotel | 768 Fifth Ave. (59th St.) | 212-546-5302 |
www.theplaza.com

Newly restored (including the installation of a copy of its original sky-light), the Plaza Hotel's "swellegant", palm-lined courtyard is "better
than ever" for "posh" New French fare or an "exquisite" afternoon tea
"accompanied by harp music"; true, it might "set off sticker shock",
but it's considered a "special treat" for "visiting guests."

Palo Santo *Pan-Latin*

22 | 23 | 21 | $42

Park Slope | 652 Union St. (bet. 4th & 5th Aves.) | Brooklyn | 718-636-6311 |
www.palosanto.us

An "ambitious" "original", this Park Slope Pan-Latin crafts "distinc-tive" "little plates" with "flair", following through with "warm hospital-ity"; with its "cool" "handmade" furniture and "tranquil" "backyard
rock garden", the "cozy" setup is just as "memorable."

NEW Pampa Grill *S American*

- | - | - | E

Williamsburg | 372 Graham Ave. (bet. Conselyea St. & Skillman Ave.) |
Brooklyn | 718-387-7405

Steaks take the spotlight at this "friendly", upscale new Williamsburg
South American that imports its prime cuts from Uruguay and serves
housemade chorizo and pastas for good measure; the water wall and
black furniture project a polished air, but they can feel a bit out of
place for the area.

	FOOD	DECOR	SERVICE	COST

Pampano *Mexican/Seafood* 24 | 22 | 21 | $56

E 40s | 209 E. 49th St. (bet. 2nd & 3rd Aves.) | 212-751-4545 |
www.modernmexican.com
You'll go far "beyond burritos" at chef Richard Sandoval and tenor
Plácido Domingo's "high-end" Midtown Mexican, where the "luscious
seafood" menu hits all the right notes; "enthusiastic" staffers and a
"sunlit upstairs" "make the tab worthwhile"; P.S. the adjacent taqueria
sells takeout inspired by the "streets of Mexico."

Pamplona *Spanish* 23 | 16 | 20 | $53

Gramercy | 37 E. 28th St. (bet. Madison Ave. & Park Ave. S.) | 212-213-2328 |
www.pamplonanyc.com
"Ingenious" chef Alex Ureña "hits the bull's-eye" with the "successful
makeover" of his namesake eatery into this "jumping" Gramercy
Spaniard, a showcase for "superior tapas" and "first-rate" Basque
bites; service is "prompt", and best of all the "price is right."

Pam Real Thai Food ⊅ *Thai* 22 | 9 | 16 | $23

W 40s | 402 W. 47th St. (bet. 9th & 10th Aves.) | 212-315-4441 ●Ⓜ
W 40s | 404 W. 49th St. (bet. 9th & 10th Aves.) | 212-333-7500
www.pamrealthai.com
As advertised, this "Thai-rific" Hell's Kitchen twosome pampers fans
of "real-deal" Siamese fare with "splendid" "spicy" cooking that
makes it "plenty popular" despite "bare-bones decor" and "amateur"
service; it's cash-only, but "so cheap you don't mind."

Panarea *Italian* ▽ 23 | 19 | 20 | $35

Staten Island | Richmond Valley Shopping Ctr. | 35A Page Ave.
(Richmond Valley Rd.) | 718-227-8582 | www.panarearistorante.com
They "don't come much classier" for SI's "high hairs" than this tasteful
Southern Italian in a "nondescript strip mall"; it's home to "delicious"
pastas and "efficient service" at prices to make a Manhattanite jealous.

Papatzul Ⓜ *Mexican* ▽ 23 | 17 | 20 | $38

SoHo | 55 Grand St. (W. B'way) | 212-274-8225 | www.papatzul.com
"Authentic" enough for "the most subtle taste", this SoHo Mexican
serves an "excellent", "reasonably priced" market menu in a "friendly",
rusticated space; the ambiance is bound to be "festive", not least because "the margaritas pack a wallop."

Papaya King *Hot Dogs* 21 | 4 | 12 | $7

E 80s | 179 E. 86th St. (3rd Ave.) | 212-369-0648 ●⊅
Harlem | 121 W. 125th St. (bet. Lenox & 7th Aves.) | 212-678-4268 🗷⊅
W Village | 200 W. 14th St. (7th Ave. S.) | 212-367-8090
www.papayaking.com
"Bliss in a bun" sums up these "standing-counter" purveyors of grilled
"red hots" that "snap" plus "fresh tropical drinks" at prices everyone
"can still afford"; you have to "brave" "sleazy" digs and "rub shoulders
with who knows who", but you haven't experienced NYC until you try it.

Pappardella ● *Italian* 19 | 14 | 18 | $39

W 70s | 316 Columbus Ave. (75th St.) | 212-595-7996 |
www.pappardella.com
A "definite staple" on the UWS, this "homey" Italian is "popular"
with the "locals" for "simple pleasures" like "tasty" pastas and "cor-

dial" service at "reasonable prices"; "nice outdoor seating" offers a breather from the "bustling" interior.

Paradou ● *French*   20 | 17 | 17 | $43

Meatpacking | 8 Little W. 12th St. (bet. Greenwich & Washington Sts.) | 212-463-8345 | www.paradounyc.com

"Less pretentious" than most in the Meatpacking District, this Gallic mini-bistro plies "elevated" Provençal "comfort food", including a "wonderful" "champagne brunch"; the year-round "garden in the back" is "lovable" even when the staff's "French temperament" isn't.

Paris Commune   *French*   17 | 18 | 16 | $41

W Village | 99 Bank St. (Greenwich St.) | 212-929-0509 | www.pariscommune.net

"Neighborhood" types commune over "solid" French bistro fare at this "busy" Villager boasting "one of the best brunches" around; even if the "loud" main room seems "overdone", the cellar wine bar is a "real find."

Park, The ● *Mediterranean*   15 | 23 | 14 | $40

Chelsea | 118 10th Ave. (bet. 17th & 18th Sts.) | 212-352-3313 | www.theparknyc.com

Scenesters admire the "amazing space" at this "sprawling" West Chelsea outpost as they gather "by the fireplace" or in the "pretty" garden for "partying" and "people-watching"; but given "underwhelming" Med fare and "lacking service", many "go to look, not to eat."

Park Avenue . . . *American*   24 | 25 | 22 | $74

E 60s | 100 E. 63rd St. (bet. Lexington & Park Aves.) | 212-644-1900 | www.parkavenyc.com

"Change is good" at this UES yearling, which "celebrates each season" with a "spectacular" quarterly "transformation" of its "gorgeous" AvroKO-designed decor and "exceptional" New American menu, as well as its name; "charming" staffers ensure the "intriguing idea" is carried out with "élan", so "pricey" tabs hardly faze its well-to-do fans.

NEW Park Avenue Bistro ⑤ *French*   20 | 19 | 22 | $57

Gramercy | 377 Park Ave. S. (bet. 26th & 27th Sts.) | 212-689-1360 | www.parkavenuebistronyc.com

After a "move across the street" and a "slight name change", Gramercy's erstwhile Park Bistro "is as terrific as ever" for "true" French fare delivered by "discreet" servers; lined with "changing artwork", it's "not nearly so homey" as before – and the prices show it.

NEW Park Room   *American/Continental*   - | - | - | VE

W 50s | Helmsley Park Lane Hotel | 36 CPS, 2nd fl. (bet. 5th & 6th Aves.) | 212-521-6655 | www.helmsleyparklane.com

From the gilded chandeliers to the 'PL' stamp on the butter pats, the era of formal hotel dining lives on at the Helmsley Park Lane's new dining room; the pricey American-Continental fare is attentively served, but it plays second fiddle to the floor-to-ceiling views of Central Park.

Park Side ● *Italian*   24 | 19 | 21 | $47

Corona | 107-01 Corona Ave. (51st Ave.) | Queens | 718-271-9321 | www.parksiderestaurant.com

"Va va voom" "never goes out of style" at this Corona "mainstay" that's a "huge favorite" for "top-of-the-line" "traditional" Italian and "white-glove service"; locals say it's "da best", but if you don't "have an edge", "you'll have to wait."

Park Terrace Bistro *French/Moroccan*

| 20 | 18 | 20 | $34 |

Inwood | 4959 Broadway (bet. Isham & 207th Sts.) | 212-567-2828 | www.parkterracebistro.com

"Devoted" locals sigh "thank goodness" for this "atmospheric" Inwood bistro as they "sip wine and indulge" in "inventive, well-spiced" French-Moroccan fare from a "friendly" staff; it's hailed as a "refreshing" "change of pace" in "a changing neighborhood."

NEW Parlor Steakhouse *Steak*

| - | - | - | E |

E 90s | 1600 Third Ave. (90th St.) | 212-423-5888 | www.parlorsteakhouse.com

Carnivores hail the arrival of this contemporary, predictably pricey new UES steakhouse that boasts plenty of prime beef, but, as its prominent raw bar suggests, also offers plenty for seafood lovers; its bi-level space features an airy, banquette-filled first floor complete with glassed-in patio plus a moody, fireplace-enhanced downstairs room.

Parma ● *Italian*

| 20 | 13 | 21 | $59 |

E 70s | 1404 Third Ave. (bet. 79th & 80th Sts.) | 212-535-3520

"Neighborhood folks" "feel at home" at this "longtime" UES "standby", where a "congenial staff" serves "above-par" Northern Italian standards; it's "costly" for a joint that "needs some fixing up", but fond followers claim "you can't beat" the "comfy" vibe.

Pascalou *French*

| 20 | 14 | 17 | $43 |

E 90s | 1308 Madison Ave. (bet. 92nd & 93rd Sts.) | 212-534-7522

"Tiny" but "big-hearted", this "quaint" Carnegie Hill "shoebox" stays "on the mark" with "wonderful" French bistro recipes and an "upbeat" feel in spite of "tight" seating; happily, the "affordable" menu finds room for a "bargain" "early-bird prix fixe."

Pasha *Turkish*

| 20 | 18 | 19 | $42 |

W 70s | 70 W. 71st St. (bet. Columbus Ave. & CPW) | 212-579-8751 | www.pashanewyork.com

This "authentic" Turk "tucked away" on the UWS "entices" with "delightful" cuisine and a "colorful" but "calm" setting that "allows conversation without a megaphone"; with "warm" service, low lights and "fair prices", it's "deservedly popular" especially "for dates."

Pasquale's Rigoletto *Italian*

| 21 | 16 | 20 | $42 |

Bronx | 2311 Arthur Ave. (Crescent Ave.) | 718-365-6644

"Patrons are part of the family" at this Arthur Avenue vet, where the "hearty" Italiano "staples" are served "with gusto" in a big, "congenial" space; sure, it's "loud" and "dated", but for the "red-sauce" "experience", this is the "real deal."

Pasticcio *Italian*

| 18 | 17 | 17 | $38 |

Murray Hill | 447 Third Ave. (bet. 30th & 31st Sts.) | 212-679-2551
Glendale | Shops at Atlas Park | 80-00 Cooper Ave. (80th St.) | Queens | 718-417-1544 Ⓜ
www.pasticciony c.com

Long a "decent" resource in Murray Hill, this "casual" Italian "fills you up" with "well-priced" repasts and uncorks "tasty" vinos at its in-

	FOOD	DECOR	SERVICE	COST

house wine bar, Prosiaccheria; the successful "routine" extends to its "underutilized" counterpart in Glendale's Shops at Atlas Park.

Pastis ● *French*

	20	20	17	$48

Meatpacking | 9 Ninth Ave. (Little W. 12th St.) | 212-929-4844 | www.pastisny.com

Worth all the "fanfare", Keith McNally's "buzzing" Meatpacking District bistro is "still the place to be" for "delish" French food and a "front-row seat" at a "fabulous" "all-hours" "scene" spanning "trendeez" to "wannabes"; granting the "waits", "madhouse" crowds and servers aspiring "to get discovered", for a "Parisian fix, nobody does it better."

Pastrami Queen *Deli*

	19	4	12	$24

E 70s | 1125 Lexington Ave. (bet. 78th & 79th Sts.) | 212-734-1500 | www.pastramiqueen.com

If you "miss the old Jewish delis", this UES "kosher nirvana" supplies "Everest-high" sandwiches stuffed with meats that "melt in your mouth" and "coagulate around your waist"; the decor is "pretty sad" and seating's "limited", so some prefer to "take out."

Patois Ⓜ *French*

	22	18	19	$39

Carroll Gardens | 255 Smith St. (bet. Degraw & Douglass Sts.) | Brooklyn | 718-855-1535

A "Smith Street trailblazer" that's "still going strong", this "chicly down-at-the-heels" Carroll Gardens bistro "stands out" with "savory" "country French fare" served "with a smile"; attractions include a "garden in summer", a "fireplace in winter" and an "excellent brunch."

Patricia's *Italian*

	24	14	20	$27

Bronx | 1080 Morris Park Ave. (bet. Haight & Lurting Aves.) | 718-409-9069
Bronx | 3764 E. Tremont Ave. (bet. Randall & Roosevelt Aves.) | 718-918-1800 | www.patriciasoftremont.com

When "you don't want to break the bank", the "wholesome" pastas and pizzas at these separately owned Bronx Italians "deliver on taste every time"; considering the "cramped quarters" have almost "no ambiance" besides "sports on the TV", "takeout" is encouraged.

Patroon Ⓩ *American/Steak*

	20	20	20	$66

E 40s | 160 E. 46th St. (bet. Lexington & 3rd Aves.) | 212-883-7373 | www.patroonrestaurant.com

"Join the dark suits" for "business" powwows at Ken Aretsky's weekdays-only Midtowner, a "classy", "conservative" New American enclave for "succulent" steaks, "smooth" service and a "fun bar" scene on the roof; it's "on the pricey side", but you'll "get what you pay for."

Patsy's *Italian*

	21	16	20	$52

W 50s | 236 W. 56th St. (bet. B'way & 8th Ave.) | 212-247-3491 | www.patsys.com

Famed as a "Sinatra hangout", this "vintage" Carnegie Hall–area Southern Italian seems "frozen in time" with its "old-style service", clientele and "classic" cooking that's "better than mama's"; partisans posit it "just gets better", though others wonder if it's "riding on reputation."

Patsy's Pizzeria *Pizza*

	20	12	15	$25

Chelsea | 318 W. 23rd St. (bet. 8th & 9th Aves.) | 646-486-7400

(continued)

(continued)

Patsy's Pizzeria

E 60s | 1312 Second Ave. (69th St.) | 212-639-1000
E 60s | 206 E. 60th St. (bet. 2nd & 3rd Aves.) | 212-688-9707
G Village | 67 University Pl. (bet. 10th & 11th Sts.) | 212-533-3500
Harlem | 2287-91 First Ave. (bet. 117th & 118th Sts.) | 212-534-9783 ⊅
Murray Hill | 509 Third Ave. (bet. 34th & 35th Sts.) | 212-689-7500
W 70s | 61 W. 74th St. (bet. Columbus Ave. & CPW) | 212-579-3000
www.patsyspizzeriany.com

Dishing up "dynamite" thin-crust pizza with "just the right amount of sauce and crunch", this brick-oven mini-chain "holds its own" despite "basic digs" and "curt" service; for best results, it's "worth venturing" to the independent East Harlem original – possibly one of "NYC's best."

Payard Bistro ☒ *Dessert/French* | 23 | 21 | 19 | $54 |

E 70s | 1032 Lexington Ave. (bet. 73rd & 74th Sts.) | 212-717-5252 | www.payard.com

"Second to none" for "irresistible desserts", François Payard's "picturesque" UES patisserie/French bistro is also "first-rate" for breakfast, "the ultimate ladies' lunch", afternoon tea or an "upscale" dinner; notwithstanding *très cher* tabs, most are content to "indulge" in this "taste of Paree" without the plane.

NEW Peaches Ⓜ *Southern* | - | - | - | M |

Bed-Stuy | 393 Lewis Ave. (bet. Decatur & MacDonough Sts.) | Brooklyn | 718-942-4162 | www.peachesbrooklyn.com

The latest from the Smoke Joint folks, this casual Southerner with an 'urban farmhouse' aesthetic is a much-needed new Bed-Stuy dining option, offering modern takes on down-home classics made with mostly local, seasonal ingredients; factor in the friendly vibe and affordable prices, and it's no wonder it's been busy from day one.

Peanut Butter & Co. *Sandwiches* | 19 | 13 | 15 | $13 |

G Village | 240 Sullivan St. (bet. Bleecker & W. 3rd Sts.) | 212-677-3995 | www.ilovepeanutbutter.com

"If you're a peanut butter lover", "go gourmet" at this Village emporium that "elevates" PB&J "to an art form" with its "creative" sandwiches; it's "pricey" compared to "your grammar school lunchbox", but the results are "too yummy to complain."

☑ Pearl Oyster Bar ☒ *Seafood* | 26 | 15 | 19 | $44 |

G Village | 18 Cornelia St. (bet. Bleecker & W. 4th Sts.) | 212-691-8211 | www.pearloysterbar.com

For "lobster roll perfection", try Rebecca Charles' "informal" Villager, a "standout" for "sensational" "New England seafood" in a "cramped" "Maine shore" setting; afishionados advise "be patient" with the "ridiculous" waits and "Manhattan prices" since the eating is "impossible to beat."

Pearl Room ❶ *Seafood* | 23 | 20 | 22 | $49 |

Bay Ridge | 8201 Third Ave. (82nd St.) | Brooklyn | 718-833-6666 | www.thepearlroom.com

"Delicious fresh seafood" is the lure at this "stylish" Bay Ridge "winner" where cooking "marked by creativity" is ferried by an "engaging" staff; rumors are it's "like a Manhattan" eatery (complete with a "noisy bar scene") and accordingly "fairly expensive" for the neighborhood.

	FOOD	DECOR	SERVICE	COST

Peasant ⓜ *Italian* | 24 | 21 | 19 | $56

NoLita | 194 Elizabeth St. (bet. Prince & Spring Sts.) | 212-965-9511 |
www.peasantnyc.com

The open kitchen at this "hospitable" NoLita Italian delivers "*delizioso*"
food at prices "no peasant can afford" in a "rustic" space with a "romantic wine bar" downstairs; still, some say having staffers "help you
navigate" that "no-English menu" is "really affected."

Peep ◑ *Thai* | 19 | 19 | 18 | $29

SoHo | 177 Prince St. (bet. Sullivan & Thompson Sts.) | 212-254-7337 |
www.peepsoho.net

A "space-age disco" setting bathed in "hot pink" neon attracts "younger"
peeps to this sceney SoHo Thai for "super" food at "decent prices";
its notorious "funky loos" with "one-way mirrored" doors ("you can
see out, they can't see in") let you "spy on your date."

Peking Duck House *Chinese* | 22 | 15 | 17 | $37

Chinatown | 28 Mott St. (bet. Mosco & Pell Sts.) | 212-227-1810
E 50s | 236 E. 53rd St. (bet. 2nd & 3rd Aves.) | 212-759-8260
www.pekingduckhousenyc.com

This "ducky" Chinese duo "can't be beat" for their "succulent" house
specialty, "skillfully carved" "right at the table" at both the "plain-
Jane" Midtowner and its "nicer looking" C-Town sire; those who flock
in for the fairly fared fowl feel everything else is "pretty standard."

Pellegrino's *Italian* | 24 | 18 | 23 | $44

Little Italy | 138 Mulberry St. (bet. Grand & Hester Sts.) | 212-226-3177
Feel the "*amore*" at this Little Italy stalwart, where the "old-fashioned"
cooking's "consistently excellent" and the "delightful" "old-style"
waiters "treat you like family"; the "homey" space is less special, but
you can "sit outside in the warm months."

Penelope ⊄ *American* | 21 | 17 | 19 | $25

Murray Hill | 159 Lexington Ave. (30th St.) | 212-481-3800 |
www.penelopenyc.com

"If you seek comfort food", the "winsome staff" at this "cozy" Murray
Hill American serves a "delightful", "well-priced" selection in "cutesy"
"country kitchen" surroundings; it's "popular" with "the girls" despite
"ridiculous brunch lines" and an "annoying" cash-only policy.

Pepe Giallo To Go *Italian* | 21 | 14 | 17 | $26

Chelsea | 253 10th Ave. (bet. 24th & 25th Sts.) | 212-242-6055
Pepe Rosso *Italian*
E Village | 127 Ave. C (8th St.) | 212-529-7747
Pepe Rosso Caffe *Italian*
E 40s | Grand Central | lower level (42nd St. & Vanderbilt Ave.) | 212-867-6054
Pepe Rosso Osteria *Italian*
W 50s | 346 W. 52nd St. (bet. 8th & 9th Aves.) | 212-245-4585
Pepe Rosso To Go *Italian*
SoHo | 149 Sullivan St. (bet. Houston & Prince Sts.) | 212-677-4555
Pepe Verde To Go *Italian*
W Village | 559 Hudson St. (bet. Perry & W. 11th Sts.) | 212-255-2221
www.peperossotogo.com

"Handy" for fill-ups "on the go", these "basic Italians" turn out "down-
to-earth" pastas "in a heartbeat" for an "amazingly" low price; the

amenities "leave something to be desired", but for a "tasty", easygoing neighborhood meal these places are a good bet.

Pepolino *Italian* 25 | 16 | 22 | $52

TriBeCa | 281 W. Broadway (bet. Canal & Lispenard Sts.) | 212-966-9983 | www.pepolino.com

A "true standout" "tucked out of the way" in TriBeCa, this Northern Italian duplex "hasn't lost its edge" for "superb" food served with "no attitude" at prices that run "high but not unrealistic"; to avoid the "noise factor", "upstairs is much better than downstairs."

Pera ⌧ *Mediterranean/Turkish* 22 | 22 | 20 | $54

E 40s | 303 Madison Ave. (bet. 41st & 42nd Sts.) | 212-878-6301 | www.peranyc.com

Med cuisine gets an "inventive" "upgrade" at this Grand Central–area "surprise", which focuses on "first-rate" "Turkish delights" in a "stylish", "modern" setting with a "vibrant after-work bar"; "commendable" service helps its "business" clientele bear the "priciness."

Perbacco ◑ *Italian* 25 | 18 | 21 | $43

E Village | 234 E. Fourth St. (bet. Aves. A & B) | 212-253-2038

It's just a "casual" "joint", but this East Village Italian "works magic" with "scrumptious" "little plates" and "fantastic" wines conveyed by "charismatic" staffers; baccers are glad they "finally accept" plastic, but given the "cramped" conditions and "constant buzz", they still "wish it were bigger."

Peri Ela *Turkish* 18 | 15 | 17 | $43

E 90s | 1361 Lexington Ave. (bet. 90th & 91st Sts.) | 212-410-4300 | www.periela.com

The quarters are "tiny", but this Carnegie Hill "Turkish haven" is a "local" "winner" thanks to its "rich" "traditional" cooking; it's apt to be "crowded" even though the decor is "hardly impressive" and the "sweet" staff is "not ready for prime time."

Perilla *American* 25 | 20 | 23 | $56

G Village | 9 Jones St. (bet. Bleecker & W. 4th Sts.) | 212-929-6868 | www.perillanyc.com

"There's a reason he won *Top Chef*" declare fans of Harold Dieterle, whose "unpretentious" Village New American is "a definite hit" for "masterful" cuisine flaunting "complex" flavors in a "small" space that's "minimalist" but "in no way cold"; overseen by "affable", "attentive" servers, it's "pricey" but the performance "doesn't disappoint."

Periyali *Greek* 23 | 20 | 21 | $57

Flatiron | 35 W. 20th St. (bet. 5th & 6th Aves.) | 212-463-7890 | www.periyali.com

"Not your run-of-the-mill" taverna, this "civilized" Flatiron "stalwart" "continues to work wonders" with its "deft" "high-end Greek" fare, "quietly stylish" setting and "wonderful service"; Hellenists insist it's "special" enough that the "expensive" outlay is "worth it."

Per Lei ◑ *Italian* 19 | 17 | 18 | $52

E 70s | 1347 Second Ave. (71st St.) | 212-439-9200 | www.perleinyc.com

"Air-kissing" "Euros" keep this UES Baraonda offshoot "loud and lively" as "tony" entourages assemble for "tasty" Italian fare in a "hip", art-lined space with streetside seating; it's a "local hot spot" even if spoilsports say the "food doesn't match the cost."

Perry Street ● *French* | 26 | 25 | 25 | $70 |

W Village | 176 Perry St. (West St.) | 212-352-1900 | www.jean-georges.com

A "cool scene" "for grown-ups", this "smooth", "subdued" far West Village "star" from Jean-Georges Vongerichten has the "'in' crowd" wowed as it pairs "exceptional", Asian-accented New French fare with "top-shelf" service in a "chic" "modern space"; the cost is equally "impressive", though streetwise sorts say the $24 lunch prix fixe "is such a steal."

☑ Per Se *American/French* | 28 | 28 | 28 | $303 |

W 60s | Time Warner Ctr. | 10 Columbus Circle, 4th fl. (60th St. at B'way) | 212-823-9335 | www.perseny.com

"In a category by itself" – it's voted No. 1 for Food and Service in NYC – Thomas Keller's French–New American "paragon" presents an "unforgettable" "gastronomical marathon" via "transcendental" prix fixe spreads served by "impeccable" "synchronized" staffers in "world-class" surroundings with "majestic" Central Park and Columbus Circle views; though it's "stunningly expensive", there's "never a regret" since once past the "daunting" reservations system, "you're in for the treat of your life."

NEW Persephone *Greek* | ▽ 22 | 19 | 21 | $66 |

E 60s | 115 E. 60th St. (bet. Lexington & Park Aves.) | 212-339-8363
Periyali's owners take "traditional Greek" to the UES at this "welcome" newcomer, already a "busy scene" serving "wonderful" Hellenic classics in a simple yet "lovely setting"; even with service "kinks", it's "successful" with "well-heeled" types who can swallow the spendy tabs.

Persepolis *Persian* | 21 | 16 | 19 | $39 |

E 70s | 1407 Second Ave. (bet. 73rd & 74th Sts.) | 212-535-1100 | www.persepolisnyc.com

"Well-prepared" food at "reasonable prices" means there's "lots to enjoy" at this "comfortable" UES "oasis", a "warm" "introduction to Persian" cuisine like its "fantastic sour cherry rice"; a regular cohort of "Iranians as customers" testifies to its authenticity.

Pershing Square *American/French* | 15 | 15 | 15 | $37 |

E 40s | 90 E. 42nd St. (Park Ave.) | 212-286-9600 | www.pershingsquare.com

Commuters and "corporate" sorts "mob" this "handy" "meeting spot" across from Grand Central, where the "standard" Franco-American brasserie eats furnish "square meals" in a "huge", "loud" space; it's a "business breakfast" fave, but otherwise "location is its biggest asset."

NEW Persimmon ☒ *Korean* | - | - | - | M |

E Village | 277 E. 10th St. (bet. Ave. A & 1st Ave.) | 212-260-9080
Neo-Korean fare takes the spotlight at this tiny new East Villager from a Momofuku alum, whose space consists of a 20-seat communal table ringed by stylish square stools, plus a few more along the open kitchen; it offers a $37 prix fixe–only menu that changes biweekly to focus on a particular ingredient.

	FOOD	DECOR	SERVICE	COST

Pescatore ❶ *Italian/Seafood* — 18 | 14 | 17 | $41

E 50s | 955 Second Ave. (bet. 50th & 51st Sts.) | 212-752-7151 | www.pescatorerestaurant.com

For a "solid meal", this Midtown Italian "steadily" supplies "decent" takes on "simple" seafood and pasta; it's "not a standout" but "not too pricey" either, and the "upstairs terrace" offers a place "in the sun."

Petaluma *Italian* — 18 | 15 | 18 | $45

E 70s | 1356 First Ave. (73rd St.) | 212-772-8800 | www.petalumanyc.com

"Reliable since forever", this "unpretentious" Yorkville Italian is a "popular" resource for "tasty" basics served by "pleasant personnel"; the "calm surroundings" fill with families and Sotheby's staffers, who say the tabs won't hurt a bit after "what you paid for your last Picasso."

⓴ Peter Luger Steak House ⊅ *Steak* — 27 | 14 | 19 | $75

Williamsburg | 178 Broadway (Driggs Ave.) | Brooklyn | 718-387-7400 | www.peterluger.com

"Bring the cash and revel in the glory" of Williamsburg's "meat lovers' paradise" that's still at the "top of the steak totem pole" (it's NYC's No. 1 chop shop for the 25th year running); "forget the menu – you know what to order": "succulent" porterhouse "fit for the gods" with "to-die-for" creamed spinach and sliced tomatoes; if a few beef about the "militant" staff's "shtick" and the quasi-"Bavarian" feel, diehards retort it's part of the "quintessential NY experience."

Pete's Downtown Ⓜ *Italian* — ▽ 18 | 18 | 20 | $40

Dumbo | 2 Water St. (Old Fulton St.) | Brooklyn | 718-858-3510 | www.petesdowntown.com

"Still holding its own in increasingly trendy" Dumbo, this "hospitable" standby serves up a "solid" Italian menu and an "almost–River Café" view "without the price"; but to most the vista "surpasses the food."

Pete's Tavern ❶ *Pub Food* — 13 | 15 | 15 | $31

Gramercy | 129 E. 18th St. (Irving Pl.) | 212-473-7676

"Rub elbows with history" over burgers and other "comforting" fare at Gramercy's "old-school haunt" where "O. Henry swilled, dined" and wrote "his knock 'em dead endings"; those who call the food "so-so" "grab a drink" at the bar – it's a "beautiful, nostalgic experience."

Petite Abeille *Belgian* — 18 | 14 | 16 | $30

Flatiron | 44 W. 17th St. (bet. 5th & 6th Aves.) | 212-727-2989
Gramercy | 401 E. 20th St. (1st Ave.) | 212-727-1505
TriBeCa | 134 W. Broadway (Duane St.) | 212-791-1360
W Village | 466 Hudson St. (Barrow St.) | 212-741-6479 ⊅
www.petiteabeille.com

"Charming Tintin" touches "warm the heart" at this "simply" appointed Belgian mini-chain known for its "vast selection of Belgian beers", "solid" moules frites and "crowded" brunch; *amis* muse "how did they re-create Belgium?" while others wonder why it's sometimes "lacking."

Petite Crevette ⊅ *Seafood* — ▽ 24 | 14 | 18 | $34

Carroll Gardens | 144 Union St. (enter on Hicks St., bet. Union & President Sts.) | Brooklyn | 718-855-2632

For "super-fresh seafood at everyday prices" check out this "wacky" Carroll Gardens BYO that's "less cramped since expanding into the neighboring flower shop"; service can be "pokey" so bring a "bottle of white and patience" – once served the "top-notch" fin fare "you'll be delighted."

Petrossian *Continental/French* | 24 | 24 | 23 | $75 |

W 50s | 182 W. 58th St. (7th Ave.) | 212-245-2214 | www.petrossian.com
"Sheer champagne-and-caviar decadence" awaits at this *magnifique* brass, glass and silver "art deco–inspired salon" near Carnegie Hall excelling at "scrumptious" French-Continental cuisine; don't let the "hedge fund manager" tabs deter you: the "sybaritic" lunch and brunch prix fixe menus are a "deal", plus the "casual" cafe next door has "some of the best baked goods in town."

Philip Marie ●Ⓜ *American* | 19 | 17 | 19 | $42 |

W Village | 569 Hudson St. (W. 11th St.) | 212-242-6200 | www.philipmarie.com
"Every neighborhood deserves" a "convivial" fallback like this West Village New American, whose "pleasing" fare tastes even better amid the "romance" of the downstairs "secret room for two"; "jazz lovers" also note that the "Wednesday evening music is truly a delight."

Philippe ● *Chinese* | 23 | 21 | 20 | $72 |

E 60s | 33 E. 60th St. (bet. Madison & Park Aves.) | 212-644-8885 | www.philippechow.com
This Eastsider from a Mr. Chow alum "continues to impress" with its "trendy" vibe and "fancy-schmancy Chinese" cuisine; however, given the prices it "helps to own a bank" – not to mention a booming voice "to be heard over" the "way-loud" acoustics.

Philoxenia Ⓜ *Greek*   ∇ | 21 | 21 | 20 | $36 |

Astoria | 32-07 34th Ave. (bet. 32nd & 33rd Sts.) | Queens | 718-626-2000
And long "may they prosper" cheer locals of this Greek "gem" that relocated within Astoria last year to "cozy" new digs that "resemble a traditional village home"; the "fresh", "wholesome" fare is as affordable as ever, while the service befits its name, which means "hospitality."

Pho Bang ⊄ *Vietnamese* | 20 | 6 | 12 | $15 |

Little Italy | 157 Mott St. (bet. Broome & Grand Sts.) | 212-966-3797
Elmhurst | 82-90 Broadway (Elmhurst Ave.) | Queens | 718-205-1500
Flushing | 41-07 Kissena Blvd. (Main St.) | Queens | 718-939-5520
At this Vietnamese noodle trio they ladle out "big bowls" of "light" but "deeply satisfying" pho soups; "no-decor" digs and "gruff" service are easy to take given the "quick" turnaround and "dirt-cheap" prices.

Phoenix Garden ⊄ *Chinese* | 23 | 7 | 12 | $29 |

E 40s | 242 E. 40th St. (bet. 2nd & 3rd Aves.) | 212-983-6666 | www.thephoenixgarden.com
It's "nothing to look at" but loyalists "would go any day, anytime" for the "flavorful", "carefully prepared" Chinese food at this "cheap" BYO "dive" in the "shadow of Tudor City"; never mind the "depressing" decor and "surly" service – "just sit down and eat."

Pho Pasteur *Vietnamese*   ∇ | 19 | 6 | 13 | $16 |

Chinatown | 85 Baxter St. (bet. Bayard & Canal Sts.) | 212-608-3656
"When on jury duty", the "super-cheap" pho at this Vietnamese noodle nook is "something to look forward to" come lunchtime; given the

"nothing-fancy" decor and service, you "may not feel as if you're in French Colonial" Hanoi – but "you're not paying for it either."

Pho Viet Huong *Vietnamese* ∇ 22 | 9 | 13 | $18

Chinatown | 73 Mulberry St. (bet. Bayard & Canal Sts.) | 212-233-8988

In the "no-frills Chinatown" mold, this Vietnamese "standby" delivers "superior", "bargain"-rate dishes to "tantalize the taste buds"; its noodle soups are the "highlight" pho sure, but the "extensive menu" boasts plenty of other choices for a "quick" lunch between court sessions.

Piadina ●⊄ *Italian* ∇ 19 | 16 | 16 | $36

G Village | 57 W. 10th St. (bet. 5th & 6th Aves.) | 212-460-8017

"Walk down the stairs" and feel "miles away" at this "tiny" Italian "candlelit" "cellar" that's "more like Europe" than Greenwich Village; "perfect" for a "low-key date" or "dinner with friends", it's among the area's increasingly rare suppliers of "tasty" basics.

❷ Piano Due ⊠ *Italian* 25 | 25 | 24 | $77

W 50s | Equitable Center Arcade | 151 W. 51st St., 2nd fl. (bet. 6th & 7th Aves.) | 212-399-9400 | www.pianoduenyc.net

A "beautiful escape from Midtown madness", Michael Cetrulo's somewhat "undiscovered" Italian supplies "exquisite" fare "seamlessly" served in a "classy" second-floor room where the tables are "well spaced" and the "noise level" rarely rises "above a murmur"; for a "before-dinner drink" hit the "vibrant" first-floor Palio Bar – and "don't miss" its "fantastic" four-walled Sandro Chia murals.

Piccola Venezia *Italian* 25 | 15 | 23 | $56

Astoria | 42-01 28th Ave. (42nd St.) | Queens | 718-721-8470 | www.piccola-venezia.com

It's "old-world charm with new-world pricing" at this Astoria Italian whose "retro" looks are straight "out of a movie set" – ditto its "cast of customers"; with its "wonderful" "tailored-to-taste" cooking "just like nonna's" and "pro" waiters who take "pride in pleasing", no wonder it's "still going strong" after all these years.

Piccolo Angolo ⓜ *Italian* 25 | 12 | 20 | $41

W Village | 621 Hudson St. (Jane St.) | 212-229-9177 | www.piccoloangolo.com

"Genial" owner Renato Migliorini and his "friendly" crew deliver "wonderfully prepared" Italian "red-sauce" staples at this "unpretentious" Village "favorite"; there's often a "line" and once inside the space is "tight" and "loud", but for "meatballs the size of your head" and the utmost in hospitality "nothing beats" it.

❷ Picholine *French/Mediterranean* 26 | 24 | 25 | $114

W 60s | 35 W. 64th St. (bet. B'way & CPW) | 212-724-8585 | www.picholinenyc.com

"Superb" prix fixe–only meals "elegantly served" in one of NYC's "most civilized rooms" is what diners find at Terry Brennan's "temple" to "fine" French-Mediterranean cuisine – and all "hail" the famously "divine" cheese cart; for a "memorable" evening, especially "followed by a short stroll to the Met", it's "as close to a sure thing as there is"; P.S. the new wine-and-fromage bar is a "wonderful" alternative.

	FOOD	DECOR	SERVICE	COST

Picket Fence *American* ▽ 20 | 17 | 19 | $29
Ditmas Park | 1310 Cortelyou Rd. (bet. Argyle & Rugby Rds.) | Brooklyn |
718-282-6661
Bringing a "little bit o' country" to "gentrifying" Ditmas Park, this New
American is "popular with families" thanks to its "friendly" vibe and
"quality" "comfort" fare in "generous", well-priced portions; a "wonderful" brunch and "cute garden" are other endearments.

PicNic Market & Café *Deli/French* 21 | 15 | 19 | $39
W 100s | 2665 Broadway (101st St.) | 212-222-8222 |
www.picnicmarket.com
"Serious eats for Francophiles" and a deli plying artisanal charcuterie
highlight this little bit of "Alsace on Upper Broadway"; *oui*, it's pricey
for a "neighborhood" nook and the "comfortable" digs are "not striking", but those "impressive" edibles make this a good pic.

Pietrasanta *Italian* 18 | 13 | 17 | $36
W 40s | 683 Ninth Ave. (47th St.) | 212-265-9471
They "knock themselves out to get you to the theater" at this "popular" Hell's Kitchen Italian known for its pasta specials and other "simple", "priced-right" fare; a recent renovation means you can now
"watch the world go by" year-round through enclosed sidewalk seating.

Pietro's ☒ *Italian/Steak* 24 | 14 | 22 | $64
E 40s | 232 E. 43rd St. (bet. 2nd & 3rd Aves.) | 212-682-9760 |
www.pietros.com
This East Side "throwback to the good ol' days" plies "classic Italian
steakhouse" dishes that "don't disappoint", delivered by "pro" waiters
in "wonderfully tacky" "men's-club" digs; upstarts say it "could use a
makeover", but longtimers like it "better than the modern" members
of the mega-meat genre.

Pigalle ◑ *French* 17 | 17 | 16 | $36
W 40s | Hilton Garden Inn Times Sq. | 790 Eighth Ave. (48th St.) |
212-489-2233 | www.pigallenyc.com
"Pretend" you're "Parisian" at this "bustling", "reliable" Hell's Kitchen
French brasserie where your "tasty" pre-curtain dinner or "after-show
dessert" comes with a side of "people-watching"; down to the "indifferent" service, it's almost the real deal.

Pig Heaven ◑ *Chinese* 19 | 14 | 19 | $35
E 80s | 1540 Second Ave. (bet. 80th & 81st Sts.) | 212-744-4333 |
www.pigheaven.biz
"Vivacious" owner Nancy Lee "makes visits enjoyable" at this "porcine-
themed" UES Chinese standby, whose supporters are also tickled pink
by its cuisine (both "pig and no-pig"); the less-enthused, who cite
"lacking" decor, wonder "what all the oinking is about."

Ping's Seafood ◑ *Chinese/Seafood* 21 | 10 | 14 | $26
Chinatown | 22 Mott St. (bet. Bayard & Pell Sts.) | 212-602-9988
Elmhurst | 83-02 Queens Blvd. (Goldsmith St.) | Queens | 718-396-1238
The "tasty Cantonese morsels" and "fresh seafood" at this "chaotic"
Elmhurst-Chinatown duo "outshine" many other "NYC dim sum palaces"; the low-cost cart-borne selection "keeps the adventurous ex-
perimenting", plus the "wait is never long" if you share a table.

	FOOD	DECOR	SERVICE	COST

Pink Tea Cup ●🌱 *Soul Food/Southern*   19 | 11 | 16 | $22

W Village | 42 Grove St. (bet. Bedford & Bleecker Sts.) | 212-807-6755 | www.thepinkteacup.com

"You ain't a NYer till" you've brunched on "eggs, grits" and the "Elvis of bacon" at this pink "Village hideaway"; the "affordable" "down-home Southern" vittles are "satisfying" – "but if you don't like smothered", mosey on ("they'd smother Jell-O if they could").

Pinocchio 🅜 *Italian*   21 | 14 | 24 | $44

E 90s | 1748 First Ave. (bet. 90th & 91st Sts.) | 212-828-5810

The "tiniest you can imagine", this UES Italian "joint" is also the "sweetest"; there's "nothing new-fangled" here, just "simple", "tasty" midpriced classics plus a "charming" staff to "take care of your every wish" – no wonder most "leave happy."

Pintaile's Pizza   *Pizza*   19 | 5 | 12 | $16

E 80s | 1573 York Ave. (bet. 83rd & 84th Sts.) | 212-396-3479
E 90s | 26 E. 91st St. (bet. 5th & Madison Aves.) | 212-722-1967

"What's not to love?" muse mavens of the "guilt-free", "veggie-laden", "paper-thin" whole wheat pizzas at this UES duo that's big with the *Gossip Girl* crowd; its "original" toppings really "think outside of the box", but the "phonebook"-size quarters don't (takeout may be best).

Piola   *Italian*   19 | 15 | 18 | $27

G Village | 48 E. 12th St. (bet. B'way & University Pl.) | 212-777-7781 | www.piola.it

For "innovative, but not weird" "thin-crust pizza" with a Brazilian accent, samba down to this "cheap", "college crowd–trendy" Village parlor; it may feel "cafeteria"-ish ("is 'Piola' Italian for 'wretched lighting'?") but the "delicious" pies and "friendly" vibe compensate.

Pio Pio   *Peruvian*   22 | 13 | 16 | $23

E 90s | 1746 First Ave. (bet. 90th & 91st Sts.) | 212-426-5800
Murray Hill | 210 E. 34th St. (bet. 2nd & 3rd Aves.) | 212-481-0034
W 90s | 702 Amsterdam Ave. (94th St.) | 212-665-3000
Bronx | 264 Cypress Ave. (bet. 138th & 139th Sts.) | 718-401-3300
Jackson Heights | 84-13 Northern Blvd. (bet. 84th & 85th Sts.) | Queens | 718-426-1010
Rego Park | 62-30 Woodhaven Blvd. (63rd Ave.) | Queens | 718-458-0606 🌱
www.piopionyc.com

There's "much to cluck about" at this "boisterous" mini-chain proffering a "Peruvian feast" of "juicy", "sinfully good" rotisserie chicken with "sublime" green sauce and sangria; "who cares" if it's "cramped" – portions are "super-huge" and prices "unbeatable."

Pipa   *Spanish*   20 | 21 | 16 | $44

Flatiron | ABC Carpet & Home | 38 E. 19th St. (bet. B'way & Park Ave. S.) | 212-677-2233 | www.abchome.com

"Low-lit chandeliers, sexy music" and a "buzzy" vibe set the "*muy romantico*" stage for an "amazing" "first date" – or "girls' night out" – at this Flatiron Spaniard; the service may be "a bit lacking", but the "creative" tapas and "addictive sangria" still "draw 'em in."

	FOOD	DECOR	SERVICE	COST

Pisticci *Italian* | 24 | 19 | 20 | $34

W 100s | 125 La Salle St. (B'way) | 212-932-3500 | www.pisticcinyc.com
Practically "part of the Columbia curriculum", this "cheery" "subterra-nean" Italian is "wonderful" for "meeting, talking and just plain enjoying yourself" over "savory", "priced-right" fare; add in "clever" decor and live-jazz Sundays, and it's no wonder the regulars are so "devoted."

Pizza Gruppo *Pizza* | ▽ 24 | 12 | 17 | $19

E Village | 186 Ave. B (bet. 11th & 12th Sts.) | 212-995-2100 |
www.gruppothincrust.com
If "you want thin and crispy, this is it" declare groupies who gobble up the "extra-tasty", "cracker-crusted" pizzas at this "tiny" East Villager; the decor's not much, but it's "cheap and easy" with "pleasant" service and a "jukebox" as a bonus.

Pizza 33 ● *Pizza* | 21 | 7 | 12 | $10

Chelsea | 268 W. 23rd St. (8th Ave.) | 212-206-0999
G Village | 527 Sixth Ave. (14th St.) | 212-255-6333
Murray Hill | 489 Third Ave. (33rd St.) | 212-545-9191
When the "post bar-hoppin' munchies" hit, there's always this "home of the late-night slice", which can be "quite the scene" in the "wee hours"; never mind the "gruff" service, when you're "craving" pizza with just the "right amount of cheese", they've got your number.

P.J. Clarke's ● *Pub Food* | 16 | 15 | 16 | $35

E 50s | 915 Third Ave. (55th St.) | 212-317-1616
P.J. Clarke's at Lincoln Square ● *Pub Food*
W 60s | 44 W. 63rd St. (Columbus Ave.) | 212-957-9700
P.J. Clarke's on the Hudson *Pub Food*
Financial District | 4 World Financial Ctr. (Vesey St.) | 212-285-1500
www.pjclarkes.com
"Burgers and beer" "reign supreme" at this "old-time" Midtown "wa-tering hole" that supplies "honest" "bar food" in digs dating from 1884; the "massive" Financial District and Lincoln Center spin-offs are "lively", but their "chainlike" feel "pales in comparison" to the original.

Place, The *American/Mediterranean* | 21 | 23 | 20 | $47

W Village | 310 W. Fourth St. (bet. Bank & 12th Sts.) | 212-924-2711 |
www.theplaceny.com
The "quintessential quaint Village" eatery, this "romantic hideaway" remains a "well-kept secret" despite its "delicious" Med–New American fare and "super-sweet" service; a "cozy" "winter dinner" near its fireplace "warms the heart" – "if you can't sweep a date off his or her feet here, "you're hopeless."

Planet Thailand ● *Japanese/Thai* | 18 | 18 | 16 | $28

Williamsburg | 133 N. Seventh St. (bet. Bedford Ave. & Berry St.) |
Brooklyn | 718-599-5758 | www.planetthailand.com
Planetthailand 212 ● *Japanese/Thai*
Flatiron | 30 W. 24th St. (bet. 5th & 6th Aves.) | 212-727-7026 |
www.pt212.com
"Thai and Japanese on the same planet" – that's the idea at this "cav-ernous" Williamsburg "spectacle" whose "funky", "loungelike" space pulses with "loud music"; the smaller Flatiron spin-off sticks to "tasty" Siamese fare and sushi, but both are beautiful "bargains."

	FOOD	DECOR	SERVICE	COST

Pó *Italian*   24 | 16 | 22 | $51

G Village | 31 Cornelia St. (bet. Bleecker & W. 4th Sts.) | 212-645-2189
Carroll Gardens | 276 Smith St. (bet. Degraw & Sackett Sts.) | Brooklyn |
718-875-1980
www.porestaurant.com

"Big flavors" come in "matchbook-size" digs at this "transcendent"
Village Italian that's always "packed" and particularly popular for its
"bargain prix fixe" (six courses for $50); now its enduring "charm" has
"easily translated" to a "worthy" new offshoot in Carroll Gardens.

Poke 🗷⇄ *Japanese*   26 | 15 | 19 | $40

E 80s | 343 E. 85th St. (bet. 1st & 2nd Aves.) | 212-249-0569

"Ethereal" rolls and other "heavenly" sushi meet with "fair prices" and
a "refreshing BYO policy" to make this East 80s standby a "neighborhood" "no-brainer"; of course most "don't dig" the "long waits" and
staff "attitude", but no one pokes fun at all that "fresh fish."

Pomaire *Chilean*   ∇ 22 | 16 | 22 | $42

W 40s | 371 W. 46th St. (bet. 8th & 9th Aves.) | 212-956-3056 |
www.pomairenyc.com

The "intimate" setting "conveys a South American flavor" to match the
"wonderful", "flavorfully spiced" Chilean fare at this "sexy" Theater
District "find"; it makes a "pleasant" "change from the usual" pre-
show choices, especially given the staff's "personal touch."

NEW Pomme de Terre *French*   ∇ 23 | 18 | 21 | $40

Ditmas Park | 1301 Newkirk Ave. (Argyle Rd.) | Brooklyn | 718-284-0005 |
www.pdtny.com

"An instant hit" in "underserved" Ditmas Park, this new "sister" to Farm
on Adderley and Patois offers "excellent" French bistro classics at
"democratic prices"; the owners' "attention" to "little things" means it
could become a "destination" as well as a "neighborhood joint."

Pomodoro Rosso *Italian*   22 | 16 | 20 | $42

W 70s | 229 Columbus Ave. (bet. 70th & 71st Sts.) | 212-721-3009

"Consistency is the hallmark" of this "hospitable" Italian, "one of the
better" "casual" options near Lincoln Center; it takes no reservations
and is "always crowded", but its moderately priced pastas ferried by
"cheerful" staffers make it worth a try.

p*ong *Dessert*   22 | 19 | 19 | $57

G Village | 150 W. 10th St. (bet. Greenwich Ave. & Waverly Pl.) |
212-929-0898 | www.p-ong.com

Pastry "genius" Pichet Ong "excels" at this "intimate" Village New
American, showcasing a "challenging" choice of savory and sweet
courses presented as "delightful" small plates; the tasting menus are
"the only way to go", and though the "grazing" "runs up the cost",
those "expecting the unexpected" can't go wr*ong.

Pongal *Indian/Vegetarian*   21 | 13 | 14 | $26

E 60s | 1154 First Ave. (bet. 63rd & 64th Sts.) | 212-355-4600
Gramercy | 110 Lexington Ave. (bet. 27th & 28th Sts.) | 212-696-9458
www.pongalnyc.com

"Out-of-this-world dosas" and other "savory" dishes make this East
Side twosome "the place to go" for "authentic" kosher South Indian

"vegetarian treats"; the settings are "simple" and the service "inatten-tive", but given the "lean prices" and "toothsome" fare, "who cares?"

Pongsri Thai *Thai*
21 | 12 | 16 | $26

Chelsea | 165 W. 23rd St. (bet. 6th & 7th Aves.) | 212-645-8808
Chinatown | 106 Bayard St. (Baxter St.) | 212-349-3132
W 40s | 244 W. 48th St. (bet. B'way & 8th Ave.) | 212-582-3392 | www.pongsri1.citysearch.com

For "titillating tastes of Thailand" at modest prices, head to this "utterly reliable" trio dispensing "fresh, fiery-hot" dishes without fanfare; the setups range from semi-"posh" to "basement"-like, but wherever you eat "you'll be in and out in a flash."

Ponticello *Italian*
▽ 23 | 19 | 22 | $50

Astoria | 46-11 Broadway (bet. 46th & 47th Sts.) | Queens | 718-278-4514 | www.ponticelloristorante.com

A "touch of elegance" in Astoria, this Italian "favorite" veers to the "old school" with its "terrific", "pricey" classics that are prepared "to your taste" and "lovingly" delivered by a pro staff; "for special occa-sions", consider its "private wine-cellar room."

Pop Burger ● *American*
18 | 14 | 11 | $20

NEW **E 50s** | 14 E. 58th St. (bet. 5th & Madison Aves.) | 212-991-6644
Meatpacking | 58-60 Ninth Ave. (bet. 14th & 15th Sts.) | 212-414-8686
www.popburger.com

The "juicy" "lil' burgers" at this "late-night", "cheap-chic" Meatpacking-Midtown twosome "go down well" "after a night of partying"; choose between the "cool" "canteen" or "swank lounge" – but "stick to takeout if you're feeling over 30."

Popover Cafe *American*
18 | 14 | 16 | $26

W 80s | 551 Amsterdam Ave. (bet. 86th & 87th Sts.) | 212-595-8555 | www.popovercafe.com

"Tried-and-true and still full of air", this "homey", "kid-friendly", "stuffed bear"–populated American "temple to the popover", aka "carb heaven", remains a "brunch-time charmer" that's also "lovely" for dinner; service is "so-so" and its "annoying popularity" spells "long lines on weekends."

Porcão Churrascaria *Brazilian/Steak*
20 | 18 | 20 | $66

Gramercy | 360 Park Ave. S. (26th St.) | 212-252-7080 | www.porcaorios.com
"Eat till you drop" is the mantra at this Gramercy Brazilian rodizio, where carnivores "pig" out on "skewered", "brilliantly seared" meats that "never stop coming"; the price is a bit "hefty", but consume "your weight in meat" – and "don't fill up" on the "tremendous salad bar" – and you'll get "great value."

Porter House New York *Steak*
23 | 24 | 23 | $79

W 60s | Time Warner Ctr. | 10 Columbus Circle, 4th fl. (60th St. at B'way) | 212-823-9500 | www.porterhousenewyork.com
The "excellent cuts" from "skilled chef" Michael Lomonaco "melt in your mouth" and the sides are like "comfort food gone to heaven" at this "quiet", "clubby", wood-paneled Time Warner Center steakhouse; en-hancing the "elegant", "expense-account" experience are an "impec-cable" staff and "divine" fourth-floor views out over Central Park.

	FOOD	DECOR	SERVICE	COST

Portofino *Italian/Seafood* — ∇ 20 | 19 | 21 | $47

Bronx | 555 City Island Ave. (Cross St.) | 718-885-1220 |
www.portofinocityisland.com

A "varied crowd" gathers at this "romantic" "old-world" City Island
Italian to drink in the "views of the NYC skyline" from the deck or sink
into the interior's "dramatic red booths"; a few sea "room for improvement", but even they salute the "caring" crew.

Portofino Grille *Italian* — 19 | 20 | 20 | $45

E 60s | 1162 First Ave. (bet. 63rd & 64th Sts.) | 212-832-4141 |
www.portofinogrille.com

Whether you find the stars on the ceiling "cute" or "cheesy", it's a
"pleasure to dine" at this "old-fashioned" East Side Italian standby; the
"tasty" dishes in "generous portions" are "served with hospitality" and
best enjoyed "by the fireplace."

Positano ● *Italian* — 22 | 18 | 21 | $39

Little Italy | 122 Mulberry St. (bet. Canal & Hester Sts.) | 212-334-9808
For an "outstanding" "taste of the Amalfi Coast" "without the feel of
touristy Little Italy", head for this "quaint" old-"faithful" Italian with
sidewalk seating; the "accommodating" staff "makes you feel" "comfortable" whether it's a "romantic" evening or a "friends' night out" –
and the bill won't change your mind.

Post House *Steak* — 24 | 20 | 22 | $76

E 60s | Lowell Hotel | 28 E. 63rd St. (bet. Madison & Park Aves.) |
212-935-2888 | www.theposthouse.com

To "experience the finer things in life" like "perfect martinis" and
"thick, juicy cuts" with "heavenly sides" try this "refined", "female-
friendly" East 60s steakhouse; the Americana-filled setting is "civilized" and the service "capable" – in short, it's one of the "classiest"
"of its ilk", and priced accordingly.

Posto *Pizza* — 23 | 14 | 17 | $26

Gramercy | 310 Second Ave. (18th St.) | 212-716-1200 |
www.postothincrust.com

Its quarters are on the "small" side, but that's part of the "charm" of
this "bustling" Gramercy pizza "gem"; the "wonderful", "thin-crust"
pies with "delightful sauce" and "gourmet-quality toppings" keep
locals "coming back" posto-haste.

Prem-on Thai *Thai* — ∇ 20 | 18 | 16 | $32

G Village | 138 W. Houston St. (bet. MacDougal & Sullivan Sts.) |
212-353-2338 | www.prem-on.com

The "fresh" dishes at this "reasonable" Village Thai have regulars rank-
ing it a "cut above" the "usual neighborhood" options; other pluses are a
"pleasant" staff and "lovely" decor that casts a "cool" colorful "glow."

Press 195 *Sandwiches* — 22 | 13 | 17 | $19

Park Slope | 195 Fifth Ave. (bet. Berkeley Pl. & Union St.) | Brooklyn |
718-857-1950 ⊠

Bayside | 40-11 Bell Blvd. (bet. 40th & 41st Aves.) | Queens | 718-281-1950
www.press195.com

Thanks to its "delicious" panini choices, this "simple" Park Slope-
Bayside sandwich duo is ideal for an affordable "casual meal"; press

on to the "cute" outdoor areas "in warmer months" and don't miss the "outstanding Belgian fries" (Queens only).

Primavera ● *Italian* | 23 | 21 | 23 | $74 |

E 80s | 1578 First Ave. (82nd St.) | 212-861-8608 | www.primaveranyc.com
"Consummate host" Nicola Civetta "makes you feel welcome every time" at this longtime "high-end" Eastside "favorite" serving "delicious" Northern Italiana; the "hushed atmosphere", "beautiful" "wood-paneled walls" and "limos parked out front" signal you're in "pricey" territory.

Prime Grill *Steak* | 22 | 19 | 19 | $69 |

E 40s | 60 E. 49th St. (bet. Madison & Park Aves.) | 212-692-9292 | www.theprimegrill.com
"You don't need" to be observant to partake in the "kosher power scene" at this "manly" Midtown steakhouse "jammed" with expense-accounters downing "excellent" beef and sushi; sure, it's "loud" and the "tables are packed too close", but for most it's purely prime.

NEW Primehouse New York *Steak* | 23 | 23 | 22 | $71 |

Gramercy | 381 Park Ave. S. (27th St.) | 212-824-2600 | www.brguestrestaurants.com
"Sexy, warm and just as inviting for women", Steve Hanson's "impressive", "predictably expensive" Gramercy newcomer "flaunts all the steakhouse classics", but with "plenty of contemporary touches" too; the "terrific" beef has just the "right amount of char", the "tableside-prepared Caesar" is "outstanding" and the tables are "roomy", producing a truly "memorable experience."

Primitivo *Italian* | ∇ 19 | 16 | 19 | $34 |

W Village | 202 W. 14th St. (bet. 7th & 8th Aves.) | 212-255-2060 | www.primitivorestaurant.com
For a "true Italian home-cooking fix", look to this "friendly" West Villager, where the "flavorful", "affordable" fare is "generously portioned" and the selection of the namesake vino "excellent"; "if only all neighborhood places were as reliable."

Primola *Italian* | 23 | 16 | 20 | $61 |

E 60s | 1226 Second Ave. (bet. 64th & 65th Sts.) | 212-758-1775
The owner "runs a tight ship", and his "clubby", "costly" Eastside Italian "bustles" with an "affluent", "celeb-sprinkled" crowd, all enjoying "excellent", "authentic" dishes; still, primo-donnas grumble "regulars are treated right, newcomers are stuck in the corner."

Provence en Boite *Bakery/French* | 18 | 17 | 16 | $33 |

Carroll Gardens | 263 Smith St. (Degraw St.) | Brooklyn | 718-797-0707 | www.provenceenboite.com
"Not slick, not a scene", this "charming" Carroll Gardens combination pastry shop/French bistro feels like a "slice of the *Sud*"; while some say "brunch is the best part", carbo-loaders melt over the "killer" croissants and "insanely good baguettes."

Prune *American* | 24 | 16 | 21 | $50 |

E Village | 54 E. First St. (bet. 1st & 2nd Aves.) | 212-677-6221 | www.prunerestaurant.com
Never mind the "crowded", "closet"-size digs of this East Village "plum", because "giant talent" Gabrielle Hamilton is in the open

kitchen whipping up "inventive, quirky" yet "simple" New American dishes; weekend brunch is "famous" for a reason, so "go early or wait with the masses."

Public *Eclectic*

| 22 | 24 | 21 | $53 |

NoLita | 210 Elizabeth St. (bet. Prince & Spring Sts.) | 212-343-7011 | www.public-nyc.com

The "elementary-school-chic" decor (card catalogs, "modern industrialist" lighting) sets the "sexy scene" at this NoLita "mainstay"; all appreciate its "imaginative" "Aussie"-accented Eclectic eats and "killer cocktails", though "high prices" mean it's "not for all of the public."

Pukk *Thai/Vegetarian*

| ∇ 23 | 21 | 21 | $21 |

E Village | 71 First Ave. (bet. 4th & 5th Sts.) | 212-253-2742 | www.pukknyc.com

Even "full-on carnivores" are "ready to return" for the "cheap", "original and delicious" vegetarian Thai offerings at this East Villager; its "spacey" decor seems "modeled after" a "YMCA swimming pool", but "in a good way" – and you "must go see the bathroom."

Pump Energy Food *Health Food*

| 18 | 5 | 13 | $14 |

E 50s | Crystal Pavilion | 805 Third Ave. (50th St.) | 212-421-3055 🅱
Flatiron | 31 E. 21st St. (bet. B'way & Park Ave. S.) | 212-253-7676
Garment District | 112 W. 38th St. (bet. B'way & 6th Ave.) | 212-764-2100
W 50s | 40 W. 55th St. (bet. 5th & 6th Aves.) | 212-246-6844
www.thepumpenergyfood.com

"It's no sacrifice" to eat "nutritiously" at these "filling stations" pumping out "tasty", "super-charged" health food and shakes; gym rats less pumped about "sweating the lines" and walls covered with "pictures of body builders with biceps bigger than your torso" tend to takeout.

Punch *Eclectic*

| 18 | 17 | 17 | $37 |

Flatiron | 913 Broadway (bet. 20th & 21st Sts.) | 212-673-6333 | www.punchrestaurant.com

"Comfy with a dose of cool", this "pleasant" loftlike Flatiron "surprise" packs a punch with its "diverse" Eclectic menu and "cheerful" decor; the "relaxing atmosphere" is made for "lingering", though oenophiles may prefer the vino lounge upstairs.

Pure Food and Wine *Vegan/Vegetarian*

| 23 | 22 | 22 | $57 |

Gramercy | 54 Irving Pl. (bet. 17th & 18th Sts.) | 212-477-1010 | www.purefoodandwine.com

"Awaken your taste buds" at Gramercy's "soothing" stove-free "oasis" that "dispels all notions" of what raw, vegan fare "can be"; its "gorgeous garden" "adds to the sense that mother nature is the maitre d'", though a few cynics quip "why so expensive? – they have no utility bill."

Puttanesca *Italian*

| 19 | 16 | 17 | $40 |

W 50s | 859 Ninth Ave. (56th St.) | 212-581-4177 | www.puttanesca.com

"Bargain prices, generous portions" and proximity to Lincoln Center keep it "hopping" at this "bright" West Side Italian with "exposed-brick" decor; however, those who find it "satisfying but unimaginative" liken it to "your old aunt – nice to visit, but just once in a while."

	FOOD	DECOR	SERVICE	COST

Pylos ● *Greek* — 25 | 23 | 21 | $45

E Village | 128 E. Seventh St. (bet. Ave. A & 1st Ave.) | 212-473-0220 |
www.pylosrestaurant.com

"Classy" and "civilized", this East Village Greek "dispenses with the
travel posters" yet still manages to "transport you to the isles"; the "divine" Hellenic wines and "modern" dishes also break with convention –
if only "your *yia yia* cooked like this"; P.S. "love the communal table."

Q Thai Bistro *Thai* — 21 | 19 | 19 | $40

Forest Hills | 108-25 Ascan Ave. (bet. Austin & Burns Sts.) | Queens |
718-261-6599 | www.qthaibistrony.com

This "tasty" Thai fusion player is "worth the trip" to Forest Hills "if
you're not local" and "a must if you are"; add in "reasonable" prices,
"efficient" service and "unexpectedly" "seductive ambiance" and
you've got a "neighborhood standby" that doubles as a "date spot."

Quaint *American* — ∇ 20 | 19 | 20 | $32

Sunnyside | 46-10 Skillman Ave. (bet. 46th & 47th Sts.) | Queens |
917-779-9220 | www.quaintnyc.com

More "stylish" than the name suggests, this "friendly" New American
in "leafy" Sunnyside "satisfies" with "creative", "upscale" yet affordable chow from an "open kitchen"; in warm weather the "little courtyard" couldn't be more, well, "quaint."

Quality Meats ● *American/Steak* — 23 | 23 | 22 | $74

W 50s | 57 W. 58th St. (bet. 5th & 6th Aves.) | 212-371-7777 |
www.qualitymeatsnyc.com

The "butcher shop" decor exudes "downtown chic" at this "dateworthy" Midtown meatery, where you should "come hungry" as the
"fantastic" steaks are *Flintstone*-size and the "housemade" ice
cream "incredible"; the service is "excellent", but beware tabs that
"run high" and acoustics "too loud to hear yourself chew."

Quantum Leap *Health Food/ Vegetarian* — 20 | 11 | 17 | $20

E Village | 203 First Ave. (bet. 12th & 13th Sts.) | 212-673-9848
G Village | 226 Thompson St. (bet. Bleecker & W. 3rd Sts.) |
212-677-8050
Flushing | 65-64 Fresh Meadow Ln. (67th Ave.) | Queens |
718-461-1307

"Inspired" "veggie goodness" awaits at this "mellow", "earnest" trio
where regulars "can't get enough" of the "creative" health food; "options are plentiful" (including fish) and "portions satisfying", but before leaping remember that you may "wait an eternity for your order."

Quatorze Bis *French* — 21 | 18 | 19 | $57

E 70s | 323 E. 79th St. (bet. 1st & 2nd Aves.) | 212-535-1414

Like a "quick stopover in Paris", this "welcoming" UES bistro is a longtime "local favorite" thanks to its "well-prepared" Gallic "classics" and
service "with a smile"; its "older, upscale" regulars "feel at home" in its
"cozy" surrounds and don't care if it's "pricey for the package."

Quattro Gatti *Italian* — 19 | 16 | 20 | $47

E 80s | 205 E. 81st St. (bet. 2nd & 3rd Aves.) | 212-570-1073

Oozing "charm", this tin-ceilinged Upper East Side trattoria is a true
slice of "old-world" Italiana; after 20-plus years, locals still consider it

a "delight", citing its "fresh, flavorful" fare and "pro" staff that never has you "feeling rushed."

Queen *Italian* | 24 | 14 | 20 | $43 |

Brooklyn Heights | 84 Court St. (bet. Livingston & Schermerhorn Sts.) | Brooklyn | 718-596-5955 | www.queenrestaurant.com

"Ask any *paesan*" – this circa-1958 Brooklyn Heights "monarch" reigns with "dazzling" "red-sauce Italian" classics; its service with "heart and soul" and "interesting cast of characters" ("politicians, newscasters") also appeal, even if the "1970s Holiday Inn" decor doesn't.

Queen of Sheba ● *Ethiopian* | ▽ 23 | 16 | 15 | $28 |

W 40s | 650 10th Ave. (bet. 45th & 46th Sts.) | 212-397-0610 | www.shebanyc.com

Like a "night in Addis Ababa", this "inexpensive" West 40s Ethiopian's "bold" dishes and "cozy", atmospheric digs create a transporting experience; however, while the flavors may be "hot", a few fume that service is "on the cool side."

Quercy *French* | 21 | 14 | 18 | $38 |

Cobble Hill | 242 Court St. (bet. Baltic & Kane Sts.) | Brooklyn | 718-243-2151

"Oh-so-comfortable" with a "sweet" atmosphere and a "patient" staff, this Cobble Hill French bistro has locals calling it their own "special secret"; its "affordable" classics "can't be beat", but "strangely" it's rarely "crowded."

Rack & Soul *BBQ/Southern* | 19 | 10 | 16 | $26 |

W 100s | 2818 Broadway (109th St.) | 212-222-4800 | www.rackandsoul.com

"Honey, these ain't your mamma's biscuits" or BBQ ribs say boosters of this "dinerlike" Columbia-area Southerner's "super-tasty", "down-home" grub deemed the "stuff dreams are made of"; still, purists shrug it's best for merely "tiding you over till you can get the real deal."

NEW Radegast Hall ● *European* | ▽ 19 | 25 | 14 | $27 |

Williamsburg | 113 N. Third St. (Berry St.) | Brooklyn | 718-963-3973 | www.radegasthall.com

Thanks to its "*wunderbar*" "true biergarten" atmosphere, "carefully chosen" beers and solid Austro-accented European fare, this "rollicking" Williamsburg newcomer has been "mobbed" from day one; its hall with a central bar and "big wooden tables" is adjoined by a 'garten' room, which is outfitted with picnic tables and a retractable roof.

☑ Rainbow Room Ⓜ *Italian* | 20 | 27 | 22 | $260 |

W 40s | GE Bldg. | 30 Rockefeller Plaza, 65th fl. (enter on 49th St., bet. 5th & 6th Aves.)

☑ Rainbow Grill *Italian*

W 40s | GE Bldg. | 30 Rockefeller Plaza, 65th fl. (enter on 49th St., bet. 5th & 6th Aves.)
212-632-5100 | www.rainbowroom.com

A "NY legend" like no other, Rock Center's "opulent" 65th-floor "landmark" offers its "almighty" panoramic views at a "skyscraping" price ($200 prix fixe–only dinner on select Fridays and Saturdays, $80 for Sunday brunch); the Northern Italian cuisine is "fine", but it's the "stunning" "art deco" setting and "spinning dance floor" that make this a "not-to-be-missed" experience; N.B. the adjacent Rainbow Grill offers a less-pricey à la carte menu every night of the week.

	FOOD	DECOR	SERVICE	COST

Rai Rai Ken ●✍ *Noodle Shop*
| | 21 | 11 | 17 | $15 |

E Village | 214 E. 10th St. (bet. 1st & 2nd Aves.) | 212-477-7030
For true "Tokyo eating" in the East Village, squeeze into this "friendly", "no-frills" "sliver" of a "noodle counter" and slurp up "delicious", "affordable" "elixirs in ramen form"; the "only thing missing" are the "Japanese company men."

Ramen Setagaya ✍ *Noodle Shop*
| | 20 | 10 | 15 | $18 |

E Village | 141 First Ave. (bet. 9th St. & St. Marks Pl.) | 212-529-2740
Blows the competition "out of the water" declare devotees of this "austere" link of a Tokyo-based chain that's heating up the East Village "ramen wars" with its "deeply flavored broth" and "chewy noodles"; still, the less-impressed respond "feh" – "too salty."

NEW R & L Restaurant ● *Coffee Shop/French*
| | - | - | - | ⁞ |

Meatpacking | 69 Gansevoort St. (bet. Greenwich & Washington Sts.) | 212-989-3863
Annexing the premises of the legendary Florent, this new 24/7 Meatpacking diner has reverted to its original 1950s name and offers much of the same cheap comfort food that its predecessor did; the maps on the wall are gone, ditto the crowds – and without the charismatic Florent Morellet on board, who knows what the future holds.

Rao's ☒✍ *Italian*
| | 23 | 18 | 23 | $71 |

Harlem | 455 E. 114th St. (Pleasant Ave.) | 212-722-6709 | www.raos.com
From "business leaders to established tough guys", "everyone's smiling" while devouring "old-school Italian" fare at Frank Pellegrino's "unforgettable" Bogart-style East Harlem hideaway; to score a table before 3001, you "gotta know the right people" – otherwise you'll have to settle for the offshoot in Vegas' Caesars Palace.

Raoul's ● *French*
| | 23 | 20 | 20 | $55 |

SoHo | 180 Prince St. (bet. Sullivan & Thompson Sts.) | 212-966-3518 | www.raouls.com
A "SoHo standby" since 1975, this "sexy" French "classic" with a dark "backstreet Paris" air sets the "gold standard" for "hip, authentic" NYC bistros; never mind if it's "a little expensive", thanks to "incredible" cooking and that "dream" of a "hideaway garden", it's "still hot."

Rare Bar & Grill *Burgers*
| | 21 | 15 | 17 | $31 |

G Village | 228 Bleecker St. (bet. Carmine St. & 6th Ave.) | 212-691-7273
Murray Hill | Shelburne Murray Hill Hotel | 303 Lexington Ave. (37th St.) | 212-481-1999
www.rarebarandgrill.com
The "burger sits on the pedestal it deserves" at these "upscale joints" where young carnivores "gorge" on "damn fine" patties and "even better" french fries; other rare refinements include weekend jazz brunches and the Murray Hill branch's "fab rooftop bar."

Rayuela *Pan-Latin*
| | 23 | 24 | 20 | $53 |

LES | 165 Allen St. (bet. Rivington & Stanton Sts.) | 212-253-8840 | www.rayuelanyc.com
"Start the night off right" with "powerful" cocktails and follow up with "complex", "savory" dishes at this LES Pan-Latin "trendsetter"; the

"dramatic" decor centered around a "live olive tree" "wows" – as do the "steep" tabs.

Real Madrid *Spanish*

| ▽ 22 | 15 | 20 | $36 |

Staten Island | 2075 Forest Ave. (Union Ave.) | 718-447-7885 | www.realmadrid-restaurant.com

Sharing its name with perhaps the "most famous soccer club in the world", this "cozy" Staten Island Spaniard inspires instant replays with its "authentic", "delicious" fare delivered by a "friendly" team; as for the atmosphere, one person's "great themed decor" is another's "big yawn."

Rectangles ● *Israeli*

| 17 | 12 | 15 | $29 |

E 70s | 1431 First Ave. (bet. 74th & 75th Sts.) | 212-744-7470 | www.rectanglesrestaurant.com

"Adds tremendously" to the UES's "kosher offerings" say regulars who circle back for "interesting" Yemenite Israeli dishes at this "homey", "pleasant" "neighborhood pick"; however, a few take a different angle, pegging it as "inconsistent" and "a bit pricey" for what it is.

Red Cat *American/Mediterranean*

| 24 | 19 | 23 | $54 |

Chelsea | 227 10th Ave. (bet. 23rd & 24th Sts.) | 212-242-1122 | www.theredcat.com

After "gallery-hopping" in Chelsea, a "cosmopolitan crowd" laps up the "scrumptious" New American–Med cuisine at this "seductive feline" with "pleasant" service and a "comfortable", "NYC-meets-Vermont" setting; it's so "popular", "you feel like a cool cat" just scoring a table.

NEW Red Egg *Chinese/Peruvian*

| - | - | - | M |

Little Italy | 202 Centre St. (Howard St.) | 212-966-1123

To the Little Italy–Chinatown border comes this new dim sum stop, whose space-age digs are decked out in white banquettes and shiny globe lighting fixtures; the lengthy Chinese menu includes dishes both classic (beef chow fun) and contemporary (Peking duck sliders), plus a few Peruvian plates like ceviche.

Redeye Grill ● *American/Seafood*

| 20 | 18 | 19 | $54 |

W 50s | 890 Seventh Ave. (56th St.) | 212-541-9000 | www.redeyegrill.com

Shelly Fireman's "funky", "airstrip-size" New American seafooder boasts "two large revolving shrimp" sculptures and a "rollicking lunchtime buzz"; culture mavens also applaud its "attentive" staff that "gets you out quickly for Carnegie Hall" concerts across the avenue.

NEW Redhead, The 🅂🅜 *American*

| - | - | - | M |

E Village | 349 E. 13th St. (bet. 1st & 2nd Aves.) | 212-533-6212 | www.theredheadnyc.com

The East Village's former Detour space had a minor face-lift and re-emerged as this neighborhood New American, where the long bar is now complemented by a faux tin ceiling; the moderately priced menu features gussied-up pub grub made with greenmarket ingredients, and there are also ambitious cocktails.

Regency *American*

| ▽ 19 | 21 | 21 | $66 |

E 60s | Loews Regency Hotel | 540 Park Ave. (61st St.) | 212-339-4050 | www.loewshotels.com

NYC's major "movers and shakers" (mayors, governors, etc.) hold their "breakfast meetings" at this Tisch-owned East Side New American – and "it helps if you're with one"; cabaret fans claim it's even "better at night" when it morphs into Feinstein's nightclub.

Regional Thai *Thai*   18 | 15 | 17 | $27

Chelsea | 208 Seventh Ave. (22nd St.) | 212-807-9872
E 70s | 1479 First Ave. (77th St.) | 212-744-6374
"Solid", low-cost Thai standards, "volcanic cocktails", "whimsical" decor and pleasantly "quirky" service add up to "beloved neighborhood institution" status for this Chelsea-UES duo; the less-enamored complain of "mediocre" fare, iffy service and sorta "seedy" digs.

Relish ● *American*   ▽ 20 | 20 | 16 | $26

Williamsburg | 225 Wythe Ave. (bet. Metropolitan Ave. & N. 3rd St.) | Brooklyn | 718-963-4546 | www.relish.com
They have "interesting, honest" New American comfort fare at this "sexy" 1950s stainless-steel "railcar diner", as well as a "spacious garden" and a view of the Williamsburg Bridge; surveyors also relish the reasonable prices, but not the merely "adequate" service.

Remi *Italian*   22 | 22 | 21 | $61

W 50s | 145 W. 53rd St. (bet. 6th & 7th Aves.) | 212-581-4242 | www.remi-ny.com
"Terrific both visually and gastronomically", this Midtown Venetian is still a "special treat" whether you're "entertaining clients" or heading to the theater; the "intimate-yet-soaring" space bedecked with "interesting" murals sets the stage for "delectable" dining, while the "charming" staff always "makes you feel welcome."

Republic *Pan-Asian*   18 | 13 | 15 | $23

Union Sq | 37 Union Sq. W. (bet. 16th & 17th Sts.) | 212-627-7172 | www.thinknoodles.com
It's "rush in, rush out" at this "hard-to-resist" Union Square Pan-Asian whose "cavernous", "modern" space is perpetually "packed"; despite the "deafening din" and "uncomfortable" benches customers clamor for the "fresh, tasty" fare priced "dirt-cheap."

Re Sette ● *Italian*   21 | 17 | 20 | $53

W 40s | 7 W. 45th St. (bet. 5th & 6th Aves.) | 212-221-7530 | www.resette.com
Its location a bit "off the Times Square path" "keeps the crowds and noise down" at this "charming" Italian plying Barese regional dishes; the King's Table upstairs is "perfect" for private parties.

Resto ● *Belgian*   20 | 15 | 17 | $42

Gramercy | 111 E. 29th St. (bet. Lexington Ave. & Park Ave. S.) | 212-685-5585 | www.restonyc.com
"Delights" including "top-notch burgers" and one of "NYC's best beer menus" produce "traffic jams" at this "small", "stark" Gramercy Belgian; for most it's "worth" the "painful wait" to get in, but a skeptical few opine it's "overhyped" and too "noisy" to provide much of a resto.

NEW Rhong-Tiam *Thai*   – | – | – | M

G Village | 541 La Guardia Pl. (bet. Bleecker & W. 3rd Sts.) | 212-477-0600 | www.rhong-tiam.com
The owners of Penang have opened this NYU-area Thai that's already gaining a following for its midpriced menu going way beyond the usual

pad Thai; the room is blandly tasteful (save for the Vespa parked up front), but the food's tongue-singeing chiles provide more than enough spice to compensate.

Rice ⊗ *Eclectic*
19 | 15 | 16 | $22

Gramercy | 115 Lexington Ave. (28th St.) | 212-686-5400
NoHo | 292 Elizabeth St. (bet. Bleecker & Houston Sts.) | 212-226-5775 ●
Dumbo | 81 Washington St. (bet. Front & York Sts.) | Brooklyn | 718-222-9880
Fort Greene | 166 DeKalb Ave. (Cumberland St.) | Brooklyn | 718-858-2700
www.riceny.com

"Multicultural, mix-and-match" rice "every way possible" is the deal at this "unassuming" Eclectic quartet where you choose the components to "create your own dinner"; it's "quick", "cheap" and "good for vegetarians" – and those who cheer "bring on the carbs!"

Rice 'n' Beans *Brazilian*
▽ 22 | 9 | 17 | $25

W 50s | 744 Ninth Ave. (bet. 50th & 51st Sts.) | 212-265-4444 | www.ricenbeansrestaurant.com

"Mounds" of "satisfying" "Brazilian home cooking" emerge from the kitchen of this "miniature", "easygoing" Hell's Kitchen "hole-in-the-wall"; the offerings are just "what the name implies", priced for "good value" – "what's not to like?"

Rickshaw Dumpling Bar *Chinese*
16 | 9 | 13 | $14

Flatiron | 61 W. 23rd St. (bet. 5th & 6th Aves.) | 212-924-9220
G Village | 53 E. Eighth St. (bet. B'way & University Pl.) | 212-461-1750
www.rickshawdumplings.com

Those needing a "dumpling fix" "in a hurry" find it at Anita Lo's "efficient" Chinese Flatiron-Village duo dispensing a "tasty assortment" plus soups and salads; "speedy service", "no-frills" digs and "cheap" tabs satisfy most surveyors, though a few insist "the idea" is a lot better than the execution.

Riingo *American/Japanese*
21 | 20 | 20 | $55

E 40s | Alex Hotel | 205 E. 45th St. (bet. 2nd & 3rd Aves.) | 212-867-4200 | www.riingo.com

"Hidden away" in Midtown's Alex Hotel, Marcus Samuelsson's "off-beat sister to Aquavit" delivers "creative" New American–Japanese dishes with "flair"; though the "quiet" room's layout strikes some as "strange" and the prices are a bit high, the "hip mood" and "enjoyable" service make it a "go-to" all the same.

Risotteria *Italian*
20 | 9 | 15 | $24

G Village | 270 Bleecker St. (Morton St.) | 212-924-6664 | www.risotteria.com

"Gluten-sensitive gourmets" gather at this "tiny" Village Italian turning out "creamy risottos" and other fare fit for "those with food restrictions" yet "terrific enough for everyone else"; there's "no decor" and little elbow room, but "squeeze in" and you'll leave "happily satiated."

☑ River Café *American*
26 | 27 | 25 | $127

Dumbo | 1 Water St. (bet. Furman & Old Fulton Sts.) | Brooklyn | 718-522-5200 | www.rivercafe.com

"Million dollar views" of Manhattan and the East River, "sublime" New American cuisine, "dignified, relaxed service" and a "flower-filled" room make a "sybaritic brew" – aka Dumbo's "grand luxe" "treat"; "it's under the Brooklyn Bridge, but over the moon", with tabs to match ($98 prix fixe–only dinners), but all agree that it's a "magical" experience "well worth the splurge"; N.B. jackets required.

Riverview *American*   ▽ 19 | 21 | 18 | $51

LIC | 2-01 50th Ave. (East River & 49th Ave.) | Queens | 718-392-5000 | www.riverviewny.com

True to its name, this "glitzy" New American in Long Island City dispenses "spectacular views" of Manhattan along with "good" eats served by a "helpful" crew; just "be sure to sit near a window" or snag a patio table in summer.

NEW Roberta's ●M⊅ *Pizza*   - | - | - | I

Bushwick | 261 Moore St. (Bogart St.) | Brooklyn | 718-417-1118 | www.robertaspizza.com

With "perfectly executed" wood-oven pizzas and "fresh, creative" toppings, this joint fills a need for postindustrial Bushwick; its "rustic" room is outfitted with "long wooden tables", while the front counter is dominated by the fire engine–red oven cranking out pies in one size only.

Z Roberto ⊠ *Italian*   26 | 18 | 21 | $51

Bronx | 603 Crescent Ave. (Hughes Ave.) | 718-733-9503

Regulars "can't rave enough" about Roberto Paciullo's "amazing" Bronx Italian, where the Salerno-style fare is *"delizioso"*, service "gracious" and the "kitschy" atmosphere "warm"; though "pricey for the area", it's "money well spent" – just "get there at the opening bell or wait forever"; P.S. if Roberto tells you to eat it, eat it.

Roberto Passon ● *Italian*   22 | 16 | 19 | $44

W 50s | 741 Ninth Ave. (50th St.) | 212-582-5599 | www.robertopasson.com

A "high quality-to-price ratio" marks this "standout" Hell's Kitchen Italian dispensing "delightful" "twists" on the "usual suspects"; there's "not much in the way of decor" in its "simple" "storefront" setting, but "pleasant", "fast" service makes it "perfect pre-theater."

Roc ● *Italian*   21 | 19 | 20 | $50

TriBeCa | 190A Duane St. (Greenwich St.) | 212-625-3333 | www.rocrestaurant.com

They "treat you well" at this "classy" TriBeCa Italian known for "fresh, flavorful" fare, "capable, kind" service and a pleasing "neighborhood feel" that extends to the "lovely" sidewalk seating; it's "not the cheapest" player around, but "you get what you pay for."

Rock Center Café *American*   18 | 21 | 19 | $48

W 50s | Rockefeller Ctr. | 20 W. 50th St. (bet. 5th & 6th Aves.) | 212-332-7620 | www.patinarestaurantgroup.com

Yes, it's "touristy", but this "casual" Rock Center American doles out "surprisingly good" food at a relatively "reasonable price"; besides that, it's "fun" on the patio in summer or "watching the skaters" in winter, especially "at Christmas."

Rocking Horse Cafe *Mexican*   21 | 16 | 18 | $37

Chelsea | 182 Eighth Ave. (bet. 19th & 20th Sts.) | 212-463-9511 | www.rockinghorsecafe.com

"Always crowded and never dull", Chelsea's "upmarket" Mexican provides a "funky" vantage from which to "watch the passing parade" while kicking back with "killer drinks" and "tasty, inventive" eats; "punishing noise" and "scrunched" seating aside, revved up regulars root "rock on!"

Rolf's German | 15 | 21 | 15 | $39 |

Gramercy | 281 Third Ave. (22nd St.) | 212-477-4750
The "truly over-the-top" "holiday lights and tinsel" are legendary at this Gramercy Park "standby" that recently morphed from traditional German to Bavarian brasserie; some carol that it has "lost its luster", and cite "nonexistent" service, but it's too soon to judge.

Roll-n-Roaster ● Sandwiches | 19 | 8 | 12 | $15 |

Sheepshead Bay | 2901 Emmons Ave. (bet. E. 29th St. & Nostrand Ave.) | Brooklyn | 718-769-5831 | www.rollnroaster.com
Brooklynites "roll on in" to this "no-fuss", low-budget Sheepshead Bay "fun fast-food" phenom for "fantastic" roast beef sandwiches and cheese fries so good they "should be illegal"; it's "authentic" as all get out, so expect a *Lords of Flatbush* feel – and "no apologies."

Room Service Thai | 17 | 17 | 16 | $27 |

Chelsea | 166 Eighth Ave. (bet. 18th & 19th Sts.) | 212-691-0299
"Bangkok disco" meets "Chelsea chic" at this "quirky" Thai turning out "tasty"-enough bites in a "hotellike" setting; it's quite a "scene", with "loud music" and "shrugging" staff, but all at "recession-proof" rates.

Roppongi Japanese | ▽ 21 | 15 | 18 | $35 |

W 80s | 434 Amsterdam Ave. (81st St.) | 212-362-8182
Upper Westsiders "looking for a comfortable neighborhood Japanese" head to this "quiet little" contender where they "can get a table" (unlike the "noisy" "competition across the street"); in sum, it's a "pleasant" place for "delicious sushi" and a "plentiful omakase" at "decent prices."

☑ Rosa Mexicano ● Mexican | 21 | 21 | 19 | $48 |

E 50s | 1063 First Ave. (58th St.) | 212-753-7407
Flatiron | 9 E. 18th St. (bet. B'way & 5th Ave.) | 212-533-3350
W 60s | 61 Columbus Ave. (62nd St.) | 212-977-7700
www.rosamexicano.com
It's "always a fiesta" at this "exuberant" trio serving "dolled-up Mexican" to a "trendy crowd"; the "made-tableside guacamole" is "justifiably famous" and the "signature pomegranate margaritas" sufficient to mask "rushed" service, "but the prices – *ay caramba!*"

Rosanjin ☒ Japanese | ▽ 27 | 27 | 26 | $153 |

TriBeCa | 141 Duane St. (bet. Church St. & W. B'way) | 212-346-0664 | www.rosanjintribeca.com
The kaiseki meals at this "peaceful" TriBeCa Japanese are "formal" multicourse extravaganzas "exquisitely presented" and "served with exceeding courtesy" – in short, an "outstanding", "super-luxurious" experience; all that's required is "time" and deep pockets to cover the $150 prix fixe (though an à la carte menu is now available too).

Rose Water American | 24 | 19 | 22 | $43 |

Park Slope | 787 Union St. (6th Ave.) | Brooklyn | 718-783-3800 | www.rosewaterrestaurant.com
"Park Slopers love" this "dazzling tribute to fresh, local" ingredients, a "tiny", "laid-back" "pearl" of a New American eatery with "wonderful"

cuisine and a "sincerely friendly" staff; most agree it "hasn't lost a step" after a recent chef change – all that's wrong is it "needs to be bigger."

Rossini's *Italian* | 23 | 18 | 24 | $60 |

Murray Hill | 108 E. 38th St. (bet. Lexington & Park Aves.) | 212-683-0135 | www.rossinisrestaurant.com

From the "terrific" Northern Italian cuisine to the "top-notch" staff and "genteel" surroundings, "they keep doing it right" at this "old-style" Murray Hill "mainstay"; nightly piano and Saturday "live opera" are a "treat" that helps make up for prices that can also hit high notes.

Rothmann's *Steak* | 23 | 19 | 21 | $70 |

E 50s | 3 E. 54th St. (bet. 5th & Madison Aves.) | 212-319-5500 | www.rothmannssteakhouse.com

Catering to "suit-wearing" "carnivores", this "big, bustling" East Midtowner provides the requisite "good ol' steakhouse atmosphere" for its "perfectly cooked" cuts delivered via "attentive" staffers; the wine list rates a "wow", while the tabs get an 'ow.'

Roth's Westside Steakhouse *Steak* | 20 | 16 | 19 | $50 |

W 90s | 680 Columbus Ave. (93rd St.) | 212-280-4103 | www.rothswestsidesteakhouse.com

A "reliable" "red-meat lovers' delight", this "comfortable" UWS "steak joint" proffers "properly done" slabs "carefully served"; with live jazz to "sweeten the ambiance" on weekends, it's a "good neighborhood choice" that's on the money.

Royal Siam *Thai* | 19 | 11 | 18 | $29 |

Chelsea | 240 Eighth Ave. (bet. 22nd & 23rd Sts.) | 212-741-1732

"Old-fashioned", "tasty" Thai arrives "a minute after you order it" at this "unassuming" Chelsea "neighborhood favorite"; some "wish they'd spruce up" a bit and lament that the "menu never changes", but no one complains about the "pleasant" service or "low prices."

Roy's New York *Hawaiian* | 24 | 20 | 22 | $54 |

Financial District | Marriott Financial Ctr. | 130 Washington St. (bet. Albany & Carlisle Sts.) | 212-266-6262 | www.roysnewyork.com

They "know their way around a fish" at this Financial District venue for Roy Yamaguchi's "memorable", "absolutely excellent" Hawaiian fusion feasts worth "going out of the way" for; "sweet servers with the aloha spirit" compensate for the "pricey" tabs and "1980s" "hotel decor."

RUB BBQ *BBQ* | 20 | 9 | 15 | $28 |

Chelsea | 208 W. 23rd St. (bet. 7th & 8th Aves.) | 212-524-4300 | www.rubbbq.net

"Real Kansas City BBQ done right", from "righteous ribs" to "lean, savory brisket", keeps this "fairly priced", "no-frills" Chelsea joint jumping; "better show up early", though, because "sometimes they run out of what you really want."

Ruby Foo's ◐ *Pan-Asian* | 19 | 21 | 17 | $44 |

W 40s | 1626 Broadway (49th St.) | 212-489-5600
W 70s | 2182 Broadway (77th St.) | 212-724-6700
www.brguestrestaurants.com

It's a "perpetual party" at these "big", "Disneyfied" Pan-Asians, where the "terrific" fare comes "fast and furious" in "overwrought", "carnival"-

style digs; "kids love 'em" and, yes, they're perfect for "out-of-towners" – but "who says tourists should have all the fun?"

	FOOD	DECOR	SERVICE	COST

Rue 57 ● French
18 | 18 | 16 | $46

W 50s | 60 W. 57th St. (6th Ave.) | 212-307-5656 | www.rue57.com
"Always buzzy", this Midtown "bistro on steroids" boasts a "crazy menu" that mixes sushi and French brasserie classics; it's "ridiculously dark" with "tables on top of each other", the servers are often "overwhelmed" and you need a "megaphone" to be heard – but "somehow it all works."

Rughetta ☒ Italian
22 | 17 | 21 | $44

E 80s | 347 E. 85th St. (bet. 1st & 2nd Aves.) | 212-517-3118 | www.rughetta.com
"Tucked away" on the UES, this midpriced Italian "exceeds expectations" with "first-rate", "perfectly understated" Roman dishes delivered by a "wonderful staff"; the "itty-bitty", "candlelit" room "fills quickly", so no wonder locals want to "keep it a secret."

Russian Samovar ● Continental
19 | 17 | 18 | $50

W 50s | 256 W. 52nd St. (bet. B'way & 8th Ave.) | 212-757-0168 | www.russiansamovar.com
Step through the door and you're in "1950s Moscow" at this "rowdy" Theater District Continental; it's full of "real Russians" partaking of "potent flavored vodkas" and "serious" "traditional" eats conveyed by an "eager staff" – all in all it's a "rollicking good time."

Russian Tea Room Continental/Russian
19 | 24 | 20 | $72

W 50s | 150 W. 57th St. (bet. 6th & 7th Aves.) | 212-581-7100 | www.russiantearoomnyc.com
After being closed for several years, this "fabulously over-the-top" Russian-accented Continental Midtown "jewel box" is back and hailed by fans as "better than ever"; however, non-fans who report "the life isn't there the way it once was" say it's "for tourists alone"; all agree it's as "hard to kill as Rasputin" and costs plenty of rubles.

Ruth's Chris Steak House Steak
24 | 20 | 23 | $69

W 50s | 148 W. 51st St. (bet. 6th & 7th Aves.) | 212-245-9600 | www.ruthschris.com
"Outrageous sizzling-butter steaks" and "well-prepared sides" star at this "hospitable" Theater District outpost of the "high-end" New Orleans steakhouse chain; the opulent, wood-paneled digs may be "dated", but the service is "everything it should be" considering you'll "spend big" for the experience.

Sac's Place Pizza
20 | 12 | 16 | $28

Astoria | 25-41 Broadway (29th St.) | Queens | 718-204-5002
"Amazing" thin-crust, coal-burning brick-oven pizza topped with "quality ingredients" is the "highlight" at this "friendly", "informal" Astoria Italian; most come for those "square pies", so never mind if the other dishes are mostly "ordinary."

Safran French/Vietnamese
▽ 21 | 19 | 20 | $40

Chelsea | 88 Seventh Ave. (bet. 15th & 16th Sts.) | 212-929-1778 | www.safran88.com
Maybe it "doesn't look special from the street", but this "comfortable, quiet", "modern" Chelsea yearling turns out "imaginative" French-

Vietnamese cuisine served by a "cordial" crew; its moderate prices are another "delightful surprise."

	FOOD	DECOR	SERVICE	COST

S'Agapo ● *Greek* ∇ 21 | 11 | 19 | $33
Astoria | 34-21 34th Ave. (35th St.) | Queens | 718-626-0303
It "doesn't get more Greek" than this "authentic", "affordable" Astoria tavern, where they "treat you as family", dishing up "perfectly simple", "mama's kitchen"–style "delights"; for those who are bothered by the "cracked-linoleum" decor, check out the "alfresco seating area."

☑ Sahara ● *Turkish* 22 | 15 | 16 | $28
Gravesend | 2337 Coney Island Ave. (bet. Aves. T & U) | Brooklyn | 718-376-8594 | www.saharapalace.com
"Everything grilled is wonderful" at this "big, noisy" Gravesend Turk turning out "ample portions" perfect for "family-style feasting"; "labyrinthine", "cavernous rooms" and "so-so service" detract, but the "outdoor dining area" and "South Brooklyn prices" make it feel like an "oasis."

Saigon Grill ● *Vietnamese* 21 | 12 | 16 | $25
G Village | 91-93 University Pl. (bet. 11th & 12th Sts.) | 212-982-3691
W 90s | 620 Amsterdam Ave. (90th St.) | 212-875-9072
"Heaping plates" of "fresh" Vietnamese eats served "super speedy" supply a "cheap thrill" at this "popular" pair; they're "crowded and noisy" and the decor "isn't fetching", yet diners "leave contented."

Sakagura ● *Japanese* 25 | 22 | 21 | $50
E 40s | 211 E. 43rd St., downstairs (bet. 2nd & 3rd Aves.) | 212-953-7253 | www.sakagura.com
The "initiated" seek out this "soothing" basement Japanese izakaya near Grand Central for "marvelous" small bites and "sake every which way"; service is "polite" and lunch a "deal", but at dinner "prices soar."

Sala *Spanish* 22 | 19 | 19 | $40
Flatiron | 35 W. 19th St. (bet. 5th & 6th Aves.) | 212-229-2300
NoHo | 344 Bowery (Great Jones St.) | 212-979-6606
www.salanyc.com
"Budget-conscious" friends gather at these "festive" NoHo-Flatiron Spaniards for the "tastiest tapas west of Barcelona" washed down with "free-flowing sangria"; the "dark, sexy" settings get "loud at happy hour", but they're less of a "scene" at lunch.

Salaam Bombay *Indian* 19 | 16 | 18 | $38
TriBeCa | 317 Greenwich St. (bet. Duane & Reade Sts.) | 212-226-9400 | www.salaambombay.com
TriBeCans "craving Indian cuisine" find fixes at this "reliably good" fallback; it's best known for its "unbeatable" $13.95 lunch buffet whose "beautiful display" lends luster to the somewhat "dowdy" digs.

Sal Anthony's Lanza *Italian* 19 | 17 | 19 | $42
E Village | 168 First Ave. (bet. 10th & 11th Sts.) | 212-674-7014
Sal Anthony's S.P.Q.R. *Italian*
Little Italy | 133 Mulberry St. (bet. Grand & Hester Sts.) | 212-925-3120
www.salanthonys.com
This East Village–Little Italy "delightful anachronism" dispenses "darngood", "old-world" Southern Italian "real red-sauce" specialties via an

"eager-to-please" staff; factor in the "family atmosphere" and "reasonable" rates, and it's "an offer you can't refuse."

Sala Thai *Thai*
FOOD	DECOR	SERVICE	COST
20	11	16	$29

E 80s | 1718 Second Ave. (bet. 89th & 90th Sts.) | 212-410-5557
A "loyal following" "counts on" this "unpretentious" UES Thai vet for "fine" fare that's "just spicy enough"; perhaps service "could improve", but tabs are "modest", and those who think the room's "tired" note "takeout's terrific."

Salt ⑧ *American*
FOOD	DECOR	SERVICE	COST
▽ 21	18	20	$44

SoHo | 58 MacDougal St. (bet. Houston & Prince Sts.) | 212-674-4968

Salt Bar ●⑧Ⓜ⇄ *American*
LES | 29A Clinton St. (bet. Houston & Stanton Sts.) | 212-979-8471
www.saltnyc.com
"Inventive", "savory" tastes are the draw at this "low-key" little SoHo New American that packs 'em in at "long communal tables"; the equally snug LES branch offers fewer main courses, focusing more on "fun" bites and beverages.

Salute! *Italian*
FOOD	DECOR	SERVICE	COST
19	18	16	$49

Murray Hill | 270 Madison Ave. (39th St.) | 212-213-3440 | www.salutenyc.com
"Hordes of suits" do "business lunch" at this "pleasant" Murray Hill Med-Italian; overall it's a "fine" choice, though even "expense-account" patrons bridle at paying "premium" prices for "subpar" service.

Sambuca *Italian*
FOOD	DECOR	SERVICE	COST
18	16	18	$40

W 70s | 20 W. 72nd St. (bet. Columbus Ave. & CPW) | 212-787-5656 | www.sambucanyc.com
Maybe the "basic", "family-style" Italian eats at this "kid-friendly" UWS "alternative to Carmine's" "won't wow you", but the "giant portions" may, so "go with a group" and "share"; waiters are "cheery", and – who woulda thunk? – there's a "gluten-free menu."

Sammy's Roumanian *Jewish*
FOOD	DECOR	SERVICE	COST
20	9	18	$53

LES | 157 Chrystie St. (Delancey St.) | 212-673-0330
"Traditional", schmaltz-laden "Jewish cuisine" means "mega-doses of cholesterol" at this "hilarious" LES "throwback" that's like a wild "Bar Mitzvah" party; its kind is an "endangered species", so just let the "frozen vodka help" you stomach the "tacky" decor and that "guy belting out musical numbers" – "more fun you cannot have."

Sandro's ● *Italian*
FOOD	DECOR	SERVICE	COST
23	16	18	$56

E 80s | 306 E. 81st St. (bet. 1st & 2nd Aves.) | 212-288-7374
"Larger-than-life" chef Sandro Fioriti is "back" on the scene with this "sophisticated" UES "new neighborhood star" delivering "off-the-charts delicious" Italian fare and "dangerous grappa" via staffers who aim "to please"; only the "plain", "very white" decor doesn't go down so well.

San Pietro ⑧ *Italian*
FOOD	DECOR	SERVICE	COST
24	21	23	$78

E 50s | 18 E. 54th St. (bet. 5th & Madison Aves.) | 212-753-9015 | www.sanpietro.net
"Superb" Southern Italian cuisine "employing luxury ingredients" plus "wonderful wines" bring "tycoons at play" to this "pretty", "high-

powered" Midtowner; service is generally "skillful", but really it's best to "go with a regular" – one who hopefully can pick up the tab.

Santa Fe   *Southwestern*

18	15	17	$38

W 70s | 73 W. 71st St. (bet. Columbus Ave. & CPW) | 212-724-0822
A "mature" UWS crowd (including a few "ABC TV personalities") gathers for "honest" Southwestern fare at this "comfy" cantina; though some still "miss the old digs" a couple of blocks away, "decent prices" and "powerhouse margaritas" "make up for a lot."

Sant Ambroeus   *Italian*

21	20	20	$60

E 70s | 1000 Madison Ave. (bet. 77th & 78th Sts.) | 212-570-2211
W Village | 259 W. Fourth St. (Perry St.) | 212-604-9254
www.santambroeus.com
"European air-kissers", "social x-rays" and other "elites" meet at these "lively" Italians proffering Milanese cooking "at its best"; perhaps "food is beside the point" given such a "scene", but the prices are "steep" "just for people-watching."

Sapori D'Ischia   Ⓜ *Italian*

25	16	19	$51

Woodside | 55-15 37th Ave. (56th St.) | Queens | 718-446-1500
"Deli by day" and dispenser of "delicious" dinners at night, this "quirky" Woodside Italian "winner" located in "the back of nowhere" is worth getting out the "GPS" to find; "charming waiters" and live opera on Thursdays await you.

Sapphire Indian   *Indian*

21	18	19	$43

W 60s | 1845 Broadway (bet. 60th & 61st Sts.) | 212-245-4444 | www.sapphireny.com
Lincoln Center–goers "applaud" this "convenient" UWS Indian for its "subtle", "savory" fare, "prompt" service and "pleasant", "calm" setting; it's more "refined" than many of its type, with matching "upscale prices", but the "lavish" $13.95 lunch buffet is a steal.

Sapporo East   ☻ *Japanese*

▽ 21	8	16	$26

E Village | 164 First Ave. (10th St.) | 212-260-1330
"Ramen done right", "passable sushi" and other "working-class Japanese comestibles" keep the "lines out the door" at this "low-key" East Village "stalwart"; though nothing to look at, it offers real "bang for your buck" in an area where bargains are increasingly hard to find.

Sarabeth's   *American*

20	17	17	$34

Chelsea | Chelsea Mkt. | 75 Ninth Ave. (bet. 15th & 16th Sts.) | 212-989-2424 | www.sarabeth.com
E 70s | Whitney Museum | 945 Madison Ave. (75th St.) | 212-570-3670 | www.sarabeth.com   Ⓜ
E 90s | 1295 Madison Ave. (bet. 92nd & 93rd Sts.) | 212-410-7335 | www.sarabeth.com
W 50s | 40 Central Park S. (bet. 5th & 6th Aves.) | 212-826-5959 | www.sarabethscps.com
W 80s | 423 Amsterdam Ave. (bet. 80th & 81st Sts.) | 212-496-6280 | www.sarabeth.com
"Home base of lunching ladies", this "cheerful" American chainlet is also a "breakfast mecca" ("even the porridge seems sexy") and "tops for brunch"; "wobbly" service and "mile-long" "queues are a pain", though "it's not such a zoo" come dinnertime.

	FOOD	DECOR	SERVICE	COST

Saravanaas *Indian* ▽ | 24 | 10 | 14 | $22 |

Gramercy | 81 Lexington Ave. (26th St.) | 212-679-0204 |
www.saravanaas.com

"Excellent", "real-deal dosas" and other "subtle" South Indian vegetarian vittles are "something to get excited about" at this Gramercy
"diamond in the rough"; patrons happily overlook "poor service",
"crowded tables" and a "plain" space given the "seriously cheap" tabs.

Sardi's Ⓜ *Continental* | 17 | 21 | 19 | $52 |

W 40s | 234 W. 44th St. (bet. B'way & 8th Ave.) | 212-221-8440 |
www.sardis.com

The "ultimate showbiz" institution and "tourist" magnet, this "retro"
Theater District Continental "legend" is famed for the "fun" "carica-
tures of celebs" that "plaster its walls" – plus some live ones sitting "at
the tables"; fans feel the kitchen's getting "its mojo back", so "choose
well, and you can dine fine" as long as you're not cash-strapped.

Sarge's Deli ◐ *Deli* | 18 | 8 | 14 | $24 |

Murray Hill | 548 Third Ave. (bet. 36th & 37th Sts.) |
212-679-0442

"It's not pretty", but this 24/7 Murray Hill "institution" is "still going
strong", pumping out "piled-high" sandwiches ("priced accordingly")
with "old-style NY deli flair"; "snippy waitresses" provide "nostalgia"
for some, but enhance the "get it to go" option for others.

Ⓩ Sasabune Ⓢ Ⓜ *Japanese* | 27 | 11 | 21 | $83 |

E 70s | 401 E. 73rd St. (bet. 1st & York Aves.) | 212-249-8583

"Sushi purists" "trust the master" at Kenji Takahashi's UES omakase-
only "gem", where the "always-changing" offerings are "guaranteed to
dazzle"; the digs are "tiny" and "minimalist" and prices "high", but
supporters say it's "not expensive considering the quality."

Ⓩ Saul *American* | 27 | 19 | 24 | $63 |

Boerum Hill | 140 Smith St. (bet. Bergen & Dean Sts.) | Brooklyn |
718-935-9844 | www.saulrestaurant.com

At once "riveting and subtle", the "nuanced" New American fare at
Saul Bolton's "upscale" Boerum Hill bistro is simply a "knockout"; the
room is "romantic", the service "stellar" and the wine list "enticing" –
in short, it's "worth the trip from anywhere."

Savann *French/Mediterranean* | 19 | 15 | 19 | $37 |

W 70s | 414 Amsterdam Ave. (bet. 79th & 80th Sts.) | 212-580-0202 |
www.savann.com

Providing an "oasis" of "quiet" for Upper Westsiders to "sit and talk",
this "homey" French-Med "standby" serves "surprisingly good" eats in
a "comfortably rustic" setting; a staff that "tries hard" and "small
checks" add to the overall "enjoyable" experience.

Savoia *Pizza* | 20 | 17 | 18 | $31 |

Carroll Gardens | 277 Smith St. (bet. Degraw & Sackett Sts.) | Brooklyn |
718-797-2727

"One of the steady places" in Carroll Gardens, this "cheerful" Italian
churns out "delicious brick-oven pizza" and gets points for "solid pastas" too; "slow" service adds to the "relaxed feel", but be warned: it
can be a "mob scene on weekends."

| | FOOD | DECOR | SERVICE | COST |

savorNY *Eclectic* ▽ 24 | 23 | 24 | $40
LES | 63 Clinton St. (bet. Rivington & Stanton Sts.) | 212-358-7125 |
www.savornyrestaurant.com
Those who've found this LES "sleeper" report that its Eclectic small-plates "blend of cuisines" packs pleasingly "bold flavors"; its "adorable", "slender" space, "personable" crew and "inexpensive wine list" have admirers declaring the area "needs more like it."

Savoy *American/Mediterranean* 23 | 20 | 22 | $58
SoHo | 70 Prince St. (Crosby St.) | 212-219-8570 | www.savoynyc.com
"Deft" chef Peter Hoffman is the "king of seasonal cooking" declare "locavores" who favor his "SoHo classic" for "fabulous", "farm-fresh" fare delivered by a "well-trained" staff; the "inviting", "country-home" decor ("sit upstairs for romance") and "superlative" wines secure his customers' support.

Scaletta *Italian* 21 | 19 | 23 | $53
W 70s | 50 W. 77th St. (bet. Columbus Ave. & CPW) | 212-769-9191 |
www.scalettaristorante.com
"Quiet and dignified", this "grown-up" Northern Italian serves Upper Westsiders "quality" fare via "experienced waiters" in a "spacious", "comfortable" setting; "some find it stodgy" – you needn't "look for trendy young 'uns" here – but that's "part of its charm."

Scalinatella ● *Italian* 26 | 17 | 21 | $79
E 60s | 201 E. 61st St. (3rd Ave.) | 212-207-8280
Step "downstairs to a hidden treasure" at this "happening" UES Italian serving "superior" Capri-style dishes in a stone cellar that exudes "relaxed chic"; you may "require a Daddy Warbucks" to settle the tab ("watch out for the specials"), but for the "lively crowd" "it's worth it."

Z Scalini Fedeli Ⓢ *Italian* 27 | 24 | 25 | $85
TriBeCa | 165 Duane St. (bet. Greenwich & Hudson Sts.) | 212-528-0400 |
www.scalinifedeli.com
"Sublime, satisfying" Northern Italian cuisine, service that "makes you feel special" and a "grand, elegant" room add up to a "lovely way to spend an evening" at this "top-shelf" TriBeCan; the $65 prix fixe "may not seem like a bargain" – but for such a "truly fine experience", it is.

Scarlatto ● *Italian* 20 | 17 | 18 | $44
W 40s | 250 W. 47th St. (bet. B'way & 8th Ave.) | 212-730-4535 |
www.scarlattonyc.com
There's "something for everyone" at this "welcoming" Theater District Northern Italian dishing up "huge" amounts of "good chow" at rates about "as affordable as it gets" in the area; it's "noisy and hectic" pre-show, but the "amicable" staff will "get you out in time."

NEW Scarpetta *Italian* 26 | 24 | 23 | $70
Chelsea | 355 W. 14th St. (bet. 8th & 9th Aves.) | 212-691-0555 |
www.scarpettanyc.com
Chef Scott Conant (ex L'Impero, Alto) "hits a home run" with this "beautiful" new Chelsea Italian where his trademark "bright, flavorful" dishes are delivered by a "hospitable" staff; the dining room features a "wow"-worthy crowd as well as a "large" "retractable" skylight, leaving "way-expensive" prices as the only rub.

	FOOD	DECOR	SERVICE	COST

Schiller's ● *Eclectic*
18 | 19 | 17 | $38

LES | 131 Rivington St. (Norfolk St.) | 212-260-4555 | www.schillersny.com

An "über-cool" crowd creates "wall-to-wall buzz" at Keith McNally's LES "Pastis East" dishing up "better-than-you-expect" Eclectic bistro fare paired with "perfect" cocktails; it's best to "be young" here so that you won't mind the "cacophony" and "so-so service."

Scottadito Osteria Toscana *Italian*
▽ 19 | 19 | 18 | $37

Park Slope | 788A Union St. (bet. 6th & 7th Aves.) | Brooklyn | 718-636-4800 | www.scottadito.com

They do a "fine job" turning out "fresh", "tasty" Tuscan at this Park Sloper done up like a "charming" farmhouse; "friendly service" and "the best value" make it "enjoyable" whether "for a date" or dining with the family.

SEA *Thai*
21 | 22 | 17 | $27

E Village | 75 Second Ave. (bet. 4th & 5th Sts.) | 212-228-5505 | www.spicenyc.net
Williamsburg | 114 N. Sixth St. (Berry St.) | Brooklyn | 718-384-8850 | www.seathairestaurant.com ●

For "excellent Thai on the cheap", try this "high-energy" duo, whose "bursting-at-the-seams" East Village location is "not as showy" as Williamsburg's "huge", "nightclub-like" branch complete with "lotus pond"; "blasting" music, "hit-or-miss" service and "crazy-busy" weekends are the deal at both.

Sea Grill ☒ *Seafood*
24 | 24 | 23 | $67

W 40s | Rockefeller Ctr. | 19 W. 49th St. (bet. 5th & 6th Aves.) | 212-332-7610 | www.theseagrillnyc.com

"Not just for tourists", this "delightful" Rock Center seafooder offers "fabulous" fin fare and "warm hospitality" to go with its "wonderful view" of "the ice rink and Christmas tree in winter"; however, as always, "location" comes at "high cost."

NEW 2nd Ave Deli ● *Deli*
22 | 12 | 16 | $28

Murray Hill | 162 E. 33rd St. (bet. Lexington & 3rd Aves.) | 212-689-9000 | www.2ndavedeli.com

Recently transplanted to Murray Hill, this black-and-white-tiled kosher deli remake "captures the spirit of the famous original" with the same "mile-high" pastrami sandwiches ("do I eat it or climb it?") and "gruff" service; the "cramped" interior accounts for the "out-the-door lines" at prime times.

Seo *Japanese*
▽ 23 | 18 | 20 | $47

E 40s | 249 E. 49th St. (bet. 2nd & 3rd Aves.) | 212-355-7722

But for its moderate prices, you "could be in Tokyo" at this "sophisticated" East Midtown Japanese that's an "aficionados'" choice for "high-quality", "inventive" sushi and "delicious" cooked dishes; the "serene tone" and "cozy back room" overlooking a garden make it "great for a date."

Serafina ● *Italian*
19 | 15 | 15 | $42

E 50s | 38 E. 58th St. (bet. Madison & Park Aves.) | 212-832-8888 ☒

(continued)

Serafina

E 60s | 29 E. 61st St. (bet. Madison & Park Aves.) | 212-702-9898
E 70s | 1022 Madison Ave., 2nd fl. (79th St.) | 212-734-2676
NoHo | 393 Lafayette St. (4th St.) | 212-995-9595
NEW **W 40s** | Time Hotel | 224. W. 49th St. (bet. B'way & 8th Ave.) |
212-247-1000
W 50s | Dream Hotel | 210 W. 55th St. (B'way) | 212-315-1700
www.serafinarestaurant.com

Despite a certain "McTrattoria" feel, these "hip", "casual" Italians are a "safe bet", plying "above-average" thin-crust pizzas, pastas and salads in "loud", "lively" environs; the "Euro"-centric crowd doesn't seem to notice if the staff seems to have "more attitude than skill."

Serendipity 3 ● Dessert | 17 | 18 | 13 | $30 |

E 60s | 225 E. 60th St. (bet. 2nd & 3rd Aves.) | 212-838-3531 |
www.serendipity3.com

At this "knickknack"-laden "amusement park" of an Eastsider, "huge, decadent" sundaes and other desserts are dished up for folks on "family outings"; "long, jostling waits" and "arrogant" service are the price for that "ever-popular frozen hot chocolate."

Sette Enoteca e Cucina Italian | 19 | 17 | 17 | $38 |

Park Slope | 207 Seventh Ave. (3rd St.) | Brooklyn | 718-499-7767 |
www.setteparkslope.com

With "20 wines under $20" and "ever-flowing champagne cocktails" at brunch, the "solid" Southern Italian eats at this Park Sloper taste all the more "satisfying"; even considering "sometimes-shoddy" service and "noisy" environs, it's "perfect for a date", especially in the "pretty" enclosed patio.

Sette Mezzo ●⇄ Italian | 23 | 16 | 20 | $65 |

E 70s | 969 Lexington Ave. (bet. 70th & 71st Sts.) | 212-472-0400

Maybe it's "not much to look at", but you "rub elbows with moguls" and their molls when dining on the "classy Italian cuisine" at this "pricey" UES trattoria; those not in "the club" knock its "rarefied snob appeal", but members consider it "cute and neighborly" – though even they lament its "archaic cash-only policy."

Seven ●🗒 American | 19 | 17 | 17 | $43 |

Chelsea | 350 Seventh Ave. (bet. 29th & 30th Sts.) | 212-967-1919 |
www.sevenbarandgrill.com

"Consistently" "decent" New American "basics" make this "peaceful" North Chelsean a "haven" for "pre-MSG" dining where "tourists are at a minimum"; it's "nothing special" and a bit "pricey" too, but still it's "one of the best" in a tough area; P.S. the bar "rocks."

718 French | 21 | 20 | 20 | $37 |

Astoria | 35-01 Ditmars Blvd. (35th St.) | Queens | 718-204-5553 |
www.718restaurant.com

Astorians "dine in style without going to Manhattan" at this "sophisticated" yet "unpretentious" bistro where the Spanish-accented French fare is as well liked as its "intimate", "loungelike" setting; thankfully, prices remain "reasonable", despite it being rather "trendy" and "fancy" for Queens.

	FOOD	DECOR	SERVICE	COST

Sevilla ◐ *Spanish*   **21** | **13** | **19** | **$39**

W Village | 62 Charles St. (W. 4th St.) | 212-929-3189 |
www.sevillarestaurantandbar.com

A "favorite haunt" for fans of "genuine paella" and other "flavorful"
Spanish fare, this West Village "garlic paradise" is a circa-1941 "oldie
but goodie"; in addition to decor dating "from year one", it boasts
"servers who care" and "bargain" prices "to boot."

Sezz Medi' *Mediterranean/Pizza*   ▽ **20** | **15** | **18** | **$32**

W 100s | 1260 Amsterdam Ave. (122nd St.) | 212-932-2901 |
www.sezzmedi.com

"Reliably tasty", "crispy-crusted" pizzas and other "brick-oven preparations" make this "informal" Morningside Heights Med a "jewel in the
neighborhood"; service is "willing", and when it gets "crowded", sitting on the "pleasant terrace" is a privilege.

Sfoglia ⊠ *Italian*   **24** | **19** | **21** | **$60**

E 90s | 1402 Lexington Ave. (92nd St.) | 212-831-1402 |
www.sfogliarestaurant.com

"Sfantastic" declare those "lucky enough to secure" a table at this
"teeny", "not-inexpensive" Carnegie Hill Italian, a "reigning hot spot"
serving "rich, robust" classics to "swoon over"; its "rustic" setting and
solid service complement the food.

Shabu-Shabu 70 *Japanese*   **20** | **12** | **21** | **$39**

E 70s | 314 E. 70th St. (bet. 1st & 2nd Aves.) | 212-861-5635

"Lots of fun" "if you don't mind making a mess", this Upper Eastsider
offers a "Japanese fondue concept" ("cook your own") as well as "excellent sushi" for non-DIY diners; an "amenable" staff and "fair" prices
compensate for digs that "could use sprucing up."

Shaffer's ⊠ *American*   **22** | **15** | **21** | **$48**

Flatiron | 5 W. 21st St. (bet. 5th & 6th Aves.) | 212-255-9827 |
www.shaffercity.com

The "raw bar" still "rocks" at Jay Shaffer's "amiable" Flatiron "hangout",
but the new name reflects a shift from seafood to American comfort
fare; unchanged is the "delightful" owner's "good humor", "helpful"
service and the "black and white-tiled" setting.

⊠ Shake Shack *Burgers*   **23** | **13** | **12** | **$14**

Flatiron | Madison Square Park | 23rd St. (Madison Ave.) | 212-889-6600 |
www.shakeshack.com

"Brilliant" burgers and hot dogs plus "shakes worth every calorie" add
up to pure "magic" at this Madison Square Park alfresco "treat", now
open year 'round and soon to expand to the UWS and beyond; one
"negative" – "half the planet" is "on line", so "check their webcam" or
"be prepared" for a "monumental" wait.

NEW Shalizar ◐ *Persian*   **-** | **-** | **-** | **M**

E 80s | 1420 Third Ave. (bet. 80th & 81st Sts.) | 212-288-0012 |
www.persepolisnyc.com

Longtime UESer Persepolis' owners have opened this new nearby offshoot, a slightly more upscale affair offering much the same traditional Iranian cooking in pleasingly restrained digs; the menu is
augmented with Persian-accented cocktails like pomegranate martinis.

	FOOD	DECOR	SERVICE	COST

Shanghai Café ⊄ *Chinese* — ▽ 22 | 12 | 12 | $19

Little Italy | 100 Mott St. (bet. Canal & Hester Sts.) |
212-966-3988

"Bring a big appetite" to this "funky" Chinese "diner" where the "to-die-for soup dumplings" are the thing to order, though there are also other "flavorful" Shanghai dishes offered "for a song"; "overlook" the "stark atmosphere" and "hurried" service and just "go for the food."

Shanghai Pavilion *Chinese* — 20 | 16 | 18 | $37

E 70s | 1378 Third Ave. (bet. 78th & 79th Sts.) | 212-585-3388

"A cut above the norm", this UES Chinese provides "delicate" Shanghai-style eats in a "grown-up" setting complete with "tablecloths"; "attentive servers" and "value" prices are other reasons there's no need for a "trek to C-town."

Sharz Cafe & Wine Bar *Mediterranean* — 19 | 14 | 18 | $40

E 80s | 435 E. 86th St. (bet. 1st & York Aves.) | 212-876-7282

"Fine Mediterranean cooking" and a "gazillion affordable wines" are the draw at this "off-the-beaten-path" UES bistro; "yes, it's tiny", and "unhip" too - "nobody's showing off" here, just enjoying the "relaxed" vibe and "terrific value."

Shelly's Tradizionale *Italian* — 19 | 19 | 21 | $57

W 50s | 41 W. 57th St. (bet. 5th & 6th Aves.) | 212-245-2422 |
www.shellysnewyork.com

"Really fresh seafood" along with "homemade pastas" and other Italian specialties are delivered by a "knowledgeable" staff at this spacious Midtowner that's "reinvented itself several times in recent years"; if it's still "missing that X factor", fans believe "Shelly will get it sooner or later."

NEW Sheridan Square *American* — ▽ 21 | 19 | 20 | $64

W Village | 138 Seventh Ave. S. (bet. Charles & W. 10th Sts.) |
212-352-2237 | www.sheridansquarenyc.com

In the wake of an early chef change, this upscale West Village arrival continues to turn out "assured" New American dishes, including many from the open kitchen's wood-fired oven and grill; the airy dining room's cushy banquettes are "best for people-watching", while the adjacent bar area is ideal for an "innovative" drink.

Shinbashi ⊠ *Japanese* — ▽ 20 | 17 | 20 | $58

E 40s | 7 E. 48th St. (bet. 5th & Madison Aves.) | 212-813-1009

After a hiatus of about seven years, this Midtown Japanese is back on the scene just a few doors west of its original location; it offers a pricey, protean menu of "traditional" dishes served up in a roomy, "modern", somewhat generic space that's already drawing area business types.

NEW Shorty's.32 *American* — 24 | 18 | 21 | $50

SoHo | 199 Prince St. (bet. MacDougal & Sullivan Sts.) | 212-375-8275 |
www.shortys32.com

Quickly becoming a SoHo "hot spot", this "tiny" American newcomer has made a "good debut" with its "quirky" combo of "classy comfort food" and "excellent" "upscale entrees"; other reasons it's already a "tough spot" to get into are "gracious service", a "comfortable room with great tunes" and "no reservations."

	FOOD	DECOR	SERVICE	COST

Shula's Steak House *Steak* | 21 | 19 | 21 | $68 |

W 40s | Westin NY Times Sq. | 270 W. 43rd St. (bet. B'way & 8th Ave.) |
212-201-2776 | www.donshula.com

"Better than expected" for a "chain", coach Don Shula's "football-themed" Times Square meatery provides a "civilized, quiet" arena for "huge", "juicy" steaks and "awesome shareable desserts"; still, considering "those prices", some give it a pass.

Shun Lee Cafe ● *Chinese* | 20 | 16 | 18 | $42 |

W 60s | 43 W. 65th St. (bet. Columbus Ave. & CPW) | 212-769-3888 |
www.shunleewest.com

"Upscale" dim sum "stars" at this "busy" Lincoln Center–area Chinese whose "efficient" service makes it perfect for a "before-show bite"; though its "black-and-white checkerboard" digs may be in "need of updating", it's "cheaper" than its "fancier" next-door sibling.

Shun Lee Palace ● *Chinese* | 24 | 20 | 22 | $56 |

E 50s | 155 E. 55th St. (bet. Lexington & 3rd Aves.) | 212-371-8844 |
www.shunleepalace.com

"Continuously classy", Michael Tong's Midtown Chinese flagship leaves diners "spoiled forever after" by its "exceptional" cuisine, "superb presentation" and "unfailingly polite" staff; sure, the prices are high by genre standards, but by any other measure they are reasonable.

Shun Lee West ● *Chinese* | 22 | 20 | 20 | $54 |

W 60s | 43 W. 65th St. (bet. Columbus Ave. & CPW) | 212-595-8895 |
www.shunleewest.com

A "chic crowd" gathers to "feast" on "haute" Chinese cuisine at this "legendary" Lincoln Center–area "classic", done up with "posh", "black and white–lacquered" dragon-motif decor; add "fabulous" service, and you'll understand why this place is often "packed."

Siam Square Ⓜ *Thai* | ▽ 23 | 18 | 20 | $30 |

Bronx | 564 Kappock St. (Henry Hudson Pkwy.) | 718-432-8200 |
www.siamsq.com

"Fresh, delicious" "twists on Thai" satisfy "demanding regulars" at this "hospitable" Riverdale "treasure"; rates are "inexpensive", while "caring", if "sometimes slow", service enhances the "soothing" ambiance.

Sip Sak *Turkish* | 19 | 12 | 15 | $32 |

E 40s | 928 Second Ave. (bet. 49th & 50th Sts.) | 212-583-1900 |
www.sip-sak.com

Among the "Turkish delights" at this "popular" U.N.-area standout are "dynamite appetizers" and an "abundance of specials", including "pleasing vegetarian" options; the "decor is nowhere" and the staff leaves something "to be desired", but you'll be "pleasantly surprised at the bill."

Sistina ● *Italian* | 24 | 18 | 21 | $77 |

E 80s | 1555 Second Ave. (bet. 80th & 81st Sts.) | 212-861-7660
"Mature" yet stylish gourmands convene at this UES Italian where the "superb" fare "screams *mangia*" while the "accommodating" staffers murmur "warm welcomes"; the wine list is "out of sight" and the digs are "elegant" enough "for special occasions", so even if you "leave broke", you'll leave happy.

	FOOD	DECOR	SERVICE	COST

67 Burger Ⓜ *Burgers* | 21 | 13 | 16 | $16

Fort Greene | 67 Lafayette Ave. (Fulton St.) | Brooklyn | 718-797-7150 | www.67burger.com

"Mouthwatering, juicy burgers", "hand-cut" fries and an "excellent beer selection" are the hallmarks of this Fort Greene patty palace that's "close to BAM"; the decor may be "industrial" and the mood "frenetic", but no one's complaining given tabs this "cheap."

S'MAC *American* | 21 | 10 | 14 | $16

E Village | 345 E. 12th St. (bet. 1st & 2nd Aves.) | 212-358-7912 | www.smacnyc.com

NEW Pinch & S'MAC *American/Pizza*

W 80s | 474 Columbus Ave. (bet. 82nd & 83rd Sts.) | 212-686-5222 | www.pinchandsmac.com

There are "no frills", just "mouthwatering" mac 'n' cheese at this East Village American "dedicated" to "diverse" iterations of the dish served in "hot skillets" "to ensure ultimate gooiness"; the UWS branch has "teamed up with Pinch" to offer "pizza by the inch" along with the M&C.

NEW Smith, The *American* | 19 | 17 | 17 | $36

E Village | 55 Third Ave. (bet. 10th & 11th Sts.) | 212-420-9800 | www.thesmithnyc.com

Already "jam-packed and loud as a frat house", this East Village arrival (a sibling to Jane) delivers "solid" New American "comfort" fare with a "bistro twist"; "amiable" service, a "homey-yet-cool" setting and "everyday prices" have most hailing it as a "wonderful addition."

Smith & Wollensky *Steak* | 22 | 17 | 20 | $70

E 40s | 797 Third Ave. (49th St.) | 212-753-1530 | www.smithandwollensky.com

"Testosterone abounds" at this duplex Midtown "carnivore's Shangri-la" complete with "huge" "doses of red meat", "wisecracking waiters" and "power suits" "showing off their credit limit"; the less-"manly" may prefer Wollensky's Grill next door, which offers "lighter meals", "better prices" and later hours.

NEW Smith's *American* | 22 | 21 | 22 | $58

G Village | 79 MacDougal St. (bet. Bleecker & Houston Sts.) | 212-260-0100 | www.smithsnyc.com

Cindy Smith (Raoul's) and Danny Abrams (Red Cat) join forces with this "bright new" Villager, already a "winner" thanks to its "terrific" New American fare and "sunny" "pro" service; its narrow dining room evoking a "railway car" and "hip" back bar "transport you to the '40s."

Smoke Joint *BBQ* | 22 | 10 | 16 | $20

Fort Greene | 87 S. Elliot Pl. (Lafayette Ave.) | Brooklyn | 718-797-1011 | www.thesmokejoint.com

'Cue fans "queue up" at this "funky" Fort Greene "cafeteria" for "succulent, tender" BBQ on the "cheap"; its "relaxed", "get-your-own-silverware" vibe includes "juke joint decor" and "harried-but-happy" service, making it "a favorite" "before or after BAM."

Smorgas Chef *Scandinavian* | 19 | 15 | 17 | $34

E 40s | 924 Second Ave. (49th St.) | 212-486-1411 ☻

(continued)

(continued)

Smorgas Chef

Financial District | 53 Stone St. (William St.) | 212-422-3500
W Village | 283 W. 12th St. (4th St.) | 212-243-7073 ◗
www.smorgaschef.com

"Meatballs are a must" at these "casual", "cozy" Scandinavians serving up "traditional" eats for "not much moola"; the setups feel a bit "thrown together" and "bipolar" service ranges from "excellent" to "snarky", but the outdoor tables down "on Stone Street" couldn't be more "pleasant."

Snack *Greek*

▽ 22	10	17	$27

SoHo | 105 Thompson St. (bet. Prince & Spring Sts.) | 212-925-1040

"Squeeze in" to this "cramped-but-cute" SoHo "cubbyhole" and you'll be treated to some of the "freshest", most "satisfying" Greek specialties "outside of Astoria"; laid-back and "very affordable" in a neighborhood short on bargains, it's well "worth" the inevitable "wait."

Snack Taverna *Greek*

22	17	19	$41

W Village | 63 Bedford St. (Morton St.) | 212-929-3499

Snack's bigger (though still "cozy"), "upscale" Village sibling offers its "refined", "delectable" Greek cuisine in an "airy corner" space; its selection of Hellenic wines "you never knew existed" and "caring" service are other reasons it's "a hidden prize worth finding."

Soba-ya *Japanese*

23	16	19	$29

E Village | 229 E. Ninth St. (bet. 2nd & 3rd Aves.) | 212-533-6966 |
www.sobaya-nyc.com

"Sublime soba" swimming in soups supported by sybaritic side dishes ensure this "high-quality", "low-key" East Village Japanese stays a "favorite"; service can be "rushed", but with its "pleasing" vibe and "inexpensive" tabs, "you can't get near the place during peak hours."

NEW Socarrat Paella Bar *Spanish*

-	-	-	M

Chelsea | 259 W. 19th St. (bet. 7th & 8th Aves.) | 212-462-1000

Named for the irresistibly crunchy golden crust that forms on the bottom of a well-made paella, this new Chelsea Spaniard plies six varieties of the classic rice dish, plus traditional tapas; communal seating at a single lengthy table makes for a convivial feeling in its stylishly laid-back digs.

Sofrito ◗ *Puerto Rican*

21	19	17	$41

E 50s | 400 E. 57th St. (bet. 1st Ave. & Sutton Pl.) | 212-754-5999 |
www.sofritony.com

A "party atmosphere" prevails at this "busy" Sutton Place Puerto Rican where the new owners still offer "copious" amounts of "fancy" food in a "pretty room"; *negativas* include "long" waits, "so-so service" and "loud" renditions of "'Happy Birthday' every seven minutes."

Solace *American*

▽ 22	20	20	$50

E 60s | 406 E. 64th St. (bet. 1st & York Aves.) | 212-750-0434 |
www.solacenyc.com

"Truly reflecting its name", David Regueiro's "quiet" UES yearling serves "savory" New American fare in a "pretty townhouse" setting with a "lovely garden" in back; overall it offers a relatively "affordable fine-dining" experience.

	FOOD	DECOR	SERVICE	COST

Solera ⌧ *Spanish*
E 50s | 216 E. 53rd St. (bet. 2nd & 3rd Aves.) | 212-644-1166 | www.solerany.com

22 | 19 | 21 | $55

"Terrific" tapas and paella are served "with a smile" at this "charming", if "expensive", East Midtown Spaniard; it's hard to beat for a "long, relaxing lunch" especially if you order "a pitcher of sangria."

Solo *Mediterranean*
E 50s | Sony Plaza Atrium | 550 Madison Ave. (bet. 55th & 56th Sts.) | 212-833-7800 | www.solonyc.com

∇ 22 | 22 | 20 | $73

Bringing "variety and elegance" to kosher cooking, this "lovely", "tucked-away" Midtown Mediterranean treats its "upscale" clientele to a "quality" experience; no surprise, the tab can induce "sticker shock", but it's "spotty service" that causes the most kvetching.

Sol y Sombra ● *Spanish*
W 80s | 462 Amsterdam Ave. (bet. 82nd & 83rd Sts.) | 212-400-4036 | www.solysombranyc.com

∇ 17 | 14 | 18 | $37

"Tapas for all palates", "real sangria" and "welcoming" staffers are the draw at this "comfortable" UWS Spaniard; partisans only wish they'd "spice the place up" – its "dark" decor is "more sombra than sol."

Son Cubano ⌧ *Cuban*
Meatpacking | 405 W. 14th St. (bet. 9th Ave. & Washington St.) | 212-366-1640 | www.soncubanonyc.com

21 | 21 | 18 | $47

At this "happening" Meatpacking District Cuban, "feel like you're in 1940s Havana" as you down "incredible" drinks and "authentic" fare; it's "always a good time", though it's "hard to *comprende*" your companions "when the live music cranks up."

Song ⊅ *Thai*
Park Slope | 295 Fifth Ave. (bet. 1st & 2nd Sts.) | Brooklyn | 718-965-1108

23 | 17 | 18 | $21

"First-class dining at Third World prices" makes this "hip" "sister to Joya" "the joint to hit for delish Thai" in Park Slope; the food's served "efficiently, if not elegantly" in a "minimalist" room that's "crowded" and "raucous", so take "earplugs" or do "takeout."

NEW Sookk *Thai*
W 100s | 2686 Broadway (bet. 102nd & 103rd Sts.) | 212-870-0253

∇ 23 | 19 | 17 | $27

"Unusual" "Thai with a twist of Chinese" (like "eating in Bangkok") makes this "lovely" new sibling to Room Service a "wonderful addition to the UWS"; its "clever", colorful digs are "a bit tight" and the staff "somewhat confused", but given the super-"reasonable" tabs, who cares?

Sosa Borella ● *Argentinean/Italian*
W 50s | 832 Eighth Ave. (50th St.) | 212-262-7774 | www.sosaborella.com

17 | 14 | 17 | $41

Providing a "change of pace" in the Theater District, this "sweet little" Italian-Argentine turns out "pleasant", sometimes "inventive", fare at moderate prices; the setting's "relaxed" and service "fast", making it "terrific" "pre-show" or just for a casual "friendly gathering."

⊠ Soto ●⌧ *Japanese*
G Village | 357 Sixth Ave. (bet. Washington Pl. & W. 4th St.) | 212-414-3088

26 | 20 | 21 | $82

Prepare to be "wowed" at Sotohiro Kosugi's "extraordinary" Village Japanese offering "adventurous" sushi and "ethereal" cooked dishes;

"mind-blowing presentations" easily eclipse the "understated store-front" setting and "minor service hiccups", so "just savor" – and try "not to worry" about the "gargantuan bill."

Sottovoce *Italian*

| 19 | 16 | 19 | $31 |

Park Slope | 225 Seventh Ave. (4th St.) | Brooklyn | 718-369-9322 | www.sottovocerestaurant.com

Moderately priced Italian classics delivered via "personable" staffers "entice" neighborhood denizens into this "cozy little" Park Slope trattoria; it can be a "romantic", "candlelit" "getaway" for love-birds, while its "appealing" "sidewalk seating" means it's "great for people-watching" too.

South Fin Grill *Seafood/Steak*

| 20 | 24 | 18 | $51 |

Staten Island | 300 Father Capodanno Blvd. (Sand Ln.) | 718-447-7679 | www.southfingrill.com

If "Staten Island had tourists", they'd flock to this "gorgeous" surf 'n' turfer "on the boardwalk" boasting "fantastic views of the Verrazano Bridge", not to mention very good "fresh seafood"; regulars suggest "train" the "young" staff and this "could be a jewel."

NEW South Gate *American*

| 24 | 25 | 22 | $81 |

E 50s | Jumeirah Essex House | 160 Central Park S. (bet. 6th & 7th Aves.) | 212-484-5120 | www.jumeirahessexhouse.com

Chef Kerry Heffernan (ex Eleven Madison Park) brings his "magic" to this Central Park South New American, sending out "exceptional" cuisine in a "modern", "sprawling" space "overlooking Central Park"; "so-licitous" service and a "dynamite bar" are two more reasons to come – as long as you can afford it.

Spanky's BBQ *BBQ*

| 15 | 11 | 14 | $27 |

W 40s | 127 W. 43rd St. (bet. B'way & 6th Ave.) | 212-575-5848 | www.spankysnyc.com

"Decent BBQ in the heart of touristy Times Square" is the deal at this "simple" standby that's "dependable" for "quick", "serviceable" meals in a "relaxed, down-home" setting; sure, it's all "a bit tacky", but those "inexpensive" prices ensure it's "always busy."

Sparks Steak House 🗷 *Steak*

| 25 | 19 | 21 | $76 |

E 40s | 210 E. 46th St. (bet. 2nd & 3rd Aves.) | 212-687-4855 | www.sparkssteakhouse.com

"Where the boys are", this "quintessential" "he-man steakhouse" is a "perennial" Midtown "champion" for "unforgettable" slabs of meat and "outstanding wines" via a well-seasoned staff; expect "ridiculous waits" as well as the occasional "celeb sighting" – oh, and bring your bankroll.

Spice *Thai*

| 20 | 15 | 16 | $28 |

Chelsea | 199 Eighth Ave. (bet. 20th & 21st Sts.) | 212-989-1116
E 70s | 1411 Second Ave. (bet. 73rd & 74th Sts.) | 212-988-5348
NEW E Village | 104 Second Ave. (6th St.) | 212-533-8900
G Village | 60 University Pl. (10th St.) | 212-982-3758

Offering "fresh", "tasty" (if "Americanized") Thai fare at "value" prices, this "always-packed" foursome is a "favorite" among "younger" types "on a tight budget"; still, "abrupt" service and settings that are "hardly elegant" have some opting for takeout.

	FOOD	DECOR	SERVICE	COST

**⛫ Spice Market ** ⚫ *SE Asian*   22 | 26 | 20 | $59

Meatpacking | 403 W. 13th St. (9th Ave.) | 212-675-2322 |
www.jean-georges.com

From the "stunning" two-floor setting to the "sublime" Southeast Asian "street vendor" cuisine, Jean-Georges Vongerichten's Meatpacking District "fantasy" market is "a feast for the senses"; with "hot" staffers in "racy outfits" serving a "cool" "eye-candy" crowd, it's a "must-visit" – and those downstairs party rooms are a must-stay.

Spicy & Tasty ⊘ *Chinese*   23 | 8 | 13 | $23

Flushing | 39-07 Prince St. (39th Ave.) | Queens | 718-359-1601

The "name says it all" about the "lip-numbingly good", "real-deal" Sichuan cooking at this "Flushing treasure"; the space is "spartan" and service "lax", but to overcome the "language barrier" just "point out what you want" and "dig in."

Spiga *Italian*   22 | 17 | 20 | $47

W 80s | 200 W. 84th St. (bet. Amsterdam Ave. & B'way) | 212-362-5506 |
www.spiganyc.com

"Don't be fooled" by the "rustic" decor, because the cuisine at this "tiny" UWS Italian is "inventive" and "modern"; add "doting" service and it's no wonder most would "go back anytime."

Spigolo *Italian*   25 | 16 | 22 | $59

E 80s | 1561 Second Ave. (81st St.) | 212-744-1100

"Delectable" Italian cuisine supported by "engaging owners" Heather and Scott Fratangelo keep this "teeny" UES "delight" "packed to the rafters"; despite the "cramped" conditions, it's "worth every penny" – assuming you ever "score a reservation" (hint: "try for an outside table" in summer).

Spitzer's Corner ⚫ *American*   ∇ 17 | 17 | 15 | $29

LES | 101 Rivington St. (Ludlow St.) | 212-228-0027 |
www.spitzerscorner.com

"Hipsters and yupsters" perch at communal tables at this "laid-back" LES gastropub purveying "simple" New American vittles and a "vast selection of draft beer"; while "earsplitting" noise and a "clueless" staff remain, hopefully the new chef may improve the just-"ok" food.

Spotted Pig ⚫ *Gastropub*   22 | 18 | 16 | $46

W Village | 314 W. 11th St. (Greenwich St.) | 212-620-0393 |
www.thespottedpig.com

"Pretty people", "celebs" and many of NYC's "top" toques "clamor to get in" to this "witty" Village gastropub for April Bloomfield's "spot-on" Modern European eats; it's "all the rage", so "hurried service" and "killer waits" are a "given", unless you "go at off hours" (fortunately, the kitchen's open till 2 AM).

Square Meal ⊠M *American*   ∇ 23 | 18 | 22 | $48

E 90s | 30 E. 92nd St. (bet. 5th & Madison Aves.) | 212-860-9872 |
www.squaremealnyc.com

"Ideal" for the Carnegie Hill "gentry", this American newcomer presents Yura Mohr's "lovely", "creative" "home cooking" in a "pleasant" room reminiscent of your UES "grandma's"; "terrific" service and "fair" prices (for the area) are other pluses.

	FOOD	DECOR	SERVICE	COST

☒ Sripraphai ⊘ *Thai* | 27 | 13 | 16 | $25 |

Woodside | 64-13 39th Ave. (bet. 64th & 65th Sts.) | Queens | 718-899-9599
Once again voted NYC's "champ of Thai food", this "fantabulous" Woodsider offers "outrageously good" dishes with an "incendiary" quotient that's "not for weaklings"; a redo recently "beefed up" its "ho-hum" decor, while the garden remains "wonderful" and the low tabs "incredible", so no surprise, the staff can get "overwhelmed" and there's "often a long wait."

Stage Deli ❶ *Deli* | 19 | 9 | 14 | $29 |

W 50s | 834 Seventh Ave. (bet. 53rd & 54th Sts.) | 212-245-7850 | www.stagedeli.com
"Mile-high sandwiches" that "could choke a horse" are the hallmark of this theatrically "old-style" Midtown deli with "sassy waiters" as "part of the shtick"; as the "throngs of tourists" "crowding" in indicate, it's a "Manhattan must" for those Texans who want to learn which is the bagel and which is the lox.

Stamatis ❶ *Greek* | 22 | 12 | 18 | $31 |

Astoria | 29-09 23rd Ave. (bet. 29th & 31st Sts.) | Queens | 718-932-8596
Astoria | 31-14 Broadway (bet. 31st & 32nd Sts.) | Queens | 718-204-8964
A "simple, no-spin" approach to "homestyle" cooking dispensed in "generous portions" links these separately owned Astoria Greeks; they also share "plain-Jane" surroundings and "rock-bottom" prices that result in "waits" on weekends.

Stand ❶ *Burgers* | 20 | 14 | 16 | $23 |

G Village | 24 E. 12th St. (bet. 5th Ave. & University Pl.) | 212-488-5900
"Delicious" burgers "jazzed up" with "outrageous sides" and "milkshakes from heaven" (spiked with "spirits") are the draws at this "casual" Village eatery; its "picnic"-style tables are "filled with families and college kids" who, given the "price point", are "not concerned" about service.

Stanton Social ❶ *Eclectic* | 23 | 22 | 19 | $52 |

LES | 99 Stanton St. (bet. Ludlow & Orchard Sts.) | 212-995-0099 | www.thestantonsocial.com
"Everything's bite-size" at this "highly social" LES Eclectic, where the "young and trendy" nibble on small plates meant "for sharing" as they "mix and mingle"; it's a "sleek", "swanky" "hangout" ("if you don't mind hollering"), and "worth every precious penny."

Stella del Mare ☒ *Italian* | ▽ 23 | 19 | 22 | $53 |

Murray Hill | 346 Lexington Ave. (bet. 39th & 40th Sts.) | 212-687-4425 | www.stelladelmareny.com
"Always on-target", this "elegant" duplex Midtown Northern Italian seafood vet makes a "comfortable, old-world" venue for "business lunches"; come evening, the "entertaining" "piano bar" turns the atmosphere "cheery" – at least until the bill arrives.

Stella Maris *European* | ▽ 20 | 18 | 18 | $40 |

Seaport | 213 Front St. (bet. Beekman St. & Peck Slip) | 212-233-2417 | www.stellamarisnyc.com
Finally, the Seaport has "the bistro every neighborhood needs" in this "sleekly modern" European purveying "landlubber choices" as well as

"creative" seafood; a "refreshing" vibe, an "unbeatable outdoor setting" and "solid wines" make it a prime "after-work spot."

STK ● *Steak*

FOOD	DECOR	SERVICE	COST
21	23	18	$68

Meatpacking | 26 Little W. 12th St. (bet. 9th Ave. & Washington St.) | 646-624-2444 | www.stkhouse.com
"Extremely cool", this Meatpacking District steakhouse feeds "better-than-average" beef to its "beautiful", "twentysomething" clientele in "club-style" quarters; though "more scene than substance", it's perfect "for a wild night out", even given the service with "attitude."

Stone Park Café *American*

FOOD	DECOR	SERVICE	COST
24	19	20	$45

Park Slope | 324 Fifth Ave. (3rd St.) | Brooklyn | 718-369-0082 | www.stoneparkcafe.com
"Artful subtlety" marks the New American cuisine at this "convivial" Park Sloper, making it a "favorite" for an "elaborate meal or just a burger"; service is usually "capable" and the "attractive" digs "always crowded", but you must "watch out for long lines" at brunch.

Strip House ● *Steak*

FOOD	DECOR	SERVICE	COST
25	21	21	$72

G Village | 13 E. 12th St. (bet. 5th Ave. & University Pl.) | 212-328-0000 | www.theglaziergroup.com
"A break from the norm", this "female-friendly" Village chop shop serves "sinfully delicious" steaks in "knockout" "bordello-ish" digs with photos of "old-time strippers" adorning the ruby red walls; factor in "fantastic service" and the "big tabs" are easy to swallow.

Suba ● *Spanish*

FOOD	DECOR	SERVICE	COST
20	24	20	$54

LES | 109 Ludlow St. (bet. Delancey & Rivington Sts.) | 212-982-5714 | www.subanyc.com
"Dramatic" decor featuring "flowing water" in a "romantic grotto" room is the highlight at this "hip" LES Spaniard, however, its "upscale riffs on classic" Iberian cuisine are also draws; add "helpful" service and a "sexy bar scene" and it's "perfect for dates."

Sueños *Mexican*

FOOD	DECOR	SERVICE	COST
22	19	19	$45

Chelsea | 311 W. 17th St. (bet. 8th & 9th Aves.) | 212-243-1333 | www.suenosnyc.com
Beyond the "dark alley–esque entrance", Sue Torres' "inviting" Chelsea "favorite" is best known for its "adventurous", "modernized" Mexican fare and "wicked-good drinks"; a few find it a tad "expensive", but they are easily outvoted.

☑ Sugiyama ●☒Ⓜ *Japanese*

FOOD	DECOR	SERVICE	COST
27	19	26	$87

W 50s | 251 W. 55th St. (bet. B'way & 8th Ave.) | 212-956-0670 | www.sugiyama-nyc.com
Chef Nao Sugiyama is the "king of kaiseki" declare "true lovers of Japanese" cuisine tucking in at his "transcendent" Midtown "jewel"; "memorable" dishes "perfectly prepared and presented" come via "classy" staffers in "simple surroundings", adding up to "one of NYC's magical experiences" – with accordingly "high prices."

Superfine Ⓜ *Mediterranean*

FOOD	DECOR	SERVICE	COST
∇ 19	19	18	$30

Dumbo | 126 Front St. (bet. Jay & Pearl Sts.) | Brooklyn | 718-243-9005
Brooklynites "feeling hip" head to this "lively" Dumbo Med, though really "more for the scene" than the "decent" "bistro-type" eats; the

"hall-like" former warehouse space is just the place to "hang and play pool", or hear "fantastic" live bluegrass at Sunday brunch.

Supper ●♥ *Italian*

25 | 19 | 18 | $36

E Village | 156 E. Second St. (bet. Aves. A & B) | 212-477-7600 | www.supperrestaurant.com

"Stunningly simple" yet "superb" Italian classics ("especially the pastas") at "affordable" rates make this "cash-only" contender a "favorite" East Village "go-to"; despite "communal tables", the "cozy" setting is somehow "romantic", and the "wine bar next door" makes "brutal" waits on weekends almost fly by.

Surya *Indian*

∇ 22 | 16 | 20 | $38

W Village | 302 Bleecker St. (bet. Grove St. & 7th Ave. S.) | 212-807-7770 | www.suryany.com

The "standout" regional Indian eats at this "calm" Village spot taste even better thanks to its classy cocktails and "attentive service"; its "take-out lunch boxes are a deal" but dining in the "peaceful, secluded garden" is the real "plus" given the somewhat plain "mod" interior.

SushiAnn 🗷 *Japanese*

24 | 17 | 21 | $61

E 50s | 38 E. 51st St. (bet. Madison & Park Aves.) | 212-755-1780 | www.sushiann.com

Maybe it's "not adventurous", but this "plain", "no-nonsense" Midtown Japanese standby draws a "big business crowd" for its "super-high-quality" sushi and "tasty cooked dishes"; also offsetting the "pricey" tab are clairvoyant staffers who "know what you need before you need it."

Sushiden *Japanese*

24 | 16 | 21 | $58

E 40s | 19 E. 49th St. (bet. 5th & Madison Aves.) | 212-758-2700
W 40s | 123 W. 49th St. (bet. 6th & 7th Aves.) | 212-398-2800 🗷
www.sushiden.com

Sushi "havens of the highest order", these "quiet" Midtown Japanese twins provide the "pinnacle of raw fish" to local "salarymen"; "first-class" service from "kimono-clad waitresses" raises the tone of the "drab digs" and takes the edge off the high "price tag."

Sushi Hana ● *Japanese*

21 | 16 | 18 | $38

E 70s | 1501 Second Ave. (78th St.) | 212-327-0582
W 80s | 466 Amsterdam Ave. (bet. 82nd & 83rd Sts.) |
212-874-0369

"Fresh, well-priced sushi" with "clever" custom rolls "hits the spot" at this separately owned Japanese twosome; patrons appreciate the recent "much-needed face-lift" and "sexy sake bar" at the more "stylish" UES outpost, but value "cordial" service at both locations.

SushiSamba ● *Brazilian/Japanese*

22 | 19 | 16 | $50

Flatiron | 245 Park Ave. S. (bet. 19th & 20th Sts.) | 212-475-9377
W Village | 87 Seventh Ave. S. (Barrow St.) | 212-691-7885
www.sushisamba.com

"Cranking out" a "quirky mix" of Japanese and Brazilian, this "high-energy" duo dispenses "bold" fusion flavors for the "adventurous"; throw in "young clubhoppers" sipping "fancy cocktails" and, despite "grumpy" staffers, you've got a "crazy night out" – especially on the West Village location's "fun" rooftop deck.

	FOOD	DECOR	SERVICE	COST

☑ Sushi Seki ●⊠ *Japanese* | 27 | 13 | 22 | $73

E 60s | 1143 First Ave. (bet. 62nd & 63rd Sts.) | 212-371-0238

"Animated" chef Seki "will blow you away" with an "out-of-this-world" omakase at his UES Japanese "standout", where "attentive" service outweighs "nondescript" decor; "mortgage-the-house" prices are "commensurate" with the "excellent quality", and sushi bar service until 3 AM is another "selling point."

Sushi Sen-nin *Japanese* | 24 | 17 | 19 | $55

Murray Hill | 30 E. 33rd St. (bet. Madison Ave. & Park Ave. S.) | 212-889-2208 | www.sushisennin.com

The "creative" rolls are "big, fresh and delicious" at this "calming" Murray Hill Japanese that has fans declaring it "deserves to be known outside its neighborhood"; "gracious" service and a "lovely setting" help locals swallow prices that seem "steep" "for the area."

Sushiya *Japanese* | 19 | 13 | 18 | $38

W 50s | 28 W. 56th St. (bet. 5th & 6th Aves.) | 212-247-5760

A "solid choice" for "old-school sushi", this nothing-fancy Japanese Midtowner keeps "regulars" regular with "enjoyable" fare at "fair prices"; the "efficient" staff is "courteous" and the simple setting "serene", except when the "hectic midday" lunch crowd files in.

☑ Sushi Yasuda ⊠ *Japanese* | 28 | 21 | 23 | $79

E 40s | 204 E. 43rd St. (bet. 2nd & 3rd Aves.) | 212-972-1001 | www.sushiyasuda.com

"If God were going out for sushi", chef Naomichi Yasuda's "peaceful" Grand Central–area "temple" – once again voted the No. 1 Japanese in NYC – might "be the place" thanks to its "pristine" bites of "pure piscatorial pleasure"; mortals enjoying the "heavenly" experience "relax" in a handsome "minimalist" space attended by a "polite" staff, preparing to tithe for this experience.

Sushi Zen ⊠ *Japanese* | 25 | 19 | 21 | $56

W 40s | 108 W. 44th St. (bet. B'way & 6th Ave.) | 212-302-0707 | www.sushizen-ny.com

Acolytes of "superior" sushi can meditate on "a menu full of wonders" at this "tiny", "refined" Theater District Japanese, where presentation is "artistic", service "gracious" and the atmosphere is, well, "Zen-like"; but remember, such "delight for the senses" doesn't come cheap.

Suteishi *Japanese* | ▽ 22 | 20 | 22 | $41

Seaport | 24 Peck Slip (Front St.) | 212-766-2344 | www.suteishi.com

A "much-needed addition" to the Seaport area, this "sophisticated", yet moderately priced, Japanese "gem" serves "original" sushi and cooked fare via a "genuinely friendly" staff; it's "cute to boot", with "modern decor" and "floor-to-ceiling glass doors" overlooking the Brooklyn Bridge.

Swagat Indian Cuisine *Indian* | 20 | 11 | 19 | $28

W 70s | 411A Amsterdam Ave. (bet. 79th & 80th Sts.) | 212-362-1400 | www.swagatupperwestside.com

"Not inventive, not fancy", just "consistently good", this "terrific" UWS "nook" tenders "tasty" Indian "comfort food" with plenty of "vegetarian choices"; though service is "warm", the "tight seating" in its "tiny" space has some suggesting it's best for "delivery or takeout"; N.B. Swagat and Zagat are not related.

Sweet Melissa   *Dessert/Sandwiches*

21	17	16	$18

Cobble Hill | 276 Court St. (bet. Butler & Douglass Sts.) | Brooklyn | 718-855-3410
Park Slope | 175 Seventh Ave. (bet. 1st & 2nd Sts.) | Brooklyn | 718-502-9153
www.sweetmelissapatisserie.com

"Crammed with tons of sweet treats", these Brooklyn patisseries are also a "charming stop" for "light lunches" or "a cuppa" at "afternoon tea"; the "passive staff" could use a "sugar rush", but "lovely" gardens "are a definite plus."

Sweet-n-Tart Cafe ●⊄ *Chinese*

19	11	13	$17

Flushing | 136-11 38th Ave. (Main St.) | Queens | 718-661-3380 | www.sweetntart.com

"Fast food, Chinese-style" is the deal at this "cheap", "reliable" Flushing Cantonese "favorite" for "authentic dim sum" and "amazing desserts"; gripes about "seen-better-days" decor have been addressed by a post-Survey overhaul, which also broadened the menu (and may outdate the above ratings).

Swifty's ● *American*

18	18	18	$61

E 70s | 1007 Lexington Ave. (bet. 72nd & 73rd Sts.) | 212-535-6000 | www.swiftysny.com

"If they know you", you'll be "coddled" at this UES American "canteen" for the "Social Register" set, aka "Palm Beach North"; if not, just "settle into your banquette", nibble on the "pricey" "Wasp country club"-esque fare and watch the "wannabes" trying to "hobnob with the old guard" – "you've gotta love it."

Sylvia's *Soul Food*

17	13	17	$31

Harlem | 328 Lenox Ave. (bet. 126th & 127th Sts.) | 212-996-0660 | www.sylviassoulfood.com

"After all these years", devotees declare that the "down-South cookin'" and gospel brunch at this "Harlem institution" still "reign supreme"; some say it "ain't what it used to be", bemoaning "tacky" decor, "slow" service and "lots of tourists", but even they say "you gotta go once."

Symposium *Greek*

19	14	21	$26

W 100s | 544 W. 113th St. (bet. Amsterdam Ave. & B'way) | 212-865-1011
Possibly the "best bang for your buck in Morningside Heights", this "friendly" Greek "taverna"-cum-"Columbia hangout" is an "oldie but goodie" where the "hearty" dishes "brim with flavor" and the "vintage" '70s decor features "wonderful funky murals"; just be ready to shout "*opa* – flaming cheese!"

Szechuan Gourmet *Chinese*

-	-	-	∎

Garment District | 21 W. 39th St. (bet. 5th & 6th Aves.) | 212-921-0233
Flushing | 135-15 37th Ave. (bet. Main & Prince Sts.) | Queens | 718-888-9388 ●

Aficionados of authentically bold Sichuan cooking look to this unpretentious twosome for sizzlingly spicy satisfaction at bargain-basement prices; the Flushing original boasts a wider menu of real-deal dishes, while its red lantern–enhanced Garment District offshoot allows Manhattanites a crack at the action.

	FOOD	DECOR	SERVICE	COST

🅉 Tabla *American* | 25 | 25 | 24 | $83

Gramercy | 11 Madison Ave. (25th St.) | 212-889-0667 | www.tablany.com
The "wow factor" remains sky-high at this Madison Square Park "stand-out", where chef Floyd Cardoz works "wonders with Indian spices" to create "sublime" New American cuisine; the "beautifully presented" food, "gorgeous" surroundings and "gracious" service naturally come with "prices to match" (prix fixe–only dinners start at $64); N.B. changes are afoot here that may recast the menu and the bi-level setup.

Table d'Hôte *French* | 18 | 15 | 18 | $47

E 90s | 44 E. 92nd St. (bet. Madison & Park Aves.) | 212-348-8125
Carnegie Hill locals and "92nd Street Y devotees" laud this "reliable" French "standby" for its "pleasant" bistro fare served by "friendly" staffers; its "intimate" "tearoom" setting may be "minuscule", but the prix fixe "bargains" are big.

🅉 Taboon *Mediterranean/Mideastern* | 25 | 20 | 21 | $50

W 50s | 773 10th Ave. (52nd St.) | 212-713-0271
"Hot-from-the-taboon" breads, "sinfully creamy" hummus and other "heavenly" Med–Middle Eastern fare at "midrange prices" are why this "out-of-the-way" Midtowner is often "packed" despite its "barren" 10th Avenue locale; "stylish" decor and "welcoming" service are other reasons it's "worth the cab ride" west.

Taci's Beyti *Mediterranean/Turkish* | ▽ 23 | 10 | 18 | $27

Midwood | 1955 Coney Island Ave. (bet. Ave. P & Kings Hwy.) | Brooklyn | 718-627-5750
"Everything is fresh, fresh, fresh" at this "festive", "friendly" Midwood Turk, beloved for its Med staples including "flavorful grilled meats" and "perfect salads"; true, the "harsh lighting does no favors", but "low" prices and a BYO policy make it "truly cheap."

Tailor ●Ⓜ *Dessert* | ▽ 23 | 23 | 20 | $66

SoHo | 525 Broome St. (bet. Sullivan & Thompson Sts.) | 212-334-5182 | www.tailornyc.com
"Avant-garde" desserts are the claim to fame of this SoHo New American–Eclectic where wd-50 disciple Sam Mason conjures "one-of-a-kind" dishes both "savory and sweet"; its "far-out" flavors "aren't for everybody", ditto the "pricey" tabs, but the "smart" vintage-apothecary look and "amazing cocktails" are universal crowd-pleasers.

Takahachi *Japanese* | 23 | 14 | 21 | $41

E Village | 85 Ave. A (bet. 5th & 6th Sts.) | 212-505-6524 ●
TriBeCa | 145 Duane St. (bet. Church St. & W. B'way) | 212-571-1830
www.takahachi.net
This "low-key" TriBeCa-East Village twosome plies the "winning" combination of "fresh" classic sushi rolls and "ever-changing specials"; the "minimalist" settings may "need an upgrade", but "efficient" service and "reasonable prices" overcome all.

Taksim *Turkish* | 20 | 10 | 18 | $26

E 50s | 1030 Second Ave. (bet. 54th & 55th Sts.) | 212-421-3004 | www.taksim.us
When you're "talking Turkey", head for this "cheap" Midtown "favorite" for "no-nonsense" meze, whose "large portions" and "just-right"

prices make for "unbelievable value"'; what it "lacks in atmosphere", it makes up for in "flavor" and "friendliness."

NEW Talay ◐ *Pan-Latin/Thai*   - | - | - | M

Harlem | 701 W. 135th St. (12th Ave.) | 212-491-8300 | www.talayrestaurant.com

Uptown hipsters mingle over cocktails and Thai-Latino small plates at this arrival to a happening stretch of Harlem's 12th Avenue that some have dubbed 'ViVa' (that's short for 'Viaduct Valley'); from the dragon statues at its entrance to the sleek bar, upstairs lounge and cavernous, dimly lit dining room, it's all about seeing and being seen – if not being heard.

Z Tamarind ◐ *Indian*   25 | 22 | 22 | $54

Flatiron | 41-43 E. 22nd St. (bet. B'way & Park Ave. S.) | 212-674-7400 | www.tamarinde22.com

Recently renovated, this Flatiron Indian boasts a "calming", "modern" atmosphere and "knowledgeable" service, but it's the "fit-for-a-maharaja" fare that "takes center stage"; yes, "it'll cost you", but then there's always the "wonderful" $24 lunch prix fixe – or the "bargain" next-door tearoom.

Tang Pavilion *Chinese*   22 | 17 | 21 | $39

W 50s | 65 W. 55th St. (bet. 5th & 6th Aves.) | 212-956-6888

This "comfortable" Midtown Chinese stalwart's menu of Shanghai delights "changes remarkably little" over time – and that's a "good thing"; its "efficient" staff, "reasonable" prices and location "convenient" to Radio City and City Center make it a no-brainer.

Z Tanoreen Ⓜ *Mediterranean/Mideastern*   26 | 11 | 21 | $28

Bay Ridge | 7704 Third Ave. (bet. 77th & 78th Sts.) | Brooklyn | 718-748-5600 | www.tanoreen.com

"Gifted cook" Rawia Bishara's "sensational", "super-cheap" Med-Middle Eastern fare bursting with "vibrant flavors and textures" makes this eatery the "pride of Bay Ridge"; though it boasts supremely "warm" service, most agree it "needs more space" – happily a move to "larger" nearby digs is in the works.

Z Tao ◐ *Pan-Asian*   22 | 26 | 19 | $60

E 50s | 42 E. 58th St. (bet. Madison & Park Aves.) | 212-888-2288 | www.taorestaurant.com

With its "loud" "dance music", "jaw-dropping" Zen-themed decor (complete with "giant Buddha") and "lively" "young" clientele, this Midtown Pan-Asian "feels more like a club" than a restaurant; even though the "pricey" food is "surprisingly good", it's the "electric energy" that the "beautiful" crowd "comes for."

Tarallucci e Vino *Italian*   21 | 17 | 18 | $36

E Village | 163 First Ave. (10th St.) | 212-388-1190 ◐
Flatiron | 15 E. 18th St. (bet. B'way & 5th Ave.) | 212-228-5400
www.tarallucievino.net

Something of an "undiscovered gem" in the Flatiron, this "relaxed", "European-style" eatery offers "delicious", "reasonable" Italian small plates and wines in "rustic"-yet-"cosmopolitan" quarters complete with a front take-out area; N.B. the smaller East Village original is counter service–only.

	FOOD	DECOR	SERVICE	COST

Tartine ⊅ *French*
22 | 13 | 16 | $30

W Village | 253 W. 11th St. (4th St.) | 212-229-2611

"Quality" bistro classics at "bargain prices" plus a "BYO policy" with "no corkage fee" add up to "long lines" at this "tiny", "adorably simple" West Village French; "come early" or "bring a bottle and a book."

Taste *American*
22 | 14 | 19 | $52

E 80s | 1413 Third Ave. (80th St.) | 212-717-9798 | www.elizabar.com

"Great, fresh ingredients lead to success every time" for Eli Zabar and his UES eatery that's cafeteria-style by day, "sophisticated place for grown-ups" come evening; its "ever-changing" New American fare and "interesting" wines are "top-quality", and surprisingly good "value" for one of Eli's places.

☑ Taverna Kyclades *Greek/Seafood*
25 | 11 | 18 | $34

Astoria | 33-07 Ditmars Blvd. (bet. 33rd & 35th Sts.) | Queens | 718-545-8666 | www.tavernakyclades.com

"Weekend lines" "longer than at Disney" hint at the "wonderful", "just-off-the-hook-fresh" seafood offered at this Astoria Greek; "large portions", "modest" prices and "cheerful" service are other reasons "people keep coming back" despite the "hokey" decor and "deadly waits."

Tavern on the Green *American*
14 | 24 | 17 | $65

W 60s | Central Park W. (bet. 66th & 67th Sts.) | 212-873-3200 | www.tavernonthegreen.com

"Glittery" as ever, this "legendary" Central Park "feast" for the eyes "amazes every time" with its "fantasyland" decor complete with "twinkling white lights" in a "beautiful garden" and "lovely party rooms"; "it's not about" the American eats ("bland" and "pricey") or the service ("mediocre") – whether it strikes you as "magical" or just plain "gaudy", it's an experience that "everyone should have once."

◼NEW T-Bar Steak & Lounge *Steak*
21 | 19 | 20 | $60

E 70s | 1278 Third Ave. (bet. 73rd & 74th Sts.) | 212-772-0404 | www.tbarnyc.com

"Spruced up and rarin' to go", the UES's former Lenox Room has been "reborn" as this "stylish" steakhouse whose "lively" crowd is "not the typical males-bonding-over-beef-and-bourbon" sort; "hands-on" owner Tony Fortuna ensures "attentive" service and "satisfying" chops in portions that are "ample" – ditto the prices.

Tea & Sympathy *British*
21 | 17 | 18 | $25

W Village | 108 Greenwich Ave. (bet. 12th & 13th Sts.) | 212-807-8329 | www.teaandsympathynewyork.com

"Anglophiles and expats" pack this "twee" West Village teahouse for frugal fixes of "English soul food" or absolutely "brill" afternoon tea service; the British staff is "sweet" but "no-nonsense", and "teany" quarters mean you must "go off-peak or prepare to wait" – "outside, dearie!"

☑ Telepan *American*
25 | 20 | 24 | $71

W 60s | 72 W. 69th St. (bet. Columbus Ave. & CPW) | 212-580-4300 | www.telepan-ny.com

At this "understated" Lincoln Center–area "wonder", chef Bill Telepan's "commitment" to "seasonal market ingredients" results in New

American dishes that tread a "wonderful middle ground between haute and homey"; some question the "odd" "cool-green" decor (think "nouveau barnyard") and "up-there" tabs, but the "caring" staff makes "every meal here a delight."

Telly's Taverna ● *Greek/Seafood*

FOOD	DECOR	SERVICE	COST
21	13	18	$37

Astoria | 28-13 23rd Ave. (bet. 28th & 29th Sts.) | Queens | 718-728-9056 | www.tellystaverna.com

Schools of fish fans ford the East River to net the "fresh" grilled *pesce* and "authentic" meze at this "friendly" "midpriced" Astoria Greek; its "spacious" digs "can get noisy", so in warm weather "opt for the back garden."

Tempo *Mediterranean*

FOOD	DECOR	SERVICE	COST
24	22	23	$49

Park Slope | 256 Fifth Ave. (bet. Carroll St. & Garfield Pl.) | Brooklyn | 718-636-2020 | www.tempobrooklyn.com

What with the "divine" Med cuisine, "extraordinary" wines, "thoughtful" service and "date-place" ambiance, it's a "mystery" that this "classy" prix fixe–only Park Sloper "isn't packed every night" – especially since its multicourse options are offered at "Brooklyn prices"; P.S. it's possible to order à la carte in the "beautiful" bar area.

Tenzan ● *Japanese*

FOOD	DECOR	SERVICE	COST
23	14	19	$33

NEW **E 50s** | 988 Second Ave. (bet. 52nd & 53rd Sts.) | 212-980-5900
E 80s | 1714 Second Ave. (89th St.) | 212-369-3600
W 70s | 285 Columbus Ave. (73rd St.) | 212-580-7300
Bensonhurst | 7116 18th Ave. (71st St.) | Brooklyn | 718-621-3238
www.tenzanrestaurants.com

For "delicious", "godzilla-size" rolls, you "can't beat the price" at this "crowded" sushi quartet; there's "no ambiance" to speak of, so you may want to opt for "quick" delivery or takeout if you "like your digs better than theirs."

Teodora *Italian*

FOOD	DECOR	SERVICE	COST
20	15	17	$49

E 50s | 141 E. 57th St. (bet. Lexington & 3rd Aves.) | 212-826-7101

"Hidden" in plain sight, this oasis of "calm" amid "Midtown's hubbub" proffers "dependable" midpriced Northern Italian fare in "family-style portions"; service can be "spotty" and the space is "starting to look run-down", but at least "you can hear yourself talk."

Teresa's *Diner*

FOOD	DECOR	SERVICE	COST
19	11	14	$22

Brooklyn Heights | 80 Montague St. (Hicks St.) | Brooklyn | 718-797-3996

"Big portions" of traditional diner fare and "hearty" Polish "comfort" dishes, perfect for a "casual brunch", have the locals returning often to this Brooklyn Heights stalwart; though a meal "won't set you back financially", "slow", "gruff" service and "tired" digs may set you back emotionally.

☑ Terrace in the Sky Ⓜ *French/Mediterranean*

FOOD	DECOR	SERVICE	COST
23	27	23	$67

W 100s | 400 W. 119th St. (bet. Amsterdam Ave. & Morningside Dr.) | 212-666-9490 | www.terraceinthesky.com

"Refined" French-Mediterranean fare and waiters in "tuxes" create an "elegant", "old-fashioned" ambiance at this Morningside Heights "special-occasion" place; however, it's the "breathtaking" cityscape views from its penthouse dining room that make this such a great place for parties and proposing.

	FOOD	DECOR	SERVICE	COST

NEW Tet *Vietnamese* — | - | - | - | I |

E Village | 83 Ave. A (bet. 5th & 6th Sts.) | 212-253-0800
From the owner of Omai and Nam comes this new East Villager, many of whose subtly updated classic Vietnamese dishes are offered in small portions intended for sharing (though there are plenty of entrees too); the simple, modern digs are comfortable enough, but here the excitement is on the plate.

Tevere *Italian* ▽ 23 | 17 | 20 | $59

E 80s | 155 E. 84th St. (bet. Lexington & 3rd Aves.) | 212-744-0210 | www.teverenyc.com
"Wish there were more like this" sigh the observant of this kosher UES Italian, which has a "long history" as a supplier of "delicious" pastas and other classics; the "intimate" setting and solid service are good for "romantic" occasions, but there's no romance about the tab.

Thai Pavilion *Thai* ▽ 21 | 12 | 20 | $23

Astoria | 37-10 30th Ave. (37th St.) | Queens | 718-777-5546 | www.thaipavilionny.com
"Not your usual" neighborhood Thai, this Astoria veteran's "delicious", "spicy" dishes are delivered "with care and pride" at "really local prices"; its "not-very-large" digs boast "no bells and whistles", so takeout or delivery are always worth considering.

Thalassa *Greek/Seafood* 24 | 24 | 21 | $65

TriBeCa | 179 Franklin St. (bet. Greenwich & Hudson Sts.) | 212-941-7661 | www.thalassanyc.com
The "all-white" space at this "refined" TriBeCa Greek seafooder is so "calming" that diners can "almost feel the Mediterranean breeze" as they tuck into "superb", "ultrafresh" fish; add a "gracious" crew and the only snare is the "expensive" "by-the-pound" pricing.

Thalia ● *American* 20 | 20 | 19 | $49

W 50s | 828 Eighth Ave. (50th St.) | 212-399-4444 | www.restaurantthalia.com
Its "convenient" Theater District location and "creative" menu that's considered a cut "above the usual Broadway fare" make this "dependable" New American a regular pre- or post-curtain "haunt"; "classy" decor contributes to the spirited vibe, though the "noise level" can be a "downer."

Thomas Beisl ● *Austrian* 18 | 16 | 17 | $39

Fort Greene | 25 Lafayette Ave. (Ashland Pl.) | Brooklyn | 718-222-5800
"Ample portions" of "hearty" Viennese classics, a "strong" "Austrian wine and beer" list and "convenience to BAM" keep this "relaxed" Fort Greene mainstay "busy"; a "disappointed" contingent cites "hit-or-miss" service and food, but when they get it right, it's a "sweet place."

Thor ● *American* 17 | 21 | 16 | $52

LES | The Hotel on Rivington | 107 Rivington St. (bet. Essex & Ludlow Sts.) | 212-796-8040 | www.hotelonrivington.com
A "late-night crowd" "noshes" on "gourmet mini-burgers" and such amid a "trendy" scene at this "sleek" LES New American; the kitchen has seen a succession of chefs but thus far "lightning hasn't struck" – overall the "pricey" experience is deemed "nothing to rave about."

	FOOD	DECOR	SERVICE	COST

Z Tía Pol *Spanish* | 24 | 15 | 19 | $40

Chelsea | 205 10th Ave. (bet. 22nd & 23rd Sts.) | 212-675-8805 |
www.tiapol.com

A "tiny place that's big on food", this "lively" Chelsea *tapería* offers an
"excellent array of Spanish nibbles" paired with "top-notch" wines;
"long waits" are the norm, but "if you can squeeze in", try "everything" –
though bear in mind that those "little snacks" "can add up."

Tides ⊠♥ *Seafood* | ∇ 24 | 22 | 24 | $41

LES | 102 Norfolk St. (bet. Delancey & Rivington Sts.) | 212-254-8855 |
www.tidesseafood.com

"Let the waters carry you" to this "lovely" LES "hideaway", whose
"must-try" lobster roll and other "simple, fresh" seafood are served
under a striking "sea grass"–like ceiling; an "attentive" staff and overall "refined" feel are other reasons it "would cost more Uptown."

Tierras Colombianas ♥ *Colombian* | 20 | 11 | 17 | $25

Astoria | 33-01 Broadway (33rd St.) | Queens | 718-956-3012
Jackson Heights | 82-18 Roosevelt Ave. (82nd St.) | Queens | 718-426-8868

"When you want something stick-to-your-ribs", these "friendly" Queens
"bargains" fill the bill with "flavorful", "down-to-earth" Colombian
dishes big enough "to feed a small horse"; the "dinerlike" digs are
"nothing fancy", but you'll "eat like a king" – or three.

Tio Pepe ❶ *Mexican/Spanish* | 18 | 15 | 18 | $32

G Village | 168 W. Fourth St. (bet. Cornelia & Jones Sts.) | 212-242-9338 |
www.tiopepenyc.com

"Decently priced" Spanish platters and Mexican "standards" share the
bill at this "reliable" Greenwich Village "staple"; "noise" issues and
"cheesy" decor aside, its "terrific" drinks and "lovely garden" keep this
"party scene" "jumping."

Tiramisu ❶ *Italian* | 19 | 14 | 17 | $38

E 80s | 1410 Third Ave. (80th St.) | 212-988-9780

If a "family vibe" is "what you're looking for", hit this "reasonably
priced" UES Italian, where, between the "decent" pastas and brick-oven
pizzas, "there's something for everyone"; it "can get loud at peak hours"
and service is variable, but its "neighborhood crowd" keeps coming.

Z Tocqueville ⊠ *American/French* | 25 | 24 | 24 | $75

Union Sq | 1 E. 15th St. (bet. 5th Ave. & Union Sq. W.) | 212-647-1515 |
www.tocquevillerestaurant.com

"Tocque about fine dining" – this "tranquil", "underappreciated"
Union Square "gem" is "all-around superb", from the "interesting flair"
of chef Marco Moreira's "dazzling" French–New American cooking to
the "elegant" "vaulted ceilings" and "wonderful" staff; "a splurge it is",
but for such "off-the-charts" experiences, it's 100% worth it.

Todai *Japanese/Seafood* | 17 | 12 | 14 | $31

Murray Hill | 6 E. 32nd St. (bet. 5th & Madison Aves.) | 212-725-1333 |
www.todainyc.com

"Smorgasbord" is the word for this "casual", "friendly" Japanese
Murray Hiller's "block-long" buffet of sushi and cooked offerings; sure,
the flavors are mostly "bland", but the sheer "variety" and "bargain"
"all-you-can-eat" setup ensure that "hearty appetites get their fill."

	FOOD	DECOR	SERVICE	COST

Tokyo Pop *Japanese*

| 18 | 15 | 14 | $34 |

W 100s | 2728 Broadway (bet. 104th & 105th Sts.) | 212-932-1000 | www.tokyopoping.com

The "Franco-Japanese fusion" at this "fun" sushi spot near Columbia may sound strange, but "the concept works", producing "better-than-expected" "combos" offered up in "funky" digs; the "Euro dude" staffers can be "amateurish", but they "make up for it in sweetness."

Toloache *Mexican*

| 23 | 18 | 19 | $46 |

W 50s | 251 W. 50th St. (bet. B'way & 8th Ave.) | 212-581-1818 | www.toloachenyc.com

Julian Medina's "fantastic" Hell's Kitchen yearling is turning "creative spins" on Nuevo Mexicana, creating "bold" flavors that "work well together" and are backed by a "vast" tequila selection; the service "needs work" and the "cute", "small" quarters get "noisy", but still – what a "Midtown find."

Tommaso *Italian*

| ▽ 24 | 17 | 22 | $48 |

Dyker Heights | 1464 86th St. (bet. 14th & 15th Aves.) | Brooklyn | 718-236-9883 | www.tommasoinbrooklyn.com

"Carefully prepared" dishes that "taste like grandma's" maintain this Dyker Heights Italian's rep as a "beloved" "old reliable"; however, fans note "there's more to this place than red sauce" – to name two, there's the "fabulous", "reasonable" wine list and owner Thomas Verdillo's "glorious" "opera-singing."

Tomoe Sushi *Japanese*

| 25 | 7 | 16 | $44 |

G Village | 172 Thompson St. (bet. Bleecker & Houston Sts.) | 212-777-9346

"No reservations" and a "deserved reputation" as "one of the best" (for less) mean there are "more people on line than sitting inside" at this "ridiculously small" Greenwich Village Japanese; still, schools of "sushi aristocats" keep stalking the "fantastically fresh" fish despite "zero atmosphere."

Tomo Sushi & Sake Bar ● *Japanese*

| 18 | 14 | 16 | $26 |

W 100s | 2850 Broadway (bet. 110th & 111th Sts.) | 212-665-2916

This "dependable" Morningside Japanese serves up "good fish" at prices "designed for" area students; no one praises the "slow" service or "cramped" setting, but its "lack of competition" keeps the college crowd from straying.

Tom's ⊠⇄ *Diner*

| 20 | 17 | 26 | $16 |

Prospect Heights | 782 Washington Ave. (Sterling Pl.) | Brooklyn | 718-636-9738

"Service is a matter of pride" at this "classic" 1930s Prospect Heights coffee shop famed for its "friendly" vibe and "killer brunches"; its "old-school" offerings like egg creams and lime rickeys match the "throwback" decor – as do the pleasingly low tabs.

Tony's Di Napoli *Italian*

| 19 | 14 | 18 | $37 |

E 80s | 1606 Second Ave. (83rd St.) | 212-861-8686
W 40s | 147 W. 43rd St. (bet. B'way & 6th Ave.) | 212-221-0100 ● www.tonysnyc.com

These bumptious "big-platter" Italians conjure lively "Sunday *famiglia* dinners" with their "tasty" portions big enough to "feed the neighborhood", "enthusiastic" waiters and "impossibly loud" noise levels; besides everything else, they're "mainstays for celebrations", and the Times Square branch is "super-speedy."

Topaz Thai *Thai*
20 | 10 | 15 | $29

W 50s | 127 W. 56th St. (bet. 6th & 7th Aves.) | 212-957-8020
"Convenient" for a "quick bite" "before Carnegie Hall", this "mom-and-pop" Thai is "reliable" for "surprisingly good", "affordable" fare in an otherwise "pricey area"; however, "slam-bam" service and "cramped", "no-decor" digs have regulars warning "don't even think of lingering."

Tosca Café ● *Italian*
20 | 22 | 18 | $31

Bronx | 4038 E. Tremont Ave. (bet. Miles & Sampson Aves.) | 718-239-3300 | www.toscanyc.com
"Cool eatery by day", "hip hangout by night", this "lively" Throgs Neck Italian boasts a "chic", "South Beach lounge" as well as "classy" drinks that fuel a "noisy" scene; the "full-bodied" fare ranges from pasta to sushi, while the mostly "local" crowd tends toward the "young" and "trendy."

Totonno's Pizzeria Napolitano *Pizza*
21 | 9 | 14 | $23

E 80s | 1544 Second Ave. (bet. 80th & 81st Sts.) | 212-327-2800
Gramercy | 462 Second Ave. (26th St.) | 212-213-8800
Coney Island | 1524 Neptune Ave. (bet. W. 15th & 16th Sts.) | Brooklyn | 718-372-8606 Ⓜ⇄
www.totonnos.com
"Exceptional", "crispy-crusted" "brick-oven" pies are the thing at these "nothing-fancy" pizza parlors; most agree the "best" one is the circa-1924 Coney Island "original", complete with "old articles and photos on the walls" and "waitresses who call you 'hon'", but all three pack serious flavor and plenty of "bang for the buck."

☑ Tournesol *French*
25 | 15 | 20 | $40

LIC | 50-12 Vernon Blvd. (bet. 50th & 51st Aves.) | Queens | 718-472-4355
Since being "discovered", this "utterly charming" LIC French bistro continues to enrapture diners with its "stellar" food and prices; the service is "so sweet" you almost forgive the "tablesthisclose" and perpetual "crowds"; P.S. "nab an outdoor table" if you can.

Town *American*
24 | 25 | 23 | $78

W 50s | Chambers Hotel | 15 W. 56th St. (bet. 5th & 6th Aves.) | 212-582-4445 | www.townnyc.com
It's easy to "feel beautiful" at Geoffrey Zakarian's "refined" Midtown New American, where "chic" patrons dine on "top-notch" cuisine delivered with "seamless" skill; the "elegant, modern" quarters are "quiet" enough for "business" – and an "expense account" is helpful since you'll want to be able to write off the cost.

Trata Estiatorio *Greek/Seafood*
21 | 17 | 18 | $56

E 70s | 1331 Second Ave. (bet. 70th & 71st Sts.) | 212-535-3800 | www.trata.com
The "freshness of the fish" is the thing at this "lively" UES Greek seafooder known for its "expertly prepared" catch, served in recently "redecorated" digs; those who don't want to get hooked by "high" by-the-pound tabs can net the $22 prix fixe lunch "buy."

	FOOD	DECOR	SERVICE	COST

Trattoria Alba ● *Italian* | 22 | 18 | 21 | $42
Murray Hill | 233 E. 34th St. (bet. 2nd & 3rd Aves.) | 212-689-3200 | www.trattoriaalba.com

"Modest" in a "pleasant" way, this "traditional" Murray Hill Italian has "been around forever" and continues to please with "solid", "moderately priced" fare and a "quiet", "take-your-time" atmosphere; no wonder its "older" "neighborhood" clientele keeps coming.

Trattoria Dell'Arte ● *Italian* | 22 | 19 | 20 | $55
W 50s | 900 Seventh Ave. (bet. 56th & 57th Sts.) | 212-245-9800 | www.trattoriadellarte.com

After 20-plus years, this "bustling" Carnegie Hall–area Northern Italian "still packs 'em in" with "exceptional antipasti and pizza", "super-fast" service and "artful" "body-parts" decor (care to "eat under a giant breast"?); however, a few critics claim the "tired" digs need a nip and tuck.

Z Trattoria L'incontro Ⓜ *Italian* | 27 | 19 | 24 | $50
Astoria | 21-76 31st St. (Ditmars Blvd.) | Queens | 718-721-3532 | www.trattorialincontro.com

"Rivals Manhattan's best" declare devotees of this "lively" (as in "noisy" and "packed") Astoria Italian renowned for its "mile-long" list of specials recited by "waiters with panache"; "schmoozy" chef Rocco Sacramone is ever-"present", making sure the room is filled with "happy diners"; P.S. "long waits" pass quickly in the "winner" of a next-door wine bar.

Trattoria Pesce & Pasta *Italian/Seafood* | 18 | 14 | 17 | $34
E 50s | 1079 First Ave. (59th St.) | 212-888-7884 ●
E 80s | 1562 Third Ave. (bet. 87th & 88th Sts.) | 212-987-4696 ●
G Village | 262 Bleecker St. (bet. 6th Ave. & 7th Ave. S.) | 212-645-2993 ●
W 90s | 625 Columbus Ave. (bet. 90th & 91st Sts.) | 212-579-7970
www.pescepasta.com

"Reasonably priced", "garlicky" Italian fare "without the b.s." keeps customers coming to these "satisfying" "standbys" specializing in seafood and pasta ("as the name suggests"); "average" service and simple, "not-much-to-look-at" digs make it that much easier to "get a table."

Trattoria Romana *Italian* | 25 | 16 | 23 | $42
Staten Island | 1476 Hylan Blvd. (Benton Ave.) | 718-980-3113 | www.trattoriaromana.com

"*Trattoria perfetto*" sigh surveyors of this Staten Islander and its "zesty", "rustic" Italian fare dished up in "ample" quantities and delivered by an "excellent" staff; it can be a "tight squeeze during peak hours", but you'll be so busy getting "stuffed" you won't notice you're "bunking elbows" with your neighbor.

Trattoria Trecolori *Italian* | 21 | 18 | 22 | $41
W 40s | 254 W. 47th St. (bet. B'way & 8th Ave.) | 212-997-4540 | www.trattoriatrecolori.com

Since a move a couple of blocks north "upgraded" its digs, this long-time "family-owned" Theater District Italian is eliciting "bravos" for its "consistently fresh" fare at "fair" rates; what's more, the "friendly" staff is "fast" enough to beat your curtain time.

	FOOD	DECOR	SERVICE	COST

NEW **Tre** *Italian* ▽ 22 | 14 | 18 | $48

LES | 173 Ludlow St. (bet. Houston & Stanton Sts.) | 212-353-3353 |
www.trenewyork.com

The early word on this new LES Italian (from the owners of the
Meatpacking District's Nero) is that it's a "romantic" "little hole-in-
the-wall" serving "delicious" fare; still, reports are that the amiable
staff sometimes "doesn't have its act together."

tre dici 🅂 *Italian* 22 | 18 | 20 | $46

Chelsea | 128 W. 26th St. (bet. 6th & 7th Aves.) | 212-243-8183
NEW **tre dici steak** 🅂 *Steak*

Chelsea | 128 W. 26th St., 2nd fl. (bet. 6th & 7th Aves.) | 212-243-2085
www.tredicinyc.com

Boasting "all the elements of a first-class hideout", this "friendly"
"find" in "nowhereland" Chelsea offers "fresh", "creative" takes on
Italian classics to all who stumble upon it; its new upstairs steakhouse
sibling, sporting a bordello-ish look, is sure to attract more attention.

Tree ● *French* ▽ 21 | 18 | 18 | $41

E Village | 190 First Ave. (bet. 11th & 12th Sts.) | 212-358-7171 |
www.treenyc.com

If you "bark up this tree" in the East Village, you'll find "delicious",
"homey" French bistro eats offered in "relaxed" environs; "moderate"
prices balance out "slightly-bigger-than-a-breadbox" dimensions that
make the garden such a "must-hit" in summer.

Trestle on Tenth *American* 20 | 18 | 20 | $49

Chelsea | 242 10th Ave. (24th St.) | 212-645-5659 | www.trestleontenth.com
"Getting better and better", this "tranquil" "neighborhood" Chelsea
New American delivers "all-around pleasant" experiences featuring
"inventive" cuisine with "Swiss" accents and "winning" service; on a
"spring night" its "peaceful" back garden is downright "magical."

Triangolo ● *Italian* 21 | 15 | 19 | $41

E 80s | 345 E. 83rd St. (bet. 1st & 2nd Aves.) | 212-472-4488 |
www.triangolorestaurant.com

You "could walk right past" this "tiny" UES Italian "if you didn't know
it was there", but locals depend on it as a neighborhood "institution"
turning out "fresh", "delicious" standards (plus "interesting specials")
at "fair prices"; "efficient" service ices the cake.

Tribeca Grill *American* 22 | 20 | 21 | $60

TriBeCa | 375 Greenwich St. (Franklin St.) | 212-941-3900 |
www.tribecagrill.com

Back in 1990, Drew Nieporent and Robert De Niro put TriBeCa "on the
map" tablewise with this "casual", "high-quality" New American;
years later, it "still shines" for "excellent people-watching" that makes
the "swoon-worthy" tabs easier to stomach.

Trinity Place *Eclectic* ▽ 18 | 22 | 17 | $43

Financial District | 115 Broadway (enter on Cedar St., bet. B'way &
Trinity Pl.) | 212-964-0939 | www.trinityplacenyc.com

Housed in an old bank vault, this Financial District Eclectic supplies a
"surprisingly well-crafted" menu to "Wall Street types", who by day
favor it for "business lunches"; come evening, once you get by the

"loud music and drunken suits" at the front bar, there's pleasant "quiet dining" in back.

Triomphe *French*

FOOD	DECOR	SERVICE	COST
24	22	22	$65

W 40s | Iroquois Hotel | 49 W. 44th St. (bet. 5th & 6th Aves.) | 212-453-4233 | www.triompheny.com

"Simply de-lovely", this "pricey" "throwback to old elegance" is a "real surprise" in Midtown, from its "wonderful" French cuisine to its "intimate" "jewel of a room" and "service to match"; for "pre-theater dining", devotees declare it an "absolute triumph."

Tsampa ● *Tibetan*

FOOD	DECOR	SERVICE	COST
▽ 20	19	19	$26

E Village | 212 E. Ninth St. (bet. 2nd & 3rd Aves.) | 212-614-3226

Cuisine "from the high Himalayas" is the province of this East Village Tibetan that pleases "vegetarians" with its "simple, delicious" dishes at the "right price"; its "dark" digs are deemed "pleasant", while service is either "slow" or "soothing", depending on your state of mind.

☒ Tse Yang *Chinese*

FOOD	DECOR	SERVICE	COST
24	23	23	$64

E 50s | 34 E. 51st St. (bet. Madison & Park Aves.) | 212-688-5447 | www.tseyangnyc.com

The crispy "skin on the Peking duck alone" inspires repeat visits to this "elegant" East Midtown Chinese, where a "well-heeled" business crowd enjoys "gourmet" fare delivered by a "white-glove" staff; the "beautiful" setting's "mesmerizing fish tanks" help distract from the "expense account–type" tab.

Turkish Cuisine ● *Turkish*

FOOD	DECOR	SERVICE	COST
19	13	18	$32

W 40s | 631 Ninth Ave. (bet. 44th & 45th Sts.) | 212-397-9650 | www.turkishcuisinenyc.com

Its "multitude" of "tasty", budget-oriented dishes make this "friendly", if "drab", Hell's Kitchen Turk a "reliable" choice pre- or post-curtain; for more elbow room and less "rushed" service, "go when everyone else is at the theater."

☒ Turkish Kitchen *Turkish*

FOOD	DECOR	SERVICE	COST
22	17	19	$40

Gramercy | 386 Third Ave. (bet. 27th & 28th Sts.) | 212-679-6633 | www.turkishkitchen.com

"Real eaters" gorge on "succulent kebabs" and other "authentic", affordable Turkish items at this Gramercy Park "classic" locally known for its beneficent brunch buffet; its "funky", "red-everywhere" decor and "rainbow of unique martinis" make it all the more "memorable."

Turks & Frogs *Turkish*

FOOD	DECOR	SERVICE	COST
20	19	19	$40

TriBeCa | 458 Greenwich St. (bet. Desbrosses & Watts Sts.) | 212-966-4774 | www.turksandfrogs.com

Appointed with antiques and enhanced with "moody lighting", this "romantic" TriBeCa Turk is a "great date spot" that's equally enjoyable for sharing "delicious" meze "with friends over wine"; "polite" service and low prices are two reasons this "little gem" is worth checking out.

Turkuaz ● *Turkish*

FOOD	DECOR	SERVICE	COST
18	19	17	$35

W 100s | 2637 Broadway (100th St.) | 212-665-9541 | www.turkuazrestaurant.com

A virtual "magic carpet ride", this UWS Turk's "dark" "tent" ambiance comes complete with "pillows, poufs" and even "mysterious belly dancers" on weekends; if you can focus on them, the midpriced meze and other classics are "decent" enough, and the servers are fine as long as they don't block your view.

Turquoise *Seafood*

FOOD	DECOR	SERVICE	COST
22	18	20	$54

E 80s | 240 E. 81st St. (bet. 2nd & 3rd Aves.) | 212-988-8222 | www.turquoiseseafood.com

The "simply prepared" fish "couldn't be fresher if you caught it yourself" at this UES seafooder, and the Mediterranean salads also appeal; "prices are on the high side", but the "entertaining", "hard-working" owner comes at "no extra charge."

Tuscany Grill *Italian*

FOOD	DECOR	SERVICE	COST
24	18	21	$47

Bay Ridge | 8620 Third Ave. (bet. 86th & 87th Sts.) | Brooklyn | 718-921-5633

A "warm" welcome "the moment you enter" sets the tone at this "hidden", "romantic" Bay Ridge Northern Italian; upmarket prices and "small" quarters notwithstanding, it's a "favorite of the neighborhood locals" for its "flavorful" food made from "fresh ingredients."

12th St. Bar & Grill *American*

FOOD	DECOR	SERVICE	COST
20	19	19	$36

Park Slope | 1123 Eighth Ave. (12th St.) | Brooklyn | 718-965-9526 | www.12thstreetbarandgrill.com

A longtime "neighborhood treasure", this Park Slope New American is known for its "solid" cooking, "casual" pricing and "excellent" weekend brunching; when it's "too crowded", regulars head for the "side-street bar" – "they serve the same food and drinks faster."

12 Chairs *American/Mideastern*

FOOD	DECOR	SERVICE	COST
▽ 19	13	16	$23

SoHo | 56 MacDougal St. (bet. Houston & Prince Sts.) | 212-254-8640

For a "refreshing" respite from busy SoHo, check out this "low-key", low-budget spot for its "basic" American–Middle Eastern bites; though equipped with "more than 12 chairs", it's still "tiny" yet "perfect for coffee and conversation" as long as decor and service are not a priority.

21 Club ⬛ *American*

FOOD	DECOR	SERVICE	COST
22	24	24	$71

W 50s | 21 W. 52nd St. (bet. 5th & 6th Aves.) | 212-582-7200 | www.21club.com

A "testament to NYC history", this erstwhile Midtown speakeasy exuding "atmosphere galore" lures "heavy hitters" with "classic" Americana served in a "clubby", jackets-required townhouse complete with 10 private rooms and a "secret" wine cellar, all overseen by an "unobtrusive" staff; for those daunted by the prices, the $40 pre-theater prix fixe may be the "deal of the century."

26 Seats Ⓜ *French*

FOOD	DECOR	SERVICE	COST
21	16	19	$39

E Village | 168 Ave. B (bet. 10th & 11th Sts.) | 212-677-4787

"As limited in space as the name implies", this "unassuming", "candlelit" French bistro near Tompkins Square Park is still "big on taste"; even better, the "bargain" tabs are "in sync with its East Village vibe."

Two Boots *Pizza*

FOOD	DECOR	SERVICE	COST
19	10	14	$16

E 40s | Grand Central | lower level (42nd St. & Vanderbilt Ave.) | 212-557-7992 | www.twoboots.com

E Village | 42 Ave. A (3rd St.) | 212-254-1919 | www.twoboots.com ●

LES | 384 Grand St. (bet. Norfolk & Suffolk Sts.) | 212-228-8685 | www.twoboots.com

(continued)

Two Boots

NoHo | 74 Bleecker St. (B'way) | 212-777-1033 | www.twoboots.com ●
W 40s | 30 Rockefeller Plaza, downstairs (bet. 49th & 50th Sts.) |
212-332-8800 | www.twoboots.com
W Village | 201 W. 11th St. (7th Ave. S.) | 212-633-9096 |
www.twoboots.com ●
Park Slope | 514 Second St. (bet. 7th & 8th Aves.) | Brooklyn | 718-499-3253 |
www.twobootsbrooklyn.com

Boot-ineers cheer this "cheap" chainlet's "creatively named", "corn-meal-crusted" pies, citing "funky" toppings and "zesty" sauce, but they jeer the "kitschy" setups and "indifferent" slice-slingers; P.S. the independently owned Park Slope outpost is "popular" (read: "over-run") with "tykes" and their handlers.

202 Cafe *Mediterranean*   19 | 19 | 16 | $37

Chelsea | Chelsea Mkt. | 75 Ninth Ave. (bet. 15th & 16th Sts.) | 646-638-1173
For a "reasonably priced" meal and the chance to "buy a pricey pair of jeans", try this Chelsea Market Med in the Nicole Farhi boutique; the "ladylike" grub is as "stylish" as the garb, while the "slow service" leaves time for "browsing" the racks.

2 West *Steak*   ∇ 23 | 22 | 25 | $64

Financial District | Ritz-Carlton Battery Park | 2 West St. (Battery Pl.) |
917-790-2525 | www.ritzcarlton.com
The Ritz's customary "attention to detail" shines through at this pricey Financial District steakhouse featuring "terrific" chops, a "good wine list" and a "wonderful high tea"; fans say the "relaxing" vibe is just the thing following a "stressful week at the trading desk."

Umberto's Clam House ● *Italian/Seafood*   19 | 14 | 17 | $41

Little Italy | 386 Broome St. (Mulberry St.) | 212-343-2053 |
www.umbertosclamhouse.com
Bronx | 2356 Arthur Ave. (186th St.) | 718-220-2526 |
www.umbertosclamhousebronx.com
These "old-time" Italians vend "reasonable" clam-centric "classics" delivered with "nothing-fancy" service; the "legendary" Little Italy original and its *Godfather*-worthy "history" attracts mobs of "tourists", leading many to opt for the Arthur Avenue offshoot instead.

Una Pizza Napoletana Ⓜ ⌷ *Pizza*   23 | 11 | 13 | $31

E Village | 349 E. 12th St. (bet. 1st & 2nd Aves.) | 212-477-9950 |
www.unapizza.com
Pizza "connoisseurs" line up at this "small", "spartan" East Village "joint" for "stunningly authentic" Neapolitan pies; "challenges" include "few choices" (just four toppings, no slices), kinda "pricey" tabs, an "autocratic" owner and "varying" hours (it "closes when they run out of dough").

Uncle Jack's Steakhouse *Steak*   23 | 19 | 22 | $70

Garment District | 440 Ninth Ave. (bet. 34th & 35th Sts.) | 212-244-0005
NEW W 50s | 44 W. 56th St. (bet. 5th & 6th Aves.) | 212-245-1550
Bayside | 39-40 Bell Blvd. (40th Ave.) | Queens | 718-229-1100
www.unclejacks.com
Now with a new Midtown location, this "testosterone"-fueled steak-house trio is home to "melt-in-your-mouth" cuts served up by "atten-

tive" waiters in "clubby", "comfortably appointed" surroundings; it's a "carnivore's delight" but, holy cow – "what a check!"

Uncle Nick's *Greek*

FOOD	DECOR	SERVICE	COST
20	10	16	$34

NEW Chelsea | 382 Eighth Ave. (29th St.) | 212-609-0500
W 50s | 747 Ninth Ave. (bet. 50th & 51st Sts.) | 212-245-7992
www.unclenicksgreekrestaurant.com

"Sizzling" fish, "flaming" cheese and a helping of "chaos" typify the "*opa!*" experience at this "affordable" Hell's Kitchen Greek taverna; apéritifs at the adjoining *ouzeria* hopefully will offset the pain of "indifferent" service and "no-decor" surroundings; N.B. the Chelsea branch opened post-Survey.

☑ Union Square Cafe *American*

FOOD	DECOR	SERVICE	COST
27	23	26	$68

Union Sq | 21 E. 16th St. (bet. 5th Ave. & Union Sq. W.) | 212-243-4020 |
www.unionsquarecafe.com

Danny Meyer's Union Square "convivial classic" is once again "top of the heap" – it's voted NYC's Most Popular – with new executive chef Carmen Quagliata now overseeing the kitchen and its "beautifully composed" New American cuisine "honoring" "seasonal" ingredients; the experience of a "fundamentally perfect meal" is completed by the service ("top-tier but down-to-earth") and setting ("lovely", "comfortable" rooms "without pretense"); N.B. if you can't score reservations, "go spur-of-the-moment" and dine at the "lively" bar.

Ushiwakamaru ●☑ *Japanese*

FOOD	DECOR	SERVICE	COST
▽ 27	15	20	$72

G Village | 136 W. Houston St. (bet. MacDougal & Sullivan Sts.) |
212-228-4181

"Aficionados" who know this "small", under-the-radar Village Japanese hail the "master" behind its sushi bar and his "Tokyo-style" preparations of fish "flown in from Japan"; "book a seat at the bar" for the omakase – but beware tabs that quickly "run up."

Uskudar *Turkish*

FOOD	DECOR	SERVICE	COST
20	9	18	$36

E 70s | 1405 Second Ave. (bet. 73rd & 74th Sts.) | 212-988-2641

"Tasty" Turkish "basics" – meze, kebabs and other "delights" – served with a smile satisfy "locals" at this Upper Eastsider; the "humble" digs are "not much larger than a breadbox", but similarly small tabs mean it's "worth the squeeze."

Utsav *Indian*

FOOD	DECOR	SERVICE	COST
21	19	19	$38

W 40s | 1185 Sixth Ave., 2nd fl. (bet. 46th & 47th Sts.) | 212-575-2525 |
www.utsavny.com

"Hidden" in Midtown, this "upmarket" Indian is a welcome "change of pace" for "pre-theater" dining thanks to its "relaxing" second-floor setting and staffers providing guidance with the "novice-friendly" fare; the lunch buffet is a "sampler's delight" at $17.95.

Uva ● *Italian*

FOOD	DECOR	SERVICE	COST
21	21	19	$40

E 70s | 1486 Second Ave. (bet. 77th & 78th Sts.) | 212-472-4552 |
www.uvawinebarnewyork.com

"Beautiful", "young" things are smitten with this "cute" Upper East Side Italian's "tasty" nibbles, "incredible" vinos and "adorable" all-weather patio, not to mention its "ogle"-worthy staff; it's even more "*romantico*" as a "dreamy date place" since you can "leave with money left in your pocket."

	FOOD	DECOR	SERVICE	COST

Valbella 🖫 *Italian* — 24 | 24 | 25 | $78

Meatpacking | 421 W. 13th St. (bet. 9th Ave. & Washington St.) | 212-645-7777 | www.valbellany.com

A "favorite" of the "well-heeled" set, this Meatpacking Northern Italian boasts "wonderful" service from a "well-trained" staff, with "stunning decor" and "excellent" food and wine "to match"; it's "impressive all-around", but just remember to "stop at the bank first."

V&T ◑ *Italian/Pizza* — 18 | 9 | 13 | $22

W 100s | 1024 Amsterdam Ave. (bet. 110th & 111th Sts.) | 212-666-8051

"Renowned" pizzas with a big dose of "nostalgia" keep 'em coming back to this "sloppy-but-lovable" Morningside Heights Italian that "hasn't changed in decades", not even the "grumpy" waiters; "cheap" tabs are the clincher for its crowd heavy on "Columbia students" and "families."

Vento ◑ *Italian* — 19 | 17 | 18 | $47

Meatpacking | 675 Hudson St. (14th St.) | 212-699-2400 | www.brguestrestaurants.com

The "fun scene" almost "overshadows the food" at Steve Hanson's "buzzing" Meatpacking Italian, where patrons "celeb-watch" from the patio while sampling "well-priced" ("for the area") small plates; service is "attentive, negligent or strung-out" depending on the night.

🛂 Veritas *American* — 26 | 22 | 25 | $107

Flatiron | 43 E. 20th St. (bet. B'way & Park Ave. S.) | 212-353-3700 | www.veritas-nyc.com

A "superlative" wine list is the highlight at this "first-class" Flatiron New American, though the "outstanding" cuisine and "impeccable" service make it an "all-around" winner; the $82 prix fixe–only menu means many "save this one for a big occasion"; N.B. Ed Cotton (ex Daniel) replaced longtime chef Scott Bryan post-Survey.

Vermicelli *Vietnamese* — 18 | 13 | 17 | $32

E 70s | 1492 Second Ave. (bet. 77th & 78th Sts.) | 212-288-8868 | www.vermicellirestaurant.com

"Vietnamese to the core" "despite the name", this "pleasant" Upper Eastsider offers a "large selection" of "flavorful" dishes, plus a "bargain" lunch-box special that "can't be beat"; it's a "solid" "neighborhood" fallback that's reliable "for eat-in or takeout."

Veselka *Ukrainian* — 18 | 11 | 14 | $20

E Village | 144 Second Ave. (9th St.) | 212-228-9682 ◑
E Village | First Park | 75 E. First St. (1st Ave.) | 347-907-3317 ⌿
www.veselka.com

"Portions are large" and prices "low" at this "bustling" "throwback to the old Ukrainian East Village"; it plies its "comforting" fare 24/7 and is equally "beloved" for "hangover brunches" and "pierogi at 2 AM", "spotty" service and "dinerlike" digs notwithstanding; P.S. the "Little Veselka" kiosk on East First Street serves a smaller sampling of "noshes."

Vespa *Italian* — 19 | 18 | 18 | $41

E 80s | 1625 Second Ave. (bet. 84th & 85th Sts.) | 212-472-2050 | www.barvespa.com

"Cute but cramped", this UES "neighborhood trattoria" is a little "hipper than its neighbors"; while it's "worth a scooter trip" for its "solid", "value-priced" Italian fare alone, the "cool Euro" staff and "fantastic garden" are "added attractions."

Vezzo *Pizza*

| 23 | 16 | 18 | $23 |

Murray Hill | 178 Lexington Ave. (31st St.) | 212-839-8300 | www.vezzothincrust.com

"Delicious", "paper thin"-crusted pizzas with "yummy toppings" are the forte of this "low-key", low-priced Murray Hill Italian boasting a "working juke"; wash them down with a "glass of Montepulciano" and you may forget that "service isn't the best" and space is "tight."

Via Brasil *Brazilian/Steak*

| 18 | 13 | 17 | $40 |

W 40s | 34 W. 46th St. (bet. 5th & 6th Aves.) | 212-997-1158 | www.viabrasilrestaurant.com

This Theater District "trip to Rio" is reliable for "solid" beef and other "traditional" Brazilian steakhouse fare in "ample portions", bolstered by a "piano player" on weekends; "modest" decor and "ok" service aside, most declare it a "real find" when going to a show.

Via Emilia 🈂🏂 *Italian*

| 21 | 15 | 18 | $37 |

Flatiron | 47 E. 21st St. (bet. B'way & Park Ave. S.) | 212-505-3072 | www.viaemilia.us

"Home cooking from Modena" is the focus of this "spacious", "unassuming" Flatiron Italian, where "tasty" pastas and other "authentic", "affordable" specialties are delivered by a "pleasant" crew; the "only drawback" is that pesky "cash-only" policy.

Viand *Coffee Shop*

| 16 | 7 | 16 | $22 |

E 60s | 673 Madison Ave. (bet. 61st & 62nd Sts.) | 212-751-6622 🏂
E 70s | 1011 Madison Ave. (78th St.) | 212-249-8250
E 80s | 300 E. 86th St. (2nd Ave.) | 212-879-9425 ◗
W 70s | 2130 Broadway (75th St.) | 212-877-2888 | www.viandnyc.com ◗

These "quintessential" "NY coffee shops" offer up "decent" "diner" standards (including "fantastic turkey clubs") at "good value" via "huge menus with specials at every meal"; manned by "fast", "long-term" waiters, they're "cramped" with "no atmosphere" and that suits the regulars fine – isn't that "Mayor Bloomberg"?

Via Oreto *Italian*

| 20 | 16 | 18 | $49 |

E 60s | 1121-23 First Ave. (bet. 61st & 62nd Sts.) | 212-308-0828 | www.viaoreto.com

"Homestyle Italian food" ("love that garlic!") and a "personal touch" endear this Upper East Side "favorite" to the locals – no wonder it's been "getting more crowded"; it may cost "bigger bucks than you'd expect" and service can be "spotty", but "you can't beat mama's meatballs" (Sundays and Mondays).

Via Quadronno *Italian*

| 21 | 14 | 17 | $40 |

E 70s | 25 E. 73rd St. (bet. 5th & Madison Aves.) | 212-650-9880 | www.viaquadronno.com

For a "quick espresso" or a "light" meal, hit this "chic" UES "little corner of Milan", where the "panini and gelato" are "as good as in *Italia*"; it also excels for "snooty people"-watching, but be ready to "sit in somebody's lap" – and bring plenty of euros.

	FOOD	DECOR	SERVICE	COST

ViceVersa ⓩ *Italian*
22 | 21 | 22 | $53

W 50s | 325 W. 51st St. (bet. 8th & 9th Aves.) | 212-399-9291 | www.viceversarestaurant.com

Perhaps the "most pleasant of the Theater District" standbys, this "reliable" Italian "continues to shine" with "thoughtfully prepared" dishes, "polished" service and a "sleek, sophisticated" room; bonus points go to the "romantic back garden" and laid-back lunches.

NEW Vicino Firenze ❶ *Italian*
- | - | - | M

E 80s | 1586 Second Ave. (bet. 82nd & 83rd Sts.) | www.vicinofirenze.com

The Upper East Side's romantic Firenze has spawned this cozy, cherrywood-paneled Italian offshoot a few doors down on Second Avenue's Restaurant Row; its midpriced Tuscan menu is similar to the original's, with the notable additions of pizzas at lunch and a porterhouse carved tableside at dinner.

Vico ❶⊟ *Italian*
20 | 15 | 19 | $60

E 90s | 1302 Madison Ave. (bet. 92nd & 93rd Sts.) | 212-876-2222

"Watch the moguls mingle" at this "always-packed" UES Italian "locals' favorite" where the "well-prepared" (if "surprisingly expensive") dishes are delivered by an "attentive" staff; some suggest it could use "a few larger tables" and "a little less air-kissing."

ⓩ Victor's Cafe ❶ *Cuban*
22 | 19 | 21 | $49

W 50s | 236 W. 52nd St. (bet. B'way & 8th Ave.) | 212-586-7714 | www.victorscafe.com

You half expect "Ricky Ricardo to begin playing the bongos" at this "lively", "upscale", circa-1963 Theater District Cuban; "delicious" "old standards" and some "contemporary creations" are served with "charm" amid the "ceiling fans" – "Fidel is out" but "Victor" is a "keeper."

VietCafé ⓩ *Vietnamese*
∇ 22 | 17 | 17 | $33

TriBeCa | 345 Greenwich St. (bet. Harrison & Jay Sts.) | 212-431-5888 | www.viet-cafe.com

Vietnamese specialties "modern" and "traditional" are a "cut above" at this "relaxed", "trendy"-looking TriBeCa eatery offering solid "value" and some popular "lunchtime options" (including "the best" "Viet sandwiches"); fans just wonder why this place "isn't busier" at dinner.

View, The *Continental*
17 | 25 | 19 | $91

W 40s | Marriott Marquis Hotel | 1535 Broadway, 47th fl. (bet. 45th & 46th Sts.) | 212-704-8900 | www.nymarriottmarquis.com

"The name says it all" about this "rotating" Continental hotel dining room, where the "breathtaking" Times Square panorama nearly equals a "Broadway show"; still, some say the "spinning is to distract you" from the "ordinary" prix fixe–only fare and vertigo-inducing tabs.

Villa Berulia *Italian*
21 | 17 | 23 | $52

Murray Hill | 107 E. 34th St. (bet. Lexington & Park Aves.) | 212-689-1970 | www.villaberulia.com

"Formal but friendly" is the mood at this "old-world" Murray Hill Northern Italian appreciated for its "solidly good" food and "unhurried" service; though upstarts call it "outdated", the "quiet" atmosphere and subdued ambiance "appeal to a mature crowd" that takes its tabs in stride.

	FOOD	DECOR	SERVICE	COST

Village *American/French* | 19 | 18 | 19 | $44 |

G Village | 62 W. Ninth St. (bet. 5th & 6th Aves.) | 212-505-3355 |
www.villagerestaurant.com

Half "French bistro", half "local tavern", this Villager is a "warm", "dependable" "standby" for "pleasant" Franco-American fare and "reasonably priced wines"; "regulars" stop for a drink at the "cheerful" bar then head back to a "table under the wonderful skylight."

Villa Mosconi ⚠ *Italian* | 21 | 15 | 22 | $44 |

G Village | 69 MacDougal St. (bet. Bleecker & Houston Sts.) | 212-673-0390 |
www.villamosconi.com

A "tradition" since 1976, this Village "classic" "continues to please" with "honest" "red-sauce" Italian standards, including housemade pastas and "meatballs like mama made"; its look may be "ordinary", but the "affable" staffers "treat you like a long lost friend."

Vincent's ⚫ *Italian* | 21 | 13 | 18 | $39 |

Little Italy | 119 Mott St. (Hester St.) | 212-226-8133 |
www.originalvincents.com

Trademark "hot sauces" and other "tasty" Italian staples plus plenty of "old-time NY" atmosphere keep 'em coming to this circa-1904 Little Italy "landmark"; it draws everyone from "tourists" to neighborhood nostalgists – i.e. everyone you expect "to see when going to Little Italy."

Virgil's Real Barbecue ⚫ *BBQ* | 20 | 13 | 16 | $34 |

W 40s | 152 W. 44th St. (bet. B'way & 6th Ave.) | 212-921-9494 |
www.virgilsbbq.com

"Yes, you can find" "succulent BBQ" near Times Square at this "barnlike" joint brimming with "tourists and locals" "pigging out" on "affordable" eats and using "towels as napkins"; all in all, it's a "fun, fast, messy" time, even if service blows "hot and cold."

Vivolo ⚠ *Italian* | 19 | 17 | 20 | $49 |

E 70s | 140 E. 74th St. (bet. Lexington & Park Aves.) | 212-737-3533 |
www.vivolonyc.com

This "charming townhouse" Italian is an "old-school" "favorite" among "mature" UESers who appreciate its "calm" vibe and "terrific $26 early-bird" deal; critics, who cry "time warp", say it "could be more inventive", but "regulars" retort "it's been around a long time for good reason."

Vong *French/Thai* | 22 | 23 | 21 | $64 |

E 50s | 200 E. 54th St. (3rd Ave.) | 212-486-9592 | www.jean-georges.com

"Still delightfully different", Jean-Georges Vongerichten's Midtown French-Thai offers "perfectly balanced" fusion dishes in "beautiful, almost otherworldly" surroundings staffed by an "attentive" team; yes, tabs can get "hefty", but the $20 lunch prix fixe is a serious "value."

Vynl *American/Thai* | 15 | 17 | 15 | $26 |

NEW Chelsea | 102 Eighth Ave. (15th St.) | 212-400-2118 ⚫
E 70s | 1491 Second Ave. (78th St.) | 212-249-6080
W 50s | 754 Ninth Ave. (51st St.) | 212-974-2003 ⚫
W 80s | 507 Columbus Ave. (bet. 84th & 85th Sts.) | 212-362-1107
www.vynl-nyc.com

Catering to a "wide array of taste buds", not to mention "'80s music" fans, this "campy" New American–Thai quartet serves everything from burgers to pad Thai in "vinyl memorabilia"-filled digs (the musical loos are a "must-see"); as for the staffers, they're "personable" but sometimes seem "stoned out."

Wakiya ● *Chinese*
▽ 19 | 25 | 19 | $70

Gramercy | Gramercy Park Hotel | 2 Lexington Ave. (21st St.) | 212-995-1330 | www.gramercyparkhotel.com

The "beautiful people" "love" the "ultramodern", "Asian-themed" decor at Ian Schrager's "swanky" Chinese in the "remodeled" Gramercy Hotel; as for chef Yuji Wakiya's "pricey" plates meant for "sharing", some say it's a "matter of style over substance", while others find plenty of gems in the mix.

Waldy's Wood Fired Pizza *Pizza*
22 | 10 | 15 | $17

Chelsea | 800 Sixth Ave. (bet. 27th & 28th Sts.) | 212-213-5042 | www.waldyspizza.com

"Gourmet pizza" with "crisp wood-fired crusts" and "fresh, interesting" toppings but "without the attitude" is the deal at Waldy Malouf's "tiny" Chelsea pie place; limited seating and service sometimes "like a *Seinfeld* episode" are part of the package.

Walker's ● *Pub Food*
17 | 13 | 17 | $29

TriBeCa | 16 N. Moore St. (Varick St.) | 212-941-0142

"Comfy as your favorite jeans", this TriBeCa "institution" is "beloved" for its "reliable" "burger-and-beer" eats at "honest" prices; it's a "wonderful holdover" from the area's pre-"yuppie" days, with a "neighborhood-tavern" vibe that affords "lots of local color."

☒ Wallsé *Austrian*
26 | 22 | 24 | $69

W Village | 344 W. 11th St. (Washington St.) | 212-352-2300 | www.wallse.com

Take a trip to "Vienna in the Village" via Kurt Gutenbrunner's "modern" Austrian cuisine "with edge"; yes, it's "pricey", but the "charming", "well-informed" staff and "calm setting" featuring "stupendous" Julian Schnabel paintings will have you "waltzing" on air.

Wasabi Lobby *Japanese*
21 | 15 | 19 | $32

E 80s | 1584 Second Ave. (82nd St.) | 212-988-8882 | www.wasabilobbynyc.com

Don't let the "cheesy name" "fool you" – there's "fresh" "innovative sushi" to be had at this "simple", low-budget UES Japanese; still, sometimes "hovering" service has a few lobbying for "takeout."

Watawa *Japanese*
▽ 25 | 18 | 23 | $30

Astoria | 33-10 Ditmars Blvd. (33rd St.) | Queens | 718-545-9596

"Exotic rolls" and other "mouthwatering", "creative" sushi is the specialty of this "trendy" Astoria Japanese; the "decor is minimal" but patrons are "treated like honored guests", and, best of all, tabs are "very reasonable" – "whatawa surprise."

Water Club *American*
22 | 25 | 22 | $64

Murray Hill | East River at 30th St. (enter on 23rd St.) | 212-683-3333 | www.thewaterclub.com

The "magnificent" river views from this "nautically themed" American set on an East River barge "can't be beat" – and the "food and service match up" to boot; yes, it's "pricey", but it's a "first-class NY dining experience" "perfect for special celebrations", and the $39 Sunday brunch buffet is just what you prayed for.

WaterFalls M Italian — ▽ 20 | 19 | 18 | $42

Staten Island | 2012 Victory Blvd. (Jewett Ave.) | 718-815-7200 | www.waterfalls-restaurant.com

A "lovely place to meet friends" for "consistently good" food at a "fair price", this Staten Island Italian is something of a "local secret"; service is variable, but the valet parking lends serious "curb appeal."

Water's Edge ⊠ American/Seafood — 22 | 25 | 23 | $65

LIC | East River & 44th Dr. (Vernon Blvd.) | Queens | 718-482-0033 | www.watersedgenyc.com

"Swoon"-worthy views of Midtown, a "formal" setting and "smooth" pro service add up to an "unparalleled romantic evening" at this LIC New American made for "marriage" proposals and "special occasions"; "wonderful" seafood and a free water-taxi to and from Manhattan make the "steep" tab easy to swallow.

Waverly Inn and Garden ◑ American — 19 | 21 | 18 | $65

W Village | 16 Bank St. (Waverly Pl.) | 212-243-7900

Packing in more models than 7th on Sixth and "more celebs than the Oscars", complete with sidewalk "paparazzi", this charmingly restored 1920s West Village tavern owned by *Vanity Fair* editor Graydon Carter offers a "homestyle" menu (think chicken pot pie) with Hollywood touches (think "truffled mac 'n' cheese"); though reservations can't be made by phone, walk-ins are accepted – as long as they go early or very late.

wd-50 ◑ American/Eclectic — 23 | 18 | 23 | $82

LES | 50 Clinton St. (bet. Rivington & Stanton Sts.) | 212-477-2900 | www.wd-50.com

"Enter with an open mind" and prepare for a "memorable" "adventure" at Wylie Dufresne's highly "experimental" LES New American-Eclectic; it's an "exciting" (some say "wacky") "dinner and science class all in one", but keep in mind that tuition is "high."

West Bank Cafe American — 20 | 17 | 19 | $43

W 40s | Manhattan Plaza | 407 W. 42nd St. (bet. 9th & 10th Aves.) | 212-695-6909 | www.westbankcafe.com

"Theatrical types" and "matinee ladies" populate this moderately priced Theater District New American "close to many of the off-Broadway" shows; there are no surprises here, just "reliably" good food served by a "cheerful" (if sometimes "harried") crew.

Westville American — 22 | 13 | 18 | $24

W Village | 210 W. 10th St. (bet. Bleecker & W. 4th Sts.) | 212-741-7971

Westville East American

E Village | 173 Ave. A (11th St.) | 212-677-2033 www.westvillenyc.com

"Upscale comfort food" with a focus on "fresh market produce" is the draw at these West Village–East Village "hipster" magnets; the something-for-everyone menu pleases all from "burger-eaters" to "vegans", with "low prices" making the "long waits" and "shabby" digs easy to endure.

	FOOD	DECOR	SERVICE	COST

Whole Foods Café *Eclectic/Health Food*   18 | 9 | 9 | $17

LES | 95 E. Houston St., 2nd fl. (Bowery) | 212-420-1320
NEW **TriBeCa** | 270 Greenwich St., 2nd fl. (bet. Murray & Warren Sts.) |
212-349-6555
Union Sq | 4 Union Sq. S. (bet. B'way & University Pl.) | 212-673-5388
W 60s | Time Warner Ctr. | 10 Columbus Circle, downstairs
(60th St. at B'way) | 212-823-9600
www.wholefoods.com

"Always a zoo", these in-supermarket cafeterias let you "grab your
own meal" from bountiful "eclectic buffets" offering everything from
"ethnic eats" to "terrific salads"; "daunting" check-out lines move
quickly enough, but you'll need to "scrum for seats" – tables "go faster
than the blink of an eye" since this is a brilliant concept.

Whym *American*   20 | 17 | 20 | $41

W 50s | 889 Ninth Ave. (bet. 57th & 58th Sts.) | 212-315-0088 |
www.whymnyc.com

This "mod" Hell's Kitchen New American fills a "local" need for "upscale
but relaxed" dining with its "eclectic menu that works", "energetic"
room and "friendly" service; prices "reasonable" "for the neighborhood" make it a prime "pre-theater" option.

'wichcraft *Sandwiches*   20 | 11 | 14 | $16

Chelsea | Terminal Warehouse | 269 11th Ave. (bet. 27th & 28th Sts.) |
212-780-0577
NEW **E 40s** | 245 Park Ave. (47th St.) | 212-780-0577 ⑤
E 40s | 555 Fifth Ave. (46th St.) | 212-780-0577 ⑤
Flatiron | 11 E. 20th St. (bet. B'way & 5th Ave.) | 212-780-0577
G Village | 60 E. Eighth St. (Mercer St.) | 212-780-0577
Murray Hill | Equinox | 1 Park Ave. (33rd St.) | 212-780-0577
SoHo | Equinox | 106 Crosby St. (Prince St.) | 212-780-0577
TriBeCa | 397 Greenwich St. (Beach St.) | 212-780-0577
W 40s | Bryant Park | Sixth Ave. (bet. 40th & 42nd Sts.) | 212-780-0577
NEW **W 50s** | 1 Rockefeller Plaza (on 50th St., bet. 5th & 6th Aves.) |
212-780-0577
www.wichcraftnyc.com

"Sublime sandwiches" with "exceptional ingredients" and "sophisticated
combinations" are the "magic" secret of this burgeoning mini-chain from
Craft's Tom Colicchio; service can be "slow" and the "price-portion ratio"
can "seem unfair", but for "upscale brown-bagging" it "can't be beat."

Wild Ginger *Thai*   18 | 17 | 16 | $27

W Village | 51 Grove St. (bet. Bleecker St. & 7th Ave. S.) | 212-367-7200 |
www.wildginger-ny.com

"Prices are low" and portions "huge" and "flavorful" at this "tranquil"
West Village Thai "budget date destination" complete with fish pond;
the service perhaps "needs work", but staffers are "helpful if you ask."

NEW Wildwood Barbeque *BBQ*   17 | 17 | 17 | $39

Flatiron | 225 Park Ave. S. (bet. 18th & 19th Sts.) | 212-533-2500 |
www.brguestrestaurants.com

Stephen Hanson's B.R. Guest (Dos Caminos, Ruby Foo's, etc.) "does
the BBQ thang" at this new "rustic-chic" "barn" of a Flatironer that's
packing in a "young" crowd; opinions are split on its "relatively pricey"
smokehouse fare ("luscious" vs. "disappointing"), but all agree the
"busy" "bar scene" is a hoot.

	FOOD	DECOR	SERVICE	COST

Wo Hop ● ⇼ *Chinese* | 21 | 5 | 13 | $18 |

Chinatown | 17 Mott St. (Canal St.) | 212-267-2536

A Chinatown "greasy spoon, er chopstick" that "never changes", this circa-1938, all-night "standby" keeps churning out "terrific", "dirt-cheap" Cantonese dishes via "disinterested waiters" in a "harshly lit" basement that resembles a "Communist-bloc bus station."

Wolfgang's Steakhouse *Steak* | 25 | 20 | 20 | $74 |

Murray Hill | 4 Park Ave. (33rd St.) | 212-889-3369
TriBeCa | 409 Greenwich St. (bet. Beach & Hubert Sts.) | 212-925-0350
www.wolfgangssteakhouse.com

"Chips off the old butcher block", these Peter Luger "imitations" put out "flavorful", costly steaks in "old school-cool" settings; drawbacks include "noise that puts the 'din' in dinner" and a habit of "not honoring" reservation times.

Wollensky's Grill ● *Steak* | 22 | 16 | 20 | $54 |

E 40s | 201 E. 49th St. (3rd Ave.) | 212-753-0444 |
www.smithandwollensky.com

"Not as fancy" and "more reasonably priced", this "little brother" of Smith & Wollensky also stays up later, offering a "clubby" atmosphere and "lots of bustle" until 2 AM; it's just the thing when you feel like "slipping in and out for a steak or a chop."

Wondee Siam *Thai* | 23 | 8 | 16 | $22 |

NEW **W 40s** | 641 10th Ave. (bet. 45th & 46th Sts.) | 212-245-4601
W 50s | 792 Ninth Ave. (bet. 52nd & 53rd Sts.) | 212-459-9057 ⇼
W 50s | 813 Ninth Ave. (bet. 53rd & 54th Sts.) | 917-286-1726

"Delectable", "dirt-cheap" Thai that's "as close to the real thing as you can get" earns this Hell's Kitchen trio a loyal fan base; aficionados happily ignore the "nonexistent decor" and variable service and focus instead on the "wondee-ful" eats.

Woo Lae Oak *Korean* | 22 | 21 | 18 | $52 |

SoHo | 148 Mercer St. (bet. Houston & Prince Sts.) | 212-925-8200 |
www.woolaeoaksoho.com

Skip the "scenesters" and just "concentrate on BBQing" at "your own table" at this "SoHo-chic" Korean that's "sleek", "dark" and great "for groups"; the "top-quality" fare and "sexy" vibe allow most to forget that they're paying "more than you'd expect in K-town."

Wu Liang Ye *Chinese* | 22 | 11 | 15 | $31 |

E 80s | 215 E. 86th St. (bet. 2nd & 3rd Aves.) | 212-534-8899
Murray Hill | 338 Lexington Ave. (bet. 39th & 40th Sts.) | 212-370-9648
W 40s | 36 W. 48th St. (bet. 5th & 6th Aves.) | 212-398-2308

"Tongue-tingling", spicy Sichuan food at "fair prices" fires up fans of this Chinese trio, where diners report being richly "rewarded" for their "incendiary" menu choices; if only the "no-decor" digs and "inconsistent" service "were as hot as the food."

X.O. ⇼ *Chinese* | 19 | 10 | 13 | $17 |

Little Italy | 148 Hester St. (bet. Bowery & Elizabeth St.) |
212-965-8645
Chinatown | 96 Walker St. (bet. Centre & Lafayette Sts.) | 212-343-8339

At this Chinatown–Little Italy "Hong Kong-style" dim sum duo, the "vast" menu is so "affordable", you can "sample" lots "without breaking the budget"; it's a "cheap", "fun" time, as long as you don't mind the "divey" digs.

Xunta ● *Spanish*

| 21 | 13 | 15 | $28 |

E Village | 174 First Ave. (bet. 10th & 11th Sts.) | 212-614-0620 | www.xuntatapasbar.com

"Memorable" tapas, "potent sangria" and "you're-in-Spain" decor keep this "lively" East Villager with "barrels" for tables "packed"; "low prices" and elevated "noise levels" mean it's a natural for the "under-30" crowd.

⌷ Yakitori Totto ● *Japanese*

| 26 | 16 | 19 | $46 |

W 50s | 251 W. 55th St., 2nd fl. (bet. B'way & 8th Ave.) | 212-245-4555

It's "Japan on a stick" at this "tiny" Midtown yakitori specialist serving "skewer after skewer" of "juicy" "grilled-to-perfection" meats that start off cheap but "rack up quickly"; its "hidden" upstairs location is "hard to find" and the "wait is long", but it's "so worth it."

Yama ☒ *Japanese*

| 23 | 12 | 17 | $40 |

E 40s | 308 E. 49th St. (bet. 1st & 2nd Aves.) | 212-355-3370
Gramercy | 122 E. 17th St. (Irving Pl.) | 212-475-0969
G Village | 38-40 Carmine St. (bet. Bedford & Bleecker Sts.) | 212-989-9330
www.yamarestaurant.com

The sushi and sashimi are "whale-size" and so "fresh" they must've just been "harpooned" at this Japanese chainlet that's also known for its "good-value" prices; a sizable "loyal following" means there's "always a long line", "no-frills" setups and "impersonal service" notwithstanding.

⌷⌷⌷ Yerba Buena *Pan-Latin*

| - | - | - | M |

E Village | 23 Ave. A (bet. Houston & 2nd Sts.) | 212-529-2919 | www.ybnyc.com

With a backlit bar plying sophisticated specialty drinks and Julian Medina (Toloache) in the kitchen turning out appealing Pan-Latin fare, this East Villager is off to a promising start; a convivial vibe prevails in its stylish space featuring a wood-burning oven, and fair prices only sweeten the mood.

York Grill *American*

| 22 | 20 | 22 | $50 |

E 80s | 1690 York Ave. (bet. 88th & 89th Sts.) | 212-772-0261

Its far Eastside location may be "remote", but this "old-fashioned" New American lures its "grown-up" clientele with "warm welcomes", "tasty" food and a "cozy" atmosphere; prices that are "slightly expensive for the neighborhood" have some saving it for "special occasions."

Yuca Bar ● *Pan-Latin*

| 21 | 16 | 16 | $30 |

E Village | 111 Ave. A (7th St.) | 212-982-9533 | www.yucabarnyc.com

Sangria and mojitos fuel a "young", "spirited" scene at this "funky" East Villager that dishes up tapas and other "reasonably priced" Pan-Latin standards; decibel levels can reach "blasting", but no one minds as this is a "place to stare and be stared at."

Yuka *Japanese*

| 21 | 10 | 18 | $28 |

E 80s | 1557 Second Ave. (bet. 80th & 81st Sts.) | 212-772-9675

"People line up" for "consistently delicious" sushi – including a "bargain" $19 all-you-can-eat deal – at this Yorkville "neighborhood joint"; the "bright", "utilitarian" decor is certainly "not fancy", and service can be "rushed", but "you get your yen's worth here."

Yuki Sushi ● *Japanese*

FOOD	DECOR	SERVICE	COST
21	15	21	$31

W 90s | 656 Amsterdam Ave. (92nd St.) | 212-787-8200 |
www.yukisushiny.com

For sushi "prepared with great care", locals look to this "gracious"
UWS Japanese "standby"; despite "spare", "tight" digs, its "basic",
"affordable" rolls and cooked dishes make it both a "family" destination and a "late-night savior" (until 11:30 nightly).

Yuva *Indian*

FOOD	DECOR	SERVICE	COST
▽ 22	17	19	$46

E 50s | 230 E. 58th St. (bet. 2nd & 3rd Aves.) | 212-339-0090 |
www.yuvanyc.com

"Sublimely spiced" specialties satisfy subcontinental sympathizers at
this "upscale" East Midtown Indian, where the "charming" (if sometimes "slow") staff delivers "authentic" standards in vaguely "corporate" quarters; sealing the deal are relatively "reasonable" prices and
a "fantastic" $14 lunch buffet.

Zabar's Cafe *Deli*

FOOD	DECOR	SERVICE	COST
19	6	11	$17

W 80s | 2245 Broadway (80th St.) | 212-787-2000 |
www.zabars.com

Acolytes "schlep" to the UWS for bagels, nova and other "affordable"
"taste-of-NY" delights at this legendary deli; sure, it's notorious for its
"grouchy" service and "crowded" space, but for the vast majority of
surveyors, it's simply "fulfilling."

Zarela *Mexican*

FOOD	DECOR	SERVICE	COST
21	16	18	$43

E 50s | 953 Second Ave. (bet. 50th & 51st Sts.) | 212-644-6740 |
www.zarela.com

Usually "packed", this Eastsider showcases Zarela Martinez's "artful"
Mexican specialties inside a "lively" bi-level space complete with
a "bustling" street-level bar; insiders warn "watch it" when it
comes to those "wicked" margaritas, or "you won't be able to climb
upstairs" to eat.

Zaytoons *Mideastern*

FOOD	DECOR	SERVICE	COST
20	13	17	$19

Carroll Gardens | 283 Smith St. (Sackett St.) | Brooklyn |
718-875-1880
Fort Greene | 472 Myrtle Ave. (bet. Hall St. & Washington Ave.) |
Brooklyn | 718-623-5522
NEW **Prospect Heights** | 594 Vanderbilt Ave. (St. Marks Pl.) | Brooklyn |
718-230-3200 ●⇗
www.zaytoonsrestaurant.com

"Straight-from-the-oven" pitas and other Mideastern specialties
make this "casual" Brooklyn trio a "favorite" standby; the setups
are "cramped" and the service "lacking", but "insanely cheap" tabs ensure they are "satisfying experiences"; N.B. Carroll Gardens and Fort
Greene are BYO.

Za Za *Italian*

FOOD	DECOR	SERVICE	COST
19	15	19	$38

E 60s | 1207 First Ave. (bet. 65th & 66th Sts.) | 212-772-9997 |
www.zazanyc.com

"Flavorful" Italian specialties, including "housemade pastas and
sauces", stand out at this "cozy" Eastsider with an "amiable" staff and
"value" prices; a somewhat "drab interior" leads many to choose the
"beautiful garden" out back.

	FOOD	DECOR	SERVICE	COST

Zebú Grill *Brazilian* | 20 | 15 | 19 | $42

E 90s | 305 E. 92nd St. (bet. 1st & 2nd Aves.) | 212-426-7500 |
www.zebugrill.com

"Brazilian standards done well" draw "young, professional" types to
this churrascaria in "quaint" UES digs; "reasonable" prices, "excellent"
caipirinhas and servers that "try hard to please" – "what a great find."

Zenkichi Ⓜ *Japanese* | ▽ 23 | 27 | 28 | $51

Williamsburg | 77 N. Sixth St. (Wythe Ave.) | Brooklyn | 718-388-8985 |
www.zenkichi.com

"If you can find the front door", prepare for a "hallucinatory but exhil-
arating experience" at this tri-level Williamsburg izakaya with "sexy"
"private alcoves" for supping on pricey, "beautifully presented" Japanese
small plates; to add a "secret-agent" vibe, you "press a button on your
table" for near-"instant" service.

Zen Palate *Vegetarian* | 19 | 14 | 17 | $28

Financial District | 104 John St. (Cliff St.) | 212-962-4208
W 40s | 663 Ninth Ave. (46th St.) | 212-582-1669
www.zenpalate.com

"Meat is missing, but not the taste" at these BYO vegetarians in Hell's
Kitchen and the Financial District offering "flavorful" tofu and vegetable dishes that "surprise" carnivores; the "brusque" staff and "not-
fancy" ambiance are offset by "generous portions" and "bargain" tabs.

NEW Zero Otto Nove Ⓜ *Italian/Pizza* | ▽ 25 | 24 | 21 | $42

Bronx | 2357 Arthur Ave. (186th St.) | 718-220-1027
Named for the area code of owner Roberto Paciullo's native Salerno,
this "bustling" new Arthur Avenue brick-oven pizzeria is a lower-
priced sibling of his nearby Roberto; it's designed to look like a back
street in Italy, with "out-of-control good" artisanal pies and "welcoming" service that "doesn't disappoint."

Zest Ⓜ *American* | ▽ 23 | 23 | 19 | $49

Staten Island | 977 Bay St. (Willow Ave.) | 718-390-8477
"City-chic on the East Shore" sums up this Staten Islander where "vibrant" French-accented New Americana complements a wine list that
"won't break the bank"; regulars say the staff "needs more training",
but given the "fantasyland patio in back", it's a "winner" all the same.

Zócalo *Mexican* | 20 | 15 | 17 | $42

E 40s | Grand Central | lower level (42nd St. & Vanderbilt Ave.) |
212-687-5666
E 80s | 174 E. 82nd St. (bet. Lexington & 3rd Aves.) | 212-717-7772
www.zocalonyc.com

A "young scene" prevails at these "high-energy", "upscale" Mexicans
in Grand Central and on the UES dishing up "zesty fare" paired with
"potent" margaritas; still, the "spotty" service and "noisy" digs make
some wonder why they're "droppin' lots of cash" here.

Zoë *American* | 19 | 19 | 18 | $53

SoHo | 90 Prince St. (bet. B'way & Mercer St.) | 212-966-6722 |
www.zoerestaurant.com

"Rest your feet" post-"shopping" at this longtime SoHo "standby" offering "dependable" New American fare (especially the "top-notch"

brunch) from an open kitchen; besides "comfortable", high-ceilinged environs, the staff is "friendly" too, but still there are grumbles about "pricey" tabs for "just-ok" experiences.

Zona Rosa ⏏ *Mexican* | 18 | 16 | 17 | $46 |

W 50s | 40 W. 56th St. (bet. 5th & 6th Aves.) | 212-247-2800 | www.zonarosarestaurant.com

"Chunky, delicious" guacamole made tableside kicks things off at this bi-level Midtown Mexican with a "dark", mirrored room downstairs and cantina upstairs; upscale prices and "tight" seating may detract, but "delicious" tequilas keep the mood "festive."

Zum Schneider ⏏ *German* | 19 | 17 | 16 | $29 |

E Village | 107 Ave. C (7th St.) | 212-598-1098 | www.zumschneider.com
"Bankers, hipsters" and "thick-accented" expats comprise the "noisy, happy" crowd at this Alphabet City German featuring "huge" steins of beer and "shockingly good brats"; it's "packed" on weekends and service can be "harried", but it's just the thing when "you're in a partying mood" and have a limited budget.

Zum Stammtisch *German* | 23 | 19 | 21 | $37 |

Glendale | 69-46 Myrtle Ave. (bet. 69th Pl. & 70th St.) | Queens | 718-386-3014 | www.zumstammtisch.com
"If you like real German food, get your heinie over" to Glendale for an "elaborate meal" in this "landmark" Bavarian-style dining room; you'll find "costumed" staffers bearing steins of beer and "huge portions" at "gentle prices"; in sum, *"sehr gut!"*

Zutto *Japanese* | 21 | 16 | 19 | $37 |

TriBeCa | 77 Hudson St. (Harrison St.) | 212-233-3287 | www.sushizutto.com
Something of a secret "hideaway", this "longtime" TriBeCa "favorite" flies under the radar with its "delicious" sushi that fans swear "has no competition in its price range"; the "quiet", "low-key" setting and "enthusiastic" service add up to an all-around "relaxing" time.

INDEXES

LOCATION MAPS

Cuisines

Includes restaurant names, locations and Food ratings.

AFGHAN

Afghan Kebab | **multi.**	19

AFRICAN

Korhogo 126 | **Carroll Gdns**	23
Les Enfants | **LES**	17
NEW Merkato 55 | **Meatpacking**	21

AMERICAN (NEW)

Abigail | **Prospect Hts**	-
Aesop's Tables | **SI**	22
Alchemy | **Park Slope**	17
Alice's Tea Cup | **multi.**	19
NEW Allen & Delancey | **LES**	24
☑ Annisa | **G Vill**	27
NEW Apiary | **E Vill**	-
applewood | **Park Slope**	25
Arabelle | **E 60s**	22
☑ Asiate | **W 60s**	24
Aspen | **Flatiron**	18
☑ Aureole | **E 60s**	27
NEW Avon Bistro | **E 50s**	-
NEW Back Forty | **E Vill**	19
Bar Americain | **W 50s**	22
barmarché | **NoLita**	19
Battery Gdns. | **Financial**	18
Beacon | **W 50s**	22
Bistro Ten 18 | **W 100s**	18
Black Duck | **Gramercy**	20
BLT Market | **W 50s**	24
☑ BLT Prime | **Gramercy**	25
☑ Blue Hill | **G Vill**	26
Blue Ribbon | **multi.**	24
Blue Ribbon Bakery | **G Vill**	24
Boathouse | **E 70s**	17
Bouchon Bakery | **W 60s**	23
NEW Brasserie 44 | **W 40s**	19
Bridge Cafe | **Financial**	21
NEW Broadway East | **LES**	21
Bull Run | **Financial**	17
Butter | **E Vill**	20
Cafe S.F.A. | **E 40s**	18
CamaJe | **G Vill**	22
Casellula | **W 50s**	21
Caviar Russe | **E 50s**	24
Chestnut | **Carroll Gdns**	24
Chop't Creative | **multi.**	19
Cibo | **E 40s**	19
Clinton St. Baking Co. | **LES**	25
NEW Commerce | **W Vill**	22
NEW Community Food | **W 100s**	23

Compass | **W 70s**	22
Cornelia St. Cafe | **G Vill**	19
Country | **Gramercy**	20
☑ Craft | **Flatiron**	26
Craftbar | **Flatiron**	21
☑ davidburke/dona. | **E 60s**	25
David Burke/Bloom. | **E 50s**	18
Deborah | **G Vill**	20
NEW Delicatessen | **NoLita**	-
Dennis Foy | **TriBeCa**	24
Devin | **TriBeCa**	18
Diner | **W'burg**	21
District | **W 40s**	20
Ditch Plains | **G Vill**	16
NEW Dovetail | **W 70s**	26
D'twn Atlantic | **Boerum Hill**	19
Dressler | **W'burg**	26
NEW Duane Park | **TriBeCa**	25
DuMont | **W'burg**	24
Eatery | **W 50s**	19
NEW eighty one | **W 80s**	26
NEW Elettaria | **G Vill**	23
elmo | **Chelsea**	16
Essex | **LES**	18
Etats-Unis | **E 80s**	24
Farm/Adderley | **Ditmas Pk**	22
57 | **E 50s**	23
5 Front | **Dumbo**	20
5 Points | **NoHo**	22
Fives | **W 50s**	23
Flatbush Farm | **Park Slope**	19
NEW Forge | **TriBeCa**	-
44/44½ | **W 40s**	22
☑ Four Seasons | **E 50s**	26
Fred's at Barneys | **E 60s**	20
Freemans | **LES**	21
☑ Garden Cafe | **Prospect Hts**	28
NEW General Greene | **Ft Greene**	-
Gilt | **E 50s**	25
Giorgio's | **Flatiron**	21
good | **W Vill**	21
☑ Gotham B&G | **G Vill**	27
☑ Gramercy Tavern | **Flatiron**	28
Greenhouse | **Bay Ridge**	18
☑ Grocery, The | **Carroll Gdns**	27
Harrison, The | **TriBeCa**	24
Hawaiian Tropic | **W 40s**	15
Hearth | **E Vill**	25
Henry's End | **Bklyn Hts**	24
Hudson Café | **Harlem**	21

Restaurant	Rating
Ici | **Ft Greene**	21
NEW Irving Mill | **Gramercy**	21
Isabella's | **W 70s**	20
Jack Horse | **Bklyn Hts**	22
NEW James | **Prospect Hts**	-
Jane | **G Vill**	21
Jimmy's 43 | **E Vill**	21
Josephina | **W 60s**	18
Kings' Carriage | **E 80s**	21
NEW Kingswood | **G Vill**	21
Klee Brass. | **Chelsea**	21
Knickerbocker | **G Vill**	19
Lady Mendl's | **Gramercy**	22
Landmark Tavern | **W 40s**	17
Lever House | **E 50s**	22
Little D | **Park Slope**	25
Little Giant | **LES**	23
Little Owl | **W Vill**	25
NEW Market Table | **G Vill**	23
Z Mas | **G Vill**	28
Melt | **Park Slope**	22
Mercer Kitchen | **SoHo**	21
Metrazur | **E 40s**	20
Z Modern, The | **W 50s**	26
Z NEW Momofuku Ko | **E Vill**	26
Momofuku Ssäm | **E Vill**	23
Morgan | **Murray Hill**	21
Morrell Wine Bar | **W 40s**	18
New Leaf | **Wash. Hts**	20
NEW Niche | **E 80s**	-
NoHo Star | **NoHo**	17
Norma's | **W 50s**	25
North Sq. | **G Vill**	22
Oceana | **E 50s**	26
NEW Olana | **Gramercy**	23
Z One if by Land | **G Vill**	24
101 | **multi.**	19
Orchard, The | **LES**	23
Z Ouest | **W 80s**	25
Park Avenue . . . | **E 60s**	24
NEW Park Room | **W 50s**	-
Patroon | **E 40s**	20
Perilla | **G Vill**	25
Z Per Se | **W 60s**	28
Philip Marie | **W Vill**	19
Picket Fence | **Ditmas Pk**	20
Place, The | **W Vill**	21
p*ong | **G Vill**	22
Pop Burger | **multi.**	18
Prune | **E Vill**	24
Quaint | **Sunnyside**	20
Quality Meats | **W 50s**	23
Red Cat | **Chelsea**	24
Redeye Grill | **W 50s**	20
NEW Redhead, The | **E Vill**	-
Regency | **E 60s**	19
Relish | **W'burg**	20
Riingo | **E 40s**	21
Z River Café | **Dumbo**	26
Riverview | **LIC**	19
Rose Water | **Park Slope**	24
Salt | **multi.**	21
Z Saul | **Boerum Hill**	27
Savoy | **SoHo**	23
Seven | **Chelsea**	19
NEW Sheridan Sq. | **W Vill**	21
NEW Smith, The | **E Vill**	19
NEW Smith's | **G Vill**	22
Solace | **E 60s**	22
NEW South Gate | **E 50s**	24
Spitzer's | **LES**	17
STK | **Meatpacking**	21
Stone Park | **Park Slope**	24
Z Tabla | **Gramercy**	25
Tailor | **SoHo**	23
Taste | **E 80s**	22
Z Telepan | **W 60s**	25
Thalia | **W 50s**	20
Thor | **LES**	17
Z Tocqueville | **Union Sq**	25
Town | **W 50s**	24
Trestle on 10th | **Chelsea**	20
Tribeca Grill | **TriBeCa**	22
12th St. B&G | **Park Slope**	20
Z Union Sq. Cafe | **Union Sq**	27
Z Veritas | **Flatiron**	26
Village | **G Vill**	19
Vynl | **multi.**	15
Water's Edge | **LIC**	22
wd-50 | **LES**	23
West Bank Cafe | **W 40s**	20
Whym | **W 50s**	20
York Grill | **E 80s**	22
Zest | **SI**	23
Zoë | **SoHo**	19

AMERICAN (TRADITIONAL)

Restaurant	Rating
Algonquin | **W 40s**	16
Alias | **LES**	21
American Girl | **E 40s**	12
Angus McIndoe | **W 40s**	17
Barking Dog | **multi.**	15
Brooklyn Diner | **multi.**	17
Brown Café | **LES**	22
Bryant Park | **W 40s**	17
Bubba Gump | **W 40s**	14

Bubby's | **multi.** — 17

Burger Shoppe | **Financial** — 18

Cafe Cluny | **W Vill** — 20

Cafeteria | **Chelsea** — 18

Chadwick's | **Bay Ridge** — 22

Coffee Shop | **Union Sq** — 15

Comfort Diner | **multi.** — 16

Cookshop | **Chelsea** — 23

Corner Bistro | **W Vill** — 22

NEW Crave | **W 40s** — 19

Dirty Bird | **W Vill** — 19

Dylan Prime | **TriBeCa** — 24

E.A.T. | **E 80s** — 19

EJ's Luncheon. | **multi.** — 16

Elaine's | **E 80s** — 12

Fairway Cafe | **multi.** — 18

Fatty's Cafe | **Astoria** — 22

Fraunces Tavern | **Financial** — 16

Friend/Farmer | **Gramercy** — 18

Good Enough/Eat | **W 80s** — 20

Hard Rock Cafe | **W 40s** — 12

Heartland | **multi.** — 14

HK | **Garment** — 17

Houston's | **multi.** — 20

Hudson Cafeteria | **W 50s** — 20

NEW Hundred Acres | **SoHo** — 18

Jackson Hole | **multi.** — 17

Joe Allen | **W 40s** — 17

Lorenzo's | **SI** — 19

Mama's Food | **E Vill** — 21

Angelo/Maxie's | **Flatiron** — 21

Moran's | **Chelsea** — 18

NEW Moxie Spot | **Bklyn Hts** — -

Odeon | **TriBeCa** — 18

O'Neals' | **W 60s** — 17

Penelope | **Murray Hill** — 21

Pershing Sq. | **E 40s** — 15

Popover Cafe | **W 80s** — 18

Rock Ctr. | **W 50s** — 18

Sarabeth's | **multi.** — 20

Shaffer's | **Flatiron** — 22

NEW Shorty's.32 | **SoHo** — 24

S'MAC/Pinch | **multi.** — 21

Square Meal | **E 90s** — 23

Swifty's | **E 70s** — 18

Tavern on Green | **W 60s** — 14

NEW T-Bar Steak | **E 70s** — 21

12 Chairs | **SoHo** — 19

21 Club | **W 50s** — 22

Walker's | **TriBeCa** — 17

Water Club | **Murray Hill** — 22

Waverly Inn | **W Vill** — 19

Westville | **multi.** — 22

ARGENTINEAN

Azul Bistro | **LES** — 23

Buenos Aires | **E Vill** — 22

Chimichurri Grill | **W 40s** — 20

Estancia | **TriBeCa** — 20

Hacienda/Argentina | **E 70s** — 18

Industria | **TriBeCa** — 19

NEW La Rural | **W 90s** — 22

NEW Lomito | **SoHo** — -

Novecento | **SoHo** — 19

NEW Pampa Grill | **W'burg** — -

Sosa Borella | **W 50s** — 17

ASIAN

Asia de Cuba | **Murray Hill** — 23

Z Asiate | **W 60s** — 24

Z Buddakan | **Chelsea** — 23

China Grill | **W 50s** — 22

Chino's | **Gramercy** — 19

Citrus B&G | **W 70s** — 19

44/44½ | **W 40s** — 22

ASIAN FUSION

Buddha Bar | **Meatpacking** — 19

Chinese Mirch | **Gramercy** — 19

Chow Bar | **W Vill** — 19

JJ's Asian Fusion | **Astoria** — 24

Nana | **Park Slope** — 20

Roy's NY | **Financial** — 24

AUSTRALIAN

Bondi Rd. | **LES** — 18

8 Mile Creek | **NoLita** — 20

NEW Kingswood | **G Vill** — 21

AUSTRIAN

Blaue Gans | **TriBeCa** — 21

NEW Café Katja | **LES** — 24

Café Sabarsky | **E 80s** — 21

Cafe Steinhof | **Park Slope** — 18

Thomas Beisl | **Ft Greene** — 18

Z Wallsé | **W Vill** — 26

BAKERIES

Amy's Bread | **multi.** — 23

Blue Ribbon Bakery | **G Vill** — 24

Bouchon Bakery | **W 60s** — 23

City Bakery | **Flatiron** — 21

Clinton St. Baking Co. | **LES** — 25

D'twn Atlantic | **Boerum Hill** — 19

Ferrara | **L Italy** — 22

La Bergamote | **multi.** — 24

La Flor Bakery | **Woodside** — 24

Le Pain Q. | **multi.** — 18

Once Upon a Tart | **SoHo** — 20

Provence/Boite | **Carroll Gdns** — 18

BARBECUE

Blue Smoke | **Gramercy**	21
Brother Jimmy | **multi.**	16
Daisy May's | **W 40s**	22
Dallas BBQ | **multi.**	14
Dinosaur BBQ | **Harlem**	22
Z Fette Sau | **W'burg**	24
Hill Country | **Chelsea**	21
Johnny Utah | **W 50s**	13
NEW Lookout Hill | **Park Slope**	-
Rack & Soul | **W 100s**	19
RUB BBQ | **Chelsea**	20
Smoke Joint | **Ft Greene**	22
Spanky's BBQ | **W 40s**	15
Virgil's BBQ | **W 40s**	20
NEW Wildwood BBQ | **Flatiron**	17

BELGIAN

B. Café | **E 70s**	22
Café de Bruxelles | **W Vill**	20
Le Pain Q. | **multi.**	18
Markt | **Flatiron**	19
Petite Abeille | **multi.**	18
Resto | **Gramercy**	20

BRAZILIAN

Cafe Colonial | **NoLita**	18
Casa | **W Vill**	24
Z Churrascaria | **multi.**	23
Circus | **E 60s**	20
Coffee Shop | **Union Sq**	15
Green Field | **Corona**	18
Malagueta | **Astoria**	23
NEW Miss Favela | **W'burg**	-
Porcão | **Gramercy**	20
Rice 'n' Beans | **W 50s**	22
SushiSamba | **multi.**	22
Via Brasil | **W 40s**	18
Zebú Grill | **E 90s**	20

BRITISH

ChipShop | **multi.**	19
Tea & Sympathy | **W Vill**	21

BURGERS

Better Burger | **multi.**	15
Big Nick's | **W 70s**	17
BLT Burger | **G Vill**	19
brgr | **Chelsea**	18
Burger Heaven | **multi.**	16
burger joint | **W 50s**	23
NEW Burger Shoppe | **Financial**	18
Corner Bistro | **W Vill**	22
Z db Bistro Moderne | **W 40s**	25
DuMont | **W'burg**	24

Five Guys | **multi.**	20
NEW 5 Napkin Burger | **W 40s**	-
goodburger | **multi.**	18
Hard Rock Cafe | **W 40s**	12
Island Burgers | **W 50s**	22
Jackson Hole | **multi.**	17
J.G. Melon | **E 70s**	21
P.J. Clarke's | **multi.**	16
Pop Burger | **multi.**	18
Rare B&G | **multi.**	21
Z Shake Shack | **Flatiron**	23
67 Burger | **Ft Greene**	21
Stand | **G Vill**	20

BURMESE

Mingala Burmese | **multi.**	19

CAJUN

Bayou | **SI**	22
NEW Bourbon St. B&G | **W 40s**	-
Bourbon St. Café | **Bayside**	18
Delta Grill | **W 40s**	19
Great Jones Cafe | **NoHo**	19
Mara's | **E Vill**	22
107 West | **multi.**	17

CALIFORNIAN

Michael's | **W 50s**	22

CAMBODIAN

NEW Cambodian Cuisine | **E 90s**	-
Kampuchea | **LES**	21

CARIBBEAN

Don Pedro's | **E 90s**	20
Ideya | **SoHo**	19
Ivo & Lulu | **SoHo**	24
Mo-Bay | **Harlem**	20

CAVIAR

Caviar Russe | **E 50s**	24
Petrossian | **W 50s**	24

CHEESE STEAKS

Carl's Steaks | **multi.**	21
99 Mi. to Philly | **E Vill**	18

CHILEAN

Pomaire | **W 40s**	22

CHINESE

(* dim sum specialist)

Amazing 66 | **Chinatown**	21
Au Mandarin | **Financial**	18
Big Wong | **Chinatown**	22
Café Evergreen* | **E 60s**	20
Chef Ho's | **E 80s**	22

Chiam | **E 40s**	22
China Fun* | **multi.**	15
Chinatown Brass.* | **NoHo**	21
Chin Chin | **E 40s**	23
Congee | **multi.**	20
Dim Sum Go Go* | **Chinatown**	21
Dumpling Man | **E Vill**	18
East Manor* | **Flushing**	19
Empire Szechuan | **multi.**	15
Evergreen* | **Murray Hill**	19
Excellent Dumpling* | **Chinatown**	19
Flor de Mayo | **multi.**	20
Fuleen | **Chinatown**	23
Golden Unicorn* | **Chinatown**	20
Grand Sichuan | **multi.**	22
HSF* | **Chinatown**	19
Jing Fong* | **Chinatown**	19
Joe's Shanghai | **multi.**	22
Joe's | **Chinatown**	20
King Yum | **Fresh Meadows**	17
Liberty View | **Financial**	19
Mandarin Court* | **Chinatown**	21
Mee Noodle | **multi.**	18
Mr. Chow | **multi.**	21
Mr. K's | **E 50s**	22
New Bo-Ky | **Chinatown**	20
Nice Green Bo | **Chinatown**	23
NoHo Star | **NoHo**	17
Ollie's | **multi.**	15
☑ Oriental Gdn.* | **Chinatown**	24
Our Place* | **multi.**	20
Pacificana* | **Sunset Pk**	21
Peking Duck | **multi.**	22
Philippe | **E 60s**	23
Phoenix Gdn. | **E 40s**	23
Pig Heaven | **E 80s**	19
Ping's Sea.* | **multi.**	21
NEW Red Egg | **L Italy**	-
Rickshaw Dumpling | **multi.**	16
Shanghai Café | **L Italy**	22
Shanghai Pavilion | **E 70s**	20
Shun Lee Cafe* | **W 60s**	20
Shun Lee Palace | **E 50s**	24
Shun Lee West | **W 60s**	22
Spicy & Tasty | **Flushing**	23
Sweet-n-Tart* | **Flushing**	19
Szechuan Gourmet | **multi.**	-
Tang Pavilion | **W 50s**	22
☑ Tse Yang | **E 50s**	24
Wakiya | **Gramercy**	19
Wo Hop | **Chinatown**	21
Wu Liang Ye | **multi.**	22
X.O.* | **multi.**	19

COFFEEHOUSES

Cafe Lalo | **W 80s**	19
Edgar's | **W 80s**	17
Edison | **W 40s**	15
Ferrara | **L Italy**	22
French Roast | **multi.**	15
Le Pain Q. | **multi.**	18
Omonia | **multi.**	18
Once Upon a Tart | **SoHo**	20

COFFEE SHOPS/DINERS

Brooklyn Diner | **multi.**	17
Burger Heaven | **multi.**	16
Clinton St. Baking Co. | **LES**	25
Comfort Diner | **multi.**	16
Diner | **W'burg**	21
Edison | **W 40s**	15
EJ's Luncheon. | **multi.**	16
Empire Diner | **Chelsea**	15
Junior's | **multi.**	17
La Taza de Oro | **Chelsea**	18
NEW R & L | **Meatpacking**	-
Teresa's | **Bklyn Hts**	19
Tom's | **Prospect Hts**	20
Veselka | **E Vill**	18
Viand | **multi.**	16

COLOMBIAN

Tierras | **multi.**	20

CONTINENTAL

Battery Gdns. | **Financial**	18
Cebu | **Bay Ridge**	21
Cole's Dock | **SI**	22
Jack's Lux. | **E Vill**	26
Lake Club | **SI**	22
NEW Luxe | **Garment**	-
NEW Park Room | **W 50s**	-
Petrossian | **W 50s**	24
Russian Samovar | **W 50s**	19
Russian Tea | **W 50s**	19
Sardi's | **W 40s**	17
View, The | **W 40s**	17

CREOLE

Bayou | **SI**	22
Delta Grill | **W 40s**	19
Mara's | **E Vill**	22

CUBAN

Asia de Cuba | **Murray Hill**	23
Cafecito | **E Vill**	21
Cafe Con Leche | **multi.**	17
Café Habana/Outpost | **multi.**	20
☑ Cuba | **G Vill**	23

Menus, photos, voting and more – free at ZAGAT.com

Cuba Cafe	**Chelsea**	20
Cubana Café	**multi.**	19
Guantanamera	**W 50s**	20
Havana Alma	**W Vill**	20
Havana Central	**multi.**	17
Son Cubano	**Meatpacking**	21
🗹 Victor's Cafe	**W 50s**	22

DELIS

Artie's Deli	**W 80s**	18
🗹 Barney Greengrass	**W 80s**	24
Ben's Kosher	**multi.**	18
Carnegie Deli	**W 50s**	21
Ess-a-Bagel	**multi.**	23
NEW Friedman's	**Chelsea**	21
🗹 Katz's Deli	**LES**	23
Lenny's	**E 50s**	18
Leo's Latticini	**Corona**	25
Liebman's	**Bronx**	20
Mill Basin Deli	**Mill Basin**	22
Pastrami Queen	**E 70s**	19
PicNic Market	**W 100s**	21
Sarge's Deli	**Murray Hill**	18
NEW 2nd Ave Deli	**Murray Hill**	22
Stage Deli	**W 50s**	19
Zabar's Cafe	**W 80s**	19

DESSERT

Cafe Lalo	**W 80s**	19
Café Sabarsky	**E 80s**	21
ChikaLicious	**E Vill**	25
Chocolate Rm.	**multi.**	25
Edgar's	**W 80s**	17
Ferrara	**L Italy**	22
Junior's	**multi.**	17
Kyotofu	**W 40s**	21
La Bergamote	**multi.**	24
Lady Mendl's	**Gramercy**	22
L & B Spumoni	**Bensonhurst**	23
Max Brenner	**multi.**	17
Omonia	**multi.**	18
Payard Bistro	**E 70s**	23
p*ong	**G Vill**	22
Serendipity 3	**E 60s**	17
Sweet Melissa	**multi.**	21
Tailor	**SoHo**	23

DOMINICAN

Cafe Con Leche	**multi.**	17
El Malecon	**multi.**	21
Hispaniola	**Wash. Hts**	20
Mamajuana	**Inwood**	21

EASTERN EUROPEAN

Sammy's	**LES**	20

ECLECTIC

🗹 Bouley Upstairs	**TriBeCa**	25
NEW Cafe Society	**Union Sq**	-
Carol's	**SI**	24
Colors	**E Vill**	18
East of 8th	**Chelsea**	17
Fatty's Cafe	**Astoria**	22
5 9th	**Meatpacking**	20
FROG	**SoHo**	19
Good Fork	**Red Hook**	25
NEW Graffiti	**E Vill**	24
Grayz	**W 50s**	23
Harry's	**Financial**	22
Hudson Cafeteria	**W 50s**	20
Josie's	**multi.**	19
Little D	**Park Slope**	25
Nook	**W 50s**	22
Public	**NoLita**	22
Punch	**Flatiron**	18
Rice	**multi.**	19
savorNY	**LES**	24
Schiller's	**LES**	18
Stanton Social	**LES**	23
Tailor	**SoHo**	23
Trinity Pl.	**Financial**	18
wd-50	**LES**	23
Whole Foods	**multi.**	18

ETHIOPIAN

Awash	**multi.**	21
Ghenet	**multi.**	21
Meskerem	**multi.**	21
Queen of Sheba	**W 40s**	23

EUROPEAN

August	**W Vill**	21
NEW Belcourt	**E Vill**	20
NEW Bobo	**W Vill**	21
🗹 Cru	**G Vill**	26
Danny Brown	**Forest Hills**	25
Don Pedro's	**E 90s**	20
Employees Only	**W Vill**	19
E.U., The	**E Vill**	18
Klee Brass.	**Chelsea**	21
Knife + Fork	**E Vill**	21
NEW Radegast Hall	**W'burg**	19
Spotted Pig	**W Vill**	22
Stella Maris	**Seaport**	20

FILIPINO

Cendrillon	**SoHo**	21
Kuma Inn	**LES**	24

FRENCH

🗹**NEW** Adour	**E 50s**	26
NEW Allegretti	**Flatiron**	-

Arabelle | **E 60s** — 22
NEW Bagatelle | **Meatpacking** — 22
Barbès | **Murray Hill** — 20
NEW Bar Blanc | **G Vill** — 23
Bistro 33 | **Astoria** — 24
Bouchon Bakery | **W 60s** — 23
Z Bouley | **TriBeCa** — 28
Breeze | **W 40s** — 21
Brick Cafe | **Astoria** — 19
Z Café Boulud | **E 70s** — 27
Z Café des Artistes | **W 60s** — 22
Café du Soleil | **W 100s** — 19
Cafe Gitane | **NoLita** — 19
Z Carlyle | **E 70s** — 22
Z Chanterelle | **TriBeCa** — 27
Chez Napoléon | **W 50s** — 21
NEW Corton | **TriBeCa** — -
Danal | **G Vill** — 20
Z Daniel | **E 60s** — 28
Darna | **W 80s** — 21
Z Degustation | **E Vill** — 27
Demarchelier | **E 80s** — 17
Django | **E 40s** — 20
Elephant, The | **E Vill** — 21
Z Eleven Madison | **Gramercy** — 27
Fives | **W 50s** — 23
Fleur de Sel | **Flatiron** — 25
Frederick's | **multi.** — 17
FROG | **SoHo** — 19
Geisha | **E 60s** — 23
Gordon Ramsay | **W 50s** — 25
Ici | **Ft Greene** — 21
Indochine | **E Vill** — 21
Ivo & Lulu | **SoHo** — 24
Jack's Lux. | **E Vill** — 26
Z Jean Georges | **W 60s** — 28
Jolie | **Boerum Hill** — 21
Kitchen Club | **NoLita** — 21
Korhogo 126 | **Carroll Gdns** — 23
La Baraka | **Little Neck** — 22
La Bergamote | **multi.** — 24
La Boîte en Bois | **W 60s** — 21
Z La Grenouille | **E 50s** — 27
La Mediterranée | **E 50s** — 19
Z L'Atelier/Robuchon | **E 50s** — 28
Z Le Bernardin | **W 50s** — 28
Z Le Cirque | **E 50s** — 24
L'Ecole | **SoHo** — 25
Le Colonial | **E 50s** — 19
Le Grainne Cafe | **Chelsea** — 19
Le Marais | **W 40s** — 20
Z Le Perigord | **E 50s** — 24
Le Refuge Inn | **Bronx** — 24

Le Rivage | **W 40s** — 20
Les Enfants | **LES** — 17
Marlow/Sons | **W'burg** — 23
Maze | **W 50s** — 25
Mercer Kitchen | **SoHo** — 21
Métisse | **W 100s** — 19
Z Modern, The | **W 50s** — 26
NEW Nizza | **W 40s** — 21
Once Upon a Tart | **SoHo** — 20
Palm Court | **W 50s** — 20
Park Terrace | **Inwood** — 20
Perry St. | **W Vill** — 26
Z Per Se | **W 60s** — 28
Petrossian | **W 50s** — 24
Z Picholine | **W 60s** — 26
PicNic Market | **W 100s** — 21
NEW R & L | **Meatpacking** — -
Safran | **Chelsea** — 21
Savann | **W 70s** — 19
718 | **Astoria** — 21
Z Terrace in Sky | **W 100s** — 23
Z Tocqueville | **Union Sq** — 25
Triomphe | **W 40s** — 24
26 Seats | **E Vill** — 21
Vong | **E 50s** — 22

FRENCH (BISTRO)

Alouette | **W 90s** — 20
A.O.C. | **multi.** — 19
Bacchus | **Boerum Hill** — 19
NEW Bar Boulud | **W 60s** — 22
Belleville | **Park Slope** — 17
NEW Benoit | **W 50s** — 18
Bistro Cassis | **W 70s** — 20
Bistro Chat Noir | **E 60s** — 19
Bistro Citron | **W 80s** — 20
Bistro du Nord | **E 90s** — 18
Bistro Les Amis | **SoHo** — 21
Bistro 61 | **E 60s** — 19
Cafe Cluny | **W Vill** — 20
Cafe Joul | **E 50s** — 18
Cafe Loup | **G Vill** — 19
Cafe Luluc | **Cobble Hill** — 20
Cafe Luxembourg | **W 70s** — 20
Cafe Un Deux | **W 40s** — 16
CamaJe | **G Vill** — 22
NEW Canaille | **Park Slope** — 23
Capsouto Frères | **TriBeCa** — 23
Casimir | **E Vill** — 20
Chez Jacqueline | **G Vill** — 20
Chez Josephine | **W 40s** — 20
Chez Oskar | **Ft Greene** — 17
Cornelia St. Cafe | **G Vill** — 19
Cosette | **Murray Hill** — 21

☑ db Bistro Moderne | **W 40s**	25
Demaré | **E 70s**	19
Deux Amis | **E 50s**	19
Félix | **SoHo**	16
Flea Mkt. Cafe | **E Vill**	19
French Roast | **multi.**	15
Gascogne | **Chelsea**	21
Gavroche | **W Vill**	17
Jarnac | **W Vill**	23
Jean Claude | **SoHo**	21
JoJo | **E 60s**	24
Jubilee | **E 50s**	22
Jules | **E Vill**	18
La Belle Vie | **Chelsea**	18
La Bonne Soupe | **W 50s**	18
La Goulue | **E 60s**	20
La Lunchonette | **Chelsea**	21
La Mangeoire | **E 50s**	19
La Mirabelle | **W 80s**	22
Landmarc | **multi.**	20
La Petite Aub. | **Gramercy**	19
La Ripaille | **W Vill**	23
Le Bilboquet | **E 60s**	22
Le Boeuf/Mode | **E 80s**	22
Le Gamin | **multi.**	19
Le Gigot | **G Vill**	24
Le Jardin | **NoLita**	19
Le Petit Marché | **Bklyn Hts**	22
Le Refuge | **E 80s**	20
Les Halles | **multi.**	19
Le Singe Vert | **Chelsea**	18
Le Veau d'Or | **E 60s**	18
L'Express | **Flatiron**	17
Loulou | **Ft Greene**	20
Lucien | **E Vill**	21
Lucky Strike | **SoHo**	16
Madison Bistro | **Murray Hill**	20
Mon Petit Cafe | **E 60s**	18
Montparnasse | **E 50s**	18
Moutarde | **Park Slope**	17
Nice Matin | **W 70s**	19
Odeon | **TriBeCa**	18
Paradou | **Meatpacking**	20
Paris Commune | **W Vill**	17
NEW Park Ave. Bistro | **Gramercy**	20
Pascalou | **E 90s**	20
Pastis | **Meatpacking**	20
Patois | **Carroll Gdns**	22
Payard Bistro | **E 70s**	23
NEW Pomme/Terre | **Ditmas Pk**	23
Provence/Boite | **Carroll Gdns**	18
Quatorze Bis | **E 70s**	21
Quercy | **Cobble Hill**	21

Raoul's | **SoHo**	23
Table d'Hôte | **E 90s**	18
Tartine | **W Vill**	22
☑ Tournesol | **LIC**	25
Tree | **E Vill**	21
Village | **G Vill**	19

FRENCH (BRASSERIE)

☑ Artisanal | **Murray Hill**	23
☑ Balthazar | **SoHo**	23
Brasserie | **E 50s**	20
NEW Brasserie Cognac | **W 50s**	19
Brasserie 8½ | **W 50s**	22
Brasserie Julien | **E 80s**	18
Brass. Ruhlmann | **W 50s**	18
Café d'Alsace | **E 80s**	20
Cercle Rouge | **TriBeCa**	19
Jacques | **multi.**	19
L'Absinthe | **E 60s**	22
Maison | **W 50s**	18
Marseille | **W 40s**	20
Metro Marché | **W 40s**	19
Orsay | **E 70s**	18
Pershing Sq. | **E 40s**	15
Pigalle | **W 40s**	17
Rue 57 | **W 50s**	18

GASTROPUB

Alchemy | Amer. | **Park Slope**	17
E.U., The | Euro. | **E Vill**	18
NEW Kingswood | Australian | **G Vill**	21
Spitzer's | Amer. | **LES**	17
Spotted Pig | Mod. Euro. | **W Vill**	22

GERMAN

Blaue Gans | **TriBeCa**	21
Hallo Berlin | **W 40s**	19
Heidelberg | **E 80s**	18
Killmeyer | **SI**	19
Nurnberger | **SI**	21
Rolf's | **Gramercy**	15
Zum Schneider | **E Vill**	19
Zum Stammtisch | **Glendale**	23

GREEK

Agnanti | **multi.**	24
Ammos | **multi.**	21
Anthos | **W 50s**	24
Avra | **E 40s**	24
Cafe Bar | **Astoria**	20
Cávo | **Astoria**	20
Eliá | **Bay Ridge**	25
Elias Corner | **Astoria**	22
Ethos | **Murray Hill**	22

Greek Kitchen | **W 50s**	20
Gus' Place | **G Vill**	19
Ithaka | **E 80s**	21
Kellari Tav./Parea | **multi.**	21
Mezzo Mezzo | **Astoria**	17
🗹 Milos | **W 50s**	27
Molyvos | **W 50s**	22
Omonia | **multi.**	18
Periyali | **Flatiron**	23
NEW Persephone | **E 60s**	22
Philoxenia | **Astoria**	21
Pylos | **E Vill**	25
S'Agapo | **Astoria**	21
Snack | **SoHo**	22
Snack Taverna | **W Vill**	22
Stamatis | **Astoria**	22
Symposium | **W 100s**	19
🗹 Taverna Kyclades | **Astoria**	25
Telly's Taverna | **Astoria**	21
Thalassa | **TriBeCa**	24
Trata Estiatorio | **E 70s**	21
Uncle Nick's | **multi.**	20

HAWAIIAN

Roy's NY | **Financial**	24

HEALTH FOOD

(See also Vegetarian)

Energy Kitchen | **multi.**	15
Josie's | **multi.**	19
Pump Energy | **multi.**	18
Whole Foods | **multi.**	18

HOT DOGS

Gray's Papaya | **multi.**	21
Papaya King | **multi.**	21
🗹 Shake Shack | **Flatiron**	23

ICE CREAM PARLORS

L & B Spumoni | **Bensonhurst**	23
Serendipity 3 | **E 60s**	17

INDIAN

Amma | **E 50s**	24
Baluchi's | **multi.**	17
Banjara | **E Vill**	22
Bay Leaf | **W 50s**	20
Bombay Palace | **W 50s**	18
Bombay Talkie | **Chelsea**	19
Brick Ln. Curry | **E Vill**	21
Bukhara Grill | **E 40s**	22
Cafe Spice | **multi.**	18
Chennai Gdn. | **Gramercy**	22
Chola | **E 50s**	23
Curry Leaf | **Gramercy**	20
Dakshin | **E 80s**	21

Darbar | **E 40s**	21
Dawat | **E 50s**	23
Delhi Palace | **Jackson Hts**	20
dévi | **Flatiron**	23
Diwan | **E 40s**	21
Earthen Oven | **W 70s**	20
Hampton Chutney | **multi.**	19
Haveli | **E Vill**	21
Indus Valley | **W 100s**	22
Jackson Diner | **Jackson Hts**	21
Jewel of India | **W 40s**	19
Kati Roll | **multi.**	22
Mint | **E 50s**	22
Mughlai | **W 70s**	19
Pongal | **multi.**	21
Salaam Bombay | **TriBeCa**	19
Sapphire | **W 60s**	21
Saravanaas | **Gramercy**	24
Surya | **W Vill**	22
Swagat Indian | **W 70s**	20
🗹 Tamarind | **Flatiron**	25
Utsav | **W 40s**	21
Yuva | **E 50s**	22

IRISH

Landmark Tavern | **W 40s**	17
Neary's | **E 50s**	14

ISRAELI

Azuri Cafe | **W 50s**	25
Hummus Pl. | **multi.**	23
Miriam | **multi.**	21
Rectangles | **E 70s**	17

ITALIAN

(N=Northern; S=Southern)

Abboccato | **W 50s**	21
Acappella | N | **TriBeCa**	24
Accademia/Vino | **E 60s**	20
Acqua | S | **W 90s**	18
Acqua/Peck Slip | **Seaport**	19
NEW Ago | N | **TriBeCa**	17
Alberto | **Forest Hills**	22
🗹 Al Di La | N | **Park Slope**	26
Aleo | **Flatiron**	19
Al Forno Pizza | **E 70s**	20
Alfredo of Rome | S | **W 40s**	18
Alto | N | **E 50s**	25
Ama | S | **SoHo**	23
Amarone | **W 40s**	18
Amorina | **Prospect Hts**	24
Angelina's | **SI**	23
Angelo's/Mulberry | S | **L Italy**	23
Angelo's Pizza | **multi.**	19
Anthony's | S | **Park Slope**	19

Menus, photos, voting and more – free at ZAGAT.com

CUISINES

Antica Venezia | **W Vill**	22
Antonucci | **E 80s**	21
ápizz | **LES**	24
Areo | **Bay Ridge**	25
Arno | N | **Garment**	20
Aroma | **NoHo**	24
Arqua | N | **TriBeCa**	22
Arté | N | **G Vill**	17
Arté Café | **W 70s**	18
Arturo's | **G Vill**	21
Aurora | **multi.**	25
A Voce | **Gramercy**	25
☑ Babbo | **G Vill**	27
Baci/Abbracci | **W'burg**	22
Baldoria | **W 40s**	21
Bamonte's | **W'burg**	22
Baraonda | **E 70s**	18
Barbetta | N | **W 40s**	20
NEW Bar Blanc | **G Vill**	23
Barbone | **E Vill**	23
Barbuto | **W Vill**	21
NEW Bar Milano | N | **Gramercy**	22
Barolo | **SoHo**	19
Bar Pitti | **G Vill**	22
Bar Stuzz. | S | **Flatiron**	20
Basilica | N | **W 40s**	20
Basso56 | S | **W 50s**	21
Basta Pasta | **Flatiron**	22
☑ Becco | **W 40s**	23
Beccofino | **Bronx**	21
Bella Blu | N | **E 70s**	20
Bella Via | **LIC**	21
Bellavitae | **G Vill**	23
NEW Bellini | **W 80s**	18
Bello | **W 50s**	20
Beppe | N | **Flatiron**	22
Bettola | **W 70s**	20
Bianca | N | **NoHo**	23
Bice | N | **E 50s**	20
Biricchino | N | **Chelsea**	19
Bocca Lupo | **Cobble Hill**	23
Bocelli | **SI**	25
Bond 45 | **W 40s**	19
Borgo Antico | **G Vill**	17
Bottega/Vino | **E 50s**	21
Bottino | N | **Chelsea**	19
Bravo Gianni | N | **E 60s**	21
Bread | **TriBeCa**	19
Bricco | **W 50s**	19
Brick Cafe | **Astoria**	19
Brio | **multi.**	18
Brioso | **SI**	24
Cacio e Pepe | S | **E Vill**	21
Cacio e Vino | S | **E Vill**	21
Cafe Fiorello | **W 60s**	20
Caffe Bondi | S | **SI**	19
Caffe Buon Gusto | **multi.**	17
Caffe Cielo | N | **W 50s**	19
Caffe Grazie | **E 80s**	18
Caffe Linda | **E 40s**	19
Caffé/Green | **Bayside**	21
Campagnola | **E 70s**	24
NEW Campo | **W 100s**	18
Canaletto | N | **E 60s**	21
Cara Mia | **W 40s**	19
Carino | S | **E 80s**	20
☑ Carmine's | S | **multi.**	20
Cascina | **W 40s**	19
Celeste | S | **W 80s**	24
Cellini | N | **E 50s**	21
Centolire | N | **E 80s**	21
Centovini | **SoHo**	20
Centro Vinoteca | **W Vill**	22
'Cesca | S | **W 70s**	23
Chianti | **Bay Ridge**	21
Cibo | N | **E 40s**	19
Cipriani Dolci | **E 40s**	19
Cipriani D'twn | **SoHo**	20
NEW Convivio | S | **E 40s**	-
Coppola's | **multi.**	19
NEW Covo | **Harlem**	24
Crispo | N | **W Vill**	23
Cucina/Pesce | **E Vill**	18
Da Andrea | N | **W Vill**	23
Da Ciro | **Murray Hill**	22
Da Filippo | N | **E 60s**	21
Da Nico | **L Italy**	21
Da Noi | N | **SI**	23
Da Silvana | **Forest Hills**	22
Da Silvano | N | **G Vill**	21
Da Tommaso | N | **W 50s**	19
Da Umberto | N | **Chelsea**	25
Dean's | **multi.**	17
DeGrezia | **E 50s**	22
NEW dell'anima | **W Vill**	24
☑ Del Posto | **Chelsea**	26
Destino | **E 50s**	20
Divino | N | **E 80s**	18
Dominick's | **Bronx**	23
Don Giovanni | **multi.**	17
Don Peppe | **Ozone Pk**	25
Due | N | **E 70s**	21
Ecco | **TriBeCa**	22
Elaine's | **E 80s**	12
Elementi | **Park Slope**	18
Elio's | **E 80s**	23

Ennio/Michael | G Vill	21
Enzo's | Bronx	23
Erminia | S | E 80s	25
Esca | S | W 40s	25
Estancia | TriBeCa	20
etc. etc. | W 40s	21
Fabio Piccolo | E 40s	22
Falai | multi.	24
F & J Pine | Bronx	21
🅩 Felidia | E 50s	26
Fiamma | SoHo	24
Filippo's | SI	26
F.illi Ponte | TriBeCa	22
Finestra | E 70s	17
Fino | N | multi.	19
Fiorentino's | S | Gravesend	20
Fiorini | S | E 50s	20
Firenze | N | E 80s	21
Forlini's | N | Chinatown	19
Fragole | Carroll Gdns	22
Frank | E Vill	23
Frankies | multi.	24
Franny's | Prospect Hts	25
Fratelli | Bronx	21
Fred's at Barneys | N | E 60s	20
Fresco | N | multi.	23
Gabriel's | N | W 60s	22
Gargiulo's | S | Coney Is	22
Gemma | E Vill	19
Gennaro | W 90s	24
Giambelli | E 50s	22
Gigino | multi.	20
Gino | E 60s	19
Giorgione | SoHo	22
Giovanni | N | E 80s	22
Girasole | E 80s	21
Gnocco Caffe | N | E Vill	22
Gonzo | G Vill	20
Grace's Tratt. | E 70s	19
Gradisca | G Vill	21
Grand Tier | W 60s	19
Grano Tratt. | G Vill	23
Grifone | N | E 40s	23
Grotta Azzurra | S | L Italy	19
Gusto | G Vill	22
Harry Cipriani | N | E 50s	19
Hearth | N | E Vill	25
I Coppi | N | E Vill	22
Il Bagatto | E Vill	23
Il Bastardo | N | Chelsea	19
Il Buco | NoHo	24
Il Cantinori | N | G Vill	22
Il Corallo | SoHo	22

Il Cortile | L Italy	23
Il Fornaio | L Italy	22
Il Gattopardo | S | W 50s	23
Il Giglio | N | TriBeCa	25
Il Menestrello | N | E 50s	21
🅩 Il Mulino | G Vill	27
Il Nido | N | E 50s	23
Il Palazzo | L Italy	22
NEW Il Passatore | W'burg	25
Il Postino | E 40s	23
Il Riccio | S | E 70s	20
Il Tinello | N | W 50s	24
Il Vagabondo | E 60s	18
Il Valentino | N | E 50s	18
'ino | G Vill	24
'inoteca | LES	23
Insieme | W 50s	24
Intermezzo | Chelsea	17
NEW I Sodi | W Vill	21
Italianissimo | E 80s	24
I Tre Merli | N | multi.	17
I Trulli | Gramercy	23
Joe & Pat's | SI	22
John's/12th St. | E Vill	19
La Bottega | Chelsea	16
La Cantina Toscana | N | E 60s	24
La Focaccia | W Vill	20
La Giara | Murray Hill	19
La Gioconda | E 50s	20
La Grolla | N | W 70s	19
La Houppa | N | E 60s	18
La Lanterna | G Vill	19
La Masseria | S | W 40s	22
La Mela | S | L Italy	19
L & B Spumoni | Bensonhurst	23
La Pizza Fresca | Flatiron	22
La Rivista | N | W 40s	21
Lattanzi | S | W 40s	22
Lavagna | E Vill	25
La Vela | N | W 70s	18
La Villa Pizzeria | multi.	21
Leo's Latticini | Corona	25
Le Zie 2000 | N | Chelsea	21
Libretto's Pizza | Murray Hill	21
Lil' Frankie Pizza | E Vill	22
Lisca | N | W 90s	19
Locale Café & Bar | Astoria	20
Locanda Vini | N | Clinton Hill	25
NEW Lomito | SoHo	-
Lumi | E 70s	18
Luna Piena | E 50s	18
Lunetta | multi.	21
🅩 Lupa | S | G Vill	25

Lusardi's | N | E 70s	23	Patricia's | Bronx	24
NEW Luxe | Garment	-	Patsy's | S | W 50s	21
Luzzo's | S | E Vill	24	Peasant | NoLita	24
Macelleria | N | Meatpacking	19	Pellegrino's | L Italy	24
Madison's | Bronx	21	Pepe | multi.	21
Malatesta | N | W Vill	23	Pepolino | N | TriBeCa	25
Manducatis | LIC	22	Perbacco | E Vill	25
Manetta's | LIC	22	Per Lei | E 70s	19
Marco Polo | Carroll Gdns	20	Pescatore | E 50s	18
Maria Pia | W 50s	19	Petaluma | E 70s	18
Marinella | G Vill	21	Pete's D'town | Dumbo	18
Mario's | S | Bronx	22	Piadina | G Vill	19
Maruzzella | N | E 70s	22	Piano Due | W 50s	25
NEW Matilda | N | E Vill	18	Piccola Venezia | Astoria	25
Max | S | multi.	22	Piccolo Angolo | W Vill	25
Mediterraneo | E 60s	18	Pietrasanta | W 40s	18
Mezzaluna | E 70s	20	Pietro's | E 40s	24
Mezzogiorno | N | SoHo	20	Pinocchio | E 90s	21
NEW Mia Dona | E 50s	21	Piola | G Vill	19
Moda | S | W 50s	19	Pisticci | S | W 100s	24
Morandi | G Vill	21	Pó | multi.	24
Nanni | N | E 40s	24	Pomodoro Rosso | W 70s	22
Naples 45 | S | E 40s	17	Ponticello | N | Astoria	23
Natsumi | W 50s	22	Portofino | Bronx	20
Nello | N | E 60s	18	Portofino Grille | E 60s	19
Nero | Meatpacking	19	Positano | S | L Italy	22
Nick's | multi.	23	Primavera | N | E 80s	23
Nicola's | E 80s	22	Primitivo | S | W Vill	19
Nino's | N | multi.	21	Primola | E 60s	23
NEW Nizza | W 40s	20	Puttanesca | W 50s	19
Nocello | N | W 50s	20	Quattro Gatti | E 80s	19
Nonna | W 80s	18	Queen | Bklyn Hts	24
Noodle Pudding | Bklyn Hts	24	Z Rainbow Room | N | W 40s	20
Notaro | N | Murray Hill	18	Rao's | S | Harlem	23
Novitá | N | Gramercy	24	Remi | W 50s	22
NEW 1 Dominick | N | SoHo	-	Re Sette | W 40s	21
One 83 | N | E 80s	20	Risotteria | G Vill	20
101 | multi.	19	NEW Roberta's | Bushwick	-
Orso | W 40s	23	Z Roberto | Bronx	26
Osso Buco | multi.	17	Roberto Passon | W 50s	22
Osteria al Doge | N | W 40s	20	Roc | TriBeCa	21
Osteria del Circo | N | W 50s	22	Rossini's | N | Murray Hill	23
Osteria Gelsi | S | Garment	22	Rughetta | S | E 80s	22
Osteria Laguna | E 40s	21	Sac's Place | Astoria	20
Otto | G Vill	23	Sal Anthony's | S | multi.	19
NEW Padre Figlio | E 40s	-	Salute! | Murray Hill	19
Palma | S | G Vill	23	Sambuca | W 70s	18
Panarea | S | SI	23	Sandro's | E 80s	23
Pappardella | W 70s	19	San Pietro | S | E 50s	24
Park Side | Corona	24	Sant Ambroeus | N | multi.	21
Parma | N | E 70s	20	Sapori D'Ischia | Woodside	25
Pasquale's | Bronx	21	Savoia | Carroll Gdns	20
Pasticcio | multi.	18	Scaletta | N | W 70s	21

CUISINES

Scalinatella | E 60s | 26
Z Scalini Fedeli | N | TriBeCa | 27
Scarlatto | N | W 40s | 20
NEW Scarpetta | Chelsea | 26
Scottadito | N | Park Slope | 19
Serafina | multi. | 19
Sette Enoteca | S | Park Slope | 19
Sette Mezzo | E 70s | 23
Sfoglia | N | E 90s | 24
Shelly's Tradizionale | W 50s | 19
Sistina | N | E 80s | 24
Sosa Borella | W 50s | 17
Sottovoce | Park Slope | 19
Spiga | W 80s | 22
Spigolo | E 80s | 25
Stella del Mare | N | Murray Hill | 23
Supper | N | E Vill | 25
Tarallucci | multi. | 21
Teodora | N | E 50s | 20
Tevere | E 80s | 23
Tiramisu | E 80s | 19
Tommaso | Dyker Hts | 24
Tony's Di Napoli | S | multi. | 19
Tosca Café | Bronx | 20
Tratt. Alba | N | Murray Hill | 22
Tratt. Dell'Arte | N | W 50s | 22
Z Tratt. L'incontro | Astoria | 27
Tratt. Pesce | multi. | 18
Tratt. Romana | SI | 25
Trattoria Trecolori | W 40s | 21
NEW Tre | LES | 22
tre dici | Chelsea | 22
Triangolo | E 80s | 21
Tuscany Grill | N | Bay Ridge | 24
Umberto's | multi. | 19
Uva | E 70s | 21
Valbella | N | Meatpacking | 24
V&T | W 100s | 18
Vento | Meatpacking | 19
Vespa | E 80s | 19
Via Emilia | N | Flatiron | 21
Via Oreto | E 60s | 20
Via Quadronno | N | E 70s | 21
ViceVersa | W 50s | 22
NEW Vicino Firenze | E 80s | -
Vico | E 90s | 20
Villa Berulia | N | Murray Hill | 21
Villa Mosconi | G Vill | 21
Vincent's | L Italy | 21
Vivolo | E 70s | 19
WaterFalls | SI | 20
Za Za | N | E 60s | 19
NEW Zero Otto | S | Bronx | 25

JAMAICAN

Maroons | Chelsea | 21
Negril | multi. | 20

JAPANESE

(* sushi specialist)

Aburiya Kinnosuke | E 40s | 25
Aki | G Vill | 26
Arirang Hibachi | multi. | 20
Asiakan* | W 90s | 19
Benihana | W 50s | 17
Bistro 33 | Astoria | 24
Blue Ginger | Chelsea | 20
Z Blue Ribbon Sushi* | multi. | 26
NEW Blue Ribbon Sushi B&G | W 50s | 24
Bond St.* | NoHo | 24
Butai | Gramercy | 21
NEW Cho Cho San* | G Vill | -
Cube 63 | multi. | 22
Dae Dong | Bayside | 18
Donguri | E 80s | 27
EN Japanese | W Vill | 23
15 East* | Union Sq | 26
Fushimi* | multi. | 25
Z Gari/Sushi* | multi. | 26
Geisha | E 60s | 23
NEW Greenwich Grill* | TriBeCa | -
Gyu-Kaku | multi. | 22
Haru* | multi. | 21
Hasaki* | E Vill | 22
Hatsuhana* | E 40s | 24
Hibino* | Cobble Hill | 26
Ichiro* | E 80s | 21
Inagiku* | E 40s | 22
NEW Ippudo | E Vill | 25
Iron Sushi* | multi. | 19
Ise* | multi. | 21
Japonais | Gramercy | 20
Japonica* | G Vill | 22
Jewel Bako* | E Vill | 25
Kai | E 60s | 25
Kanoyama* | E Vill | 26
Katsu-Hama | E 40s | 22
Ki Sushi* | Boerum Hill | 26
Kitchen Club | NoLita | 21
Kodama* | W 40s | 19
Koi* | W 40s | 24
Ko Sushi* | multi. | 20
NEW Kouzan* | W 90s | 20
Kuruma Zushi* | E 40s | 28
Kyotofu | W 40s | 21
Kyo Ya | E Vill | 29
Lan* | E Vill | 25

☑ Masa/Bar Masa* | **W 60s**	27
NEW Matsugen | **TriBeCa**	21
Matsuri* | **Chelsea**	23
Megu | **multi.**	24
Menchanko-tei | **multi.**	20
Minca | **E Vill**	22
Mishima* | **Murray Hill**	22
Mizu Sushi* | **Flatiron**	23
Momoya* | **multi.**	22
Monster Sushi* | **multi.**	17
Morimoto | **Chelsea**	25
Natsumi | **W 50s**	22
Nëo Sushi* | **W 80s**	23
Ninja | **TriBeCa**	16
Nippon* | **E 50s**	22
☑ Nobu* | **TriBeCa**	27
☑ Nobu 57* | **W 50s**	26
Omen | **SoHo**	23
Omido* | **W 50s**	24
Ono* | **Meatpacking**	19
Planet Thai | **multi.**	18
Poke* | **E 80s**	26
Rai Rai Ken | **E Vill**	21
Ramen Setagaya | **E Vill**	20
Riingo | **E 40s**	21
Roppongi* | **W 80s**	21
Rosanjin | **TriBeCa**	27
Sakagura | **E 40s**	25
Sapporo East* | **E Vill**	21
☑ Sasabune* | **E 70s**	27
Seo* | **E 40s**	23
Shabu-Shabu 70* | **E 70s**	20
Shinbashi | **E 40s**	20
Soba-ya | **E Vill**	23
☑ Soto* | **G Vill**	26
☑ Sugiyama | **W 50s**	27
SushiAnn* | **E 50s**	24
Sushiden* | **multi.**	24
Sushi Hana* | **multi.**	21
SushiSamba* | **multi.**	22
☑ Sushi Seki* | **E 60s**	27
Sushi Sen-nin* | **Murray Hill**	24
Sushiya* | **W 50s**	19
☑ Sushi Yasuda* | **E 40s**	28
Sushi Zen* | **W 40s**	25
Suteishi* | **Seaport**	22
Takahachi* | **multi.**	23
Tenzan* | **multi.**	23
Todai | **Murray Hill**	17
Tokyo Pop* | **W 100s**	18
Tomoe Sushi* | **G Vill**	25
Tomo Sushi* | **W 100s**	18
Ushiwakamaru* | **G Vill**	27

Wasabi Lobby* | **E 80s**	21
Watawa* | **Astoria**	25
☑ Yakitori Totto | **W 50s**	26
Yama* | **multi.**	23
Yuka* | **E 80s**	21
Yuki Sushi* | **W 90s**	21
Zenkichi | **W'burg**	23
Zutto* | **TriBeCa**	21

JEWISH

Artie's Deli | **W 80s**	18
☑ Barney Greengrass | **W 80s**	24
Ben's Kosher | **multi.**	18
Carnegie Deli | **W 50s**	21
Edison | **W 40s**	15
NEW Friedman's | **Chelsea**	21
☑ Katz's Deli | **LES**	23
Lattanzi | **W 40s**	22
Liebman's | **Bronx**	20
Mill Basin Deli | **Mill Basin**	22
Pastrami Queen | **E 70s**	19
Sammy's | **LES**	20
Sarge's Deli | **Murray Hill**	18
NEW 2nd Ave Deli | **Murray Hill**	22
Stage Deli | **W 50s**	19

KOREAN

(* barbecue specialist)

Bann | **W 50s**	24
Cho Dang Gol* | **Garment**	23
Dae Dong* | **Bayside**	18
Do Hwa* | **G Vill**	21
Dok Suni's | **E Vill**	22
Franchia | **Murray Hill**	19
Gahm Mi Oak | **Garment**	20
☑ Hangawi | **Murray Hill**	24
Kang Suh* | **Garment**	21
Korea Palace* | **E 50s**	18
Kum Gang San* | **multi.**	21
Mandoo Bar | **Garment**	20
Mill Korean | **W 100s**	18
Moim | **Park Slope**	24
Momofuku Ssäm | **E Vill**	23
NEW Persimmon | **E Vill**	-
Woo Lae Oak* | **SoHo**	22

KOSHER

Abigael's | **Garment**	19
Azuri Cafe | **W 50s**	25
Ben's Kosher | **multi.**	18
Caravan/Dreams | **E Vill**	20
Chennai Gdn. | **Gramercy**	22
Darna | **W 80s**	21
NEW Friedman's | **Chelsea**	21
Le Marais | **W 40s**	20

Levana | **W 60s**	20
Liebman's | **Bronx**	20
Mill Basin Deli | **Mill Basin**	22
Pastrami Queen | **E 70s**	19
Pongal | **multi.**	21
Prime Grill | **E 40s**	22
Rectangles | **E 70s**	17
NEW 2nd Ave Deli | **Murray Hill**	22
Solo | **E 50s**	22
Tevere | **E 80s**	23

LEBANESE

Al Bustan | **E 50s**	19
NEW ilili | **Gramercy**	23

MALAYSIAN

Fatty Crab | **W Vill**	21
Nyonya | **multi.**	22

MEDITERRANEAN

Aesop's Tables | **SI**	22
Aleo | **Flatiron**	19
Alta | **G Vill**	23
Amalia | **W 50s**	21
Amaranth | **E 60s**	18
Ammos | **multi.**	21
Barbounia | **Flatiron**	20
Beast | **Prospect Hts**	22
Bello Sguardo | **W 70s**	19
Bodrum | **W 80s**	20
Cafe Bar | **Astoria**	20
Cafe Centro | **E 40s**	19
Café du Soleil | **W 100s**	19
Cafe Ronda | **W 70s**	19
Conviv. Osteria | **Park Slope**	25
Danal | **G Vill**	20
Dee's Pizza | **Forest Hills**	22
Django | **E 40s**	20
Epices/Traiteur | **W 70s**	21
Extra Virgin | **W Vill**	21
Fig & Olive | **multi.**	20
5 Points | **NoHo**	22
Frederick's | **multi.**	17
NEW Greenwich Grill | **TriBeCa**	-
Gus' Place | **G Vill**	19
House | **Gramercy**	20
Il Buco | **NoHo**	24
NEW ilili | **Gramercy**	23
Isabella's | **W 70s**	20
Jarnac | **W Vill**	23
Levana | **W 60s**	20
Little Owl | **W Vill**	25
NEW Lokal | **Greenpt**	22
Mangia | **multi.**	19

Marseille | **W 40s**	20
Miriam | **multi.**	21
Moda | **W 50s**	19
Nice Matin | **W 70s**	19
Nick & Toni's | **W 60s**	17
Olea | **Ft Greene**	23
Olives | **Union Sq**	22
Palma | **G Vill**	23
Park, The | **Chelsea**	15
Pera | **E 40s**	22
☑ Picholine | **W 60s**	26
Place, The | **W Vill**	21
Red Cat | **Chelsea**	24
Savann | **W 70s**	19
Savoy | **SoHo**	23
Sezz Medi' | **W 100s**	20
Sharz Cafe | **E 80s**	19
Solo | **E 50s**	22
Superfine | **Dumbo**	19
☑ Taboon | **W 50s**	25
Taci's Beyti | **Midwood**	23
☑ Tanoreen | **Bay Ridge**	26
Tempo | **Park Slope**	24
☑ Terrace in Sky | **W 100s**	23
202 Cafe | **Chelsea**	19

MEXICAN

Alma | **Carroll Gdns**	20
NEW Barrio | **Park Slope**	19
Blockhead Burrito | **multi.**	16
Bonita | **multi.**	19
NEW Cabrito | **G Vill**	-
Café Frida | **W 70s**	20
Café Habana/Outpost | **multi.**	20
Centrico | **TriBeCa**	19
Chiles/Chocolate | **Park Slope**	18
Chipotle | **multi.**	18
Crema | **Chelsea**	22
Dos Caminos | **multi.**	20
El Centro | **W 50s**	20
El Parador Cafe | **Murray Hill**	22
El Paso Taqueria | **multi.**	22
Gabriela's | **W 90s**	18
Hell's Kitchen | **W 40s**	23
Itzocan | **multi.**	24
La Esquina | **L Italy**	22
La Flor Bakery | **Woodside**	24
La Palapa | **multi.**	19
La Taqueria/Rachel | **Park Slope**	20
Los Dados | **Meatpacking**	19
NEW Mad Dog | **Financial**	19
Mamá Mexico | **multi.**	19
Maria's | **Park Slope**	19
NEW Matilda | **E Vill**	18

Maya	**E 60s**	24
Maz Mezcal	**E 80s**	21
Mercadito	**multi.**	23
Mexicana Mama	**multi.**	24
Mexican Radio	**NoLita**	18
Mi Cocina	**W Vill**	21
Noche Mex.	**W 100s**	23
Pampano	**E 40s**	24
Papatzul	**SoHo**	23
Rocking Horse	**Chelsea**	21
🆕 Rosa Mexicano	**multi.**	21
Sueños	**Chelsea**	22
Tio Pepe	**G Vill**	18
Toloache	**W 50s**	23
Zarela	**E 50s**	21
Zócalo	**multi.**	20
Zona Rosa	**W 50s**	18

MIDDLE EASTERN

🆕 Gazala Place	**W 40s**	25
Moustache	**multi.**	21
🆕 Taboon	**W 50s**	25
🆕 Tanoreen	**Bay Ridge**	26
12 Chairs	**SoHo**	19
Zaytoons	**multi.**	20

MOROCCAN

Barbès	**Murray Hill**	20
Cafe Gitane	**NoLita**	19
Cafe Mogador	**E Vill**	21
Darna	**W 80s**	21
Park Terrace	**Inwood**	20

NEW ENGLAND

Black Pearl	**Chelsea**	18
Ed's Lobster	**NoLita**	23
🆕 Pearl Oyster	**G Vill**	26

NOODLE SHOPS

Bao Noodles	**Gramercy**	18
Donguri	**E 80s**	27
Great NY Noodle	**Chinatown**	22
🆕 Ippudo	**E Vill**	25
Kampuchea	**LES**	21
🆕 Matsugen	**TriBeCa**	21
Mee Noodle	**multi.**	18
Menchanko-tei |-**multi.**	20
Minca	**E Vill**	22
🆕 Momofuku Noodle	**E Vill**	23
New Bo-Ky	**Chinatown**	20
Pho Bang	**multi.**	20
Pho Pasteur	**Chinatown**	19
Pho Viet Huong	**Chinatown**	22
Rai Rai Ken	**E Vill**	21
Ramen Setagaya	**E Vill**	20

Republic	**Union Sq**	18
Soba-ya	**E Vill**	23

NORTH AFRICAN

Nomad	**E Vill**	20

NUEVO LATINO

Cabana	**multi.**	21
Calle Ocho	**W 80s**	22
Citrus B&G	**W 70s**	19
Esperanto	**E Vill**	20
Luz	**Ft Greene**	24
Mamajuana	**Inwood**	21
Paladar	**LES**	19

PAN-ASIAN

Abigael's	**Garment**	19
Aja	**multi.**	20
Amber	**multi.**	20
Aquamarine	**Murray Hill**	20
Asiakan	**W 90s**	19
🆕 bar Q	**W Vill**	20
bluechili	**W 50s**	20
Blue Ginger	**Chelsea**	20
Cendrillon	**SoHo**	21
Chance	**Boerum Hill**	20
🆕 Chop Suey	**W 40s**	15
🆕 Moxie Spot	**Bklyn Hts**	-
Republic	**Union Sq**	18
Ruby Foo's	**multi.**	19
🆕 Tao	**E 50s**	22

PAN-LATIN

Boca Chica	**E Vill**	20
Bogota	**Park Slope**	20
Lucy	**Flatiron**	20
Palo Santo	**Park Slope**	22
Rayuela	**LES**	23
🆕 Talay	**Harlem**	-
🆕 Yerba Buena	**E Vill**	-
Yuca Bar	**E Vill**	21

PERSIAN

Persepolis	**E 70s**	21
🆕 Shalizar	**E 80s**	-

PERUVIAN

Chimu	**W'burg**	23
Coco Roco	**multi.**	21
Flor de Mayo	**multi.**	20
Lima's Taste	**W Vill**	21
Mancora	**E Vill**	22
🆕 Nobu	**TriBeCa**	27
🆕 Nobu 57	**W 50s**	26
Pio Pio	**multi.**	22
🆕 Red Egg	**L Italy**	-

CUISINES

PIZZA

Adrienne's | **Financial**	24
Al Forno Pizza | **E 70s**	20
Amorina | **Prospect Hts**	24
Angelo's Pizza | **multi.**	19
Anthony's | **Park Slope**	19
ápizz | **LES**	24
🆕 Artichoke Basille | **E Vill**	24
Arturo's | **G Vill**	21
Baci/Abbracci | **W'burg**	22
Bella Blu | **E 70s**	20
Bella Via | **LIC**	21
Bettola | **W 70s**	20
Cacio e Vino | **E Vill**	21
Cafe Fiorello | **W 60s**	20
Coals | **Bronx**	23
🆕 Covo | **Harlem**	24
Da Ciro | **Murray Hill**	22
Dean's | **multi.**	17
Dee's Pizza | **Forest Hills**	22
Denino's | **SI**	25
☑ Di Fara | **Midwood**	27
Don Giovanni | **multi.**	17
Fornino | **W'burg**	23
Franny's | **Prospect Hts**	25
Gigino | **multi.**	20
Gonzo | **G Vill**	20
Grimaldi's | **Dumbo**	25
Joe & Pat's | **SI**	22
Joe's Pizza | **multi.**	23
John's Pizzeria | **multi.**	22
La Bottega | **Chelsea**	16
L & B Spumoni | **Bensonhurst**	23
La Pizza Fresca | **Flatiron**	22
La Villa Pizzeria | **multi.**	21
Lil' Frankie Pizza | **E Vill**	22
Lombardi's | **NoLita**	24
☑ Lucali | **Carroll Gdns**	27
Luzzo's | **E Vill**	24
Mediterraneo | **E 60s**	18
Mezzaluna | **E 70s**	20
Naples 45 | **E 40s**	17
Nick's | **multi.**	23
Nino's | **E 40s**	21
Otto | **G Vill**	23
Patsy's Pizzeria | **multi.**	20
Pintaile's Pizza | **multi.**	19
Pizza Gruppo | **E Vill**	24
Pizza 33 | **multi.**	21
Posto | **Gramercy**	23
🆕 Roberta's | **Bushwick**	-
Sac's Place | **Astoria**	20
Savoia | **Carroll Gdns**	20

Sezz Medi' | **W 100s**	20
S'MAC/Pinch | **W 80s**	21
Tiramisu | **E 80s**	19
Totonno Pizza | **multi.**	21
Two Boots | **multi.**	19
Una Pizza | **E Vill**	23
V&T | **W 100s**	18
Vezzo | **Murray Hill**	23
Waldy's Pizza | **Chelsea**	22
🆕 Zero Otto | **Bronx**	25

POLISH

Teresa's | **Bklyn Hts**	19

POLYNESIAN

King Yum | **Fresh Meadows**	17

PORTUGUESE

Alfama | **W Vill**	21

PUB FOOD

Elephant & Castle | **G Vill**	18
Heartland | **multi.**	14
J.G. Melon | **E 70s**	21
Landmark Tavern | **W 40s**	17
Neary's | **E 50s**	14
Pete's Tavern | **Gramercy**	13
P.J. Clarke's | **multi.**	16
Walker's | **TriBeCa**	17

PUERTO RICAN

La Taza de Oro | **Chelsea**	18
Sofrito | **E 50s**	21

RUSSIAN

FireBird | **W 40s**	19
Russian Samovar | **W 50s**	19
Russian Tea | **W 50s**	19

SANDWICHES

Amy's Bread | **multi.**	23
☑ Barney Greengrass | **W 80s**	24
Bôi | **E 40s**	19
Bouchon Bakery | **W 60s**	23
Bread | **NoLita**	19
Brennan | **Sheepshead**	20
Chop't Creative | **multi.**	19
Così | **multi.**	16
Dishes | **multi.**	21
DuMont | **W'burg**	24
E.A.T. | **E 80s**	19
Ess-a-Bagel | **multi.**	23
Hale/Hearty | **multi.**	19
☑ Katz's Deli | **LES**	23
Lenny's | **multi.**	18
Liebman's | **Bronx**	20

Mangia | multi.	19
Nicky's | multi.	22
Pastrami Queen | E 70s	19
Peanut Butter Co. | G Vill	19
Press 195 | multi.	22
Roll-n-Roaster | Sheepshead	19
Sarge's Deli | Murray Hill	18
NEW 2nd Ave Deli | Murray Hill	22
67 Burger | Ft Greene	21
Stage Deli | W 50s	19
Sweet Melissa | multi.	21
'wichcraft | multi.	20
Zabar's Cafe | W 80s	19

SCANDINAVIAN

AQ Cafe | Murray Hill	22
Z Aquavit | E 50s	25
Smorgas Chef | multi.	19

SEAFOOD

Ammos | multi.	21
Z Aquagrill | SoHo	26
Artie's | Bronx	23
Atlantic Grill | E 70s	23
Avra | E 40s	24
Black Duck | Gramercy	20
Black Pearl | Chelsea	18
BLT Fish | Flatiron	23
Blue Fin | W 40s	21
Z Blue Water | Union Sq	23
Brooklyn Fish | Park Slope	22
Bubba Gump | W 40s	14
Christos | Astoria	24
City Crab | Flatiron	17
City Hall | TriBeCa	20
City Is. Lobster | Bronx	20
City Lobster | W 40s	18
Cole's Dock | SI	22
Ditch Plains | G Vill	16
Docks Oyster | multi.	19
Ed's Lobster | NoLita	23
Elias Corner | Astoria	22
Esca | W 40s	25
Fish | G Vill	20
Francisco's | Chelsea	22
fresh | TriBeCa	25
Fuleen | Chinatown	23
Hudson Café | Harlem	21
Ithaka | E 80s	21
Jack's Lux. | E Vill	26
Kellari Tav./Parea | W 40s	21
Lake Club | SI	22
Z 'Le Bernardin | W 50s	28
Lobster Box | Bronx	19

London Lennie's | Rego Pk	21
Lure Fishbar | SoHo	23
Marina Cafe | SI	20
Mary's Fish Camp | W Vill	24
McCormick/Schmick | W 50s	20
Mermaid Inn | multi.	21
Z Milos | W 50s	27
Neptune Rm. | W 80s	21
Oceana | E 50s	26
Ocean Grill | W 70s	23
Z Oriental Gdn. | Chinatown	24
Oyster Bar | E 40s	21
Pampano | E 40s	24
Z Pearl Oyster | G Vill	26
Pearl Room | Bay Ridge	23
Pescatore | E 50s	18
Petite Crev. | Carroll Gdns	24
Ping's Sea. | multi.	21
Portofino | Bronx	20
Redeye Grill | W 50s	20
Sea Grill | W 40s	24
Shelly's Tradizionale | W 50s	19
South Fin | SI	20
Stamatis | Astoria	22
Stella del Mare | Murray Hill	23
Z Taverna Kyclades | Astoria	25
Telly's Taverna | Astoria	21
Thalassa | TriBeCa	24
Tides | LES	24
Todai | Murray Hill	17
Trata Estiatorio | E 70s	21
Tratt. Pesce | multi.	18
Turquoise | E 80s	22
Umberto's | multi.	19
Water's Edge | LIC	22

SERBIAN

NEW Kafana | E Vill	-

SMALL PLATES

(See also Spanish tapas specialist)

Alta | Med. | G Vill	23
Bar Stuzz. | Italian | Flatiron	20
Beast | Med. | Prospect Hts	22
Bellavitae | Italian | G Vill	23
Bello Sguardo | Med. | W 70s	19
Beyoglu | Turkish | E 80s	21
Bocca Lupo | Italian | Cobble Hill	23
NEW Bún | Viet. | SoHo	21
Butai | Japanese | Gramercy	21
Centro Vinoteca | Italian | W Vill	22
Chino's | Asian | Gramercy	19
Z Degustation | French/Spanish | E Vill	27

EN Japanese | Japanese | **W Vill** 23
Frankies | Italian | **multi.** 24
NEW General Greene | Amer. | - |
Ft Greene
Grayz | Amer. | **W 50s** 23
House | Med. | **Gramercy** 20
NEW ilili | Lebanese/Med. | 23
Gramercy
'inoteca | Italian | **LES** 23
Jimmy's 43 | Amer. | **E Vill** 21
Kuma Inn | SE Asian | **LES** 24
Z L'Atelier/Robuchon | French | 28
E 50s
Little D | Eclectic | **Park Slope** 25
Marlow/Sons | French | **W'burg** 23
Maze | French | **W 50s** 25
Mercadito | Mex. | **multi.** 23
Perbacco | Italian | **E Vill** 25
p*ong | Dessert | **G Vill** 22
Sakagura | Japanese | **E 40s** 25
savorNY | Eclectic | **LES** 24
Stanton Social | Eclectic | **LES** 23
Tarallucci | Italian | **multi.** 21
Uncle Nick's | Greek | **W 50s** 20
Vento | Italian | **Meatpacking** 19
Zenkichi | Japanese | **W'burg** 23

SOUL FOOD

Amy Ruth's | **Harlem** 21
Charles' Kitchen | **Harlem** 22
Londel's | **Harlem** 20
Miss Mamie/Maude | **Harlem** 21
Mo-Bay | **Harlem** 20
Pink Tea Cup | **W Vill** 19
Sylvia's | **Harlem** 17

SOUP

Hale/Hearty | **multi.** 19
La Bonne Soupe | **W 50s** 18

SOUTH AFRICAN

NEW Braai | **W 50s** - |

SOUTH AMERICAN

Cafe Ronda | **W 70s** 19
Empanada Mama | **W 50s** 22

SOUTHEAST ASIAN

Cafe Asean | **G Vill** 20
Z Spice Market | **Meatpacking** 22

SOUTHERN

Amy Ruth's | **Harlem** 21
Bourbon St. Café | **Bayside** 18
B. Smith's | **W 40s** 18
Charles' Kitchen | **Harlem** 22

Egg | **W'burg** 24
Kitchenette | **multi.** 19
Londel's | **Harlem** 20
NEW Madeleine Mae | **W 80s** 16
Maroons | **Chelsea** 21
Miss Mamie/Maude | **Harlem** 21
NEW Peaches | **Bed-Stuy** - |
Pink Tea Cup | **W Vill** 19
Rack & Soul | **W 100s** 19

SOUTHWESTERN

Agave | **W Vill** 19
Canyon Road | **E 70s** 19
Cilantro | **multi.** 17
Cowgirl | **W Vill** 16
Johnny Utah | **W 50s** 13
Z Mesa Grill | **Flatiron** 23
Miracle Grill | **multi.** 18
Santa Fe | **W 70s** 18

SPANISH

(* tapas specialist)
Alcala* | **E 40s** 22
Boqueria* | **Flatiron** 22
Cafe Español | **G Vill** 20
Z Casa Mono | **Gramercy** 25
Z Degustation | **E Vill** 27
El Charro Español | **G Vill** 22
El Faro* | **W Vill** 21
El Pote | **Murray Hill** 22
El Quijote | **Chelsea** 19
NEW El Quinto Pino* | **Chelsea** 23
Euzkadi* | **E Vill** 19
Flor de Sol* | **TriBeCa** 21
Francisco's | **Chelsea** 22
La Paella* | **E Vill** 19
Las Ramblas* | **G Vill** 24
Mercat* | **NoHo** 22
Oliva* | **LES** 20
Pamplona* | **Gramercy** 23
Pipa* | **Flatiron** 20
Real Madrid | **SI** 22
Sala* | **multi.** 22
Sevilla | **W Vill** 21
NEW Socarrat | **Chelsea** - |
Solera* | **E 50s** 22
Sol y Sombra* | **W 80s** 17
Suba | **LES** 20
Z Tía Pol* | **Chelsea** 24
Tio Pepe | **G Vill** 18
Xunta* | **E Vill** 21

STEAKHOUSES

A.J. Maxwell's | **W 40s** 22
Angelo/Maxie's | **Flatiron** 21

Arirang Hibachi | **multi.**	20
Artie's | **Bronx**	23
Austin's Steak | **Bay Ridge**	21
Ben & Jack's | **E 40s**	23
Ben Benson's | **W 50s**	23
Benihana | **W 50s**	17
Benjamin Steak | **E 40s**	23
☑ BLT Prime | **Gramercy**	25
BLT Steak | **E 50s**	24
Bobby Van's | **multi.**	22
Buenos Aires | **E Vill**	22
Bull & Bear | **E 40s**	19
Capital Grille | **E 40s**	23
Chimichurri Grill | **W 40s**	20
Christos | **Astoria**	24
☑ Churrascaria | **multi.**	23
City Hall | **TriBeCa**	20
Craftsteak | **Chelsea**	23
☑ Del Frisco's | **W 40s**	25
Delmonico's | **Financial**	22
DeStefano | **W'burg**	23
Dylan Prime | **TriBeCa**	24
Embers | **Bay Ridge**	21
Erawan | **Bayside**	23
Fairway Cafe | **W 70s**	18
Frankie/Johnnie | **multi.**	21
Gallagher's | **W 50s**	21
Green Field | **Corona**	18
Hacienda/Argentina | **E 70s**	18
Harry's | **Financial**	22
Il Bastardo | **Chelsea**	19
Industria | **TriBeCa**	19
Jake's | **Bronx**	23
Keens | **Garment**	24
Knickerbocker | **G Vill**	19
Kobe Club | **W 50s**	23
Le Marais | **W 40s**	20
Les Halles | **multi.**	19
Macelleria | **Meatpacking**	19
Maloney/Porcelli | **E 50s**	22
MarkJoseph | **Financial**	24
Michael Jordan | **E 40s**	21
Morton's | **E 40s**	24
Nick & Stef's | **Garment**	21
Novecento | **SoHo**	19
Old Homestead | **Meatpacking**	24
Outback | **multi.**	15
☑ Palm, The | **multi.**	24
NEW Pampa Grill | **W'burg**	-
NEW Parlor Steak | **E 90s**	-
Patroon | **E 40s**	20
☑ Peter Luger | **W'burg**	27
Pietro's | **E 40s**	24

Porção | **Gramercy**	20
Porter House NY | **W 60s**	23
Post House | **E 60s**	24
Prime Grill | **E 40s**	22
NEW Primehouse | **Gramercy**	23
Quality Meats | **W 50s**	23
Rothmann's | **E 50s**	23
Roth's Westside | **W 90s**	20
Ruth's Chris | **W 50s**	24
Shula's | **W 40s**	21
Smith & Wollensky | **E 40s**	22
South Fin | **SI**	20
Sparks | **E 40s**	25
STK | **Meatpacking**	21
Strip House | **G Vill**	25
NEW T-Bar Steak | **E 70s**	21
tre dici | **Chelsea**	22
2 West | **Financial**	23
Uncle Jack's | **multi.**	23
Via Brasil | **W 40s**	18
Wolfgang's | **multi.**	25
Wollensky's | **E 40s**	22

TEAROOMS

Alice's Tea Cup | **multi.**	19
American Girl | **E 40s**	12
Franchia | **Murray Hill**	19
Lady Mendl's | **Gramercy**	22
Sweet Melissa | **multi.**	21
Tea & Sympathy | **W Vill**	21

TEX-MEX

Burritoville | **multi.**	17
Lobo | **multi.**	15
Mary Ann's | **multi.**	14
107 West | **multi.**	17

THAI

Bann Thai | **Forest Hills**	19
Breeze | **W 40s**	21
Elephant, The | **E Vill**	21
Erawan | **Bayside**	23
Highline | **Meatpacking**	19
Holy Basil | **E Vill**	21
Jaiya Thai | **Gramercy**	22
Jasmine | **E 80s**	19
Joya | **Cobble Hill**	23
☑ Kittichai | **SoHo**	22
Klong | **E Vill**	21
Kuma Inn | **LES**	24
Land | **multi.**	22
Lemongrass | **multi.**	16
Long Tan | **Park Slope**	18
Pam Real Thai | **W 40s**	22
Peep | **SoHo**	19

Planet Thai | **multi.**	18
Pongsri Thai | **multi.**	21
Prem-on Thai | **G Vill**	20
Pukk | **E Vill**	23
Q Thai Bistro | **Forest Hills**	21
Regional Thai | **multi.**	18
NEW Rhong-Tiam | **G Vill**	-
Room Service | **Chelsea**	17
Royal Siam | **Chelsea**	19
Sala Thai | **E 80s**	20
SEA | **multi.**	21
Siam Sq. | **Bronx**	23
Song | **Park Slope**	23
NEW Sookk | **W 100s**	23
Spice | **multi.**	20
Z Sripraphai | **Woodside**	27
NEW Talay | **Harlem**	-
Thai Pavilion | **Astoria**	21
Topaz Thai | **W 50s**	20
Vong | **E 50s**	22
Vynl | **multi.**	15
Wild Ginger | **W Vill**	18
Wondee Siam | **multi.**	23

TIBETAN

Tsampa | **E Vill**	20

TUNISIAN

Epices/Traiteur | **W 70s**	21

TURKISH

Akdeniz | **W 40s**	21
A La Turka | **E 70s**	18
Ali Baba | **multi.**	22
Bereket | **LES**	19
Beyoglu | **E 80s**	21
Bodrum | **W 80s**	20
Dervish | **W 40s**	19
Pasha | **W 70s**	20
Pera | **E 40s**	22
Peri Ela | **E 90s**	18
Z Sahara | **Gravesend**	22
Sip Sak | **E 40s**	19
Taci's Beyti | **Midwood**	23
Taksim | **E 50s**	20
Turkish Cuisine | **W 40s**	19
Z Turkish Kitchen | **Gramercy**	22
Turks & Frogs | **TriBeCa**	20
Turkuaz | **W 100s**	18
Uskudar | **E 70s**	20

UKRAINIAN

Veselka | **E Vill**	18

URUGUAYAN

NEW Pampa Grill | **W'burg**	-

VEGETARIAN

(* vegan)

Angelica Kit.* | **E Vill**	20
Blossom* | **multi.**	22
NEW Broadway East | **LES**	21
Candle Cafe* | **E 70s**	23
Z Candle 79* | **E 70s**	23
Caravan/Dreams* | **E Vill**	20
Chennai Gdn. | **Gramercy**	22
Counter* | **E Vill**	21
Franchia | **Murray Hill**	19
Gobo* | **multi.**	22
Z Hangawi | **Murray Hill**	24
Hummus Pl. | **multi.**	23
Pongal | **multi.**	21
Pukk | **E Vill**	23
Pure Food/Wine* | **Gramercy**	23
Quantum Leap | **multi.**	20
Saravanaas | **Gramercy**	24
Zen Palate | **multi.**	19

VENEZUELAN

Caracas | **E Vill**	25

VIETNAMESE

Bao Noodles | **Gramercy**	18
Bôi | **E 40s**	19
NEW Bún | **SoHo**	21
Doyers | **Chinatown**	21
Indochine | **E Vill**	21
Le Colonial | **E 50s**	19
Mai House | **TriBeCa**	20
Nam | **TriBeCa**	21
New Bo-Ky | **Chinatown**	20
Nha Trang | **Chinatown**	21
Nicky's | **multi.**	22
Omai | **Chelsea**	23
Pho Bang | **multi.**	20
Pho Pasteur | **Chinatown**	19
Pho Viet Huong | **Chinatown**	22
Safran | **Chelsea**	21
Saigon Grill | **multi.**	21
NEW Tet | **E Vill**	-
Vermicelli | **E 70s**	18
VietCafé | **TriBeCa**	22

YEMENITE

Rectangles | **E 70s**	17

Manhattan Neighborhoods

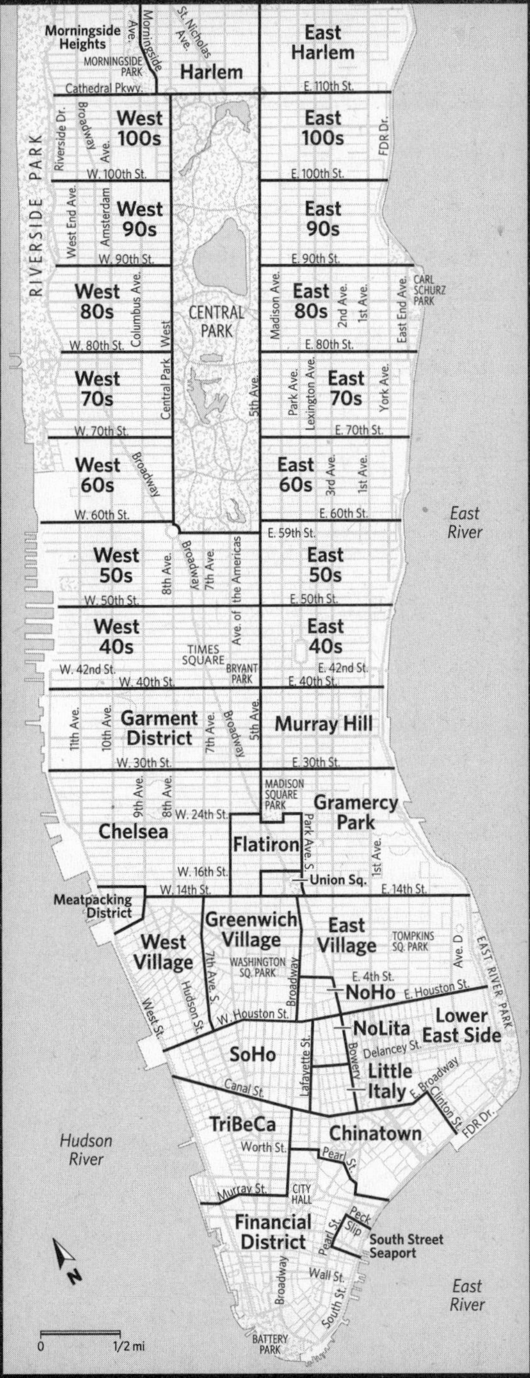

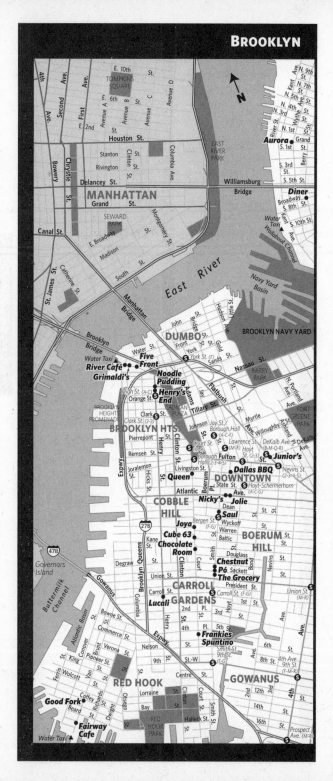

BROOKLYN

MANHATTAN

DUMBO

BROOKLYN NAVY YARD

East River

Aurora

Diner

Five
Front

River Café
Grimaldi's

Noodle
Pudding

Henry's
End

BROOKLYN HTS.

Junior's

Queen

Dallas BBQ

DOWNTOWN

**COBBLE
HILL**

Nicky's

Jolie

Saul

Joya

**BOERUM
HILL**

Cube 63
Chocolate
Room

Chestnut

Pó
The Grocery

**CARROLL
GARDENS**

Lucali

Governors
Island

Frankies
Spuntino

GOWANUS

RED HOOK

Good Fork

Fairway
Cafe

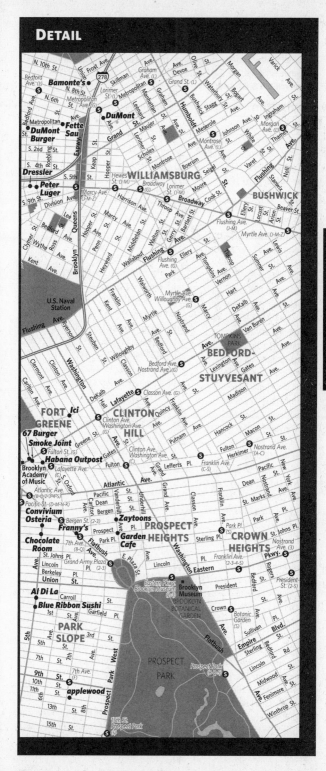

N. 10th St.
Frost Ave.
Union Ave.
278
Skillman Ave.
Devoe
Olive
Morgan
Varick

Bedford Ave. (L)
N. 8th St.
Bamonte's
Lorimer
Graham Ave. (L)
Ave.
Bogart
Ingraham

N. 6th St.
Metropolitan St.
Metropolitan Ave. (G)
Leonard
Graham
Waterbury
Bushwick
Stagg
White
Morgan Ave. (L)
Thames

DuMont
Ave.
Mayjer
Scholes
Meserole
Johnson Ave.
Varet

Metropolitan
Fette Sau
Grand
Lorimer
St.
Montrose Ave. (L)
Gates

DuMont Burger
Roebling
Keap
Hooper
Montrose
Boerum
Siegel
Flushing
Stanwix

S. 2nd St.
Ave.
Hewes
WILLIAMSBURG
Moore
Cook St.
BUSHWICK
Beaver St.

S. 4th St.
Dressler
S. 5th St.
Broadway (G)
Lorimer St. (J-M)
Broadway
Ellery
Locust
Aron
St.

Peter Luger
Marcy Ave. (J-M-Z)
Harrison Ave.
Throop
Bartlett St.
Flushing Ave. (J-M)
Lewis

S. 9th St.
Division Ave.
Marcy
Ave.
Walton
Gerry
Ave.
Myrtle Ave. (J-M-Z)

Clymer
Bedford
Lees
Hooper
Penn
Middleton
St.
Flushing Ave. (G)
Sumner
Ave.

Wythe
Ross
Brooklyn
Heyward
Wallabout
Flushing Ave. (G)
Hart
DeKalb

Kent
Ave.
Franklin
Kent
Myrtle
Nostrand
Marcy
Van Buren

U.S. Naval Station
Iverson
Steuben
St.
Myrtle Ave. Willoughby Ave. (G)
TOMPKINS PARK

Flushing Ave.
Clermont
Willoughby
Bedford
Ave.
Ave.
Lexington Ave. (G)

Clinton
Washington
Classon
BEDFORD-STUYVESANT
Madison

Carlton
Ave.
DeKalb
Bedford Ave. Nostrand Ave. (G)
Quincy

Carroll
FORT GREENE
Ici
Lafayette
Classon Ave. (G)
Franklin
Hancock
Macon

67 Burger
Smoke Joint
Clinton Ave. Washington Ave. (G)
CLINTON HILL
Putnam
Fulton
Herkimer
Nostrand Ave. (A-C)

Habana Outpost
Greene
Gates
Clinton Ave. Washington Ave. (C)
Lafayette Ave.
Fulton St. (G)
Lefferts Pl.
Franklin Ave. (C-S)
Pacific

Brooklyn Academy of Music
Lafayette Ave.
Fulton
Grand Ave.
Dean
Nostrand
New York
St. Marks

Atlantic Ave. (B-Q-2-3-4-5)
Atlantic
Ave.
Vanderbilt
Underhill
St.
Classon
Park
York

Pacific St. (D-M-N-R)
Carlton
Dean
Bergen
Franklin
St.
PROSPECT HEIGHTS
Park Pl. (S)
CROWN HEIGHTS

Convivium Osteria
Bergen St. (2-3)
Zaytoons
Sterling Pl.
St. Johns Pl.
Nostrand

Franny's
Prospect
Flatbush
Garden Cafe
Washington
Franklin Ave. (2-3-4-5)
Pkwy.

Chocolate Room
7th Ave.
Prospect Pl.
Lincoln
Eastern
Pkwy.
Rogers
President St. (2-5)

St. Johns Pl.
Grand Army Plaza (2-3)
Eastern
President

Lincoln
E. Plaza St.
Brooklyn Museum
Crown
Bedford

Al Di La
Berkeley
Union St.
Eastern Pkwy. Brooklyn Museum (2-3)
BROOKLYN BOTANICAL GARDEN
Botanic Garden (S)

Blue Ribbon Sushi
1st St.
Garfield St.
Flatbush
Sullivan
Blvd.

PARK SLOPE
3rd St.
Crown
Empire
Sterling
Bedford
Rd.

5th
5th St.
PROSPECT PARK
Lincoln
Midwood

7th
7th Ave. (F)
Fenimore
Ave.

applewood
9th
10th
11th
St.
6th
8th
Prospect Park (B-Q)
Winthrop

13th St.
15th St. Prospect Park (F)

Locations

Includes names, Food ratings and street locations. Abbreviations key: a=Avenue, s=Street, e.g. 1a/116s=First Ave. at 116th St.; 3a/82-3s=Third Ave. between 82nd & 83rd Sts.

Manhattan

CHELSEA

(24th to 30th Sts., west of 5th; 14th to 24th Sts., west of 6th)

Amy's Bread	9a/15-16s	23
Better Burger	8a/19s	15
Biricchino	29s/8a	19
Black Pearl	26s/Bway-6a	18
Blossom	9a/21-22s	22
Blue Ginger	8a/15-16s	20
Bombay Talkie	9a/21-22s	19
Bottino	10a/24-25s	19
brgr	7a/26-27s	18
☑ Buddakan	9a/16s	23
Burritoville	23s/7-8a	17
Cafeteria	7a/17s	18
Cookshop	10a/20s	23
Craftsteak	10a/15-16s	23
Crema	17s/6-7a	22
Cuba Cafe	8a/20-21s	20
Dallas BBQ	8a/23s	14
Da Umberto	17s/6-7a	25
☑ Del Posto	10a/16s	26
Don Giovanni	10a/22-23s	17
East of 8th	23s/7-8a	17
elmo	7a/19-20s	16
El Quijote	23s/7-8a	19
NEW El Quinto Pino	24s/9a	23
Empire Diner	10a/22s	15
Energy Kitchen	17s/8-9a	15
Francisco's	23s/6-7a	22
NEW Friedman's	9a/15-16s	21
Gascogne	8a/17-18s	21
Grand Sichuan	9a/24s	22
Hale/Hearty	9a/15-16s	19
Hill Country	26s/Bway-6a	21
Il Bastardo	7a/21-22s	19
Intermezzo	8a/20-21s	17
Klee Brass.	9a/22-23s	21
La Belle Vie	8a/19-20s	18
La Bergamote	9a/20s	24
La Bottega	9a/17s	16
La Lunchonette	10a/18s	21
La Taza de Oro	8a/14-15s	18
Le Grainne Cafe	9a/21s	19
Le Singe Vert	7a/19-20s	18
Le Zie 2000	7a/20-21s	21
Maroons	16s/7-8a	21

Mary Ann's	8a/16s	14
Matsuri	16s/9a	23
Momoya	7a/21s	22
Monster Sushi	23s/6-7a	17
Moran's	10a/19s	18
Morimoto	10a/15-16s	25
Negril	23s/8-9a	20
Omai	9a/19-20s	23
Park, The	10a/17-18s	15
Patsy's Pizzeria	23s/8-9a	20
Pepe	10a/24-25s	21
Pizza 33	23s/8a	21
Pongsri Thai	23s/6-7a	21
Red Cat	10a/23-24s	24
Regional Thai	7a/22s	18
Rocking Horse	8a/19-20s	21
Room Service	8a/18-19s	17
Royal Siam	8a/22-23s	19
RUB BBQ	23s/7-8a	20
Safran	7a/15-16s	21
Sarabeth's	9a/15-16s	20
NEW Scarpetta	14s/8-9a	26
Seven	7a/29-30s	19
NEW Socarrat	19s/7-8a	-
Spice	8a/20-21s	20
Sueños	17s/8-9a	22
☑ Tía Pol	10a/22-23s	24
tre dici	26s/6-7a	22
Trestle on 10th	10a/24s	20
202 Cafe	9a/15-16s	19
Uncle Nick's	8a/29s	20
Vynl	8a/15s	15
Waldy's Pizza	6a/27-28s	22
'wichcraft	11a/27-28s	20

CHINATOWN

(Canal to Pearl Sts., east of B'way)

Amazing 66	Mott/Bayard	21
Big Wong	Mott/Bayard-Canal	22
Dim Sum Go Go	E Bway/Chatham	21
Doyers	Doyers/Chatham	21
Excellent Dumpling	Lafayette/Canal-Walker	19
Forlini's	Baxter/Walker	19
Fuleen	Division/Bowery	23
Golden Unicorn	E Bway/Catherine	20
Grand Sichuan	Canal/Chrystie	22
Great NY Noodle	Bowery/Bayard	22
HSF	Bowery/Bayard-Canal	19

Jing Fong	*Elizabeth/Bayard*	19
Joe's Shanghai	*Pell/Bowery*	22
Joe's	*Pell/Doyers*	20
Mandarin Court	*Mott/Bayard*	21
New Bo-Ky	*Bayard/Mott*	20
Nha Trang	*multi.*	21
Nice Green Bo	*Bayard/Elizabeth*	23
Z Oriental Gdn.	*Elizabeth/Bayard-Canal*	24
Peking Duck	*Mott/Mosco-Pell*	22
Pho Pasteur	*Baxter/Bayard*	19
Pho Viet Huong	*Mulberry/Bayard-Canal*	22
Ping's Sea.	*Mott/Bayard-Pell*	21
Pongsri Thai	*Bayard/Baxter*	21
Wo Hop	*Mott/Canal*	21
X.O.	*Walker/Centre-Lafayette*	19

EAST 40s

Aburiya Kinnosuke	*45s/2-3a*	25
Alcala	*46s/1-2a*	22
Ali Baba	*2a/46s*	22
American Girl	*5a/49s*	12
Ammos	*Vanderbilt/44-45s*	21
Avra	*48s/Lex-3a*	24
Ben & Jack's	*44s/2-3a*	23
Benjamin Steak	*41s/Mad-Park*	23
Bobby Van's	*Park/46s*	22
Bôi	*multi.*	19
Brother Jimmy	*42s/Vanderbilt*	16
Bukhara Grill	*49s/2-3a*	22
Bull & Bear	*Lex/49s*	19
Burger Heaven	*multi.*	16
Cafe Centro	*Park/45s*	19
Cafe S.F.A.	*5a/49-50s*	18
Cafe Spice	*42s/Vanderbilt*	18
Caffe Linda	*49s/Lex-3a*	19
Capital Grille	*42s/Lex-3a*	23
Chiam	*48s/Lex-3a*	22
Chin Chin	*49s/2-3a*	23
Chipotle	*44s/Lex-3a*	18
Cibo	*2a/41s*	19
Cipriani Dolci	*42s/Vanderbilt*	19
Comfort Diner	*45s/2-3a*	16
NEW Convivio	*42s/1-2a*	-
Così	*45s/Mad-Vanderbilt*	16
Darbar	*46s/Lex-3a*	21
Dean's	*2a/42-43s*	17
Dishes	*multi.*	21
Diwan	*48s/Lex-3a*	21
Django	*Lex/46-47s*	20
Docks Oyster	*3a/40s*	19
Energy Kitchen	*41s/2a*	15
Fabio Piccolo	*44s/2-3a*	22

goodburger	*2a/42s*	18
Grifone	*46s/2-3a*	23
Gyu-Kaku	*3a/50s*	22
Hale/Hearty	*multi.*	19
Haru	*Park/48s*	21
Hatsuhana	*multi.*	24
Il Postino	*49s/1-2a*	23
Inagiku	*49s/Lex-Park*	22
Ise	*49s/Lex-3a*	21
Junior's	*42s/Vanderbilt*	17
Katsu-Hama	*47s/5a-Mad*	22
Kuruma Zushi	*47s/5a-Mad*	28
Mamá Mexico	*49s/2-3a*	19
Mangia	*48s/5a-Mad*	19
Mee Noodle	*2a/49s*	18
Megu	*1a/47s*	24
Menchanko-tei	*45s/Lex-3a*	20
Metrazur	*42s/Vanderbilt*	20
Michael Jordan	*42s/Vanderbilt*	21
Morton's	*5a/45s*	24
Nanni	*46s/Lex-3a*	24
Naples 45	*Park/45s*	17
Nino's	*multi.*	21
Osteria Laguna	*42s/2-3a*	21
Oyster Bar	*42s/Vanderbilt*	21
NEW Padre Figlio	*44s/1-2a*	-
Z Palm, The	*2a/44-45s*	24
Pampano	*49s/2-3a*	24
Patroon	*46s/Lex-3a*	20
Pepe	*42s/Vanderbilt*	21
Pera	*Mad/41-42*	22
Pershing Sq.	*42s/Park*	15
Phoenix Gdn.	*40s/2-3a*	23
Pietro's	*43s/2-3a*	24
Prime Grill	*49s/Mad-Park*	22
Riingo	*45s/2-3a*	21
Sakagura	*43s/2-3a*	25
Seo	*49s/2-3a*	23
Shinbashi	*48s/5a-Mad*	20
Sip Sak	*2a/49-50s*	19
Smith & Wollensky	*3a/49s*	22
Smorgas Chef	*2a/49s*	19
Sparks	*46s/2-3a*	25
Sushiden	*49s/5a-Mad*	24
Z Sushi Yasuda	*43s/2-3a*	28
Two Boots	*42s/Vanderbilt*	19
'wichcraft	*multi.*	20
Wollensky's	*49s/3a*	22
Yama	*49s/1-2a*	23
Zócalo	*42s/Vanderbilt*	20

EAST 50s

Z NEW Adour	*55s/5a-Mad*	26
Aja	*1a/58s*	20

LOCATIONS

Al Bustan | *3a/50-51s*	19
Alto | *53s/5a-Mad*	25
Amma | *51s/2-3a*	24
Angelo's Pizza | *2a/55s*	19
⚡ Aquavit | *55s/Mad-Park*	25
NEW Avon Bistro | *52s/Lex-3a*	-
Baluchi's | *53s/2-3a*	17
Bice | *54s/5a-Mad*	20
Blockhead Burrito | *2a/50-51s*	16
BLT Steak | *57s/Lex-Park*	24
Bobby Van's | *54s/Lex-Park*	22
Bottega/Vino | *59s/5a-Mad*	21
Brasserie | *53s/Lex-Park*	20
Burger Heaven | *multi.*	16
Burritoville | *3a/52s*	17
Cafe Joul | *1a/58-59s*	18
Caffe Buon Gusto | *2a/53-54s*	17
Caviar Russe | *Mad/54-55s*	24
Cellini | *54s/Mad-Park*	21
Chipotle | *52s/Lex-3a*	18
Chola | *58s/2-3a*	23
Chop't Creative | *multi.*	19
Così | *56s/Mad-Park*	16
David Burke/Bloom. | *59s/Lex*	18
Dawat | *58s/2-3a*	23
DeGrezia | *50s/2-3a*	22
Destino | *1a/50s*	20
Deux Amis | *51s/1-2a*	19
Dishes | *Park/53s*	21
Dos Caminos | *3a/50-51s*	20
Energy Kitchen | *2a/57-58s*	15
Ess-a-Bagel | *3a/50-51s*	23
⚡ Felidia | *58s/2-3a*	26
57 | *57s/Mad*	23
NEW Fig & Olive | *52s/5a-Mad*	20
Fiorini | *56s/2-3a*	20
⚡ Four Seasons | *52s/Lex-Park*	26
Fresco | *52s/Mad-Park*	23
Giambelli | *50s/Mad-Park*	22
Gilt | *Mad/50-51s*	25
goodburger | *Lex/54s*	18
Grand Sichuan | *2a/55-56s*	22
Harry Cipriani | *5a/59-60s*	19
Houston's | *3a/54s*	20
Il Menestrello | *50s/Mad-Park*	21
Il Nido | *53s/2-3a*	23
Il Valentino | *56s/1-2a*	18
Jubilee | *54s/1-2a*	22
Korea Palace | *54s/Lex-Park*	18
La Gioconda | *53s/2-3a*	20
⚡ La Grenouille | *52s/5a-Mad*	27
La Mangeoire | *2a/53-54s*	19
La Mediterranée | *2a/50-51s*	19

⚡ L'Atelier/Robuchon | *57s/Mad*	28
⚡ Le Cirque | *58s/Lex-3a*	24
Le Colonial | *57s/Lex-3a*	19
Lenny's | *2a/54s*	18
⚡ Le Perigord | *52s/FDR-1a*	24
Lever House | *53s/Mad-Park*	22
Luna Piena | *53s/2-3a*	18
Maloney/Porcelli | *50s/Mad*	22
NEW Mia Dona | *58s/2-3a*	21
Mint | *50s/Lex-3a*	22
Montparnasse | *51s/2-3a*	18
Mr. Chow | *57s/1-2a*	21
Mr. K's | *Lex/51s*	22
Neary's | *57s/1a*	14
Nippon | *52s/Lex-3a*	22
Oceana | *54s/Mad-Park*	26
Our Place | *55s/Lex-3a*	20
Outback | *56s/2-3a*	15
Peking Duck | *53s/2-3a*	22
Pescatore | *2a/50-1s*	18
P.J. Clarke's | *3a/55s*	16
Pop Burger | *58s/5a-Mad*	18
Pump Energy | *3a/50s*	18
⚡ Rosa Mexicano | *1a/58s*	21
Rothmann's | *54s/5a-Mad*	23
San Pietro | *54s/5a-Mad*	24
Serafina | *58s/Mad-Park*	19
Shun Lee Palace | *55s/Lex-3a*	24
Sofrito | *57s/1a-Sutton*	21
Solera | *53s/2-3a*	22
Solo | *Mad/55-56s*	22
NEW South Gate | *CPS/6-7a*	24
SushiAnn | *51s/Mad-Park*	24
Taksim | *2a/54-55s*	20
⚡ Tao | *58s/Mad-Park*	22
Tenzan | *2a/52-53a*	23
Teodora | *57s/Lex-3a*	20
Tratt. Pesce | *1a/59s*	18
⚡ Tse Yang | *51s/Mad-Park*	24
Vong | *54s/3a*	22
Yuva | *58s/2-3a*	22
Zarela | *2a/50-51s*	21

EAST 60s

Accademia/Vino | *3a/63-64s*	20
Alice's Tea Cup | *64s/Lex*	19
Amaranth | *62s/5a-Mad*	18
Arabelle | *64s/Mad-Park*	22
⚡ Aureole | *61s/Mad-Park*	27
Bistro Chat Noir | *66s/5a-Mad*	19
Bistro 61 | *1a/61s*	19
Bravo Gianni | *63s/2-3a*	21
Brio | *61s/Lex*	18

Burger Heaven	*Lex/62s*	16
Cabana	*3a/60-61s*	21
Café Evergreen	*1a/69-70s*	20
Canaletto	*60s/2-3a*	21
China Fun	*2a/64s*	15
Circus	*61s/Lex-Park*	20
Da Filippo	*2a/69-70s*	21
☑ Daniel	*65s/Mad-Park*	28
☑ davidburke/dona.	*61s/Lex*	25
Fig & Olive	*Lex/62-63s*	20
Frederick's	*Mad/65-66s*	17
Fred's at Barneys	*Mad/60s*	20
Geisha	*61s/Mad-Park*	23
Gino	*Lex/60-61s*	19
Hale/Hearty	*Lex/64-65s*	19
Il Vagabondo	*62s/1-2a*	18
Jackson Hole	*64s/2-3a*	17
John's Pizzeria	*64s/1a-York*	22
JoJo	*64s/Lex-3a*	24
Kai	*Mad/68-69s*	25
L'Absinthe	*67s/2-3a*	22
La Cantina Toscana	*1a/60-61s*	24
La Goulue	*Mad/64-65s*	20
La Houppa	*64s/5a-Mad*	18
Le Bilboquet	*63s/Mad-Park*	22
Lenny's	*1a/68s*	18
Le Pain Q.	*Lex/63-64s*	18
Le Veau d'Or	*60s/Lex-Park*	18
Maya	*1a/64-65s*	24
Mediterraneo	*2a/66s*	18
Mon Petit Cafe	*Lex/62s*	18
Nello	*Mad/62-63s*	18
Park Avenue . . .	*63s/Lex*	24
Patsy's Pizzeria	*multi.*	20
NEW Persephone	*60s/Lex*	22
Philippe	*60s/Mad-Park*	23
Pongal	*1a/63-64s*	21
Portofino Grille	*1a/63-64s*	19
Post House	*63s/Mad-Park*	24
Primola	*2a/64-65s*	23
Regency	*Park/61s*	19
Scalinatella	*61s/3a*	26
Serafina	*61s/Mad-Park*	19
Serendipity 3	*60s/2-3a*	17
Solace	*64s/1a-York*	22
☑ Sushi Seki	*1a/62-63s*	27
Viand	*Mad/61-62s*	16
Via Oreto	*1a/61-62s*	20
Za Za	*1a/65-66s*	19

EAST 70s

Afghan Kebab	*2a/70-71s*	19
A La Turka	*2a/74s*	18
Al Forno Pizza	*2a/77-78s*	20
Atlantic Grill	*3a/76-77s*	23
Baraonda	*2a/75s*	18
Barking Dog	*York/77s*	15
B. Café	*75s/2-3a*	22
Bella Blu	*Lex/70-71s*	20
Boathouse	*Central Pk Dr N*	17
Brother Jimmy	*2a/77-78s*	16
Burritoville	*2a/77-78s*	17
☑ Café Boulud	*76s/5a-Mad*	27
Caffe Buon Gusto	*77s/2-3a*	17
Campagnola	*1a/73-74s*	24
Candle Cafe	*3a/74-75s*	23
☑ Candle 79	*79s/Lex-3a*	23
Canyon Road	*1a/76-77s*	19
☑ Carlyle	*76/Mad*	22
Cilantro	*1a/71s*	17
Dallas BBQ	*3a/72-73s*	14
Demaré	*78s/Lex-3a*	19
Due	*3a/79-80s*	21
EJ's Luncheon.	*3a/73s*	16
Finestra	*York/73s*	17
☑ Gari/Sushi	*78s/1a-York*	26
Grace's Tratt.	*71s/2-3a*	19
Hacienda/Argentina	*75s/1-2a*	18
Haru	*3a/76s*	21
Il Riccio	*79s/Lex-3a*	20
Iron Sushi	*78s/1-2a*	19
J.G. Melon	*3a/74s*	21
Ko Sushi	*2a/70s*	20
Lenny's	*2a/77s*	18
Le Pain Q.	*77s/2-3a*	18
Lumi	*Lex/70s*	18
Lusardi's	*2a/77-78s*	23
Maruzzella	*1a/77-78s*	22
Mezzaluna	*3a/74-75s*	20
Mingala Burmese	*2a/72-73s*	19
Nino's	*1a/72-73s*	21
Orsay	*Lex/75s*	18
Parma	*3a/79-80s*	20
Pastrami Queen	*Lex/78-79*	19
Payard Bistro	*Lex/73-74s*	23
Per Lei	*2a/71s*	19
Persepolis	*2a/73-74s*	21
Petaluma	*1a/73s*	18
Quatorze Bis	*79s/1-2a*	21
Rectangles	*1a/74-75s*	17
Regional Thai	*1a/77s*	18
Sant Ambroeus	*Mad/77-78s*	21
Sarabeth's	*Mad/75s*	20
☑ Sasabune	*73s/1a-York*	27
Serafina	*Mad/79s*	19
Sette Mezzo	*Lex/70-71s*	23
Shabu-Shabu 70	*70s/1-2a*	20

LOCATIONS

Shanghai Pavilion	3a/78-79s	20
Spice	2a/73-74s	20
Sushi Hana	2a/78s	21
Swifty's	Lex/72-73s	18
NEW T-Bar Steak	3a/73-74s	21
Trata Estíatorio	2a/70-71s	21
Uskudar	2a/73-74s	20
Uva	2a/77-78s	21
Vermicelli	2a/77-78s	18
Viand	Mad/78s	16
Via Quadronno	73s/5a-Mad	21
Vivolo	74s/Lex-Park	19
Vynl	2a/78s	15

EAST 80s

Alice's Tea Cup	81s/2-3a	19
Amber	3a/80s	20
Antonucci	81s/Lex-3a	21
Baluchi's	2a/89-90s	17
Beyoglu	3a/81s	21
Blockhead Burrito	2a/81-82s	16
Brasserie Julien	3a/80-81s	18
Brio	2a/89s	18
Burger Heaven	3a/86-87s	16
Café d'Alsace	2a/88s	20
Café Sabarsky	5a/86s	21
Caffe Grazie	84s/5a-Mad	18
Carino	2a/88-89s	20
Centolire	Mad/85-86s	21
Chef Ho's	2a/89-90s	22
Cilantro	2a/88-89s	17
Dakshin	1a/88-89s	21
Demarchelier	86s/Mad-Park	17
Divino	2a/80-81s	18
Donguri	83s/1-2a	27
E.A.T.	Mad/80-81s	19
Elaine's	2a/88-89s	12
Elio's	2a/84s	23
Erminia	83s/2a	25
Etats-Unis	81s/2-3a	24
Firenze	2a/82-83s	21
Giovanni	83s/5a-Mad	22
Girasole	82s/Lex-3a	21
Gobo	3a/81s	22
Heidelberg	2a/85-86s	18
Ichiro	2a/87-88s	21
Italianissimo	84s/1-2a	24
Ithaka	86s/1-2a	21
Jackson Hole	2a/83-84s	17
Jacques	85s/2-3a	19
Jasmine	2a/84s	19
Josie's	2a/84s	19
Kings' Carriage	82s/2-3a	21
Ko Sushi	York/85s	20

Land	2a/81-82s	22
Le Boeuf/Mode	81s/E End	22
Le Pain Q.	Mad/84-85s	18
Le Refuge	82s/Lex-3a	20
Maz Mezcal	86s/1-2a	21
NEW Niche	2a/82-83s	-
Nicola's	84s/Lex-3a	22
One 83	1a/83-84s	20
Our Place	3a/82s	20
Papaya King	86s/3a	21
Pig Heaven	2a/80-81s	19
Pintaile's Pizza	York/83-84s	19
Poke	85s/1-2a	26
Primavera	1a/82s	23
Quattro Gatti	81s/2-3a	19
Rughetta	85s/1-2a	22
Sala Thai	2a/89-90s	20
Sandro's	81s/1-2a	23
NEW Shalizar	3a/80-81s	-
Sharz Cafe	86s/1a-York	19
Sistina	2a/80-81s	24
Spigolo	2a/81s	25
Taste	3a/80s	22
Tenzan	2a/89s	23
Tevere	84s/Lex-3a	23
Tiramisu	3a/80s	19
Tony's Di Napoli	2a/83s	19
Totonno Pizza	2a/80-81s	21
Tratt. Pesce	3a/87-88s	18
Triangolo	83s/1-2a	21
Turquoise	81s/2-3a	22
Vespa	2a/84-85s	19
Viand	86s/2a	16
NEW Vicino Firenze	2a/82-3s	-
Wasabi Lobby	2a/82s	21
Wu Liang Ye	86s/2-3a	22
York Grill	York/88-89s	22
Yuka	2a/80-81s	21
Zócalo	82s/Lex-3a	20

EAST 90s & 100s

(90th to 110th Sts.)

Barking Dog	3a/94s	15
Bistro du Nord	Mad/93s	18
Brother Jimmy	3a/92s	16
NEW Cambodian Cuisine	3a/93-94s	-
Don Pedro's	2a/96s	20
El Paso Taqueria	multi.	22
Itzocan	Lex/101s	24
Jackson Hole	Mad/91s	17
Nick's	2a/94s	23
Osso Buco	3a/93s	17
NEW Parlor Steak	3a/90s	-

Pascalou | *Mad/92-93s*	20
Peri Ela | *Lex/90-91s*	18
Pinocchio | *1a/90-91s*	21
Pintaile's Pizza | *91s/5a-Mad*	19
Pio Pio | *1a/90-91s*	22
Sarabeth's | *Mad/92-93s*	20
Sfoglia | *Lex/92s*	24
Square Meal | *92s/5a-Mad*	23
Table d'Hôte | *92s/Mad-Park*	18
Vico | *Mad/92-93s*	20
Zebú Grill | *92s/1-2a*	20

EAST VILLAGE

(14th to Houston Sts., east of B'way,
excluding NoHo)

Angelica Kit. | *12s/1-2a*	20
NEW Apiary | *3a/10-11s*	-
NEW Artichoke Basille | *14s/1a*	24
Awash | *6s/1-2a*	21
NEW Back Forty | *Ave B/11-12s*	19
Banjara | *1a/6s*	22
Barbone | *Ave B/11-12s*	23
NEW Belcourt | *4s/2a*	20
Boca Chica | *1a/1s*	20
Brick Ln. Curry | *6s/2a*	21
Buenos Aires | *6s/Aves A-B*	22
Butter | *Lafayette/Astor-4s*	20
Cacio e Pepe | *2a/11-12s*	21
Cacio e Vino | *2a/4-5s*	21
Cafecito | *Ave C/11-12s*	21
Cafe Mogador | *St Marks/Ave A*	21
Caracas | *multi.*	25
Caravan/Dreams | *6s/1a*	20
Casimir | *Ave B/6-7s*	20
ChikaLicious | *10s/1-2a*	25
Chipotle | *St Marks/2-3a*	18
Colors | *Lafayette/Astor-4s*	18
Counter | *1a/6-7s*	21
Cucina/Pesce | *4s/Bowery-2a*	18
Dallas BBQ | *2a/St Marks*	14
Z Degustation | *5s/2-3a*	27
Dok Suni's | *1a/St Marks-7s*	22
Dumpling Man | *St Marks/Ave A*	18
Elephant, The | *1s/1-2a*	21
Esperanto | *Ave C/9s*	20
E.U., The | *4s/Aves A-B*	18
Euzkadi | *4s/1-2a*	19
Flea Mkt. Cafe | *Ave A/9s*	19
Frank | *2a/5-6s*	23
Gemma | *Bowery/2-3s*	19
Gnocco Caffe | *10s/Aves A-B*	22
NEW Graffiti | *10s/1-2a*	24
Grand Sichuan | *St Marks/2-3a*	22
Gyu-Kaku | *Cooper/Astor-4s*	22

Hasaki | *9s/2-3a*	22
Haveli | *2a/5-6s*	21
Hearth | *12s/1a*	25
Holy Basil | *2a/9-10s*	21
Hummus Pl. | *St Marks/Ave A*	23
I Coppi | *9s/Ave A-1a*	22
Il Bagatto | *2s/Aves A-B*	23
Indochine | *Lafayette/Astor-4s*	21
NEW Ippudo | *4a/9-10s*	25
Itzocan | *9s/Ave A-1a*	24
Jack's Lux. | *2a/5-6s*	26
Jewel Bako | *5s/2-3a*	25
Jimmy's 43 | *7s/Bowery-2a*	21
John's/12th St. | *12s/2a*	19
Jules | *St Marks/1-2a*	18
NEW Kafana | *Ave C/7-8s*	-
Kanoyama | *2a/11s*	26
Klong | *St Marks/2-3a*	21
Knife + Fork | *4s/1-2a*	21
Kyo Ya | *7s/1a*	29
Lan | *3a/10-11s*	25
La Paella | *9s/2-3a*	19
La Palapa | *St Marks/1-2a*	19
Lavagna | *5s/Aves A-B*	25
Le Gamin | *5s/Aves A-B*	19
Lil' Frankie Pizza | *1a/1-2s*	22
Lucien | *1a/1s*	21
Luzzo's | *1a/12-13s*	24
Mama's Food | *3s/Aves A-B*	21
Mancora | *1a/6s*	22
Mara's | *6s/1-2a*	22
Mary Ann's | *2a/5s*	14
NEW Matilda | *11s/Aves B-C*	18
Max | *Ave B/3-4s*	22
Max Brenner | *2a/9s*	17
Mercadito | *multi.*	23
Mermaid Inn | *2a/5-6s*	21
Minca | *5s/Aves A-B*	22
Mingala Burmese | *7s/2-3a*	19
Z **NEW** Momofuku Ko | *1a/10s*	26
Z Momofuku Noodle | *1a/10s*	23
Momofuku Ssäm | *2a/13s*	23
Moustache | *10s/Ave A-1a*	21
Nicky's | *2s/Ave A*	22
99 Mi. to Philly | *3a/12-13s*	18
Nomad | *2a/4s*	20
Pepe | *Ave C/8s*	21
Perbacco | *4s/Aves A-B*	25
NEW Persimmon | *10s/Ave A*	-
Pizza Gruppo | *Ave B/11-12s*	24
Prune | *1s/1-2a*	24
Pukk | *1a/4-5s*	23
Pylos | *7s/Ave A-1a*	25

LOCATIONS

Quantum Leap | *1a/12-13s* `20`
Rai Rai Ken | *10s/1-2a* `21`
Ramen Setagaya | *1a/9s* `20`
NEW Redhead, The | *13s/1-2a* `-`
Sal Anthony's | *1a/10-11s* `19`
Sapporo East | *1a/10s* `21`
SEA | *2a/4-5s* `21`
S'MAC/Pinch | *12s/1-2a* `21`
NEW Smith, The | *3a/10-11s* `19`
Soba-ya | *9s/2-3a* `23`
Spice | *2a/6s* `20`
Supper | *2s/Aves A-B* `25`
Takahachi | *Ave A/5-6s* `23`
Tarallucci | *1a/10s* `21`
NEW Tet | *Ave A/5-6s* `-`
Tree | *1a/11-12s* `21`
Tsampa | *9s/2-3a* `20`
26 Seats | *Ave B/10-11s* `21`
Two Boots | *Ave A/3s* `19`
Una Pizza | *12s/1-2a* `23`
Veselka | *multi.* `18`
Westville | *Ave A/11s* `22`
Xunta | *1a/10-11s* `21`
NEW Yerba Buena | *Ave A/Houston-2s* `-`
Yuca Bar | *Ave A/7s* `21`
Zum Schneider | *Ave C/7s* `19`

FINANCIAL DISTRICT

(South of Murray St.)

Adrienne's | *Pearl/Coenties* `24`
Au Mandarin | *Vesey/West* `18`
Battery Gdns. | *Battery Pk* `18`
Bobby Van's | *Broad/Exchange* `22`
Bridge Cafe | *Water/Dover* `21`
Bull Run | *William/Pine* `17`
NEW Burger Shoppe | *Water/Broad* `18`
Burritoville | *multi.* `17`
Chipotle | *Bway/Stone* `18`
Così | *Vesey/West* `16`
Delmonico's | *Beaver/William* `22`
Energy Kitchen | *Nassau/Fulton* `15`
Fino | *Wall/Pearl* `19`
Fraunces Tavern | *Pearl/Broad* `16`
Fresco | *Pearl/Hanover* `23`
Gigino | *Battery/West* `20`
Hale/Hearty | *Broad/Beaver* `19`
Harry's | *multi.* `22`
Haru | *Wall/Beaver-Pearl* `21`
Ise | *Pine/Pearl-William* `21`
Lemongrass | *William/Maiden* `16`
Lenny's | *John/Cliff-Pearl* `18`
Les Halles | *John/Bway-Nassau* `19`
Liberty View | *S End/3pl-Thames* `19`

NEW Mad Dog | *Pearl/Hanover* `19`
Mangia | *Wall/Nassau-William* `19`
MarkJoseph | *Water/Peck* `24`
P.J. Clarke's | *World Fin/Vesey* `16`
Roy's NY | *Wash/Albany-Carlisle* `24`
Smorgas Chef | *Stone/William* `19`
Trinity Pl. | *Cedar/Bway-Trinity* `18`
2 West | *West/Battery* `23`
Zen Palate | *John/Cliff* `19`

FLATIRON DISTRICT

(14th to 24th Sts., 6th Ave. to
Park Ave. S., excluding Union Sq.)

Aleo | *20s/5a* `19`
NEW Allegretti | *22s/5-6a* `-`
Angelo/Maxie's | *multi.* `21`
Aspen | *22s/5-6a* `18`
Barbounia | *Park/20s* `20`
Bar Stuzz. | *Bway/21-22s* `20`
Basta Pasta | *17s/5-6a* `22`
Beppe | *22s/Bway-Park* `22`
BLT Fish | *17s/5-6a* `23`
Boqueria | *29s/5-6a* `22`
Chipotle | *6a/21-22s* `18`
City Bakery | *18s/5-6a* `21`
City Crab | *Park/19s* `17`
Comfort Diner | *23s/5-6a* `16`
Così | *6a/22-23s* `16`
Z Craft | *19s/Bway-Park* `26`
Craftbar | *Bway/19-20s* `21`
dévi | *18s/Bway-5a* `23`
Fleur de Sel | *20s/Bway-5a* `25`
Giorgio's | *21s/Bway-Park* `21`
goodburger | *Bway/17-18s* `18`
Z Gramercy Tavern | *20s/Bway* `28`
Haru | *Park/18s* `21`
Kellari Tav./Parea | *20s/Bway* `21`
La Pizza Fresca | *20s/Bway-Park* `22`
Lenny's | *23s/5a* `18`
Le Pain Q. | *19s/Bway-Park* `18`
L'Express | *Park/20s* `17`
Lucy | *18s/Bway-Park* `20`
Lunetta | *Bway/21s* `21`
Mangia | *23s/5-6a* `19`
Markt | *6a/21s* `19`
Z Mesa Grill | *5a/15-16s* `23`
Mizu Sushi | *20s/Bway-Park* `23`
Outback | *23s/5-6a* `15`
Periyali | *20s/5-6a* `23`
Petite Abeille | *17s/5-6a* `18`
Pipa | *19s/Bway-Park* `20`
Planet Thai | *24s/5-6a* `18`
Pump Energy | *21s/Bway-Park* `18`
Punch | *Bway/20-21s* `18`

Menus, photos, voting and more – free at ZAGAT.com

Rickshaw Dumpling | 23s/5-6a `16`
Z Rosa Mexicano | 18s/Bway-5a `21`
Sala | 19s/5-6a `22`
Shaffer's | 21s/5-6a `22`
Z Shake Shack | 23s/Mad sq `23`
SushiSamba | Park/19-20s `22`
Z Tamarind | 22s/Bway-Park `25`
Tarallucci | 18s/Bway-5a `21`
Z Veritas | 20s/Bway-Park `26`
Via Emilia | 21s/Bway-Park `21`
'wichcraft | 20s/Bway-5a `20`
NEW Wildwood BBQ | Park/18s `17`

GARMENT DISTRICT

(30th to 40th Sts., west of 5th)
Abigael's | Bway/38-39s `19`
Arno | 38s/Bway-7a `20`
Ben's Kosher | 38s/7-8a `18`
Brother Jimmy | 8a/31s `16`
Burritoville | 39s/9a `17`
Cho Dang Gol | 35s/5-6a `23`
Così | 7a/36-37s `16`
Frankie/Johnnie | 37s/5-6a `21`
Gahm Mi Oak | 32s/Bway-5a `20`
Gray's Papaya | 8a/37s `21`
Hale/Hearty | 7a/35s `19`
Heartland | 5a/34s `14`
HK | 9a/39s `17`
Kang Suh | Bway/32s `21`
Kati Roll | 39s/5-6a `22`
Keens | 36s/5-6a `24`
Kum Gang San | 32s/Bway-5a `21`
NEW Luxe | 35s/7-8a `-`
Mandoo Bar | 32s/Bway-5a `20`
Nick & Stef's | 33s/7-8a `21`
Osteria Gelsi | 9a/38s `22`
Pump Energy | 38s/Bway-6a `18`
Szechuan Gourmet | 39s/5-6a `-`
Uncle Jack's | 9a/34-35s `23`

GRAMERCY PARK

(24th to 30th Sts., east of 5th;
14th to 24th Sts., east of Park)
A Voce | Mad/26s `25`
Baluchi's | 3a/24-25s `17`
Bao Noodles | 2a/22-23s `18`
NEW Bar Milano | 3a/24s `22`
Black Duck | 28s/Lex-Park `20`
Z BLT Prime | 22s/Lex-Park `25`
Blue Smoke | 27s/Lex-Park `21`
Butai | 18s/Irving-Park `21`
Z Casa Mono | Irving/17s `25`
Chennai Gdn. | 27s/Park `22`
Chinese Mirch | Lex/28s `19`
Chino's | 3a/16-17s `19`

Coppola's | 3a/27-28s `19`
Country | Mad/26-27s `20`
Curry Leaf | Lex/27s `20`
Dos Caminos | Park/26-27s `20`
Z Eleven Madison | Mad/24s `27`
Ess-a-Bagel | 1a/21s `23`
Friend/Farmer | Irving/18-19s `18`
House | 17s/Irving-Park `20`
Houston's | Park/27s `20`
NEW ilili | 5a/27-28s `23`
NEW Irving Mill | 16s/Irving `21`
I Trulli | 27s/Lex-Park `23`
Jaiya Thai | 3a/28s `22`
Japonais | 18s/Irving-Park `20`
Lady Mendl's | Irving/17-18s `22`
La Petite Aub. | Lex/27-28s `19`
Les Halles | Park/28-29s `19`
Novitá | 22s/Lex-Park `24`
NEW Olana | Mad/27-28s `23`
Pamplona | 28s/Mad-Park `23`
NEW Park Ave. Bistro |
    Park/26-27s `20`
Pete's Tavern | 18s/Irving `13`
Petite Abeille | 20s/1a `18`
Pongal | Lex/27-28s `21`
Porcão | Park/26s `20`
Posto | 2a/18s `23`
NEW Primehouse | Park/27s `23`
Pure Food/Wine | Irving/17s `23`
Resto | 29s/Lex-Park `20`
Rice | Lex/28s `19`
Rolf's | 3a/22s `15`
Saravanaas | Lex/26s `24`
Z Tabla | Mad/25s `25`
Totonno Pizza | 2a/26s `21`
Z Turkish Kitchen | 3a/27-28s `22`
Wakiya | Lex/21s `19`
Yama | 17s/Irving `23`

GREENWICH VILLAGE

(Houston to 14th Sts., west of
B'way, east of 7th Ave. S.)
Aja | 6a/9-10s `20`
Aki | 4s/Barrow-Jones `26`
Alta | 10s/5-6a `23`
Amy's Bread | Blkr/Carmine `23`
Z Annisa | Barrow/7a-4s `27`
Arté | 9s/5a-Uni `17`
Arturo's | Houston/Thompson `21`
Z Babbo | Waverly/MacDougal `27`
Baluchi's | multi. `17`
NEW Bar Blanc | 10s/7a `23`
Bar Pitti | 6a/Blkr-Houston `22`
Bellavitae | Minetta/MacDougal `23`

BLT Burger	6a/11-12s	19
☑ Blue Hill	Wash pl/MacDougal	26
Blue Ribbon Bakery	Downing/Bedford	24
Borgo Antico	13s/5a-Uni	17
NEW Cabrito	Carmine/Blkr	-
Cafe Asean	10s/Greenwich a	20
Cafe Español	multi.	20
Cafe Loup	13s/6-7a	19
Cafe Spice	Uni/10-11s	18
CamaJe	MacDougal/Blkr	22
Chez Jacqueline	MacDougal/Blkr	20
Chipotle	8s/Bway-Uni	18
NEW Cho Cho San	8s/5-6a	-
Cornelia St. Cafe	Cornelia/4s	19
Così	multi.	16
☑ Cru	5a/9-10s	26
☑ Cuba	Thompson/Blkr-3s	23
Cubana Café	Thompson/Prince	19
Danal	5a/12-13s	20
Da Silvano	6a/Blkr	21
Deborah	Carmine/Bedford-Blkr	20
Ditch Plains	Bedford/Downing	16
Do Hwa	Carmine/Bedford	21
El Charro Español	Charles/Greenwich a	22
Elephant & Castle	Greenwich a/Perry	18
NEW Elettaria	8s/5-6a	23
Empire Szechuan	multi.	15
Ennio/Michael	La Guardia/3s	21
Fish	Blkr/Jones	20
Five Guys	La Guardia/Blkr	20
French Roast	11s/5-6a	15
Gobo	6a/8s-Waverly	22
Gonzo	13s/6-7a	20
☑ Gotham B&G	12s/5a-Uni	27
Gradisca	13s/6-7a	21
Grand Sichuan	7a/Carmine	22
Grano Tratt.	Greenwich a/10s	23
Gray's Papaya	6a/8s	21
Gus' Place	Blkr/MacDougal-6a	19
Gusto	Greenwich a/Perry	22
Hummus Pl.	multi.	23
Il Cantinori	10s/Bway-Uni	22
☑ Il Mulino	3s/Sullivan	27
'ino	Bedford/Downing-6a	24
Jane	Houston/La Guardia	21
Japonica	Uni/12s	22
Joe's Pizza	Carmine/Blkr-6a	23
John's Pizzeria	Blkr/6-7a	22
Kati Roll	MacDougal/Blkr-3s	22
NEW Kingswood	10s/6a	21
Knickerbocker	Uni/9s	19
La Lanterna	MacDougal/3-4s	19
La Palapa	6a/Wash pl-4s	19
Las Ramblas	4s/Cornelia-Jones	24
Le Gamin	Houston/MacDougal	19
Le Gigot	Cornelia/Blkr-4s	24
Lenny's	6a/9s	18
Le Pain Q.	multi.	18
☑ Lupa	Thompson/Blkr	25
Marinella	Carmine/Bedford	21
NEW Market Table	Carmine/Bedford	23
☑ Mas	Downing/Bedford	28
Max Brenner	Bway/13-14s	17
Meskerem	MacDougal/Blkr-3s	21
Mexicana Mama	12s/Bway	24
Morandi	Waverly/Charles	21
Negril	3s/La Guardia	20
North Sq.	Waverly/MacDougal	22
☑ One if by Land	Barrow/7a	24
Osso Buco	Uni/11-12s	17
Otto	8s/5a-Uni	23
Palma	Cornelia/Blkr-6a	23
Patsy's Pizzeria	Uni/10-11s	20
Peanut Butter Co.	Sullivan/3s	19
☑ Pearl Oyster	Cornelia/Blkr	26
Perilla	Jones/Blkr-4s	25
Piadina	10s/5-6a	19
Piola	12s/Bway-Uni	19
Pizza 33	6a/14s	21
Pó	Cornelia/Blkr-4s	24
p*ong	10s/Greenwich a	22
Prem-on Thai	Houston/MacDougal	20
Quantum Leap	Thompson/3s	20
Rare B&G	Blkr/Carmine-6a	21
NEW Rhong-Tiam	La Guardia/3s	-
Rickshaw Dumpling	8s/Bway	16
Risotteria	Blkr/Morton	20
Saigon Grill	Uni/11-12s	21
NEW Smith's	MacDougal/Blkr	22
☑ Soto	6a/Wash-4s	26
Spice	Uni/10s	20
Stand	12s/5a-Uni	20
Strip House	12s/5a-Uni	25
Tio Pepe	4s/Cornelia-Jones	18
Tomoe Sushi	Thompson/Blkr	25
Tratt. Pesce	Blkr/6-7a	18
Ushiwakamaru	Houston/MacDougal	27
Village	9s/5-6a	19
Villa Mosconi	MacDougal/Blkr	21
'wichcraft	8s/Mercer	20
Yama	Carmine/Bedford-Blkr	23

Menus, photos, voting and more – free at ZAGAT.com

HARLEM/EAST HARLEM

(110th to 157th Sts., excluding Columbia U. area)

Amy Ruth's | 116s/Lenox-7a	21
Charles' Kitchen | Douglass/151s	22
NEW Covo | 135s/12a	24
Dinosaur BBQ | 131s/12a	22
El Paso Taqueria | 116s/3a	22
Hudson Café | 133s/12a	21
Londel's | Douglass/139-140s	20
Miss Mamie/Maude | multi.	21
Mo-Bay | 125s/5a-Lenox	20
Papaya King | 125s/Lenox-7a	21
Patsy's Pizzeria | 1a/117-118s	20
Rao's | 114s/Pleasant	23
Sylvia's | Lenox/126-127s	17
NEW Talay | 135s/12a	-

LITTLE ITALY

(Canal to Kenmare Sts., Bowery to Lafayette St.)

Angelo's/Mulberry | Mulberry/Grand	23
Congee | Bowery/Grand-Hester	20
Da Nico | Mulberry/Broome	21
Ferrara | Grand/Mott-Mulberry	22
Grotta Azzurra | Mulberry/Broome	19
Il Cortile | Mulberry/Canal	23
Il Fornaio | Mulberry/Grand	22
Il Palazzo | Mulberry/Grand	22
La Esquina | Kenmare/Cleveland	22
La Mela | Mulberry/Broome	19
Nyonya | Grand/Mott-Mulberry	22
Pellegrino's | Mulberry/Grand	24
Pho Bang | Mott/Broome-Grand	20
Positano | Mulberry/Canal	22
NEW Red Egg | Centre/Howard	-
Sal Anthony's | Mulberry/Grand	19
Shanghai Café | Mott/Canal	22
Umberto's | Broome/Mulberry	19
Vincent's | Mott/Hester	21
X.O. | Hester/Bowery-Elizabeth	19

LOWER EAST SIDE

(Houston to Canal Sts., east of Bowery)

Alias | Clinton/Riv	21
NEW Allen & Delancey | Allen/Delancey	24
ápizz | Eldridge/Riv-Stanton	24
Azul Bistro | Stanton/Suffolk	23
Bereket | Houston/Orchard	19
Bondi Rd. | Riv/Clinton-Suffolk	18
NEW Broadway East | Bway/Jefferson-Rutgers	21
Brown Café | Hester/Essex	22

NEW Café Katja | Orchard/Broome	24
Clinton St. Baking Co. | Clinton/Houston	25
Congee | multi.	20
Cube 63 | Clinton/Riv-Stanton	22
Essex | Essex/Riv	18
Falai | Clinton/Riv	24
Frankies | Clinton/Houston	24
Freemans | Riv/Bowery-Chrystie	21
'inoteca | Riv/Ludlow	23
Kampuchea | Riv/Allen	21
⊠ Katz's Deli | Houston/Ludlow	23
Kuma Inn | Ludlow/Delancey	24
Les Enfants | Canal/Ludlow	17
Little Giant | Orchard/Broome	23
Oliva | Houston/Allen	20
Orchard, The | Orchard/Riv	23
Paladar | Ludlow/Houston	19
Rayuela | Allen/Riv-Stanton	23
Salt | Clinton/Houston-Stanton	21
Sammy's | Chrystie/Delancey	20
savorNY | Clinton/Riv-Stanton	24
Schiller's | Riv/Norfolk	18
Spitzer's | Riv/Ludlow	17
Stanton Social | Stanton/Ludlow	23
Suba | Ludlow/Delancey-Riv	20
Thor | Riv/Essex-Ludlow	17
Tides | Norfolk/Delancey-Riv	24
NEW Tre | Ludlow/Houston	22
Two Boots | Grand/Norfolk	19
wd-50 | Clinton/Riv-Stanton	23
Whole Foods | Houston/Grand	18

MEATPACKING

(Gansevoort to 15th Sts., west of 9th Ave.)

NEW Bagatelle | 13s/9a-Wash	22
Buddha Bar | Little W 12s/9a	19
Fig & Olive | 13s/9a-Wash	20
5 9th | 9a/Gansevoort	20
Highline | Wash/Little W 12s	19
Los Dados | Gansevoort/Wash	19
Macelleria | Gansevoort/Greenwich s	19
NEW Merkato 55 | Gansevoort/Greenwich s	21
Nero | Gansevoort/Greenwich s	19
Old Homestead | 9a/14-15s	24
Ono | 9A/13s	19
Paradou | Little W 12s/Greenwich s	20
Pastis | 9a/Little W 12s	20
Pop Burger | 9a/14-15s	18
NEW R & L | Gansevoort/Greenwich s	-

Son Cubano | *14s/9a-Wash* | 21
Ƶ Spice Market | *13s/9a* | 22
STK | *Little W 12s/9a-Wash* | 21
Valbella | *13s/9a-Wash* | 24
Vento | *Hudson/14s* | 19

MURRAY HILL

(30th to 40th Sts., east of 5th)

Ali Baba | *34s/2-3a* | 22
AQ Cafe | *Park/37-38s* | 22
Aquamarine | *2a/38-39s* | 20
Ƶ Artisanal | *32s/Mad-Park* | 23
Asia de Cuba | *Mad/37-38s* | 23
Barbès | *36s/5a-Mad* | 20
Barking Dog | *34s/Lex-3a* | 15
Better Burger | *3a/37s* | 15
Blockhead Burrito | *3a/33-34s* | 16
Brother Jimmy | *Lex/31s* | 16
Carl's Steaks | *3a/34s* | 21
Chipotle | *5a/34s* | 18
Cosette | *33s/Lex-3a* | 21
Da Ciro | *Lex/33-34s* | 22
El Parador Cafe | *34s/1-2a* | 22
El Pote | *2a/38-39s* | 22
Ethos | *3a/33-34s* | 22
Evergreen | *38s/5a-Mad* | 19
Fino | *36s/5a-Mad* | 19
Franchia | *Park/34-35s* | 19
Grand Sichuan | *Lex/33-34s* | 22
Ƶ Hangawi | *32s/5a-Mad* | 24
Iron Sushi | *3a/30-31s* | 19
Jackson Hole | *3a/35s* | 17
Josie's | *3a/37s* | 19
La Giara | *3a/33-34s* | 19
Lemongrass | *34s/Lex-3a* | 16
Libretto's Pizza | *3a/36s* | 21
Madison Bistro | *Mad/37-38s* | 20
Mee Noodle | *2a/30-31s* | 18
Mishima | *Lex/30-31s* | 22
Morgan | *Mad/363-7s* | 21
Notaro | *2a/34-35s* | 18
Pasticcio | *3a/30-31s* | 18
Patsy's Pizzeria | *3a/34-35s* | 20
Penelope | *Lex/30s* | 21
Pio Pio | *34s/2-3a* | 22
Pizza 33 | *3a/33s* | 21
Rare B&G | *Lex/37s* | 21
Rossini's | *38s/Lex-Park* | 23
Salute! | *Mad/39s* | 19
Sarge's Deli | *3a/36-37s* | 18
NEW 2nd Ave Deli | *33s/Lex-3a* | 22
Stella del Mare | *Lex/39-40s* | 23
Sushi Sen-nin | *33s/Mad-Park* | 24
Todai | *32s/5a-Mad* | 17

Tratt. Alba | *34s/2-3a* | 22
Vezzo | *Lex/31s* | 23
Villa Berulia | *34s/Lex-Park* | 21
Water Club | *E River/23s* | 22
'wichcraft | *Park/33s* | 20
Wolfgang's | *Park/33s* | 25
Wu Liang Ye | *Lex/39-40s* | 22

NOHO

(Houston to 4th Sts., Bowery to B'way)

Aroma | *4s/Bowery-Lafayette* | 24
Bianca | *Blkr/Bowery-Elizabeth* | 23
Bond St. | *Bond/Bway-Lafayette* | 24
Chinatown Brass. | *Lafayette/Gr Jones* | 21
5 Points | *Gr Jones/Bowery* | 22
Great Jones Cafe | *Gr Jones/Bowery* | 19
Il Buco | *Bond/Bowery-Lafayette* | 24
Mercat | *Bond/Bowery-Lafayette* | 22
NoHo Star | *Lafayette/Blkr* | 17
Rice | *Elizabeth/Blkr-Houston* | 19
Sala | *Bowery/Gr Jones* | 22
Serafina | *Lafayette/4s* | 19
Two Boots | *Blkr/Bway* | 19

NOLITA

(Houston to Kenmare Sts., Bowery to Lafayette St.)

barmarché | *Spring/Elizabeth* | 19
Bread | *Spring/Elizabeth-Mott* | 19
Cafe Colonial | *Elizabeth/Houston* | 18
Cafe Gitane | *Mott/Prince* | 19
Café Habana/Outpost | *Prince/Elizabeth* | 20
NEW Delicatessen | *Prince/Lafayette* | -
Ed's Lobster | *Lafayette/Spring* | 23
8 Mile Creek | *Mulberry/Prince* | 20
Ghenet | *Mulberry/Houston* | 21
Jacques | *Prince/Elizabeth-Mott* | 19
Kitchen Club | *Prince/Mott* | 21
Le Jardin | *Cleveland/Kenmare* | 19
Lombardi's | *Spring/Mott* | 24
Mexican Radio | *Cleveland/Kenmare* | 18
Peasant | *Elizabeth/Prince* | 24
Public | *Elizabeth/Prince-Spring* | 22

SOHO

(Canal to Houston Sts., west of Lafayette St.)

Ama | *MacDougal/King-Prince* | 23
Ƶ Aquagrill | *Spring/6a* | 26
Aurora | *Broome/Thompson* | 25
Ƶ Balthazar | *Spring/Bway* | 23
Baluchi's | *Spring/Sullivan* | 17

Barolo | *W Bway/Broome-Spring* | 19
Bistro Les Amis | *Spring/Thompson* | 21
Blue Ribbon | *Sullivan/Prince* | 24
🆉 Blue Ribbon Sushi | | 26
Sullivan/Prince
NEW Bún | *Grand/Crosby* | 21
Cendrillon | *Mercer/Broome* | 21
Centovini | *Houston/Greene* | 20
Chipotle | *Varick/Houston-King* | 18
Cipriani D'twn | *W Bway/Broome* | 20
Dos Caminos | *W Bway/Houston* | 20
Falai | *Lafayette/Prince* | 24
Félix | *W Bway/Grand* | 16
Fiamma | *Spring/6a-Sullivan* | 24
FROG | *Spring/Crosby-Lafayette* | 19
Giorgione | *Spring/Greenwich s* | 22
Hampton Chutney | *Prince/Crosby* | 19
NEW Hundred Acres | | 18
MacDougal/Prince
Ideya | *W Bway/Broome-Grand* | 19
Il Corallo | *Prince/Sullivan* | 22
I Tre Merli | *W Bway/Houston* | 17
Ivo & Lulu | *Broome/6a-Varick* | 24
Jean Claude | *Sullivan/Houston* | 21
🆉 Kittichai | *Thompson/Broome* | 22
L'Ecole | *Bway/Grand* | 25
Le Pain Q. | *Grand/Greene* | 18
NEW Lomito | *Spring/Hudson* | –
Lucky Strike | *Grand/W Bway* | 16
Lure Fishbar | *Mercer/Prince* | 23
Mercer Kitchen | *Prince/Mercer* | 21
Mezzogiorno | *Spring/Sullivan* | 20
Novecento | *W Bway/Broome* | 19
Omen | *Thompson/Prince* | 23
Once Upon a Tart | | 20
Sullivan/Houston
NEW 1 Dominick | *Dominick/6a* | –
Papatzul | *Grand/W Bway* | 23
Peep | *Prince/Sullivan-Thompson* | 19
Pepe | *Sullivan/Houston* | 21
Raoul's | *Prince/Sullivan* | 23
Salt | *MacDougal/Houston* | 21
Savoy | *Prince/Crosby* | 23
NEW Shorty's.32 | | 24
Prince/MacDougal
Snack | *Thompson/Prince-Spring* | 22
Tailor | *Broome/Sullivan* | 23
12 Chairs | *MacDougal/Prince* | 19
'wichcraft | *Crosby/Prince* | 20
Woo Lae Oak | *Mercer/Houston* | 22
Zoë | *Prince/Bway-Mercer* | 19

SOUTH STREET SEAPORT

Acqua/Peck Slip | *Peck/Water* | 19
Cabana | *South/Fulton* | 21

Heartland | *South/Fulton* | 14
Stella Maris | *Front/Beekman* | 20
Suteishi | *Peck/Front* | 22

TRIBECA

(Canal to Murray Sts.,
west of B'way)

Acappella | *Hudson/Chambers* | 24
NEW Ago | *Greenwich s/Moore* | 17
Arqua | *Church/White* | 22
Baluchi's | *Greenwich s/Warren* | 17
Blaue Gans | *Duane/Church* | 21
🆉 Bouley | *W Bway/Duane* | 28
🆉 Bouley Upstairs | | 25
W Bway/Duane
Bread | *Church/Walker* | 19
Bubby's | *Hudson/N Moore* | 17
Burritoville | *Chambers/Church* | 17
Capsouto Frères | *Wash/Watts* | 23
Carl's Steaks | *Chambers/Bway* | 21
Centrico | *W Bway/Franklin* | 19
Cercle Rouge | *W Bway/Beach* | 19
🆉 Chanterelle | *Harrison/Hudson* | 27
🆉 Churrascaria | *W Bway/Franklin* | 23
City Hall | *Duane/Church* | 20
NEW Corton | *W Bway/Walker* | –
Dean's | *Greenwich s/Harrison* | 17
Dennis Foy | *Church/Lispenard* | 21
Devin | *Greenwich s/Franklin* | 18
NEW Duane Park | | 25
Duane/Hudson-W Bway
Dylan Prime | *Laight/Greenwich s* | 24
Ecco | *Chambers/Church* | 22
Estancia | *Greenwich* | 20
s/Desbrosses
F.illi Ponte | *Desbrosses/Wash* | 22
Flor de Sol | *Greenwich s/Franklin* | 21
NEW Forge | *Reade/Greenwich s* | –
fresh | *Reade/Church-W Bway* | 25
Gigino | *Greenwich s/Duane* | 20
NEW Greenwich Grill | | –
Greenwich s/Laight
Harrison, The | | 24
Greenwich s/Harrison
Il Giglio | *Warren/Greenwich s* | 25
Industria | *Greenwich s/Duane* | 19
Kitchenette | | 19
Chambers/Greenwich s
Landmarc | *W Bway/Leonard* | 20
Mai House | *Duane/Greenwich s* | 20
Mary Ann's | *W Bway/Chambers* | 14
NEW Matsugen | *Church/Leonard* | 21
Max | *Duane/Greenwich s* | 22
Megu | *Thomas/Church-W Bway* | 24
Mr. Chow | *Hudson/N Moore* | 21
Nam | *Reade/W Bway* | 21

Ninja | *Hudson/Duane-Reade* 16

☑ Nobu | *multi.* 27

Odeon | *W Bway/Duane* 18

Pepolino | *W Bway/Canal* 25

Petite Abeille | *W Bway/Duane* 18

Roc | *Duane/Greenwich s* 21

Rosanjin | *Duane/Church* 27

Salaam Bombay | 19
Greenwich s/Duane-Reade

☑ Scalini Fedeli | 27
Duane/Greenwich s

Takahachi | *Duane/Church* 23

Thalassa | *Franklin/Greenwich s* 24

Tribeca Grill | *Greenwich s/Franklin* 22

Turks & Frogs | 20
Greenwich s/Desbrosses

VietCafé | *Greenwich s/Jay* 22

Walker's | *N Moore/Varick* 17

Whole Foods | 18
Greenwich s/Murray

'wichcraft | *Greenwich s/Beach* 20

Wolfgang's | *Greenwich s/Beach* 25

Zutto | *Hudson/Harrison* 21

UNION SQUARE

(14th to 17th Sts., 5th Ave. to
Union Sq. E.)

☑ Blue Water | *Union sq/16s* 23

NEW Cafe Society | *16s/5a* -

Chop't Creative | *17s/Bway-5a* 19

Coffee Shop | *Union sq/16s* 15

15 East | *15s/5a-Union sq* 26

Havana Central | *17s/Bway-5a* 17

Heartland | *Union sq/16-17s* 14

Olives | *Park/17s* 22

Republic | *Union sq/16-17s* 18

☑ Tocqueville | *15s/5a-Union sq* 25

☑ Union Sq. Cafe | *16s/5a* 27

Whole Foods | *Union sq/Bway* 18

WASHINGTON HTS./ INWOOD

(North of W. 157th St.)

Dallas BBQ | *Bway/165-166s* 14

El Malecon | *Bway/175s* 21

Empire Szechuan | *Bway/170s* 15

Hispaniola | *181s/Cabrini* 20

Mamajuana | *Dyckman/Payson* 21

New Leaf | *Corbin/190s* 20

107 West | *187s/Ft Wash* 17

Park Terrace | *Bway/Isham-207s* 20

WEST 40s

A.J. Maxwell's | *48s/5-6a* 22

Akdeniz | *46s/5-6a* 21

Alfredo of Rome | *49s/5-6a* 18

Algonquin | *44s/5-6a* 16

Amarone | *9a/47-48s* 18

Amy's Bread | *9a/46-47s* 23

Angus McIndoe | *44s/Bway-8a* 17

Baldoria | *49s/Bway-8a* 21

Barbetta | *46s/8-9a* 20

Basilica | *9a/46-47s* 20

☑ Becco | *46s/8-9a* 23

Better Burger | *9a/42-43s* 15

Blue Fin | *Bway/47s* 21

Bond 45 | *45s/6-7a* 19

NEW Bourbon St. B&G | *46s/8a* -

NEW Brasserie 44 | *44s/5-6a* 19

Breeze | *9a/45-46s* 21

Brooklyn Diner | *43s/Bway-6a* 17

Bryant Park | *40s/5-6a* 17

B. Smith's | *46s/8-9a* 18

Bubba Gump | *Bway/43-44s* 14

Burritoville | *9a/44s* 17

Cafe Un Deux | *44s/Bway-6a* 16

Cara Mia | *9a/45-46s* 19

☑ Carmine's | *44s/Bway-8a* 20

Cascina | *9a/45-46s* 19

Chez Josephine | *42s/9-10a* 20

Chimichurri Grill | *9a/43-44s* 20

Chipotle | *42s/5-6a* 18

NEW Chop Suey | *7a/47-48s* 15

☑ Churrascaria | *49s/8-9a* 23

City Lobster | *49s/6a* 18

Così | *42s/5-6a* 16

NEW Crave | *42s/11-12s* 19

Daisy May's | *11a/46s* 22

Dallas BBQ | *42s/7-8a* 14

☑ db Bistro Moderne | *44s/5a* 25

☑ Del Frisco's | *6a/48-49s* 25

Delta Grill | *9a/48s* 19

Dervish | *47s/6-7a* 19

District | *46s/6-7a* 20

Don Giovanni | *44s/9a* 17

Edison | *47s/Bway-8a* 15

Energy Kitchen | *47s/9a* 15

Esca | *43s/9a* 25

etc. etc. | *44s/8-9a* 21

FireBird | *46s/8-9a* 19

NEW 5 Napkin Burger | *9a/45s* -

44/44½ | *multi.* 22

Frankie/Johnnie | *45s/Bway-8a* 21

☑ Gari/Sushi | *46s/8-9a* 26

NEW Gazala Place | *9a/48-49s* 25

goodburger | *45s/5-6a* 18

Hale/Hearty | *multi.* 19

Hallo Berlin | *10a/44-45s* 19

Hard Rock Cafe | *Bway/43s* 12

Haru | *43s/Bway-8a* 21

Havana Central | 46s/6-7a	17
Hawaiian Tropic | 7a/49s	15
Heartland | 43s/Bway-6a	14
Hell's Kitchen | 9a/46-47s	23
Jewel of India | 44s/5-6a	19
Joe Allen | 46s/8-9a	17
John's Pizzeria | 44s/Bway-8a	22
Junior's | 45s/Bway-8a	17
Kellari Tav./Parea | 44s/5-6a	21
Kodama | 45s/8-9a	19
Koi | 40s/5-6a	24
Kyotofu | 9a/48-49s	21
La Masseria | 48s/Bway-8a	22
Landmark Tavern | 11a/46s	17
La Rivista | 46s/8-9a	21
Lattanzi | 46s/8-9a	22
Le Marais | 46s/6-7a	20
Lenny's | multi.	18
Le Rivage | 46s/8-9a	20
Marseille | 9a/44s	20
Meskerem | 47s/9-10a	21
Metro Marché | 8a/41s	19
Monster Sushi | 46s/5-6a	17
Morrell Wine Bar | 49s/5-6a	18
NEW Nizza | 9a/44-45s	20
Ollie's | 42s/9-10a	15
Orso | 46s/8-9a	23
Osteria al Doge | 44s/Bway-6a	20
Pam Real Thai | multi.	22
Pietrasanta | 9a/47s	18
Pigalle | 8a/48s	17
Pomaire | 46s/8-9a	22
Pongsri Thai | 48s/Bway-8a	21
Queen of Sheba | 10a/45-46s	23
Z Rainbow Room | 49s/5-6a	20
Re Sette | 45s/5-6a	21
Ruby Foo's | Bway/49s	19
Sardi's | 44s/Bway-8a	17
Scarlatto | 47s/Bway-8a	20
Sea Grill | 49s/5-6a	24
Serafina | 49s/Bway-8a	19
Shula's | 43s/Bway-8a	21
Spanky's BBQ | 43s/Bway-6a	15
Sushiden | 49s/6-7a	24
Sushi Zen | 44s/Bway-6a	25
Tony's Di Napoli | 43s/Bway-6a	19
Trattoria Trecolori | 47s/Bway	21
Triomphe | 44s/5-6a	24
Turkish Cuisine | 9a/44-45s	19
Two Boots | Rock plz/49-50s	19
Utsav | 6a/46-47s	21
Via Brasil | 46s/5-6a	18
View, The | Bway/45-46s	17

Virgil's BBQ | 44s/Bway-6a	20
West Bank Cafe | 42s/9-10a	20
'wichcraft | 6a/40-42s	20
Wondee Siam | 10a/45-46s	23
Wu Liang Ye | 48s/5-6a	22
Zen Palate | 9a/46s	19

WEST 50s

Abboccato | 55s/6-7a	21
Afghan Kebab | 9a/51-52s	19
Amalia | 55s/Bway-7a	21
Angelo's Pizza | multi.	19
Anthos | 52s/5-6a	24
Azuri Cafe | 51s/9-10a	25
Baluchi's | 56s/Bway-8a	17
Bann | 50s/8-9a	24
Bar Americain | 52s/6-7a	22
Basso56 | 56s/Bway-8a	21
Bay Leaf | 56s/5-6a	20
Beacon | 56s/5-6a	22
Bello | 9a/56s	20
Ben Benson's | 52s/6-7a	23
Benihana | 56s/5-6A	17
NEW Benoit | 55s/5-6a	18
Blockhead Burrito | 50s/8-9a	16
BLT Market | 6a/CPS	24
bluechili | 51s/Bway-8a	20
NEW Blue Ribbon Sushi B&G | 58s/8-9a	24
Bobby Van's | 50s/6-7a	22
Bombay Palace | 52s/5-6a	18
NEW Braai | 51s/8-9a	-
NEW Brasserie Cognac | Bway/55s	19
Brasserie 8½ | 57s/5-6a	22
Brass. Ruhlmann | 50s/5-6a	18
Bricco | 56s/8-9a	19
Brooklyn Diner | 57s/Bway-7a	17
burger joint | 56s/6-7a	23
Caffe Cielo | 8a/52-53s	19
Carnegie Deli | 7a/55s	21
Casellula | 52s/9-10a	21
Chez Napoléon | 50s/8-9a	21
China Grill | 53s/5-6a	22
Chop't Creative | 51s/6a	19
Così | Bway/50s	16
Da Tommaso | 8a/53-54s	19
Eatery | 9a/53s	19
El Centro | 9a/54s	20
Empanada Mama | 9a/51-52s	22
Five Guys | 55s/5-6a	20
Fives | 5a/55s	23
Gallagher's | 52s/Bway-8a	21
Gordon Ramsay | 54s/6-7a	25

Grayz | 54s/5-6a	23
Greek Kitchen | 10a/58s	20
Guantanamera | 8a/55-56s	20
Hale/Hearty | 56s/5-6a	19
Heartland | 6a/51s	14
Hudson Cafeteria | 58s/8-9a	20
Il Gattopardo | 54s/5-6a	23
Il Tinello | 56s/5-6a	24
Insieme | 7a/50-51s	24
Ise | 56s/5-6a	21
Island Burgers | 9a/51-52s	22
Joe's Shanghai | 56s/5-6a	22
Johnny Utah | 51s/5-6a	13
Kobe Club | 58s/5-6a	23
La Bergamote | 52s/10-11a	24
La Bonne Soupe | 55s/5-6a	18
☑ Le Bernardin | 51s/6-7a	28
Le Pain Q. | 7a/58s	18
Maison | Bway/53s	18
Mangia | 57s/5-6a	19
Maria Pia | 51s/8-9a	19
Maze | 54s/6-7a	25
McCormick/Schmick | 52s/6a	20
Mee Noodle | 9a/53s	18
Menchanko-tei | 55s/5-6a	20
Michael's | 55s/5-6a	22
☑ Milos | 55s/6-7a	27
Moda | 52s/6-7a	19
☑ Modern, The | 53s/5-6a	26
Molyvos | 7a/55-56s	22
Natsumi | 50s/Bway-8a	22
Nino's | 58s/6-7a	21
☑ Nobu 57 | 57s/5-6a	26
Nocello | 55s/Bway-8a	20
Nook | 9a/50-51s	22
Norma's | 57s/6-7a	25
Omido | Bway/53-54s	24
Osteria del Circo | 55s/6-7a	22
☑ Palm, The | 50s/Bway-8a	24
Palm Court | 5a/59s	20
NEW Park Room | CPS/5-6a	-
Patsy's | 56s/Bway-8a	21
Pepe | 52s/8-9a	21
Petrossian | 58s/7a	24
☑ Piano Due | 51s/6-7a	25
Pump Energy | 55s/5-6a	18
Puttanesca | 9a/56s	19
Quality Meats | 58s/5-6a	23
Redeye Grill | 7a/56s	20
Remi | 53s/6-7a	22
Rice 'n' Beans | 9a/50-51s	22
Roberto Passon | 9a/50s	22
Rock Ctr. | 50s/5-6a	18

Rue 57 | 57s/6a	18
Russian Samovar | 52s/Bway	19
Russian Tea | 57s/6-7a	19
Ruth's Chris | 51s/6-7a	24
Sarabeth's | CPS/5-6a	20
Serafina | 55s/Bway	19
Shelly's Tradizionale | 57s/5-6a	19
Sosa Borella | 8a/50s	17
Stage Deli | 7a/53-4s	19
☑ Sugiyama | 55s/Bway-8a	27
Sushiya | 56s/5-6a	19
☑ Taboon | 10a/52s	25
Tang Pavilion | 55s/5-6a	22
Thalia | 8a/50s	20
Toloache | 50s/Bway-8a	23
Topaz Thai | 56s/6-7a	20
Town | 56s/5-6a	24
Tratt. Dell'Arte | 7a/56-57s	22
21 Club | 52s/5-6a	22
Uncle Jack's | 56s/5-6a	23
Uncle Nick's | 9a/50-51s	20
ViceVersa | 51s/8-9a	22
☑ Victor's Cafe | 52s/Bway-8a	22
Vynl | 9a/51s	15
Whym | 9a/57-58s	20
'wichcraft | 50s/5-6a	20
Wondee Siam | multi.	23
☑ Yakitori Totto | 55s/Bway-8a	26
Zona Rosa | 56s/5-6a	18

WEST 60s

☑ Asiate | 60s/Bway	24
NEW Bar Boulud | Bway/63-64s	22
Bouchon Bakery | 60s/Bway	23
☑ Café des Artistes | 67s/Colum	22
Cafe Fiorello | Bway/63-64s	20
Empire Szechuan | Colum/68s	15
Gabriel's | 60s/Bway-Colum	22
Grand Tier | Lincoln Ctr/63-65s	19
☑ Jean Georges | CPW/60-61s	28
Josephina | Bway/63-64s	18
La Boîte en Bois | 68s/Colum	21
Landmarc | 60s/Bway	20
Le Pain Q. | 65s/Bway-CPW	18
Levana | 69s/Bway-Colum	20
☑ Masa/Bar Masa | 60s/Bway	27
Nick & Toni's | 67s/Bway	17
Ollie's | Bway/67-68s	15
O'Neals' | 64s/Bway-CPW	17
☑ Per Se | 60s/Bway	28
☑ Picholine | 64s/Bway-CPW	26
P.J. Clarke's | 63s/Colum	16
Porter House NY | 60s/Bway	23
☑ Rosa Mexicano | Colum/62s	21

Sapphire | *Bway/60-61s*	21
Shun Lee Cafe | *65s/Colum*	20
Shun Lee West | *65s/Colum*	22
Tavern on Green | *CPW/66-67s*	14
☑ Telepan | *69s/Colum-CPW*	25
Whole Foods | *60s/Bway*	18

WEST 70s

Alice's Tea Cup | *73s/Amst*	19
Amber | *Colum/70s*	20
Arté Café | *73s/Amst-Colum*	18
Bello Sguardo | *Amst/79-80s*	19
Bettola | *Amst/79-80s*	20
Big Nick's | *multi.*	17
Bistro Cassis | *Colum/70-71s*	20
Burritoville | *72s/Amst-Colum*	17
Café Frida | *Colum/77-78s*	20
Cafe Luxembourg | *70s/Amst*	20
Cafe Ronda | *Colum/71-72s*	19
'Cesca | *75s/Amst*	23
China Fun | *Colum/71-72s*	15
Citrus B&G | *Amst/75s*	19
Compass | *70s/Amst-W End*	22
Coppola's | *W 79s/Amst-Bway*	19
Così | *Bway/76-77s*	16
Dallas BBQ | *72s/Colum-CPW*	14
NEW Dovetail | *77s/Colum*	26
Earthen Oven | *72s/Colum*	20
Epices/Traiteur | *70s/Colum*	21
Fairway Cafe | *Bway/74s*	18
☑ Gari/Sushi | *Colum/77-78s*	26
Gray's Papaya | *Bway/72s*	21
Hummus Pl. | *Amst/74-75s*	23
Isabella's | *Colum/77s*	20
Josie's | *Amst/74s*	19
La Grolla | *Amst/79-80s*	19
La Vela | *Amst/77-78s*	18
Lenny's | *Colum/74s*	18
Le Pain Q. | *72s/Colum-CPW*	18
Mughlai | *Colum/75s*	19
Nice Matin | *79s/Amst*	19
Ocean Grill | *Colum/78-79s*	23
Pappardella | *Colum/75s*	19
Pasha | *71s/Colum-CPW*	20
Patsy's Pizzeria | *74s/Colum*	20
Pomodoro Rosso | *Colum/70s*	22
Ruby Foo's | *Bway/77s*	19
Sambuca | *72s/Colum-CPW*	18
Santa Fe | *71s/Colum-CPW*	18
Savann | *Amst/79-80s*	19
Scaletta | *77s/Colum-CPW*	21
Swagat Indian | *Amst/79-80s*	20
Tenzan | *Colum/73s*	23
Viand | *Bway/75s*	16

WEST 80s

Artie's Deli | *Bway/82-83s*	18
☑ Barney Greengrass | *Amst/86s*	24
NEW Bellini | *Colum/83-84s*	18
Bistro Citron | *Colum/82-83s*	20
Bodrum | *Amst/88-89s*	20
Brother Jimmy | *Amst/80-81s*	16
Blossom | *Colum/82-83s*	22
Cafe Con Leche | *Amst/80-81s*	17
Cafe Lalo | *83s/Amst-Bway*	19
Calle Ocho | *Colum/81-82s*	22
Celeste | *Amst/84-85s*	24
Cilantro | *Colum/83-4s*	17
Darna | *Colum/89s*	21
Dean's | *85s/Amst-Bway*	17
Docks Oyster | *Bway/89-90s*	19
Edgar's | *84s/Bway-West End*	17
NEW eighty one | *81s/Colum*	26
EJ's Luncheon. | *Amst/81-82s*	16
Flor de Mayo | *Amst/83-84s*	20
French Roast | *Bway/85s*	15
Good Enough/Eat | *Amst/83s*	20
Hampton Chutney | *Amst/82s*	19
Haru | *Amst/80-81s*	21
Jackson Hole | *Colum/85s*	17
La Mirabelle | *86s/Amst-Colum*	22
Land | *Amst/81-82s*	22
Lenny's | *Colum/84s*	18
NEW Madaleine Mae | *Colum/82s*	16
Mermaid Inn | *Amst/87-88s*	21
Momoya | *Amst/80-81s*	22
Nëo Sushi | *Bway/83s*	23
Neptune Rm. | *Amst/84-85s*	21
Nonna | *Colum/85s*	18
Ollie's | *Bway/84s*	15
☑ Ouest | *Bway/83-84s*	25
Popover Cafe | *Amst/86-87s*	18
Roppongi | *Amst/81s*	21
Sarabeth's | *Amst/80-81s*	20
S'MAC/Pinch | *Colum/82-83s*	21
Sol y Sombra | *Amst/82-83s*	17
Spiga | *84s/Amst-Bway*	22
Sushi Hana | *Amst/82-83s*	21
Vynl | *Colum/84-85s*	15
Zabar's Cafe | *Bway/80s*	19

WEST 90s

Acqua | *Amst/94-95s*	18
Alouette | *Bway/97-98s*	20
Asiakan | *Amst/94-95s*	19
Cafe Con Leche | *Amst/95-96s*	17
☑ Carmine's | *Bway/90-91s*	20
El Malecon | *Amst/97-98s*	21

Gabriela's | Colum/93-94s	18
Gennaro | Amst/92-93s	24
NEW Kouzan | Amst/93s	20
NEW La Rural | Amst/97-98s	22
Lemongrass | Bway/94-95s	16
Lisca | Amst/92-93s	19
Pio Pio | Amst/94s	22
Roth's Westside | Colum/93s	20
Saigon Grill | Amst/90s	21
Tratt. Pesce | Colum/90-91s	18
Yuki Sushi | Amst/92s	21

WEST 100s

(See also Harlem/East Harlem)

Awash | Amst/106-107s	21
Bistro Ten 18 | Amst/110s	18
Blockhead Burrito | Amst/106s	16
Café du Soleil | Bway/104s	19
NEW Campo | Bway/112-113s	18
NEW Community Food | Bway/112-113s	23
Empire Szechuan | Bway/100s	15
Flor de Mayo | Bway/100-101s	20
Havana Central | Bway/113s	17
Indus Valley | Bway/100s	22
Kitchenette | Amst/122-123s	19
Mamá Mexico | Bway/102s	19
Max | Amst/123s	22
Métisse | 105s/Amst-Bway	19
Mill Korean | Bway/112-113s	18
Noche Mex. | Amst/101-102s	23
Ollie's | Bway/116s	15
107 West | Bway/107-108s	17
PicNic Market | Bway/101s	21
Pisticci | La Salle/Bway	24
Rack & Soul | Bway/109s	19
Sezz Medi' | Amst/122s	20
NEW Sookk | Bway/102-103s	23
Symposium | 113s/Amst-Bway	19
Z Terrace in Sky | 119s/Amst	23
Tokyo Pop | Bway/104-105s	18
Tomo Sushi | Bway/110-111s	18
Turkuaz | Bway/100s	18
V&T | Amst/110-111s	18

WEST VILLAGE

(Houston to 14th Sts., west of 7th Ave. S., excluding Meatpacking District)

Agave | 7a/Charles-10s	19
Alfama | Hudson/Perry	21
Antica Venezia | West/10s	22
A.O.C. | Blkr/Grove	19
August | Blkr-Charles-10s	21
Barbuto | Wash/Jane-12s	21

NEW bar Q | Blkr/Grove-7a	20
NEW Bobo | 10s/7a	21
Burritoville | Blkr/7a	17
Cafe Cluny | 12s/4s	20
Café de Bruxelles | Greenwich a/13s	20
Casa | Bedford/Commerce	24
Centro Vinoteca | 7a/Barrow	22
Chow Bar | 4s/10s	19
NEW Commerce | Commerce/Barrow	22
Corner Bistro | 4s/Jane	22
Cowgirl | Hudson/10s	16
Crispo | 14s/7-8a	23
Da Andrea | Hudson/Perry-11s	23
NEW dell'anima | 8a/Jane-12s	24
Dirty Bird | 14s/7a	19
El Faro | Greenwich s/Horatio	21
Employees Only | Hudson/Christopher	19
Energy Kitchen | Christopher/7a	15
EN Japanese | Hudson/Leroy	23
Extra Virgin | 4s/Charles-Perry	21
Fatty Crab | Hudson/Gansevoort	21
Five Guys | Blkr/7a	20
Frederick's | Hudson/Horation	17
Gavroche | 14s/7-8a	17
good | Greenwich a/Bank-12s	21
Havana Alma | Christopher/Bedford	20
NEW I Sodi | Christopher/Blkr	21
I Tre Merli | 10s/4s	17
Jarnac | 12s/Greenwich s	23
La Focaccia | Bank/4s	20
La Ripaille | Hudson/Bethune	23
Lima's Taste | Christopher/Bedford	21
Little Owl | Bedford/Grove	25
Malatesta | Wash/Christopher	23
Mary's Fish Camp | Charles/4s	24
Mercadito | 7a/Blkr-Grove	23
Mexicana Mama | Hudson/Charles	24
Mi Cocina | Jane/Hudson	21
Miracle Grill | Blkr/Bank-11s	18
Monster Sushi | Hudson/Charles	17
Moustache | Bedford/Barrow	21
Papaya King | 14s/7a	21
Paris Commune | Bank/Greenwich s	17
Pepe | Hudson/Perry-11s	21
Perry St. | Perry/West	26
Petite Abeille | Hudson/Barrow	18
Philip Marie | Hudson/11s	19
Piccolo Angolo | Hudson/Jane	25
Pink Tea Cup | Grove/Bedford	19

Place, The | *4s/Bank-12s* `21`
Primitivo | *14s/7-8a* `19`
Sant Ambroeus | *4s/Perry* `21`
Sevilla | *Charles/4s* `21`
NEW Sheridan Sq. | *7a/Charles* `21`
Smorgas Chef | *12s/4s* `19`
Snack Taverna | *Bedford/Morton* `22`
Spotted Pig | *11s/Greenwich s* `22`
Surya | *Blkr/Grove-7a* `22`
SushiSamba | *7a/Barrow* `22`
Tartine | *11s/4s* `22`
Tea & Sympathy | `21`
  Greenwich a/12-13s
Two Boots | *11s/7a* `19`
Z Wallsé | *11s/Wash* `26`
Waverly Inn | *Bank/Waverly* `19`
Westville | *10s/Blkr-4s* `22`
Wild Ginger | *Grove/Blkr-7a* `18`

Bronx

Artie's | *City Is/Ditmars* `23`
Beccofino | *Mosholu/Fieldston* `21`
City Is. Lobster | *Bridge/City Is* `20`
Coals | *Eastchester/Morris Pk* `23`
Dominick's | *Arthur/Crescent* `23`
El Malecon | *Bway/231s* `21`
Enzo's | *multi.* `23`
F & J Pine | *Bronxdale/Matthews* `21`
Fratelli | *Eastchester/Mace* `21`
Jake's | *Bway/242s* `23`
Le Refuge Inn | *City Is/Beach* `24`
Liebman's | *235s/Johnson* `20`
Lobster Box | *City Is/Belden* `19`
Madison's | *Riverdale/259s* `21`
Mario's | *Arthur/184-186s* `22`
Pasquale's | *Arthur/Crescent* `21`
Patricia's | *multi.* `24`
Pio Pio | *Cypress/138-139s* `22`
Portofino | *City Is/Cross* `20`
Z Roberto | *Crescent/Hughes* `26`
Siam Sq. | *Kappock/Henry* `23`
Tosca Café | *Tremont/Miles* `20`
Umberto's | *Arthur/186s* `19`
NEW Zero Otto | *Arthur/186s* `25`

Brooklyn

BAY RIDGE

Agnanti | *5a/78s* `24`
Areo | *3a/84-85s* `25`
Arirang Hibachi | *4a/88-89s* `20`
Austin's Steak | *5a/90s* `21`
Cebu | *3a/88s* `21`
Chadwick's | *3a/89s* `22`

Chianti | *3a/85-86s* `21`
ChipShop | *3a/72-73s* `19`
Eliá | *3a/86-87s* `25`
Embers | *3a/95-96s* `21`
Fushimi | *4a/93-94s* `25`
Greenhouse | *3a/77-78s* `18`
Omonia | *3a/76-77s* `18`
101 | *4a/100-101s* `19`
Pearl Room | *3a/82s* `23`
Z Tanoreen | *3a/77-78s* `26`
Tuscany Grill | *3a/86-87s* `24`

BEDFORD-STUYVESANT

NEW Peaches | *Lewis/Decatur* `-`

BENSONHURST

L & B Spumoni | *86s/10-11s* `23`
Tenzan | *18a/71s* `23`

BOERUM HILL

Bacchus | *Atlantic/Bond-Nevins* `19`
Chance | *Smith/Butler* `20`
D'ṭwn Atlantic | *Atlantic/Bond* `19`
Jolie | *Atlantic/Hoyt-Smith* `21`
Ki Sushi | *Smith/Dean-Pacific* `26`
Lunetta | *Smith/Dean-Pacific* `21`
Nicky's | *Atlantic/Hoyt-Smith* `22`
Z Saul | *Smith/Bergen-Dean* `27`

BROOKLYN HEIGHTS

Caffe Buon Gusto | `17`
  Montague/Clinton-Henry
Chipotle | *Montague/Clinton* `18`
ChipShop | *Atlantic/Clinton* `19`
Five Guys | *Montague/Clinton* `20`
Hale/Hearty | *Court/Remsen* `19`
Henry's End | *Henry/Cranberry* `24`
Jack Horse | *Hicks/Cranberry* `22`
Le Petit Marché | *Henry/Cranberry* `22`
NEW Moxie Spot | `-`
  Atlantic/Henry-Hicks
Noodle Pudding | *Henry/Cranberry* `24`
Queen | *Court/Livingston* `24`
Teresa's | *Montague/Hicks* `19`

BUSHWICK

NEW Roberta's | *Moore/Bogart* `-`

CARROLL GARDENS

Alma | *Col/Degraw* `20`
Chestnut | *Smith/Degraw* `24`
Cubana Café | *Smith/Degraw* `19`
Fragole | *Court/1pl* `22`
Frankies | *Court/4pl* `24`
Z Grocery, The | *Smith/Sackett* `27`
Korhogo 126 | *Union/Col-Hicks* `23`

Z Lucali | Henry/Carroll-1pl `27`
Marco Polo | Court/Union `20`
Patois | Smith/Degraw-Douglass `22`
Petite Crev. | Union/Hicks `24`
Pó | Smith/Degraw-Sackett `24`
Provence/Boite | Smith/Degraw `18`
Savoia | Smith/Degraw-Sackett `20`
Zaytoons | Smith/Sackett `20`

CLINTON HILL

Locanda Vini | Gates/Cambridge `25`

COBBLE HILL

Bocca Lupo | Henry/Warren `23`
Cafe Luluc | Smith/Baltic `20`
Chocolate Rm. | Court/Butler `25`
Coco Roco | Smith/Bergen-Dean `21`
Cube 63 | Court/Baltic-Warren `22`
Hibino | Henry/Pacific `26`
Joya | Court/Warren `23`
Lemongrass | Court/Dean `16`
Lobo | Court/Baltic-Warren `15`
Miriam | Court/Baltic-Warren `21`
Quercy | Court/Baltic-Kane `21`
Sweet Melissa | Court/Butler `21`

CONEY ISLAND

Gargiulo's | 15s/Mermaid-Surf `22`
Totonno Pizza | Neptune/15-16s `21`

DITMAS PARK

Farm/Adderley | `22`
   Cortelyou/Stratford
Picket Fence | Cortelyou/Argyle `20`
NEW Pomme/Terre | `23`
   Newkirk/Argyle

DOWNTOWN

Dallas BBQ | Livingston/Hoyt `14`
Junior's | Flatbush/DeKalb `17`

DUMBO

Bubby's | Main/Plymouth-Water `17`
5 Front | Front/Old Fulton `20`
Grimaldi's | Old Fulton/Front `25`
Pete's D'town | Water/Old Fulton `18`
Rice | Wash/Front-York `19`
Z River Café | Water/Furman `26`
Superfine | Front/Jay-Pearl `19`

DYKER HEIGHTS

Outback | 86s/15a `15`
Tommaso | 86s/14-15a `24`

FORT GREENE

Bonita | DeKalb/Vanderbilt `19`
Chez Oskar | DeKalb/Adelphi `17`
NEW General Greene | `-`
   DeKalb/Clermont

Café Habana/Outpost | `20`
   Fulton/Portland
Ici | DeKalb/Clermont-Vanderbilt `21`
Loulou | DeKalb/Adelphi `20`
Luz | Vanderbilt/Myrtle `24`
Olea | Lafayette/Adelphi `23`
Rice | DeKalb/Cumberland `19`
67 Burger | Lafayette/Fulton `21`
Smoke Joint | Elliot/Lafayette `22`
Thomas Beisl | Lafayette/Ashland `18`
Zaytoons | Myrtle/Hall-Wash `20`

GRAVESEND

Fiorentino's | Ave U/McDonald `20`
Z Sahara | Coney Is/Aves T-U `22`

GREENPOINT

NEW Lokal | Lorimer/Bedford `22`

MIDWOOD

Z Di Fara | Ave J/14-15s `27`
Joe's Pizza | Kings/16s `23`
Taci's Beyti | Coney Is/Ave P `23`

MILL BASIN

La Villa Pizzeria | Ave U/66-67s `21`
Mill Basin Deli | Ave T/59s `22`

PARK SLOPE

Alchemy | 5a/Bergen-St Marks `17`
Z Al Di La | 5a/Carroll `26`
Anthony's | 7a/14-15s `19`
A.O.C. | 5a/Garfield `19`
applewood | 11s/7-8a `25`
NEW Barrio | 7a/3s `19`
Belleville | 5a/5s `17`
Blue Ribbon | 5a/1s-Garfield `24`
Z Blue Ribbon Sushi | 5a/1s `26`
Bogota | 5a/Lincoln-St Johns `20`
Brooklyn Fish | 5a/Degraw `22`
Cafe Steinhof | 7a/14s `18`
NEW Canaille | 5a/Prospect `23`
Chiles/Chocolate | 7a/Lincoln `18`
ChipShop | 5a/6-7s `19`
Chocolate Rm. | 5a/Propsect `25`
Coco Roco | 5a/6-7s `21`
Conviv. Osteria | 5a/Bergen `25`
Elementi | 7a/Carroll `18`
Five Guys | 7a/6-7s `20`
Flatbush Farm | St Marks/Flatbush `19`
Ghenet | Douglass/4-5a `21`
Joe's Pizza | 7a/Carroll-Garfield `23`
La Taqueria/Rachel | multi. `20`
La Villa Pizzeria | 5a/1s-Garfield `21`
Lemongrass | 7a/Berkeley `16`
Little D | 7a/14-15s `25`
Lobo | 5a/Lincoln `15`

Long Tan | *5a/Berkeley-Union* `18`
NEW Lookout Hill | *5a/President* `-`
Maria's | *Union/4-5a* `19`
Melt | *Bergen/5s-Flatbush* `22`
Miracle Grill | *7a/3s* `18`
Miriam | *5a/Prospect* `21`
Moim | *Garfield/7-8a* `24`
Moutarde | *5a/Carroll* `17`
Nana | *5a/Lincoln-St Johns* `20`
Palo Santo | *Union/4-5a* `22`
Press 195 | *5a/Berkeley-Union* `22`
Rose Water | *Union/6a* `24`
Scottadito | *Union/6-7a* `19`
Sette Enoteca | *7a/3s* `19`
Song | *5a/1-2s* `23`
Sottovoce | *7a/4s* `19`
Stone Park | *5a/3s* `24`
Sweet Melissa | *7a/1-2s* `21`
Tempo | *5a/Carroll-Garfield* `24`
12th St. B&G | *8a/12s* `20`
Two Boots | *2s/7-8a* `19`

PROSPECT HEIGHTS

Abigail | *Classon/St Johns* `-`
Amorina | *Vanderbilt/Prospect* `24`
Beast | *Bergen/Vanderbilt* `22`
Franny's | *Flatbush/Prospect* `25`
Z Garden Cafe | `28`
  Vanderbilt/Prospect
NEW James | *Carlton/St Marks* `-`
Le Gamin | *Vanderbilt/Bergen* `19`
Tom's | *Wash/Sterling* `20`
Zaytoons | *Vanderbilt/St Marks* `20`

RED HOOK

Fairway Cafe | *Van Brunt/Reed* `18`
Good Fork | *Van Brunt/Coffey* `25`

SHEEPSHEAD BAY

Brennan | *Nostrand/Ave U* `20`
Roll-n-Roaster | *Emmons/29s* `19`

SUNSET PARK

Nyonya | *8a/54s* `22`
Pacificana | *55s/8a* `21`

WILLIAMSBURG

Aurora | *Grand/Wythe* `25`
Baci/Abbracci | *Grand/Bedford* `22`
Bamonte's | *Withers/Lorimer* `22`
Bonita | *Bedford/S 2-3s* `19`
Chimu | *Union/Bond-Nevins* `23`
DeStefano | *Conselyea/Leonard* `23`
Diner | *Bway/Berry* `21`
Dressler | *Bway/Bedford-Driggs* `26`

DuMont | *multi.* `24`
Egg | *N 5s/Bedford-Berry* `24`
Z Fette Sau | *Metro/Havemeyer* `24`
Fornino | *Bedford/N 6-7s* `23`
NEW Il Passatore | `25`
  Bushwick/Devoe
Marlow/Sons | *Bway/Berry* `23`
NEW Miss Favela | *S 5s/Wythe* `-`
NEW Pampa Grill | `-`
  Graham/Conselyea
Z Peter Luger | *Bway/Driggs* `27`
Planet Thai | *N 7s/Bedford-Berry* `18`
NEW Radegast Hall | *N 3s/Berry* `19`
Relish | *Wythe/Metro-N 3s* `20`
SEA | *N 6s/Berry* `21`
Zenkichi | *N 6s/Wythe* `23`

Queens

ASTORIA

Agnanti | *Ditmars/19s* `24`
Ammos | *Steinway/20a-20r* `21`
Bistro 33 | *Ditmars/21s* `24`
Brick Cafe | *33s/31a* `19`
Cafe Bar | *36s/34a* `20`
Cávo | *31a/42-43s* `20`
Christos | *23a/41s* `24`
Elias Corner | *31s/24a* `22`
Fatty's Cafe | *Ditmars/Crescent* `22`
JJ's Asian Fusion | *31a/37-38s* `24`
Locale Café & Bar | *34a/33s* `20`
Malagueta | *36a/28s* `23`
Mezzo Mezzo | *Ditmars/32-33s* `17`
Omonia | *Bway/33s* `18`
Philoxenia | *34a/32-33s* `21`
Piccola Venezia | *28a/42s* `25`
Ponticello | *Bway/46-47s* `23`
Sac's Place | *Bway/29s* `20`
S'Agapo | *34a/35s* `21`
718 | *Ditmars/35s* `21`
Stamatis | *multi.* `22`
Z Taverna Kyclades | *Ditmars/33s* `25`
Telly's Taverna | *23a/28-29s* `21`
Thai Pavilion | *30a/37s* `21`
Tierras | *Bway/33s* `20`
Z Tratt. L'incontro | *31s/Ditmars* `27`
Watawa | *Ditmars/33s* `25`

BAYSIDE

Ben's Kosher | *26a/211s* `18`
Bourbon St. Café | *Bell/40-41a* `18`
Caffé/Green | *Cross Is/Clearview* `21`
Dae Dong | *Northern/220s* `18`
Erawan | *multi.* `23`

Jackson Hole | *Bell/35a* — 17

Outback | *Bell/26a* — 15

Press 195 | *Bell/40-41a* — 22

Uncle Jack's | *Bell/40a* — 23

COLLEGE POINT

Five Guys | *14a/132s* — 20

CORONA

Green Field | *Northern/108s* — 18

Leo's Latticini | *104s/46a* — 25

Park Side | *Corona/51a* — 24

ELMHURST

Outback | *Queens/56a* — 15

Pho Bang | *Bway/Elmhurst* — 20

Ping's Sea. | *Queens/Goldsmith* — 21

FLUSHING

East Manor | *Kissena/Kalmia* — 19

Joe's Shanghai | *37a/Main* — 22

Kum Gang San | *Northern/Bowne* — 21

Pho Bang | *Kissena/Main* — 20

Quantum Leap | *Fresh Meadow/67a* — 20

Spicy & Tasty | *Prince/39a* — 23

Sweet-n-Tart | *38s/Main* — 19

Szechuan Gourmet | *37a/Main-Prince* — -

FOREST HILLS

Alberto | *Metro/70a* — 22

Baluchi's | *Queens/76a-76r* — 17

Bann Thai | *Austin/Yellowstone* — 19

Cabana | *70r/Austin-Queens* — 21

Danny Brown | *Metro/71dr* — 25

Da Silvana | *Yellowstone/Clyde* — 22

Dee's Pizza | *Metro/74a* — 22

Nick's | *Ascan/Austin-Burns* — 23

Q Thai Bistro | *Ascan/Austin* — 21

FRESH MEADOWS

King Yum | *Union/181s* — 17

GLENDALE

Pasticcio | *Cooper/80s* — 18

Zum Stammtisch | *Myrtle/69pl* — 23

HOWARD BEACH

La Villa Pizzeria | *153a/82s* — 21

JACKSON HEIGHTS

Afghan Kebab | *37a/74-75s* — 19

Delhi Palace | *74s/37a-37r* — 20

Jackson Diner | *74s/Roosevelt* — 21

Jackson Hole | *Astoria/70s* — 17

Pio Pio | *Northern/84-85s* — 22

Tierras | *Roosevelt/82s* — 20

LITTLE NECK

La Baraka | *Northern/Little Neck* — 22

LONG ISLAND CITY

Bella Via | *Vernon/48a* — 21

Manducatis | *Jackson/47a* — 22

Manetta's | *Jackson/49a* — 22

Riverview | *E River-49a* — 19

☑ Tournesol | *Vernon/50-51a* — 25

Water's Edge | *E River/44dr* — 22

OZONE PARK

Don Peppe | *Lefferts/135-149a* — 25

REGO PARK

Grand Sichuan | *Queens/66r* — 22

London Lennie's | *Woodhaven/Fleet* — 21

Pio Pio | *Woodhaven/63a* — 22

SUNNYSIDE

Quaint | *Skillman/46-47s* — 20

WOODSIDE

La Flor Bakery | *Roosevelt/53s* — 24

Sapori D'Ischia | *37a/56s* — 25

☑ Sripraphai | *39a/64-65s* — 27

Staten Island

Aesop's Tables | *Bay/Maryland* — 22

Angelina's | *multi.* — 23

Arirang Hibachi | *Nelson/Locust* — 20

Bayou | *Bay/Chestnut* — 22

Bocelli | *Hylan/Clove-Old Town* — 25

Brioso | *New Dorp/9s* — 24

Caffe Bondi | *Hylan/Buel* — 19

Carol's | *Richmond/Four Corners* — 24

Cole's Dock | *Cleveland/Hylan* — 22

Da Noi | *multi.* — 23

Denino's | *Port Richmond/Hooker* — 25

Filippo's | *Richmond/Buel* — 26

Fushimi | *Richmond/Lincoln* — 25

Joe & Pat's | *Victory/Manor* — 22

Killmeyer | *Arthur Kill/Sharrotts* — 19

Lake Club | *Clove/Victory* — 22

Lorenzo's | *South/Lois* — 19

Marina Cafe | *Mansion/Hillside* — 20

Nurnberger | *Castleton/Davis* — 21

101 | *Richmond/Amboy* — 19

Panarea | *Page/Richmond* — 23

Real Madrid | *Forest/Union* — 22

South Fin | *Father Capodanno/Sand* — 20

Tratt. Romana | *Hylan/Benton* — 25

WaterFalls | *Victory/Jewett* — 20

Zest | *Bay/Willow* — 23

Menus, photos, voting and more – free at ZAGAT.com

Special Features

Listings cover the best in each category and include names, locations and Food ratings. Multi-location restaurants' features may vary by branch.

BREAKFAST

(See also Hotel Dining)

☑ Balthazar | **SoHo**	23
☑ Barney Greengrass | **W 80s**	24
Brasserie | **E 50s**	20
Bubby's | **TriBeCa**	17
Cafe Colonial | **NoLita**	18
Cafe Con Leche | **W 80s**	17
Cafe Luxembourg | **W 70s**	20
Cafe Mogador | **E Vill**	21
Café Sabarsky | **E 80s**	21
Carnegie Deli | **W 50s**	21
City Bakery | **Flatiron**	21
City Hall | **TriBeCa**	20
Clinton St. Baking Co. | **LES**	25
E.A.T. | **E 80s**	19
Edgar's | **W 80s**	17
Egg | **W'burg**	24
EJ's Luncheon. | **multi.**	16
Good Enough/Eat | **W 80s**	20
HK | **Garment**	17
☑ Katz's Deli | **LES**	23
Kitchenette | **multi.**	19
Landmarc | **W 60s**	20
Le Pain Q. | **multi.**	18
Michael's | **W 50s**	22
Morandi | **G Vill**	21
Naples 45 | **E 40s**	17
Nice Matin | **W 70s**	19
NoHo Star | **NoHo**	17
Pastis | **Meatpacking**	20
Payard Bistro | **E 70s**	23
Penelope | **Murray Hill**	21
Pershing Sq. | **E 40s**	15
Popover Cafe | **W 80s**	18
Rue 57 | **W 50s**	18
Sant Ambroeus | **multi.**	21
Sarabeth's | **multi.**	20
Tartine | **W Vill**	22
Taste | **E 80s**	22
Teresa's | **Bklyn Hts**	19
Veselka | **E Vill**	18

BRUNCH

A.O.C. | **W Vill**	19
applewood | **Park Slope**	25
☑ Aquagrill | **SoHo**	26
☑ Aquavit | **E 50s**	25
Arté Café | **W 70s**	18

☑ Artisanal | **Murray Hill**	23
Atlantic Grill | **E 70s**	23
☑ Balthazar | **SoHo**	23
NEW Bar Milano | **Gramercy**	22
Beacon | **W 50s**	22
Blue Ribbon Bakery | **G Vill**	24
☑ Blue Water | **Union Sq**	23
Bubby's | **multi.**	17
Cafe Con Leche | **multi.**	17
Café de Bruxelles | **W Vill**	20
☑ Café des Artistes | **W 60s**	22
Cafe Luxembourg | **W 70s**	20
Cafe Mogador | **E Vill**	21
Cafe Ronda | **W 70s**	19
Cafeteria | **Chelsea**	18
Cafe Un Deux | **W 40s**	16
Caffe Cielo | **W 50s**	19
Capsouto Frères | **TriBeCa**	23
☑ Carlyle | **E 70s**	22
☑ Carmine's | **W 40s**	20
Cebu | **Bay Ridge**	21
Celeste | **W 80s**	24
Chez Oskar | **Ft Greene**	17
Clinton St. Baking Co. | **LES**	25
Cornelia St. Cafe | **G Vill**	19
☑ davidburke/dona. | **E 60s**	25
Delta Grill | **W 40s**	19
Diner | **W'burg**	21
Eatery | **W 50s**	19
Elephant & Castle | **G Vill**	18
☑ Eleven Madison | **Gramercy**	27
elmo | **Chelsea**	16
Essex | **LES**	18
Extra Virgin | **W Vill**	21
Félix | **SoHo**	16
5 Points | **NoHo**	22
Friend/Farmer | **Gramercy**	18
Gascogne | **Chelsea**	21
good | **W Vill**	21
Good Enough/Eat | **W 80s**	20
Great Jones Cafe | **NoHo**	19
Isabella's | **W 70s**	20
Jackson Diner | **Jackson Hts**	21
Jane | **G Vill**	21
JoJo | **E 60s**	24
Le Gigot | **G Vill**	24
Les Halles | **multi.**	19
L'Express | **Flatiron**	17
☑ Mesa Grill | **Flatiron**	23

SPECIAL FEATURES

Miracle Grill | **multi.**	18
Miriam | **Park Slope**	21
Miss Mamie/Maude | **Harlem**	21
Mon Petit Cafe | **E 60s**	18
Nice Matin | **W 70s**	19
Norma's | **W 50s**	25
Ocean Grill | **W 70s**	23
Odeon | **TriBeCa**	18
Olea | **Ft Greene**	23
Z Ouest | **W 80s**	25
Paradou | **Meatpacking**	20
Paris Commune | **W Vill**	17
Pastis | **Meatpacking**	20
Patois | **Carroll Gdns**	22
Penelope | **Murray Hill**	21
Petrossian | **W 50s**	24
Pietrasanta | **W 40s**	18
Pink Tea Cup | **W Vill**	19
Pipa | **Flatiron**	20
Popover Cafe | **W 80s**	18
Prune | **E Vill**	24
Public | **NoLita**	22
Punch | **Flatiron**	18
Z Rainbow Room | **W 40s**	20
Z River Café | **Dumbo**	26
Rocking Horse | **Chelsea**	21
Rose Water | **Park Slope**	24
Sarabeth's | **multi.**	20
Schiller's | **LES**	18
Sette Enoteca | **Park Slope**	19
718 | **Astoria**	21
Spotted Pig | **W Vill**	22
Stanton Social | **LES**	23
Stone Park | **Park Slope**	24
Sylvia's | **Harlem**	17
Tartine | **W Vill**	22
Taste | **E 80s**	22
Z Telepan | **W 60s**	25
Teresa's | **Bklyn Hts**	19
Thalia | **W 50s**	20
Tribeca Grill | **TriBeCa**	22
Z Turkish Kitchen | **Gramercy**	22
Z Wallsé | **W Vill**	26
Water Club | **Murray Hill**	22
Zoë | **SoHo**	19

BUFFET

(Check availability)

Z Aquavit | **E 50s**	25
Arabelle | **E 60s**	22
Bay Leaf | **W 50s**	20
Beacon | **W 50s**	22
Bombay Palace | **W 50s**	18
Brasserie 8½ | **W 50s**	22

Brick Ln. Curry | **E Vill**	21
Bukhara Grill | **E 40s**	22
Z Carlyle | **E 70s**	22
Charles' Kitchen | **Harlem**	22
Chennai Gdn. | **Gramercy**	22
Chola | **E 50s**	23
Dakshin | **E 80s**	21
Darbar | **E 40s**	21
Darna | **W 80s**	21
Delhi Palace | **Jackson Hts**	20
Diwan | **E 40s**	21
Green Field | **Corona**	18
Hudson Cafeteria | **W 50s**	20
Jackson Diner | **Jackson Hts**	21
Jewel of India | **W 40s**	19
Killmeyer | **SI**	19
La Baraka | **Little Neck**	22
Lake Club | **SI**	22
Lorenzo's | **SI**	19
Mamajuana | **Inwood**	21
Mangia | **multi.**	19
Z One if by Land | **G Vill**	24
NEW Park Room | **W 50s**	-
NEW Persephone | **E 60s**	22
Z Rainbow Room | **W 40s**	20
Roy's NY | **Financial**	24
Salaam Bombay | **TriBeCa**	19
Sapphire | **W 60s**	21
South Fin | **SI**	20
NEW South Gate | **E 50s**	24
Surya | **W Vill**	22
Taste | **E 80s**	22
Todai | **Murray Hill**	17
Z Turkish Kitchen | **Gramercy**	22
Turkuaz | **W 100s**	18
2 West | **Financial**	23
Utsav | **W 40s**	21
View, The | **W 40s**	17
Water Club | **Murray Hill**	22
Yuva | **E 50s**	22

BYO

Afghan Kebab | **W 50s**	19
Amy Ruth's | **Harlem**	21
Angelica Kit. | **E Vill**	20
Baluchi's | **Gramercy**	17
NEW Bellini | **W 80s**	18
Bereket | **LES**	19
Comfort Diner | **E 40s**	16
Cube 63 | **LES**	22
NEW Gazala Place | **W 40s**	25
Grand Sichuan | **G Vill**	22
Ivo & Lulu | **SoHo**	24
Kuma Inn | **LES**	24

☑ Lucali | **Carroll Gdns**	27
Meskerem | **G Vill**	21
NEW Moxie Spot | **Bklyn Hts**	–
Nook | **W 50s**	22
NEW 1 Dominick | **SoHo**	–
NEW Pampa Grill | **W'burg**	–
NEW Peaches | **Bed-Stuy**	–
Peking Duck | **Chinatown**	22
NEW Persimmon | **E Vill**	–
Petite Crev. | **Carroll Gdns**	24
Phoenix Gdn. | **E 40s**	23
Poke | **E 80s**	26
Quantum Leap | **multi.**	20
NEW R & L | **Meatpacking**	–
NEW Roberta's | **Bushwick**	–
NEW Socarrat | **Chelsea**	–
Square Meal | **E 90s**	23
Taci's Beyti | **Midwood**	23
☑ Tanoreen | **Bay Ridge**	26
Tartine | **W Vill**	22
Wondee Siam | **W 40s**	23
Zaytoons | **multi.**	20
Zen Palate | **multi.**	19

CELEBRATIONS

(Special prix fixe meals offered on major holidays)

☑ **NEW** Adour | **E 50s**	26
NEW Allegretti | **Flatiron**	–
☑ Aureole | **E 60s**	27
Beacon | **W 50s**	22
BLT Fish | **Flatiron**	23
☑ BLT Prime | **Gramercy**	25
Bond 45 | **W 40s**	19
☑ Bouley | **TriBeCa**	28
☑ Buddakan | **Chelsea**	23
☑ Café des Artistes | **W 60s**	22
'Cesca | **W 70s**	23
☑ Cru | **G Vill**	26
☑ Daniel | **E 60s**	28
NEW Duane Park | **TriBeCa**	25
NEW eighty one | **W 80s**	26
FireBird | **W 40s**	19
☑ Four Seasons | **E 50s**	26
Fresco | **E 50s**	23
Gallagher's | **W 50s**	21
☑ Gotham B&G | **G Vill**	27
☑ La Grenouille | **E 50s**	27
☑ Le Bernardin | **W 50s**	28
☑ Le Cirque | **E 50s**	24
☑ Mas | **G Vill**	28
Matsuri | **Chelsea**	23
Megu | **TriBeCa**	24
Mercer Kitchen | **SoHo**	21

☑ Modern, The | **W 50s**	26
Molyvos | **W 50s**	22
☑ Nobu 57 | **W 50s**	26
Olives | **Union Sq**	22
☑ One if by Land | **G Vill**	24
☑ Ouest | **W 80s**	25
☑ Palm, The | **multi.**	24
☑ Peter Luger | **W'burg**	27
Petrossian | **W 50s**	24
☑ Rainbow Room | **W 40s**	20
Raoul's | **SoHo**	23
Redeye Grill | **W 50s**	20
☑ River Café | **Dumbo**	26
Rock Ctr. | **W 50s**	18
☑ Rosa Mexicano | **multi.**	21
Ruby Foo's | **multi.**	19
NEW Scarpetta | **Chelsea**	26
Sea Grill | **W 40s**	24
Tavern on Green | **W 60s**	14
☑ Terrace in Sky | **W 100s**	23
Tratt. Dell'Arte | **W 50s**	22
View, The | **W 40s**	17
Water Club | **Murray Hill**	22
Water's Edge | **LIC**	22

CELEBRITY CHEFS

Julieta Ballesteros	
Crema | **Chelsea**	22
Dan Barber	
☑ Blue Hill | **G Vill**	26
Lidia Bastianich	
☑ Del Posto | **Chelsea**	26
☑ Felidia | **E 50s**	26
Mario Batali	
☑ Babbo | **G Vill**	27
☑ Casa Mono | **Gramercy**	25
☑ Del Posto | **Chelsea**	26
Esca | **W 40s**	25
☑ Lupa | **G Vill**	25
Otto | **G Vill**	23
April Bloomfield	
Spotted Pig | **W Vill**	22
Saul Bolton	
☑ Saul | **Boerum Hill**	27
David Bouley	
☑ Bouley | **TriBeCa**	28
☑ Bouley Upstairs | **TriBeCa**	25
Daniel Boulud	
NEW Bar Boulud | **W 60s**	22
☑ Café Boulud | **E 70s**	27
☑ Daniel | **E 60s**	28
☑ db Bistro Moderne | **W 40s**	25
Anthony Bourdain	
Les Halles | **Gramercy**	19

SPECIAL FEATURES

Antoine Bouterin
  Le Perigord | **E 50s** — 24

Jimmy Bradley
  Red Cat | **Chelsea** — 24

Terrance Brennan
  Artisanal | **Murray Hill** — 23
  Picholine | **W 60s** — 26

David Burke
  davidburke/dona. | **E 60s** — 25
  David Burke/Bloom. | **E 50s** — 18
  Hawaiian Tropic | **W 40s** — 15

Anne Burrell
  Centro Vinoteca | **W Vill** — 22
  Gusto | **G Vill** — 22

Marco Canora
  Hearth | **E Vill** — 25
  Insieme | **W 50s** — 24

Floyd Cardoz
  Tabla | **Gramercy** — 25

Michael Cetrulo
  Piano Due | **W 50s** — 25
  Scalini Fedeli | **TriBeCa** — 27

Ian Chalermkittichai
  Kittichai | **SoHo** — 22

David Chang
  Momofuku Ko | **E Vill** — 26
  Momofuku Noodle | **E Vill** — 23
  Momofuku Ssäm | **E Vill** — 23

Rebecca Charles
  Pearl Oyster | **G Vill** — 26

Tom Colicchio
  Craft | **Flatiron** — 26
  Craftbar | **Flatiron** — 21
  Craftsteak | **Chelsea** — 23
  'wichcraft | **multi.** — 20

Harold Dieterle
  Perilla | **G Vill** — 25

Alain Ducasse
  Adour | **E 50s** — 26
  Benoit | **W 50s** — 18

Wylie Dufresne
  wd-50 | **LES** — 23

Todd English
  Olives | **Union Sq** — 22

Sandro Fioriti
  Sandro's | **E 80s** — 23

Bobby Flay
  Bar Americain | **W 50s** — 22
  Mesa Grill | **Flatiron** — 23

Amanda Freitag
  Harrison, The | **TriBeCa** — 24

Shea Gallante
  Cru | **G Vill** — 26

Kurt Gutenbrunner
  Blaue Gans | **TriBeCa** — 21
  Café Sabarsky | **E 80s** — 21
  Wallsé | **W Vill** — 26

Gabrielle Hamilton
  Prune | **E Vill** — 24

Peter Hoffman
  Back Forty | **E Vill** — 19
  Savoy | **SoHo** — 23

Daniel Humm
  Eleven Madison | **Gramercy** — 27

Thomas Keller
  Bouchon Bakery | **W 60s** — 23
  Per Se | **W 60s** — 28

Gabriel Kreuther
  Modern, The | **W 50s** — 26

Gray Kunz
  Grayz | **W 50s** — 23

Paul Liebrandt
  Corton | **TriBeCa** — –

Anita Lo
  Annisa | **G Vill** — 27
  bar Q | **W Vill** — 20
  Rickshaw Dumpling | **Flatiron** — 16

Michael Lomonaco
  Porter House NY | **W 60s** — 23

Pino Luongo
  Centolire | **E 80s** — 21

Waldy Malouf
  Beacon | **W 50s** — 22
  Waldy's Pizza | **Chelsea** — 22

Zarela Martinez
  Zarela | **E 50s** — 21

Sam Mason
  Tailor | **SoHo** — 23

Nobu Matsuhisa
  Nobu | **TriBeCa** — 27
  Nobu 57 | **W 50s** — 26

Henry Meer
  City Hall | **TriBeCa** — 20

Marco Moreira
  15 East | **Union Sq** — 26
  Tocqueville | **Union Sq** — 25

Masaharu Morimoto
  Morimoto | **Chelsea** — 25

Marc Murphy
  Ditch Plains | **G Vill** — 16
  Landmarc | **multi.** — 20

Tadashi Ono
  Matsuri | **Chelsea** — 23

Charlie Palmer
  Aureole | **E 60s** — 27
  Metrazur | **E 40s** — 20

David Pasternack
Esca | **W 40s** — 25

François Payard
Payard Bistro | **E 70s** — 23

Zak Pelaccio
Fatty Crab | **W Vill** — 21

Alfred Portale
🅩 Gotham B&G | **G Vill** — 27

Michael Psilakis
Anthos | **W 50s** — 24
🆕 Mia Dona | **E 50s** — 21

Gordon Ramsay
Gordon Ramsay | **W 50s** — 25
Maze | **W 50s** — 25

Mary Redding
Brooklyn Fish | **Park Slope** — 22
Mary's Fish Camp | **W Vill** — 24

Cyril Renaud
Fleur de Sel | **Flatiron** — 25

Eric Ripert
🅩 Le Bernardin | **W 50s** — 28

Joël Robuchon
🅩 L'Atelier/Robuchon | **E 50s** — 28

Marcus Samuelsson
AQ Cafe | **Murray Hill** — 22
🅩 Aquavit | **E 50s** — 25
Riingo | **E 40s** — 21

Aarón Sanchez
Centrico | **TriBeCa** — 19
Paladar | **LES** — 19

Suvir Saran, Hemant Mathur
dévi | **Flatiron** — 23

Gari Sugio
🅩 Gari/Sushi | **multi.** — 26

Nao Sugiyama
🅩 Sugiyama | **W 50s** — 27

Masayoshi Takayama
🅩 Masa/Bar Masa | **W 60s** — 27

Bill Telepan
🅩 Telepan | **W 60s** — 25

Sue Torres
Los Dados | **Meatpacking** — 19
Sueños | **Chelsea** — 22

Laurent Tourondel
BLT Burger | **G Vill** — 19
BLT Fish | **Flatiron** — 23
BLT Market | **W 50s** — 24
🅩 BLT Prime | **Gramercy** — 25
BLT Steak | **E 50s** — 24
Brass. Ruhlmann | **W 50s** — 18

Alex Ureña
Pamplona | **Gramercy** — 23

Tom Valenti
🅩 Ouest | **W 80s** — 25

Jean-Georges Vongerichten
🅩 Jean Georges | **W 60s** — 28
JoJo | **E 60s** — 24
🆕 Matsugen | **TriBeCa** — 21
Mercer Kitchen | **SoHo** — 21
Perry St. | **W Vill** — 26
🅩 Spice Market | **Meatpacking** — 22
Vong | **E 50s** — 22

Yuji Wakiya
Wakiya | **Gramercy** — 19

David Waltuck
🅩 Chanterelle | **TriBeCa** — 27

Jonathan Waxman
Barbuto | **W Vill** — 21
🆕 Madeleine Mae | **W 80s** — 16

Michael White
Alto | **E 50s** — 25
🆕 Convivio | **E 40s** — –

Roy Yamaguchi
Roy's NY | **Financial** — 24

Naomichi Yasuda
🅩 Sushi Yasuda | **E 40s** — 28

Orhan Yegen
Sip Sak | **E 40s** — 19

Geoffrey Zakarian
Town | **W 50s** — 24

Galen Zamarra
🅩 Mas | **G Vill** — 28

CHEESE TRAYS

🅩🆕 Adour | **E 50s** — 26
🆕 Allen & Delancey | **LES** — 24
applewood | **Park Slope** — 25
🅩 Artisanal | **Murray Hill** — 23
🅩 Babbo | **G Vill** — 27
🆕 Bar Boulud | **W 60s** — 22
BLT Market | **W 50s** — 24
Casellula | **W 50s** — 21
🅩 Chanterelle | **TriBeCa** — 27
🅩 Craft | **Flatiron** — 26
🅩 Daniel | **E 60s** — 28
🅩 db Bistro Moderne | **W 40s** — 25
🅩 Eleven Madison | **Gramercy** — 27
Gordon Ramsay | **W 50s** — 25
🅩 Gramercy Tavern | **Flatiron** — 28
'inoteca | **LES** — 23
🅩 Jean Georges | **W 60s** — 28
🅩 La Grenouille | **E 50s** — 27
🅩 Modern, The | **W 50s** — 26
Otto | **G Vill** — 23
🅩 Per Se | **W 60s** — 28
🅩 Picholine | **W 60s** — 26
Savoy | **SoHo** — 23

SPECIAL FEATURES

CHEF'S TABLE

Abigael's | **Garment**	19
Ama | **SoHo**	23
☑ Aquavit | **E 50s**	25
Aurora | **W'burg**	25
Avra | **E 40s**	24
Barbounia | **Flatiron**	20
Barbuto | **W Vill**	21
Brasserie Julien | **E 80s**	18
Fiorini | **E 50s**	20
Fratelli | **Bronx**	21
Gordon Ramsay | **W 50s**	25
Grayz | **W 50s**	23
Hearth | **E Vill**	25
House | **Gramercy**	20
Il Buco | **NoHo**	24
Kai | **E 60s**	25
Kyo Ya | **E Vill**	29
Maloney/Porcelli | **E 50s**	22
Megu | **TriBeCa**	24
Mercadito | **E Vill**	23
Mercat | **NoHo**	22
Olives | **Union Sq**	22
Palma | **G Vill**	23
Park Avenue . . . | **E 60s**	24
Patroon | **E 40s**	20
Remi | **W 50s**	22
Resto | **Gramercy**	20
Smith & Wollensky | **E 40s**	22
NEW Talay | **Harlem**	-
Valbella | **Meatpacking**	24
Yuva | **E 50s**	22
Zoë | **SoHo**	19

CHILD-FRIENDLY

(See also Theme Restaurants;
* children's menu available)

Alice's Tea Cup* | **W 70s**	19
American Girl* | **E 40s**	12
Amy Ruth's* | **Harlem**	21
Antica Venezia | **W Vill**	22
Arirang Hibachi* | **multi.**	20
Artie's Deli* | **W 80s**	18
Bamonte's | **W'burg**	22
Barking Dog* | **multi.**	15
Belleville* | **Park Slope**	17
Benihana* | **W 50s**	17
Blue Smoke* | **Gramercy**	21
Boathouse* | **E 70s**	17
Brennan | **Sheepshead**	20
Bubby's* | **multi.**	17
Cafe Un Deux* | **W 40s**	16
☑ Carmine's | **W 40s**	20
Comfort Diner* | **multi.**	16

Cowgirl* | **W Vill**	16
Dallas BBQ | **multi.**	14
Da Nico | **L Italy**	21
EJ's Luncheon.* | **multi.**	16
Friend/Farmer* | **Gramercy**	18
Gargiulo's | **Coney Is**	22
Good Enough/Eat* | **W 80s**	20
Café Habana/Outpost | **Ft Greene**	20
Hard Rock Cafe* | **W 40s**	12
Jackson Hole* | **multi.**	17
Junior's* | **multi.**	17
L & B Spumoni* | **Bensonhurst**	23
Landmarc* | **multi.**	20
La Villa Pizzeria | **multi.**	21
London Lennie's* | **Rego Pk**	21
Miss Mamie/Maude* | **Harlem**	21
NEW Moxie Spot | **Bklyn Hts**	-
Nick's | **multi.**	23
Ninja | **TriBeCa**	16
Otto | **G Vill**	23
NEW Peaches | **Bed-Stuy**	-
Peanut Butter Co. | **G Vill**	19
Picket Fence* | **Ditmas Pk**	20
Pig Heaven | **E 80s**	19
Rack & Soul* | **W 100s**	19
Rock Ctr.* | **W 50s**	18
Rossini's | **Murray Hill**	23
Sarabeth's | **multi.**	20
Savoia | **Carroll Gdns**	20
Serendipity 3 | **E 60s**	17
☑ Shake Shack | **Flatiron**	23
Sylvia's* | **Harlem**	17
Tavern on Green* | **W 60s**	14
Tony's Di Napoli | **multi.**	19
Two Boots* | **multi.**	19
View, The* | **W 40s**	17
Virgil's BBQ* | **W 40s**	20
Whole Foods | **multi.**	18
NEW Zero Otto | **Bronx**	25
Zum Stammtisch* | **Glendale**	23

CLASS OF '79

(In our original 1979 NYC guide and
still in today)

Algonquin | **W 40s**	16
Barbetta | **W 40s**	20
Brasserie | **E 50s**	20
☑ Café des Artistes | **W 60s**	22
☑ Chanterelle | **TriBeCa**	27
Da Silvano | **G Vill**	21
El Faro | **W Vill**	21
El Parador Cafe | **Murray Hill**	22
☑ Four Seasons | **E 50s**	26
Giambelli | **E 50s**	22

Gino | **E 60s**	19
Grotta Azzurra | **L Italy**	19
HSF | **Chinatown**	19
Kuruma Zushi | **E 40s**	28
☑ La Grenouille | **E 50s**	27
Landmark Tavern | **W 40s**	17
☑ Le Cirque | **E 50s**	24
Le Veau d'Or | **E 60s**	18
Nanni | **E 40s**	24
☑ One if by Land | **G Vill**	24
Oyster Bar | **E 40s**	21
☑ Palm, The | **E 40s**	24
☑ Peter Luger | **W'burg**	27
Phoenix Gdn. | **E 40s**	23
Pietro's | **E 40s**	24
P.J. Clarke's | **E 50s**	16
Raoul's | **SoHo**	23
☑ River Café | **Dumbo**	26
Russian Tea | **W 50s**	19
Sardi's | **W 40s**	17
Shun Lee Palace | **E 50s**	24
Tavern on Green | **W 60s**	14
21 Club | **W 50s**	22
☑ Victor's Cafe | **W 50s**	22

COMMUTER OASES

Grand Central	
Ammos | **E 40s**	21
Bobby Van's | **E 40s**	22
Brother Jimmy | **E 40s**	16
Burger Heaven | **E 40s**	16
Cafe Centro | **E 40s**	19
Cafe Spice | **E 40s**	18
Capital Grille | **E 40s**	23
Cipriani Dolci | **E 40s**	19
Dishes | **E 40s**	21
Django | **E 40s**	20
Docks Oyster | **E 40s**	19
Hale/Hearty | **E 40s**	19
Hatsuhana | **E 40s**	24
Junior's | **E 40s**	17
Menchanko-tei | **E 40s**	20
Metrazur | **E 40s**	20
Metro Marché | **W 40s**	19
Michael Jordan | **E 40s**	21
Morton's | **E 40s**	24
Nanni | **E 40s**	24
Oyster Bar | **E 40s**	21
Patroon | **E 40s**	20
Pepe | **E 40s**	21
Pershing Sq. | **E 40s**	15
☑ Sushi Yasuda | **E 40s**	28
Two Boots | **E 40s**	19
Zócalo | **E 40s**	20

Penn Station	
Gray's Papaya | **Garment**	21
Nick & Stef's | **Garment**	21
Uncle Jack's | **Garment**	23
Port Authority	
Angus McIndoe | **W 40s**	17
Better Burger | **W 40s**	15
Chez Josephine | **W 40s**	20
Chimichurri Grill | **W 40s**	20
Dallas BBQ | **W 40s**	14
Don Giovanni | **W 40s**	17
Esca | **W 40s**	25
etc. etc. | **W 40s**	21
HK | **Garment**	17
John's Pizzeria | **W 40s**	22
Marseille | **W 40s**	20
Shula's | **W 40s**	21
West Bank Cafe | **W 40s**	20

CRITIC-PROOF

(Gets lots of business despite so-so food)

Algonquin | **W 40s**	16
Barking Dog | **multi.**	15
Better Burger | **multi.**	15
Blockhead Burrito | **multi.**	16
Brother Jimmy | **multi.**	16
Bubba Gump | **W 40s**	14
Burger Heaven | **multi.**	16
Cafe Un Deux | **W 40s**	16
China Fun | **multi.**	15
Coffee Shop | **Union Sq**	15
Comfort Diner | **multi.**	16
Così | **multi.**	16
Cowgirl | **W Vill**	16
Dallas BBQ | **multi.**	14
Edison | **W 40s**	15
Elaine's | **E 80s**	12
elmo | **Chelsea**	16
Empire Diner | **Chelsea**	15
Empire Szechuan | **multi.**	15
Fraunces Tavern | **Financial**	16
French Roast | **multi.**	15
Hard Rock Cafe | **W 40s**	12
Heartland | **multi.**	14
Mary Ann's | **multi.**	14
Ollie's | **multi.**	15
Outback | **multi.**	15
Park, The | **Chelsea**	15
Pershing Sq. | **E 40s**	15
Pete's Tavern | **Gramercy**	13
Rickshaw Dumpling | **multi.**	16
Tavern on Green | **W 60s**	14
Viand | **multi.**	16
Vynl | **multi.**	15

SPECIAL FEATURES

DANCING

Cávo	**Astoria**	20
☑ Rainbow Room	**W 40s**	20
Sofrito	**E 50s**	21
Son Cubano	**Meatpacking**	21
Suba	**LES**	20
Tavern on Green	**W 60s**	14

ENTERTAINMENT

(Call for days and times of performances)

Alfama	varies	**W Vill**	21
Algonquin	cabaret	**W 40s**	16
Blue Fin	jazz	**W 40s**	21
Blue Smoke	jazz	**Gramercy**	21
☑ Blue Water	jazz	**Union Sq**	23
Chez Josephine	piano	**W 40s**	20
Cornelia St. Cafe	varies	**G Vill**	19
Delta Grill	varies	**W 40s**	19
Flor de Sol	flamenco	**TriBeCa**	21
Ideya	jazz	**SoHo**	19
Jules	jazz	**E Vill**	18
Knickerbocker	jazz	**G Vill**	19
La Lanterna	jazz	**G Vill**	19
La Lunchonette	varies	**Chelsea**	21
Londel's	varies	**Harlem**	20
☑ Rainbow Room	varies	**W 40s**	20
☑ River Café	piano	**Dumbo**	26
Son Cubano	Cuban/DJs	**Meatpacking**	21
Sylvia's	varies	**Harlem**	17
Tavern on Green	varies	**W 60s**	14
Tommaso	varies	**Dyker Hts**	24
Walker's	jazz	**TriBeCa**	17

FIREPLACES

Ali Baba	**Murray Hill**	22
Alta	**G Vill**	23
Antica Venezia	**W Vill**	22
applewood	**Park Slope**	25
Arté	**G Vill**	17
Aspen	**Flatiron**	18
Benjamin Steak	**E 40s**	23
Beppe	**Flatiron**	22
Bistro Ten 18	**W 100s**	18
Black Duck	**Gramercy**	20
NEW Brasserie 44	**W 40s**	19
Caffé/Green	**Bayside**	21
Cebu	**Bay Ridge**	21
Christos	**Astoria**	24
Cornelia St. Cafe	**G Vill**	19
Cucina/Pesce	**E Vill**	18
Darna	**W 80s**	21
Dee's Pizza	**Forest Hills**	22
Delta Grill	**W 40s**	19

Devin	**TriBeCa**	18
Eliá	**Bay Ridge**	25
Employees Only	**W Vill**	19
Fairway Cafe	**W 70s**	18
F & J Pine	**Bronx**	21
Fatty's Cafe	**Astoria**	22
57	**E 50s**	23
FireBird	**W 40s**	19
5 9th	**Meatpacking**	20
Frankie/Johnnie	**Garment**	21
Fraunces Tavern	**Financial**	16
Freemans	**LES**	21
Friend/Farmer	**Gramercy**	18
Geisha	**E 60s**	23
Giorgione	**SoHo**	22
Grayz	**W 50s**	23
Greenhouse	**Bay Ridge**	18
Hacienda/Argentina	**E 70s**	18
House	**Gramercy**	20
Ici	**Ft Greene**	21
I Trulli	**Gramercy**	23
Keens	**Garment**	24
Lady Mendl's	**Gramercy**	22
Lake Club	**SI**	22
La Lanterna	**G Vill**	19
La Ripaille	**W Vill**	23
Lattanzi	**W 40s**	22
Le Refuge Inn	**Bronx**	24
Lobster Box	**Bronx**	19
Lorenzo's	**SI**	19
Lumi	**E 70s**	18
Manducatis	**LIC**	22
Manetta's	**LIC**	22
Marco Polo	**Carroll Gdns**	20
Mezzo Mezzo	**Astoria**	17
Moran's	**Chelsea**	18
Notaro	**Murray Hill**	18
Nurnberger	**SI**	21
NEW Olana	**Gramercy**	23
☑ One if by Land	**G Vill**	24
Park, The	**Chelsea**	15
Patois	**Carroll Gdns**	22
Pearl Room	**Bay Ridge**	23
☑ Per Se	**W 60s**	28
Piccola Venezia	**Astoria**	25
Place, The	**W Vill**	21
Portofino Grille	**E 60s**	19
Public	**NoLita**	22
Quality Meats	**W 50s**	23
Santa Fe	**W 70s**	18
Savoy	**SoHo**	23
Serafina	**NoHo**	19
Shaffer's	**Flatiron**	22

NEW South Gate | **E 50s** | 24
STK | **Meatpacking** | 21
Z Telepan | **W 60s** | 25
Telly's Taverna | **Astoria** | 21
Z Terrace in Sky | **W 100s** | 23
Tiramisu | **E 80s** | 19
Tosca Café | **Bronx** | 20
Triomphe | **W 40s** | 24
21 Club | **W 50s** | 22
Uncle Jack's | **Garment** | 23
Vivolo | **E 70s** | 19
Water Club | **Murray Hill** | 22
Water's Edge | **LIC** | 22
Waverly Inn | **W Vill** | 19
wd-50 | **LES** | 23

GRACIOUS HOSTS

Angelina's | *Angelina Malerba* | **SI** | 23
Angus McIndoe | *Angus McIndoe* | **W 40s** | 17
Anthos | *Donatella Arpaia* | **W 50s** | 24
Barbetta | *Laura Maioglio* | **W 40s** | 20
Z Blue Hill | *Franco Serafin* | **G Vill** | 26
Bricco | *Nino Cituogno* | **W 50s** | 19
Z Chanterelle | *Karen Waltuck* | **TriBeCa** | 27
Chez Josephine | *Jean-Claude Baker* | **W 40s** | 20
Chin Chin | *James Chin* | **E 40s** | 23
Z Degustation | *Grace & Jack Lamb* | **E Vill** | 27
Deux Amis | *Bucky Yahiaoui* | **E 50s** | 19
Due | *Ernesto Cavalli* | **E 70s** | 21
Eliá | *Christina & Pete Lekkas* | **Bay Ridge** | 25
Z Four Seasons | *Julian Niccolini, Alex von Bidder* | **E 50s** | 26
Fresco | *Marion Scotto* | **E 50s** | 23
Z Garden Cafe | *Camille Policastro* | **Prospect Hts** | 28
Z Jean Georges | *P. Vongerichten* | **W 60s** | 28
Jewel Bako | *Grace & Jack Lamb* | **E Vill** | 25
Kitchen Club | *Marja Samsom* | **NoLita** | 21
Klee Brass. | *Lori Mason* | **Chelsea** | 21
La Baraka | *Lucette Sonigo* | **Little Neck** | 22
Z La Grenouille | *Charles Masson* | **E 50s** | 27
La Mirabelle | *Annick Le Douaron* | **W 80s** | 22
Z Le Cirque | *Sirio Maccioni* | **E 50s** | 24
Z Le Perigord | *Georges Briguet* | **E 50s** | 24

Le Zie 2000 | *Claudio Bonotto* | **Chelsea** | 21
Loulou | *Christine & William Snell* | **Ft Greene** | 20
Neary's | *Jimmy Neary* | **E 50s** | 14
Nino's | *Nino Selimaj* | **E 70s** | 21
Patroon | *Ken Aretsky* | **E 40s** | 20
Piccolo Angolo | *R. Migliorini* | **W Vill** | 25
Pig Heaven | *Nancy Lee* | **E 80s** | 19
Primavera | *Nicola Civetta* | **E 80s** | 23
Rao's | *Frank Pellegrino* | **Harlem** | 23
San Pietro | *Gerardo Bruno* | **E 50s** | 24
Shaffer's | *Jay Shaffer* | **Flatiron** | 22
Sistina | *Giuseppe Bruno* | **E 80s** | 24
Spigolo | *Heather Fratangelo* | **E 80s** | 25
Z Tamarind | *Avtar & Gary Walia* | **Flatiron** | 25
Z Tocqueville | *Jo-Ann Makovitzky* | **Union Sq** | 25
Tommaso | *Thomas Verdillo* | **Dyker Hts** | 24
Z Tratt. L'incontro | *Rocco Sacramone* | **Astoria** | 27
Tratt. Romana | *V. Asoli, A. Lobianco* | **SI** | 25
Turquoise | *Sam Marelli* | **E 80s** | 22

HISTORIC PLACES

(Year opened; * building)

1762 | Fraunces Tavern | **Financial** | 16
1794 | Bridge Cafe* | **Financial** | 21
1853 | Morgan* | **Murray Hill** | 21
1864 | Pete's Tavern | **Gramercy** | 13
1868 | Landmark Tavern* | **W 40s** | 17
1868 | Old Homestead | **Meatpacking** | 24
1884 | P.J. Clarke's | **E 50s** | 16
1885 | Keens | **Garment** | 24
1887 | Peter Luger | **W'burg** | 27
1888 | Katz's Deli | **LES** | 23
1890 | Walker's* | **TriBeCa** | 17
1892 | Ferrara | **L Italy** | 22
1896 | Rao's | **Harlem** | 23
1900 | Bamonte's | **W'burg** | 22
1902 | Algonquin | **W 40s** | 16
1902 | Angelo's/Mulberry | **L Italy** | 23
1904 | Sal Anthony's* | **E Vill** | 19
1904 | Trinity Pl.* | **Financial** | 18
1904 | Vincent's | **L Italy** | 21
1907 | Gargiulo's* | **Coney Is** | 22
1908 | Barney Greengrass | **W 80s** | 24
1908 | John's/12th St. | **E Vill** | 19
1910 | Wolfgang's* | **Murray Hill** | 25
1911 | Havana Central* | **W 100s** | 17

SPECIAL FEATURES

1913	Oyster Bar*	**E 40s**	21
1917	Café des Artistes	**W 60s**	22
1919	Mario's	**Bronx**	22
1920	Leo's Latticini	**Corona**	25
1920	Waverly Inn*	**W Vill**	19
1921	Sardi's	**W 40s**	17
1922	Tosca Café	**Bronx**	20
1924	Totonno Pizza	**Coney Is**	21
1925	El Charro Español	**G Vill**	22
1926	Frankie/Johnnie	**W 40s**	21
1926	Palm, The	**E 40s**	24
1927	Diner*	**W'burg**	21
1927	El Faro	**W Vill**	21
1927	Gallagher's	**W 50s**	21
1929	Empire Diner*	**Chelsea**	15
1929	John's Pizzeria	**G Vill**	22
1929	Russian Tea*	**W 50s**	19
1929	21 Club	**W 50s**	22
1930	Carlyle	**E 70s**	22
1930	El Quijote	**Chelsea**	19
1932	Pietro's	**E 40s**	24
1933	Patsy's Pizzeria	**Harlem**	20
1934	Papaya King	**E 80s**	21
1934	Rainbow Room	**W 40s**	20
1936	Tom's	**Prospect Hts**	20
1937	Carnegie Deli	**W 50s**	21
1937	Denino's	**SI**	25
1937	Le Veau d'Or	**E 60s**	18
1937	Stage Deli	**W 50s**	19
1938	Brennan	**Sheepshead**	20
1938	Heidelberg	**E 80s**	18
1938	Wo Hop	**Chinatown**	21
1939	L & B Spumoni	**Bensonhurst**	23
1941	Commerce*	**W Vill**	22
1941	Sevilla	**W Vill**	21
1943	Forlini's	**Chinatown**	19
1944	Patsy's	**W 50s**	21
1945	Gino	**E 60s**	19
1945	V&T	**W 100s**	18
1946	Lobster Box	**Bronx**	19
1950	Junior's	**Downtown Bklyn**	17
1953	King Yum	**Fresh Meadows**	17
1953	Liebman's	**Bronx**	20
1954	Pink Tea Cup	**W Vill**	19
1954	Serendipity 3	**E 60s**	17
1954	Veselka	**E Vill**	18
1957	Arturo's	**G Vill**	21
1957	Giambelli	**E 50s**	22
1957	La Taza de Oro	**Chelsea**	18
1957	Moran's	**Chelsea**	18
1958	Queen	**Bklyn Hts**	24

HOTEL DINING

Affinia Dumont		
Barking Dog	**Murray Hill**	15
Alex Hotel		
Riingo	**E 40s**	21
Algonquin Hotel		
Algonquin	**W 40s**	16
Amsterdam Court Hotel		
Natsumi	**W 50s**	22
Blakely Hotel		
Abboccato	**W 50s**	21
Bowery Hotel		
Gemma	**E Vill**	19
Bryant Park Hotel		
Koi	**W 40s**	24
Carlton Hotel		
Country	**Gramercy**	20
Carlyle Hotel		
Z Carlyle	**E 70s**	22
Chambers Hotel		
Town	**W 50s**	24
City Club Hotel		
Z db Bistro Moderne	**W 40s**	25
Club Quarters Hotel		
Bull Run	**Financial**	17
Dream Hotel		
Serafina	**W 50s**	19
Edison Hotel		
Edison	**W 40s**	15
Excelsior Hotel		
NEW eighty one	**W 80s**	26
Flatotel		
Moda	**W 50s**	19
Four Seasons Hotel		
57	**E 50s**	23
Z L'Atelier/Robuchon	**E 50s**	28
Gansevoort Hotel		
Ono	**Meatpacking**	19
Gramercy Park Hotel		
Wakiya	**Gramercy**	19
Greenwich Hotel		
NEW Ago	**TriBeCa**	17
Helmsley Middletowne		
Diwan	**E 40s**	21
Helmsley Park Lane Hotel		
NEW Park Room	**W 50s**	-
Hilton Garden Inn		
Lorenzo's	**SI**	19
Hilton Garden Inn Times Sq.		
Pigalle	**W 40s**	17
Hotel on Rivington		
Thor	**LES**	17

Hudson Hotel
  Hudson Cafeteria | **W 50s**   20

Inn at Irving Pl.
  Lady Mendl's | **Gramercy**   22

Iroquois Hotel
  Triomphe | **W 40s**   24

Jumeirah Essex House
  🆕 South Gate | **E 50s**   24

Le Parker Meridien
  burger joint | **W 50s**   23
  Norma's | **W 50s**   25

Le Refuge Inn
  Le Refuge Inn | **Bronx**   24

Loews Regency Hotel
  Regency | **E 60s**   19

London NYC
  Gordon Ramsay | **W 50s**   25
  Maze | **W 50s**   25

Lowell Hotel
  Post House | **E 60s**   24

Mandarin Oriental Hotel
  🅩 Asiate | **W 60s**   24

Maritime Hotel
  La Bottega | **Chelsea**   16
  Matsuri | **Chelsea**   23

Marriott Financial Ctr.
  Roy's NY | **Financial**   24

Marriott Marquis Hotel
  View, The | **W 40s**   17

Mercer Hotel
  Mercer Kitchen | **SoHo**   21

Michelangelo Hotel
  Insieme | **W 50s**   24

Morgans Hotel
  Asia de Cuba | **Murray Hill**   23

Muse Hotel
  District | **W 40s**   20

NY Palace Hotel
  Gilt | **E 50s**   25

Park South Hotel
  Black Duck | **Gramercy**   20

Peninsula Hotel
  Fives | **W 50s**   23

Plaza Athénée Hotel
  Arabelle | **E 60s**   22

Plaza Hotel
  Palm Court | **W 50s**   20

Pod Hotel
  Montparnasse | **E 50s**   18

Renaissance Times Square Hotel
  🆕 Chop Suey | **W 40s**   15

Ritz-Carlton
  BLT Market | **W 50s**   24

Ritz-Carlton Battery Park
  2 West | **Financial**   23

Royalton Hotel
  🆕 Brasserie 44 | **W 40s**   19

San Carlos Hotel
  Mint | **E 50s**   22

Shelburne Murray Hill Hotel
  Rare B&G | **Murray Hill**   21

Sherry Netherland
  Harry Cipriani | **E 50s**   19

6 Columbus Hotel
  🆕 Blue Ribbon Sushi B&G | 24
  W 50s

60 Thompson
  🅩 Kittichai | **SoHo**   22

St. Regis Hotel
  🅩🆕 Adour | **E 50s**   26

Surrey Hotel
  🅩 Café Boulud | **E 70s**   27

Sutton Place Hotel
  Il Valentino | **E 50s**   18

Time Hotel
  Serafina | **W 40s**   19

Trump Int'l Hotel
  🅩 Jean Georges | **W 60s**   28

Waldorf-Astoria
  Bull & Bear | **E 40s**   19
  Inagiku | **E 40s**   22

Washington Square Hotel
  North Sq. | **G Vill**   22

Westin NY Times Sq.
  Shula's | **W 40s**   21

Wingate by Wyndham
  🆕 Luxe | **Garment**   -

W Times Sq.
  Blue Fin | **W 40s**   21

W Union Sq.
  Olives | **Union Sq**   22

JACKET REQUIRED

(* Tie also required)

🅩 Carlyle | **E 70s**   22
🅩 Daniel | **E 60s**   28
🅩 Four Seasons | **E 50s**   26
🅩 Jean Georges | **W 60s**   28
🅩 La Grenouille | **E 50s**   27
🅩 Le Bernardin | **W 50s**   28
🅩 Le Cirque | **E 50s**   24
🅩 Le Perigord | **E 50s**   24
🅩 Modern, The | **W 50s**   26
🅩 Per Se | **W 60s**   28
🅩 Rainbow Room* | **W 40s**   20
🅩 River Café | **Dumbo**   26
21 Club* | **W 50s**   22

SPECIAL FEATURES

JURY DUTY

(Near Foley Sq.)

Acappella | **TriBeCa**	24
Arqua | **TriBeCa**	22
Big Wong | **Chinatown**	22
Blaue Gans | **TriBeCa**	21
Z Bouley | **TriBeCa**	28
Z Bouley Upstairs | **TriBeCa**	25
Bread | **TriBeCa**	19
Carl's Steaks | **TriBeCa**	21
Centrico | **TriBeCa**	19
City Hall | **TriBeCa**	20
Dim Sum Go Go | **Chinatown**	21
Doyers | **Chinatown**	21
Ecco | **TriBeCa**	22
Excellent Dumpling | **Chinatown**	19
fresh | **TriBeCa**	25
Fuleen | **Chinatown**	23
Golden Unicorn | **Chinatown**	20
Great NY Noodle | **Chinatown**	22
HSF | **Chinatown**	19
Jing Fong | **Chinatown**	19
Joe's | **Chinatown**	20
Mandarin Court | **Chinatown**	21
Nam | **TriBeCa**	21
New Bo-Ky | **Chinatown**	20
Nha Trang | **Chinatown**	21
Nice Green Bo | **Chinatown**	23
Odeon | **TriBeCa**	18
Z Oriental Gdn. | **Chinatown**	24
Peking Duck | **Chinatown**	22
Petite Abeille | **TriBeCa**	18
Pho Pasteur | **Chinatown**	19
Pho Viet Huong | **Chinatown**	22
Ping's Sea. | **Chinatown**	21
Pongsri Thai | **Chinatown**	21
NEW Red Egg | **L Italy**	-
Takahachi | **TriBeCa**	23
Wo Hop | **Chinatown**	21

LATE DINING

(Weekday closing hour)

A.O.C. | 1 AM | **Park Slope**	19
NEW Artichoke Basille | 3 AM | **E Vill**	24
Arturo's | 1 AM | **G Vill**	21
Baraonda | 1 AM | **E 70s**	18
NEW Bar Milano | 3 AM | **Gramercy**	22
Bereket | 24 hrs. | **LES**	19
Big Nick's | varies | **W 70s**	17
Blue Ribbon | varies | **SoHo**	24
Z Blue Ribbon Sushi | varies | **SoHo**	26
NEW Blue Ribbon Sushi B&G | 2 AM | **W 50s**	24
Brennan | 1 AM | **Sheepshead**	20
NEW Bún | 24 hrs. | **SoHo**	21
Cafe Lalo | 2 AM | **W 80s**	19
Cafe Mogador | 1 AM | **E Vill**	21
NEW Cafe Society | 1 AM | **Union Sq**	-
Cafeteria | 24 hrs. | **Chelsea**	18
Carnegie Deli | 3:30 AM | **W 50s**	21
Casellula | 2 AM | **W 50s**	21
Cávo | 2 AM | **Astoria**	20
Cebu | 3 AM | **Bay Ridge**	21
Chez Josephine | 1 AM | **W 40s**	20
Coffee Shop | varies | **Union Sq**	15
Corner Bistro | 3:30 AM | **W Vill**	22
Così | 1 AM | **G Vill**	16
NEW Delicatessen | 1 AM | **NoLita**	-
Ditch Plains | 2 AM | **G Vill**	16
DuMont | 2 AM | **W'burg**	24
Edgar's | 1 AM | **W 80s**	17
Elaine's | 2 AM | **E 80s**	12
El Malecon | varies | **Wash. Hts**	21
El Paso Taqueria | 1 AM | **E 100s**	22
Empire Diner | 24 hrs. | **Chelsea**	15
Empire Szechuan | varies | **multi.**	15
Employees Only | 3:30 AM | **W Vill**	19
Frank | 1 AM | **E Vill**	23
French Roast | 24 hrs. | **multi.**	15
Fuleen | 3 AM | **Chinatown**	23
Gahm Mi Oak | 24 hrs. | **Garment**	20
Gray's Papaya | 24 hrs. | **multi.**	21
Great NY Noodle | 4 AM | **Chinatown**	22
Hawaiian Tropic | 1 AM | **W 40s**	15
HK | 1 AM | **Garment**	17
House | 3 AM | **Gramercy**	20
Hummus Pl. | varies | **G Vill**	23
'ino | 2 AM | **G Vill**	24
'inoteca | 3 AM | **LES**	23
Jackson Hole | varies | **multi.**	17
J.G. Melon | 2:30 AM | **E 70s**	21
Joe's Pizza | 5 AM | **G Vill**	23
Johnny Utah | 2 AM | **W 50s**	13
Kang Suh | 24 hrs. | **Garment**	21
Kati Roll | varies | **G Vill**	22
Knickerbocker | 1 AM | **G Vill**	19
Kum Gang San | 24 hrs. | **multi.**	21
La Esquina | 2 AM | **L Italy**	22
La Lanterna | 3 AM | **G Vill**	19
La Mela | 2 AM | **L Italy**	19
Landmarc | 2 AM | **multi.**	20
L'Express | 24 hrs. | **Flatiron**	17
Lil' Frankie Pizza | 2 AM | **E Vill**	22

Lucky Strike | varies | **SoHo**	16		Barbuto | **W Vill**	21
Macelleria | 1 AM | **Meatpacking**	19		**NEW** Belcourt | **E Vill**	20
NEW Mad Dog | 2 AM | **Financial**	19		Better Burger | **multi.**	15
Maison | 24 hrs. | **W 50s**	18		Blossom | **Chelsea**	22
Momofuku Ssäm | 2 AM | **E Vill**	23		BLT Market | **W 50s**	24
Neary's | 1 AM | **E 50s**	14		**Z** Blue Hill | **G Vill**	26
NEW Nizza | 2 AM | **W 40s**	20		**NEW** Broadway East | **LES**	21
Odeon | 1 AM | **TriBeCa**	18		Brown Café | **LES**	22
Ollie's | varies | **W 100s**	15		Candle Cafe | **E 70s**	23
Omonia | 4 AM | **multi.**	18		**Z** Candle 79 | **E 70s**	23
Pastis | varies | **Meatpacking**	20		Caravan/Dreams | **E Vill**	20
P.J. Clarke's | varies | **multi.**	16		Chennai Gdn. | **Gramercy**	22
Pop Burger | varies | **multi.**	18		Chestnut | **Carroll Gdns**	24
NEW R & L | 24 hrs. | **Meatpacking**	-		City Bakery | **Flatiron**	21
Raoul's | 1 AM | **SoHo**	23		Clinton St. Baking Co. | **LES**	25
Roll-n-Roaster | 1 AM | **Sheepshead**	19		**NEW** Community Food | **W 100s**	23
			Cookshop | **Chelsea**	23
Z Sahara | 2 AM | **Gravesend**	22		Counter | **E Vill**	21
Sarge's Deli | 24 hrs. | **Murray Hill**	18		**Z** Craft | **Flatiron**	26
Schiller's | 1 AM | **LES**	18		**Z** Degustation | **E Vill**	27
Spitzer's | 4 AM | **LES**	17		Dressler | **W'burg**	26
Spotted Pig | 2 AM | **W Vill**	22		Egg | **W'burg**	24
Stage Deli | 2 AM | **W 50s**	19		**NEW** eighty one | **W 80s**	26
Stamatis | varies | **Astoria**	22		**Z** Eleven Madison | **Gramercy**	27
Stanton Social | 3 AM | **LES**	23		Esca | **W 40s**	25
SushiSamba | varies | **multi.**	22		Falai | **LES**	24
Z Sushi Seki | 3 AM | **E 60s**	27		**Z** Fette Sau | **W'burg**	24
Tio Pepe | 1 AM | **G Vill**	18		57 | **E 50s**	23
Tosca Café | 1 AM | **Bronx**	20		5 Points | **NoHo**	22
Two Boots | varies | **multi.**	19		Flatbush Farm | **Park Slope**	19
Umberto's | 4 AM | **L Italy**	19		Fleur de Sel | **Flatiron**	25
Uva | 2 AM | **E 70s**	21		Fornino | **W'burg**	23
Veselka | varies | **E Vill**	18		Frankies | **multi.**	24
Viand | varies | **multi.**	16		Franny's | **Prospect Hts**	25
Vincent's | 1:30 AM | **L Italy**	21		FROG | **SoHo**	19
Walker's | 1 AM | **TriBeCa**	17		**Z** Garden Cafe | **Prospect Hts**	28
Wollensky's | 2 AM | **E 40s**	22		Gobo | **multi.**	22

NATURAL/ORGANIC/ LOCAL

(Places specializing in organic, local ingredients)			Good Enough/Eat | **W 80s**	20
Accademia/Vino | **E 60s**	20		Good Fork | **Red Hook**	25
Ammos | **E 40s**	21		**Z** Gramercy Tavern | **Flatiron**	28
Amy's Bread | **multi.**	23		**Z** Grocery, The | **Carroll Gdns**	27
Angelica Kit. | **E Vill**	20		Harrison, The | **TriBeCa**	24
applewood | **Park Slope**	25		Hearth | **E Vill**	25
Arabelle | **E 60s**	22		**NEW** Hundred Acres | **SoHo**	18
Aroma | **NoHo**	24		Ici | **Ft Greene**	21
Z Aureole | **E 60s**	27		Il Buco | **NoHo**	24
Aurora | **multi.**	25		**NEW** Irving Mill | **Gramercy**	21
Z Babbo | **G Vill**	27		Isabella's | **W 70s**	20
NEW Back Forty | **E Vill**	19		Ivo & Lulu | **SoHo**	24
Barbetta | **W 40s**	20		**NEW** James | **Prospect Hts**	-
NEW Bar Boulud | **W 60s**	22		Jewel Bako | **E Vill**	25
			Josephina | **W 60s**	18
			Josie's | **multi.**	19

SPECIAL FEATURES

L'Ecole | **SoHo** — 25
Le Pain Q. | **Flatiron** — 18
Little Giant | **LES** — 23
NEW Market Table | **G Vill** — 23
Marlow/Sons | **W'burg** — 23
NEW Peaches | **Bed-Stuy** — ‑
Z Per Se | **W 60s** — 28
NEW Persimmon | **E Vill** — ‑
PicNic Market | **W 100s** — 21
Pure Food/Wine | **Gramercy** — 23
NEW Redhead, The | **E Vill** — ‑
Rose Water | **Park Slope** — 24
Z Saul | **Boerum Hill** — 27
Savoy | **SoHo** — 23
Z Telepan | **W 60s** — 25
Z Tocqueville | **Union Sq** — 25
Z Union Sq. Cafe | **Union Sq** — 27
Whole Foods | **multi.** — 18
Zen Palate | **multi.** — 19

NOTEWORTHY NEWCOMERS

Z Adour | **E 50s** — 26
Ago | **TriBeCa** — 17
Allegretti | **Flatiron** — ‑
Allen & Delancey | **LES** — 24
Apiary | **E Vill** — ‑
Artichoke Basille | **E Vill** — 24
Avon Bistro | **E 50s** — ‑
Back Forty | **E Vill** — 19
Bagatelle | **Meatpacking** — 22
Bar Blanc | **G Vill** — 23
Bar Boulud | **W 60s** — 22
Bar Milano | **Gramercy** — 22
bar Q | **W Vill** — 20
Barrio | **Park Slope** — 19
Belcourt | **E Vill** — 20
Bellini | **W 80s** — 18
Benoit | **W 50s** — 18
Blue Ribbon Sushi B&G | **W 50s** — 24
Bobo | **W Vill** — 21
Bourbon St. B&G | **W 40s** — ‑
Braai | **W 50s** — ‑
Brasserie Cognac | **W 50s** — 19
Brasserie 44 | **W 40s** — 19
Broadway East | **LES** — 21
Bún | **SoHo** — 21
Burger Shoppe | **Financial** — 18
Cabrito | **G Vill** — ‑
Café Katja | **LES** — 24
Cafe Society | **Union Sq** — ‑
Cambodian Cuisine | **E 90s** — ‑
Campo | **W 100s** — 18
Canaille | **Park Slope** — 23

Cho Cho San | **G Vill** — ‑
Chop Suey | **W 40s** — 15
Commerce | **W Vill** — 22
Community Food | **W 100s** — 23
Convivio | **E 40s** — ‑
Corton | **TriBeCa** — ‑
Covo | **Harlem** — 24
Crave | **W 40s** — 19
Delicatessen | **NoLita** — ‑
dell'anima | **W Vill** — 24
Dovetail | **W 70s** — 26
Duane Park | **TriBeCa** — 25
eighty one | **W 80s** — 26
Elettaria | **G Vill** — 23
El Quinto Pino | **Chelsea** — 23
5 Napkin Burger | **W 40s** — ‑
Forge | **TriBeCa** — ‑
Friedman's | **Chelsea** — 21
Gazala Place | **W 40s** — 25
General Greene | **Ft Greene** — ‑
Graffiti | **E Vill** — 24
Greenwich Grill | **TriBeCa** — ‑
Hundred Acres | **SoHo** — 18
ilili | **Gramercy** — 23
Il Passatore | **W'burg** — 25
Ippudo | **E Vill** — 25
Irving Mill | **Gramercy** — 21
I Sodi | **W Vill** — 21
James | **Prospect Hts** — ‑
Kafana | **E Vill** — ‑
Kingswood | **G Vill** — 21
Kouzan | **W 90s** — 20
La Rural | **W 90s** — 22
Lokal | **Greenpt** — 22
Lomito | **SoHo** — ‑
Lookout Hill | **Park Slope** — ‑
Luxe | **Garment** — ‑
Madaleine Mae | **W 80s** — 16
Mad Dog | **Financial** — 19
Market Table | **G Vill** — 23
Matilda | **E Vill** — 18
Matsugen | **TriBeCa** — 21
Merkato 55 | **Meatpacking** — 21
Mia Dona | **E 50s** — 21
Miss Favela | **W'burg** — ‑
Z Momofuku Ko | **E Vill** — 26
Moxie Spot | **Bklyn Hts** — ‑
Niche | **E 80s** — ‑
Nizza | **W 40s** — 20
Olana | **Gramercy** — 23
1 Dominick | **SoHo** — ‑
Padre Figlio | **E 40s** — ‑
Pampa Grill | **W'burg** — ‑

Park Ave. Bistro | **Gramercy**	20
Park Room | **W 50s**	-
Parlor Steak | **E 90s**	-
Peaches | **Bed-Stuy**	-
Persephone | **E 60s**	22
Persimmon | **E Vill**	-
Pomme/Terre | **Ditmas Pk**	23
Primehouse | **Gramercy**	23
Radegast Hall | **W'burg**	19
R & L | **Meatpacking**	-
Red Egg | **L Italy**	-
Redhead, The | **E Vill**	-
Rhong-Tiam | **G Vill**	-
Roberta's | **Bushwick**	-
Scarpetta | **Chelsea**	26
2nd Ave Deli | **Murray Hill**	22
Shalizar | **E 80s**	-
Sheridan Sq. | **W Vill**	21
Shorty's.32 | **SoHo**	24
Smith, The | **E Vill**	19
Smith's | **G Vill**	22
Socarrat | **Chelsea**	-
Sookk | **W 100s**	23
South Gate | **E 50s**	24
Talay | **Harlem**	-
T-Bar Steak | **E 70s**	21
Tet | **E Vill**	-
Tre | **LES**	22
Vicino Firenze | **E 80s**	-
Wildwood BBQ | **Flatiron**	17
Yerba Buena | **E Vill**	-
Zero Otto | **Bronx**	25

OUTDOOR DINING

(G=garden; P=patio; S=sidewalk; T=terrace)

Aesop's Tables | G | **SI**	22
Aleo | G | **Flatiron**	19
Alma | T | **Carroll Gdns**	20
A.O.C. | G | **W Vill**	19
☑ Aquagrill | T | **SoHo**	26
Barbetta | G | **W 40s**	20
NEW Bar Milano | S | **Gramercy**	22
Barolo | G | **SoHo**	19
Bar Pitti | S | **G Vill**	22
NEW Barrio | P | **Park Slope**	19
Battery Gdns. | G, P, T | **Financial**	18
☑ Blue Hill | G | **G Vill**	26
☑ Blue Water | T | **Union Sq**	23
Boathouse | T | **E 70s**	17
NEW Bobo | T | **W Vill**	21
Bottino | G | **Chelsea**	19
Bryant Park | G | **W 40s**	17
Cabana | T | **Seaport**	21

Cacio e Pepe | G, S | **E Vill**	21
Cafe Centro | S | **E 40s**	19
Cafe Fiorello | S | **W 60s**	20
Cávo | G, P | **Astoria**	20
Coffee Shop | S | **Union Sq**	15
NEW Convivio | P | **E 40s**	-
Conviv. Osteria | G | **Park Slope**	25
Da Nico | G, S | **L Italy**	21
Da Silvano | S | **G Vill**	21
East of 8th | G | **Chelsea**	17
Employees Only | G | **W Vill**	19
Esca | P | **W 40s**	25
Farm/Adderley | G | **Ditmas Pk**	22
5 Front | G | **Dumbo**	20
Flatbush Farm | G | **Park Slope**	19
Gascogne | G | **Chelsea**	21
Gavroche | G | **W Vill**	17
Gemma | S | **E Vill**	19
Gigino | P, S | **multi.**	20
Gnocco Caffe | G | **E Vill**	22
☑ Grocery, The | G | **Carroll Gdns**	27
I Coppi | G | **E Vill**	22
Il Gattopardo | P | **W 50s**	23
Il Palazzo | S | **L Italy**	22
Isabella's | S | **W 70s**	20
I Trulli | G | **Gramercy**	23
Jolie | G | **Boerum Hill**	21
La Bottega | T | **Chelsea**	16
Lake Club | G | **SI**	22
La Lanterna | G | **G Vill**	19
La Mangeoire | S | **E 50s**	19
L & B Spumoni | G | **Bensonhurst**	23
Lattanzi | G, T | **W 40s**	22
Le Jardin | G | **NoLita**	19
Le Refuge | G | **E 80s**	20
Long Tan | G | **Park Slope**	18
Loulou | G | **Ft Greene**	20
Marina Cafe | T | **SI**	20
Markt | S | **Flatiron**	19
New Leaf | P | **Wash. Hts**	20
Ocean Grill | S | **W 70s**	23
Ono | G, S | **Meatpacking**	19
Pampano | T | **E 40s**	24
Paradou | G | **Meatpacking**	20
Park, The | G | **Chelsea**	15
Pastis | S | **Meatpacking**	20
Patois | G | **Carroll Gdns**	22
Pete's Tavern | S | **Gramercy**	13
Portofino | T | **Bronx**	20
NEW Primehouse | S | **Gramercy**	23
Pure Food/Wine | G | **Gramercy**	23
Relish | G | **W'burg**	20
☑ River Café | G | **Dumbo**	26

SPECIAL FEATURES

Riverview | P | **LIC**	19
Rock Ctr. | T | **W 50s**	18
☑ Sahara | G | **Gravesend**	22
Sea Grill | G | **W 40s**	24
☑ Shake Shack | G | **Flatiron**	23
🆕 Sheridan Sq. | S | **W Vill**	21
☑ Sripraphai | G | **Woodside**	27
Surya | G | **W Vill**	22
Sweet Melissa | G | **Cobble Hill**	21
☑ Tabla | S | **Gramercy**	25
Tartine | S | **W Vill**	22
Tavern on Green | G | **W 60s**	14
☑ Terrace in Sky | T | **W 100s**	23
Tree | G | **E Vill**	21
Vento | S | **Meatpacking**	19
ViceVersa | G | **W 50s**	22
Water Club | P | **Murray Hill**	22
Water's Edge | P | **LIC**	22
Wollensky's | S | **E 40s**	22
Zum Schneider | S | **E Vill**	19

POWER SCENES

☑🆕 Adour | **E 50s**	26
Bar Americain | **W 50s**	22
Ben Benson's | **W 50s**	23
☑ BLT Prime | **Gramercy**	25
Bobby Van's | **E 40s**	22
Bull & Bear | **E 40s**	19
☑ Carlyle | **E 70s**	22
China Grill | **W 50s**	22
City Hall | **TriBeCa**	20
☑ Daniel | **E 60s**	28
Delmonico's | **Financial**	22
☑ Del Posto | **Chelsea**	26
Elio's | **E 80s**	23
☑ Four Seasons | **E 50s**	26
Fresco | **E 50s**	23
Gallagher's | **W 50s**	21
Gilt | **E 50s**	25
☑ Gotham B&G | **G Vill**	27
Harry's | **Financial**	22
☑ Jean Georges | **W 60s**	28
Keens | **Garment**	24
☑ La Grenouille | **E 50s**	27
☑ Le Bernardin | **W 50s**	28
☑ Le Cirque | **E 50s**	24
Lever House | **E 50s**	22
Michael's | **W 50s**	22
Morton's | **E 40s**	24
☑ Nobu | **TriBeCa**	27
☑ Nobu 57 | **W 50s**	26
Norma's | **W 50s**	25
Patroon | **E 40s**	20
☑ Peter Luger | **W'burg**	27

Rao's | **Harlem**	23
Regency | **E 60s**	19
Russian Tea | **W 50s**	19
Sant Ambroeus | **multi.**	21
Smith & Wollensky | **E 40s**	22
Solo | **E 50s**	22
Sparks | **E 40s**	25
21 Club | **W 50s**	22
Wakiya | **Gramercy**	19
Waverly Inn | **W Vill**	19

PRIVATE ROOMS/PARTIES

(Restaurants charge less at off times; call for capacity)

Arabelle | **E 60s**	22
Barbetta | **W 40s**	20
Battery Gdns. | **Financial**	18
Beacon | **W 50s**	22
Ben & Jack's | **E 40s**	23
BLT Fish | **Flatiron**	23
☑ BLT Prime | **Gramercy**	25
BLT Steak | **E 50s**	24
☑ Blue Hill | **G Vill**	26
Blue Smoke | **Gramercy**	21
☑ Blue Water | **Union Sq**	23
☑ Buddakan | **Chelsea**	23
Capital Grille | **E 40s**	23
Cellini | **E 50s**	21
Centolire | **E 80s**	21
City Hall | **TriBeCa**	20
Compass | **W 70s**	22
Country | **Gramercy**	20
☑ Craft | **Flatiron**	26
☑ Daniel | **E 60s**	28
☑ Del Frisco's | **W 40s**	25
Delmonico's | **Financial**	22
☑ Del Posto | **Chelsea**	26
☑ Eleven Madison | **Gramercy**	27
EN Japanese | **W Vill**	23
☑ Felidia | **E 50s**	26
Fiamma | **SoHo**	24
F.illi Ponte | **TriBeCa**	22
FireBird | **W 40s**	19
☑ Four Seasons | **E 50s**	26
Fresco | **E 50s**	23
Gabriel's | **W 60s**	22
Geisha | **E 60s**	23
☑ Gramercy Tavern | **Flatiron**	28
Grayz | **W 50s**	23
Il Buco | **NoHo**	24
Il Cortile | **L Italy**	23
'inoteca | **LES**	23
☑ Jean Georges | **W 60s**	28
Keens | **Garment**	24

☑ La Grenouille | **E 50s**	27
Landmark Tavern | **W 40s**	17
☑ Le Bernardin | **W 50s**	28
☑ Le Cirque | **E 50s**	24
☑ Le Perigord | **E 50s**	24
Lever House | **E 50s**	22
Le Zie 2000 | **Chelsea**	21
Maloney/Porcelli | **E 50s**	22
Matsuri | **Chelsea**	23
Megu | **TriBeCa**	24
Michael's | **W 50s**	22
Mi Cocina | **W Vill**	21
☑ Milos | **W 50s**	27
☑ Modern, The | **W 50s**	26
Moran's | **Chelsea**	18
Mr. Chow | **E 50s**	21
Mr. K's | **E 50s**	22
☑ Nobu | **TriBeCa**	27
☑ Nobu 57 | **W 50s**	26
Oceana | **E 50s**	26
Park, The | **Chelsea**	15
NEW Parlor Steak | **E 90s**	-
Patroon | **E 40s**	20
Periyali | **Flatiron**	23
☑ Per Se | **W 60s**	28
☑ Picholine | **W 60s**	26
Primavera | **E 80s**	23
Raoul's | **SoHo**	23
Redeye Grill | **W 50s**	20
Remi | **W 50s**	22
Re Sette | **W 40s**	21
Riingo | **E 40s**	21
☑ River Café | **Dumbo**	26
Rock Ctr. | **W 50s**	18
Sambuca | **W 70s**	18
Shun Lee Palace | **E 50s**	24
Solo | **E 50s**	22
Sparks | **E 40s**	25
☑ Spice Market | **Meatpacking**	22
☑ Tabla | **Gramercy**	25
☑ Tao | **E 50s**	22
Tavern on Green | **W 60s**	14
☑ Terrace in Sky | **W 100s**	23
Thalassa | **TriBeCa**	24
☑ Tocqueville | **Union Sq**	25
Tribeca Grill | **TriBeCa**	22
21 Club | **W 50s**	22
Vento | **Meatpacking**	19
Water Club | **Murray Hill**	22

PUBS/MICROBREWERIES

(See Zagat NYC Nightlife)

Chadwick's | **Bay Ridge**	22
ChipShop | **Bklyn Hts**	19

Corner Bistro | **W Vill**	22
8 Mile Creek | **NoLita**	20
E.U., The | **E Vill**	18
Heartland | **multi.**	14
Jackson Hole | **multi.**	17
J.G. Melon | **E 70s**	21
Joe Allen | **W 40s**	17
Landmark Tavern | **W 40s**	17
O'Neals' | **W 60s**	17
Pete's Tavern | **Gramercy**	13
P.J. Clarke's | **multi.**	16
Spotted Pig | **W Vill**	22
Walker's | **TriBeCa**	17
Wollensky's | **E 40s**	22

QUIET CONVERSATION

☑ NEW Adour | **E 50s**	26
NEW Allegretti | **Flatiron**	-
Alto | **E 50s**	25
Arabelle | **E 60s**	22
Aroma | **NoHo**	24
☑ Asiate | **W 60s**	24
☑ Chanterelle | **TriBeCa**	27
Fleur de Sel | **Flatiron**	25
Giovanni | **E 80s**	22
Il Gattopardo | **W 50s**	23
Jarnac | **W Vill**	23
☑ Jean Georges | **W 60s**	28
Kai | **E 60s**	25
Kings' Carriage | **E 80s**	21
Knife + Fork | **E Vill**	21
Kyotofu | **W 40s**	21
☑ La Grenouille | **E 50s**	27
☑ Le Bernardin | **W 50s**	28
Lumi | **E 70s**	18
☑ Masa/Bar Masa | **W 60s**	27
Mr. K's | **E 50s**	22
North Sq. | **G Vill**	22
Palm Court | **W 50s**	20
Papatzul | **SoHo**	23
NEW Park Room | **W 50s**	-
☑ Per Se | **W 60s**	28
Petite Crev. | **Carroll Gdns**	24
Petrossian | **W 50s**	24
☑ Picholine | **W 60s**	26
Provence/Boite | **Carroll Gdns**	18
Rosanjin | **TriBeCa**	27
savorNY | **LES**	24
Seo | **E 40s**	23
Sfoglia | **E 90s**	24
Square Meal | **E 90s**	23
☑ Terrace in Sky | **W 100s**	23
☑ Tocqueville | **Union Sq**	25

Tree	**E Vill**	21
Tsampa	**E Vill**	20
12 Chairs	**SoHo**	19
Zenkichi	**W'burg**	23

RAW BARS

Angus McIndoe	**W 40s**	17
🛛 Aquagrill	**SoHo**	26
Arabelle	**E 60s**	22
Arté	**G Vill**	17
Atlantic Grill	**E 70s**	23
Baldoria	**W 40s**	21
🛛 Balthazar	**SoHo**	23
Bar Americain	**W 50s**	22
NEW bar Q	**W Vill**	20
Ben & Jack's	**E 40s**	23
Black Pearl	**Chelsea**	18
BLT Fish	**Flatiron**	23
bluechili	**W 50s**	20
Blue Fin	**W 40s**	21
Blue Ribbon	**multi.**	24
Blue Smoke	**Gramercy**	21
🛛 Blue Water	**Union Sq**	23
Bond 45	**W 40s**	19
Brooklyn Fish	**Park Slope**	22
City Crab	**Flatiron**	17
City Hall	**TriBeCa**	20
City Lobster	**W 40s**	18
Craftsteak	**Chelsea**	23
Docks Oyster	**multi.**	19
Ed's Lobster	**NoLita**	23
Esca	**W 40s**	25
E.U., The	**E Vill**	18
NEW Fig & Olive	**E 50s**	20
Fish	**G Vill**	20
Flor de Sol	**TriBeCa**	21
fresh	**TriBeCa**	25
Giorgione	**SoHo**	22
Jack's Lux.	**E Vill**	26
La Houppa	**E 60s**	18
Le Singe Vert	**Chelsea**	18
London Lennie's	**Rego Pk**	21
Lure Fishbar	**SoHo**	23
Marlow/Sons	**W'burg**	23
Mercer Kitchen	**SoHo**	21
Mermaid Inn	**E Vill**	21
Natsumi	**W 50s**	22
Neptune Rm.	**W 80s**	21
Ocean Grill	**W 70s**	23
Olea	**Ft Greene**	23
Oyster Bar	**E 40s**	21
NEW Parlor Steak	**E 90s**	-
🛛 Pearl Oyster	**G Vill**	26
Pearl Room	**Bay Ridge**	23

P.J. Clarke's	**multi.**	16
NEW Primehouse	**Gramercy**	23
Riverview	**LIC**	19
Shaffer's	**Flatiron**	22
Shelly's Tradizionale	**W 50s**	19
Shula's	**W 40s**	21
South Fin	**SI**	20
Spitzer's	**LES**	17
Stella Maris	**Seaport**	20
NEW T-Bar Steak	**E 70s**	21
Thalia	**W 50s**	20
Tides	**LES**	24
Todai	**Murray Hill**	17
Trata Estiatorio	**E 70s**	21
21 Club	**W 50s**	22
Umberto's	**multi.**	19
Uncle Jack's	**Garment**	23
Water Club	**Murray Hill**	22
Water's Edge	**LIC**	22

ROMANTIC PLACES

Aleo	**Flatiron**	19
Algonquin	**W 40s**	16
NEW Allen & Delancey	**LES**	24
Alma	**Carroll Gdns**	20
Alta	**G Vill**	23
🛛 Asiate	**W 60s**	24
🛛 Aureole	**E 60s**	27
🛛 Balthazar	**SoHo**	23
Barbetta	**W 40s**	20
Barolo	**SoHo**	19
Battery Gdns.	**Financial**	18
🛛 Blue Hill	**G Vill**	26
Blue Ribbon Bakery	**G Vill**	24
Boathouse	**E 70s**	17
Bottino	**Chelsea**	19
🛛 Bouley	**TriBeCa**	28
🛛 Café des Artistes	**W 60s**	22
Caffé/Green	**Bayside**	21
CamaJe	**G Vill**	22
NEW Canaille	**Park Slope**	23
Capsouto Frères	**TriBeCa**	23
Caviar Russe	**E 50s**	24
🛛 Chanterelle	**TriBeCa**	27
Chez Josephine	**W 40s**	20
Conviv. Osteria	**Park Slope**	25
🛛 Daniel	**E 60s**	28
🛛 davidburke/dona.	**E 60s**	25
🛛 Del Posto	**Chelsea**	26
NEW Duane Park	**TriBeCa**	25
🛛 Eleven Madison	**Gramercy**	27
Erminia	**E 80s**	25
FireBird	**W 40s**	19

Firenze | **E 80s** — 21
5 Front | **Dumbo** — 20
Fleur de Sel | **Flatiron** — 25
Flor de Sol | **TriBeCa** — 21
Ⓩ Four Seasons | **E 50s** — 26
Frankies | **LES** — 24
Ⓩ Garden Cafe | **Prospect Hts** — 28
Gascogne | **Chelsea** — 21
Gigino | **Financial** — 20
Ⓩ Grocery, The | **Carroll Gdns** — 27
House | **Gramercy** — 20
I Coppi | **E Vill** — 22
Il Buco | **NoHo** — 24
Il Valentino | **E 50s** — 18
I Trulli | **Gramercy** — 23
Jack's Lux. | **E Vill** — 26
NEW James | **Prospect Hts** — -
JoJo | **E 60s** — 24
Jolie | **Boerum Hill** — 21
Kings' Carriage | **E 80s** — 21
Kitchen Club | **NoLita** — 21
Kyotofu | **W 40s** — 21
L'Absinthe | **E 60s** — 22
Lady Mendl's | **Gramercy** — 22
Ⓩ La Grenouille | **E 50s** — 27
La Lanterna | **G Vill** — 19
La Mangeoire | **E 50s** — 19
La Ripaille | **W Vill** — 23
Las Ramblas | **G Vill** — 24
Le Gigot | **G Vill** — 24
Le Refuge | **E 80s** — 20
Le Refuge Inn | **Bronx** — 24
Maria Pia | **W 50s** — 19
Ⓩ Mas | **G Vill** — 28
Mr. K's | **E 50s** — 22
Nino's | **E 70s** — 21
Oliva | **LES** — 20
Ⓩ One if by Land | **G Vill** — 24
Pam Real Thai | **W 40s** — 22
Pasha | **W 70s** — 20
Patois | **Carroll Gdns** — 22
Periyali | **Flatiron** — 23
Petrossian | **W 50s** — 24
Philip Marie | **W Vill** — 19
Ⓩ Piano Due | **W 50s** — 25
Piccola Venezia | **Astoria** — 25
Pinocchio | **E 90s** — 21
Place, The | **W Vill** — 21
Portofino Grille | **E 60s** — 19
Primavera | **E 80s** — 23
Quercy | **Cobble Hill** — 21
Ⓩ Rainbow Room | **W 40s** — 20
Raoul's | **SoHo** — 23

Ⓩ River Café | **Dumbo** — 26
Riverview | **LIC** — 19
Roc | **TriBeCa** — 21
Savoy | **SoHo** — 23
Ⓩ Scalini Fedeli | **TriBeCa** — 27
Sistina | **E 80s** — 24
NEW Smith's | **G Vill** — 22
Ⓩ Spice Market | **Meatpacking** — 22
Suba | **LES** — 20
Teodora | **E 50s** — 20
Ⓩ Terrace in Sky | **W 100s** — 23
Ⓩ Tocqueville | **Union Sq** — 25
Town | **W 50s** — 24
Uva | **E 70s** — 21
View, The | **W 40s** — 17
Ⓩ Wallsé | **W Vill** — 26
Water Club | **Murray Hill** — 22
Water's Edge | **LIC** — 22
Zenkichi | **W'burg** — 23

SENIOR APPEAL

NEW Allegretti | **Flatiron** — -
Arabelle | **E 60s** — 22
Arté | **G Vill** — 17
Artie's Deli | **W 80s** — 18
Ⓩ Aureole | **E 60s** — 27
Baldoria | **W 40s** — 21
Bamonte's | **W'burg** — 22
Barbetta | **W 40s** — 20
Ⓩ Barney Greengrass | **W 80s** — 24
Borgo Antico | **G Vill** — 17
Bravo Gianni | **E 60s** — 21
Ⓩ Café des Artistes | **W 60s** — 22
Caffé/Green | **Bayside** — 21
Campagnola | **E 70s** — 24
Capsouto Frères | **TriBeCa** — 23
Chadwick's | **Bay Ridge** — 22
Chez Napoléon | **W 50s** — 21
Dawat | **E 50s** — 23
DeGrezia | **E 50s** — 22
Ⓩ Del Posto | **Chelsea** — 26
Elaine's | **E 80s** — 12
Embers | **Bay Ridge** — 21
Ⓩ Felidia | **E 50s** — 26
Fiorini | **E 50s** — 20
Gallagher's | **W 50s** — 21
Giovanni | **E 80s** — 22
Grifone | **E 40s** — 23
Il Nido | **E 50s** — 23
Il Tinello | **W 50s** — 24
Il Valentino | **E 50s** — 18
Ⓩ Jean Georges | **W 60s** — 28
La Bonne Soupe | **W 50s** — 18

SPECIAL FEATURES

La Goulue | **E 60s**	20	Bryant Park | **W 40s**	17
La Mangeoire | **E 50s**	19	Ⓩ Buddakan | **Chelsea**	23
La Mediterranée | **E 50s**	19	Buddha Bar | **Meatpacking**	19
La Mirabelle | **W 80s**	22	Butter | **E Vill**	20
La Petite Aub. | **Gramercy**	19	Cabana | **multi.**	21
Lattanzi | **W 40s**	22	Canyon Road | **E 70s**	19
Le Boeuf/Mode | **E 80s**	22	Cercle Rouge | **TriBeCa**	19
Le Marais | **W 40s**	20	Chinatown Brass. | **NoHo**	21
Ⓩ Le Perigord | **E 50s**	24	Citrus B&G | **W 70s**	19
Levana | **W 60s**	20	Coffee Shop | **Union Sq**	15
Lusardi's | **E 70s**	23	Ⓩ Del Frisco's | **W 40s**	25
MarkJoseph | **Financial**	24	NEW Delicatessen | **NoLita**	-
Montparnasse | **E 50s**	18	Dos Caminos | **multi.**	20
Mr. K's | **E 50s**	22	East of 8th | **Chelsea**	17
Nicola's | **E 80s**	22	Elephant, The | **E Vill**	21
Nippon | **E 50s**	22	NEW Elettaria | **G Vill**	23
Palm Court | **W 50s**	20	elmo | **Chelsea**	16
Pastrami Queen | **E 70s**	19	NEW El Quinto Pino | **Chelsea**	23
Piccola Venezia | **Astoria**	25	Employees Only | **W Vill**	19
Pietro's | **E 40s**	24	Essex | **LES**	18
Ponticello | **Astoria**	23	Félix | **SoHo**	16
Primola | **E 60s**	23	Flor de Sol | **TriBeCa**	21
Quattro Gatti | **E 80s**	19	Freemans | **LES**	21
Rao's | **Harlem**	23	Heartland | **multi.**	14
Ⓩ River Café | **Dumbo**	26	Houston's | **multi.**	20
Rossini's | **Murray Hill**	23	Hudson Cafeteria | **W 50s**	20
Rughetta | **E 80s**	22	Ideya | **SoHo**	19
Russian Tea | **W 50s**	19	'inoteca | **LES**	23
Sal Anthony's | **E Vill**	19	Isabella's | **W 70s**	20
San Pietro | **E 50s**	24	Jane | **G Vill**	21
Sardi's | **W 40s**	17	Japonais | **Gramercy**	20
Ⓩ Saul | **Boerum Hill**	27	Joya | **Cobble Hill**	23
Scaletta | **W 70s**	21	NEW Kingswood | **G Vill**	21
Shun Lee West | **W 60s**	22	Kobe Club | **W 50s**	23
Tavern on Green | **W 60s**	14	Koi | **W 40s**	24
Teresa's | **Bklyn Hts**	19	La Esquina | **L Italy**	22
12 Chairs | **SoHo**	19	La Goulue | **E 60s**	20
		Lure Fishbar | **SoHo**	23
SINGLES SCENES		Maloney/Porcelli | **E 50s**	22
		Markt | **Flatiron**	19
Angelo/Maxie's | **Flatiron**	21	NEW Merkato 55 | **Meatpacking**	21
Asia de Cuba | **Murray Hill**	23	Ⓩ Mesa Grill | **Flatiron**	23
Aspen | **Flatiron**	18	Otto | **G Vill**	23
Atlantic Grill | **E 70s**	23	Pam Real Thai | **W 40s**	22
Baraonda | **E 70s**	18	Pastis | **Meatpacking**	20
NEW Bar Blanc | **G Vill**	23	Peep | **SoHo**	19
NEW Bar Milano | **Gramercy**	22	Pete's Tavern | **Gramercy**	13
NEW Barrio | **Park Slope**	19	Pipa | **Flatiron**	20
Blue Fin | **W 40s**	21	Punch | **Flatiron**	18
Blue Ribbon | **multi.**	24	Ruby Foo's | **multi.**	19
Ⓩ Blue Water | **Union Sq**	23	Schiller's | **LES**	18
NEW Bobo | **W Vill**	21	Ⓩ Spice Market | **Meatpacking**	22
Boca Chica | **E Vill**	20	STK | **Meatpacking**	21
Brasserie 8½ | **W 50s**	22		
Brother Jimmy | **multi.**	16		

Suba	**LES**	20
SushiSamba	**multi.**	22
Z Tao	**E 50s**	22
Thor	**LES**	17
Tribeca Grill	**TriBeCa**	22
Xunta	**E Vill**	21
Zarela	**E 50s**	21

SLEEPERS

(Fine food, but little known)

Alcala	**E 40s**	22
AQ Cafe	**Murray Hill**	22
Bistro 33	**Astoria**	24
Brown Café	**LES**	22
NEW Canaille	**Park Slope**	23
Chimu	**W'burg**	23
Coals	**Bronx**	23
Cole's Dock	**SI**	22
Da Silvana	**Forest Hills**	22
DeStefano	**W'burg**	23
Fabio Piccolo	**E 40s**	22
Filippo's	**SI**	26
Ivo & Lulu	**SoHo**	24
JJ's Asian Fusion	**Astoria**	24
Kai	**E 60s**	25
Korhogo 126	**Carroll Gdns**	23
La Ripaille	**W Vill**	23
NEW Lokal	**Greenpt**	22
Luz	**Ft Greene**	24
Mancora	**E Vill**	22
Minca	**E Vill**	22
Mint	**E 50s**	22
Natsumi	**W 50s**	22
Nippon	**E 50s**	22
Omen	**SoHo**	23
Omido	**W 50s**	24
Palma	**G Vill**	23
Papatzul	**SoHo**	23
Petite Crev.	**Carroll Gdns**	24
Pizza Gruppo	**E Vill**	24
Queen of Sheba	**W 40s**	23
Rosanjin	**TriBeCa**	27
Saravanaas	**Gramercy**	24
savorNY	**LES**	24
Seo	**E 40s**	23
Siam Sq.	**Bronx**	23
Stella del Mare	**Murray Hill**	23
Suteishi	**Seaport**	22
Tevere	**E 80s**	23
Tides	**LES**	24
Ushiwakamaru	**G Vill**	27
Watawa	**Astoria**	25
Zenkichi	**W'burg**	23
Zest	**SI**	23

SUNDAY BEST BETS

(See also Hotel Dining)

Z Aquagrill	**SoHo**	26
Z Aquavit	**E 50s**	25
Z Artisanal	**Murray Hill**	23
Z Balthazar	**SoHo**	23
Bar Americain	**W 50s**	22
Z Blue Hill	**G Vill**	26
Blue Ribbon	**SoHo**	24
Z Blue Water	**Union Sq**	23
Z Bouley	**TriBeCa**	28
Café de Bruxelles	**W Vill**	20
Z Café des Artistes	**W 60s**	22
Chez Oskar	**Ft Greene**	17
Z davidburke/dona.	**E 60s**	25
Demarchelier	**E 80s**	17
5 Points	**NoHo**	22
Z Gotham B&G	**G Vill**	27
Z Gramercy Tavern	**Flatiron**	28
La Mediterranée	**E 50s**	19
Lucky Strike	**SoHo**	16
Z Lupa	**G Vill**	25
Z Mesa Grill	**Flatiron**	23
Mi Cocina	**W Vill**	21
Moran's	**Chelsea**	18
Odeon	**TriBeCa**	18
Z Ouest	**W 80s**	25
Our Place	**E 50s**	20
Z Peter Luger	**W'burg**	27
Piccolo Angolo	**W Vill**	25
Z Picholine	**W 60s**	26
Pomaire	**W 40s**	22
Prune	**E Vill**	24
Z River Café	**Dumbo**	26
Solo	**E 50s**	22
Tratt. Dell'Arte	**W 50s**	22
Tribeca Grill	**TriBeCa**	22
Z Union Sq. Cafe	**Union Sq**	27
Water Club	**Murray Hill**	22
Zoë	**SoHo**	19

TASTING MENUS

($ minimum)

Z NEW Adour	$110	**E 50s**	26
Aki	$55	**G Vill**	26
Alto	$136	**E 50s**	25
Amma	$50	**E 50s**	24
Z Annisa	$75	**G Vill**	27
Anthos	$95	**W 50s**	24
applewood	$55	**Park Slope**	25
Z Aquavit	$115	**E 50s**	25
Z Asiate	$125	**W 60s**	24
Z Aureole	$115	**E 60s**	27
Aurora	$60	**W'burg**	25

SPECIAL FEATURES

Ⓩ Babbo	$75	**G Vill**	27
Barbone	$37	**E Vill**	23
NEW Bar Milano	$85	**Gramercy**	22
Ⓩ Blue Hill	$72	**G Vill**	26
Bond St.	$80	**NoHo**	24
Caviar Russe	$95	**E 50s**	24
Ⓩ Chanterelle	$140	**TriBeCa**	27
Chestnut	$60	**Carroll Gdns**	24
Chiam	$45	**E 40s**	22
NEW Corton	$110	**TriBeCa**	-
Ⓩ Craft	$110	**Flatiron**	26
Ⓩ Cru	$125	**G Vill**	26
Ⓩ Daniel	$175	**E 60s**	28
Ⓩ davidburke/dona.	$75	**E 60s**	25
Dawat	$65	**E 50s**	23
Ⓩ Degustation	$50	**E Vill**	27
Ⓩ Del Posto	$175	**Chelsea**	26
dévi	$65	**Flatiron**	23
Django	$75	**E 40s**	20
Donguri	$85	**E 80s**	27
Ⓩ Eleven Madison	$145	**Gramercy**	27
EN Japanese	$65	**W Vill**	23
Esca	$75	**W 40s**	25
Falai	$90	**LES**	24
Ⓩ Felidia	$85	**E 50s**	26
Fiamma	$105	**SoHo**	24
15 East	$120	**Union Sq**	26
Fleur de Sel	$89	**Flatiron**	25
Ⓩ Gari/Sushi	$85	**multi.**	26
Gilt	$110	**E 50s**	25
Gordon Ramsay	$135	**W 50s**	25
Ⓩ Gramercy Tavern	$110	**Flatiron**	28
Ⓩ Grocery, The	$75	**Carroll Gdns**	27
Hearth	$90	**E Vill**	25
Insieme	$67	**W 50s**	24
NEW Irving Mill	$54	**Gramercy**	21
Jack's Lux.	$50	**E Vill**	26
Ⓩ Jean Georges	$148	**W 60s**	28
Jewel Bako	$95	**E Vill**	25
JoJo	$65	**E 60s**	24
Ⓩ La Grenouille	$155	**E 50s**	27
Ⓩ L'Atelier/Robuchon	$190	**E 50s**	28
Ⓩ Le Bernardin	$135	**W 50s**	28
Ⓩ Le Cirque	$145	**E 50s**	24
Locanda Vini	$45	**Clinton Hill**	25
Ⓩ Mas	$95	**G Vill**	28
Maze	$75	**W 50s**	25
Megu	$95	**E 40s**	24
Melt	$25	**Park Slope**	22
Ⓩ Modern, The	$125	**W 50s**	26

Ⓩ NEW Momofuku Ko	$100	**E Vill**	26
Morimoto	$120	**Chelsea**	25
Ⓩ Nobu	$100	**TriBeCa**	27
Ⓩ Nobu 57	$100	**W 50s**	26
Oceana	$110	**E 50s**	26
NEW Olana	$69	**Gramercy**	23
Ⓩ One if by Land	$95	**G Vill**	24
Payard Bistro	$72	**E 70s**	23
Perilla	$70	**G Vill**	25
Ⓩ Per Se	$275	**W 60s**	28
NEW Persimmon	$37	**E Vill**	-
Ⓩ Piano Due	$85	**W 50s**	25
Ⓩ Picholine	$115	**W 60s**	26
Pó	$50	**multi.**	24
Pure Food/Wine	$69	**Gramercy**	23
Ⓩ River Café	$125	**Dumbo**	26
Rosanjin	$150	**TriBeCa**	27
Rose Water	$56	**Park Slope**	24
Ⓩ Saul	$85	**Boerum Hill**	27
Ⓩ Scalini Fedeli	$90	**TriBeCa**	27
Sea Grill	$72	**W 40s**	24
Ⓩ Soto	$80	**G Vill**	26
Spigolo	$70	**E 80s**	25
Ⓩ Sugiyama	$58	**W 50s**	27
Ⓩ Sushi Seki	$50	**E 60s**	27
Sushi Zen	$150	**W 40s**	25
Ⓩ Tabla	$89	**Gramercy**	25
Tailor	$90	**SoHo**	23
Takahachi	$30, $55	**multi.**	23
Ⓩ Telepan	$64	**W 60s**	25
Ⓩ Tocqueville	$95	**Union Sq**	25
Town	$65	**W 50s**	24
Triomphe	$75	**W 40s**	24
Ⓩ Tse Yang	$50	**E 50s**	24
21 Club	$85	**W 50s**	22
Ⓩ Wallsé	$85	**W Vill**	26
wd-50	$140	**LES**	23
Zenkichi	$44	**W'burg**	23

TEA SERVICE

Abigael's	**Garment**	19
Alice's Tea Cup	**multi.**	19
American Girl	**E 40s**	12
Arabelle	**E 60s**	22
Cafe S.F.A.	**E 40s**	18
Danal	**G Vill**	20
NEW Duane Park	**TriBeCa**	25
Franchia	**Murray Hill**	19
Kings' Carriage	**E 80s**	21
Lady Mendl's	**Gramercy**	22
Morgan	**Murray Hill**	21
North Sq.	**G Vill**	22
Palm Court	**W 50s**	20

NEW Park Room | **W 50s**	–
Payard Bistro | **E 70s**	23
Sant Ambroeus | **multi.**	21
Sarabeth's | **multi.**	20
Sweet Melissa | **multi.**	21
Tavern on Green | **W 60s**	14
Tea & Sympathy | **W Vill**	21
202 Cafe | **Chelsea**	19
2 West | **Financial**	23

THEME RESTAURANTS

NEW Braai | **W 50s**	–
Bubba Gump | **W 40s**	14
Cowgirl | **W Vill**	16
Hard Rock Cafe | **W 40s**	12
Hawaiian Tropic | **W 40s**	15
Johnny Utah | **W 50s**	13
Ninja | **TriBeCa**	16

TRANSPORTING EXPERIENCES

Z Asiate | **W 60s**	24
Z Balthazar | **SoHo**	23
Boathouse | **E 70s**	17
Z Buddakan | **Chelsea**	23
Buddha Bar | **Meatpacking**	19
Z Café des Artistes | **W 60s**	22
Chez Josephine | **W 40s**	20
FireBird | **W 40s**	19
Fraunces Tavern | **Financial**	16
Il Buco | **NoHo**	24
NEW ilili | **Gramercy**	23
Keens | **Garment**	24
Z La Grenouille | **E 50s**	27
Le Colonial | **E 50s**	19
Z Masa/Bar Masa | **W 60s**	27
Matsuri | **Chelsea**	23
Megu | **TriBeCa**	24
Ninja | **TriBeCa**	16
Z One if by Land | **G Vill**	24
Z Per Se | **W 60s**	28
Z Rainbow Room | **W 40s**	20
Rao's | **Harlem**	23
Suba | **LES**	20
Z Tao | **E 50s**	22
Tavern on Green | **W 60s**	14
Water's Edge | **LIC**	22

VIEWS

Alma | **Carroll Gdns**	20
Angelina's | **SI**	23
Antica Venezia | **W Vill**	22
Z Asiate | **W 60s**	24
Battery Gdns. | **Financial**	18

Boathouse | **E 70s**	17
Bouchon Bakery | **W 60s**	23
Bryant Park | **W 40s**	17
Bubby's | **Dumbo**	17
Cabana | **Seaport**	21
Cafe S.F.A. | **E 40s**	18
Caffé/Green | **Bayside**	21
NEW Chop Suey | **W 40s**	15
Cipriani Dolci | **E 40s**	19
Fairway Cafe | **Red Hook**	18
F.illi Ponte | **TriBeCa**	22
Gigino | **Financial**	20
Heartland | **Seaport**	14
Hispaniola | **Wash. Hts**	20
Hudson Café | **Harlem**	21
Lake Club | **SI**	22
Le Refuge Inn | **Bronx**	24
Liberty View | **Financial**	19
Lobster Box | **Bronx**	19
Marina Cafe | **SI**	20
Metrazur | **E 40s**	20
Michael Jordan | **E 40s**	21
Z Modern, The | **W 50s**	26
NEW Park Room | **W 50s**	–
Z Per Se | **W 60s**	28
Pete's D'town | **Dumbo**	18
P.J. Clarke's | **Financial**	16
Porter House NY | **W 60s**	23
Portofino | **Bronx**	20
Z Rainbow Room | **W 40s**	20
Z River Café | **Dumbo**	26
Riverview | **LIC**	19
Roc | **TriBeCa**	21
Rock Ctr. | **W 50s**	18
Sea Grill | **W 40s**	24
South Fin | **SI**	20
NEW South Gate | **E 50s**	24
Suteishi | **Seaport**	22
Tavern on Green | **W 60s**	14
Z Terrace in Sky | **W 100s**	23
2 West | **Financial**	23
View, The | **W 40s**	17
Water Club | **Murray Hill**	22
Water's Edge | **LIC**	22

VISITORS ON EXP. ACCT.

Z NEW Adour | **E 50s**	26
Anthos | **W 50s**	24
Z Babbo | **G Vill**	27
Z Bouley | **TriBeCa**	28
Z Buddakan | **Chelsea**	23
Z Café Boulud | **E 70s**	27
Z Carlyle | **E 70s**	22

Z Chanterelle	TriBeCa	27
Z Craft	Flatiron	26
Z Daniel	E 60s	28
Z Del Frisco's	W 40s	25
Z Del Posto	Chelsea	26
NEW eighty one	W 80s	26
Z Eleven Madison	Gramercy	27
Z Four Seasons	E 50s	26
Z Gari/Sushi	W 40s	26
Gordon Ramsay	W 50s	25
Z Gramercy Tavern	Flatiron	28
Harry Cipriani	E 50s	19
Z Il Mulino	G Vill	27
Z Jean Georges	W 60s	28
Keens	Garment	24
Kuruma Zushi	E 40s	28
Z La Grenouille	E 50s	27
Z Le Bernardin	W 50s	28
Z Le Cirque	E 50s	24
Z Masa/Bar Masa	W 60s	27
Z Milos	W 50s	27
Z Modern, The	W 50s	26
Z Nobu	TriBeCa	27
Z Nobu 57	W 50s	26
Z Palm, The	multi.	24
Z Per Se	W 60s	28
Z Peter Luger	W'burg	27
Petrossian	W 50s	24
Z Picholine	W 60s	26
Z River Café	Dumbo	26
NEW Scarpetta	Chelsea	26
Smith & Wollensky	E 40s	22
Z Spice Market	Meatpacking	22
Z Sushi Yasuda	E 40s	28
Z Union Sq. Cafe	Union Sq	27
Z Veritas	Flatiron	26

WATERSIDE

Alma	Carroll Gdns	20
Battery Gdns.	Financial	18
Boathouse	E 70s	17
Cabana	Seaport	21
City Is. Lobster	Bronx	20
Cole's Dock	SI	22
Lake Club	SI	22
Marina Cafe	SI	20
Pete's D'town	Dumbo	18
Portofino	Bronx	20
Z River Café	Dumbo	26
Riverview	LIC	19
South Fin	SI	20
Water Club	Murray Hill	22
Water's Edge	LIC	22

WINNING WINE LISTS

Accademia/Vino	E 60s	20
Z NEW Adour	E 50s	26
Alfama	W Vill	21
NEW Allegretti	Flatiron	-
Alto	E 50s	25
Z Annisa	G Vill	27
Z Aquavit	E 50s	25
Arno	Garment	20
Z Artisanal	Murray Hill	23
Z Asiate	W 60s	24
Z Aureole	E 60s	27
A Voce	Gramercy	25
Z Babbo	G Vill	27
Bacchus	Boerum Hill	19
Z Balthazar	SoHo	23
Barbetta	W 40s	20
NEW Bar Boulud	W 60s	22
NEW Bar Milano	Gramercy	22
Barolo	SoHo	19
Z Becco	W 40s	23
Ben Benson's	W 50s	23
BLT Steak	E 50s	24
Z Blue Hill	G Vill	26
Blue Ribbon	multi.	24
Bottega/Vino	E 50s	21
Z Bouley	TriBeCa	28
Z Café Boulud	E 70s	27
Capital Grille	E 40s	23
Z Casa Mono	Gramercy	25
'Cesca	W 70s	23
Z Chanterelle	TriBeCa	27
Chiam	E 40s	22
City Hall	TriBeCa	20
Compass	W 70s	22
Conviv. Osteria	Park Slope	25
Counter	E Vill	21
Z Craft	Flatiron	26
Z Cru	G Vill	26
Z Daniel	E 60s	28
Z db Bistro Moderne	W 40s	25
Z Del Frisco's	W 40s	25
NEW dell'anima	W Vill	24
Z Del Posto	Chelsea	26
NEW eighty one	W 80s	26
Z Eleven Madison	Gramercy	27
Falai	LES	24
Fatty Crab	W Vill	21
Z Felidia	E 50s	26
Fiamma	SoHo	24
Fleur de Sel	Flatiron	25
Gabriel's	W 60s	22
Gilt	E 50s	25

ⓩ Gotham B&G | **G Vill**	27	
ⓩ Gramercy Tavern | **Flatiron**	28	
Harrison, The | **TriBeCa**	24	
Hearth | **E Vill**	25	
Il Buco | **NoHo**	24	
'ino | **G Vill**	24	
'inoteca | **LES**	23	
I Trulli | **Gramercy**	23	
ⓩ Jean Georges | **W 60s**	28	
Landmarc | **multi.**	20	
La Pizza Fresca | **Flatiron**	22	
Lavagna | **E Vill**	25	
ⓩ Le Bernardin | **W 50s**	28	
ⓩ Le Cirque | **E 50s**	24	
ⓩ Lupa | **G Vill**	25	
ⓩ Mas | **G Vill**	28	
Megu | **TriBeCa**	24	
Michael Jordan | **E 40s**	21	
Michael's | **W 50s**	22	
ⓩ Milos | **W 50s**	27	
ⓩ Modern, The | **W 50s**	26	
Morrell Wine Bar | **W 40s**	18	
Nice Matin | **W 70s**	19	
Nick & Stef's | **Garment**	21	
Oceana | **E 50s**	26	
Orsay | **E 70s**	18	
Osteria del Circo | **W 50s**	22	
Otto | **G Vill**	23	
ⓩ Ouest | **W 80s**	25	
ⓩ Per Se | **W 60s**	28	
ⓩ Picholine | **W 60s**	26	
Pomaire | **W 40s**	22	
Post House | **E 60s**	24	
NEW Primehouse | **Gramercy**	23	
Raoul's | **SoHo**	23	
Ruth's Chris | **W 50s**	24	
San Pietro | **E 50s**	24	
ⓩ Scalini Fedeli | **TriBeCa**	27	
NEW Scarpetta | **Chelsea**	26	
Sea Grill | **W 40s**	24	
Sette Enoteca | **Park Slope**	19	
Sharz Cafe | **E 80s**	19	
Smith & Wollensky | **E 40s**	22	
Solera | **E 50s**	22	
NEW South Gate | **E 50s**	24	
Sparks | **E 40s**	25	
Strip House | **G Vill**	25	
Supper | **E Vill**	25	
ⓩ Tabla | **Gramercy**	25	
ⓩ Telepan | **W 60s**	25	
ⓩ Tocqueville | **Union Sq**	25	
Tommaso | **Dyker Hts**	24	
Town | **W 50s**	24	
Tribeca Grill | **TriBeCa**	22	
ⓩ Tse Yang | **E 50s**	24	
21 Club | **W 50s**	22	
ⓩ Union Sq. Cafe | **Union Sq**	27	
Uva | **E 70s**	21	
ⓩ Veritas | **Flatiron**	26	
ⓩ Wallsé | **W Vill**	26	
West Bank Cafe | **W 40s**	20	
Zoë | **SoHo**	19	

Wine Vintage Chart

This chart, based on our 0 to 30 scale, is designed to help you select wine. The ratings (by **Howard Stravitz,** a law professor at the University of South Carolina) reflect the vintage quality and the wine's readiness to drink. We exclude the 1991–1993 vintages because they are not that good. A dash indicates the wine is either past its peak or too young to rate. Loire ratings are for dry white wines.

Whites	89	90	94	95	96	97	98	99	00	01	02	03	04	05	06	07
French:																
Alsace	24	25	24	23	23	22	25	23	25	26	22	21	24	25	24	-
Burgundy	23	22	-	27	26	23	21	25	25	24	27	23	26	27	25	23
Loire Valley	-	-	-	-	-	-	-	24	25	26	22	23	27	24	-
Champagne	26	29	-	26	27	24	23	24	24	22	26	21	-	-	-	-
Sauternes	25	28	-	21	23	25	23	24	24	29	25	24	21	26	23	27
California:																
Chardonnay	-	-	-	-	-	-	24	23	26	26	25	26	29	25	-
Sauvignon Blanc	-	-	-	-	-	-	-	-	-	26	27	26	27	26
Austrian:																
Grüner Velt./ Riesling	-	-	-	25	21	26	26	25	22	23	25	26	26	25	24	-
German:	26	27	24	23	26	25	26	23	21	29	27	24	26	28	24	-

Reds	89	90	94	95	96	97	98	99	00	01	02	03	04	05	06	07
French:																
Bordeaux	25	29	21	26	25	23	25	24	29	26	24	26	24	28	25	23
Burgundy	24	26	-	26	27	25	22	27	22	24	27	25	24	27	25	-
Rhône	28	28	23	26	22	24	27	26	27	26	-	26	24	27	25	-
Beaujolais	-	-	-	-	-	-	-	-	-	22	24	21	27	25	23
California:																
Cab./Merlot	-	28	29	27	25	28	23	26	-	27	26	25	24	26	23	-
Pinot Noir	-	-	-	-	-	-	24	23	25	28	26	27	25	24	-
Zinfandel	-	-	-	-	-	-	-	-	25	23	27	22	23	23	-
Oregon:																
Pinot Noir	-	-	-	-	-	-	-	-	-	27	25	26	27	26	-
Italian:																
Tuscany	-	25	23	24	20	29	24	27	24	27	-	25	27	25	24	-
Piedmont	27	27	-	-	26	27	26	25	28	27	-	24	23	26	25	24
Spanish:																
Rioja	-	-	26	26	24	25	-	25	24	27	-	24	25	26	24	-
Ribera del Duero/Priorat	-	-	26	26	27	25	24	25	24	27	20	24	27	26	24	-
Australian:																
Shiraz/Cab.	-	-	24	26	23	26	28	24	24	27	27	25	26	26	24	-
Chilean:	-	-	-	-	-	24	-	25	23	26	24	25	24	26	25	24

Menus, photos, voting and more – free at ZAGAT.com

Zagat Products

Available wherever books are sold or at ZAGAT.com. To customize Zagat guides as gifts or marketing tools, call 800-540-9609.

RESTAURANTS & MAPS

America's Top Restaurants
Atlanta
Beijing
Boston
Brooklyn
California Wine Country
Cape Cod & The Islands
Chicago
Connecticut
Europe's Top Restaurants
Hamptons (incl. wineries)
Hong Kong
Las Vegas
London
Long Island (incl. wineries)
Los Angeles I So. California
(guide & map)
Miami Beach
Miami I So. Florida
Montréal
New Jersey
New Jersey Shore
New Orleans
New York City (guide & map)
Palm Beach
Paris
Philadelphia
San Diego
San Francisco (guide & map)
Seattle
Shanghai
Texas
Tokyo
Toronto
Vancouver
Washington, DC I Baltimore
Westchester I Hudson Valley
World's Top Restaurants

LIFESTYLE GUIDES

America's Top Golf Courses
Movie Guide
Music Guide
NYC Gourmet Shop./Entertaining
NYC Shopping

NIGHTLIFE GUIDES

Los Angeles
New York City
San Francisco

HOTEL & TRAVEL GUIDES

Beijing
Hong Kong
Las Vegas
London
New Orleans
Montréal
Shanghai
Top U.S. Hotels, Resorts & Spas
Toronto
U.S. Family Travel
Vancouver
Walt Disney World Insider's Guide
World's Top Hotels, Resorts & Spas

WEB & WIRELESS SERVICES

ZAGAT TO GO℠ for handhelds
ZAGAT.com℠ • ZAGAT.mobi℠

ZAGATMAP

Manhattan Subway Map

Most Popular Restaurants

Map coordinates follow each name. Sections A–H lie south of 34th Street (see adjacent map). Sections I–P lie north of 34th Street (see reverse side of map).

1 Union Square Cafe (B-4)

2 Gramercy Tavern (B-4)

3 Babbo (C-3)

4 Le Bernardin (O-3)

5 Gotham Bar & Grill (C-4)

6 Jean Georges (N-3)

7 Daniel (M-5)

8 Peter Luger (E-7)

9 Bouley (F-4)

10 Eleven Madison Park (B-4)

11 Balthazar (E-4)

12 Blue Water Grill (B-4)

13 Per Se (N-3)

14 Del Posto (C-2)

15 Becco (O-3)

16 Atlantic Grill (L-5)

17 Rosa Mexicano (B-4, N-3, N-6)

18 Modern, The (O-4)

19 Café Boulud (L-4)

20 Aureole (N-4)

21 Nobu (F-3)

22 Carmine's (K-2, P-3)

23 Felidia (N-5)

24 Buddakan (C-2)

25 Palm, The (O-3, P-5, P-5)

26 Picholine (N-3)

27 Artisanal (A-4)

28 Four Seasons (O-5)

29 Aquagrill (E-3)

30 Del Frisco's (O-4)

31 Tabla (B-4)

32 Chanterelle (F-3)

33 Aquavit (N-5)

34 Blue Hill (D-3)

35 Telepan* (M-3)

36 Il Mulino (D-4)

37 Ouest (K-2)

38 Spice Market (C-2)

39 davidburke & donatella (N-5)

40 Café des Artistes (M-3)

41 Lupa (D-4)

42 Craft (B-4)

43 Bar Americain (O-3)

44 One if by Land (D-3)

45 Al Di La (G-7)

46 La Grenouille (O-4)

47 db Bistro Moderne (P-4)

48 Sushi Yasuda (P-5)

49 Mesa Grill (C-4)

50 L'Atelier de Joël Robuchon (N-4)

*Indicates tie with above